**The Interface Descriptive Language:
Definition and Use**

PRINCIPLES OF COMPUTER SCIENCE SERIES

Series Editors
Alfred V. Aho, Bell Telephone Laboratories, Murray Hill, New Jersey
Jeffrey D. Ullman, Stanford University, Stanford, California

Computer Organization
Michael Andrews
Trends in Theoretical Computer Science
Egon Borger, Editor
Advanced C: Food for the Educated Palate
Narain Gehani
C: An Advanced Introduction
Narain Gehani
C: An Advanced Introduction, Ansi C Version
Narain Gehani
C for Personal Computers: IBM PC, AT&T PC 6300, and Compatibles
Narain Gehani
Theory of Relational Databases
David Maier
An Introduction to Solid Modeling
Martti Mantyla
Principles of Computer Design
Leonard R. Marino
UNIX: The Minimal Manual
Jim Moore
The Theory of Database Concurrency Control
Christos Papadimitriou
Algorithms for Graphics and Image Processing
Theo Pavlidis
The Interface Description Language: Definition and Use
Richard Snodgrass
Data Compression: Methods and Theory
James A. Storer
The Elements of Artificial Intelligence
Steven Tanimoto
Computational Aspects of VLSI
Jeffrey D. Ullman
Principles of Database and Knowledge-Base Systems, Vol. I & II
Jeffrey D. Ullman
Algorithmic Studies in Mass Storage Systems
C. K. Wong

OTHER BOOKS OF INTEREST

Jewels of Formal Language Theory
Arto Salomaa
Fuzzy Sets, Natural Language Computations, and Risk Analysis
Kurt J. Schmucker
LISP: An Interactive Approach
Stuart C. Shapiro
Principles of Database Systems, Second Edition
Jeffrey D. Ullman

The Interface Description Language: Definition and Use

Richard Snodgrass
University of North Carolina at Chapel Hill

With contributing authors:

Karen P. Shannon
University of North Carolina

Jerry S. Kickenson
AT&T

Michael A. Shapiro
Data General Corporation

Dean D. Throop
Data General Corporation

William B. Warren
The MAC Group

David A. Lamb
Queen's University

John R. Nestor
Consultant

William A. Wulf
University of Virginia

COMPUTER SCIENCE PRESS

Library of Congress Cataloging-in-Publication Data
Snodgrass, Richard.
   The interface description language: definition and use / Richard Snodgrass; with contributing authors, Karen P. Shannon...[et al.].
   p.   cm.
   Bibliography: p.
   Includes index.
   ISBN 0-7167-8198-0
   1. IDL (Computer program language)   I. Shannon, Karen P.   II. Title.
QA76.73.I194S66 1988   88-29956
005.13'3—dc19   CIP

UNIX® is a registered trademark of AT&T; DEC and VAX, are trademarks of Digital Equipment Corporation; Ada is a registered trademark of the U.S. government (Ada Joint Program Office); T_EX is a trademark of the American Mathematical Society.

Copyright © 1989 Computer Science Press

No part of this book may be reproduced by any mechanical, photographic, or electronic process, or in the form of a phonographic recording, nor may it be stored in a retrieval system, transmitted, or otherwise copied for public or private use, without written permission from the publisher.

Printed in the United States of America

Computer Science Press
1803 Research Boulevard
Rockville, MD 20850

An imprint of W. H. Freeman and Company
41 Madison Avenue, New York, NY 10010
20 Beaumont Street, Oxford OX1 2NQ, England

1 2 3 4 5 6 7 8 9 0   RRD   7 6 5 4 3 2 1 0 8 9

Contents

Preface	xi
Chapter 1 Introduction	**1**
1.1 Data Instances	5
1.2 Using IDL	6
1.3 Benefits of IDL	9
1.4 IDL Variants	11
1.5 Conventions	11
1.6 Why Is This Book So Long?	12
Exercises	13
Bibliographic Notes	14
Part I Two Introductory Examples	**17**
Chapter 2 The Steps in Using IDL	**19**
2.1 The IDL Specification	20
2.2 Translating the Specification	42
2.3 Writing the Algorithm	56
2.4 Compiling the Process	60
2.5 Running the Process	60
2.6 Checking the Assertions	66
2.7 Summary	69
Exercises	69
Bibliographic Notes	69
Chapter 3 A Second Example	**71**
3.1 Example Problem	71
3.2 The IDL Specification	75
3.3 Translating the Specification	84

3.4 Writing the Algorithm 88
3.5 Compiling the Process 91
3.6 Running the Process 91
3.7 Summary 97
Exercises 102
Bibliographic Notes 102

Part II Language Definition   103

Chapter 4 IDL Language Definition   105
4.1 Structure Specifications 108
4.2 Process Specifications 116
4.3 Import Specifications 121
4.4 Instantiation of IDL Specifications 122
Exercises 125
Bibliographic Notes 125

Chapter 5 Assertion Language Definition   129
5.1 The Assertion Statement 130
5.2 Expressions 130
5.3 Literals 131
5.4 Infix Operations on Values 132
5.5 Prefix Operations on Values 133
5.6 Infix Operations on Object Collections 133
5.7 Prefix Operations on Collections 135
5.8 Object Collections As Values 135
5.9 If Expressions 135
5.10 Quantifiers 136
5.11 Case Expressions 136
5.12 Definitions 137
Exercises 138
Bibliographic Notes 138

Chapter 6 The ASCII External Representation   141
6.1 Lexical Rules 142
6.2 Syntactic Rules 142
6.3 Readers and Writers 143
Exercises 143
Bibliographic Notes 144

Chapter 7 Using IDL with C — 145
- 7.1 Target Clause — 145
- 7.2 Data Types — 146
- 7.3 Processes — 167
- Exercises — 170
- Bibliographic Notes — 170

Chapter 8 Using IDL with Pascal — 173
- 8.1 Target Clause — 173
- 8.2 Data Types — 174
- 8.3 Processes — 193
- Exercises — 196
- Bibliographic Notes — 196

Chapter 9 Using IDL in a Compiler — 199
- 9.1 The Frontend — 199
- 9.2 The Frontend in C — 206
- 9.3 The Frontend in Pascal — 209
- 9.4 Semantic Analysis — 212
- 9.5 Constant Folding — 218
- 9.6 Converting Source Positions — 218
- 9.7 Merging IDL Processes — 219
- Exercises — 225
- Bibliographic Notes — 228

Chapter 10 Writing IDL Specifications — 231
- 10.1 Coarse Structuring — 231
- 10.2 Abstract Syntax Trees — 234
- 10.3 Use of Classes — 237
- 10.4 The Symbol Table — 240
- 10.5 Attribute Placement — 248
- 10.6 Invariant Structures — 252
- 10.7 Miscellaneous — 253
- Bibliographic Notes — 254

Part III   Example: A Cross-Referencer — 257

Chapter 11 An Introduction to XRef — 259
- 11.1 Tokens — 260
- 11.2 Basic XRef Primitives — 260
- 11.3 Additional Primitives — 264

11.4 A Second Example	265
11.5 Conclusion	266
Exercises	266

Chapter 12 XRef Language Definition — 267

12.1 Lexical Conventions	267
12.2 XRef Grammar	269
12.3 Semantics	272
12.4 Predicates	275
12.5 Scope Rules	275
Exercises	276
Bibliographic Notes	277

Chapter 13 xref Implementation — 279

13.1 The Preprocessor	279
13.2 The Frontend	281
13.3 Semantic Analysis	283
13.4 Summary	295
13.5 The Syntax Tree Structure	296
13.6 The Attributed Syntax Tree Structure	299
Bibliographic Notes	300
Exercises	300

Part IV Example: The IDL Translator — 303

Chapter 14 Overview of the IDL Translator — 305

14.1 IDL Translator Architecture	305
14.2 The Prelude	309
Bibliographic Notes	310

Chapter 15 The Candle Structure — 311

15.1 Design Principles	311
15.2 Constructing a Candle Instance	315
15.3 Rationale	334
15.4 Statistics on the Specification	365
Bibliographic Notes	366

Chapter 16 candlewalk Implementation — 369

16.1 Regenerating the IDL Source	369
16.2 Generating Formatted Source	377
16.3 Variants of Formatted Source	379

16.4	Calculating Source Positions	380
16.5	Summary	381
	Bibliographic Notes	382

Chapter 17 idlc Implementation   383

17.1	Implementation Overview	384
17.2	The Frontend	389
17.3	Semantic Analysis	390
17.4	Independent Representation Analysis	409
17.5	Dependent Representation Analysis	412
17.6	Code Generation	416
17.7	Error Handling	417
17.8	Evaluation	417
	Bibliographic Notes	420

Chapter 18 idlcheck Implementation   421

18.1	Code Generation	422
18.2	Interpretation	426
18.3	Error Log Generation	431
18.4	Summary	434
	Bibliographic Notes	434

Part V   Appendices   435

A   Glossary   437

B   IDL Syntax   445

B.1	Lexical Conventions	445
B.2	IDL Grammar	448
B.3	Implementation-defined Aspects	452
B.4	Syntactic Differences	454
B.5	Semantic Differences	465
	Bibliographic Notes	467

C   C Interface Details   469

C.1	Prefixes	469
C.2	Representations	471
C.3	Runtime Support Routines	474
C.4	Representation Specifications	483
C.5	Restrictions	484

D	**Pascal Interface Details**	**485**
	D.1 Prefixes	485
	D.2 Representations	487
	D.3 Runtime Support Routines	490
	D.4 Representation Specifications	496
	D.5 Restrictions	497
E	**Function Language Compiler**	**499**
	E.1 Language Definition	501
	E.2 The IDL Specifications	501
	E.3 The Implementation in C	501
	E.4 The Implementation in Pascal	512
	E.5 Function Language Cross Referencers	524
	E.6 Specification Concordances	524
	E.7 XRef Specifications	529
F	**The Candle Specification**	**535**
	F.1 The `CandleSyntax` Structure	535
	F.2 The `CandleSemantic` Structure	541
	F.3 The `CandleRep` Structure	543
	F.4 The CANDLE Structure	544
	F.5 The `UNCCandle` Structure	544
	F.6 The `CandlePos` Structure	544
	F.7 The `UNCCandlePos` Structure	545
	F.8 The `CandleContext` Structure	545
	F.9 The `CandleSymbolTable` Structure	547
G	**idlcheck Instructions**	**549**
	G.1 Literals	550
	G.2 Binary Operators	551
	G.3 Unary Operators	555
	G.4 Miscellaneous Instructions	555
	Bibliographic Notes	558
H	**Answers to Exercises**	**559**
	Bibliography	**573**
	Author Index	**591**
	Index	**597**

Preface

This book presents both a specification language, the *Interface Description Language* (IDL), describing data structures and their movement between tools, and a set of meta-tools, the *IDL Toolkit*, used to manipulate specifications expressed in IDL. IDL is a notation for describing the characteristics of data structures passed among a collection of cooperating processes. A tool, the IDL translator, maps these descriptions into code fragments in one of several target programming languages. These code fragments contain declarations of data structures in the target programming language that are functionally equivalent to those described in the IDL specification. The code fragments also define utilities for in-core manipulation and input and output of instances of the data structures. The IDL user writes programs in terms of the target programming language data declarations and utilities produced by the IDL translator. These programs process instances of the IDL-specified data structures residing in main memory or on external storage. The first use of IDL was to specify DIANA, an intermediate representation of Ada programs. IDL has since been used to specify the internal data structures of many academic and commercial compilers. The IDL Toolkit implemented at the University of North Carolina at Chapel Hill consists of an IDL translator generating C and Pascal code, an assertion checker, and several other tools.

    This book is intended for those who are interested in using the toolkit and for those who are interested in using IDL independently of the toolkit. The book may be used by professional compiler and programming environment designers and implementors and by researchers in programming environments and compiler design. The book can also be used as a primary text for a graduate level software systems course or as a secondary text for an upper-level undergraduate compiler construction course. Finally, it is a tutorial and reference manual for those using the IDL Toolkit.

Organization and Content

This book is organized around four examples of IDL. Part I introduces IDL through two examples. IDL structures, assertions, and processes are introduced. The IDLC and IDLCHECK tools and the C and Pascal interfaces are demonstrated. Part I contains a billing example as well as a simple constant folding compiler phase. In this part, as well as in Part II and in the appendices, the sections on C and Pascal are parallel—either can be read independently of the other and they contain similar material, in content and in presentation. All source code for these two examples is provided in both C and Pascal. Experience with C or Pascal and with designing small to medium programs is assumed. Knowledge of the overall structure of a compiler is also assumed. Part I presents enough of IDL for readers to begin using IDL to solve elementary problems.

Part II defines the language and its interfaces to the C and Pascal programming languages. It serves as a reference manual for IDL and its implementation. A complete frontend is given for the toy language introduced in Part I, including full source in Pascal and C. This frontend is composed of phases performing lexical, syntactic, and semantic analysis. A detailed understanding of compiler construction is not assumed until the last chapter of Part II.

Part III presents a comprehensive use of IDL. The XRef language, in which a cross referencer may be specified, is defined and a translator to intermediate code and an interpreter for this intermediate code are described. The intermediate code is in fact an instance of an IDL structure. All specifications are included.

Part IV examines the central tools of the IDL Toolkit: IDLC and IDLCHECK. The two tools are each composed of several IDL processes. A third tool, CANDLEWALK, manipulating IDL instances produced by IDLC, is also discussed. IDL is used extensively in the implementation of these tools; a thorough understanding of IDL may be gained by studying this example.

Guide to Readers

This book is organized so that it can be read in different ways by different classes of readers. All readers should read Parts I and II to gain an understanding of IDL and its use. Students in an upper level undergraduate compiler course using this book as a secondary text may find the material in Parts III and IV too advanced or too detailed; instead, they might want to refer to Part II while using the IDL Toolkit in their own compiler project. Others using the toolkit may find the material in Part III to be of greater interest. For professional compiler and programming environment designers, implementors, and researchers, the material in Part IV will probably be of the most interest, after the previous parts have been read.

Exercises

The exercises have been designed for self-study. They generally progress from easy (e.g., "What is..."), to moderate (e.g., "Extend the implementation to..."), to hard (e.g., "Design and implement..."). Solutions to most of the exercises appear in Appendix H. Please use them wisely; they will be of most benefit if a solution is at least attempted before the answer is consulted. Often the solution given will be sketchy, with the details to be provided by the reader.

The IDL Toolkit

A collection of IDL tools, including an IDL translator that generates C and Pascal (IDLC), an assertion checker (IDLCHECK), a generator of cross referencers (XREF), a listing generator (CANDLEWALK) and several additional utilities, is available. The IDL Toolkit may be obtained from

> UniPress Software
> 2025 Lincoln Highway
> Edison, NJ 08817
> (201) 985-8000

Sources for the examples in this book are included with the distribution. The examples have been tested on release 4.0 of the toolkit.

Contributors

Richard Snodgrass is a faculty member in the Department of Computer Science, University of North Carolina at Chapel Hill. He directed the SoftLab Project which developed the IDL Toolkit, and wrote Chapters 9, 10, 13, and 16 and Appendices B, E, and H. He also wrote portions of the remaining chapters and edited the entire book. Karen P. Shannon is completing her Ph.D. in the Department of Computer Science, University of North Carolina at Chapel Hill. She designed and implemented most of the IDL translator, including second versions of the semantic analysis and code generator phases, implemented the second version of the assertion checker, implemented some of the C runtime library for IDL, helped design the CANDLE IDL specification, and implemented many of the auxiliary tools included in the IDL Toolkit. She wrote Chapters 7, 14, 15, and 17 and Appendices C, and F. Jerry S. Kickenson is a member of the technical staff at AT & T in Lincroft, New Jersey. As part of his Master's thesis work, he implemented the first version of the assertion code generator, interpreter, and the semantic analysis of assertions. He wrote Sections 2.6, 3.2.2, and 3.2.2, Chapters 5 and 18, and Appendix G. Michael A. Shapiro and Dean D. Throop are Senior Software Engineers in the Data Communications Section of the RTP Laboratory, Data General Corporation, Research Triangle Park, North Carolina. Michael Shapiro designed and implemented the Pascal representation and the initial Pascal code generator of IDLC and wrote Chapter 8 and Appendix D. Dean Throop designed and implemented the initial version of XREF and wrote Chapters 11 and 12. William B. Warren is a consultant with the MAC Group, Cambridge, Massachusetts. He wrote most of Chapters 2 and 3 and much of Appendix A. David A. Lamb is a faculty member in the Department of Computing and Information Science, Queen's University, Kingston, Ontario, Canada. John R. Nestor is an independent consultant based in Pittsburgh, Pennsylvania. William A. Wulf is a faculty member in the Department of Computer Science, University of Virginia, Charlottesville. David Lamb, John Nestor, and William Wulf designed the IDL language, including the assertion language, and wrote Section 1.1 and Chapters 4–6. The current "standard" definition of IDL was copyrighted in 1982 by John R. Nestor, David A. Lamb, and William A. Wulf. The material in Chapters 4 and 6 and Appendices B.1 and B.2 is covered under that copyright. John Nestor also wrote Section 3.7.

The Cover

The cover shows three processes, illustrated as circles, and three IDL structure specifications, illustrated as rectangles. The middle big process on the front reads an instance of structure A (the rectangle on the back) from a file (shown as a database on the back) and produces two instances, one of structure A' (derived from structure A and shown as a double-bordered rectangle on the front) read by the bottom process, and one of the unrelated structure B (the upper-right thin rectangle) read by the process in the upper-right-hand corner.

Acknowledgments

It is a pleasure to acknowledge the help of those who contributed to this book and helped in the development of the IDL Toolkit. Tim Maroney was a great help during the initial stages of the implementation of the IDL Toolkit. He designed the first version of the C and Pascal representations, implemented the first version of much of the IDL translator, implemented the first version of the C and Pascal runtime libraries for IDL, and wrote

PREFACE

the initial draft of Chapter 7 and Appendix C. Others contributing to the IDL Toolkit implementation either through code development or constructive criticism include Vikram Biyani, Nancy Butler, James Chou, Ralph Cook, Joan Curry, Srinivas Desirazu, Arthur Evans, Jr., Michael Foster, Robert France, Helen Gill Chuck Howell, Bharadwaj Jayaraman, Mick Jordan, Steven Konstant, Alex Nelson, Joseph Newcomer, Con O'Connell, Daniel Pettingill, Jeff Raynes, Lawrence Ross, Dore Rosenblum, Karsten Schwan, Yen-Ping Shan, Frank Silbermann, Robert Stam, Donald Stone, and Sundar Varadarajan. Ilsoo Ahn, Anund Lie, Edwin McKenzie, and Richard Rubin, as well as many listed above, provided comments on the text. Pamela Payne converted most of the text from troff to TEX, and then to LATEX. Leigh Pittman, Vernon Chi, Peter Calingaert, and Graham Gash helped with the formatting. Figures were produced by Pamela Payne and Ellyn Palermo. Pamela Payne developed the initial index and greatly helped with the innumerable details involved in producing a book; without her help, the process would have been a lot less fun.

The Department of Computer Science at the University of North Carolina at Chapel Hill has provided an excellent research environment for the development of the tools and the concepts encapsulated in them, and has continued to support the SoftLab project through the provision of research assistants and other resources. The National Science Foundation has recently supported SoftLab through its Institutional Infrastructure Program. IBM and the Software Engineering Institute at Carnegie-Mellon University have also indirectly provided support.

R.T.S.
Chapel Hill, North Carolina
December 1988

Chapter 1

Introduction

This book presents the *Interface Description Language* (IDL), a mechanism for specifying properties of structured data, and the *IDL Toolkit*, a set of tools used to manipulate specifications expressed in IDL. The objective of such specifications is to permit the data to be communicated safely and efficiently among related programs. Before considering the mechanism itself we shall briefly discuss the motivation that led to its design.

Compilers are conceptually partitioned into *phases*, each of which transforms the source program from one representation into another. Figure 1.1 shows the typical decomposition of a compiler, identifying six phases. The lexical analyzer phase scans the source program character by character, generating a sequence of tokens, representing keywords, integer constants, identifiers, etc. The syntax analyzer builds a parse tree from this sequence of tokens. Subsequent phases perform further analysis, with target code as the end result. Partitioning the compiler into phases aids in understanding this complex program; each phase performs specific tasks, using algorithms tailored to its tasks.

Programming environments are a natural evolution from multi-phase compilers. A programming environment is a computer-aided design system for software. Programming environments are viewed by many as a promising approach to the high cost of producing software, a cost that is rising dramatically in the aggregate. Programming environments provide a set of tools within a uniform framework. They take advantage of the underlying structure of programs that is more than a string of characters, and they use this structure as an organizational device. A compiler can be viewed as a very simple programming environment, with each phase considered to be a simple tool. Most programming environments are more comprehensive in their support of software design and implementation. They consist of a

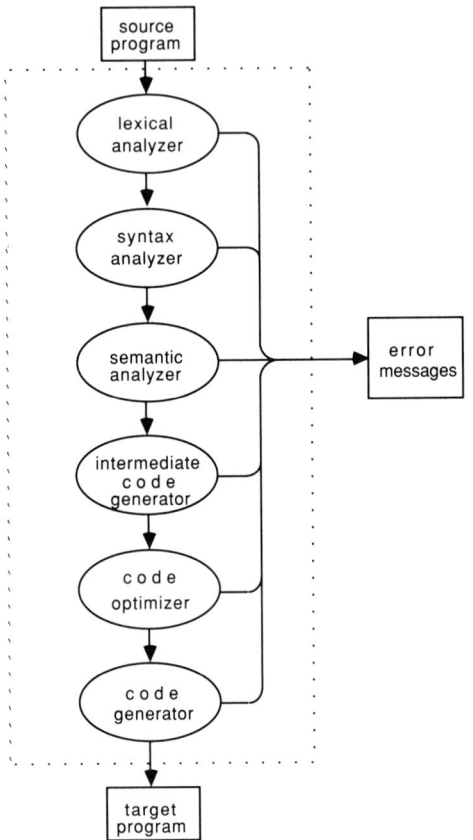

Figure 1.1: Typical Phases of a Compiler

CHAPTER 1. INTRODUCTION

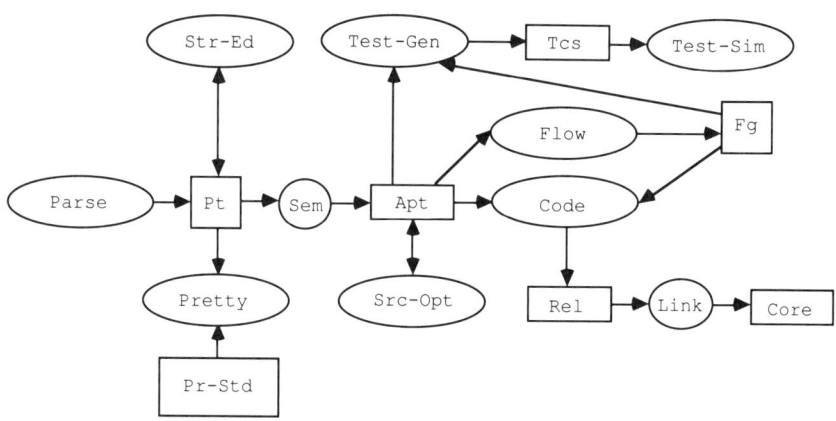

Figure 1.2: An Example Collection of Programs

number of tools that assist a programmer in the program construction, test, and validation process. These tools include editors, debuggers, compilers, pretty-printers, test-case generators, various kinds of analysis aids, and so on. Many of these tools operate on some intermediate representation of the program: a form that is below the level of the source text. Some of them also need access to data that is derived from the source text, but not explicit in it: procedure call graphs, data flow graphs, symbol tables, and various semantic attributes. Finally, some of the tools will need to access data that is specific to the installation or target machine but not otherwise related to a particular program: tables that define coding or reporting standards, tables that define local pretty-printing conventions, tables of simulated on-line testing data, and so on. The situation we envision is illustrated in Figure 1.2.

In this figure, rectangular boxes represent data and oval represent programs; both boxes and ovals contain labels to suggest their roles. So, for example, a parser, **Parse**, produces a parse tree, **Pt**. A pretty-printer program, **Pretty**, accepts **Pt** and produces a listing using conventions defined in a database called **Pr-Std**. A screen-oriented language-based editor, **Str-Ed**, operates on the parse tree and produces another valid parse tree. A semantic analyzer, **Sem**, generates an attributed parse tree, **Apt**, from the simpler tree generated by the parser and/or editor. Several tools operate from the attributed tree: **Flow** creates a flow graph, **Fg**; a source level optimizer, **Src-Opt**, performs program transformations that are again represented as valid attributed trees; a test-case generator, **Test-Gen**, uses the attributed tree as well as the flow graph to produce a form, **Tcs**, that can be used by the test-case simulator, Test-Sim; finally, a code generator, Code, uses the flow graph and attributed parse tree to generate a relocatable file, Rel. A linker, Link, converts relocatable code into an executable core image, Core. The Parse, Sem, Src-Opt, Flow, Code, and Link tools together form a large tool, a compiler, with an architecture similar to that shown in Figure 1.1.

To work together harmoniously, the various programs must have a precise and compatible definition of the data structures they use to communicate with each other. The primary purpose of IDL is to provide such a definition.

Diagrams such as that in Figure 1.2 may be helpful in illustrating the relation between data and the programs that process it, but they are totally inadequate as a specification technique. One must be careful not to read too much into such a diagram. One might easily infer, for example, that each of the boxes representing data is a file, or that each of the ovals is a separate program. Perhaps neither of these is intended. One might also infer that there is a single internal representation for the data denoted by a box. This may also be incorrect. We need a specification technique that allows all these things, as well as many other possibilities.

An IDL specification describes a data structure without forcing a particular representation on the structure. Individual instances of structures satisfying the specification may be implemented in a way that is appropriate for the particular program, or portion of the program, that manipulates the data. The well-known methodology of *abstract data types* has these characteristics.

We shall adopt the view that each box in Figure 1.2 denotes an instance of an abstract data type about which we can make various *assertions*. Each oval denotes an instance of an abstract process, which accepts one or more instances of a data abstraction as its "input" and yields instances of other abstractions as its "output." In effect, the boxes in Figure 1.2 can be viewed as input-output assertions on the ovals. For example, we can specify that, if the input to Sem satisfies the definition of Pt, then its output will satisfy Apt. Similarly, we can define the effect of the code generator, Code, by specifying that, if the inputs to Code satisfy Apt and Fg, the output will satisfy Rel. Saying these relationships another way, the input to Code must satisfy both specifications Apt and Fg, and the output of Code is guaranteed to satisfy Rel.

This view of the diagram in Figure 1.2 is obviously abstract. For pragmatic reasons an implementation of the various programs in a specific situation will need to be concerned with lower-level representation details, and later chapters of this book will deal with these legitimate concerns. For the moment, however, we will stick with the abstract view for several reasons. First, this view provides the basis for the level of precision we are seeking. Second, it provides complete representation and language independence. Finally, coupled with a well-engineered specification technique, it allows for easy maintenance, and hence ensures compatibility in the face of evolution. We will later show how the abstract view taken here can be mechanically mapped into efficient implementations.

IDL may also be used to specify interfaces between components of a single tool. Later chapters examine the use of IDL in constructing three compilers, an assertion checker, and several other tools. IDL is appropriate if a tool or tool component communicates complex data structures with another tool or tool component.

1.1 Data Instances

As noted above, we shall view each of the boxes in Figure 1.2 as an abstract data type; data input to the programs represented by the ovals are instances of these types. The first step in an IDL specification will be to define the abstract types under discussion.

An *abstract data type* consists of a set of *values* (the *domain* of the type), and a set of *operations* on these values. Any specification of an abstract type must define both of these; in IDL the *abstract modeling* technique is used. In this technique one specifies the domain of the type in terms of previously defined mathematical entities; the operations of the abstract type are then specified in terms of their effect on these entities.

All specifications written with IDL must use the same model. The model must therefore be a very general one, but it must have straightforward and efficient implementations. IDL uses typed, attributed directed graphs as its data model. Informally, this domain is a collection of *objects*. Each object has a type, a location, and a value. One category of types in the model are *node types*; the other categories are scalars (integers, rationals, booleans, and strings), sets, and sequences. The value of a node object is a collection of *attributes*; the particular attributes associated with a node object are a property of its type. No two attributes of the same node type have the same name; each attribute of a node object has an associated location. Attributes are also typed; the objects form a graph because some of the attributes may reference other objects.

Note that we have not specified how each node and link is represented. A node might be implemented by a record in some programming language with components to represent its attributes, and a link represented with a pointer. This implementation would be an adequate one—but it is not the only one, and is certainly not the best one under many circumstances. For instance, while some node objects might be represented as records, others that are referenced only once might be "upmerged" to become components of the records corresponding to the node objects that reference them.

1.2 Using IDL

The steps in using IDL are shown in Figure 1.3. You first write an IDL specification describing the characteristics of data structures passed among a collection of cooperating processes. A tool, the IDL translator, maps these descriptions into code fragments in one of several target programming languages. These code fragments contain declarations of data structures in the target programming language that are functionally equivalent to those described in the IDL specification. The code fragments also define utilities for manipulation of main-memory data and input and output of instances of the data structures. You proceed to program the algorithm (i.e., a particular phase of a compiler) in the selected target programming language in terms of the data declarations produced by the IDL translator. While programming, you use the tailored set of runtime support routines to allocate new instances of data structures, to maintain sets and sequences composed of them, and to read and write them from external storage. You then compile and link the code for the algorithm along with the IDL-produced data declarations and runtime support routines to produce an executable program. Finally, you execute this program to process instances of data structures that are represented externally in the ASCII External Representation Language. Tools communicate when a data instance produced by one tool is later read by another tool.

To illustrate the part IDL plays, let us consider how a compiler is implemented with and without IDL. In either case, we must determine how to physically partition the phases of the compiler into *passes*, each of which reads an input file and writes an output file. Each phase may be a single pass, or several phases might be combined into a single pass. Historically, early compilers consisted of many passes, because main memories were small; recent compilers consist of only a few passes, to reduce the time required to write the data from one pass and read it into the next pass. Phases are a conceptual device and passes reflect the physical organization.

Let's initially assume that, since main memory prices are steadily decreasing, a single-pass organization is adopted. In such a compiler, the lexical analyzer will coordinate with the syntax analyzer through coroutines. The parse tree will be constructed in main memory, then augmented with attributes by the semantic analyzer. The intermediate code generator will create a list of low-level statements, such as triples, also in main

1.2. USING IDL

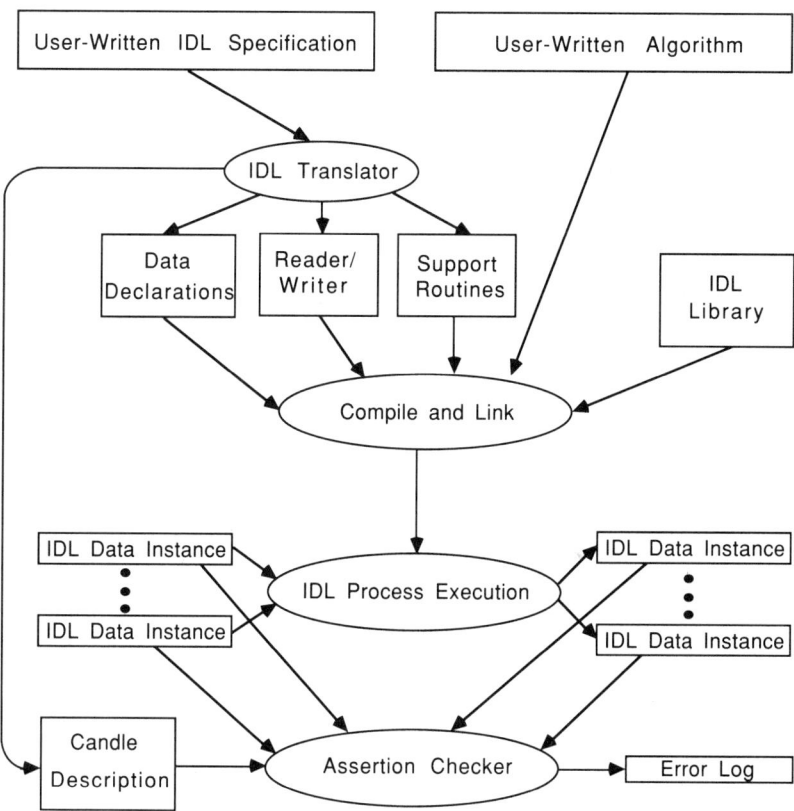

Figure 1.3: Steps in Using IDL

memory, which will be rearranged by the code optimizer. Finally, the code generator will traverse the list, emitting target code as it proceeds.

The advantage of this organization is good performance. Since the intermediate data structures, the parse tree, intermediate code, and symbol table, all reside in main memory, there is no expensive input or output of these structures. The users of the compiler benefit. The disadvantages are felt by the compiler developers. A specification of the phases does not exist in any explicit form. Such a specification is only implicit in the data structure declarations and the pattern of access to variables in the code for the phases. The lack of such a specification makes adding programmers to the development team difficult. Alternatively, the organization may be documented separately, with the ever-present danger that the documentation and the code become inconsistent. Secondly, debugging the compiler is difficult: all the phases must be debugged simultaneously (unless the bug is known to reside in an early phase). The debugger is usually the only tool available for displaying the data structures in main memory. Most debuggers are able to display only simple data types, and thus can display complex parse trees or symbol tables only one node or even one field at a time. Finally, there is nothing preventing one phase from accessing or corrupting data used in another phase, which increases the likelihood of such bugs.

To avoid these problems, a multi-pass organization, with each phase a separate pass, is adopted. Each phase writes its output data structures to a file, to be read in by the next phase. Debugging is now much easier. Each phase can be executed separately, and the output of that phase examined to ensure that the phase did the correct things with the input data. Since each phase is a separate process, the phases cannot corrupt each other; access to improper fields or variables will be detected at compile-time.

Three drawbacks remain. The first is performance, which was the primary reason the multi-pass organization was initially rejected. The second drawback is that the compiler developers must write the code to read and write the intermediate data structures. For the compiler illustrated in Figure 1.1, five readers and five writers are required. While such code is not conceptually difficult (unless it is highly optimized for performance), it is voluminous and tedious. Even worse, each time a data structure is changed (and such changes will be frequent, at least during initial implementation), the readers and writers must be updated and debugged, before any of the code that references that data structure can itself be debugged. Finally, there is still no specification of the organization of the compiler; such a specification is implicit in the code for the readers and writers.

For a simple compiler, these drawbacks may not be critical. In many cases, a single-pass organization may be indicated, and the reliability and debugging difficulties simply accepted. For a complex compiler, or for a programming environment composed of many tools, the drawbacks of both the single-pass and multi-pass approaches may significantly increase the cost and development time.

IDL allows substantial technology to be applied to resolve this quandary. The compiler is first specified in IDL, identifying both the tools (i.e., the phases) and the data structures passed between the tools. The IDL specification documents the compiler organization in sufficient detail to aid newcomers to the development team or compiler maintainers. The IDL translator maps this specification into code fragments implementing the reader(s), writer(s) and access functions, as well as data declarations to be used by the code implementing the phase. Since the declarations are generated directly from the specifications, the two are guaranteed to be consistent. During development, the IDL translator is directed to map each phase to a separate process, thereby aiding in debugging. The compiler will be slow, but runtime efficiency of the compiler is not particularly important during implementation. No additional code need be written, since this IDL translator provides this code. Specialized tools are available for formatting the data while it resides in files, and for checking the data for correctness. The needs of the compiler developers have been met. Once the phases have been debugged, the IDL translator is directed to map all the phases into one process, thereby achieving good performance, and meeting the needs of the compiler users.

1.3 Benefits of IDL

In summary, using IDL simplifies the development of complex software systems. Designing the system is easier because IDL permits a higher level of data abstraction than that provided by most programming languages. Abstract data types such as sets and sequences for any type, complete with all necessary data declarations and data manipulation routines, are supported by IDL. Consequently, you may more naturally express the algorithm in terms of these abstractions without becoming mired in implementation detail.

Building the system is faster because there is less code to write and debug. Since a large portion of the data manipulation utility routines are provided bug-free by the IDL system, the implementor must write and debug only the code for the algorithm. This approach in turn makes for fast prototyping of the system, which permits an iterative design approach.

Making the structure of data passed between portions of the system explicit also simplifies building the system. The implementor is forced to consider what information is required by each portion and what information is produced. Once the code is working, the data instances used and produced by each portion can be examined to determine their correctness.

Finally, the software system that has been developed using the IDL system is better documented and thus easier to maintain. Data structures specified with IDL are documented by their specifications. The IDL-supplied data manipulation routines are documented in the IDL system documentation.

While providing a definition of the data structures that tools communicate with, IDL also has the following characteristics:

- *Precision*: The IDL definition is sufficiently precise to be used as a formal specification by those who are writing programs to process the data.

- *Representation independence*: The IDL specification does not unduly constrain the internal representation of the data. Individual tools must be able to use internal representations that reflect their special processing requirements.

- *Language independence*: The IDL mechanism is not restricted to specifying data structures to be manipulated by a single target language. The tools in a programming environment may be written in different languages.

- *Maintainability*: The tools in a programming environment, like programs in general, will be developed incrementally and will be enhanced through experience in using them. The various data structures through which they communicate will consequently also evolve. To retain compatibility in the face of this evolution, IDL provides means for coping with changes that are both easy to use and amenable to automatic analysis.

- *Communication form*: Data described in IDL may be communicated between arbitrary programs and, indeed, between arbitrary computers. IDL supports a standard representation of the data and the ability to map between this form and the internal one chosen by specific tools.

That these characteristics are desirable and are associated with IDL will become apparent as we examine, in the next two chapters, two tools built using IDL.

When is IDL *not* appropriate? Other strategies are relevant when the advantages that IDL provides are outweighed by the overhead of learning

IDL and its associated tools, or when assumptions inherent in the use of IDL are not satisfied. Specifically, IDL should probably not be used

- if data communicated between tools is very simple (although IDL has been profitably used to specify one data structure, an error instance used in the IDL translator itself consisting of only two integers and one sequence of arguments, each of which could be either an integer or a string);
- if the data is accessed more as a database, with incremental modification, than as instances passed between tools (this limitation is imposed by existing IDL implementations; there is nothing in the language itself precluding efficient database access to IDL instances);
- if the tool must be implemented in a language not supported by an IDL translator, or if, for some reason, the IDL runtime library has unresolvable conflicts with existing code (again, this limitation is imposed by existing IDL implementations, rather than by IDL itself); or
- if much of the tool has already been written without using IDL, and the cost of converting the existing code to use IDL is prohibitive (although techniques have been developed to integrate IDL and non-IDL tools).

The many tools discussed in this book illustrate the wide class of applications for which IDL is appropriate.

1.4 IDL Variants

Implicit in any implementation of IDL are assumptions about how the instances of IDL structures are used. These assumptions may affect the language supported by the tools. For instance, some tools might restrict the operations slightly to achieve reasonable efficiency. Each implementation unavoidably defines a variant of the specification language that may differ from that supported by another implementation. The language described in this book is the one supported by the IDL Toolkit. This language is generally but not completely a superset of the standard definition of IDL; differences are listed in Appendix B.

1.5 Conventions

Words or phrases that denote important concepts will be printed in *italics* on first appearance. These words and phrases are collected in a glossary

(Appendix A) and in the index at the end of the text with the page number of the definition appearing in **boldface**. File names also appear in **boldface**.

In the programming language and IDL specification examples appearing in the running text, all IDL, C, and Pascal reserved words (e.g., `Structure`, `union`, `record`) as well as IDL predefined types (e.g., `Rational`), parameters (e.g., `Runtime Version`), and operation names (e.g., `appendfrontSEQ`) appear in `slanted typewriter` font. User-defined identifiers are shown in `typewriter` font. Comments in programs and in specifications appear in *italics*. A SMALL CAPITALIZED font is used for names of programs that can be executed (e.g., IDLC, XREF); major IDL specifications are in the same font yet have at least an initial capital letter (e.g., CANDLE). Names of languages (e.g., Pascal, IDL, XRef) appear in Roman and are capitalized. The virtual machine instructions for the assertion checker appear in a sans-serif font.

All syntactic definitions are given in an extended version of the Backus-Naur Form (BNF). Angle brackets ("⟨ ⟩") surround the name of a nonterminal. Braces ("{ }") are used to group elements of a production; a trailing asterisk ("}*") denotes zero or more occurrences; a trailing plus ("}$^+$") denotes one or more occurrences; and a trailing question mark ("}$^?$") denotes an optional item. The construct "$\{a \mid b\}$" specifies that either a or b is present. Special characters that are lexemes, such as a semicolon, are quoted with single quotation marks (e.g., ' ; '). In running text, these characters will be quoted normally, with double quotes. Keywords in a `slanted typewriter` font are not quoted.

1.6 Why Is This Book So Long?

The focus of this book, specifying interfaces between tools in a programming environment, is but one concern in building such an environment. Other aspects include

- the tools themselves must be designed and implemented;
- the user interface must be determined;
- the tool algorithms must be developed;
- interfaces to existing tools and operating system(s) are required; and
- documentation, tutorials, and installation instructions must be written.

Given these tasks, why is such a thick book required just on the interface between the tools?

One answer is that the interface itself must inevitably inherit some of the complexity and diversity of the tools it connects. Hence, the language used to describe the interface must be able to specify complex entities. The Interface Description Language, while containing at its core only a few basic linguistic constructs, nevertheless is not a simple language. Actually, IDL is at least three languages: a structural description language, an assertion language, and an instance description language. Because IDL is capable of expressing complicated entities, it is itself complicated, requiring a careful explanation of the language. However, the language definition occupies only about a sixth of this book.

This book is also long because an expressive language such as IDL requires several examples to show the reader how the language may be employed. This book is organized around four examples. The commentary for these examples forms half of the book.

This book is long because it not only introduces the language, but also serves as a reference manual for the use of the IDL Toolkit, an implementation of IDL. The book explains how IDL was used in the implementation of the Toolkit, and gives an example of a production system built using the techniques presented in this book. This description added several chapters and many appendices, contributing about a sixth of the book.

Finally, this book is long because we wanted to show that IDL is language-independent, that IDL could express the interface between tools written in different programming languages. We also wanted the book to be accessible to readers knowledgeable in only Pascal or C. Hence, some sections and chapters are parallel, with identical material in each, but using Pascal or C. This repetition added a final sixth to the length of the book.

The bad news is that we've taken what should be a simple topic, tool interfaces, and made it appear to be a complicated, involved topic. The good news is that much of the material will be optional to most readers, and some of the material need never be read, but is there to be consulted infrequently, perhaps late at night when you want to know whether a particular Pascal record contains a certain field.

Exercises

1.1 Explain how the data structures illustrated in Figure 1.2 relate. Are some a superset or a subset of others?

1.2 List all sentences in the language specified as follows.

⟨sentence⟩ ::= { 'a' | 'b' } Is '::=' { 'd' | 'e' }? { 'f' }⁺ { 'g' }*

Bibliographic Notes

Barstow, Shrobe, and Sandewall [1984] is a slightly outdated, but otherwise excellent survey of work in programming environments.

Two de facto standard intermediate representations have been defined as IDL specifications. DIANA (Goos and Wulf [1981]) is an intermediate representation for Ada [1983] programs. DIANA has been used in compilers implemented at Ada Group Ltd. (Harrison [1983]), Bell Labs (Quinn [1982]), Burroughs, University of California, Berkeley (Zorn [1985]), Intermetrics (Avakian et al. [1982]), the University of Karlsruhe (Persch [1983], Kirchgässner et al. [1987]), Rational (Archer and Devlin [1986]), Rolm, SofTech Microsystems (Simpson [1982] and Wolfe [1981]), Stanford (Rosenblum [1985]), Systeam (Howell et al. [1988]), and Verdix (Butler [1983]). Both the Army and Air Force Ada Programming Support Environments base their program representations on DIANA (Intermetrics [1981] and Lamb [1987b]).

IVAN is an intermediate representation, specified in IDL, of programs written in VHDL (the VHSIC Hardware Description Language, defined by Shahdad et al. [1985]). IVAN is being used as the basis of an environment supporting that language (Gilman [1986]).

Finally, Burroughs, Carnegie-Mellon University, Intermetrics, Sperry Univac, Stanford, Tartan Labs and the University of North Carolina have used IDL as the basis for many of their tools (Lamb [1987b], Leverett [1982], Luckham, Neff, and Rosenblum [1987], Nestor and Beard [1981], Nestor et al. [1989], and Wulf [1980]).

IDL is similar to module interconnection languages (MILs), as defined by DeRemer and Kron [1976]. MILs define the form of modules and the resources (e.g., variables, types, procedures, exceptions) exported and imported by each module. Narayanaswamy and Scacchi [1987], Purtilo [1985, 1986], Tichy [1979], and Wolf, Clarke, and Wileden [1985, 1989] describe representative MILs. Most modern languages, such as Ada [1983], Mesa (Mitchell, Maybury, and Sweet [1979]), and Wirth's [1983] Modula-2 include constructs that perform similar functions. These approaches focus on controlling the visibility of operations and in-memory data structures contained in a single tool. IDL concerns a coarser granularity: inter-tool

1.6. WHY IS THIS BOOK SO LONG? 15

rather than intra-tool, and focuses purely on data flowing between tools. The Odin System, implemented by Clemm [1986], applies at an even coarser granularity: tools communicate typed objects whose internal structure is not known to the system.

Snodgrass [1987] describes the difficulties of using a conventional debugger to display complex data structures residing in main memory. Persch [1987] describes an editor for IDL instances, which is helpful in tool debugging. IDL is similar to remote procedure call (RPC) facilities, such as those implemented by Birrell and Nelson [1984] and Sun Microsystems [1988], which allow parameters to be passed from a client machine to a server machine, where the procedure executed and the results sent back to the client machine. In heterogeneous RPC systems, such as those implemented by Bershad et al. [1987], Jones and Rashid [1986], and Notkin et al. [1988], the client and server machines may be of different architectures. Heterogeneous RPC is similar to IDL in that both involve specifications of the data passed between processes, often running on different machines (in fact, the specifications in remote procedure call implementations are written in an interface description language that is often called IDL!) The primary difference is that of data granularity: IDL is oriented towards complex data structures whereas RPC is oriented towards passing elementary data such as single integers. Varadarajan [1988] describes how to connect IDL readers and writers to XDR, allowing IDL processes to interact via Sun's RPC. He also shows how a popular programming environment, the Cornell Program Synthesizer implemented by Reps and Teitelbaum [1987], can be modified to read and write IDL instances. Finally, he provides an approach to integrating existing software into a programming environment based on IDL.

Feiler [1987] compares IDL with structure editor generation technology, which emphasizes incremental modification. Conradi, Didriksen, and Lie [1986] propose that IDL be used to describe the interface between tools and a programming environment database. Newcomer [1987a] describes various approaches to connecting tools together, including the IDL approach, and examines how the concepts embodied in IDL might be generalized to include programming environments and databases [1986].

The language described in this book is a minor variant of the standard definition of IDL, as defined by Nestor, Lamb, and Wulf [1982]. IDL Version 3 has recently been defined by Nestor and described and formalized by Nestor et al. [1989]. IDL Version 3 is a significant redesign of IDL, and should be considered to be a new language, distinct from standard IDL.

Figure 1.3 is from Lamb [1983]. Aho, Sethi, and Ullman [1986] motivate the decomposition of a compiler into phases as shown in Figure 1.1.

Part I

Two Introductory Examples

Part I of this book is a tutorial introduction to using IDL. Chapter 2 gives a step-by-step method for using the elementary capabilities of IDL. As each step is examined, the relevant components of the IDL system will be introduced and explained. While IDL supports several target programming languages, the examples in this book use the C and Pascal programming languages. Chapter 3 uses IDL to implement a compiler phase.

Chapter 2

The Steps in Using IDL

IDL is used to specify data structures in a language-independent manner. It is oriented towards data structures employed in a programming environment, e.g., parse trees, symbol tables, intermediate code, but is also more generally applicable.

In this chapter we demonstrate this generality by using it to implement a tool far removed from programming environments: a batch billing program, illustrated in Figure 2.1. This tool reads a list of customers and a sequence of transactions. It steps through the transactions, either crediting the customer (if the transaction indicates the customer has paid a bill) or generating a bill (if the transaction indicates the customer was debited). It then writes the updated customer list and the list of generated bills.

This chapter will walk through the steps shown in Figure 1.3, first specifying the billing program in IDL, then implementing it, and finally executing it on test data. As each step is discussed, the relevant parts of the IDL system are explained. The next chapter examines each step once again in the context of a second example.

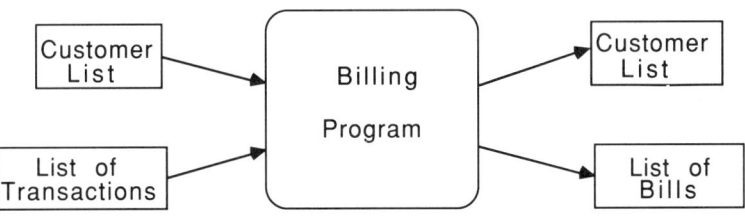

Figure 2.1: The Billing Program

2.1 The IDL Specification

The first step involves writing a specification of the collection of cooperating processes that compose the system being developed and of the data structures those processes share. Figure 2.2 identifies this portion of the whole process of using the IDL system. The specification is written in IDL. The specifications for one or more data structures and one or more processes constitute a complete specification. For this example, we define three data structures, those depicted in Figure 2.1, and two functionally equivalent processes, one implemented in C and one in Pascal. This section incrementally defines the data structures and processes for the billing program.

2.1.1 Specifying the Data Structures

The fundamental data structure building blocks of IDL are nodes and classes. Nodes and classes are organized into named collections called structures.

Nodes

A *node* is a named collection of zero or more named values called *attributes* that are treated as a unit. Attributes actually hold the data values; nodes are a grouping device. Nodes are analogous to records found in many programming languages; their attributes are analogous to the fields of a record. It is important to note that nodes need not actually *be* records—they just act like they are. In particular, in some implementations the values for attributes may be stored outside the node, or may not be stored at all, instead being recomputed whenever the attribute is accessed. IDL is an *abstract specification* capable of being mapped onto a myriad of representations.

A declaration for a node, termed an *attribute production*, consists of the name of the node followed by a "=>", and a list of zero or more comma-separated attribute-type pairs which end with a semicolon. The syntax for declaring a node is given below.

⟨node name⟩ '=>' { ⟨attribute name⟩ ':' ⟨type⟩
    { ',' ⟨attribute name⟩ ':' ⟨type⟩ }* }? ';'

The ordering of the attributes within a node is not significant. Names for nodes and attributes and for any other named IDL objects are contiguous sequences of letters, digits, and the underscore character "_". The first

2.1. THE IDL SPECIFICATION

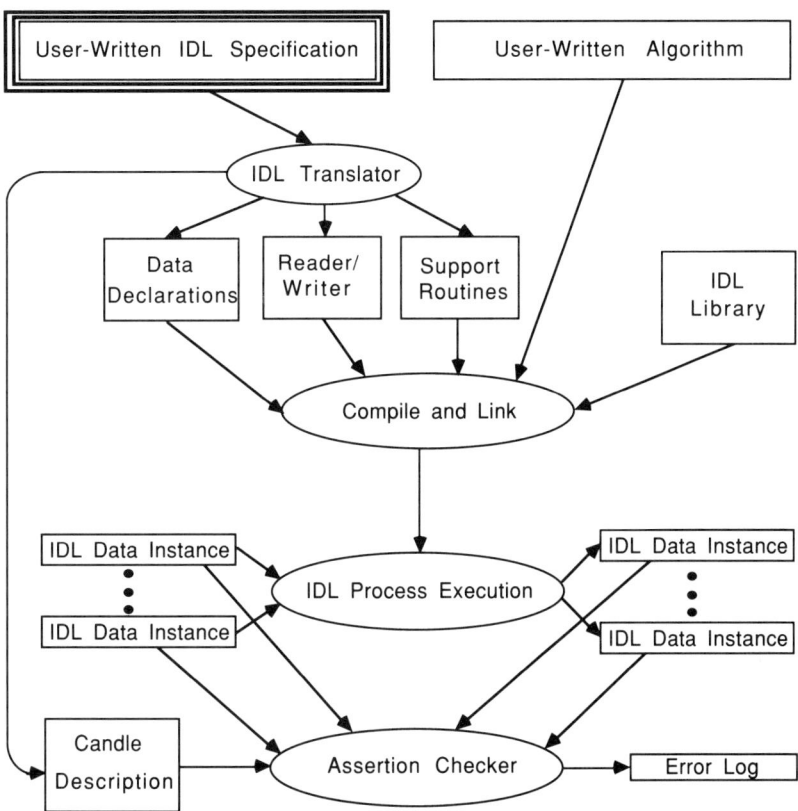

Figure 2.2: The Specification Step

```
commercial_customer  => industry_code:  Integer;
state_customer       => state_code:     Integer;
federal_customer     => agency_code:    Integer;
bill                 => amount:         Rational;
```

Figure 2.3: A Node Type Declaration

character must be a letter or an underscore; case is significant. All characters in a name are considered significant. All IDL keywords (introduced below) are reserved and must be spelled exactly as they appear; case is not significant for keywords. The various parts of a declaration may be separated by any amount of white space, that is, blanks, tabs, and newline characters.

An attribute's *type* specifies the domain of values that the attribute can hold. IDL provides four *basic types* and two kinds of *structured types*. The IDL keywords Boolean, Integer, Rational, and String name the basic types. Booleans can have values True and False. Integers are theoretically unbounded; all implementations have a practical limit. Rationals are technically fractions with integral numerator and denominator; this definition encompasses conventional floating point representations such as Pascal's real and C's float, as well as the fixed point types of PL/1 and Ada. A String is a sequence of characters. Some languages such as C support them directly; in others, such as Pascal, they are often represented as records. The attribute productions given in Figure 2.3 specifies four nodes, each with one attribute. The first three describe various kinds of customers: commercial companies, state agencies, and federal agencies. The last node describes a bill to be sent to a customer.

IDL provides two kinds of structured types, indicated by the keywords Set Of and Seq Of. A Set Of ⟨type⟩ is an unordered collection of objects of ⟨type⟩. Here, ⟨type⟩ stands for any valid attribute type, other than sets or sequences. Duplication of objects is not permitted within a set. A Seq Of ⟨type⟩ is an ordered collection (sequence) of objects of ⟨type⟩. Duplication of objects *is* allowed in a sequence. The IDL system automatically supplies a collection of runtime support routines to manipulate sets and sequences consistent with their expected behavior.

The bill_list node contains one attribute, a sequence of nodes of type bill:

```
bill_list => list:  Seq of bill;
```

As with the basic types and nodes, there are many possible representations

2.1. THE IDL SPECIFICATION

for sets and sequences, from mundane ones such as arrays and linked lists to more interesting ones such as threaded sequences, where an attribute in the node is used as a pointer (perhaps abstractly, say through a hash table) to the next node of the set or sequence. Whatever the representation, appropriate support routines are provided.

Nodes may be declared without any attributes. The following definition of `local_sales_tax` is an example of such a node.

```
local_sales_tax => ;
```

We will see the utility of such nodes later.

In addition to the four basic and two structured types supplied by IDL, an attribute may have a node or class (defined below) declared as its type. An attribute with a type that is the name of a node has a value that is a reference to a node of that type. Nodes may be self-referential through their attributes.

Attributes within the same node must have different names. Attributes in different node types may share identical names without conflict. Attributes with the same name that appear in different node types may even have different types.

Classes

An attribute of a *class* type can hold a reference to one of a set of nodes or other classes. The nodes or other classes that a class attribute can refer to are called its *members*. A class is used to state some common aspect of its members, such as the fact that all contain a particular attribute. As with nodes, there are a great many ways to represent classes. Possible implementations of IDL classes are Pascal variant `record`s, C `union`s, and Simula-2 and Smalltalk classes.

A declaration of a class, termed a *class production*, consists of the name of the new class followed by a "::=" and a list of one or more node or other class names separated by alternation signs, "|", and ending with a semicolon.

⟨class name⟩ '::=' { ⟨class name⟩ | ⟨node name⟩ }
            { '|' { ⟨class name⟩ | ⟨node name⟩ } }* ';'

There is no significance to the ordering of the nodes and classes on the right-hand side of a declaration. Restrictions on classes will be discussed below.

As Figure 2.4 illustrates, `Customer` is a class with two members, a `commercial_customer` node and a `Government_customer` class. The Gov-

```
Customer            ::= commercial_customer
                      | Government_customer;

Government_customer ::= state_customer | federal_customer;
```

Figure 2.4: A Class Declaration

ernment_customer class is declared to have two members, a state_customer node and a federal_customer node, which we have seen before.

The members of a class that are listed in its declaration are said to be *direct class members*. In the example above, the commercial_customer node and the Government_customer class are the direct class members of the Customer class. These are not the only members of the Customer class, however. Through a process call *class membership inheritance*, the members of the Government_customer class are also considered to be members of the Customer class. This process of membership inheritance repeats indefinitely. The members of a class that are inherited through other classes in this manner are said to be *indirect class members* of the class.

The class membership tree for the example in Figure 2.4 is as follows.

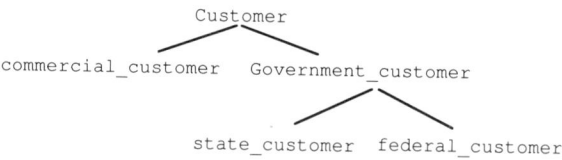

The interior branches are the Customer and Government_customer classes and the leaves are the commercial_customer, state_customer, and federal_customer nodes. The Government_customer class in this figure has the state_customer and federal_customer nodes as its only members.

An attribute of a node may have a type that is a class declared elsewhere. An example is shown below.

```
bill => billee: Customer;
```

Classes can also be used in sets and sequences, as shown below.

```
customer_list => list: Seq Of Customer;
```

When all the direct or indirect class member nodes of a particular class share one or more attributes, you should assign the shared attributes to all of the direct or indirect class member nodes simultaneously through the

2.1. THE IDL SPECIFICATION

class rather than making assignments of the common attributes to each of those nodes individually. In this way, similarities among the member nodes are clearly stated, and unintentional differences are avoided. More importantly, the assertion language and some target language implementations of IDL, including the C and Pascal interfaces to be discussed shortly, will not allow attributes of variables of a class type to be accessed or shared unless the attribute is associated with that class, or with a class of which it is a member.

The syntax for assigning attributes to all direct and indirect class member nodes through a class, also termed an *attribute production*, is given below.

⟨class_name⟩ '=>' { ⟨attribute_name⟩ ':' ⟨type⟩
    { ',' ⟨attribute_name⟩ ':' ⟨type⟩ }* }? ';'

Examples of attributes declared for classes and for nodes are given below.

```
Customer => name:             String,
            address:          String,
            active:           Boolean,
            customer_number   Integer,
            balance:          Rational;
```

The `name`, `address`, `active`, `customer_number`, and `balance` attributes are assigned to `commercial_customer`, `state_customer`, and `federal_customer` nodes through the `Customer` class. These attributes propagate through the `Government_customer` class to the `state_customer` and `federal_customer` nodes. In this form, it is easy to see how the `commercial_customer`, `state_customer`, and `federal_customer` nodes are similar and how they differ. Also, if another node is added to the `Customer` class, it will automatically inherit the `name`, `address`, `active`, `customer_number`, and `balance` attributes.

IDL allows a node or class to be declared all in one place or for its declaration to be split into several parts. The effect of a multipart declaration is cumulative. The attributes of the `Customer` class node declared in Figure 2.3, for example, could have been declared in two different places as in the following example.

```
Customer => name:              String,
            address:           String;
Customer => active:            Boolean,
            customer_number:   Integer,
            balance:           Rational;
```

The effective declaration of the Customer class is the union of both declaration "pieces." The parts of a node or class declaration may be grouped in the order that enhances clarity.

Structures

All node and class declarations in an IDL specification are grouped into named collections termed *structures*. A declaration of a structure starts with the keyword Structure followed by the structure's name, then by the identification of a node or class as its root introduced by the keyword Root, and then by a list of the one or more node and class declarations between the keywords Is and End (the more complicated derived and refined structures will be discussed in Sections 2.1.1 and 4.1.5, respectively).

> Structure ⟨structure name⟩ { Root ⟨type⟩ }$^?$ Is
>   { ⟨node or class declaration⟩ }*
> End

Within a structure, the ordering of the node and class declarations is not significant; node and class declarations may be listed without regard to forward references.

The declarations concerning customers are collected in a structure in Figure 2.5.

A second example of a structure specification is shown in Figure 2.6. A structure named transactions is declared in this example consisting of two classes, Transaction and Tax_code, and six nodes, transaction_list, credit, debit, local_sales_tax, state_sales_tax, and federal_sales_tax. The credit and debit nodes have identical attributes, customer_number, date, amount, and tax_status, which have been inherited through the Transaction class. The local_sales_tax, state_sales_tax and federal_sales_tax nodes are examples of unattributed nodes. The transaction_list node has been specified as the root of the structure.

Structure Writing Details

Just as the node defines a scope for the names of its attributes, the structure defines a scope for the names of its nodes and classes. The names of different nodes and classes within the same structure must be different. Only those nodes and classes that have been declared within a structure may be referenced as attribute types within that structure.

2.1. THE IDL SPECIFICATION

```
Structure customers Root customer_list Is

   customer_list       =>  list:             Seq Of Customer;

   Customer            ::= commercial_customer
                        |  Government_customer;
   Customer            =>  name:             String,
                           address:          String,
                           active:           Boolean,
                           customer_number:  Integer,
                           balance:          Rational;

   commercial_customer =>  industry_code:    Integer;

   Government_customer ::= state_customer
                        |  federal_customer;

   state_customer      =>  state_code:       Integer;

   federal_customer    =>  agency_code:      Integer;
End
```

Figure 2.5: The customers Structure

```
Structure transactions Root transaction_list Is
    transaction_list  =>  list:              Seq Of Transaction;

    Transaction           ::= credit | debit;
    Transaction           =>  customer_number: Integer,
                              date:            Integer,
                              amount:          Rational,
                              tax_status:      Set Of Tax_code;

    credit                =>  ;
    debit                 =>  ;

    Tax_code              ::= local_sales_tax
                              | state_sales_tax
                              | federal_sales_tax;
    local_sales_tax       =>  ;
    state_sales_tax       =>  ;
    federal_sales_tax     =>  ;
End
```

Figure 2.6: The transactions Structure

2.1. THE IDL SPECIFICATION

All nodes and classes must be *reachable* from the root node or class of the structure (the two exceptions are the invariant structure of a process, discussed in Section 4.2.3, and intermediate structures participating in a derivation, to be discussed shortly). It must be possible to trace a path from the root node or class type to all other node and class types declared in the structure. A path is traced through a node to other nodes and classes via the attributes of the original node that have a type that is another node or class. A path is traced through a class to other nodes and classes via its direct class member nodes or classes. For example, in Figure 2.6, the `Transaction` class is reachable directly from the `transaction_list` node through the type of its `list` attribute. The `credit` and `debit` nodes are then indirectly reachable from the `transaction_list` node through the `Transaction` class.

The concept of a path in this context differs from that discussed in the section on classes with regards to class membership. In determining class membership, only those paths that we can trace through direct and indirect class membership are of interest. For deciding reachability, however, one may consider paths traced through either attribute types or class membership or through a combination of both. The reachability requirement guards against spelling mistakes, missing class membership declarations, and missing attribute declarations.

At runtime, the root of a structure serves much like the root of a tree. Instances of the IDL-specified data structures, whether internal to a program or on external storage, consist of an instance of the root node or class with instances of one or more of the other nodes or classes attached. The attachments of the other nodes or classes to the root are made through the attributes. For example, an actual instance of the `transactions` structure specified in Figure 2.6 would consist of a single instance of the `transaction_list` node with an attached list of zero or more instances of members of the `Transaction` class, either `credits` or `debits`. The node or class that is named as the root is used as a handle to the rest of the data structure.

At this point, it may appear to the reader to be a difficult task to determine from a specification the objects within a structure that are nodes and the objects that are classes. However, differentiating nodes and classes can be easily done. The classes within a structure are those objects that appear on the left-hand side of at least one class production no matter how many times they may appear on the left-hand side of class productions. The nodes within a structure are those objects that appear on the left-hand side of one or more attribute productions. Appearances of classes on the left-hand side of class productions, if there are any, are attribute assignments to its member nodes.

```
             Structure bills Root bill_list From customers Is

               Without customer_list;
                   Customer => active;
                   Customer => balance;

               bill_list    => list:   Seq Of bill;

               bill         => billee: Customer,
                               amount: Rational;
             End
```

Figure 2.7: An Example of Structure Derivation

Derivation

Derivation allows a new data structure to be declared in terms of one or more previously declared data structures, and makes the relationships between different data structures clearer. It also avoids multiple copies of the same information and the attendant problems in keeping all copies consistent with one another. A set of declarations may be recorded in just one place, with derivation and refinement used to declare related data structures. In declaring a derived structure, the node and class declarations from several structures may be copied, and then node types, class types, members to class types, attributes to node types, or attributes to class types can be added or deleted. An example of the usefulness of derivation is the bills data structure, shown in Figure 2.7.

In this example, the derivation of the bills data structure from the customers data structure is signaled by the IDL keyword *From*. The three statements beginning with the IDL keyword *Without* delete parts of the customers data structure. The first *Without* statement deletes the customer_list node from the new data structure entirely. The next two delete the active and balance attributes of the node members of the Customer class. The two attribute productions add the bill_list and bill nodes to the new data structure. Note how the relationship between the customers and bills data structures is shown.

2.1.2 Specifying the Processes

A *process* is the IDL model for a computation. An instance of a process reads and writes instances of IDL-specified data structures to and from

2.1. THE IDL SPECIFICATION

main memory through a collection of ports. Each process has a master data structure, called the *invariant*, that is the union of all data structures used in that process.

Ports

A *port* is an association between an IDL-specified data structure and a name for the IDL-supplied implementation of the routines for reading or writing that structure to or from a process. There are two kinds of ports: *Pre* ports for input of instances of the associated data structure and *Post* ports for output. The declaration of a port consists of the type of port followed by a comma-separated list of (port name, structure name) pairs. The list ends with a semicolon.

>   *Pre* ⟨port name⟩ ':' ⟨structure name⟩
>   { ',' ⟨port name⟩ ':' ⟨structure name⟩ }* ';'
>   *Post* ⟨port name⟩ ':' ⟨structure name⟩
>   { ',' ⟨port name⟩ ':' ⟨structure name⟩ }* ';'

An example will be given below.

Processes

Processes are analogous to C programs. An instance of a process reads zero or more instances of IDL-specified data structures from external storage or another process, performs some computation on its inputs, and writes out instances of zero or more new or transformed IDL-specified data structures to external storage or another process. Figure 1.2 illustrated this model of a process. The process declaration specifies the name of the process, the names of the collection of IDL-specified data structures read and written by an instance of the process, and the target language for the process. The IDL declaration does not describe the manipulation of the data structures performed during the computation.

A declaration of a process starts with the IDL keyword *Process* followed by the process's name, then by a list of the declarations of the ports used by the process that begins with the IDL keyword *Is* and ends with the IDL keyword *End*.

>   *Process* ⟨process name⟩ *Is*
>   { ⟨process statement⟩ }*
>   *End*

```
Process billing_process Is
  Pre customers_in:     customers;
  Pre transactions_in:  transactions;
  Post customers_out:   customers;
  Post bills_out:       bills;
End
```

Figure 2.8: A Process Declaration

An example of a process declaration is shown in Figure 2.8. The more complicated refined process is discussed below.

In this example, a process named `billing_process` is declared. This process has two *Pre* ports named `customers_in` and `transactions_in` that read instances of the `customers` and `transactions` data structures, respectively, and two *Post* ports named `customers_out` and `bills_out` that write instances of the `customers` and `bills` data structures, respectively.

This process reads in two data structures, creates a new data structure, and writes out the new data structure and a modified version of one of the data structures it read in. The `transactions` data structure is discarded after being processed. Many other combinations of input and output behavior of structures are possible. In the next chapter we will see an example of a process that reads in a single data structure, modifies it, and writes out the modified data structure.

Within a process declaration, each port name must differ from all other port names referred to within that process. There may be any number of *Pre* or *Post* port declaration sequences within the same process declaration as in Figure 2.8. The order of port declarations within a process is not significant.

An instance of an IDL-specified process may perform input or output other than that specified in the process specification. The process specification only captures the I/O behavior of the process concerning reading and writing instances of IDL-specified data structures.

Target Languages

IDL supports several *target languages*, that is, languages in which the process is implemented. The external form of an instance can be language-independent, allowing it to be written by a process implemented in one language and read by a second process implemented in a different language. The syntax for specifying the target language is shown below.

2.1. THE IDL SPECIFICATION

> *Target Language* ⟨language name⟩ ' ; '

Related constructs allow one to specify the operating system, machine, and even the version of the runtime system.

Imported Structures and Processes

When a specification includes several structure and/or process declarations, it is often convenient to place these structures and processes in separate files to permit sharing. To access a specification in one file with a second file, the Import clause is used.

> *Import* ⟨name⟩ { ' , ' ⟨name⟩ }* *From* ⟨file name⟩ *End*

The name(s) identify structures or processes to be found in the indicated file.

Refined Processes

A process may be *refined* from another process through the *Refines* clause. The refined process inherits all ports from its ancestor process. A target language and/or target language version may be specified in the refined process (other aspects can also be added; these will be covered in Chapter 4).

C Target Language

In the specification in Figure 2.9, the billing_process (and all the structures and processes it depends on, i.e., customers, transactions, and bills) is extracted from the **billingproc.idl** file (the suffix ".idl" is appended automatically). billing differs from billing_process only in that a target language and target language version has been specified. Version B specifies that additional macros should be generated by the IDL translator; these macros will be discussed in Section 2.2.2.

Pascal Target Language

The specification for the Pascal target language is shown in Figure 2.10. billing_process (and all the structures and processes it depends on, i.e., customers, transactions, and bills) is extracted from the **billingproc.idl** file (the suffix ".idl" is appended automatically). billing differs from billing_process only in that a target language and target language

```
-- file: billing/C/billing.idl

Import billing_process From billingproc End

Process billing Refines billing_process Is
    Target Language C;
    Target Language Version B;
End
```

Figure 2.9: The billing Process in C

```
-- file: billing/Pascal/billing.idl

Import billing_process From billingproc End

Process billing Refines billing_process Is
    Target Language Pascal;
    Target Language Version B;
End
```

Figure 2.10: The billing Process in Pascal

version has been specified. Version B specifies that additional functions should be generated; these functions will be discussed in Section 2.2.3.

2.1.3 Specifying the Assertions

IDL permits assertions to be made concerning IDL structures and the values of attributes within those structures. A program called IDLCHECK can then automatically check the validity of these assertions on particular structure instances. Assertions can be associated with structures and with processes.

The Purpose of Assertions

The assertion language is meant to provide both specification and verification facilities to IDL.

As a specification language, the assertions provide a means for the programmer to specify precisely what is true about the data structures speci-

2.1. THE IDL SPECIFICATION

fied in IDL. Using the assertion language improves communication between members of a programming team or between future and present programmers. Maintenance of large programs is eased, since the maintainer may look at the assertions to ascertain exactly what is done by the program, rather than attempting to determine this by directly reading code or comments (which are often sparse, incomplete, and imprecise). In addition, writing assertions serves to hone the programmer's thinking about a particular problem, since writing assertions requires a thorough understanding of the tasks being performed. Finally, the assertions provide a guide to the writing of the code. Assertions are given in terms of the IDL structures. Programming in the IDL system involves manipulating instances of these structures. Thus, well written assertions state precisely what changes of the IDL instances must be performed by the code.

As a verification language, assertions provide a debugging aid. Once the assertions are written, instances of data structures can be checked automatically to ensure that they satisfy their assertions.

Basic Assertions With Quantifiers

Assertions begin with the keyword `Assert`, preceded by an optional name for the assertion. The simplest assertions to make concern the values of specified attributes within a structure. These assertions may appear anywhere within the structure to which they refer, although it is often clearer to group assertions with the declarations of the nodes and classes to which they refer. Assertions can be made about a property of a single object or a property that should hold for many objects. For example, to assert in the `customers` structure that the customer list is not empty, we would write

```
-- There is at least one customer
Assert Size(Root.list) ~= 0;
```

`Root` refers to the root of the structure in which the assertion appears. Here, the root of the `customers` structure is of type `customer_list`. Thus, `Root.list` is a sequence of `Customer`. The symbol "`~=`" means "not equal to." The assertion states that the size of this sequence is not zero. This example also illustrates an IDL comment, which is preceded by the characters "`--`" and which extends to the end of the line.

Often one wishes to make an assertion about all objects of a certain type. *Quantifiers* may be used to accomplish this task. There are two quantifiers in the language. The `ForAll` variant asserts that the body is true for all objects of the specified type. For example, we might wish to make some assertions about the `customers` structure. First, all customer numbers should be greater than or equal to 1. A negative customer number would signify an input error. We would assert this constraint as

Assert ForAll C *In* Customer *Do* C.customer_number >= 1 *Od*;

The name C is an *iterator* which will take on successive values of the specified object type, which here is Customer. The body of the quantifier states that the customer_number attribute of C (C is of type Customer) is greater than or equal to 1. The period (".") denotes the extraction of an attribute. (This usage parallels the "=>" symbol in the IDL specification.) Since the *ForAll* variant is used, we are asserting that the customer_number attribute of all objects of type Customer have the described property.

The *Exists* variant asserts that the body is true for at least one object of the specified type. For example, to assert that at least one customer is active, we would write

Assert Exists C *In* Customer *Do* C.active *Od*;

The body of a quantifier, whether *ForAll* or *Exists*, is a boolean expression. Despite the use of the *Do...Od* form, nothing is *done*. We are asserting what must be true. The type of the iterator, specified immediately after the keyword *In*, must be a valid type in the IDL specification. A valid type is any node or class name (but not attribute name) or a basic type (*Integer*, *Rational*, *String*, *Seq Of* ⟨type⟩, or *Set Of* ⟨type⟩).

Boolean operators such as *And*, *Or*, and *Not* may be used. For example, we wish to assert that the state_code of every state_customer is between 1 and 50, inclusive. We could write

Assert ForAll sc *In* state_customer *Do*
    sc.state_code >= 1 *And* sc.state_code <= 50
Od;

Nesting of quantifiers is allowed. For example, we wish to assert that no two distinct customers have the same customer number, to avoid confusing bills and credits. We would assert the following.

    -- *No duplicate customer numbers*
    Assert ForAll c1 *In* Customer *Do*
        ForAll c2 *In* Customer *Do*
            If c1 ~= c2
            Then c1.customer_number ~= c2.customer_number
            Else True Fi
    Od Od;

2.1. THE IDL SPECIFICATION

The two iteration identifiers must be distinct when using nested quantifiers. Here the names used are c1 and c2. *Od* appears twice at the end; each occurrence of a quantifier must end with its own *Od*.

Similar assertions on attribute values might be made in the **transactions** structure and the **bills** structure. For instance, we could assert in the **transactions** structure

-- All transactions contain a valid customer number
Assert ForAll t *In* Transaction *Do* t.customer_number >= 1 *Od*;

In the **bills** structure, we might wish to be certain that the amount of all bills is positive. We could then assert in the **bills** structure

   Assert ForAll b *In* bill *Do* b.amount > 0 *Od*;

The assertion language supplies a few built-in functions which are useful. The function *Size* was used above. It returns the number of objects in a set, sequence, or collection (described below) or the number of characters in a string. Other functions will be introduced below. String constants are characters enclosed within quotes. For example, we wish to be certain that an important customer named IBM is in our customer list. We would then assert

-- IBM is a customer
IBMExists *Assert Exists* C *In* Customer *Do* C.name = "IBM" *Od*;

This example also illustrates an optional name for the assertion, here "IBMExists".

Assertions Within Processes

The above assertions concern particular structures. They are thus placed inside the structure to which they refer. It is also possible to make assertions within process specifications. In this way, one can make assertions about the relation of output structures to input structures.

For example, in the process **billing** defined in Section 2.1.2, there is an instance of the **customers** structure read in and an instance of the **customers** structure written out. The information within these instances should remain unaltered, except perhaps for the balance attribute of **Customer**. We could assert this consistency constraint as follows (within the process specification).

```
Assert ForAll c_in In customers_in:Customer Do
    ForAll c_out In customers_out:Customer Do
        If c_in.customer_number = c_out.customer_number
        Then c_in.name = c_out.name And
            c_in.address = c_out.address And
            c_in.active = c_out.active
        Else True Fi
    Od Od;
```

The specified iterator types (Customer) in the above quantifiers are prefixed with a port name followed by a colon. The prefix specifies the name of the port associated with the structure instance the assertion is referring to. In the above example, the first quantifier is referring to all objects of type Customer in the structure associated with the port named customer_in. The second quantifier is referring to all objects of type Customer in the structure associated with the port named Customer_out. These structures must both contain the type specified (here, Customer). The use of these *port prefixes* is allowed only in an assertion within a process specification, since structure specifications do not have ports. Clearly, a port with the name specified in the prefix should exist if the assertion is to make sense.

In the last example the balance attribute was not mentioned, because this attribute may be legitimately altered due to transactions being processed. In addition, the industry_code, state_code, and agency_code attributes were not mentioned. These should remain unaltered also, but they are not attributes of the entire class Customer. They are attributes of particular node members of that class. Thus statements about them cannot be made within the context of the entire class. For example, to assert

```
Assert ForAll c In Customer Do  -- Bad Assertion!
    c.customer_number > 0 And
    c.industry_code > 0 Od;
```

would result in a compile-time typing error, because c is of type Customer, which does not necessarily have an industry_code attribute. If one wishes to make an assertion about such an attribute, one must write an assertion specifically targeted toward that class of node containing the attribute. For example, we could assert

```
Assert ForAll cc_in In customers_in:commercial_customer Do
    ForAll cc_out In customers_out:commercial_customer Do
        If cc_in.customer_number = cc_out.customer_number
        Then cc_in.industry_code = cc_out.industry_code
        Else True Fi
    Od Od;
```

2.1. THE IDL SPECIFICATION

Since commercial_customer is a member of the Customer class, we can refer to the customer_number attribute of cc_in and cc_out which are of type Customer. Since we have specified cc_in and cc_out as type commercial_customer, we can now also refer to an industry_code attribute. Similar assertions could be made about the state_code for objects of type state_customer and the agency_code for objects of type federal_customer.

As another example, we can assert that every transaction refers to an existing customer.

```
-- Each transaction refers to an existing customer
Assert ForAll t In transactions_in:.Transaction Do
    Exists c In customers_in:Customer Do
        t.customer_number = c.customer_number
    Od Od;
```

Assertions can get more complicated than the examples above. To simplify the formation of these assertions, the assertion language allows one to create definitions, and then use these definitions in assertions.

Value-returning Definitions

The simplest kind of definition returns a value. For example, we wish to assert that the balance of a customer on output from our billing process is equal to the balance the customer had on input plus any credit received through transactions. The total credit a customer receives is the sum of all credit transactions for that customer. This analysis suggests creating a definition that will take a customer and the list of transactions and return the total amount of credit for that customer. Such a definition would then be used in the assertion we wish to make about the customer's balance. The definition could take the following form:

```
Define Total_Credit(c: Customer, TList: Seq Of Transaction) =
    If Size(TList) = 0 Then 0
    OrIf Head(TList).customer_number = c.customer_number
        And Head(TList) Is credit
    Then Head(TList).amount + Total_Credit(c,Tail(TList))
    Else Total_Credit(c,Tail(TList))
    Fi;
```

The keyword *Define* introduces a definition. The definition takes two arguments. The first is of type Customer and the second is a sequence of Transaction. If the size of the transaction sequence is 0, then there are no transactions. The definition then returns 0. Otherwise, if the transaction at the head of the sequence has the same customer number as the customer, meaning that this transaction deals with this customer, and the transaction is of type `credit`, we add the amount of this transaction to the total credit of the remaining transactions (the `Tail` function returns the sequence that is the argument without its head). If the transaction does not concern this particular customer or the transaction is not a credit, then we return the total credit of the remaining transactions only.

The definition of `Total_Credit` is recursive. It is guaranteed to terminate since the definition is applied to a smaller collection each time it is called (the `Tail` of a sequence is always smaller than the sequence itself, if the sequence is nonempty), and the definition does not call itself when an empty sequence (of size 0) is encountered.

In this definition, `OrIf` was used. The `OrIf` form is a shorthand which is recommended. Every use of `If` must be ended with a `Fi`. Use of `OrIf` does not require a preceding `Fi`. Thus `OrIf` is preferable to `Else If`.

With this definition in hand, we can now make the assertion that the balance of a customer at output is the balance the customer had at input plus any credit received.

```
-- All customers are properly credited.
ProperCredit Assert ForAll c_out In customers_out:Customer Do
     ForAll c_in In customers_in:Customer Do
         If c_in.customer_number = c_out.customer_number
         Then c_out.balance = c_in.balance +
             Total_Credit(c_in, transactions_in:Root.list)
         Else True Fi
     Od Od;
```

The meaning of the above assertion should be clear except for two points. First, note the *Else True*. Every *If* clause must have an *Else* clause attached. If the customer numbers are not equal, then the program is fine. So we assert *True* in the *Else* clause (sometimes it makes sense to assert *False*). Second, the reserved word *Root* was used. Here, the port prefix `transactions_in` specifies that we mean the root of the structure associated with the port `transactions_in`, which is the `transactions` structure. The root of this structure is of type `transaction_list`. This type has an attribute of type *Seq Of* Transaction. That is why the *Root*.list is specified as an argument. This dotted expression has type *Seq Of* Transaction since the specified root has an attribute called `list` which has this type.

As another example of the use of definitions, we can use a definition to help us assert that the number of bills generated equals the number of debit transactions. We can create a definition that will return the number of debit transactions.

2.1. THE IDL SPECIFICATION

```
Define Num_debits(TList: Seq Of Transaction) =
    If Size(Tlist) = 0 Then 0
    OrIf Type(Head(TList)) Is debit
    Then 1 + Num_debits(Tail(TList))
    Else Num_debits(Tail(TList)) Fi;
```

With this definition, we can now assert

```
Assert Size(bills_out:Root.list)
       = Num_debits(transactions_in:Root.list);
```

Assertions may often be written in several ways. For instance, the above assertion could have been written without using the Num_debits definition.

```
Assert Size(bills_out:Root.list)
       = Size(transactions_in:debit);
```

Collection-returning Definitions

Definitions may also return *collections* of objects. A collection is similar to an IDL set, differing in three important ways. First, an attribute may have an IDL set as a value, but may not have a collection as a value. Second, an IDL set is declared explicitly using "*Set Of*"; a collection is determined implicitly by the IDL translator. Finally, collections exist only within assertions.

We have already used collections. In one of the earlier assertions,

`Assert ForAll C In Customer Do C.customer_number >= 1 Od;`

Customer is actually an expression denoting the collection of all nodes belonging to the Customer class. Any expression evaluating to a collection may be used in a quantifier.

One may define a collection of objects and then make assertions about the objects in the collection. For example, we wish to assert that a bill is generated for each debit transaction. First we can define a definition that returns the collection of all objects that are debit transactions. Then we can assert that there exists a bill for each of these transactions.

```
Define Debits(TList: Seq Of Transaction) =
    If Size(TList) = 0 Then Empty
    OrIf Type(Head(TList)) Is debit
    Then Head(TList) Union Debits(Tail(TList))
    Else Debits(Tail(TList)) Fi;
```

The usual set operations (including *Union*, used above) are available to use with collections of objects that exist explicitly in the IDL structure specification or that are defined in the assertion language. If the transaction sequence is empty, the definition returns `Empty`, denoting the empty collection, or the collection of no objects. Returning 0 would not make sense in this context, since the definition is returning a collection of objects.

In fact, there is a cleaner, nonrecursive way of stating this constraint.

```
Define Debits(TList: Seq Of Transaction) =
    Members(TList) Intersect debit;
```

We may now make our assertion

```
-- A bill is generated for every debit transaction
Assert ForAll deb In Debits(transactions_in:Root.list) Do
    Exists b In Members(bills_out:Root.list) Do
        b.billee.customer_number = deb.customer_number
        And b.amount = deb.amount
    Od Od;
```

The above assertion makes use of the collection-returning definition, `Debits`. `b.billee` is of type `Customer`, and thus has an attribute named `customer_number`, and the reference to `b.billee.customer_number` is permitted. `Members` is a supplied function which takes a set or sequence (as here) and produces the collection containing all objects in that set or sequence. `Members` should be used to access the objects contained in a set or sequence, rather than manipulating the set or sequence as a single object.

With the `Debits` definition above, there is yet another way to assert that the number of bills equals the number of debit transactions.

```
Assert Size(bills_out:Root.list)
    = Size(Debits(transactions_in:Root.list));
```

2.2 Translating the Specification

The second step in using IDL is to translate the collection of data and process specifications with the IDL translator into declarations and runtime support routines in the target programming language. The runtime support routines will be tailored for manipulating target language versions of the declared data structures. Figure 2.11 shows this portion of the process of using the IDL system. Here, and throughout the book, we use the IDL Toolkit, introduced in Section 1.4, as a concrete example. All discussion of the commands to invoke the various tools, as well as information about the output produced by these tools, is necessarily specific to the IDL Toolkit,

2.2. TRANSLATING THE SPECIFICATION

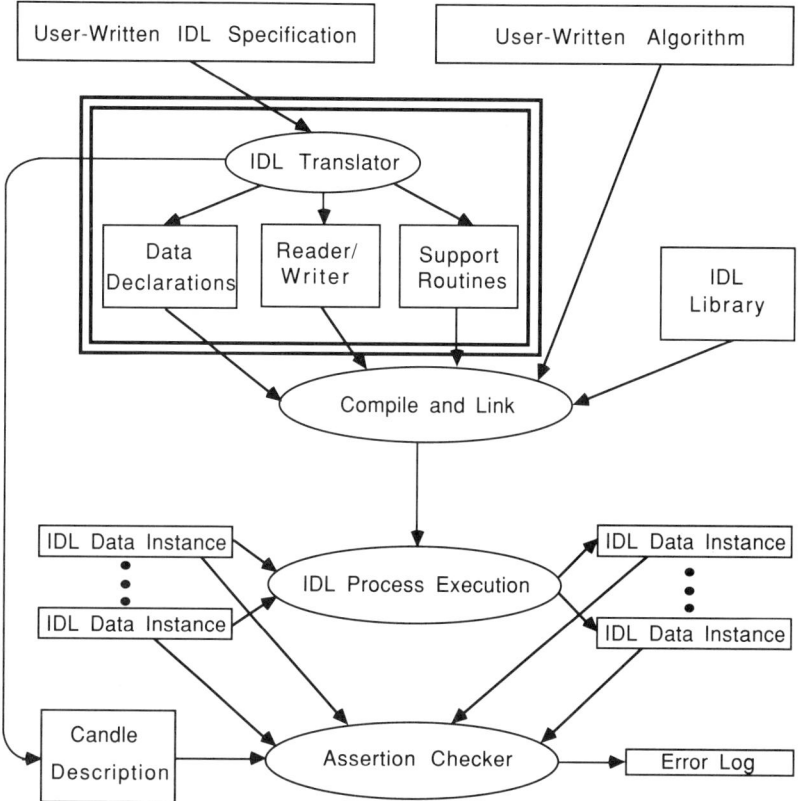

Figure 2.11: The Specification Translation Step

and to one operating system, Unix. Information available with the toolkit discusses how to run these tools under other operating systems.

2.2.1 Using the IDL Translator

To invoke the IDL translator, enter a command line of the following form.

   idlc { ⟨option⟩ }* ⟨file⟩ { ⟨file⟩ }*

The ⟨option⟩s portion of the command specifies zero or more options to change the default behavior of the translator. The list of one or more files contains the IDL structure and process specifications to be processed as a unit. Usually a single file is named, and related structure and process declarations found in other files are imported by that file.

By default, the IDL translator parses the input file or files and checks for syntactic and semantic correctness. For each process specification encountered, the IDL translator creates several files containing the declarations of the data types and the definitions of the process-specific code for the runtime support routines.

If the file(s) do not contain process specifications, the IDL translator will simply check the syntactic and semantic correctness of the specifications. Similarly, if additional structures are included in the collection that are not referred to by any process, they will be checked by the IDL translator for syntactic and semantic correctness.

2.2.2 The C Target Language

The algorithm is expressed in terms of the data declarations produced by the IDL translator. While programming, the tailored set of runtime support routines may be used to allocate new instances of data structures, to maintain sets and sequences, and to read and write them from main memory. The organization will follow that of Section 2.1.1. Chapter 7 discusses these aspects in greater detail. Pascal is also available as a target language, and is discussed in the next section.

For each process specification encountered, the IDL translator creates two files: a "⟨process name⟩.h" file containing the declarations of the data types and a "⟨process name⟩.c" file containing the definitions of process-specific code for the runtime support routines. If Version B is specified, the additional macros are placed in a "⟨process name⟩**Macros.h**" file. At the end of the generation of the ".h" and ".c" files, the IDL translator compiles each ".c" file with the C compiler into a ".o" file and deletes the ".c" files. Several options exist for changing the default behavior.

As an example, to process the specification developed so far, enter the command shown below.

```
idlc -v -C billing.Cdl billing.idl
```

In response to this command, the IDL translator creates the **billing.h**, **billingMacros.h**, and **billing.c** files (since the process was named billing) and then compiles **billing.c** into **billing.o**. After the compilation, **billing.c** is deleted. The -v option requests messages from the IDL translator indicating what it is doing, and the -C option instructs the IDL translator to produce an output file, **billing.Cdl**, which will be shown to be of use in Section 2.6.

2.2. TRANSLATING THE SPECIFICATION

The Data Declarations

The "⟨process⟩.h" file produced by the IDL translator is usually long and repetitious. However, with a little experience you need not look at the contents of the file to use the declarations contained in it. Each IDL construct is mapped into a C declaration in a consistent fashion: all names follow the convention of a capital letter followed by the identifier. Appendix C lists the meaning of all the single letter prefixes. We will give the names for the various identifiers declared in **billing.h** and **billingMacros.h**, but will not examine their definitions. Chapter 7 discusses the internal representation in C at length.

Basic Types and Nodes

IDL constructs are mapped to a combination of C declarations and macro and constant declarations. Nodes are mapped to C *struct*s, and their attributes are mapped to members of the *struct*. The basic types of *Integer* and *Rational* are mapped to the C types *int* and *float*. *Boolean* is mapped to *char*, taking on the values 0 (*False*) and 1 (*True*). *String* is mapped to String, a new type effectively encapsulating a pointer to a null-terminated character string. Finally, an initialization macro and a manifest constant specifying the type are defined. The node contains both direct and propagated attributes. Node references are represented as pointers to the appropriate *struct*. A second representation of unattributed nodes, as integers, is not used here.

For attributed nodes (e.g., state_customer), four identifiers are declared: the struct Rstate_customer, the pointer state_customer, the manifest constant Kstate_customer, and the initialization macro Nstate_customer. The manifest constant is returned by the typeof function, when given a particular node of that type. The initialization macro returns a reference to the node. The names of these constants, structs, pointers, and macros follow the convention described earlier.

Variables can be declared to be of a node type.

```
state_customer thisSC;
```

Such variables can then be initialized.

```
thisSC = Nstate_customer;
```

The typeof operator is not interesting when applied to expressions of a node type: typeof(thisSC) will always return Kstate_customer. However, it is useful with class variables.

An instance of a structure may form a graph by having nodes reference other nodes through attribute values. The structures defined in Section 2.1.1 are rather simple, in that the only node references are in lists. However, sharing is still possible in this example between structures. For instance, a `Customer` referenced in the `billee` attribute of a `bill` in the `bills` structure may be one of the `Customers` found on the list referenced by the `list` attribute of a `customer_list` in the `customers` structure (the algorithm discussed in Section 2.3 causes `Customer` nodes to be shared in this way).

Version B generates an macro for each attribute, direct or inherited, to access its value.

```
nameOfstate_customer
addressOfstate_customer
customer_numberOfstate_customer
activeOfstate_customer
balanceOfstate_customer
state_codeOfstate_customer
```

These macros, which all take a single argument of type `state_customer`, can be used on either side of an assignment statement.

```
if (balanceOfstate_customer(thisSC)==0)
    activeOfstate_customer(thisSC) = false;
```

Sets and Sequences

Sets and sequences have various representations, such as linked lists, binary trees, arrays, and bitvectors. Over a dozen macros specific to the sequence are defined for each sequence; sets are accompanied by similar macros. Each macro name is structured as a verb followed by the characters "SEQ" followed by the IDL identifier, say, "bill". The `initializeSEQbill` macro must be called before an attribute or variable of type *Seq Of* bill is accessed. The attribute or variable appears as the one argument of the macro. The `appendrearSEQbill` macro takes two arguments: an attribute or variable of type *Seq Of* bill, and an expression of type bill. The bill is added to the end of the sequence. Finally, the `foreachinSEQbill` macro is an iterator in the fashion of a `for` statement. It takes three arguments: a *Seq Of* bill to iterate over, a variable of type *Seq Of* bill used to keep track of the iteration, and a variable of type bill, which will be successively assigned a bill in the sequence. It is used in this way.

2.2. TRANSLATING THE SPECIFICATION

```
bill_list ABL;
SEQbill tempSEQbill;
bill abill;
...
foreachinSEQbill(listOfbill_list(ABL), tempSEQbill, abill) {
        /* do something with abill */
}
```

If the sequence `listOfbill_list(ABL)` contained five nodes, then "do something" would be executed five times, each with a different node referenced by `abill`.

Classes

Classes are mapped into C unions. For each class, an identifier, the name of the class, is declared.

Version B of the C target language provides macros that manipulate classes. These macros allow the full generality of classes to be used when programming in C. Attribute accessing macros are generated for each node and class. For example, the following macros are among those generated for the billing process.

```
activeOffederal_Customer
activeOfstate_Customer
activeOfcommercial_Customer
activeOfCustomer
```

Using these macros, inherited attributes are accessed identically to attributes associated directly with a node.

Attributes associated with subclasses are *not* directly available to variables of a class. Hence, the attribute `state_code` cannot be directly accessed through a variable of type `Customer`.

Version B also generates conversion macros, a subset of which follows.

```
state_customerToCustomer
state_customerToGovernment_customer
Government_customerToCustomer
```

The value returned by the `typeof` operator when applied to an expression of a class type, designating the specific node type actually present, can vary at runtime. To illustrate, we first create a class variable and two node variables.

```
Customer thisC;
state_customer thisSC;
federal_customer thisFC;
...
thisSC = Nstate_customer;
thisFC = Nfederal_customer;
```

When we assign a node to `thisC`

```
thisC = state_customerToCustomer(thisSC);
```

then `typeof(thisC)` will be `Kstate_customer`. However, after the following assignment:

```
thisC = federal_customerToCustomer(thisFC);
```

then `typeof(thisC)` will return `Kfederal_customer`.

The conversion macros presented thus far go "up" the class hierarchy, in that a node or class is converted into one of its superclasses. Macros are also generated to go the other way.

```
CustomerToGovernment_customer
Government_customerTostate_customer
CustomerTostate_customer
```

These macros must be used with caution. If the argument is not the target class (or node) type, an error routine will be invoked. One correct usage is written with an *if* statement. To access the `state_code` attribute, use

```
if (typeof(thisC)==Kstate_customer){
    ... state_codeOfstate_customer(
            CustomerTostate_customer(thisC)) ...
}
```

The if statement uses the `typeof` function to determine that the `Customer` referenced by the variable `thisCustomer` was indeed a `state_customer` node. Such a test is necessary to avoid a runtime error in `CustomerTostate_customer`. If the test succeeds, though, the node is first considered to be a `state_customer`, through the conversion macro, then the `state_code` attribute is accessed.

The conversion macros are also useful when calling routines expecting subclasses or superclasses of a given class. If a subclass (e.g., `state_customer`) is expected, a runtime type check is required. If a superclass is expected (an example is calling a routine expecting a `Government_customer`, passing a `federal_customer` as a parameter), the runtime type check is not required.

2.2. TRANSLATING THE SPECIFICATION

To pass the variable `thisCustomer` to a routine expecting a subclass, e.g.,

```
ProcessStateCustomer(aSC)
state_customer aSC;
```

use

```
if (typeof(thisC)==Kstate_customer)
    ProcessStateCustomer(CustomerTostate_customer(thisC));
```

To call a routine expecting a superclass, e.g.,

```
ProcessGovernment_customer(aGC)
Government_customer aGC;
```

with a variable of type `federal_customer`, the type test is not required.

```
federal_customer afc;
...
ProcessGovernment_customer(
            federal_customerToGovernment_customer(afc));
```

Classes are used as variable types in the C program. Only node instances exist in main memory. To illustrate, we first define two variables.

```
Customer ACustomer;
state_customer Astate_customer;
...
Astate_customer = Nstate_customer;
nameOfstate_customer(Astate_customer) = ...
```

Since `state_customer` is a subclass of `Customer`, the following assignment is valid:

```
ACustomer = state_customerToCustomer(Astate_customer);
```

and the following predicate would be true.

```
(typeof(ACustomer)==Kstate_customer)
```

However, in a later portion of the C code, a node instance of a different node type (say, a `federal_customer`) could be assigned to the variable `ACustomer`, and the predicate would then be false.

```
ACustomer = federal_customerToCustomer(thisFC);
```

Finally, the following assignment is not correct.

```
bill Abill;
...
ACustomer = billToCustomer(Abill);
```

The C compiler would flag it as an error, because `bill` is not a subclass of `Customer`. Declaring the `ACustomer` variable to be of type `Customer` effectively limits the nodes that can be assigned to that variable.

Processes

Each IDL process is mapped to a C program. The structures used by the process are mapped to *struct* and *union* declarations for that program. Ports are mapped to C functions. Input ports (*Pre*) are mapped to functions taking a file pointer and returning a node of the root type for the structure. Output ports (*Post*) are mapped to functions taking a file pointer and a node for the root of the structure instance. The four ports declared in Figure 2.8 on page 32 would be mapped to these declarations

```
transaction_list transactions_in(f);
FILE *f;
customer_list customers_in(f);
FILE *f;
void bills_out(f, n);
FILE *f;
bills n;
void customers_out(f, n);
FILE *f;
customers n;
```

2.2.3 The Pascal Target Language

Pascal is also available as a target language, and the IDL translator can produce declarations in Pascal. While programming, you can use the tailored set of runtime support routines to allocate new instances of data structures, to maintain sets and sequences, and to read and write them from main memory. The organization will follow that of Section 2.1.1. In Chapter 8 these aspects are discussed in greater detail.

For each process specification encountered, the IDL translator creates three files; a "⟨process name⟩.**h**" file containing the declarations of the data types, a "⟨process name⟩.**i**" file containing the signatures of routines generated by the translator, and a "⟨process name⟩.**p**" file containing the definitions of process-specific code for the runtime support routines. If

2.2. TRANSLATING THE SPECIFICATION 51

Version B is specified, the additional routines are placed in a "⟨process name⟩**Functions.h**" file. At the end of the generation of the ".**h**", ".**i**" and ".**p**" files, the IDL translator compiles each ".**p**" file with the Pascal compiler into a ".**o**" file and deletes the ".**p**" files. Several options exist for changing the default behavior.

As an example, to process the specification developed so far, enter the command shown below.

    idlc -v -C billing.Cdl billing.idl

In response to this command, the IDL translator creates the **billing.h**, **billing.i**, **billingFunctions.h**, and **billing.p** files (since the process was named **billing**) and then compiles **billing.p** into **billing.o**. After the compilation, **billing.p** is deleted. The -v option requests messages indicating what the IDL translator is doing and the -C option instructs the IDL translator to produce an output file **billing.Cdl**, which will be shown to be of use in Section 2.6.

The Data Declarations

The "⟨process⟩.**h**" file produced by the IDL translator is usually long and repetitious. However, with a little experience you need not look at the contents of the file to use the declarations contained in it. Each IDL construct is mapped into a Pascal declaration in a consistent fashion: all names follow the convention of a capital letter followed by the identifier. Appendix D lists the meaning of all the single-letter prefixes. We will give the names for the various identifiers declared in **billing.h**, **billing.i** and **billingFunctions.h**, but will not examine their definitions. Chapter 8 discusses the internal representation in Pascal at length.

Basic Types, Nodes, and Classes

IDL constructs are mapped to Pascal declarations. Nodes are mapped to Pascal *record*s, and their attributes are mapped to fields of the *record*. The basic types of Integer and Rational are mapped to the Pascal types of integer and real. Boolean is mapped to boolean. String is mapped to String, which is a new type effectively encapsulating a pointer to an array of characters. Nodes and classes are represented using variant *record*s. Finally, an initialization function and an integer constant specifying the type are defined for each node. Node references are represented as pointers to the appropriate *record*.

Four identifiers are declared for each node (e.g., statecustomer): the *record* Rstatecustomer, the pointer statecustomer, the constant

Kstatecustomer, and the initialization function Nstatecustomer (underscores are stripped from identifiers used in an IDL specification to form valid Pascal identifiers). The initialization function returns a reference to the node. The names of these constants, records, pointers, and routines follow the convention described above.

Variables can be declared with a node type.

>   var thisSC: statecustomer;

Such variables can then be initialized.

>   thisSC := Nstatecustomer;

An instance of a structure may form a graph by having nodes reference other nodes through attribute values. The structures defined in Section 2.1.1 are simple, in that the only node references are in lists. However, sharing is still possible in this example between structures. For instance, a Customer referenced in the billee attribute of a bill in the bills structure may be one of the Customers found on the list referenced by the list attribute of a customerlist in the customers structure (the algorithm discussed in Section 2.3 causes Customer nodes to be shared in this way).

Version B generates an function for each attribute, direct or inherited, to access its value.

>   nameOfstatecustomer
>   addressOfstatecustomer
>   customernumberOfstatecustomer
>   activeOfstatecustomer
>   balanceOfstatecustomer
>   statecodeOfstatecustomer

These functions, which all take a single argument of type statecustomer, can be used on either side of an assignment statement.

>   if balanceOfstatecustomer(thisSC) = 0
>   then activeOfstatecustomer(thisSC) := *false*;

Sets and Sequences

Sets and sequences have various representations, such as linked lists, arrays, binary tress, and bitvectors. Over a dozen routines specific to the sequence are also defined for each sequence; sets are accompanied by similar routines. Each routine name is structured as a verb followed by the characters "SEQ" followed by the IDL identifier, say, "bill." The initializeSEQbill procedure must be called before an attribute or variable of type *Seq Of* bill

2.2. TRANSLATING THE SPECIFICATION

is accessed. The attribute or variable appears as the one argument of the procedure. The `appendrearSEQbill` procedure takes two arguments: an attribute or variable of type `Seq Of bill`, and an expression of type `bill`. The `bill` is added to the end of the sequence. Finally, the `ithinSEQbill` takes as arguments an expression of type `Seq of bill` and an integer expression, and selects the `bill` whose position is specified by the integer.

Class Routines

Version B of the Pascal target language provides additional functions that manipulate classes. These functions allow the full generality of classes to be exploited when programming in Pascal. Attribute-accessing functions are generated for each node and class. For example, the following functions are among those generated for the `billing` process.

```
activeOffederalCustomer
activeOfstateCustomer
activeOfcommercialCustomer
activeOfCustomer
```

Using these functions, inherited attributes are accessed identically to attributes associated directly with a node.

Attributes associated with subclasses are *not* directly available to variables of a class. Hence, the attribute `statecode` cannot be directly accessed through a variable of type `Customer`.

Version B also generates conversion functions, a subset of which follows.

```
statecustomerToCustomer
statecustomerToGovernmentcustomer
GovernmentcustomerToCustomer
```

The value in the E⟨class name⟩ field in an expression of a class type, designating the specific member of the class actually present, can vary at runtime. To illustrate, we first create a class variable and two node variables.

```
var thisC: Customer;
    thisSC: statecustomer;
    thisCC: commercialcustomer;
...
thisSC := Nstatecustomer;
thisCC := Ncommercialcustomer;
```

When we assign a node to `thisC`.

```
thisC = statecustomerToCustomer(thisSC);
```

then thisC^.ECustomer will be KCustomerstatecustomer. However, after the following assignment:

```
thisC = commercialcustomerToCustomer(thisCC);
```

then thisC^.ECustomer will return KCustomercommercialcustomer.

The conversion functions presented thus far go "up" the class hierarchy, in that a node or class is converted into one of its superclasses. Functions are also generated to go the other way.

```
CustomerToGovernmentcustomer
GovernmentcustomerTostatecustomer
CustomerTostatecustomer
```

These functions must be used with caution. If the argument is not in fact the target class (or node) type, an error routine will be invoked. One correct usage is written with an *if* statement. To access the industrycode attribute, use

```
if thisC^.ECustomer = KCustomercommercialcustomer
then begin
   ... industrycodeOfcommercialcustomer(
           CustomerTocommercialcustomer(thisC)) ...
end
```

The if statement first determines that the Customer referenced by the variable thisCustomer was indeed a commercialcustomer node. Such a test is necessary to avoid a runtime error in CustomerTocommercialcustomer. If the test succeeds, though, the node is first considered to be a commercialcustomer, through the conversion function, then the industrycode attribute is accessed.

These conversion routines are also useful when calling routines expecting subclasses or superclasses of a given class. If a subclass (e.g., commercialcustomer) is expected, a runtime type check is required. If a superclass is expected (an example is calling a routine expecting a Governmentcustomer, passing a federalcustomer as a parameter), the runtime type check is not required.

To pass the variable thisCustomer to a routine expecting a subclass, e.g.,

procedure ProcessCommercialCustomer(aCC: commercialcustomer);

use

2.2. TRANSLATING THE SPECIFICATION

```
if thisC^.ECustomer = KCustomercommercialcustomer
then ProcessCommercialCustomer(
                CustomerTocommercialcustomer(thisC));
```

To call a routine expecting a superclass, e.g.,

```
procedure ProcessCustomer(aC: Customer);
```

with a variable of type commercialcustomer, the type test is not required.

```
var aCC: commercialcustomer;
...
ProcessCustomer(commercialcustomerToCustomer(aCC));
```

Classes are used as variable types in the Pascal program. To illustrate, we first define two variables.

```
var aC: Customer;
    aCC: commercialcustomer;
...
aCC := Ncommercialcustomer;
industrycodeOfcommercialcustomer(aCC) := 15;
ACustomer := commercialcustomerToCustomer(aCC);
```

The last assignment is valid because statecustomer is a subclass of Customer, and the following predicate is true.

```
ACustomer^.ECustomer = KCustomercommercialcustomer
```

However, in a later portion of the Pascal code, a node instance of a different node type (say, a statecustomer) could be assigned to the variable ACustomer, and the predicate would then be false.

```
Acustomer := statecustomerToCustomer(thisSC);
```

Finally, the following assignment is not correct.

```
var Abill: bill;
...
ACustomer := billToCustomer(Abill);
```

The Pascal compiler would flag it as an error, because bill is not a subclass of Customer. Declaring the ACustomer variable to be of type Customer effectively limits the nodes that can be assigned to that variable.

Processes

Each IDL process is mapped to a Pascal program. The structures used by the process are mapped to declarations. Ports are mapped to Pascal routines. Input ports (*Pre*) are mapped to functions taking a file pointer and returning a node of the root type for the structure. A flag is also set indicating whether errors were detected during reading. Output ports (*Post*) are mapped to procedures taking a file pointer and a node for the root of the structure instance. The four ports declared in Figure 2.8 on page 32 would be mapped to these declarations.

```
function transactionsin(var f: text;
            var readerok: boolean): transactionlist;
function customersin(var f: text;
            var readerok: boolean): customerlist;
procedure billsout(var f: text; root: billlist);
procedure customersout(var f: text; root: customerlist);
```

2.3 Writing the Algorithm

Writing the algorithm for the process in the target programming language is the next step. Figure 2.12 illustrates this portion of the process of using the IDL system. The composition of the billing program, illustrated below, is a refinement of Figure 2.1.

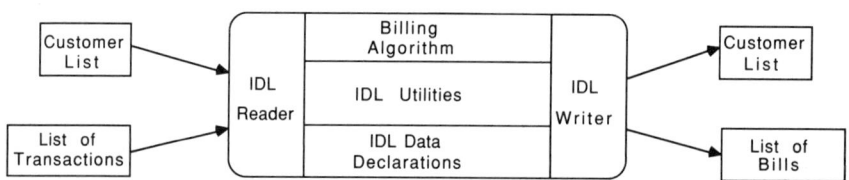

The algorithm in this example is a simple one. It reads a customer list and a sequence of transactions, through the `customers_in` and `transactions_in` ports, respectively. Then it steps through the transactions, either crediting the customer or generating a bill, according to the type of the transaction. Finally, it writes the updated customer list and the list of bills, through the `customers_out` and `bills_out` ports, respectively. The algorithm as coded in C is given in Figure 2.13 and in Pascal in Figure 2.14.

The code is fairly self-explanatory, so we will only make a few observations here. Since a `bill_list` is being created, it must be allocated (`Nbill_list`) and the sequence attribute initialized (`initializeSEQbill`). The outer `foreachinSEQTransaction` successively assigns transactions to `thisTransaction`; the inner `foreachinSEQCustomer` successively assigns

2.3. WRITING THE ALGORITHM

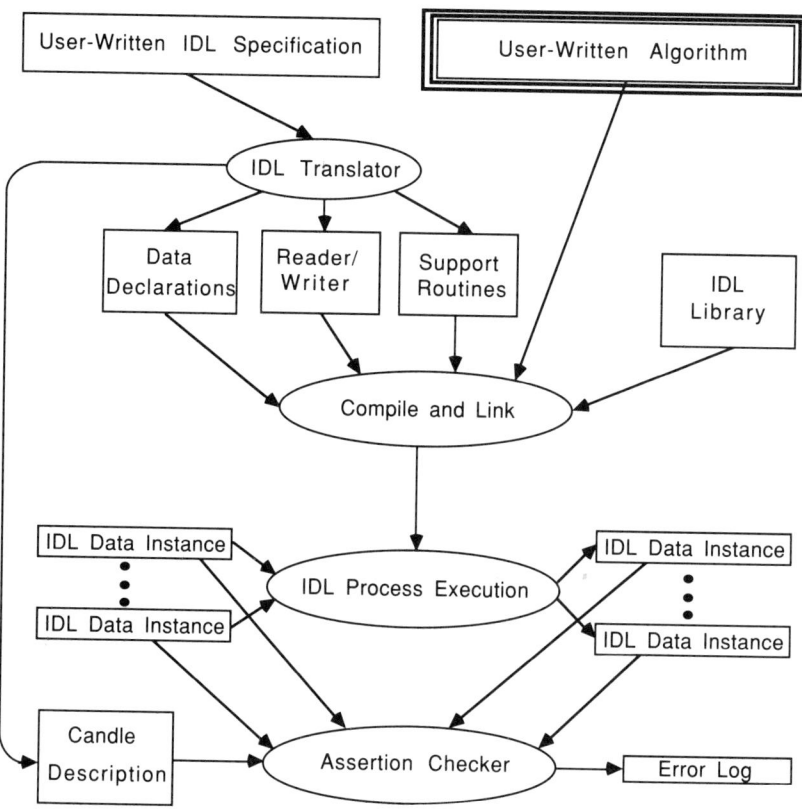

Figure 2.12: The Algorithm Writing Step

```c
/* file: billing/C/algorithm.c */
#include <stdio.h>
#include "billing.h"
#include "billingMacros.h"

main ()
{
      customer_list       thisCL;
      transaction_list    thisTL;
      bill_list           thisBL;
      Customer            thisCustomer;
      Transaction         thisTransaction;
      bill                thisbill;
      SEQCustomer         remainingCustomers;
      SEQTransaction      remainingTransactions;
      FILE                *c_in, *t_in, *c_out, *b_out;
/* input the initial customer list */
      c_in = fopen("customers.in", "r");
      thisCL = customers_in(c_in);
/* input the transactions list */
      t_in = fopen("transactions.in", "r");
      thisTL = transactions_in(t_in);
/* initialize bills */
      thisBL = Nbill_list;
      initializeSEQbill(listOfbill_list(thisBL));

/* process the transactions */
      foreachinSEQTransaction(listOftransaction_list(thisTL),
                        remainingTransactions, thisTransaction) {
                  /* find the Customer mentioned in the transaction */
            foreachinSEQCustomer(listOfcustomer_list(thisCL),
                        remainingCustomers, thisCustomer)
              if (customer_numberOfCustomer(thisCustomer)
                  == customer_numberOfTransaction(thisTransaction)) break;
            switch (typeof(thisTransaction)) {
            case Kcredit:     /* credit the Customer */
              balanceOfCustomer(thisCustomer)
                  += amountOfTransaction(thisTransaction);
              break;
            case Kdebit:      /* generate a bill */
              thisbill = Nbill;
              billeeOfbill(thisbill) = thisCustomer;
              amountOfbill(thisbill) = amountOfTransaction(thisTransaction);
              appendrearSEQbill(listOfbill_list(thisBL), thisbill);
              break;
            /* can't be anything else */
            }
      }

/* write out the updated customer list */
      c_out = fopen("customers.out", "w");
      customers_out(c_out, thisCL);
/* write out the list of bills */
      b_out = fopen("bills.out", "w");
      bills_out(b_out, thisBL);
      exit(0);
}
```

Figure 2.13: The C Algorithm for the Billing Process

2.3. WRITING THE ALGORITHM

```pascal
(* file: billing/Pascal/algorithm.p *)
program main;
#include "billing.h"
#include "billingMacros.h"
var
      thisCL: customerlist;
      thisTL: transactionlist;
      thisBL: billlist;
      thisCustomer, foundCustomer: Customer;
      thisTransaction: Transaction;
      thisbill: bill;
      CustomerSeq: SEQCustomer;
      TransactionSeq: SEQTransaction;
      cIn, tIn, cOut, bOut: text;
      i, j: integer;
      readerOK: boolean;
#include "billing.i"
begin
(* input the initial customer list *)
      reset(cIn, 'customers.in');
      thisCL := customersin(cIn, readerOK);
      if not readerOK then halt;
(* input the transactions list *)
      reset(tIn, 'transactions.in');
      thisTL := transactionsin(tIn, readerOK);
      if not readerOK then halt;
(* initialize bills *)
      thisBL := Nbilllist;
      initializeSEQbill(listOfbilllist(thisBL));
(* process the transactions *)
      TransactionSeq := listOftransactionlist(thisTL);
      for i := 1 to lengthSEQTransaction(TransactionSeq) do begin
          thisTransaction := ithinSEQTransaction(TransactionSeq, i);
          CustomerSeq := listOfcustomerlist(thisCL);
              (* find the Customer mentioned in the transaction *)
          foundCustomer := nil;
          for j := 1 to lengthSEQCustomer(CustomerSeq) do begin
              thisCustomer := ithinSEQCustomer(CustomerSeq, i);
              if customernumberOfCustomer(thisCustomer)
                    = customernumberOfTransaction(thisTransaction)
              then foundCustomer := thisCustomer
              end;
          case thisTransaction^.ETransaction of
          KTransactioncredit: (* credit the Customer *)
              balanceOfCustomer(thisCustomer) := balanceOfCustomer(thisCustomer)
                   + amountOfTransaction(thisTransaction);
          KTransactiondebit: begin (* generate a bill *)
              thisbill := Nbill;
              billeeOfbill(thisbill) := thisCustomer;
              amountOfbill(thisbill) := amountOfTransaction(thisTransaction);
              appendrearSEQbill(listOfbilllist(thisBL), thisbill);
              end
          end;
      end;    (* of iteration over transactions *)
(* write out the updated customer list *)
      rewrite(cOut, 'customers.out');
      customersout(cOut, thisCL);
(* write out the list of bills *)
      rewrite(bOut, 'bills.out');
      billsout(bOut, thisBL);
end.
```

Figure 2.14: The Pascal Algorithm for the Billing Process

customers to `thisCustomer`, attempting to find the customer with the correct `customer_number` (it is assumed to exist). The Pascal code doesn't have `foreachinSEQ` available, so it insteads uses a traditional *for* loop and `ithinSEQ`. To generate a bill, one is first allocated, then its attributes are filled in, then it is appended to the list of bills. Finally, both output ports are called. The declarations, constants, and macro definitions produced by the IDL translator are used extensively. Because of the consistent naming, a programmer experienced with IDL would need only the IDL specification to code the algorithm.

2.4 Compiling the Process

The fourth step involves compiling and linking the code for the algorithm along with the IDL-produced data declarations and runtime support routines to produce an executable program (see Figure 2.15).

In the compilation stage, you compile the code and link it with the code produced by the IDL translator and with a library of generic IDL system routines. For example, a command to compile and link the C code would be the following:

```
cc algorithm.c billing.o /usr/lib/libidl.a -o billing
```

To compile and link the Pascal code, do the following:

```
pc algorithm.c billing.o /usr/lib/libidlP.a -o billing
```

In the examples, the code for the algorithm is assumed to reside in a file named **algorithm.c** (or **algorithm.p**), the IDL-generated routines reside in the file named **billing.o**, and the library of generic IDL system routines reside in **libidl.a** and **libidlP.a**. The output of this command will be an executable command in the file named **billing**. The specific pathnames for the library files will vary from system to system.

2.5 Running the Process

The fifth step in using the IDL system runs the program to process instances of the data structures represented externally in the ASCII External Representation Language (see Figure 2.16).

Before this step can be performed, instances of the input structures must be available. The billing process references two input structures: `customers` and `transactions`. Normally, instances of input structures

2.5. RUNNING THE PROCESS

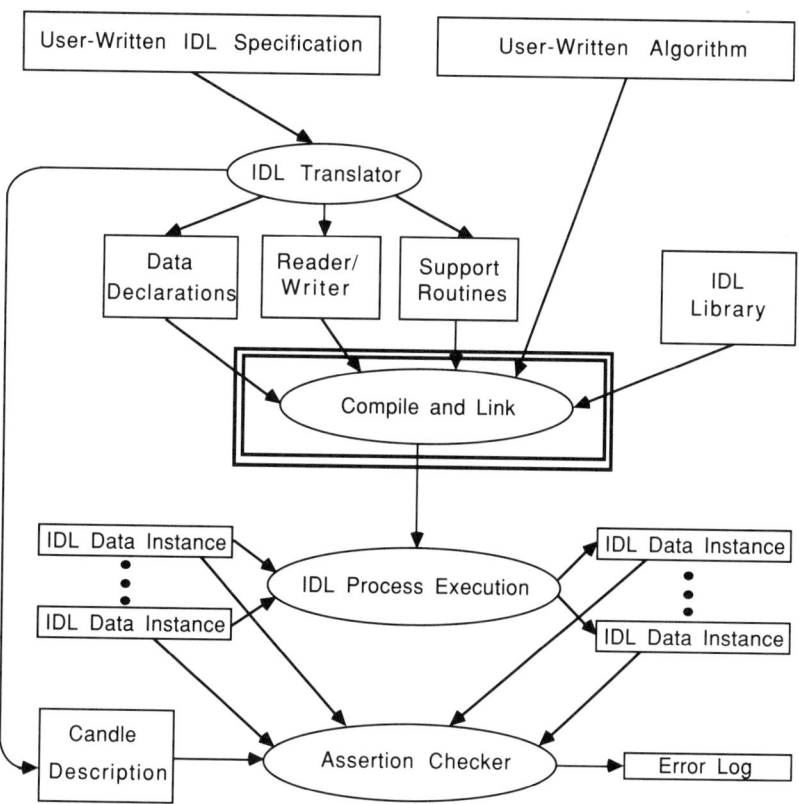

Figure 2.15: The Process Compilation Step

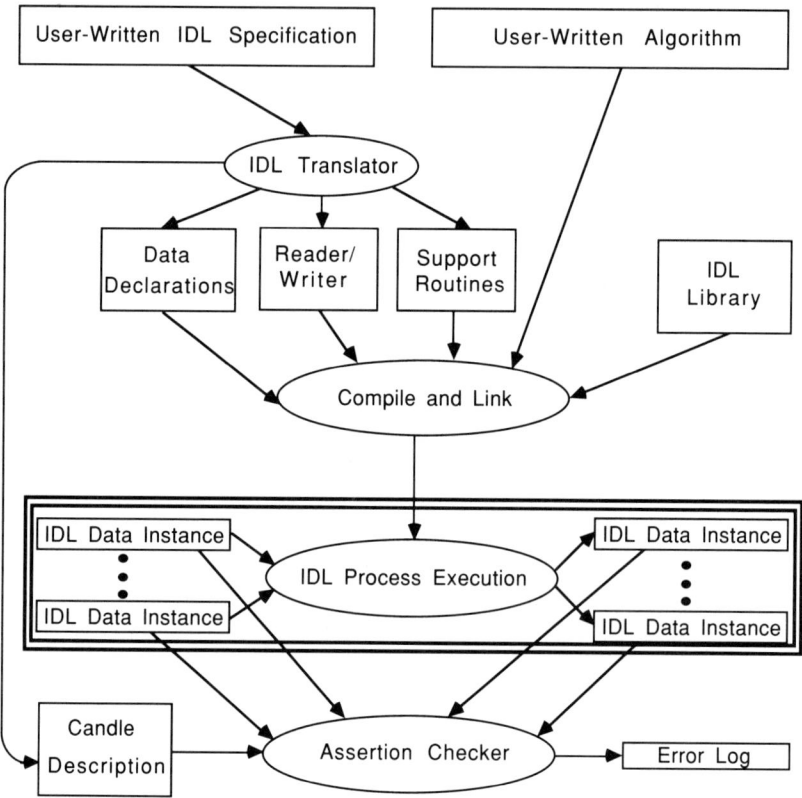

Figure 2.16: The Process Execution Step

2.5. RUNNING THE PROCESS

are written by other processes. In this example, they have been manually constructed.

The IDL ASCII External Representation Language (ERL) is the standard representation scheme for external instances of IDL data structures. Instances are data values consistent with a specific data structure. The external representation of an instance of a data structure consists of a list of the nodes in the instance. Some of the nodes in the list are given a unique label. The external representation begins with a reference to the root node. The order of subsequent nodes in the list is not significant. The "#" sign as the first character of a line signals the end of the instance. Hence, more than one instance of one or more structures may reside in the same file. Each call to the port routine will read one instance. The first call will read the first instance (up to and including the "#"); the second call passed the same file identifier will read the second instance, and so on.

A node is represented as the name of the node type followed by a list of attribute-reference pairs. Each attribute is explicitly named and the name is followed by a reference to the corresponding attribute value. The name of an attribute is the name specified in the structure declaration.

The value of an attribute of IDL basic type is the external representation of that value. The representation is machine independent, and may be created or modified by a text editor. While string values can contain any of the 128 ASCII characters, the external representation only contains printable characters within double-quotes. Nonprintable characters are represented using escaped printable characters (that is, printable characters preceded by "~"). A carriage return is represented with "~J", the cancel character (decimal 24) is represented with "~X", and the tilde character is represented with "~~".

The value of an attribute of node type is a node or an indirect reference to a node. A reference to a node consists of the label of that node followed by a "^" character. Forward references are permitted. A list of types or nodes bracketed with braces "{}" represents a set-valued attribute. A list of types bracketed with angle brackets "<>" represents a sequence-valued attribute. Comments are preceded with "-- " and extend to the end of the line. Details of the ASCII ERL are given in Chapter 6.

Classes are not represented explicitly in the external representation. If an attribute has a class type, then the value associated with that attribute will be a reference to a node whose type is a member of that class.

An example of an instance of the `customers` structure cast in the ASCII ERL is shown below.

```
-- file billing/customers.in
L1: customer_list [list < L2^L3^L4^>]
L2: commercial_customer [
      name "Innovation, Inc.";
      address "Freedom Trail";
      active TRUE;
      customer_number 1;
      balance 9546782.00;
      industry_code 12]
L3: state_customer [
      name "Department of Obfuscation";
      address "Bureaucracy Boulevard";
      active FALSE
      customer_number 2;
      balance -1000000000.85;
      state_code 50
    ]
L4: federal_customer [
      name "Office of the Director, OMB";
      address "Wonderland";
      active FALSE
      customer_number 3;
      balance -1000000000000.13;
      agency_code 1348903
    ]
#
```

In this example a list of three customers is shown. The name of the first customer is "Innovation, Inc.", the second, "Department of Obfuscation", and the last, "Office of the Director, OMB". Only the nodes in this instance are represented externally. Classes for the internal representation can be reconstructed by the reader generated by the IDL translator solely from its knowledge of the structure specification.

We also need an instance of the **transactions** structure.

```
-- file billing/transactions.in
L1: transaction_list [list <L2^ L3^ >]
L2: credit [
      customer_number 2;
      date 31285;
      amount 22354.44;
      tax_status {}
    ]
```

2.5. RUNNING THE PROCESS

```
      L3: debit [
              customer_number 1;
              date 31485;
              amount 332.12;
              tax_status {state_sales_tax}
          ]
      #
```

This instance contains two transactions, a `credit` to customer number 2 and a `debit` from customer number 1.

After we execute the billing process (either the Pascal or C variant)

```
      billing
```

we note that two files have been created: **customers.out** and **bills.out** (the file names are embedded in the code). The first (after adding spaces and line breaks to make it easier to read) contains

```
      customer_list[list <
          commercial_customer[name "Innovation,Inc.";
              address "Freedom Trail";
              customer_number 1;
              active TRUE;
              balance 9.54678E+06;
              industry_code 12]
          state_customer[name "Department of Obfuscation";
              address "Bureaucracy Boulevard";
              customer_number 2;
              active FALSE
              balance -9.9978E+08;
              state_code 50]
          federal_customer[name "Office of the Director, OMB";
              address "Wonderland";
              customer_number 3;
              active FALSE
              balance 1.1E+13;
              agency_code 1348903]
      >]
      #
```

and the second file contains the following instance.

```
bill_list[list <
   bill[billee
      commercial_customer[name"Innovation, Inc.";
          address "Freedom Trail";
          customer_number 1;
          industry_code 12];
      amount 332.12]
   >]
#
```

2.6 Checking the Assertions

The sixth and final step of using the IDL system is to check to ensure that the Pascal or C algorithm executed correctly. This step, shown in Figure 2.17, examines the validity of both the input and output instances, checking that they meet all the assertions specified in their structure definitions.

Assertions are first processed by the IDL translator. The translator checks the assertions themselves for syntactic and semantic correctness (e.g., no spelling errors, no type mismatches). The translator produces an encoded form of the assertions when the -C option is used. In Section 2.2, we specified that the file **billing.Cdl** was to be created to store this information.

We now check the assertions.

```
idlcheck -v -C billing.Cdl customers_in customers.in \
         transactions_in transactions.in \
         customers_out customers.out \
         bills_out bills.out
```

The "\" indicates that the next line is considered part of the command. Each port name is followed by the name of a file containing an instance read or written by that port. Again, we use the -v option so that the checker tells us what it is doing. Figure 2.18 shows the output generated by IDLCHECK.

Three assertions were not satisfied. **IBMExists**, given on page 37, was not satisfied for either the input **customers** structure nor for the output **customers** structure, simply because no customer has the name 'IBM'. The **ProperCredit** assertion in the **billing** process, shown on page 40, was also not satisfied. In the analysis, '>' should be read as "because" and '&' as "and". This analysis states that, for the output customer corresponding to the input customer labeled L3 (the Department of Obfuscation), the

2.6. CHECKING THE ASSERTIONS

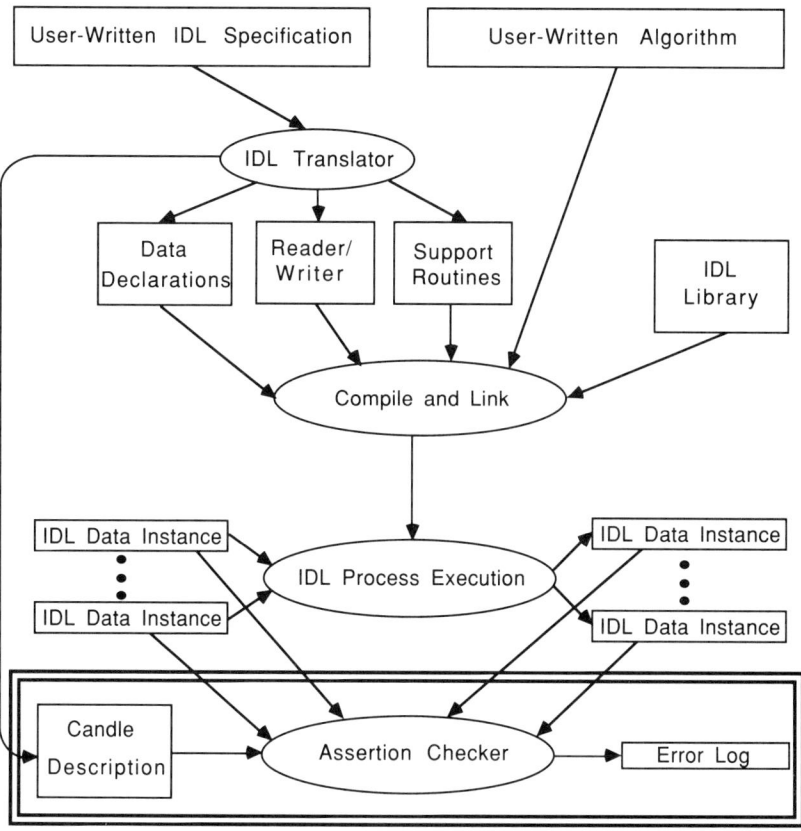

Figure 2.17: The Assertion Checker Step

```
reading instance for port 'customers_in'
reading instance for port 'customers_out'
reading instance for port 'bills_out'
reading instance for port 'transactions_in'
interpreting assertions for process 'billing'
interpreting assertions for structure 'transactions' in port 'transactions_in'
      unnamed assertion in transactions is true.
interpreting assertions for structure 'customers' in port 'customers_in'
      unnamed assertion in customers is true.
      unnamed assertion in customers is true.
      unnamed assertion in customers is true.
      unnamed assertion in customers is true.
      unnamed assertion in customers is true.
      assertion IBMExists in customers is false.
> EXISTS is not satisfied.
      unnamed assertion in customers is true.
interpreting assertions for structure 'customers' in port 'customers_out'
      unnamed assertion in customers is true.
      unnamed assertion in customers is true.
      unnamed assertion in customers is true.
      unnamed assertion in customers is true.
      unnamed assertion in customers is true.
      assertion IBMExists in customers is false.
> EXISTS is not satisfied.
      unnamed assertion in customers is true.
interpreting assertions for structure 'bills' in port 'bills_out'
      unnamed assertion in bills is true.
interpreting assertions for process 'billing_process'
      unnamed assertion in billing_process is true.
      unnamed assertion in billing_process is true.
      unnamed assertion in billing_process is true.
      unnamed assertion in billing_process is true.
      assertion ProperCredit in billing_process is false.
> FORALL is not satisfied when c_out is <no label>:state_customer
   & FORALL is not satisfied when c_in is L3:state_customer
      & Conditional is not satisfied.
            > Equality is satisfied.
                  > .customer_number is { 2 }
                        > c_in is { L3:state_customer }
                  & .customer_number is { 2 }
                        > c_out is { <no label>:state_customer }
            & Equality not satisfied.
                  > .balance is { -999977984.000000 }
                        > c_out is { <no label>:state_customer }
                  & Sum is -999977646.410000.
                        > .balance is { -1000000000.850000 }
                              > c_in is { L3:state_customer }
      unnamed assertion in billing_process is true.
      unnamed assertion in billing_process is true.
      unnamed assertion in billing_process is true.
```

Figure 2.18: Error Listing Generated by IDLCHECK

balance is incorrect. It should be -999,977,646.41, but is -999,977,984.00, an error of almost $340.00. Further analysis shows that the code calculates balances in single precision, which is incapable of representing the exact balance in this case. The assertions have uncovered a fairly subtle bug.

2.7 Summary

In this chapter we specified the billing process in IDL, implemented it in C and Pascal, executed it on test input, and checked its output to ensure that it satisfied the specified assertions. Only enough of the features of the IDL system have been presented above to allow the reader to begin using IDL quickly. The syntax for many of the declarations has been simplified. The next chapter will show a complete example of using the IDL system to solve a simple problem in compiler implementation.

Exercises

2.1 Demonstrate that all nodes and classes in the `bills` structure, specified in Figure 2.7, are reachable.

2.2 The number of macros generated is highly dependent on the specification. Keeping this in mind, how many C macros are generated for the `billing` process, specified in Figure 2.9 on page 34, in each of the following categories: node identifiers, node allocators and destroyers (both user and internal), set and sequence operations, attribute accessing (both node and class), widening, narrowing, and miscellaneous? Which of these macros are generated by the **Version B** target language?

Bibliographic Notes

The class concept in IDL is similar to that of the same name in Simula-67 (Birtwistle et al. [1973]), Smalltalk (Goldberg and Robson [1983]), CommonLoops (Bobrow [1986] C++ (Stroustrup [1986]), Objective-C (Cox [1986]), and Eiffel (Meyer [1988]). It is also similar to Wirth's [1988] type extensions and Mesa's traits (Curry et al. [1982]). These languages all support the definition of a hierarchical collection of classes and support inheritance in subclasses of attributes defined in superclasses. IDL, Smalltalk (Borning and Ingalls [1982]), C++, Eiffel, type extensions, and traits allow multiple hierarchies, which have also been proposed for Simula by Krogdahl [1984]. Lie [1984] compares IDL and Simula in some detail.

IDL differs from these languages in four ways. IDL deals only with data and not with computations; IDL is independent of the target language used to express these computations. The other languages allow procedures to be attached to classes. A second difference is that IDL emphasizes the automatic construction of readers and writers; the other languages require the user to implement the readers and writers, although Smalltalk, Objective-C, and Eiffel support methods that read and write entire objects, as well as objects reachable from the initial object, to and from files. IDL supports a larger unit of granularity, the IDL structure, than do most object-oriented languages, whose primary unit of modularization is the class. Finally, IDL is strongly typed at compile-time (except for some of the conversion routines), while those of Smalltalk and CommonLoops are solely type-checked at runtime.

Additional material on specifying data structures in IDL may be found in Lamb's [1983] dissertation . This chapter is a revised version of Warren, Kickenson, and Snodgrass [1987]. Intermetrics [1985] is another tutorial on IDL. The figures appearing in this chapter were adapted from those appearing in Nestor, Wulf, and Lamb [1982] and Lamb [1983].

Chapter 3

A Second Example

The previous chapter introduced IDL by specifying and implementing a batch billing program. In this chapter we examine some of IDL's more advanced features, while also staying closer to IDL's original application, that of programming environments. We consider here the implementation of one phase of a compiler for a simple language. Chapter 9 will discuss the remaining phases. The compiler's architecture, consisting of four phases, is shown in Figure 3.1. This chapter will discuss the optimization phase, which performs constant folding. One benefit of IDL is that it allows portions of a tool to be implemented in parallel. Hence, we can implement and test this interior phase while, concurrently or later, the other processes are themselves implemented and tested. As with the billing example, we will go through each of the steps in using the IDL system and look at the inputs that must be supplied by you.

3.1 Example Problem

The example language that our compiler will process is a toy language called the "function language." The function language permits the definition of named integer functions that take zero or more formal parameters and return the results of the evaluation of their defining expressions. A complete syntax for the function language is given in Figure 3.2.

Functions may not call other functions in their defining expression nor may they call themselves recursively. The operators allowed in expressions are "+", "-", "*", "/". They have the usual precedence and associativity: "*" and "/" are of equal and higher precedence than "+" and "-". All four operators associate left to right. Of still higher precedence are unary "+"

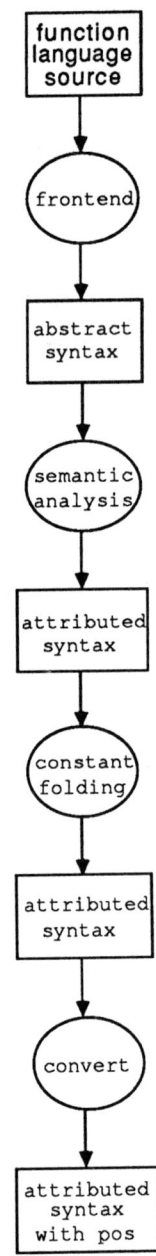

Figure 3.1: Architecture of the Function Language Compiler

3.1. EXAMPLE PROBLEM

⟨program⟩   ::= { ⟨function⟩ }*
⟨function⟩   ::= *function* ⟨head⟩ '=' ⟨expression⟩ ';'
⟨head⟩   ::= ⟨name⟩ ⟨parameters⟩ ':' ⟨type⟩
⟨parameters⟩ ::= ϵ | '(' ⟨parameter⟩ { ',' ⟨parameter⟩ }* ')'
⟨parameter⟩   ::= ⟨name⟩ ':' ⟨type⟩
⟨type⟩   ::= *integer* | *real*
⟨expression⟩ ::= ⟨expression⟩ '+' ⟨term⟩ | ⟨expression⟩ '-' ⟨term⟩
              | ⟨term⟩
⟨term⟩   ::= ⟨term⟩ '*' ⟨factor⟩ | ⟨term⟩ '/' ⟨factor⟩ | ⟨factor⟩
⟨factor⟩   ::= '+' ⟨factor⟩ | '-' ⟨factor⟩ | ⟨name⟩
              | ⟨integer⟩ | ⟨real⟩ | '(' ⟨expression⟩ ')'

Figure 3.2: The Syntax for the Function Language

```
function cube(A: integer): integer = A * A * A;
function poly_2d(A: real, B: real, C: real, X: real): real
       = C + A * (B + X * A);
```

Figure 3.3: Examples of Functions

and "-", which associate right to left. Expressions inside parentheses are of the highest precedence. Values and expressions can be of an integer or real type.

Examples of typical functions in the function language are given in Figure 3.3. Two functions are defined in this example. First, a function called cube is defined to take one argument and return that argument raised to the third power. Second, a function called poly_2d is defined to take four arguments representing the coefficients and the functional argument of a second-degree polynomial and return the value of that polynomial computed with Horner's method.

Our compiler for this language starts with lexical and syntactic analysis. In this phase, the function definition(s) are read in and parsed. If the source language input was lexically and syntactically correct, a parse tree is produced for the next phase, semantic analysis. In the semantic analysis phase, the parse tree is analyzed to ascertain whether the semantic rules had been followed. An example of such a rule requires that every name used

Before Constant Folding:

```
function foo(A: integer): integer
   = -A * (28 + 13);
```

After Constant Folding:

```
function foo(A: integer): integer
   = -A * 41;
```

Figure 3.4: An Example of Constant Folding

in the body of a function (e.g., "A" used in the cube function) was the name of a formal parameter of that function. If the parse tree met all semantic requirements, it is augmented with additional information (such as which formal parameter each name references) and passed on to the optimization phase. In this phase, the parse tree is rewritten into an equivalent, but more efficient, alternate form. The final phase of the function language compiler, the convert phase, is discussed in Chapter 9.

One of the simplest optimizations that could be made to expressions in the function language is *constant folding*. Constant folding consists of evaluating at compilation time any subexpression whose operands are entirely constants and replacing that subexpression with the result of the evaluation. The resulting expression is more efficiently evaluated at runtime because we have done as much of the evaluation as possible at compile time. The speed of execution of the code generated by the compiler is increased at the expense of reduced compilation speed.

Suppose we had a function such as foo in the "before" portion of Figure 3.4. After constant folding, we would like to have the equivalent but more efficient expression for foo as in the "after" portion of that figure in which the subexpression "(28 + 13)" has been replaced with the constant 41, the sum of 28 and 13. These two definitions for foo yield the same value for all inputs but the second form is more efficiently executed since an addition has been eliminated.

Constant folding is a recursive process. If we have a function such as bar in the before portion of Figure 3.5, we want to perform constant folding in as complete a fashion as possible.

The incomplete portion of Figure 3.5 shows the results of incomplete constant folding applied to the original definition for "bar". The subexpression "(4 + 1)" has been replaced with the sum, 5, which generates a new opportunity for constant folding. The complete portion of Figure 3.5 shows the resulting expression when all possible constant folding has been

3.2. THE IDL SPECIFICATION

Before Constant Folding:
    `function bar(A: integer): real = 30 / (4 + 1);`
After Incomplete Constant Folding:
    `function bar(A: integer): real = 30 / 5;`
After Complete Constant Folding:
    `function bar(A: integer): real = 6;`

Figure 3.5: Incomplete and Complete Constant Folding

done.

The conceptual flow of the constantfolding process is shown below.

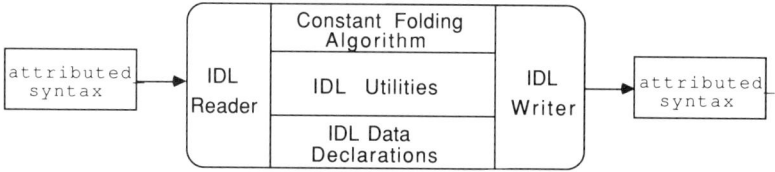

It reads an attributed syntax tree for one or more functions from the semantic analysis phase of the compiler, performs constant folding on the defining expression of the functions, and writes the modified but functionally equivalent attributed syntax tree for the next phase of the compiler.

3.2 The IDL Specification

The IDL specification describes the structures, assertions, and processes associated with the program.

3.2.1 Structure Specifications

The first step of developing our constant folding program is to write an IDL specification for the input data: attributed parse tree to be read. To do this, we first specify the abstract syntax tree (essentially a parse tree without keywords) produced by the frontend. The specification for such a parse tree is shown in Figure 3.6. We then specify the attributed parse tree in terms of this simpler structure. The assertions present in these structures are discussed in the next section.

The root of the `abstract_syntax` structure is the `functions` node, with one attribute: a sequence of function definitions. The attributes of the `function` node are the name of the function, which is an `Identifier`,

-- *file: specs/functionsyntax.idl*
```
Structure abstract_syntax Root functions Is

    -- private type declaration and type representation information
    Type source_position;
    For source_position Use External Integer;

    identifier            =>   lex_token:        String,
                               lex_pos:          source_position;
    functions             =>   syn_func_seq:     Seq Of function;

    function              =>   syn_name:         identifier,
                               syn_return_type:  types,
                               syn_parameters:   Seq Of formal_parameter,
                               syn_definition:   expression;
    NumParams Assert ForAll f In function Do
        Size(f.syn_parameters) > 0 Od;
    formal_parameter      =>   syn_name:         identifier,
                               syn_param_type:   types;

    types                 ::=  int | real;
    int =>;   real =>;

    expression            ::=  constant | formal_parameterRef | operation;
    constant              ::=  integer_constant | real_constant;
    integer_constant      =>   lex_value:        Integer;
    real_constant         =>   lex_value:        Rational;
    formal_parameterRef   =>   syn_name:         identifier;
    operation             ::=  binary_operation | unary_operation;
    binary_operation      =>   syn_op:           binaryoperator,
                               syn_left:         expression,
                               syn_right:        expression;
    binaryoperator        ::=  plus | minus | times | divide;
    plus =>;  minus =>;  times =>;  divide =>;
    unary_operation       =>   syn_op:           unaryoperator,
                               syn_argument:     expression;
    unaryoperator         ::=  unaryplus | unaryminus;
    unaryplus =>;  unaryminus =>;

    -- There are no cross branches in any parse trees
    NoCrossBranches Assert ForAll n In binary_operation
        Do (Reach(n.syn_left) Intersect Reach(n.syn_right))
            Same Empty Od;
    -- There are no cycles in any parse trees
    NoCycles Assert ForAll n In expression Do Not(n Sub Desc(n)) Od;
    -- All expressions are reachable from the root.
    NoDisconnectedComponents Assert ForAll e In expression Do
        Exists f In Members(Root.syn_func_seq)
            Do e In Reach(f.syn_definition) Od
        Od;
    Define IDesc(n: constant) = Empty;
    Define IDesc(n: formal_parameterRef) = Empty;
    Define IDesc(n: unary_operation) = n.syn_argument;
    Define IDesc(n: binary_operation) = n.syn_left Union n.syn_right;
    Cyclic Define Desc(n: expression) Returns expression
        = Reach(IDesc(n));
    Cyclic Define Reach(n: expression) Returns expression
        = n Union Desc(n);
End
```

Figure 3.6: The Specification for the abstract_syntax Structure

3.2. THE IDL SPECIFICATION

a sequence of the formal parameters of the function, the return type of the function, and the defining expression of the function. The type of the function is either `int` or `real` (we don't use `integer` because that conflicts with the IDL keyword *Integer*). Each `formal_parameter` is a node with its name and specified type as attributes.

The type of the `syn_definition` attribute, `expression`, is a class. A reference to an `expression` can be either a constant, a reference to a formal parameter, or an operation. We differentiate here and throughout the book between the *declaration* of a formal parameter and a *reference* to a formal parameter. `constants` have a single attribute, `lex_value`, of type *Integer* for `integer_constants` and of type *Rational* for `real_constants`, to hold the value of the constant.

Members of the `operation` class are the `binary_operation` and `unary_operation` nodes, both of which have a `syn_op` attribute. The `unary_operation` has a single argument as well, and the `binary_operation` node contains left and right subexpressions. The type of the `syn_op` attribute is the `binaryoperator` class, for binary operations, and the `unaryoperator` class, for unary operations. Members are the unattributed nodes `plus`, `minus`, `times`, and `div` for the `binaryoperator` class and `unaryplus` and `unaryminus` for the `unaryoperator` class.

One private type, `source_position`, appears in the structure. The private type facility allows the standard set of attribute types provided by IDL to be extended. You first declares a name to identify the private type. An external representation for the private type is also specified in terms of the standard set of attribute types provided by IDL as well as node and class types previously declared. As constant folding will not manipulate the `lex_pos` attribute, we will delay further discussion of the `source_position` private type until Chapter 9. We will discuss the assertions shortly.

An instance of the parse tree for function `foo` shown in Figure 3.4 is pictured as the tree in Figure 3.7.

Semantic analysis computes two important pieces of information: the formal parameter each name (i.e., `formal_parameterRef`) references, and the type of each subexpression. The result of semantic analysis, the `attributed_syntax` structure, is shown in Figure 3.8. This structure is *derived* from the `abstract_syntax` structure, indicating that all nodes and classes specified in `abstract_syntax` are also in `attributed_syntax`. Defining this new structure via derivation focuses on the action of the semantic analysis phase; the two attributes it computes are clearly identified.

No new structure specification is needed for the output of constant folding, since the algorithm simply restructures the instance of the abstract syntax tree into an equivalent, but more efficient, form.

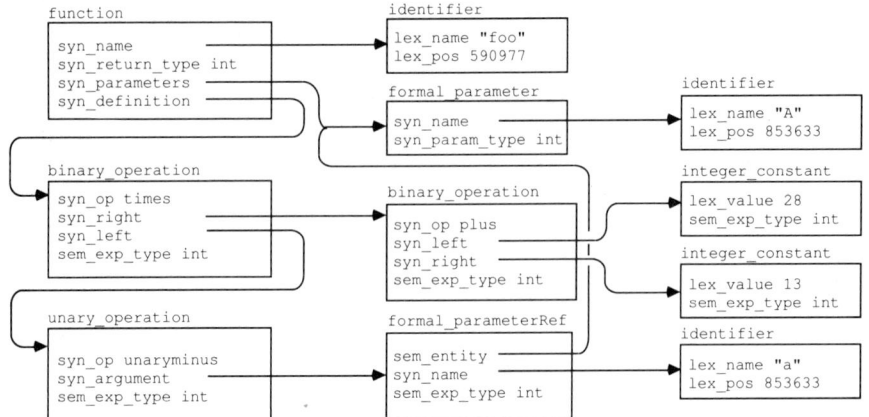

Figure 3.7: The Parse Tree for Function foo of Figure 3.4

-- *file*: *specs/functionsem.idl*

Import abstract_syntax From functionsyntax End

Structure attributed_syntax From abstract_syntax Is

   -- *additional semantic attributes*

   formal_parameterRef => sem_entity: formal_parameter;
   CorrectSemEntity Assert ForAll f In formal_parameterRef
      Do f.syn_name = f.sem_entity.syn_name Od;

   expression   => sem_exp_type: types;
   CorrectIntConstType Assert ForAll ic In integer_constant
      Do ic.sem_exp_type Is int Od;
   CorrectRealConstType Assert ForAll rc In real_constant
      Do rc.sem_exp_type Is real Od;
   CorrectFormParamType Assert ForAll f In formal_parameterRef
      Do f.sem_exp_type = f.sem_entity.syn_param_type Od;

End

Figure 3.8: The Specification of the attributed_syntax Structure

3.2. THE IDL SPECIFICATION

3.2.2 Assertions

We first discuss the process assertions, and then examine the assertions found in the structure specifications.

Basically, we wish to assert that the structure output is actually folded. We make the following assertion.

```
OutputFolded Assert ForAll s In
        Members(outputport:Root.syn_func_seq).syn_definition
    Do Folded(s) Od;
```

The prefix `outputport` before `Root` indicates that we are asserting something about the root of the structure at the port called `outputport`, and not about the root of all structures. In particular, we don't assert that the input is folded!

In order for the definition to make sense, we must define what we mean by *folded*. The following definition of `Folded` does this:

```
Define Folded(e: expression) =
    Case t Is e
        constant Do True Od
        formal_parameterRef Do True Od
        unary_operation Do If t.syn_argument Is constant
                Then False
                Else Folded(t.syn_argument)
                Fi
            Od
        binary_operation Do If t.syn_left Is constant And
                    t.syn_right Is constant
                Then False
                Else Folded(t.syn_left) And
                    Folded(t.syn_right)
                Fi
            Od
        Otherwise Do True Od
    End;
```

The `Case` statement selects an expression to evaluate based on the type of the initial expression, which here is simply e. If e is just a constant, then it is clearly folded. If e consists of only a formal name, then we also assert that it is folded. If e is a `unary_operation`, then its value is assigned to the case name t, which is given the type `unary_operation` within the following expression. If the argument of t is a constant, then the expression is not folded. If the argument is not a constant, then the unary expression is folded if its argument is folded. Similarly, if e is a `binary_operation`, then t is given that type within the following expression. If the operands are both constants, then the expression is not folded. Otherwise, the binary expression is folded if both its operand expressions are folded.

Next, we would like to assert that in the constant folding process, the value of the function has not been inadvertently changed. So we assert

```
SameValue Assert ForAll f In Members(inputport:Root.syn_func_seq)
    Do Exists f2 In Members(outputport:Root.syn_func_seq) Do
        f.syn_name.lex_token = f2.syn_name.lex_token
        And Value(f) = Value(f2) Od
    Od;
```

We must now define what we mean by the value of an expression. We use an overloaded definition, where multiple *versions* of the definition exist, differentiated by the type(s) of their parameters. Each version of the definition takes care of one kind of expression.

```
Define Value(e: integer_constant) = e.lex_value;
Define Value(e: real_constant) = e.lex_value;
```

The value of a constant is stored in its `lex_value` attribute.

```
Define Value(e: formal_parameterRef) = 1;
```

The value of a `formal_parameterRef` node is set to 1. This is done because the value of a formal name is not known. Any integer will do.

```
Cyclic Define Value(e: unary_operation) Returns Rational =
    If e.syn_op Is plus
    Then Value(e.syn_argument)
    Else - Value(e.syn_argument)
    Fi;
```

The value of a unary expression is the value of the unary operator's argument if the operator is unary plus. Otherwise the operator must be unary minus, and the value of the expression is the additive inverse of the value of the argument. We discuss the need for the keyword *Cyclic* below. Note that for such definitions the return type must be specified.

```
Cyclic Define Value(e: binary_operation) Returns Rational =
    If e.syn_op Is plus
    Then Value(e.syn_left) + Value(e.syn_right)
    OrIf e.syn_op Is minus
    Then Value(e.syn_left) - Value(e.syn_right)
```

3.2. THE IDL SPECIFICATION

```
    OrIf e.syn_op Is times
    Then Value(e.syn_left) * Value(e.syn_right)
    Else Value(e.syn_left) / Value(e.syn_right)
    Fi;
```

The value of a binary expression is the value resulting from applying the particular binary operator to the values of the operands. Note that we could have also used a `Case` expression here.

The above definition of `Value` is recursive in two of its versions. It is guaranteed to terminate since all expressions are trees of finite size.

`Value` must be defined for each kind of expression. Thus `Value` is overloaded. Each version will take care of one kind of expression. `Value` is called in the process specification with an argument of type `expression`. Since every node type in the `expression` class (`integer_constant`, `real_constant`, `formal_parameterRef`, `unary_operation`, and `binary_operation`) appears as a formal argument of a version of `Value`, all is well. Overloaded definitions allow one to use the same name for a related group of definitions that serve the same purpose, but for different types of arguments.

The use of an overloaded definition is preferable to writing one definition version that contains `If` clauses. One might have defined `Value` as

```
    -- This is bad style!
    Define Value(e: expression) =
        If e Is integer_constant Then e.lex_value
        OrIf e Is real_constant Then e.lex_value
        OrIf e Is formal_parameterRef Then 1
        OrIf e Is unary_operation Then ...
        Else ...
        Fi;
```

This method will lead to semantic type errors. For example, `e.lex_value` is incorrect, because not all `expressions` have a `lex_value` attribute—the translator is unable to determine that the type of `e` in this case must in fact be `integer_constant`. An alternative would be to use the `Case` expression, as was done with the `Fold` definition. In these situations, we recommend the use of overloading, because it is simpler in not requiring a `Case` expression. If the type of more than one argument must be examined, then overloading is far superior to multiple, nested `Case` expressions.

The function parse trees that the constant folding process takes as input and produces as output must indeed be trees. However, without the assertions, the IDL specification for the parse tree wouldnot restrict the structure to a tree. The `unary_operation` node has an attribute `syn_argument` of type `expression`. The specification does not guarantee that the particular expression referenced to by this attribute is not an instance of expression closer to the parse tree root or on the other side of the root. In other words, cycles and cross-branches are permitted, if not intended by the structure specification. In effect, there is nothing to prevent the parse "tree" from not actually being a tree. Such a strange instance of a parse tree could cause problems. Thus we wish to assert that each instance of the abstract_syntax structure is a tree.

Forming a precise assertion that a graph fulfills the requirements of a tree is not a trivial task. A few definitions will be useful. First, the immediate descendants of a node will be defined. This definition will take as an argument a node of type expression. Since expression is a class, and different kinds of expression have different definitions of immediate descendants, an overloaded definition is indicated. expression nodes of type constant and formal_parameterRef are leaves, and thus have no immediate descendants. The immediate descendant of a unary_operation node is its syn_argument attribute. The immediate descendants of a binary_operation node are its syn_left and syn_right attributes. This is reflected in the following overloaded definition.

```
Define IDesc(n: constant) = Empty;
Define IDesc(n: formal_parameterRef) = Empty;
Define IDesc(n: unary_operation) = n.syn_argument;
Define IDesc(n: binary_operation) = n.syn_left Union n.syn_right;
```

In the tree shown below

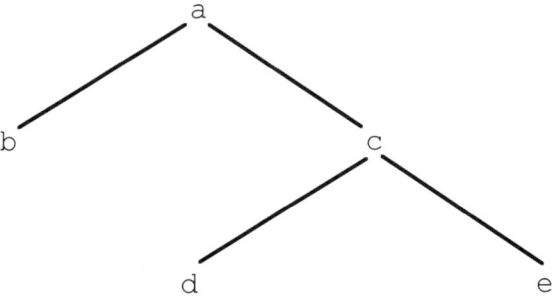

the immediate descendants of a are ⟨b, c⟩ (where ⟨ ⟩ specifies an object collection). The immediate descendants of c are ⟨d, e⟩. Nodes b, d, and e have no immediate descendants.

Next we will define the descendants of a node as the *reach* of its immediate descendants. The reach of a node will be defined as the union of the

3.2. THE IDL SPECIFICATION

node itself with its (immediate *and* indirect) descendants. For example, in the tree pictured above, the descendants of a are ⟨b, c, d, e⟩. The reach of a includes the nodes ⟨b, c, d, e, a⟩. To define descendants, we make use of the definition of reach, and to define reach, we make use of the definition of descendants. Such definitions are called *cyclic*. Under certain restrictions, such definitions are guaranteed to terminate on any specific instance; the IDL translator ensures that these restrictions are not violated. These definitions should be prefixed by the keyword *Cyclic*. The definitions would be expressed as follows.

Cyclic Define Desc(n: expression) *Returns* expression
    = Reach(IDesc(n));
Cyclic Define Reach(n: expression) *Returns* expression
    = n *Union* Desc(n);

Asserting that the structure is a tree may be expressed as three subsidiary assertions. First, we assert that the reach of the syn_left and syn_right attributes of a binary_operation node do not intersect. This will guarantee that no cross branches exist.

NoCrossBranches *Assert ForAll* n *In* binary_operation
    Do (Reach(n.syn_left) *Intersect* Reach(n.syn_right))
        Same Empty Od;

In the example tree, nodes a and c are of type binary_operation, since they have two children each. The reach of a.syn_left is the reach of b, which is ⟨ ⟩. The reach of a.syn_right is the reach of c, which is ⟨c, d, e⟩. Thus the assertion is true for node a. The reach of c.syn_left and the reach of c.syn_right are both ⟨ ⟩, and so the assertion holds for c also.

Second, we assert that no node is a descendant of itself. This will guarantee the absence of cycles.

NoCycles *Assert ForAll* n *In* expression *Do Not*(n *Sub* Desc(n)) *Od*;

The reserved word *Sub* denotes the collection subset operator. A quick look at the example tree shows that this assertion is true for that tree.

Finally, we assert that all nodes are reachable from the root. This will guarantee that there are no disjoint components in the tree.

NoDisconnectedComponents *Assert* Reach(*Root*.def) *Same* expression;

The reach of the root of the example tree (a) was listed above. Indeed, it is the entire tree (i.e., all expressions, denoted by expression).

The IDL translator will automatically check for cyclic definitions. Thus, if the *Cyclic* keyword is left out, but should have been specified, the translator will insert it and issue a warning message. Cyclic definitions carry with them two important restrictions. First, they must return collections, not values. Second, they cannot contain an *If* clause within their bodies, for a technical reason involving ensuring termination. The IDL translator will flag violations of these restrictions.

Cyclic definitions are useful, as shown above in asserting that a structure is a tree. However, their use is not always necessary. Most assertions are realizable without resort to cyclic definitions.

3.2.3 Process Specifications

As with the billing example, we first specify a generic process, then define two target-language-specific processes. The generic process specification for the constant_fold process, including the assertions just discussed, is given in Figure 3.9. The refined processes for C and Pascal are given in Figure's 3.10 and 3.11, respectively. These processes both import the generic process from **cf.idl**. They differ only in the target language they specify.

3.3 Translating the Specification

The next step in developing the constant folding program is to translate the specification for the attributed_syntax data structure and the constant_fold process into the target language. The data and process specifications reside in a file named **constant_fold.idl**, so the command for processing the specification is the following.

```
idlc -v -C constant_fold.Cdl constant_fold.idl
```

As with the billing example, we capture the CANDLE representation for use later with IDLCHECK.

The C Target Language

The output from the IDL translator consists of three files: the header file named **constant_fold.h**, the runtime support routine source code file named **constant_fold.c**, and a compiled version of that file named **constant_fold.o**.

Since no target language version is specified, the default (Version A) is used. This version differs from Version B discussed in Chapter 2 only in that the accessing and conversion macros are not generated. For large specifications, the quantity of macros generated in Version B can easily overwhelm most C compilers.

3.3. TRANSLATING THE SPECIFICATION

-- *file: functionlang/constantfold/cf.idl*

```
Import attributed_syntax From functionsem End

Process cf Is

    Pre inputport: attributed_syntax;
    Post outputport: attributed_syntax;

    -- Output tree is actually constant folded
    OutputFolded Assert ForAll s In
            Members(outputport:Root.syn_func_seq).syn_definition
        Do Folded(s) Od;

    -- Value of input expression is not altered by
    -- constant folding process
    SameValue Assert ForAll f In Members(inputport:Root.syn_func_seq)
        Do Exists f2 In Members(outputport:Root.syn_func_seq) Do
            f.syn_name.lex_token = f2.syn_name.lex_token
            And Value(f) = Value(f2) Od
        Od;

    -- Auxiliary definitions
    Define Folded(e: expression) =
        Case t Is e
            constant Do True Od
            formal_parameterRef Do True Od
            unary_operation Do If t.syn_argument Is constant
                    Then False
                    Else Folded(t.syn_argument)
                    Fi
                Od
            binary_operation Do If t.syn_left Is constant And
                        t.syn_right Is constant
                    Then False
                    Else Folded(t.syn_left) And
                        Folded(t.syn_right)
                    Fi
                Od
            Otherwise Do True Od
        End;

    Define Value(e: integer_constant) = e.lex_value;
    Define Value(e: real_constant) = e.lex_value;
    Define Value(e: formal_parameterRef) = 1;
    Cyclic Define Value(e: unary_operation) Returns Rational =
        If e.syn_op Is plus
            Then Value(e.syn_argument)
        Else - Value(e.syn_argument)
        Fi;

    Cyclic Define Value(e: binary_operation) Returns Rational =
        If e.syn_op Is plus
            Then Value(e.syn_left) + Value(e.syn_right)
        OrIf e.syn_op Is minus
            Then Value(e.syn_left) - Value(e.syn_right)
        OrIf e.syn_op Is times
            Then Value(e.syn_left) * Value(e.syn_right)
        Else Value(e.syn_left) / Value(e.syn_right)
        Fi;
    Cyclic Define Value(f: function) Returns Rational
            = Value(f.syn_definition);
End
```

Figure 3.9: The Specification for the Generic Process

```
-- file: functionlang/constantfold/C/constant_fold.idl

Import cf From cf End

Process constant_fold Refines cf Is
    Target Language C;
End
```

Figure 3.10: The Specification for the `constant_fold` Process For C


```
-- file: functionlang/constantfold/Pascal/constant_fold.idl

Import cf From cf End

Process constant_fold Refines cf Is
    Target Language Pascal;
End
```

Figure 3.11: The Specification for the `constant_fold` Process For Pascal

Node attributes can be accessed through the fields of the `struct` declared for each node.

```
binary_operation abinary_operation;
    .
    .
    .
abinary_operation->syn_op = Nplus;
```

For those variables of a class type, the `IDLclassCommon` member of the C `union` representing the class contains those attributes common to the class. The `sem_exp_type` attribute of the `expression` class is an example. This attribute can be accessed directly in a node

```
abinary_operation->sem_exp_type = Nreal;
```

which is permitted since `binary_operation` is a member of the `expression` class. Variables and expressions of a class type can also access such attributes.

3.3. TRANSLATING THE SPECIFICATION

```
operation anoperation;
...
anoperation.IDLclassCommon->sem_exp_type = Nreal;
```

Conversion of a node to a superclass uses a member in the union.

```
anoperation.Vbinary_operation = abinary_operation;
```

You must keep the class membership tree in mind when doing these casts. Errors in such conversions will be flagged by the C compiler. Conversion of a class to a superclass also uses a member in the *union*.

```
expression anexpression;
...
anexpression.Voperation = anoperation;
```

A conversion in the other direction, from a class to a subclass or to a node, is similar, except that the member is used on the right-hand side of the assignment statement:

```
if (typeof(anoperation)==Kbinary_operation)
    abinary_operation = anoperation.Vbinary_operation;
```

Such conversions should *always* be done in the context of an *if* or *switch* statement, to ensure that the conversion is a valid one.

The Pascal Target Language

The output from the IDL translator consists of four files: the header file named **constant_fold.h**, the signature declaration file named **constant_fold.i**, the runtime support routine source code file named **constant_fold.p**, and a compiled version of that file named **constant_fold.o**.

Since no target language version is specified, the default (Version A) is used. This version differs from Version B discussed in Chapter 2 only in that the accessing and conversion functions are not generated. For large specifications, the number of functions generated in Version B may overwhelm the Pascal compiler.

Direct attributes in nodes can be accessed through the fields of the *record* declared for each node.

```
var abinaryoperation: abinaryoperation;
...
abinaryoperation^.synop := Nplus;
```

Variables contained in the node but declared in a superclass of a node require a little more work to access. Since classes are also represented with records, and the attributes declared in a class reside in these records, the Pascal code must "walk up" the class hierarchy to access attributes declared with classes. The `sem_exp_type` attribute of the `expression` class is an example. This attribute can be accessed directly in a node through perhaps multiple levels of indirection.

```
abinaryoperation^.Poperation^.Pexpression^.semexptype := Nreal;
```

Variables of a class type can also access such attributes, with possibly fewer steps.

```
var anoperation: operation;
...
anoperation^.Pexpression^.semexptype := Nreal;
```

The class that is directly associated with the attribute has an easier time.

```
var anexpression: expression;
...
anexpression^.semexptype := Nreal;
```

Conversion of a node to a superclass also requires traversing the class hierarchy.

```
anexpression = abinaryoperation^.Poperation^.Pexpression;
```

Conversion of a class to a superclass is handled in the same way.

```
anexpression := anoperation^.Pexpression;
```

A conversion in the other direction, from a class to a subclass, is similar, but uses a (variant) field with a "V" prefix.

```
if anoperation^.Eoperation = Koperationbinaryoperation
   then abinaryoperation := anoperation^.Vbinaryoperation;
```

Such conversions should *always* be done in the context of an `if` or `case` statement, to ensure that the conversion is a valid one.

3.4 Writing the Algorithm

The third step is to write the algorithm for the constant folding in the target programming language. Our algorithm consists of a postorder walk of the expression tree. Whenever a node of the expression tree consists of a binary or unary operation, the attached subexpression(s) are constant

3.4. WRITING THE ALGORITHM

```
/* file: functionlang/constantfold/C/main.c */
#include <stdio.h>
#include "constant_fold.h"

main()
{
        SEQfunction Sfunction;
        function Afunction;
        functions thefunctions;

        /* input the attributed syntax tree of a function */
        thefunctions = inputport(stdin);

        /* perform constant folding on defining expression */
        foreachinSEQfunction(thefunctions->syn_func_seq, Sfunction,
                             Afunction) {
           fold(&(Afunction->syn_definition));
        }

        /* output the parse tree of the equivalent function */
        outputport(stdout, thefunctions, TWOPASS);

        exit(0);
}
```

Figure 3.12: C Code for the `main` Function

```
(* file: functionlang/constantfold/Pascal/const2.h *)
procedure fold (var exp: expression); external;
```

Figure 3.13: Pascal Declaration of the `fold` Procedure

folded before checking whether constant folding can be applied to the current expression node. Two routines are required: a main routine to control the process and a routine to do the constant folding.

The code for the main routine is shown in Figures 3.12 (in the C target language) and 3.14 (in the Pascal target language). The signature of the `fold` routine is provided in Figure 3.13. An instance of a `attributed_syntax` data structure is read, revised according to the constant folding algorithm, and written to the next phase. The parameter is passed the function definition by reference, so that it may be replaced with a folded definition.

The code for the recursive postorder tree walk routine is shown in Figures 3.15 and 3.16 (in the C target language) and 3.17 and 3.18 (in the Pascal target language). If the current expression is an operation, the subexpression(s) are constant folded in recursive call(s). The current expression is then constant folded if possible. When all the operands are constant, the operation is invoked on the values of the operands, at compile-time. A

(* file: functionlang/constantfold/Pascal/main.p *)

```pascal
program constantfold (input, output);

#include "constant_fold.h"

var   ATfunction: Tfunction;
      thefunctions: functions;
      i: integer;
      ReaderOK: boolean;

#include "const2.h"
#include "constant_fold.i"

begin
      (* input the attributed syntax tree of a function *)
      thefunctions := inputport(input, ReaderOK);
      if not ReaderOK then halt;

      (* perform constant folding on defining expression *)
      for i := 1 to lengthSEQTfunction(thefunctions^.synfuncseq) do begin
          ATfunction:= ithinSEQTfunction(thefunctions^.synfuncseq, i);
              fold(ATfunction^.syndefinition);
          end;

      (* output the parse tree of the equivalent function *)
      outputport(output, thefunctions);
end.
```

Figure 3.14: Pascal Code for the main Function

new `constant` node is allocated, the value inserted, and the `constant` node substituted for the parameter value. In the C code note the extensive use of ".V" to select a subclass once the `typeof` operator has determined that this is appropriate. In the Pascal code, note the analogous use of "^.P" to go through a subclass.

3.5 Compiling the Process

The last step is to compile and link our program. If the C code for the constant folding algorithm resides in a file named **algorithm.c** and the main program is in **main.c**, the command to compile and link the application is as follows.

```
cc -o constant_fold algorithm.c main.c constant_fold.o \
        /usr/lib/libidl.a
```

If the Pascal code for the constant folding algorithm resides in a file named **algorithm.p** and the main program is in **main.p**, the command to compile and link the application would be

```
pc -o constant_fold algorithm.p main.p constant_fold.o \
        /usr/lib/libidlP.a
```

The files **libidl.a** and **libidlP.a** are libraries of generic routines that form a portion of the IDL runtime support routines. The pathname for this file will vary from system to system. The result of this command will be in an executable program in the file named **constant_fold**.

3.6 Running the Process

We now run the constant folding program on the parse tree for the function `foo` first introduced in Figure 3.4. Since the program processes parse trees cast in the ASCII ERL, it is necessary to first convert the function language representation of `foo` into the parse tree introduced in Figure 3.7 and then into the ASCII ERL. The ASCII external representation of `foo` is shown in Figure 3.19.

Once the parse tree for `foo` had been cast into the ASCII ERL, it could be processed by the program. If the external representation of `foo` resides in a file named **foo.aer**, the command to process it would be

```
        constant_fold < foo.aer > foo_after.aer
```

```
/* file: constantfold/C/algorithm.c */

#include <stdio.h>
#include "constant_fold.h"

float get_constant_value (theConstant)
constant (theConstant);
{
    if (typeof (theConstant) == Kinteger_constant)
            return (theConstant.Vinteger_constant->lex_value);
    else return (theConstant.Vreal_constant->lex_value);
}

fold (exp)
expression* exp;
{
    binary_operation   theBinaryOperation;
    binaryoperator     theBinaryOperator;
    unary_operation    theUnaryOperation;
    unaryoperator      theUnaryOperator;
    expression         leftOperand;
    expression         rightOperand;
    expression         theOperand;
    float              x, y, z;

    switch (typeof (*exp)) {
    case Kbinary_operation:
        fold (&((*exp).Vbinary_operation->syn_left ));
        fold (&((*exp).Vbinary_operation->syn_right));

        theBinaryOperation = (*exp).Vbinary_operation;
        theBinaryOperator = theBinaryOperation->syn_op;
        leftOperand = theBinaryOperation->syn_left;
        rightOperand = theBinaryOperation->syn_right;

        if (((typeof (leftOperand ) == Kinteger_constant)
                || (typeof (leftOperand ) == Kreal_constant))
            && ((typeof (rightOperand) == Kinteger_constant)
                || (typeof (rightOperand) == Kreal_constant)))
        {
            x = get_constant_value (leftOperand);
            y = get_constant_value (rightOperand);

            switch (typeof (theBinaryOperator)) {
            case Kplus:   z = (x + y); break;
            case Kminus:  z = (x - y); break;
            case Kdivide: z = (x / y); break;
            case Ktimes:  z = (x * y); break;
            }
```

Figure 3.15: C Code for the `fold` Function, Part 1

```
            switch (typeof (theBinaryOperation->sem_exp_type)) {
            case KTint:
                (*exp).Vinteger_constant = Ninteger_constant;
                (*exp).Vinteger_constant->sem_exp_type.VTint = NTint;
                (*exp).Vinteger_constant->lex_value = z;
                break;

            case Kreal:
                (*exp).Vreal_constant = Nreal_constant;
                (*exp).Vreal_constant->sem_exp_type.Vreal = Nreal;
                (*exp).Vreal_constant->lex_value = z;
                break;
            }
        }

        break;

    case Kunary_operation:
        fold (&((*exp).Vunary_operation->syn_argument));

        theUnaryOperation = (*exp).Vunary_operation;
        theUnaryOperator = theUnaryOperation->syn_op;
        theOperand = theUnaryOperation->syn_argument;

        if ((typeof (theOperand ) == Kinteger_constant)
            || (typeof (theOperand ) == Kreal_constant))
        {
            x = get_constant_value (theOperand);

            switch (typeof (theUnaryOperator)) {
            case Kunaryplus:  z = ( x); break;
            case Kunaryminus: z = (- x); break;
            }

            switch (typeof (theUnaryOperation->sem_exp_type)) {
            case KTint:
                (*exp).Vinteger_constant = Ninteger_constant;
                (*exp).Vinteger_constant->sem_exp_type.VTint = NTint;
                (*exp).Vinteger_constant->lex_value = z;
                break;

            case Kreal:
                (*exp).Vreal_constant = Nreal_constant;
                (*exp).Vreal_constant->sem_exp_type.Vreal = Nreal;
                (*exp).Vreal_constant->lex_value = z;
                break;
            }
        }

        break;

    default:
        /* can only constant fold operations */
        break;
    }
}
```

Figure 3.16: C Code for the `fold` Function, Part 2

(* file: functionlang/constantfold/Pascal/algorithm.p *)

```
#include "constant_fold.h"
#include "const2.h"
#include "constant_fold.i"

function getconstantvalue (theconstant: constant): real;
begin
      if theconstant^.Econstant = Kconstantintegerconstant
      then getconstantvalue := theconstant^.Vintegerconstant^.lexvalue
      else getconstantvalue := theconstant^.Vrealconstant^.lexvalue;
end;

procedure fold (*var exp: expression*);
var   thebinaryoperation: binaryoperation;
      thebinaryoperator: binaryoperator;
      theunaryoperation: unaryoperation;
      theunaryoperator: unaryoperator;
      leftOperand: expression;
      rightOperand: expression;
      theOperand: expression;
      x, y, z: real;
      tempintegerconstant: integerconstant;
      tempint: int;
      temprealconstant: realconstant;
      tempTreal: Treal;

begin
      case exp^.Eexpression of
      KexpressionformalparameterRef: (* do nothing *);
      Kexpressionconstant: (* do nothing *);
      Kexpressionoperation: case exp^.Voperation^.Eoperation of
          Koperationbinaryoperation: begin
                fold (exp^.Voperation^.Vbinaryoperation^.synleft);
                fold (exp^.Voperation^.Vbinaryoperation^.synright);

                thebinaryoperation := exp^.Voperation^.Vbinaryoperation;
                thebinaryoperator := thebinaryoperation^.synop;
                leftOperand := thebinaryoperation^.synleft;
                rightOperand := thebinaryoperation^.synright;

                if (leftOperand^.Eexpression = Kexpressionconstant)
                     and (rightOperand^.Eexpression = Kexpressionconstant)
                then begin
                     x := getconstantvalue (leftOperand^.Vconstant);
                     y := getconstantvalue (rightOperand^.Vconstant);

                     case thebinaryoperator^.Ebinaryoperator of
                     Kbinaryoperatorplus: z := (x + y);
                     Kbinaryoperatorminus: z := (x - y);
                     Kbinaryoperatordivide: z := (x / y);
                     Kbinaryoperatortimes: z := (x * y);
                     end;
```

Figure 3.17: Pascal Code for the fold Procedure, Part 1

3.6. RUNNING THE PROCESS 95

```
              case thebinaryoperation^.Poperation^.Pexpression
                  ^.semexptype^.Etypes of
              Ktypesint: begin
                  tempintegerconstant := Nintegerconstant;
                  exp := tempintegerconstant^.Pconstant^.Pexpression;
                  tempint := Nint;
                  tempintegerconstant^.Pconstant^.Pexpression^.semexptype
                     := tempint^.Ptypes;
                  tempintegerconstant^.lexvalue := trunc(z);
                  end;
              KtypesTreal: begin
                  temprealconstant := Nrealconstant;
                  exp := temprealconstant^.Pconstant^.Pexpression;
                  tempTreal := NTreal;
                  temprealconstant^.Pconstant^.Pexpression^.semexptype
                     := tempTreal^.Ptypes;
                  temprealconstant^.lexvalue := z;
                  end;
              end
           end
        end;

   Koperationunaryoperation: begin
        fold (exp^.Voperation^.Vunaryoperation^.synargument);
        theunaryoperation := exp^.Voperation^.Vunaryoperation;
        theunaryoperator := theunaryoperation^.synop;
        theOperand := theunaryoperation^.synargument;
        if theOperand^.Eexpression = Kexpressionconstant
        then begin
            x := getconstantvalue (theOperand^.Vconstant);
            case theunaryoperator^.Eunaryoperator of
            Kunaryoperatorunaryplus: z := ( x);
            Kunaryoperatorunaryminus: z := (- x);
            end;

            case theunaryoperation^.Poperation^.Pexpression
                ^.semexptype^.Etypes of
            Ktypesint: begin
                tempintegerconstant := Nintegerconstant;
                exp := tempintegerconstant^.Pconstant^.Pexpression;
                tempint := Nint;
                exp^.semexptype:= tempint^.Ptypes;
                tempintegerconstant^.lexvalue := trunc(z);
                end;
            KtypesTreal: begin
                temprealconstant := Nrealconstant;
                exp := temprealconstant^.Pconstant^.Pexpression;
                tempTreal := NTreal;
                exp^.semexptype:= tempTreal^.Ptypes;
                temprealconstant^.lexvalue := z;
                end;
            end
          end;
       end
     end
   end
end;
```

Figure 3.18: Pascal Code for the fold Procedure, Part 2

The Function Language Representation:

```
function foo(A: integer): integer
    = -A * (28 + 13);
```

The ASCII External Representation:

```
-- structure attributed_syntax
functions[syn_func_seq <
    function
        [syn_name identifier[lex_token "foo"; lex_pos 590977];
        syn_return_type int;
        syn_parameters <
            L1:formal_parameter[syn_name
                    identifier[lex_token "A"; lex_pos 853633];
                syn_param_type L2:int]
        >;
        syn_definition binary_operation[
            syn_op times;
            syn_left unary_operation[syn_op unaryminus;
                syn_argument formal_parameterRef[syn_name
                        identifier[lex_token "A"; lex_pos 2490882];
                    sem_exp_type L2^;
                    sem_entity L1^];
                sem_exp_type int;
                ];
            syn_right binary_operation[syn_op plus;
                syn_left integer_constant[lex_value 28;
                    sem_exp_type int];
                syn_right integer_constant[lex_value 13;
                    sem_exp_type int];
                sem_exp_type int];
            sem_exp_type int;
        ]
    ]
>]
#
```

Figure 3.19: Function foo Before Constant Folding

3.7. SUMMARY

The Function Language Representation:

```
        function foo(A: integer): integer
            = -A * 41;
```

The ASCII External Representation:

```
--   structure attributed_syntax
functions[syn_func_seq <
    function
        [syn_name identifier[lex_token "foo"; lex_pos 590977]
        syn_return_type int;
        syn_parameters <
            L1:formal_parameter[syn_name
                        identifier[lex_token "A"; lex_pos 853633]
                syn_param_type L2:int]
            >;
        syn_definition binary_operation[
            syn_op times;
            syn_left unary_operation[syn_argument
                formal_parameterRef[
                    syn_name identifier[lex_token "A";
                        lex_pos 2490882];
                    sem_exp_type L2^;
                    sem_entity L1^;
                    ];
                syn_op unaryminus;
                sem_exp_type int];
            syn_right integer_constant[lex_value 41;
                sem_exp_type int];
            sem_exp_type int;
            ];
        ]
>]
#
```

Figure 3.20: Function foo After Constant Folding

After processing, the output would be an equivalent definition for foo residing in **foo_after.aer**, shown after slight formatting in Figure 3.20. The input and output instances could then be sent to IDLCHECK to ensure that all the assertions were met.

3.7 Summary

It is worth noting several characteristics of this solution. It was easy to design, quick to implement, and, in large part, documents itself. The design was made easy because IDL permits a natural expression of the attributed_syntax data structure that omits unnecessary detail such as the specific representation chosen to implement the sequence of the formal_parameterRef nodes. The implementation was quick since the IDL translator automatically generated most of the necessary code from the specification of the constant folding process. And, finally, the solution substantially documents itself.

One way to characterize IDL is by viewing it from several different angles. In the following, we consider IDL from eight viewpoints, each contributing towards a complete definition, and compare it with other approaches. In the next part, where we give a complete definition of the language and its support in the C and Pascal target languages, we will elaborate on the points made here; the bibliographic notes found there will make more specific comparisons.

3.7.1 IDL Is A Specification Language

The heart of IDL is a notation for specifying the properties of major data structures used in programs and of data interfaces within and between programs. The ability to concisely and precisely specify such interfaces is a key step in the design and modularization of large programs and the integration of cooperating collections of programs. A practical system such as the IDL toolkit supporting such interface specifications can be an effective means of reducing the costs of software at all stages of the software life cycle.

The IDL data specification language provides a high level, simple and elegant, representation-independent way of describing complex data structures. The specification language includes a refinement mechanism that permits incremental specification of concrete representations for a data structure. As such IDL is an abstract data type mechanism.

Traditional abstract data type mechanisms (such as Ada packages and axiomatic and algebraic specifications) work well when the abstract data structures involved are fairly simple. Some examples of these simple data structures are stacks, linked lists, and hash tables. These mechanisms, however, fail to provide any effective methodology for dealing with abstract types where the structural relationships of the data is the dominant abstract characteristic. Important examples of these kinds of data structures include parse trees, symbol tables, flow graphs, relational networks and many other examples in the area of system software. For these structures, IDL provides a concise notation and an effective methodology that is complementary to traditional abstract data type mechanisms.

3.7.2 IDL Supports Arbitrary Data Structures

The basis of an IDL data structure is a directed attributed graph. This data structure is fully general and subsumes all the data structures found in programming. As such, IDL can be thought of as an abstraction of the

3.7. SUMMARY

union of the data type structuring facilities found in procedural programming languages.

At the simplest level, primitive domains support boolean, numeric and character data. At the next level, support is provided for sets, sequences, enumerations, records and variants. At the highest level, nodes and arcs connecting nodes (abstract "pointers") provide support for trees, linked lists, graphs, as well as arbitrarily complex data relationships.

3.7.3 IDL Supports Representation Selection

IDL is not only a specification language, but can be used as a practical software implementation tool. The key component is the translator that automatically selects representations for an IDL data structure and produces code to create and process the data structure within conventional procedural programming languages. Experience with IDL shows that even though the level of an IDL specification is quite abstract, the automatically produced representations have practical efficiency comparable to more traditional manually specified data structures. A real advantage here is that IDL frees the programmer from the more tedious and error-prone aspects of the specification of complex data structures.

Even though the automatic representation selection system is usually sufficient, in some cases more explicit programmer control is needed. IDL provides an explicit representation specification mechanism for such cases. Representation specifications can be incrementally added; they need only be given for those parts of the data structure where explicit control is needed. Representation specifications provide a range of control starting with very general statements about space-time tradeoffs to very specific statements that indicate specific bit fields where data is to be placed.

3.7.4 IDL Supports Data Interchange

Since IDL is a superset of the data structuring capabilities of procedural languages, the IDL translator can map a single IDL specification into multiple target languages. It is possible for a program to be constructed with separate parts written in different implementation languages. In this way, IDL is able to transcend the type system of a single specific procedural language and provide a single common point for the data definition for the mixed language system.

Although mixed language systems have long been possible, they make it necessary to define the same data structure in each language separately and place a considerable burden on the programmer to make sure that these independent data representations are compatible. Compatibility becomes even more severe when the program is to be ported to another computer because the data layout for many languages is a property of the compiler for the language and will almost certainly change when a different host machine is used. These problems have served to discourage the use of mixed language systems in practice. IDL solves these problems making mixed language systems much easier to develop, maintain, and port.

A key contribution of the external text form is that it is able to represent not only simple data but also data that involves arbitrary cycles. An advantage of the IDL system is that the IDL translator produces the port routines. Many existing software systems incorporate parts that are similar in role to ports but are written manually with considerable development and debugging effort. The IDL system provides this capability automatically.

The external representation language provides a means to transfer data between separate programs, even when they reside on entirely different computers. This facility considerably simplifies the development of cooperating systems of programs. Transfer may be via a shared file system, networked file system, or an arbitrary communications path; the machines could be as dissimilar as a large mainframe and a microcomputer.

3.7.5 IDL Supports Data Debugging

Most current software development systems provide only minimal support for debugging simple data structures. In the most primitive form commonly available, the data structure is displayed in octal or hexadecimal format, leaving the decoding to the programmer. When the data structures become complex, debugging becomes exceedingly tedious and time consuming at best. Errors in interpretation of the data can lead to much lost time. In an IDL-based system, however, an entire complex data structure can be examined by invoking an output port and manually examining the resulting text file.

3.7.6 IDL Supports Modular Specifications

Derivation is another key concept of IDL. It allows you to specify closely related data structures. Two uses of derivation mechanisms are effective. The first of these allows a new data specification to be constructed that is the union of multiple separate specifications. For example, a structure which is the union of an abstract parse tree, a symbol table, and a flow graph may be produced from independently-specified structures, while allowing them to reference each other.

The second use states that a new specification is "just like" a previous specification but with a selected set of additions and deletions. *Multiple*

3.7. SUMMARY

views is thereby supported. A restricted view in effect supports information hiding, a key component of data abstraction. The implementor of a package may export one view of a data structure to users while maintaining another, typically richer, view for the implementation.

If we place a further interpretation that multiple views represent different disjoint "times" during the processing of a data structure, it is possible to use the same piece of memory to represent different attributes that have disjoint "lifetimes". This can, in many systems, result in a considerable savings in main memory space consumption. Although this overlap can be achieved in many programming languages, it is difficult to express because type-system defeats are generally required and because the possibilities for human error becomes severe with usually disastrous consequences, IDL provides a much more convenient, human manageable, and safe way of achieving this important optimization.

3.7.7 IDL Supports Data Validation

Another part of IDL is the assertion language and the associated assertion checker. The IDL specification language permits you to specify the data domains and connection information for an IDL data structure. The IDL assertion language permits even more detailed specifications to be made, ranging from simple assertions that specify the required relationship of several attributes to complex assertions. While many restrictions can be enforced by careful use of the specification language (the specification making it impossible to construct certain "incorrect" structures), more complicated semantic restrictions, such as asserting that some particular substructure is cycle-free, cannot be handled at the specification level. For this, the assertion language allows greater scope in stating the restrictions.

Automatic checking of the assertions is provided by the assertion checker. This tool may be used for system integration, since it is can detect when a program or program component is in violation of its interface specification.

3.7.8 IDL Has Similarities With Data Bases

When an IDL data structure is recorded on secondary storage, a primitive data base system results. Data is entered into the data base by an output port and accessed by an input port. The IDL data specification language shows a family resemblance to the data definition languages found in many data base systems. Similarly, the IDL derivation mechanism is closely related to the data base concept of multiple views; the assertion language is related to data base integrity constraint languages.

Exercises

3.1 Compare and contrast the concepts of a *class hierarchy* and a *parse tree*.

3.2 If function calls were permitted in the function language, what additional opportunities are available for constant folding?

Bibliographic Notes

Chou and Ganapathi [1983] and Ottenstein [1984] provide bibliographies on intermediate representations in compiler construction. Intermediate representations passed between phases of a compiler are of two basic types: n-address tuples (generally, $n = 0$: stack machine code and Polish notation, $n = 3$: 3-address code (Aho, Sethi, and Ullman [1986]), n arbitrary: N-address code (Frailey [1979]) or attributed graphs (e.g., parse trees, abstract syntax trees, computation graphs (Waite and Goos [1984])).

External linear representations include quadruples, triples, indirect triples ([Aho, Sethi, and Ullman [1986]), postfix, prefix and attributed-prefix (Ganapathi et al. [1981]). In this context, IDL instances are attributed graphs with a generalized attributed-prefix external linear representation.

Part II

Language Definition

Part II of this book consists of a reference manual for IDL and the IDL Toolkit. Chapter 4 defines the syntax and semantics of an IDL specification. Chapter 5 defines the sublanguage used to make assertions about components of an IDL specification. In Chapter 6 we discuss an external (ASCII) representation of the data defined by an IDL specification; this representation is essential for communication of data between computing systems. Chapter 7 outlines how the abstract specification of IDL can be mechanically converted into a concrete implementation in the C programming language; Chapter 8 covers the same ground for the Pascal programming language. Chapters 7 and 8 can be read independently; they cover the same material in the same manner, but for different programming languages. Chapter 9 contains a description of a compiler written in both C and Pascal. Finally, Chapter 10 looks at the broader issue of how IDL should be used in a compiler.

Chapter 4

IDL Language Definition

An IDL specification of a program is a precise statement of the environment and its associated programs, as shown, for example, in Figure 1.2 on page 3. The specification defines both the data—denoted by boxes—and the processes or programs—denoted by ovals. Data is viewed as an instance of an abstract data type about which various assertions can be made. Processing components are viewed as accepting one or more data types that satisfy these assertions; in turn, these components establish other assertions. We shall refer to descriptions of data as *structures* and to descriptions of programs as *processes*.

We will also occasionally speak of *structure instances* and *process instances*. A structure instance is a particular data structure that meets the assertions contained in a particular structure specification. A process instance is a particular program that fits a particular process specification. We will sometimes speak about a structure or process when we mean "all structure instances satisfying some structure specification" or "all programs satisfying some process specification"; the meaning should be clear from the context.

Although IDL takes an abstract view of data and programs, we intend it to be a *practical* tool in the construction and maintenance of collections of real systems. Hence we must be ultimately concerned with implementation issues and with the paramount need to keep the formal IDL specification synchronized with implementations of it. More will be said about implementation below; for the moment we will simply assert that we intend for implementations to be mechanically derived from the formal definition, thus forcing synchrony. Information about the intended implementation strategy must be present in the IDL specification.

For methodological reasons, it must be possible to include representational information in a manner that is disjoint from the logical portion of the specification; that is, we want a separation similar to the separation of specification and implementation in data abstraction languages. *Abstract* structure and process specifications would describe logical properties; *concrete* specifications would provide implementation-specific properties. However, a rigid enforcement of this distinction would reduce the usefulness of IDL as a tool; it is easy to imagine other methodologies that involve hierarchies of specifications, with lower levels having more concrete details.

An IDL specification, then, contains four kinds of information.

- *Structure Specifications*

    - *Abstract*: Here we define the structures in terms of the abstract model (typed attributed directed graphs) discussed in Chapter 1. Each abstract structure specification defines the domain of a single abstract data type by giving the node types that can be used for objects in the domain. Defining a node type involves specifying the names and types of its attributes. A structure specification can also include assertions that specify constraints on instances of the structure. This level of data specification makes no commitment to representational details.

    - *Concrete Level*: Here we provide details of the representation of abstract structures. For each structure specification that satisfies certain constraints as to the level of detail it embodies, as will specified later in this chapter, there is a standard ASCII external representation for the data described by that specification.

- *Process Specifications*

    - *Abstract Level*: Here we define each of the processes (the programs), in terms of what structures they expect as input and what structures they produce as output (termed "ports"). A process specification can also include assertions relating instances of the input and output data structures. These specifications attempt to capture the logical properties of a program without unduly constraining implementations.

    - *Concrete Level*: Here we provide implementation-specific details for the abstract processes. This information includes bindings of port specifications to particular port realizations, and restrictions on the set of operations the process may perform on the data.

Structures (and, independently, processes) can be organized into hierarchies, with lower levels providing more representational details. We speak of a lower-level declaration as being a *refinement* of its parent in the hierarchy. In each of these specifications, IDL provides a notation to describe certain structural properties of the component being specified. In addition, an extensible assertion language is defined for expressing properties other than those captured by the structural and typing notation. The checking of these assertions is defined by each implementation, and may occur when data is read from (written to) external media, when the data is being manipulated, or at some other time.

Although we intend that IDL be processible by machine, another important use is to communicate specifications among people. IDL allows much flexibility in the way a specification is written. Order of specifications is never significant; portions of declarations may be written separately and merged by the IDL processor. The order in which the rules are written and the use of comments and indentation is important for human understanding. Various orders and styles will make good sense in certain contexts. Unfortunately, sloppy use, poor mnemonics, and poor factorization of the specification can all detract from readability.

Two of the operations defined for each structure are reading and writing external representations. The external ASCII representation language, defined in Chapter 6, is intended to allow for communication among arbitrary tools, written in arbitrary languages for arbitrary machines. Within a particular host environment there may also be several binary representations used to communicate among tools written in different languages but running on the same machine.

The following sections define IDL. The syntactic definition of IDL is given in the extended BNF introduced in Section 1.5. The syntax is collected in Appendix B. Lexical conventions are also given there.

An IDL specification consists of a sequence of structure, process, and import specifications.

⟨specification⟩ ::= { ⟨structure decl⟩ | ⟨process decl⟩ | ⟨import decl⟩ }*

The declarations are not required to be in any particular order, and there may be more than one of each of them. You may group related portions of a specification in ways that enhance readability.

We will discuss each kind of declaration in turn. Assertions are covered in Chapter 5.

4.1 Structure Specifications

A structure specification is divided into a set of structural constraints, a set of assertions, and a set of representational specifications. Structural constraints specify the node types included in the structure, together with their set of possible attributes. Assertions capture all the other significant properties of the structure.

⟨structure decl⟩ ::= **Structure** ⟨str_name⟩ { **Root** ⟨type⟩ }$^?$
{ **Refines** ⟨str_name⟩ }$^?$
{ **From** ⟨str_name⟩ { ',' ⟨str_name⟩ }* }$^?$
Is { ⟨structure stmt⟩ ';' }* **End**

⟨structure stmt⟩ ::= ⟨production⟩ | ⟨type decl⟩ | ⟨without clause⟩
| ⟨attribute rep⟩ | ⟨type rep⟩ | ⟨assertion stmt⟩

Each structure declaration defines a new structure whose name follows the keyword **Structure**. Each structure must have a distinct name. If the **Root** clause is present, the ⟨type⟩ following the **Root** keyword specifies a node, class, set, sequence, or private type that is the type of the root object of the data structure; the root object is a distinguished object from which all others in the structure can be reached. The order in which ⟨structure stmt⟩s appear is not significant.

A structure can be specified in one of three ways.

- As a new structure. Here, the **Refines** and **From** clauses are omitted and no **Without** clauses are permitted.

- As a *refinement* of another structure. Here the **Refines** clause names the structure from which the new structure is refined, and no **Without** clauses, productions, or type declarations are permitted.

- As a modification or *derivation* of other structures. The **From** clause names the other structures. The new structure is defined by copying and editing the old structures.

Derived or refined structures are termed *dependent structures*, and the structures from which they are derived or refined are termed *ancestor structures*.

4.1.1 Productions and Type Declarations

Productions and type declarations define structural constraints. Node productions define names and types of attributes for each node type. Type declarations define *private types*, which are types whose structure is not specified within the structure specification. *Classes* are names for collections of node types; when used as types for attributes, they specify that the attribute may reference objects of any of the node types in the class. Private type names, class type names, and node type names must all be distinct.

⟨production⟩ ::= ⟨class production⟩ | ⟨attribute production⟩

The "::=" form of production is used to define class names.

⟨class production⟩ ::= ⟨class_name⟩ ' ::= '
 { ⟨class_node_name⟩
 { ' | ' ⟨class_node_name⟩ }* }?

The names to the right of the "::=" must be class or node names. The new class consists of the union of all node types that are in any classes named on the right hand side. The same class name may appear on the left of several class productions. Here, the class consists of the union of the node types defined in all such productions. Class names may not depend on themselves in a circular fashion involving only class productions. A class production with no names after the "::=" declares the ⟨class_name⟩ as a class without (as yet) any node or class members.

The "=>" form of production is used to associate sets of attributes with node and class types. Each attribute is given a name and a type.

⟨attribute production⟩ ::= { ⟨node_name⟩ | ⟨class_name⟩ } ' => '
 { ⟨attribute⟩ { ' , ' ⟨attribute⟩ }* }?
⟨attribute⟩ ::= ⟨attribute_name⟩ ' : ' ⟨type⟩

The name to the left of the "=>" is defined as a node type name if it is not defined elsewhere as a class name (i.e., on the left hand side of a class production). An ⟨attribute production⟩ with no names after the "=>" declares the name as a node without (as yet) any attributes. No node type can appear on the left-hand side of a class production (otherwise, it would be considered a class type). The ⟨attribute⟩s to the right of the "=>" define a set of attributes that are to be associated with the node types belonging to the class whose name appears on the left. The same node or class name may appear on the left of several attribute productions. The attributes of a node type are the union of the attributes specified for all classes that contain the node type. The attributes of a node type must all have different names; however, attribute names need not be disjoint from node, class, and private names. Different node types may have attributes of the same name.

The type declaration is used to define private names.

⟨type decl⟩ ::= Type ⟨private_name⟩

Private types name implementation-specific data structures that are inappropriate to specify as an abstract structure. For instance, a structure specification describing a compiler's parse tree might wish to include information in each node object about the position in the source file corresponding to that object. The notion of what constitutes a source position could be different in different environments.

Each node, class, and private type must be declared explicitly. There are no default types for undeclared names in the semantics of IDL. However particular implementations may choose to use a default type as an error recovery strategy for resolving undefined references.

4.1.2 Basic Types

In this section we define the set of permitted attribute types.

⟨atomic type⟩ ::= Boolean | Integer | Rational | String
              | ⟨atomic_name⟩
⟨type⟩   ::= ⟨atomic type⟩ | { Set | Seq } Of ⟨atomic_type⟩

These basic types are.

- **Boolean** — the boolean type with values true and false.

- **Integer** — the integer type, containing both positive and negative numbers.

- **String** — ASCII strings. Any ASCII character may be represented, including printing characters, blanks, and nonprinting control characters. Nonprinting characters are represented using an escape character as described in detail in Appendix B.1.

- **Rational** — the type containing all ratios of two integers. This type includes all values typically found in computer integer, floating point and fixed point types.

4.1. STRUCTURE SPECIFICATIONS

- *Set Of* ⟨atomic_name⟩ — an unordered collection (set) of values of ⟨atomic_name⟩, where ⟨atomic_name⟩ is the name of a node, class, private type, or the predefined types *Boolean*, *Integer*, *String*, and *Rational*. Duplication of values (i.e. multisets) is not permitted.

- *Seq Of* ⟨atomic_name⟩ — an ordered collection (sequence) of values of type ⟨⟩*atomic_name*, with the same restriction on permitted ⟨atomic_name⟩s as sets.

- ⟨atomic_name⟩ — a node, class, or private type. A value of a class type is a node object whose type is an element of the class.

There are no enumeration types per se; a class of node types having no attributes can serve this purpose. Sets and sequences of sets or sequences are not permitted.

4.1.3 Type Representations

A structure specification can contain attribute representations and type representations.

An attribute representation can be used to specify some aspect of the implementation of an attribute.

⟨attribute rep⟩ ::= *For* ⟨name⟩ '.' ⟨attribute_name⟩
    Use { ⟨parameter⟩ }⁺

⟨parameter⟩ ::= ⟨name⟩ | ⟨integer⟩ | ⟨rational⟩ | ⟨string⟩

The first name in the type reference must be a class or node name. The name after the dot must be the name of an attribute declared in some "=>" production. The ⟨parameter⟩s specify some aspect of the representation. Each IDL implementation may extend the syntax of the ⟨attribute rep⟩ to provide additional implementation-specific details; such extensions add new combinations of valid ⟨parameter⟩s. The IDL Toolkit implements several variants of ⟨attribute rep⟩; see Appendices C and D for a list of the valid options. As an example, the size of an attribute can be specified as

For ⟨name⟩.⟨attribute_name⟩ *Use Representation* ⟨integer⟩ *Bits*;

Several other variants are permitted by each target language. For instance, C permits integer-valued attributes to be defined as signed (the default) or unsigned.

For ⟨name⟩.⟨attribute_name⟩ *Use Representation Unsigned*;

A type representation may be used to define the way in which a type is to be represented.

⟨type rep⟩ ::= *For* ⟨type⟩ *Use* { ⟨parameter⟩ }⁺

Again, the allowable combinations of ⟨parameter⟩(s) are specific to the implementation. The IDL Toolkit supports several different kinds of ⟨type rep⟩. The *Representation* variant discussed above can be applied to all attributes of a particular type through a ⟨type rep⟩. Each variant is limited in its applicability. For example, *Representation Unsigned* can only be associated with the *Integer* type.

When a class, node, attribute, or private type has a name that conflicts with a reserved word in the target language (e.g., *float* in C or *function* in Pascal), the name is renamed by IDLC, but a warning is issued. A second variant is used to eliminate the warning message and to specify the replacement name.

> *For* ⟨type⟩ *Use Name* ⟨name⟩ ;

Examples with the C target language follow.

> *For* float *Use Name* real;
> *For* auto *Use Name* car;

The remaining five variants apply only to private types. Two primary aspects must be specified: how the private type is represented externally, while being communicated between processes, and how the private type is represented internally, within a process. The statement

> *For* ⟨private_name⟩ *Use External* ⟨type⟩;

specifies that the ⟨private_name⟩ be represented externally as if it had been of the named ⟨type⟩, which can be either a basic, node, class, or other private type. If the external representation is another private type, then that type must either be a nonprivate type, or have an eventual external representation that is a nonprivate type.

The internal representation of a private type can either be that of another IDL type, or be defined in a *package*, a collection of declarations and executable code that you provide. To specify the internal representation of a private type, if it is an IDL type, use

> *For* ⟨private_name⟩ *Use Internal* ⟨type⟩;

4.1. STRUCTURE SPECIFICATIONS

If an external representation, but no internal representation, is given, then the internal representation defaults to the external representation. Similarly, if an internal representation, but no external representation, is given, then the external representation defaults to the internal representation.

The other option is a representation defined in a package. To identify the package supporting the ⟨private_type⟩, use

> For ⟨private_name⟩ Use Package ⟨package_name⟩;

This package, written in the target language, will define a target language type. Normally this type will have the same name as the private type; otherwise, the following must be specified.

> For ⟨private_name⟩ Use Name ⟨internal_name⟩;

The size of the internal representation, if not an IDL type, must also be specified.

> For ⟨private_name⟩ Use Size ⟨integer⟩ { Bits | Bytes } ;

Finally, the alignment of a private type must also be specified, if it is different from its size:

> For ⟨private_name⟩ Use Alignment ⟨integer⟩ { Bits | Bytes } ;

All attributes are positioned to start at a location (bit of byte number) that is an integral multiple of the alignment of the type of the attribute.

4.1.4 Derivation

There are two ways in which structures may be defined in terms of other structures.

- *Derivation*: Here, the new structure is viewed as a modification of the old structure. This form is intended when a designer has created several structures of similar properties.

- *Refinement*: Here, the new structure is a more detailed representation of the old.

The description makes use of the *derives* and *refines* relations defined by: A *refines* B if and only if B appears after the Refines keyword in the declaration for A; A *derives* B if and only if B appears in the `From` list in the declaration for A. B is a *refines*-parent or *derives*-parent of A. The transitive closures of these relations are *refines** and *derives**, respectively. The ultimate *refines*-ancestor of A is the unique structure B such that A *refines** B and there is no C such that B *refines* C.

When a structure declaration has a `From` clause it is defined in terms of the other structures whose names appear after the `From`; we require that the `Refines` clause not be present. The new structure is derived in a three-step process.

Copying. All types, representations, operations, named assertions, and definitions from each *derives*-parent are copied (assertions and definitions will be defined in the next chapter). Information duplicated in several structures is copied only once. Specifically,

- If structure C is derived from structures A and B and both A and B contain a node with the same name, then a node is created for structure C containing the union of the attributes in the two ancestor nodes with no duplicate information. Furthermore, structures A and B must both be derived from an ancestor structure D containing the original specification of the node. A similar constraint holds for two classes or two privates with the same name. The representations for the node, class, or private type in structure C are those specified in structure A followed by those specified in structure B.

- If there is a node and a class with the same name, a node and a private with the same name, or a class and a private with the same name, then an error is reported.

- If two assertions have the same name, only one is copied. The two assertions must be derived from the same original assertion in a common ancestor structure, and hence are identical. Unnamed assertions are not copied.

- If two definitions have the same name, the instances of the definitions are combined. The two definitions must be derived from the same original definition in a common ancestor structure. Any duplicate instances are added once.

Deletions. The `Without` clauses described below are used to delete some parts of the result of the copy step.

Additions. The productions, type declarations, representations, and assertions specified as part of the new structure are added to the result of the deletion step.

4.1. STRUCTURE SPECIFICATIONS

The Without clause is used to remove various types, subclasses, attributes, assertions, and definitions in a derived structure.

⟨without clause⟩ ::= **Without** ⟨without item⟩ { ',' ⟨without item⟩ }*

⟨without item⟩ ::= **Assert** { ⟨assertion_name⟩ | '*' }
  | **Define** { ⟨def_name⟩ | '*' }
  | **Type** ⟨type⟩
  | { ⟨atomic_name⟩ | '*' } { '=>' | '::=' }
    { ⟨name⟩ | '*' }?

If the **Without** clause contains multiple ⟨without items⟩ then it is equivalent to a sequence of **Without** clauses, one for each ⟨without item⟩. The "::=" and "=>" forms of the **Without** clause remove the class name or attribute name, respectively, given on the right from those productions with the same left-hand side. If an asterisk ("*") appears to the right of the "::=" or "=>", then all productions of the corresponding type with the specified left-hand side are deleted. If the left-hand side is an asterisk then this construct is equivalent to replicating the item for all names that appear on the left-hand sides of the specified kind of production. The "**Type** ⟨type⟩" form of the ⟨without item⟩ removes the class, node, or private type with the specified name. The **Assert** ⟨name⟩ form removes the assertion with the specified name, or all assertions if an asterisk is used; the "**Define** ⟨def_name⟩" form similarly removes one or all assertion definitions.

4.1.5 Refinement

If a structure specification contains a **Refines** clause, then the new structure is a refinement of the old. The new structure specification contains the information of the old structure, together with new specifications given by the ⟨structure stmt⟩ list following the **Is** keyword. Refinement differs from derivation in that the new structure is considered to be a representation of the old; any assertions about the old structure are presumed to hold for the new.

Informally, the semantics of refinement are

- Copy all declarations and assertions from the parent structure.

- Add new representation specifications and assertions to the new structure.

- Report errors if any *Without* clauses, type declarations, attribute productions, or class productions are found in the new structure.

Specifying structures in terms of other structures organizes them into a hierarchy, with lower levels of the hierarchy being more implementation-specific than higher levels. There are two interesting boundaries in any such hierarchy.

- *Externally adequate* level: At this point, enough information has been provided to define an external representation for all instances of the structure. This level is reached when a structure supplies a representation for all types defined in the structure from which it is descended. See Chapter 6 for a discussion of external representations.

- *Internally adequate* level: At this point, enough information is present to specify internal representations for all node types and attributes defined in the structure. Internal representations for types may be given by naming packages that define the types; such clauses may be applied to predefined types as well as to user-defined types.

A structure can be internally adequate without being externally adequate, if implementation packages are given for private types without giving external representations. The reverse is not possible, since an external representation implies a default internal representation if no specific internal representation is given.

4.1.6 Inheritance of Roots

If a root clause of a derived structure is omitted, the root of the first *derives*-parent that is still present (i.e., has not been deleted by a without clause) is made the root of the derived structure. If the root clause of a refined structure is omitted, the root of the *refines*-parent, if it is still present, is used. If a structure has no root, it cannot be associated with a port in some process. Further, an IDL compiler will be unable to check that there is some way for each type of node to be reached from the root, a common symptom of typographic errors in declarations.

4.2 Process Specifications

A process specification defines the input and output data structures of a program.

4.2. PROCESS SPECIFICATIONS

⟨process decl⟩ ::= **Process** ⟨process_name⟩
    { **Refines** ⟨process_name⟩ }?
    { **Inv** ⟨str_name⟩ }?
    Is { ⟨process stmt⟩ ';' }* **End**

⟨process stmt⟩ ::= ⟨port definition⟩ | ⟨port assoc⟩ | ⟨target⟩
    | ⟨restriction⟩ | ⟨assertion stmt⟩

The ⟨name⟩ of the process follows the keyword **Process**. All process names must be distinct from each other. As with structures, it is possible to refine more abstract processes into more concrete processes.

4.2.1 Ports

The **Pre** and **Post** statements are used to specify *ports*.

⟨port definition⟩ ::= { **Pre** | **Post** } ⟨port⟩ { ',' ⟨port⟩ }*

⟨port⟩ ::= ⟨port_name⟩ ':' ⟨str_name⟩

A routine is generated for each port; this routine is called to read in an instance (if a pre port) or write out an instance (if a post port). A pre or post port is not necessarily a connection to an I/O device, a file, or even an interprocess message-communication mechanism (e.g., a "mailbox" or "pipe")—although in particular cases it may be implemented as any of these, or simply as an in-core data structure. Each ⟨port decl⟩ specifies a port name (before the ":") and an abstract structure name (after the ":"). All the port names of an abstract process must be disjoint. The abstract structure associated with a port serves as a precondition (postcondition) of the data structure bound to the port. These preconditions and postconditions are expected to hold only before or after the execution of any instance of the abstract process.

Assertions in an abstract process declaration may be used to express relationships between two or more ports.

4.2.2 The Target Clause

The language, operating system and version, and machine in which IDLC is to generate code is termed the *target* of the process.

⟨target⟩ ::= **Target** { ⟨parameter⟩ }⁺

The valid ⟨parameter⟩s are implementation-specific. The IDL Toolkit supports several target languages, operating systems and machines. For example, the target clauses required to generate C code extended with macros for a Vax running the 4.2 Berkeley Standard Distribution of Unix are

```
Target Language C;
Target Language Version B;
Target Operating System Unix;
Target Operating System Version 4.2 BSD;
Target Machine Vax;
Target Runtime System Version A;
```

Defaults supported by the IDL translator obviate the need for using most of these clauses.

4.2.3 Process Invariant

The *Inv* clause, if present, names a structure that describes properties of the data within the running process. This structure must contain all the node and class types and attributes in all the port structures, and may contain additional node types and attributes that the process needs internally to perform its work. *Inv* is short for "invariant"; the concrete structure serves as an invariant assertion about the process in the same way that structures associated with ports provide preconditions and postconditions of the process.

The purpose of the invariant data structure is to permit the automatic generation of routines to manipulate instances of the node and class types for use within an instance of an IDL process and to specify access to the data values within instances of the node and class types. Within an IDL process, only one implementation of a node or class type exists. The declaration of the node or class type that is actually implemented is that appearing in the invariant data structure, no matter how many different declarations are given in the port data structures referred to by the process.

You need not worry about generating the invariant structure for a process. Unless an invariant is specified, the IDL translator will automatically generate the invariant. On the other hand, you may define new nodes and classes that do not appear in any of the other structures referred to by the process, or add attributes and members to nodes and classes already defined in those structures. These new nodes and classes or attributes and members can be used for intermediate calculations within the process without cluttering the external definition of the structures read and written by the process.

4.2.4 Port Associations

A port association constrains the realization of a port in a similar fashion to a ⟨type rep⟩ constraining the representation of a type

⟨port assoc⟩ ::= *For* ⟨port_name⟩ *Use* { ⟨parameter⟩ }+

In particular, the ⟨parameter⟩(s) may name a representation for the external IDL instance. The allowable combinations of ⟨parameter⟩s is implementation-specific. Every implementation should at least support the ASCII External Representation Language.

4.2.5 Restriction of Operations

Restriction specifications provide information about the operations a concrete process is allowed to perform. The IDL translator may exploit this information to generate shorter or more efficient code and data structures.

⟨restriction⟩ ::= *Restrict* { ⟨type⟩ | '*' }
{ '.' { ⟨attribute_name⟩ | '*' } }?
{ *To* | *From* } ⟨oper_name⟩ { ',' ⟨oper_name⟩ }*

Restrictions are specified in two ways. The first is to restrict the generated operations for a type or a specific attribute *to* a specified set (the *To* variant). The second way is to restrict the generated operations *from* certain operations in the default set of operations (the *From* variant). Restrictions can be applied

- to a particular ⟨type⟩ (*Restrict* ⟨type⟩),

- to a particular attribute (*Restrict* ⟨atomic_name⟩.⟨attribute_name⟩),

- to all relevant types (*Restrict* *),

- to all attributes of the same name (*Restrict* *.⟨attribute_name⟩),

- to all attributes of a particular node or class (*Restrict* ⟨type⟩.*), and

- to all relevant attributes (*Restrict* *.*).

The valid ⟨oper_name⟩s are implementation-specific. A complete list of those supported by the IDL Toolkit for C and Pascal are given in Appendices C and D, respectively. Most of these operations are macros, functions, or procedures defined on sets (e.g., `sizeSET`) or sequences (e.g., `lengthSEQ`). The other four operations are defined on nodes:

- `Create`, to create an instance of this node type;

- `Destroy`, to deallocate an instance of this node type;

- `DefaultInitialize`, to perform only the default initialization on attributes within the node: `FALSE` for `Boolean` attributes, 0 for `Integer` and `Rational` attributes, `Null` or `Empty` for `String` attributes, `Null` or `Nil` for pointer types, and system-specific values for private types. If this operation is `Restrict`ed `From`, or *not* `Restrict`ed `To`, you must provide a node-type-specific initializer to be called by the IDL runtime system whenever an instance is created.

- `DefaultFinalize`, to perform minimal finalization of attributes of a node when deallocated. If this operation is `Restrict`ed `From`, or *not* `Restrict`ed `To`, you must provide a node-type-specific finalizer to be called by the IDL runtime system whenever an instance is destroyed.

For multiple restriction clauses, the operations defined on any entity (type, node, or attribute) is calculated as follows.

- If the process is a *base process*, that is, is not refined from another process, then start with the default set of operations. For the IDL Toolkit, this is the largest set possible. If the process is a refined process, start with the operations defined on that entity in the parent process.

- Take the intersection of the operation sets specified by each `Restrict To` clause for that entity, and intersect this set with the set identified above.

- Take the union of the operator sets specified by each `Restrict From` clause for that entity, and subtract this set from the set calculated in the previous step.

4.2.6 Refinement

When a process has a `Refines` clause, it is defined in terms of the process whose name appears after the `Refines`. The new process is constructed from the old in three steps.

1. Copying. All ports from the *refines*-parent are copied. Any representations associated with the ports are also copied. The invariant structure is copied. The target language is copied if specified. Any assertions or definitions are copied.

2. Additions. Port associations and target statements are added to the result of step 1. Duplicate target statements are checked for. New port definitions are not allowed. Assertions and definitions may be added. Assertions and definitions with the same name are handled the same as with derived structures.

3. Deletions. The Restrict clauses described in the previous section are used to delete operations resulting from steps 1 and 2.

4.2.7 Private Types in Processes

The process invariant, whether specified explicitly with an *Inv* clause or computed automatically, may contain private types. The internal representation specifies how the private type is encoded in main memory in the process. Each private type in a port structure must also be in the invariant, and must also have an external representation. A private type need not have an external representation, if it doesn't appear in any of the port structures, and may have several possibly different external representations, if it appears in several port structures. If the internal representation is declared in a user-provided package, or if the internal and external representations differ, then this same package must provide target-language-specific conversion routines to and from the external representation.

4.3 Import Specifications

The import specification allows declarations from another file to be included with the other declarations, thereby eliminating the need for multiple copies of a specification.

⟨import decl⟩ ::= **Import** { ⟨str_name⟩ | ⟨process_name⟩ }
  { ',' { ⟨str_name⟩ | ⟨process_name⟩ } }*
  From ⟨file_name⟩ **End**

The **Import** specification names a structure or process and the file that contains the declaration. The full file name is generated from ⟨file_name⟩ in an implementation-specific fashion. The structure or process is extracted from the file and made available to be referenced in a later structure or process declaration.

The named file may itself contain one or more import declarations. The semantics of the import declaration supports structures and processes to be implicitly imported, with the following restriction. Only those structures and processes that contribute (in the sense of derivation or refinement) to the structure or process being imported will be implicitly imported. As an example, assume that a file contained the declaration

> **Import** SymbolTable **From** ST **End**;

and that the file **ST** contained

> **Import** IdentifierTable **From** IT **End**;

If the SymbolTable structure was derived or refined directly or indirectly from IdentifierTable, then that structure would be implicitly imported from the file **IT**.

A process or structure may be imported explicitly or implicitly several times without error. Two structures or processes of the same name may not be imported from different files.

4.4 Instantiation of IDL Specifications

A prime purpose of IDL is to provide a notation for describing data structures so that the IDL translator can generate a variety of data declarations, data structures, and code segments from the description. From the IDL description of a system, it is possible to generate

- the specification of a package that defines the operations a concrete process may perform on the internal data structures. An example of an Ada package is given in the DIANA report.

- the implementation of the operations for manipulating the internal representation of a concrete structure.

4.4. INSTANTIATION OF IDL SPECIFICATIONS 123

- tables or code for a reader that inputs the external representation described in Chapter 6 and maps it into whatever internal representation is needed for a particular concrete process, and for a writer that performs the opposite transformation.

- Tables or code for a checker that verifies that a particular data structure satisfies the assertions (described in the next chapter) of some structure.

This section discusses the issues involved in instantiating an IDL description, specifically the concrete process package specification and implementation. Chapters 7 and 8 discuss the implementation of concrete structures for the C and Pascal programming languages. The specific implementation of the readers and writers will not be discussed, because the details are involved and beyond the scope of this book, and because the details are not relevant to the use of IDL with these languages.

Implementing a concrete structure involves deciding how to represent IDL nodes, IDL classes, and attributes of IDL nodes. Because IDL supports a wide range of target languages, the implementation of IDL data structures will vary from one target language to another. When provided by the target language, use of an abstract type facility is the preferred approach. The IDL internal level will be divided into two parts: one for the abstract specification (i.e., the externally visible types and operations) and a second part for the implementation. For languages lacking an abstract type facility, an attempt should be made to follow the abstract type methodology.

The straightforward implementation of an IDL structure is to define an implementation language record type for each IDL node type, and to represent IDL attributes as fields of the records. IDL classes complicate this view, since they are used as types of attributes. In a language that allows untyped pointers there is no need for a representation of classes, since node-valued attributes can be represented as untyped pointers. In a language with union types, each IDL class can be represented as a union of the node types in the class. In a strongly typed language with variant records, it might be convenient to represent all node types as variants of a single type.

The record implementation is one among many alternative implementations allowed by the abstract/concrete split in IDL. The following paragraphs discuss some of the implementation options.

A Coroutine Organization. It is common for the frontends and backends of a compiler to be organized as coroutines; the frontend produces a portion of the intermediate representation, after which the backend produces code for this portion and then discards the unneeded pieces of the intermediate representation. In this organization there would never be a complete representation for the entire structure used to communicate between the two phases. Instead, only a consistent subgraph for the portion being communicated is needed. To use this style of compiler organization, the you need only to ensure that the values of the attributes for that portion of the tree being communicated are defined properly.

Nontree Structures. IDL is oriented toward graph-structured and tree-structured data. Many simple compilers use a linear representation, such as postfix. Such a representation simplifies certain tree traversals, and indeed may be obtained from a tree representation by such a traversal. Such representations may also have an advantage in that they are more efficient where storage is limited or paging overheads are high. An IDL description might suggest a tree structure, but a linear representation is entirely within the spirit of IDL. Where an IDL description requires a (conceptual) pointer it may be replaced by an index into the linear representation.

Attributes Outside the Nodes. There is no need for the attributes of a node to be stored contiguously. There are many variations on this theme, but we will illustrate just one here. Suppose that the general storage representation to be used involves storing each node as a record in the heap and using pointers to encode structural attributes. Because there are several different attributes associated with each node type, one may not wish to store these attributes directly in the records representing the nodes. Instead, one might define a number of vectors (of records) where the records in each vector are tailored to the various groupings of attribute types in IDL nodes. Using this scheme, the nodes themselves need only contain indices into the relevant vectors. Such a scheme has the advantage of making nodes of uniform size as well as enabling the sharing of identical sets of attribute values.

Nodes Inside Other Nodes. An attribute of a node may "reference" another node, but a pointer is not necessarily required; the referenced node may be directly included in the storage structure of the outer node so long as the referenced node need not be shared. If a class consists entirely of node types with no attributes, and node objects within the class are never shared, then the class can be implemented as an enumerated type, with the node types in the class as literals of the enumerated type.

Exercises

4.1 Justify the assertion that the Rational type includes all values typically found in computer integer, floating point, and fixed point types.

4.2 Assume that the default operations for a particular entity were {A, B, C, D}. What operations do the following restrict clauses result in?

> Restrict $\cdots$ To A, B, C;
> Restrict $\cdots$ From C;
> Restrict $\cdots$ To A, C;

4.3 List all the processes and structures imported when the constant_fold process shown in Figure 3.10 on page 86 is processed.

Bibliographic Notes

The concept of a visible external representation was present in some early compilers designed to be portable across target machines. This concept was refined starting in early 1977 in connection with the Production Quality Compiler-Compiler project of the Computer Science Department of Carnegie-Mellon University under the direction of William A. Wulf (Leverett et al. [1980]). At this time, this representation, termed *linear graph notation* (LG), was defined by Newcomer and Hilfinger and support software was implemented by Hobbs (Newcomer et al. [1980]). The software included a program called REQUIR that accepted a definition of nodes (in LG) and produced a set of data structure definitions in Bliss (a programming language similar to C and defined by Wulf, Russell, and Haberman [1971]) as well as initialization tables for the LG reader and writer. Other LG packages were implemented at Intermetrics [1980] for the Pascal, C, Fortran and PL/1 languages (Avakian et al. [1982] and Marshall [1982]).

A family of intermediate languages collectively called TCOL were expressed in LG. One member, for the preliminary Ada language, was TCOL$_{Ada}$, described by Brosgol [1980] and Brosgol et al. [1980]. A second intermediate representation for Ada programs, AIDA, was developed independently at the University of Karlsruhe by Dausmann et. al. [1980] and Persch et al. [1980] In an effort to merge the best attributes of TCOL$_{Ada}$ and AIDA, the developers of these two representations met in December 1980 and January 1981 to design a new intermediate representation, with DIANA as the result (Butler [1983], Goos and Wulf [1981], and Persch and Dausmann [1983])

Roughly concurrent with the design of DIANA, a successor to LG was being designed by Nestor and William Wulf, later joined by David Lamb, to address some of the problems that had been identified in LG. This successor, based on the concept of representation- and language-independent data definition, evolved into IDL. This language was further refined at the joint meeting (one change being the use of a BNF-like syntactic form suggested by Gerhard T. Goos) and was used to specify DIANA. The original IDL system consisted of the definition, by Nestor, Wulf, and Lamb [1981], of two languages, one for describing data structures, processes, and assertions, and the other, called the ASCII External Representation Language (ERL), for representing instances of IDL-specified data structures on external storage. It also included a denotational semantics of IDL graphs, IDL types, productions, and the external form. Later that year, David Lamb implemented a minimal translator for IDL. Within another year, a formal definition of the IDL language, the external representation language, and the assertion language had been completed, including a denotational semantics of the entire language, by Nestor, Wulf, and Lamb [1982].

In May 1983, David Lamb published his Ph.D. dissertation [1983] in which he presented the results of his investigations into the practicality of using IDL as a tool for connecting the components of large software systems. His work focused on developing a design for a translator of the full IDL language, including the assertion language. He demonstrated that systems built with IDL were feasible and could be made acceptably efficient.

In May, 1986 a workshop on IDL was held, out of which a special issue of SIGPlan Notices resulted, edited by Morgan [1987]. More recently, Giannini [1986] tightened up the semantics. IDL Version 3 has recently been defined by Nestor and described and formalized by Nestor et al. [1989]. This language generalizes the port concept, supports composite processes that contain processes, defines a statement to change the type of an attribute, and makes many alterations to the syntax. IDL Version 3 is a significant redesign of IDL, and should be considered to be a new language, distinct from standard IDL. Lamb [1986] has also suggested a new type constructor, maps, to be added to the four already present in IDL: sets, sequences, nodes, and classes.

A more detailed history of IDL appears in Stone and Nestor [1987].

As part of the Arcadia environment, Clarke, Wileden, and Wolf [1986] designed GDL (graph description language) and GRAPHITE (GRAPH Interface Tool for Environments), a translator for GDL into Ada. This language shares much with IDL, both describing tool interconnection via instances of attributed graphs. GDL syntactically resembles Ada. GRAPHITE is notable in that it produces both development-supportive and production-supportive forms of the Ada code from a GDL specification. PGRAPHITE, described

4.4. INSTANTIATION OF IDL SPECIFICATIONS 127

by Wileden et al. [1988], is a significant extension that supports full persistence of graphs, including automatic storage management and controlled concurrent access.

DOSE, a Display-Oriented Structure Editor defined by Feiler and Kaiser [1983] and Feiler, Jalili, and Schlichter [1986], uses representations specified in a Representation Description Language (RDL) (Feiler [1987] and Kaiser and Feiler [1982]) similar to IDL.

Our approach to private types, including the specific representation and restriction clauses we support, is motivated by Snodgrass and Shannon [1988].

Wirth [1988] combines modules and data type extension in a manner somewhat analogous to IDL's derivation and class productions. Derivation in IDL is more general, in that attributes can be removed as well as added.

The distinct language describing the interaction between the Data Mapping Control System (essentially the data base management system) and the operating system in the Data Architectural Framework Task Group reference model is also called iDL (internal Data Language) (Gersting et al. [1988]). IDL is also an acronym for Britton-Lee's Intelligent Database Language, which is a fairly conventional database query language, as well as a registered trademark of Research Systems, Inc., concerning their interactive analysis and visualization package.

An IDL port may be placed on a spectrum of access to disk-based data, between traditional database query languages integrated with a programming language, such as Equel (designed by Allman, Held, and Stonebraker [1976]), PascalR (designed by Schmidt [1977]), Portals (designed by Stonebraker and Rowe [1984]), and Plain (designed by Wasserman [1979]), in which each access makes available a small amount of information to the application program, at one end of the spectrum, and persistent languages such as PS-Algol (Atkinson, Chisholm, and Cockshott [1982], Cockshott et al. [1984]), GemStone (Maier, Stein, and Otis [1986]), Mneme (Moss and Sinofsky [1988]), and extensions to C++ proposed by Dixon and Shrivastava [1987], in which memory and disk resident data are not even distinguished at the language level, at the other end of the spectrum. Atkinson and Buneman [1987] discuss this spectrum in detail.

An IDL derivation using only *Without* statements is similar to a relational database view (Chamberlin, Gray, and Traiger [1975] and Ullman [1982]). Relational views are simpler than IDL derived structures, but permit concurrent access. Garlan [1986, 1987a] takes the opposite approach, merging tool views to obtain a global structure, a technique similar to that of computing a process' invariant from its port structures. Garlan [1987b] proposes extensions to IDL that permit concurrent access and modification, while supporting more complex derivation.

Chapter 5

Assertion Language Definition

An IDL specification consists of structure, process, and import specifications. The constructs presented in Chapter 4 are *structural*, in that they specify constraints of the composition of instances. For example, by specifying the attributes of a particular node type, all valid instances of that structure are constrained so that all nodes of that node type have the same attributes. The specific values of those attributes are of no concern (as long as they are of the correct type). Process specifications are also structural, in that they ignore both the process' algorithm as well as the specific attribute values.

The assertion sublanguage of IDL provides a means to express more general constraints both on isolated instances as well as between instances read and written by a process. Contrasted with the constructs in Chapter 4, assertions are *value-oriented*, in that constraints are placed on the values of attributes. These constraints, taken together, can effectively restrict the scope of an instance or can relate an input instance to an output instance associated with a process.

In this chapter, we take a mixture of bottom-up and top-down approaches to presenting assertions. After examining the general structure of assertions, we consider the low-level constituents of expressions, the literals, then work our way up through the operators to the more involved conditional, quantification, and case expressions. Definitions are considered last.

5.1 The Assertion Statement

The syntax of assertions is as follows.

⟨assertion stmt⟩ ::= ⟨assertion⟩ | ⟨definition⟩
⟨assertion⟩ ::= { ⟨name⟩ }? **Assert** ⟨expression⟩

A definition is a user-created entity that returns some value. Definitions are discussed in Section 5.12. The optional assertion name is used to permit the appearance of the assertion in a **Without** clause, to specify that the assertion is valid in derived and refined structures and processes, and to identify the assertion for humans, as it is used in error messages, The expression must be of type boolean, since assertions are either true or false.

5.2 Expressions

Expressions form a conventional expression grammar with operator precedence levels. **Or** and **Union** have the lowest precedence and "*" and "/" have the highest precedence. The syntax is as follows.

⟨expression⟩ ::= ⟨1exp⟩ | ⟨expression⟩ ⟨1op⟩ ⟨1exp⟩
⟨1op⟩ ::= **Or** | **Union**
⟨1exp⟩ ::= ⟨2exp⟩ | ⟨1exp⟩ ⟨2op⟩ ⟨2exp⟩
⟨2op⟩ ::= **And** | **Intersect**
⟨2exp⟩ ::= { **Not** }? ⟨3exp⟩
⟨3exp⟩ ::= ⟨4exp⟩ | ⟨3exp⟩ ⟨3op⟩ ⟨4exp⟩
  | ⟨4exp⟩ **Is** ⟨atomic type⟩
⟨3op⟩ ::= '=' | '~=' | '<' | '<=' | '>' | '>=' | **In**
  | **Same** | **Psub** | **Sub**
⟨4exp⟩ ::= { ⟨4op⟩ }? ⟨5exp⟩ | ⟨4exp⟩ ⟨4op⟩ ⟨5exp⟩
⟨4op⟩ ::= '+' | '−'
⟨5exp⟩ ::= ⟨primary exp⟩ | ⟨5exp⟩ ⟨5op⟩ ⟨primary exp⟩
⟨5op⟩ ::= '*' | '/'
⟨primary exp⟩ ::= { ⟨port_name⟩ ':' }? ⟨type⟩ | ⟨literal⟩
  | '(' ⟨expression⟩ ')'
  | ⟨primary exp⟩ '.' ⟨attribute_name⟩

5.3. LITERALS 131

$$
\begin{aligned}
&\mid \langle \text{def\_name} \rangle \text{ `(' } \langle \text{actuals} \rangle \text{ `)'} \\
&\mid \langle \text{if exp} \rangle \mid \langle \text{quantified exp} \rangle \mid \langle \text{case exp} \rangle \\
&\mid \langle \text{class\_name} \rangle \text{ `(' } \langle \text{expression} \rangle \text{ `)'}
\end{aligned}
$$

⟨actuals⟩   ::= ⟨expression⟩ { ',' ⟨expression⟩ }*

Each expression has a type. There are two broad kinds of types an expression may have. *IDL types* include integer, boolean, rational, string, set, sequence, and node. The other kind of type is an *object collection type*.

An object collection is produced by assertions. It consists of objects of any IDL type. Its properties are similar to the IDL set type, but operations associated with the object collection type are distinct from those associated with the IDL set type. A set is an IDL object that consists of an unordered group of IDL objects of some type. A sequence is an ordered list of IDL objects of some type. The component type of a set or sequence cannot be a set or sequence.

5.3 Literals

The syntax of literals is

⟨literal⟩   ::= True | False | { ⟨port_name⟩ ':' }? Root | Empty
            | ⟨integer⟩ | ⟨rational⟩ | ⟨string⟩
            | ⟨control_name⟩ | ⟨formal_name⟩ | ⟨case_name⟩

The following literals are allowed.

- Boolean — denotes the constant values True or False.

- Root — denotes the collection containing only the root node object of the structure in which the expression appears. For assertions appearing in process specifications, the ⟨port name⟩ identifies the root.

- Empty — denotes the empty object collection.

- Integer — the standard integer constant; the syntax is identical to that in the ASCII External Representation Language (termed the *ASCII ERL*; see Chapter 6 and Appendix B.1).

- Rational — the standard floating point constant; the syntax is identical to that in the ASCII ERL.

- String — sequence of ASCII characters between quotes. Any ASCII character may be represented, including printable characters, blanks, and nonprintable control characters; the syntax is identical to that in the ASCII ERL.

- ⟨control_name⟩ — denotes the value currently assigned to the quantifier in which it appears.

- ⟨formal_name⟩ — denotes the value assigned to the formal in the context of a definition invocation.

- ⟨case_name⟩ — denotes the value assigned to the name in the context of a case expression.

5.4 Infix Operations on Values

Operations on values of IDL types are straightforward. They include

- boolean: '=', '~=', *And*, *Or*, *Not*, *Is*
- integer & rational: '=', '~=', '<', '<=', '>', '>=', '+', '-', '*', '/', *Is*
- string: '=', '~=', '<', '<=', '>', '>=', *Is*
- set: '=', '~=', *In*
- sequence: '=', '~=', *In*
- collection: *In*
- node & class: '=', '~=', *Is*, '.'

Most of these operations should be clear. Two booleans, integers, or rationals are equal if they have the same value. Two strings are equal if they contain the same characters in the same order. Integers, when they are compared with rationals or have binary arithmetic operations applied to them with rationals, are implicitly coerced to rational values. Two sets are equal if they contain the same objects. Two sequences are equal if they contain the same objects in the same order. Two nodes are equal if they are the same object. A string is less than a second string if it is lexicographically less than the second string, using the lexicographic ordering defined by the ASCII character set. An object is *In* a set or sequence if it is an element of that set or sequence. An object is *In* a collection if it is contained in the collection. An object *Is* a particular ⟨atomic_type⟩ if the value is of that type. The value of this predicate can be determined at compile time unless the type of the object, as known at compile-time, is a class.

5.5 Prefix Operations on Values

Unary plus and minus may be applied to expressions of an integer or rational type. The remaining prefix operations have the syntax of definition calls, in that the parentheses are required. This expression denotes an application of a supplied or user-defined definition on an ordered list of arguments.

- ⟨def_name⟩ (⟨expression⟩ ...) — denotes the value or collection returned after the body of the appropriate version of the definition is evaluated on the values of the parameters.

The following are supplied functions that take values as parameters.

- *Head* (⟨expression⟩) — ⟨expression⟩ must be of type sequence. *Head* returns the first object in ⟨expression⟩.

- *Members* (⟨expression⟩) — ⟨expression⟩ must be of type set or sequence. *Members* returns the object collection containing the objects in the set or sequence ⟨expression⟩.

- *Size* (⟨expression⟩) — ⟨expression⟩ may be of type string, set, sequence, or collection. If a string, *Size* returns the length of the string. If a set, sequence or arbitrary collection, *Size* returns the number of objects in the set, sequence or collection. If a singleton collection (a collection that must contain exactly one object), then *Size* returns the size of the object contained in ⟨expression⟩, which must be a string, set, or sequence.

- *Tail* (⟨expression⟩) — ⟨expression⟩ must be of type sequence. *Tail* returns the sequence obtained by removing the first object in ⟨expression⟩.

- ⟨class_name⟩ (⟨expression⟩) — the type of ⟨expression⟩ must be a class or node contained in ⟨class_name⟩. The ⟨expression⟩ is considered to be of type ⟨class_name⟩ for type checking, effecting a widening to the ⟨class_name⟩ type.

5.6 Infix Operations on Object Collections

Typically, you will create definitions (described below) using object collection operations to create a collection of objects, and then make some assertion about the collection.

The following forms specify object collections:

- ⟨port_name⟩ : ⟨type⟩ — denotes the collection of all objects in a structure of the specified type. The expression must appear in a process declaration and refers to the structure associated with the named port.

- ⟨type⟩ — denotes the collection of all objects of the specified type in the structure in which the expression appears. If the expression appears in a process declaration, then the specified type must be associated with one of the port structures.

- ⟨port_name⟩ : `Root` — denotes a collection containing only the root node object of a structure. The expression must appear in a process declaration and refers to the structure associated with the named port.

- `Union` — object collection union. The operands must contain objects of the same type.

- `Intersect` — object collection intersection. The operands must contain objects of the same type.

- ⟨primary exp⟩ . ⟨attribute_name⟩ — of an object collection containing only node objects returns an object collection containing all objects associated with the specified attribute of all nodes in the original object collection. The node or class type of ⟨primary exp⟩ must have ⟨attribute_name⟩ declared explicitly as an attribute.

- `Same` — two object collections are the same if and only if they contain exactly the same objects. The assertion language forces one to distinguish between object collections and IDL types. If a and b are object collections, then the form $a = b$ is semantically incorrect.

- `Sub` — object collection subset.

- `Psub` — object collection proper subset.

A value of an IDL type is considered to be a collection, termed a *singleton collection*, containing one object, the value, when used as an argument to `Union`, `Intersect`, `Same`, `Sub`, and `Psub`. Also, the left hand and right hand arguments to these infix operations may be different types, as long as one type is more general than the other type. In this context, if node or class A is a subclass of class B, then B is *more general* than A. Also, the

Rational type is more general than the Integer type. All other types are not related by the general relation.

The result type of these infix operations is Boolean for Same, Sub, and PSub, the more general participating type for Union, and the less general participating type for Intersect.

5.7 Prefix Operations on Collections

There is only one prefix operation on a collection.

- Type (⟨expression⟩) — ⟨expression⟩ must be an object collection. Type returns the object collection containing all objects in that structure with the same type(s) as those in the object collection ⟨expression⟩.

5.8 Object Collections As Values

Value operations may operate on object collections if it can be determined at compile-time that the collection will consist of exactly one object. The value of such a collection, termed a *singleton collection*, is the value of the object in the collection. Only the following object collections may be used as operands of value operations: a quantifier name (see Section 5.10), a formal parameter within a definition body, the "{ ⟨name⟩ ' : ' }$^?$ Root" form, the Head form, the dot qualification of one of these forms, and If expressions where all expressions following Then and Else are one of these forms.

5.9 If Expressions

An If expression has the syntax

⟨if exp⟩ ::= If ⟨expression⟩ Then ⟨expression⟩
            { OrIf ⟨expression⟩ Then ⟨expression⟩ }*
            Else ⟨expression⟩ Fi

The OrIf clause is semantically equivalent to an Else If. Syntactically, though, the OrIf clause does not need to be closed by a Fi while each Else If clause does. The expressions following If and OrIf must be of type boolean. The type of an If expression is the most general type of its constituent expressions (those following Then and Else), and must exist for the expression to be type correct.

5.10 Quantifiers

Quantified expressions have the syntax

⟨quantified exp⟩ ::= { ForAll | Exists } ⟨control_name⟩
                          In ⟨expression⟩ Do ⟨expression⟩ Od

The expression following In must be an object collection type. The ⟨name⟩ is an iterator which is assigned individual objects from the collection returned by the ⟨expression⟩ following In and may be used only within the Do – Od expression. Despite the Do, the expression between Do and Od must be of type boolean. Nothing is "done." It simply expresses a property that all objects (the ForAll variant) or at least one object (the Exists variant) in an object collection must have. The expression following In must be an object collection type. The expression between Do and Od must be of type boolean.

5.11 Case Expressions

A case expression allows different expressions to be evaluated, depending on the type of another expression.

⟨case exp⟩   ::= Case ⟨case_name⟩ Is ⟨expression⟩
                    { ⟨case select⟩ }* { ⟨case other⟩ }? End
⟨case select⟩ ::= ⟨atomic type⟩ Do ⟨expression⟩ Od
⟨case other⟩ ::= Otherwise Do ⟨expression⟩ Od

The ⟨case_name⟩, a name local to the case expression, is bound to the value of the first ⟨expression⟩. The type of the value of ⟨case_name⟩ is compared with each of the ⟨atomic_type⟩s in the ⟨case select⟩s (these ⟨type⟩s must be subclass types or node types contained in the class type of ⟨expression⟩ and must not overlap). If one ⟨type⟩ matches, the associated ⟨expression⟩ is evaluated, and its value becomes the value of the case expression (as with quantified expressions, nothing is "done.") If no type matches, the otherwise ⟨expression⟩ is evaluated. Within this ⟨expression⟩, ⟨case_name⟩ has the type of the first ⟨expression⟩. A ⟨case other⟩ is required if the ⟨type⟩s in the ⟨case select⟩s do not cover the type of the first ⟨expression⟩. The type of the case expression is the most general type of the constituent ⟨expression⟩s in the ⟨case select⟩s, and must exist for the case expression to be type correct.

5.12 Definitions

Definitions may take parameters, and return values or collections of objects about which assertions may be made. The syntax is

⟨definition⟩ ::= ⟨private Definition⟩ | ⟨IDL definition⟩
⟨private Definition⟩ ::= `Define` ⟨def_name⟩ { ⟨formals⟩ }$^?$
   `Returns` ⟨type⟩
⟨IDL definition⟩ ::= { `Cyclic` }$^?$ `Define` ⟨def_name⟩ { ⟨formals⟩ }$^?$
   { `Returns` ⟨type⟩ }$^?$ '=' ⟨expression⟩
⟨formals⟩ ::= '(' ⟨formal⟩ { ',' ⟨formal⟩ }* ')'
⟨formal⟩ ::= ⟨formal_name⟩ ':' ⟨type⟩

There are three kinds of definitions.

- A *private definition* specifies a *return type* and its body is expressed directly in a target programming language, such as C.

- *Noncyclic definitions*, in which the keyword `Cyclic` is omitted, return values or object collections. Recursion is permitted, but the definition may not be cyclic, that is, its evaluation must not involve a (direct or indirect) recursive call with the identical arguments as on a previous call, termed a *cyclic identical call*.

- *Cyclic definitions*, in which the keyword `Cyclic` is specified, return object collections. A return type must be specified for cyclic definitions. A cyclic definition may call itself directly or indirectly while evaluating its body. Cyclic identical calls are permitted. The result of a cyclic definition call is the minimum fixed point solution. The ⟨expression⟩ of a cyclic definition may not include an `If` expression. This restriction ensures monotonicity and thus the existence of a minimum fixed point result.

A definition need not have any parameters.

Overloading of definitions, in which the meaning of the definition depends on the types of its arguments, is allowed, provided the different versions of the definition can be distinguished by formal parameters. Two definition versions are distinguishable if there is no set of arguments whose types match all of the formal parameter types of both versions.

The return type of an overloaded definition is the most general return type of its versions, and must exist for the overloaded definition to be type correct. The specified return type of a definition, overloaded or cyclic, must be identical or more general than the type of the ⟨expression⟩ forming the body of the definition. The return type of a non-overloaded definition *is* the type of its body, and the specified return type, if provided, must be identical to this type.

Definitions are invoked with the "⟨name⟩ (⟨actuals⟩)" form of ⟨primary exp⟩ (see Section 5.5). The type of each actual expression must match the specified type of the corresponding formal parameter of exactly one version of the declared definition.

The type of a definition is the type following **Returns** if the definition is private, or the type of the expression, the definition body, following the "=" sign if the definition is an IDL definition.

Exercises

5.1 What are the values, in standard scientific notation, of the following *Rational* numbers: 925/32, 57.8125, 14#4A1/4#200, 2#0.1110011101#E6?

5.2 How many times can an assertion of the form "`Assert Exists ...`" fail? "`Assert ForAll ...`"? Other assertions?

Bibliographic Notes

Assertions are similar to attribute grammar specifications, introduced by Knuth [1968]; both specify in a nonprocedural fashion the values of attributes. Assertions are less constraining, in that they are not required to specify the exact value of an attribute. The two specifications, IDL assertions and attribute grammars, can naturally coexist. A tool could be specified using IDL assertions, and could be implemented using a semantic analysis generator such as GAG (Kastens, Hutt, and Zimmermann [1982]), LILA (Lewi et al. [1979a, 1979b]), SSAGS (Payton et al. [1983]), or ATG (Nestor et al. [1983]), from an attribute grammar specification. It may even be possible to prove *a priori* from an attribute grammar specification that the assertions will always be satisfied.

PLEASE, described by Terwilliger and Campbell [1988], and Anna (Sankar, Rosenblum, and Neff [1985]) both allow Ada programs, data objects as well as executable code, to be annotated with predicate logic assertions. Eiffel, defined by Meyer [1988], allows programs and data objects to be associated with boolean expression predicates. These specifications may be used in correctness proofs or as executable pre- and post-conditions to be evaluated at run-time. IDL assertions also have these characteristics.

5.12. DEFINITIONS

Support of assertions in IDL on data is substantially more comprehensive, while support of assertions on code is indirect, relating the output data to the input data.

The greatest use of assertions to data have been those given by Uhl [1983] to formalize the DIANA structure.

The *Case* statement is analogous to the Typecase statement in Modula-2+ (Rovner, Levin, and Wick [1985]). The *Is* construct is analogous to Wirth's [1988] type test.

Chapter 6

The ASCII External Representation

To communicate data between arbitrary programs, possibly written in different languages and running on different computers, there must be a canonical external representation for each concrete structure. We chose an ASCII encoding to maximize the portability of the data. This chapter defines that encoding.

The package that provides the interface between a process instance and data on its ports is required to provide operations for mapping to and from the ASCII representation. Programs are not required to use this representation, however, and operations to map to other, more efficient representations are permitted. Indeed, these alternative representations would be the preferred means of communication between production versions of the various processes.

The external representation of a concrete structure is completely defined by the abstract structure except for the representation of private types. The syntax of the external representation has free form lexical rules, so that variations based on spacing and comments are not significant. The representation of an object can be nested within the representation of the node that references it or placed at the highest level to produce a "flat" form. The distinction between nested and flat representations can be made on a object-by-object basis and is not significant.

Each private type must have an external representation consistent with the syntax given below. The representation is specified by private type representations with **External** clauses in concrete structures derived from the abstract structure defining the type. For two programs to communicate via the external representation, they must use concrete structures descendent from the same externally adequate concrete structure.

6.1 Lexical Rules

The lexemes permitted in the external representation are similar to those of the IDL Language, as presented in Appendix B.1. There are a few differences between that and the lexemes permitted in the external representation. Unlike the IDL specification, the external representation is not case sensitive, except for characters appearing in a ⟨string⟩. A constraint is implied on the use of case sensitivity in an IDL specification: two names differing only in case of letters may not be used if both might appear in an external representation. The same holds for two attribute names within a node. Only node type names and attribute names appear in the external representation; there is no representation of class names. Thus node and attribute names may have the same spelling, ignoring case, as class names. The languages differ in the permitted keywords, in the punctuation, and in the characters considered as white space. Integer, rational, and string constants are identical in the two languages.

⟨basic token⟩ ::= TRUE | FALSE | ⟨name⟩ | ⟨integer⟩ | ⟨rational⟩
                     | ⟨string⟩

⟨punctuation⟩ ::= '#' | '{' | '}' | '<' | '>' | ';' | ':' | '^'
                 | '[' | ']'

⟨white space⟩ ::= ⟨space⟩ | ⟨end of line⟩ | ⟨horizontal tab⟩
                 | '-' '-' { ⟨comment character⟩ }* ⟨end of line⟩

6.2 Syntactic Rules

The syntax of the external representation is given here, using the lexical tokens specified above.

⟨ASCII rep⟩ ::= ⟨reference⟩ { ⟨label⟩ ':' ⟨node⟩ }* { '#' }?
⟨node⟩ ::= ⟨name⟩ { '[' ⟨attributes⟩ ']' }?
⟨attributes⟩ ::= ⟨attribute⟩ { ';' ⟨attribute⟩ }* { ';' }?
⟨label⟩ ::= ⟨name⟩ | ⟨integer⟩
⟨attribute⟩ ::= ⟨name⟩ ⟨reference⟩

6.3. READERS AND WRITERS

⟨reference⟩ ::= { ⟨label⟩ ':' }? ⟨value⟩ | ⟨label⟩ '^'
⟨value⟩ ::= TRUE | FALSE | ⟨integer⟩ | ⟨string⟩ | ⟨rational⟩
 | ⟨node⟩
 | '{' { ⟨reference⟩ }* '}'
 | '<' { ⟨reference⟩ }* '>'

The external representation of a data structure consists of a reference to the root node followed by a sequence of labeled nodes. The root must have the root node type for its specified structure.

The initial ⟨name⟩ in a ⟨node⟩ must be a node type name. Following the node type there can be a list of attribute-reference pairs; each attribute is explicitly named and the name is followed by a reference to the corresponding attribute value.

A list bracketed with braces represents a set-valued attribute. A list bracketed with angle brackets represents a sequence-valued attribute.

Any value may be labeled by preceding it with "⟨label⟩ :". All labels must be unique. The "⟨label⟩ ^" form references a labeled value. Forward references are permitted. Labels are used to record the sharing relationships, which must be preserved.

6.3 Readers and Writers

Every package instantiated from an IDL definition will include a pair of reader/writer operations for mapping to/from the external representation.

The reader must be able to accept any legal form for its input; it must be able to read nested forms, "flat" forms, and mixtures of these.

There are a wide variety of choices for how the writer decides on output format. A particular implementation might provide defaults via site-specific extensions to the concrete process descriptions, or might have the writer driven by run-time options. It is not necessary that a writer be able to produce all possible variations between fully nested and completely flat; it may chose to implement only one preferred form.

Exercises

6.1 What are the possible initial characters in an ERL instance? What are the possible final characters?

6.2 Which ASCII characters are not permitted anywhere in an ERL instance?

Bibliographic Notes

ASCII stands for the set of 128 characters in the American National Standard Code for Information Exchange, as defined by ANSI [1977]. The external ASCII representation is a redesign of linear graph notation (Newcomer et al. [1980]). A conversion into EBCDIC was defined at Intermetrics by Avakian et al. [1982]. Biyani [1987], Lamb [1983, 1987b, 1989] and Newcomer [1987b] each describe in detail the implementation of readers and writers for the external ASCII representation and also for several more efficient binary encodings. Lie [1984] has implemented in Pascal a table-driven, incremental reader and writer for the ASCII ERL. Snodgrass [1987] describes several tools provided with the IDL Toolkit for formatting IDL instances in the external ASCII representation language. The approach used to communicate values of IDL private types is similar to that espoused by Herlihy and Liskov [1982] for transmitting values of abstract data types.

Lamb [1983] describes alternatives to the ASCII ERL, and discusses the improvements they elicit to file size and to I/O costs, ranging over factors of 5 and 25, respectively.

Sun Microsystem's [1987, 1988] XDR (external data representation) is a byte-oriented machine-independent protocol used in Sun's remote procedure call (RPC) facility. DeSchon [1986] compares XDR with four other data representation standards. Three of the standards, as well as the ASCII ERL, employ explicit type definitions, in which the type is communicated with the data. XDR and one other standard employ implicit type definitions, in which the sender and receiver must agree on the type of data communicated. Varadarajan [1988] describes how to connect IDL readers and writers to XDR, allowing IDL processes to interact via Sun's RPC.

Gutknecht [1986, 1987] describes a specific linearization of Modula-2 symbol tables. Atkinson [1977] describes a notation, also called IDL (for Intermediate Data Language), used to exchange data between programs running on different machines in a network. Linearizations of Eiffel (Meyer [1988]), Objective-C (Cox [1986]), and Smalltalk (Goldberg and Robson [1983]) objects have been implemented. The activity of writing the information contained in main memory in a data structure to secondary storage has been termed "passivation" by Wulf, Levin, and Harbison [1981] and by Cox [1986] and "pickling" by Birrell, Jones, and Wobber [1988]. Lamb [1987c] provides techniques for efficiently reading and writing graphs (termed *graph deltas*) that are modifications of other graphs.

Howell et al. [1988] and Smith et al. [1988] discuss how the ASCII ERL can be used to create software engineering environments that are "plug-compatible" with multiple-vendor external tools, and identify the technical and political obstacles to achieving this goal.

Chapter 7

Using IDL with C

This chapter describes the interface of IDL with the C programming language implemented in the IDL Toolkit, including representation and support routines for IDL data types and support of IDL processes. In addition, several appendices give summaries of the various representations and operations provided by the interface. In Appendix B is a table of the representation clauses that can be used to generate specific C representations. Appendix C contains a table of the various prefixes used in the C interface and their meaning, a summary of the C interface conversions of IDL data types to their corresponding C types, and a summary of the support routines provided for the various data types.

7.1 Target Clause

To specify the C programming language, use the following within a process specification.

    `Target Language C;`

There are several versions of this interface; the default is

    `Target Language Version A;`

One alternative is

    `Target Language Version B;`

Version B generates additional macros for attribute accessing, type conversion, and class membership testing. This chapter will focus on Version A, occasionally pointing out differences found in Version B.

7.2 Data Types

We first describe the internal representations of the various data types defined in IDL, as they are used with C. A declarations file is produced by the IDL translator for inclusion with user-written programs. This section describes the C representations that appear in the declarations file.

7.2.1 Scalar Data Types

IDL notation provides four scalar data types: *Boolean*, *Integer*, *Rational*, and *String*. The IDL translator maps these IDL types to their C representations.

Representation

The interface provides a new C type named Boolean to represent the IDL data type *Boolean*. The interface also provides two literals, TRUE and FALSE, with numeric values 1 and 0 respectively.

The identifier *Integer* in IDL is replaced in the C declarations file by the C declarator keyword *int*. That is, any attribute declared to be of IDL type *Integer* will be declared to be of C type *int*. You may specify a specific representation of an *Integer* for an attribute type. For example, the size of the representation of an integer typed attribute may be specified as

> *For* ⟨node_name⟩.⟨attribute_name⟩ *Use*
> *Representation* ⟨integer⟩ { *Bits* | *Bytes* };

In this way, *short* and *long* declarations may be specified (the declarator selected is machine-specific). For unsigned integers, use the following representation specification.

> *For* ⟨node_name⟩.⟨attribute_name⟩ *Use Representation Unsigned*;

The identifier *Rational* in IDL is replaced in the C declarations file by the C declarator keyword *float*. The *double* declarator can be indicated with the following representation specification.

> *For* ⟨node_name⟩.⟨attribute_name⟩ *Use Double Precision*;

The interface provides a new C type named String to represent the IDL data type *String*. Each String is maintained in a hash table to guarantee that pointer equivalence is an adequate test for String equivalence.

7.2. DATA TYPES

Operations

As integers and rationals are represented as standard C types, the operations in C are available for these types. Booleans can be manipulated in C as *char*s, the conventional way they are handled in C. In particular, they can be used in *if* statements in the same way that *char*s are used in such statements.

All string manipulation takes place through routines available in the runtime library. A new *String* is allocated and added to the hash table by the function *NewString* which takes as a single argument a pointer to a (null-terminated) array of characters. A *String* is converted back to an array of characters by the function *StringToChar*. This function takes a single argument of type *String* and returns a pointer to a (null-terminated) array of characters.

7.2.2 Node Types

IDL notation provides two different node types: attributed nodes and unattributed nodes. *Attributed nodes* are node types with at least one attribute. *Unattributed node* are nodes without any attributes. The following describes how the IDL translator maps these node types into C declarations and then describes the various support routines provided.

Representation

Attributed nodes are represented by pointers to C *struct* types. Each node type name is made into a *typedef* name for a pointer to a C a *struct* that corresponds to the node type defined in IDL. The name of each *struct* is formed by prefixing the node name with the letter "*R*".

Each attributed node type is associated with a unique even integer, which is bound to a manifest constant related to the node type name. (A manifest constant is an identifier that has been associated with a constant through use of the *#define* compiler control line in C.) The name of the manifest constant is found by attaching the prefix "*K*" to the node type name. These internal tokens are used with classes, described in the next section, to identify the type of a node used in a class variable.

The members of the C *struct* correspond precisely to the attributes of the IDL node. The attributes are stored differently depending on their type. The scalar data types *Boolean*, *Integer*, *Rational*, and *String* are stored directly in the *struct*. Node types are represented by node pointers in the *struct*. Classes and private types are stored directly like the scalar data types. Sequences and sets with the standard linked-list representation are represented as pointers to the first list cell in the sequence or set. Other representations of sequences and sets are stored differently and will be discussed below. The *struct* also contains extra members generated for internal use by the runtime system. These are contained in the IDLhidden field of the C *struct*. No guarantees are made about the ordering of the members of the *struct*. It is likely that the members will be reordered for storage efficiency.

The C representation for the node type defined by

```
function => name:       String,
            thistype:   function_type,
            parameter:  Seq Of formal_parameter,
            definition: expression;
```

might be

```
struct Rfunction { IDLnodeHeader IDLhidden;
    String name;
    function_type thistype;
    SEQformal_parameter parameters;
    expression definition;
};
struct Rfunction * function;
#define Kfunction 6
```

Unattributed nodes are node types declared without any attributes. There are two different C representations for them. The first representation is similar to the representation for attributed nodes. The difference is that the *struct* only contains the member, IDLhidden, generated for use by the runtime system.

The C representation for the unattributed node type defined by

```
plus =>;
```

would be

```
struct Rplus { IDLnodeHeader IDLhidden;
};
typedef struct Rplus * plus;
#define Kplus 12
```

A second representation for unattributed nodes is as an enumerated type (i.e., as an integer). Only one copy of each enumerated type will exist. Unattributed nodes are represented as enumerated types by giving a representation specification of the form

7.2. DATA TYPES

> *For* ⟨node_name⟩ *Use Representation Enumerated;*

An alternative specification is to name the class whose members should be represented as enumerated types. This class must be an unattributed class (see Section 7.2.3).

> *For* ⟨class_name⟩ *Use Representation Enumerated;*

No structure declarations are created for enumerated types. However, the internal token constant described above is still created. This constant is always an odd integer. In addition, a *typedef* of *int* is created for the unattributed node name. This allows enumerated types to be attribute types.

If the IDL file contains the declaration:

> unaryoperator ::= unaryplus | unaryminus;
> unaryplus => ; unaryminus => ;
> *For* unaryoperator *Use Representation Enumerated;*

then no structure declarations for unaryplus and unaryminus will appear in the IDL declarations file (provided no attributes are declared for unaryoperator). However, there will be a *typedef* for each of the nodes and definitions of the manifest constants.

> *typedef int* unaryplus;
> #define Kunaryplus 1
>
> *typedef int* unaryminus;
> #define Kunaryminus 3

Operations

The operations on nodes are node allocation, node deallocation, attribute accessing, and attribute storage. Widening of a node to a class will be discussed in Section 7.2.3.

Attributes may be accessed and stored in the conventional C syntax.

> function Afunction;
>
> Afunction->name = NewString("defaultname");
> ... Afunction->name ...

Nodes are created explicitly by the user, or implicitly by the routine associated with an input port. Storage for nodes is allocated by macros which are generated for each node by the IDL translator. The macro name is formed by prefixing the node name with "*N*" (for "New"). The macro takes no arguments, and its value is a pointer to a newly allocated node of the proper type. Local variables of a node type should be assigned a reference to an existing node or to a new node generated by a storage allocation macro. Do not use any means other than this macro for dynamic allocation of nodes; it may cause anomalous and inconsistent behavior.

Local variables of a node or class type must first be initialized, either by assigning an existing node to the variable or allocating a new node with the "*N*" macro, before accessing attributes through the variable.

If you do not want to create any nodes of a particular node type, specify

    Restrict ⟨node_name⟩ From Create;

and the node creation macro will not be made available. Nodes will still be created by readers if they are part of a Pre port structure.

The following steps are performed by the node creation macro.

- Memory for the node is allocated from the heap. The node size is determined by IDLC using the specified size and alignment of each attribute contained in the node.

- Default initialization is performed on all attributes, specifically, setting all values to 0.

- For each attribute of a private type in the node, an initialization function for the private type is called, if specified, to supply a value for that attribute. This function, named *I*⟨private name⟩, is discussed in Section 7.2.6.

- If specified, a user-supplied node initialization function is called that performs further initialization. This function is named *I*⟨node name⟩.

A *node initialization* function initializes the values of attributes when a new node is created. To ensure that the user-defined node initialization function is invoked, a restriction specification must be given, of the following form.

    Restrict ⟨node_name⟩ From DefaultInitialize;

The initializer function must be compiled separately from the IDL-generated code file and linked with the IDL process. It must have a name that is the same as the node name with a prefix of "*I*". Finally, it must accept as its single argument a pointer of the appropriate node type, and return that same pointer. It will be called each time the allocation macro

7.2. DATA TYPES

for the node is called. When the node is passed to the initialization function, it has already had type information bound to it, and all attribute fields have been set to their default values.

For example, if the IDL file contained a representation clause of the form

  Restrict function *From DefaultInitialize;*

then the declaration

  function Ifunction();

would appear in the C declarations file and you would write a routine similar to the following.

```
function Ifunction(AfunctionInstance)
function AfunctionInstance;
{
    AfunctionInstance->name = NewString("defaultname");
          .
          .
    return (AfunctionInstance);
}
```

Dynamically allocated nodes should be freed after they are no longer needed. This is done by invoking a *node deletion* macro generated by IDL. The macro name is formed by prefixing the node type name with "*D*". The single argument is a pointer to an object. This macro only frees the storage allocated for the node structure. String deletion, set deletion, and sequence deletion do not occur when the node deletion macro is called. The node deletion macro simply frees the storage used by the node and its ancestor classes.

If you do not want to delete any nodes of a particular node type, specify

  Restrict ⟨node_name⟩ *From Destroy;*

and the node deletion macro will not be generated.

The actions of the deletion macro are the reverse of those occurring during allocation.

- A user-provided attribute finalization function is called, if requested for the node. This function, named *F*⟨node name⟩, is discussed below.

- A user-provided private type finalization function is called, if requested, for each attribute of a private type in the node. This function, named *F*⟨private name⟩, is discussed in Section 7.2.6.

- The node itself is deallocated, returning its storage to the heap.

You can write *attribute finalization* functions which are called each time a node is freed. To do this, a restriction specification of the following form must be given.

    Restrict ⟨node_name⟩ From DefaultFinalize;

The finalization function must be compiled separately from the IDL-generated code file and linked with the IDL process. It must have a name that is the same as the node name with an "*F*" prefix attached. Finally, it must accept as its single argument a pointer of the appropriate node type, and its return type must be *void*. The function should delete only the storage for attributes, not the storage for the node itself.

For example, if the IDL file contained a representation clause of the form

    Restrict function From DefaultFinalize;

then the declaration

    void Ffunction();

would appear in the C declarations file and you would write a routine similar to the following.

    void Ffunction(AfunctionInstance)
    function AfunctionInstance;
    {

    }

You should take special care not to leave dangling pointers when freeing nodes and attributes of nodes.

Version B Macros

In Version B of the target language, a macro is generated for each attribute of each node. For example, four such macros would be generated for the function node.

    String nameOffunction(f);
    function_type thistypeOffunction(f);
    SEQformal_parameter parameterOffunction(f);
    expression definitionOffunction(f);

7.2. DATA TYPES

Each macro takes one parameter f, a node of type function, and returns the value of that attribute. These macros allow a functional (prefix) notation to be used when accessing attributes.

$$\cdots \text{ nameOffunction(thisfunction) } \cdots$$

7.2.3 Classes

IDL notation provides two different class types: plain classes and unattributed classes. A *plain class* is a class that contains at least one attributed node. An *unattributed class* contains all unattributed nodes. This section describes how the IDL translator maps these class types into C declarations and then describes how the type of a class may be determined at runtime.

Representation

Each plain class is represented by a union of the node types that comprise the class. This means that each class is represented by a union of pointers to structs. The members of the union have names that are formed by prefixing the node type names with "V" (for "Variant").

Instances of descendant classes may be assigned to instances of their ancestor classes. In the implementation of classes, all descendants of a descendant class are contained in the union of the ancestor class. The class member names are formed by prefixing the member type name with "V".

If the IDL declaration file contained the following class declarations:

```
expression        ::= constant | operation;
expression        => exp_type: types;
constant          ::= integer_constant | real_constant;
integer_constant  => value: Integer;
real_constant     => value: Integer;
operation         ::= binary_operation | unary_operation;
operation         => op: operator;
```

where integer_constant, real_constant, binary_operation, and unary_operation are attributed node types, types and operator are other class types, then the C declaration file would contain the following excerpt.

```
typedef struct CAconstant * CPconstant;
typedef struct CAoperation * CPoperation;
typedef struct CAexpression * CPexpression;
```

```c
typedef union {
    int IDLinternal;
    CPoperation IDLclassCommon;
    binary_operation Vbinary_operation;
    unary_operation Vunary_operation;
} operation;

typedef union {
    int IDLinternal;
    CPconstant IDLclassCommon;
    integer_constant Vinteger_constant;
    real_constant Vreal_constant;
} constant;

typedef union {
    int IDLinternal;
    CPexpression IDLclassCommon;
    constant Vconstant;
    operation Voperation;
    formal_parameter Vformal_parameter;
    integer_constant Vinteger_constant;
    real_constant Vreal_constant;
    binary_operation Vbinary_operation;
    unary_operation Vunary_operation;
} expression;

struct CAconstant {
    IDLnodeHeader IDLhidden;
    types exp_type;
};
struct CAoperation {
    IDLnodeHeader IDLhidden;
    types exp_type;
    operator op;
};
struct CAexpression {
    IDLnodeHeader IDLhidden;
    types exptype;
};
```

7.2. DATA TYPES

Operations

Operations that can be performed on classes are attribute accessing, narrowing, widening, and type query. Classes may not be allocated nor deallocated. A variable of a class type may be assigned a value of a particular node type that is a member of that class, as will be discussed below.

Information in a class is assigned and accessed through the class members except for common attributes. For example, the following code assigns an `integer_constant` node type to the variable of type `expression` and sets the value to 5. Later that value is accessed for printing.

```
expression anexp;

anexp.Vinteger_constant = Ninteger_constant;
anexp.Vinteger_constant->value = 5;

printf("Constant =%d", anexp.Vinteger_constant->value);
```

Class attributes are propagated to all class descendants by the IDL translator. Frequently, one may want to access a common attribute of a class without knowing which node type has been assigned to that class. This can be done by accessing the attribute through the `IDLclassCommon` field of the class. This field is a structure containing all the common attributes for the class. The name of the structure is the name of the class prefixed with an "*CP*" (for "Class Pointer"). This field can be used the same as any member field.

For example, if the IDL specification file contained a declaration of the form

```
operation ::= binary_operation | unary_operation;
operation => op: operator;
```

then the attribute op could be accessed through a value of a class type as follows.

```
operation Anoperation;
operator newoperator;

Anoperation.IDLclassCommon->op = newoperator;
```

If we knew that the type of the node stored in `Anoperation` was in fact a `binary_operation`, we could also do the following.

```
Anoperation.Vbinary_operation->op = newoperator;
```

However, this is not recommended, since it depends on knowledge that may later be invalidated by changes elsewhere to the code.

An unattributed class consists completely of unattributed nodes. It is also represented by a *union* so that it can be used as an argument to the operator *typeof*.

For example, if the IDL declarations file contained a declaration of the form

```
operator ::= plus | minus;
plus => ; minus => ;
```

then the C declaration file would contain a declaration of the form

```
typedef union {
    int IDLinternal;
    CPgenericHeader IDLclassCommon;
    plus Vplus;
    minus Vminus;
} operator;
```

The IDLinternal field of an unattributed class is a generic structure used by the runtime library routines. It is not meant to be used by the programmer. Classes do not have allocation or deallocation routines.

Type Information

A runtime operator called typeof is provided specifically for use with classes. The operator returns the integer constant associated with the node type. Its result is defined only if its argument is of an IDL class type, and only if the node referred to has been properly allocated (i.e., allocated with the generated allocation routine) or is NULL. The argument for typeof must be parenthesized.

Narrowing

A C variable whose type is an IDL class can have as a value a reference to a node whose type is a member of that class. In the example above, a variable of type operation can have as a value a reference to either a binary_operation or unary_operation node, with the type possibly varying at runtime. Assigning this node to a variable whose type is a subclass is termed *narrowing*, and is done through the appropriate "V" member, after a runtime type check.

7.2. DATA TYPES

```
      operation Anoperation;
      binary_operation B;
      unary_operation U;
         .
         .
      if (typeof(Anoperation) == Kbinary_operation)
          B = Anoperation.Vbinary_operation;
      else U = Anoperation.Vunary_operation;
```

Another example of the use of the *typeof* operator and narrowing may be found in the attribute finalization routine example.

```
void Ffunction(AfunctionInstance)
function AfunctionInstance;
{/* deletes storage for the attributes but not for the node itself */
switch (typeof(AfunctionInstance>expression)) {
  case Kinteger_constant:
    Finteger_constant(AfunctionInstance.Vinteger_constant);
    break;
  case Kreal_constant:
    Freal_constant(AfunctionInstance.Vreal_constant);
    break;
  case Kformal_parameter:
    Fformal_parameter(AfunctionInstance.Vformal_parameter);
    break;
  case Kbinary_operation:
    Fbinary_operation(AfunctionInstance.Vbinary_operation);
    break;
  case Kunary_operation:
    Funary_operation(AfunctionInstance.Vunary_operation);
    break;
  default: /* error: class does not contain valid instance */
  break;
  }
}
```

Widening

Widening is the inverse of narrowing, and never requires a runtime type check. Widening is performed by using the "*V*" member on the *left hand side* of the assignment

```
Anoperation.Vbinary_operation = B;
    .
    .
Anoperation.Vunary_operation = U;
```
or by explicit casting, which is less safe
```
Anoperation = (operation)B;
    .
    .
Anoperation = (operation)U;
```
Explicit casting is required when widening occurs during parameter passing in a function call.

Version B Macros

In Version B of the C target language, several macros are generated for each class. By using these macros, you may ignore many of the peculiar aspects of the implementation of class types in the C language, which doesn't directly support such types.

One macro is generated for each attribute of each class. These macros have the same form as those generated for nodes.

```
operator opOfoperation(O);
operation O;
```

This macro replaces the use of the IDLclassCommon member.

Widening and narrowing are both performed by the following macro.

⟨class name$_2$⟩ ⟨class name$_1$⟩To⟨class name$_2$⟩(c);
⟨class name$_1$⟩ c;

If ⟨class name$_1$⟩ is a subclass of ⟨class name$_2$⟩ (e.g., if ⟨class name$_1$⟩ is plus and ⟨class name$_2$⟩ is operator; that is plusTooperator), then this routine widens the argument node to be of type ⟨class name$_2$⟩ (here, operator). Since the validity of this conversion can be checked by the IDL translator, this macro results in only a type conversion; no runtime checking is necessary.

If ⟨class name$_1$⟩ is a *superclass* of ⟨class name$_2$⟩ (e.g., if ⟨class name$_1$⟩ is operator and ⟨class name$_2$⟩ is minus; that is, operatorTominus), then this routine narrows the argument node to be of type ⟨class name$_2$⟩ (here, minus). The validity of this conversion must be checked at runtime (e.g., the argument may be a plus node). If the runtime check fails, the routine

7.2. DATA TYPES

`ConversionError` is called, with the specified class names as character string arguments, here

```
ConversionError("operator", "minus");
```

More complicated variants are possible. For the following IDL specification

```
A ::= X | Y;
B ::= Y | Z;
```

the following macros would be generated

- the widening macros `XToA`, `YToA`, `YToB`, and `ZToB`;
- the narrowing macros `AToX`, `AToY`, `BToY`, and `BToZ`, and
- the macro `AToB`.

The last macro performs a conversion that is neither narrowing nor widening. It would succeed only if its argument were in `Y`.

These macros are also generated when $\langle$class name$_1\rangle$ is a node name (this would be a widening type conversion) and when $\langle$class name$_2\rangle$ is a node name (this would be a narrowing type conversion), but not when both are node names (such a conversion is always illegal). The use of these conversion macros obviates the need for using the "*V*" members explicitly.

One final macro is generated for each class.

   Boolean Is$\langle$class name$\rangle$ (c);

This macro returns `TRUE` if the type of the node passed as an argument is a member of $\langle$class name$\rangle$. Only expressions of a class type can be passed to this macro.

7.2.4 Sequences

The IDL translator generates a representation and sequence operation routines for each attribute type that is a sequence. Sequence components can be node or class types as well as scalar types. This section describes the representations and operations for sequences. All operations are available for all representations of sequences.

Linked List Representation

A sequence of $\langle$type_name$\rangle$ is by default a linked list of objects of the type. A linked list is made up of list cells, defined as follows.

```
typedef struct ⟨unique label⟩ {
    struct ⟨unique label⟩ * next;
    ⟨type_name⟩ value;
} C⟨type_name⟩, * L⟨type_name⟩;
#define SEQ⟨type_name⟩ L⟨type_name⟩
```

The ⟨value type⟩ is a node or class type. The ⟨unique label⟩ tags are identifiers generated by the IDL translator to allow recursive structures with the awkward C rules. They are not meant to be seen or used by the programmer. In particular, the sequence operations defined below do not require an understanding of the linked list implementation.

For example, if the IDL declarations file contained a declaration of the form

```
function ::= parameters: Seq Of formal_parameter;
```

then the C declaration file would contain the declaration

```
typedef struct IDLtag1 {
    struct IDLtag1 *next;
    formal_parameter value;
} Cformal_parameter, *Lformal_parameter;
#define SEQformal_parameter Lformal_parameter;
```

Declarations for all sequences of scalar types used in the specification will be included in every generated header file. SEQBoolean and SEQInteger are typedef names for pointers to list cells of types CBoolean and CInteger, with value types Boolean and int. SEQString, SEQdouble, and SEQfloat are pointers to list cells of types CString, Cdouble, and Cfloat, with value types of String, double, and float.

Array Representation

At times the linked list representation of a sequence is too slow or wastes too much space for a particular application. In these cases, you may specify an array representation for the sequence. The contents of the sequence is stored in an array referenced by the node, filling the first i locations, where the count i is contained in the array structure. The syntax of these representation specifications is

```
For Seq Of ⟨type_name⟩ Use Representation Array;
```

The array structure generated is of the form

7.2. DATA TYPES

```
typedef struct {
    int size;
    int length;
    ⟨type_name⟩ * array;
} A⟨type_name⟩;
#define SEQ⟨type_name⟩ A⟨type_name⟩
```

The size field is the size of the array. The length field is the current number of elements in the array. These fields are not meant to be seen or used by the programmer. The storage for the array is allocated by the initializeSEQ macro or by the first append to the array. If an attempt is made to add elements to a full array, a new, larger array will be allocated on the heap, and the elements will be copied from the old array to the new array. To avoid this expensive copying, use

For Seq Of ⟨type_name⟩ *Use Maximum* ⟨integer⟩ *Elements;*

The array is allocated initially to be of ⟨integer⟩ elements. Attempts to add elements to a full array are ignored.

Operations

The IDL translator provides 17 sequence operations for each generated sequence. These operations are provided regardless of the representation of the sequence. The operations are all macros that invoke the IDL generic list or array routines. These operations are also provided for each sequence of scalar types. The following is a list of the operations that would be generated for a sequence of a data type named flag. In each operation, flagseq is a sequence and flagvalue an instance of the data type flag. The types must match exactly; use widening or narrowing if necessary to achieve this. Allocation and deallocation of list cells are done by each routine but no allocation or deallocation of the data types is performed (you should create an instance before, say, appending it to the sequence). A complete description of each routine is given in Appendix C.

```
void appendfrontSEQflag (flagseq, flagvalue)
void appendrearSEQflag (flagseq, flagvalue)
SEQflag copySEQflag (flagseq)
Boolean emptySEQflag (flagseq)
foreachinSEQflag(flagseq, flagrem, flagvalue) ⟨stmtseq⟩
void initializeSEQflag (flagseq)
Boolean inSEQflag (flagseq, flagvalue)
void ithinSEQflag (flagseq, index, flagvalue)
```

```
int lengthSEQflag (flagseq)
void orderedinsertSEQflag (flagseq, flagvalue, comparison)
void removefirstSEQflag (flagseq)
void removelastSEQflag (flagseq)
void removeSEQflag (flagseq, flagvalue)
void retrievefirstSEQflag (flagseq, flagvalue)
void retrievelastSEQflag (flagseq)
sortSEQflag (flagseq, comparison)
SEQflag tailSEQflag (flagseq)
```

Restrictions

If macros for all sequence operations for all sequence types are generated (the default action), then potentially many macros will be defined, requiring excessive processing time and symbol table space in the preprocessor. Usually only a few operations are needed for each sequence type. Restriction specifications can reduce the number of macros generated. Each operation can be named in a restriction specification. For example, if the length is never interrogated for a sequence, the `lengthSEQ` macro needn't be generated.

```
Restrict * From lengthSEQ;
```

On the other hand, we can ensure that a particular operation is present with

```
Restrict Seq Of flag To ithinSEQ;
```

7.2.5 Sets

The IDL translator generates a representation and set operation routines for each attribute type that is declared as a set of a data type. Data types of sets can be node or class types as well as scalar types. The following sections describe the representations and operations for sets of the various types. All operations are available for all representations of sequences.

Representation

There is no single straightforward representation of IDL sets in C. The IDL translator uses different representations, depending on the data type of the elements of the set. The default representation for each data type is a linked list.

7.2. DATA TYPES

Representation (Integer): Sets of **Integer** can be represented as bitvectors with the following specification.

```
For Set Of Integer Use Representation Bitvector;
```

Bitvectors are stored directly in the node as an integral number of integers, each containing a machine-specific number of bits, 1 bit per integer value.

The storage requirements for sets will grow by roughly 1 bit per element allowed; the default size of the set depends on the default size of an *int*, which is machine-specific but is at least 16 bits, implying that the default bitvector contains 2^{16} bits. Where possible, you should use small sets and use arithmetic to convert to the desired integer. The syntax is

```
For Set Of Integer Use Maximum ⟨integer⟩ Elements;
```

As an example, the declarations

```
A => b: Set Of Integer;
For Set Of Integer Use Representation Bitvector;
For Set of Integer Use Maximum 40 Elements;
Target Machine VAX;
```

would generate the following

```
#define SETBitArray int
#define SETInteger SETBitArray
#define MAXSIZESETinteger 40
        .
struct RA {
        .
    SETInteger b[2];
        .
};
```

Since *int*s are 32 bits long on a DEC VAX machine, two *int*s are necessary to encode a set of 40 elements.

Representation (Rational, String): Sets of **Rational** and **String** are represented as linked lists. The set types are SETfloat, SETdouble, and SETString.

Representation (Nodes, Classes): Sets of a node or class type are represented in exactly the same way as sequences of the type except that the ⟨set type name⟩ is from the ⟨value type⟩ prefixed with "*SET*". The array representation specifications for sequences are also allowed for these sets.

Operations

The IDL translator provides eight set operations for each generated set. These operations are all macro substitutions for the IDL generic list or array routines or are special routines (for bitvector or structure manipulation). The following is a list of the operations that would be generated for a set of a data type named `flag`. In each operation, `flagset` is a set of the data type `flag` and `flagvalue` is an instance of the data type `flag`. Allocation and deallocation of list cells are done by each routine but no allocation or deallocation of the data types is performed. A complete description of each routine is given in Appendix C.

```
void addSETflag (flagset, flagvalue)
SETflag copySETflag(flagset)
Boolean emptySETflag (flagset)
foreachinSETflag(flagset, flagptr, flagvalue) ⟨stmtseq⟩
void initializeSETflag (flagset)
Boolean inSETflag (flagset, flagvalue)
void removeSETflag (flagset, flagvalue)
int sizeSETflag (flagset, flagvalue)
```

Restrictions

As with sequences, each set operation can be named in a restriction specification. An example is the following.

```
Restrict Set Of flag To removeSET;
```

7.2.6 Private Types

IDL private types allow the programmer to use private representation for a particular type. The following sections describe the representation and reader/writer interfacing for private types used with C.

Representation

Private types are specified with up to seven IDL statements which may appear in any order. The form of the first statement is

Type ⟨private_name⟩;

This statement tells the IDL translator that the type called ⟨private_name⟩ will be a private type rather than a node or class type.

7.2. DATA TYPES

The second and third IDL statements tell the IDL translator where the user-defined representation for the type exists. The form of these statements are

> For ⟨private_name⟩ Use Package ⟨module_name⟩;
>
> For ⟨private_name⟩ Use Name ⟨name⟩;

The first statement specifies the module name and the second statement specifies the name of the type within the module that will be used internally in the process. The ⟨module_name⟩ specifies a file that contains the declaration of the ⟨private_name⟩. More specifically, the ⟨module_name⟩ will be transformed into the name of a file with an appended suffix of ".**h**", and the IDL declaration file for each C process that uses the ⟨private_name⟩ will be made to #include the file specified by the ⟨module_name⟩. An include file will be included in the IDL declaration file only once.

If the second statement is used, then each instance of the ⟨private_name⟩ in the structure declaration is replaced with ⟨name⟩.

One of two statements are required to specify the form of the internal representation of a private type. The following

> For ⟨private_name⟩ Use Internal ⟨type⟩;

is useful when a process does not need to deal with the private type internal representation and can just treat it as an IDL type. The second form

> For ⟨private_name⟩ Use Size ⟨integer⟩ { Bits | Bytes } ;

is used when the internal representation is found in a package. The *Size* variant is redundant when used with the *Internal* variant.

The alignment in main memory, if different than the size, is specified with

For ⟨private_name⟩ Use Alignment ⟨integer⟩ { Bits | Bytes } ;

The last statement specifies the external representation for the private type. An external representation can be an IDL scalar type or any defined node type. This is the representation that will be used when reading or writing the private type. The form of this statement is

> For ⟨private_name⟩ Use External ⟨type⟩;

Reader/Writer Interfacing

The programmer who implements a private type must define an interface with the reader and writer. The interface is defined in C by the implementor—it provides a way for IDL to read and write the data type without knowing what the implementation is.

This interface takes the form of a separately compiled C file which must be linked into the final process. It must contain definitions for functions used by the reader and writer. Only those functions that are used must be defined; that is, if a private type is only to be written and not read, none of the input functions are needed, and you may omit them. The reverse is true as well, and if the private type is to be neither read nor written, no interface code is needed.

The following interface functions are needed.

- *Input Mapper:* A function returning a pointer to an instance of the internal representation of the private type. Its single argument is of the external type for the private type. The name of the function is "⟨external type⟩To⟨internal type⟩".

- *Output Mapper:* A function returning an instance of the external representation of the private type. The argument is an instance of the internal representation for the data type. The function name is "⟨internal type⟩To⟨external type⟩".

- *Initializer:* A function taking as a parameter a private type residing in a newly created node. This function initializes the value of the private type. The function name is the name of the private type prefixed by "*I*".

- *Finalizer:* A function taking as a parameter a private type residing in a node to be deallocated. This function frees the storage of the private type. The function name is the name of the private type prefixed by "*F*".

An example of the use of a private type and interface routines for a private type can be found in Chapter 9.

7.2.7 Name-Space Conflicts

An IDL declaration might have node, class, private type, port or attribute names that are identical to C keywords. An example would be the use of "int" as a node name. These nodes will be read and written with the names given in the IDL declaration, but you will have to use a modified version of the name in C code. The IDL translator will issue an informative message, as a warning, on the standard error output informing you of the translation and of the new form of the name, which is the name prepended with the letter "*T*". The modified form of the name will be used wherever the node name is normally prefixed. For example, if the IDL node int was modified to Tint by the IDL translator, the internal token KTint, and not Kint, would be generated. The same renaming occurs when a port name conflicts with a node, class, or private type name. If a Set Of int were used, then Tint would also appear in the generated routine names, such as sizeSEQTint. The warning message can be avoided through an appropriate representation specification, such as

> For int Use Name Tint;

7.2.8 Sharing

The C data instantiating an IDL structure within the memory of a process has the form of a graph. A single node or class may appear multiple times in a traversal of the graph. In input and output, labels are used to resolve such references. Within an IDL process, sharing detection in output data is resolved by making two passes over the data structure. The first pass determines which nodes are shared, marking them for the second pass; the second does the output, erasing the first pass's marks as it goes.

C equivalence (the "==" operator) of nodes or classes (i.e., pointer equivalence) is an adequate test for node or class equivalence. For basic types (Integer, Boolean, Rational, and String) C equivalence is an adequate test for value equivalence of basic types. In particular, there is only one copy of each String within a process. If an attribute's value (whose type is a basic type) is modified, other nodes, sets, and sequences containing the same value are unaltered. For sets and sequences, C (pointer) equivalence is not an adequate test for value equivalence: two sets can contain the same elements and not be equal. Values of sets and sequences implemented as linked lists (the default) permit sharing, in that modification of the shared set or sequence will, as a side effect, modify the values of other attributes sharing the set or sequence.

7.3 Processes

IDL processes are associated with C programs. The Target clause names the programming language the program will use. The ports correspond to the input and output for the program (specifically, they are routines invoked by the program). Finally, the invariant structure represents the collection of data types the program will use. This section describes port representation and functions, storage management for a process, generated files for a process, and the use of the IDL translator.

7.3.1 Ports

Representation

Each port in the IDL specification for a process corresponds to a C function generated by the IDL translator. The name used for the port in the IDL specification will be the name used for the automatically generated port function. When the function is called, the appropriate modifications (if any) to the process's invariant structure will be performed.

Input ports return an instance of the root type, through which the entire structure instance may be accessed. Ports take one argument, a pointer to a *FILE* from which data will be read. The file should already be open for reading; an end of file or a top-level pound sign ("#") must be seen at the end of the data, after any amount of white space. Multiple structures may be read from the same file if they are separated with pound signs. *Output ports* take two arguments, both mandatory.

- a pointer to a *FILE* to which data will be written (the argument could of course be stdout or a reference to a pipe)

- an instance of the root type, indicating the data structure to be written.

A pound sign ("#") will be written when the port's writing is complete. The caller is responsible for initially opening the file and finally closing the file. Multiple structures may be written sequentially to the file. Output ports use a first pass over the data structure to detect instances of sharing, and a second pass to erase sharing marks and to write the data. The output is in a nested form with labels used only when necessary.

For example, given the declaration

```
Process Test Is
    Target Language C;
    Pre customers_in: customers;
    Post bills_out: bills;
End
```

two routines will be generated, one for the input port and one for the output port.

7.3. PROCESSES 169

```
customers customers_in(f, readerok)
FILE *f;
boolean readerok;

void bills_out(f, root)
FILE *f;
bills root;
```

External Format

The external format of a structure associated with a port of a process is selected at translation time by a port representation clause. Every implementation must support the "ASCII External Representation Language," as described in Chapter 6. This is the default output format for any process. Other formats may also be available.

7.3.2 Storage Management

Automatically generated C functions in the IDL code file allocate storage for strings, nodes, list cells, and system data. The same macros that are used in generated code for allocation of nodes and list cells are meant to be used by the programmer. When nodes are created by the system, the user-defined initialization function will also be called. The C programmer should always use the node-type-specific, string-type-specific, and list-type-specific macros for managing node, string, and list storage.

7.3.3 Restrictions

You may restrict the generated operations for a node or class to a specified set by using restrictions. This is especially useful for decreasing the size of the generated declarations file.

Restrictions are specified in two ways. The first is to restrict the generated operations for a node or class *to* a specified set. The second way is to restrict the generated operations *from* certain operations in the default set of operations. The detailed syntax is given in Chapter 4, and the complete list of operations is given in Appendix B. By default all sequence operations are provided for each generated sequence, all set operations are provided for each generated set, and allocation, deallocation, default initializer, and default finalizer routines are provided for each node type. You should specify which operations from this group are wanted. Invalid operations given in restriction clauses are ignored.

7.3.4 Files

Two files are created by the IDL translator for every process, a declarations file and an object file. The declarations file will be named after the process, with a suffix of ".h". The code file will also be named after the process, but with a suffix of ".o". If Version B is specified, a third file, with a suffix of "**Macros.h**", containing the additional macros, is created. The declarations file is meant to be included in all files that use the data declared in the IDL specification (by #include). The object file is meant to be linked into the process along with your code for the process and C interface library code.

7.3.5 Translation of an IDL Process

To translate an IDL specification for a process into an object file and a declaration file, invoke the program the IDL translator with one argument, the name of the file containing the IDL declarations for the process. Several files can be processed by the IDL translator in one invocation.

Your C code files (which must #include the generated declarations file for the process) may be compiled after the declaration file is emitted by the IDL translator. An object code library known as the C interface library must be linked with the generated object files and your object files to produce the final program.

Exercises

7.1 Show how the IDL specification discussed in Chapter 2 may be changed to cause the ProperCredit assertion on page 40 to be satisfied.

7.2 Compare the support of the IDL type model by the runtime system and code generated by IDLC in C with that of Pascal as described in the next chapter.

Bibliographic Notes

The C programming language is described by Kernighan and Ritchie [1988] and Harbison and Steele [1987].

A similar set of creation, iteration, data access, set and sequence macros was defined in BLISS for the linear graph package (Newcomer et al. [1980]). General strategies for representing IDL structures in target languages have been proposed by Goos et al. [1983] and by Nestor, Wulf, and Lamb [1982].

7.3. PROCESSES

Shannon and Snodgrass [1986] evaluate the C interface, comparing it with (a) the Ada representation of DIANA, a specific IDL structure, implemented in the Ada-in-Ada compiler by Taft [1982], (b) the DIANA package implemented in C by Quinn [1982], a component of the Ada Breadboard Compiler (Wetherell [1982]), (c) an Ada package specification proposed by Goos et al. [1983], (d) PLUM, a C package for managing abstract data types specified in a language resembling IDL implemented by Reiss [1984, 1985], and (e) GRAPHITE, a tool that takes a structure specification similar to IDL and produces two kinds of interface packages in Ada, one that permits specification modifications without requiring modification or even recompilation of user code, and one that is less flexible but more efficient at runtime, designed by Clarke, Wileden, and Wolf [1986]. Howell et al. [1988] have implemented several interface packages in Ada for DIANA.

Lamb [1987a, 1987b, 1987d] gives principles for implementing IDL data structures in C and Pascal. Lamb and Dawes [1988] and Lie [1984] discuss efficient implementations of the Is⟨class name⟩ predicate. Snodgrass and Shannon [1988] discuss in greater detail how private types are supported by the runtime system, and exactly how user-implemented code interfaces with the runtime system. Biyani [1987] implemented a C runtime library that supports the functional interface discussed in this chapter, along with garbage collection and binary reader/writers. Nestor and Stone implemented a Mini IDL system in C supporting a subset of Version 3 IDL (a new language based on IDL) along with garbage collection (Nestor et al. [1989]).

Wirth's [1988] type extensions are similar to the support of IDL classes in C. In particular, the narrowing and widening operators (⟨class name$_1$⟩-To⟨class name$_2$⟩) is identical to Wirth's type guard, and the Is⟨class name⟩ operator is identical to Wirth's type test. The major difference is that Wirth also allows classes to be allocated.

Chapter 8

Using IDL with Pascal

This chapter describes the interface of IDL with the Pascal programming language implemented in the IDL Toolkit, including representation and support routines for IDL data types and support of IDL processes. In addition, several appendices give summaries of the various representations and operations provided by the interface. In Appendix B is a table of the representation clauses that can be used to generate specific Pascal representations. Appendix D contains a table of the various prefixes used in the Pascal interface and their meaning, a summary of the Pascal interface conversions of IDL data types to their corresponding Pascal types, and a summary of the support routines provided for the various data types.

8.1 Target Clause

To specify the Pascal programming language, use the following within a process specification.

> Target Language Pascal;

There are several versions of this interface; the default is

> Target Language Version A;

One alternative is

> Target Language Version B;

Version B generates additional functions for attribute accessing, type conversion, and class membership testing. This chapter will focus on Version A, occasionally pointing out differences found in Version B.

8.2 Data Types

We first describe the internal representations of the various data types defined in IDL, as they are used with Pascal. A declarations file is produced by the IDL translator for inclusion with user-written programs. This section describes the Pascal representations that appear in the declaration file.

8.2.1 Scalar Data Types

IDL notation provides four scalar data types: *Boolean*, *Integer*, *Rational*, and *String*. The IDL translator maps these types to their Pascal representations.

Representation

All occurrences of *Boolean* IDL data type definitions are represented by Pascal *boolean* data type. The interface also makes use of the Pascal-defined constants *true* and *false*.

The identifier *Integer* in IDL is replaced in the Pascal declarations file by the Pascal declarator keyword *integer*. That is, any attribute declared to be of IDL type *Integer* will be declared to be of Pascal type *integer*. You may specify a subrange for an attribute type, by using

For ⟨node_name⟩.⟨attribute_name⟩ *Use*
        Representation ⟨integer⟩ { *Bits* | *Bytes* };

For unsigned integers, use the following representation specification.

For ⟨node_name⟩.⟨attribute_name⟩ *Use Representation Unsigned*;

The specification

        For A.b *Use Representation* 6 *Bits*;
        For A.b *Use Representation Unsigned*;

would generate the following type declaration

        type ⟨unique label⟩ = 0..63;

The identifier *Rational* in IDL is replaced in the Pascal declarations file by the Pascal declarator keyword *real*.

The interface provides a new Pascal type named *String* to represent the IDL data type *String*. This is a pointer to an internally defined Pascal representation of strings.

8.2. DATA TYPES

Operations

As booleans, integers, and rationals are represented as standard Pascal types, operations in Pascal are available for these types. All string manipulation takes place through routines available in the runtime library. Strings are allocated by the Pascal function NewString, which takes a two arguments, the first of type *integer*, telling the maximum number of characters in the String, and the second of type packedArrayType.

```
function NewString(length: integer;
        value: packedArrayType): String;
```

and returns a pointer of type String.

There exists only one copy of each String in main memory. Two values of type String may be compared with the standard Pascal equality operator ('='). The characters in a String may be extracted with the following function.

```
function StringTopacked (source: String): packedArrayType;
```

The following routines are also defined on values of type String.

```
function StringAppend(source, added: String): String;
function StringLength(stringInstance: String): integer;
```

8.2.2 Node Types

IDL notation provides two different node types: attributed nodes and unattributed nodes. *Attributed nodes* are node types with at least one attribute. *Unattributed nodes* are nodes without any attributes. The following section describes how the IDL translator maps these node types into Pascal declarations and then describes the various support routines provided.

Representation

Both attributed nodes and unattributed nodes are represented by pointers to Pascal *record* types. Each node name is used to define a type name for a pointer to a Pascal *record* that corresponds to the node type defined in IDL. The name of each *record* is formed by prefixing the node name with the letter "R".

Each attributed node type is associated with a unique even integer, which is bound to a constant whose name is generated by attaching the prefix "K" to the node type name. These internal tokens are used with classes, described in the next section, to identify the type of a node used in a class variable.

The members of the Pascal *record* correspond to the attributes of the IDL node. The scalar data types (*Boolean*, *Integer*, and *Rational*) are stored directly into the node *record*. A *String*, represented by a pointer to the internally defined string representation, may also be stored directly in the node *record*. Sequences and sets with the standard linked-list representation are represented as pointers to the first list cell in the sequence or set. These pointers are also stored directly into the node *record*. No guarantees are made about the ordering of the members of the *record*. It is likely that the members will be reordered for storage efficiency. In addition to the node's attributes, a field called IDLhidden is also stored in the node *record*. IDLhidden contains information required by the IDL runtime system.

The Pascal representation for the IDL node type defined by

```
function => name:        String,
            thistype:    functionType,
            parameter:   Seq of formalParameter,
            definition:  expression;
```

might be:

```
const Kfunction = 2;
type Tfunction = ^RTfunction;
    RTfunction = record
            IDLhidden: IDLinternal;
            name: String;
            thistype: functionType;
            parameter: SEQparameter;
            definition: expression;
        end;
```

Since "function" is a reserved word in Pascal, it is converted by the IDL translator into Tfunction. This conversion is discussed further in Section 8.2.7. Unattributed nodes are node types declared without any attributes. Record declarations are created for them, containing only the relevant class pointers, to be discussed shortly. If there are no ancestor classes, unattributed nodes are represented by *record*s containing only the IDLhidden field.

The Pascal representation for the unattributed node type defined by

```
plus => ;
```

8.2. DATA TYPES

would be
```
const Kplus = 4;
type plus = ^Rplus;
     Rplus = record
        IDLhidden: IDLinternal
     end;
```
if there are no ancestor classes for plus.

Each node *record* also contains a class pointer for each direct class ancestor of the node. The names for these class pointers are formed by prefixing the class name with the letter "V" (for "Variant"). These class pointers are used with classes, described in the next section.

Operations

The operations on nodes are node allocation, node deallocation, attribute accessing, and attribute storage. Widening of a node to a class will be discussed in Section 8.2.3.

Attributes may be accessed and stored in the conventional Pascal syntax of pointer dereferencing followed by field selection.

```
var Afunction: function;

Afunction^.name = NewString('defaultname');
... Afunction^.name ...
```

A node allocation function and a deallocation procedure are generated for each node declared in an IDL declaration file. Storage for nodes is managed by these procedures.

Nodes are created explicitly by the user, or implicitly by the routine associated with an input port. The name for a node's allocation function is formed by prefixing the node name with "N" (for "New"). A node allocation function takes no arguments; its return value is a pointer to a newly allocated node of the proper type. Do not use any other means for dynamic allocation of nodes; it may cause anomalous and inconsistent behavior.

Local variables of a node or class type must first be initialized, either by assigning an existing node to the variable or allocating a new node with the "N" function, before accessing attributes through the variable.

If you do not want to create any nodes of a particular node type, specify

Restrict ⟨node_name⟩ **From Create**;

and the node creation function will not be made available. Nodes will still be created by readers if they are part of a Pre port structure.

The following steps are performed by the node creation function.

- Memory for the node is allocated from the heap. The node size is determined by IDLC using the specified size and alignment of each attribute contained in the node. The associated class *records* are allocated at the same time, and linked together using pointers, as described in Section 8.2.3.

- Default initialization is performed on all attributes, specifically, setting all values to 0.

- For each attribute of a private type in the node, an initialization procedure for the private type is called, if specified, to supply a value for that attribute. This procedure, named *I*⟨private name⟩, is discussed in Section 8.2.6.

- If specified, a user-supplied node initialization function is called that performs further initialization. This function is named *I*⟨node name⟩.

A *node initialization function* initializes the values of attributes when a new node is created. To ensure that the user-defined node initialization function is invoked, a restriction specification must be given, of the following form.

Restrict ⟨node_name⟩ *From DefaultInitialize*;

The initializer function must be compiled separately from the IDL-generated code file and linked with the IDL process. It must have a name that is the same as the node name with a "*I*" prefix. Finally, it must accept as its single argument a pointer of the appropriate node type, and return that same pointer. It is called each time the allocation function for the node is called. When the node is passed to the initialization function, it has had type information bound to it, and all attribute fields have been set to their default values.

For example, if the IDL file contained a representation clause of the form

For function *Use Initializer*;

then the declaration

function ITfunction (AfunctionInstance: Tfunction): Tfunction;

would appear in the Pascal declarations file and you would write a function similar to the following.

8.2. DATA TYPES

```
function ITfunction;
begin
    nameOfTfunction(AfunctionInstance) := NewString('default');
    .
    .
end;
```

Dynamically allocated nodes should be freed after they are no longer needed. This is done by invoking a *node deletion* procedure generated by the IDL translator. The procedure name is formed by prefixing the node type name with "*D*". The single argument is the node type. This procedure frees the storage allocated for the node record and all ancestor class records. String deletion, set deletion, and sequence deletion do not occur when the node deletion procedure is called. The node deletion procedure simply frees the storage used by the node and its ancestor classes.

If you do not want to delete any nodes of a particular node type, specify

> Restrict ⟨node_name⟩ From Destroy;

and the node deletion procedure will not be generated.

The actions of the deletion procedure are the reverse of those occurring during allocation.

- A user-provided attribute finalization function is called, if requested for the node. This function, named *F*⟨node name⟩, is discussed below.

- A user-provided private type finalization procedure is called, if requested, for each attribute of a private type in the node. This procedure, named *F*⟨private name⟩, is discussed in Section 7.2.6.

- The node itself, as well as its associated class *record*s, are deallocated, returning their storage to the heap.

You can write *attribute finalization functions* which are called each time a node is freed. To do this, a restriction specification of the following form must be given.

> Restrict ⟨node_name⟩ From DefaultFinalize;

The finalization procedure must be compiled separately from the IDL-generated code file and linked with the IDL process. It must have a name that is the same as the node name with an "*F*" prefix attached. Finally, it must accept as its single argument a pointer of the appropriate node type. Any inherited class attributes should also be finalized in this procedure.

For example, if the IDL file contained a representation clause of the form

```
Restrict function From DefaultFinalize;
```

then the declaration

```
procedure FTfunction(ATfunctionInstance: Tfunction);
```

would appear in the Pascal declarations file and you would write a function similar to the following.

```
procedure FTfunction;
begin
    .
    .
    .
end;
```

You should take special care not to leave dangling pointers when freeing nodes and attributes of nodes.

Version B Functions

In Version B of the target language, a function is generated for each attribute of each node. For example, four such functions would be generated for the function node

```
function nameOfTfunction(f: Tfunction): String;
function thistypeOfTfunction(f: Tfunction): functionType;
function parameterOfTfunction(f: Tfunction): SEQformalParameter;
function definitionOffunction(f: Tfunction): expression;
```

Each function takes one parameter f, a node of type Tfunction, and returns the value of that attribute. These functions allow a functional (prefix) notation to be used when accessing attributes.

```
            ··· nameOffTfunction(thisfunction) ···
```

8.2. DATA TYPES

8.2.3 Classes

IDL notation provides two different class types: plain classes and unattributed classes. A *plain class* is a class that contains at least one attributed node and no null nodes. An *unattributed class* contains all unattributed nodes. There is a common representation for both plain and unattributed classes in the Pascal representation. This section describes how the IDL translator maps these class types into Pascal declarations and then describes how the type of a class may be determined at runtime.

Representation

Each class is represented by a pointer to a Pascal *record* looseness=2that contains the class representation. Each class *record* contains the common attributes of all nodes that are in the class. A Pascal variant is also part of the class *record*. The variant structure defines the nodes and classes that may be direct descendents of the class. For each descendent, a pointer to the node or class for that descendent is defined. The tag field for the variant *record* is an enumerated type whose name is formed by prefixing the class name with "*Q*". The tag field's name in the variant portion of the class' *record* is formed by prefixing the class name with "*E*". The names for the members of the set type are formed by prefixing each descendant class or node name with "*K*" followed by the class name. The descendant node and class pointers in the variant *record* have names that are formed by prefixing the node type names with "*V*". This representation applies to all classes, both plain and unattributed. Class attributes are propagated to all class descendants by the IDL translator. Frequently, one may want to access a common attribute of a class without knowing which node type has been assigned to that class. This can be done by accessing the attribute directly in the class *record*. If the following IDL class declarations were defined in an IDL declaration file

```
expression      ::= constant | formalParameter;
constant        ::= IntegerConstant | RealConstant;
IntegerConstant => value:      Integer;
RealConstant    => value:      Rational;
expression      => lineNumber: Integer;
```

then the Pascal declaration file would contain the following.

```
const KIntegerConstant = 2;
      KRealConstant = 4;
      KformalParameter = 6;

type expression = ^Rexpression;
constant= ^Rconstant;
IntegerConstant = ^RIntegerConstant;
RealConstant = ^RRealConstant;
formalParameter = ^RformalParamter;

Qexpression = (Kexpressionconstant,KexpressionformalParameter);
Rexpression = record
      IDLhidden: IDLinternal;
      lineNumber: integer;
      case Eexpression: Qexpression of
          Kexpressionconstant: (Vconstant: constant);
          KexpressionformalParameter:
                  (VformalParameter: formalParameter);
end;

Qconstant = (KconstantIntegerConstant, KconstantRealConstant);
Rconstant = record
      IDLhidden: IDLinternal;
      Pexpression: expression;
      case Econstant: Qconstant of
          KconstantRealConstant: (VRealConstant: RealConstant);
          KconstantIntegerConstant:
                  (VIntegerConstant: IntegerConstant)
end;

RIntegerConstant = record
      IDLhidden: IDLinternal;
      Pconstant: constant;
      value: integer;
end;

RRealConstant = record
      IDLhidden: IDLinternal;
      Pconstant: constant;
      value: real;
end;
```

8.2. DATA TYPES

The Pascal *record*s that collectively form an instance of an Integer-Constant node are shown below.

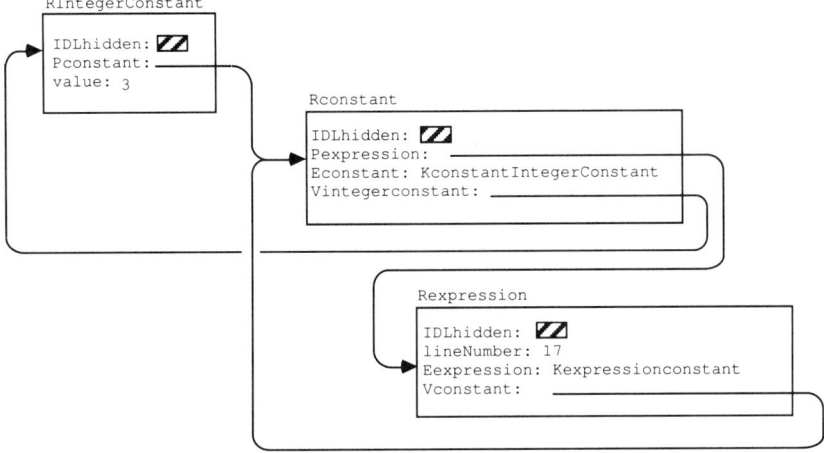

Operations

Operations that can be performed on classes are attribute accessing, narrowing, widening, and type query. Classes may not be allocated nor deallocated. A variable of a class type may be assigned a value of a particular node type that is a member of that class, as will be discussed below.

The correct *record* must first be located before an attribute may be accessed or stored. Access and storage of common class attributes is the most straightforward. As an example of storing a common class attribute without knowing the node type, you might write

```
var real1:  RealConstant;
    int1:   IntegerConstant;
    const1: constant;
    exp1:   expression;
     .
     .
    exp1^.lineNumber := 5;
```

The common class attribute may also be accessed from the node

```
    linenum := int1^.Pexpression^.lineNumber;
```

A node variable may be used to assign a class variable

```
const1 := real1^.Pconstant;
```

A node is created using the provided creation function

```
real1 := NRealConstant;
```

This function creates all the associated class records and initializes the "*P*", "*E*", "*V*" and IDLhidden fields. Classes do not have allocation or deallocation procedures.

Type Information

Class type information is available for programmer use through the "*E*" fields.

```
if const1^.Econstant = KconstantRealConstant then ...
```

Multiple levels may be involved.

```
if exp1^.Eexpression = Kexpressionconstant
then if exp1^Vconstant^.Econstant = KconstantRealConstant
then ...
```

Narrowing

A Pascal variable whose type is an IDL class can have as a value a reference to a node whose type is a member of that class. In the example above, a variable of type operation can have as a value a reference to either a BinaryOperation or UnaryOperation node with the particular node type possibly varying at runtime. Assigning this node to a variable whose type is a subclass is termed *narrowing*, and is done through the appropriate "*V*" member, after a runtime type check.

```
var Aconstant: constant;
I: IntegerConstant;
R: RealConstant;
      .
      .
      .
if Aconstant^.Econstant = KconstantIntegerConstant
then I := Aconst^.VIntegerConstant
else R = Aconst^.VRealConstant;
```

8.2. DATA TYPES

Widening

Widening is the inverse of narrowing, and never requires a runtime type check. Widening is performed by using the "P" member.

    `Aconstant := I^.Pconstant;`

          .

    `Aconstant := R^.Pconstant;`

Version B Functions

In Version B of the Pascal target language, several functions are generated for each class. By using these functions, you may ignore many of the peculiar aspects of the implementation of class types in Pascal, which doesn't directly support such types.

One function is generated for each attribute of each class. These functions have the same form as those generated for nodes.

function `lineNumberOfRealConstant(R: RealConstant): ` *Integer;*

This function replaces the use of the `Pexpression` fields.

Widening and narrowing are both supported by the following function.

function ⟨class name$_1$⟩To⟨class name$_2$⟩(c: ⟨class name$_1$⟩): ⟨class name$_2$⟩;

If ⟨class name$_1$⟩ is a subclass of ⟨class name$_2$⟩ (e.g., if ⟨class name$_1$⟩ is `IntegerConstant` and ⟨class name$_2$⟩ is `constant`; i.e., `IntegerConstant-Toconstant`), then this function widens the argument node to be of type ⟨class name$_2$⟩ (here, `constant`). Since the validity of this conversion can be checked by the IDL translator, this function results in only a type conversion; no runtime checking is necessary.

If ⟨class name$_1$⟩ is a *superclass* of ⟨class name$_2$⟩ (e.g., if ⟨class name$_1$⟩ is `constant` and ⟨class name$_2$⟩ is `IntegerConstant`; i.e., `constantToIntegerConstant`), then this function narrows the argument node to be of type ⟨class name$_2$⟩ (here, `IntegerConstant`). The validity of this conversion must be checked at runtime (for instance, the argument may be a `plus` node). If the runtime check fails, the procedure `ConversionError` is called, with the specified class names as character string arguments.

    `ConversionError("constant", "IntegerConstant");`

More complicated variants are possible. For the following IDL specification

```
A ::= X | Y;
B ::= Y | Z;
```

the following functions would be generated

- the widening functions XToA, YToA, YToB, and ZToB;
- the narrowing functions AToX, AToY, BToY, and BToZ, and
- the function AToB.

The last function performs a conversion which is neither narrowing nor widening. It would succeed only if its argument were in Y.

These functions are also generated when ⟨class name$_1$⟩ is a node name (this would be a widening type conversion) and when ⟨class name$_2$⟩ is a node name (this would be a narrowing type conversion), but not when both are node names (such a conversion is always illegal). The use of these conversion functions obviates the need for using the "*E*", "*V*" and "*P*" fields explicitly.

8.2.4 Sequences

The IDL translator generates a representation and sequence operation routines for each attribute type that is a sequence. Sequence types can be node or class types as well as scalar types. This section describes the representation and operations for sequences in Pascal. All operations are available for all representations of sequences.

Linked List Representation

A sequence of ⟨type name⟩ is represented by a linked list of objects of the type. A linked list is made up of list cells, defined as follows.

```
type SEQ⟨type name⟩ = ^CQ⟨type name⟩;
    CQ⟨type name⟩ = record
        next: ^CQ⟨type name⟩;
        value: ⟨type name⟩
    end;
```

8.2. DATA TYPES

The ⟨type name⟩ may be a node, class, string or scalar type. The sequence operations defined below allow most operations to be performed without an understanding of the linked list implementation. Programmers should avoid nonprocedural manipulation of sequences to insulate themselves from modifications to the sequence implementation.

For example, if the IDL declarations file contained a declaration of the form

```
function => parameters: Seq Of formalParameter;
```

then the Pascal declaration file would contain the declaration

```
type SEQformalParameter = ^CQformalParameter;
     CQformalParameter = record
        next: ^CQformalParameter;
        value: formalParameter
     end;
```

Declarations for all sequences of scalar types are found in the generated header file. SEQboolean and SEQinteger are names for pointers to list cells of types Cboolean and Cinteger, with value types boolean and integer. SEQString, and SEQreal are pointers to list cells of types CQString, and CQreal, with value types of String and real, respectively.

Operations

The IDL translator provides 16 sequence operations for each generated sequence type. These operations are also provided for each sequence of scalar types. The following is a list of the operations that are supplied for sequences of values of type flag. In each operation, SEQflag is a sequence of flags and value is an flag value. Allocation and deallocation of list cells are done by each routine but no allocation or deallocation of the data types is performed (you should create an instance before, say, appending it to the sequence). A complete description of each routine is given in Appendix D.

```
procedure appendfrontSEQflag(var seq: SEQflag; value: flag);
procedure appendrearSEQflag(var seq: SEQflag; value: flag);
function copySEQflag(seq: SEQflag): SEQflag;
function emptySEQflag(seq: SEQflag): boolean;
procedure initializeSEQflag(var seq: SEQflag);
function inSEQflag(seq: SEQflag; value: flag): boolean;
function ithinSEQflag(seq: SEQflag; index: flag): flag;
function lengthSEQflag(seq: SEQflag): integer;
procedure orderedinsertSEQflag(var seq: SEQflag;
         member: flag; function comparison: boolean);
```

```
procedure removefirstSEQflag(var seq: SEQflag);
procedure removelastSEQflag(var seq: SEQflag);
procedure removeSEQflag(var seq: SEQflag; value: flag);
function retrievefirstSEQflag(seq: SEQflag): flag;
function retrievelastSEQflag(seq: SEQflag): flag;
procedure sortSEQflag(var seq: SEQflag;
         function comparison: boolean);
function tailSEQflag(seq: SEQflag): SEQflag;
```

Restrictions

If functions for all sequence operations for all sequence types are generated (the default action), then potentially many functions will be defined, requiring excessive processing time and symbol table space in the preprocessor. Usually only a few operations are needed for each sequence type. Restriction specifications can reduce the number of functions generated. Each operation can be named in a restriction specification. For example, if the length is never interrogated for a sequence, the lengthSEQ function needn't be generated.

> *Restrict * From* lengthSEQ;

On the other hand, we can ensure that a particular operation is present with

> *Restrict Seq Of* flag *To* ithinSEQ;

8.2.5 Sets

The IDL translator generates a representation and set operations for each attribute type that is declared as a set of a data type. Data types of sets can be node or class types as well as scalar types. This section describes the representations and operations for sets of the various types. All operations are available for all representations of sets.

Linked List Representation

The IDL translator uses a linked list representation identical to the sequence representation just described. A set of a data type is represented by a linked list of objects of the type. A linked list is made up of list cells, defined as follows.

> *type* SET⟨type name⟩ = ^CT⟨type name⟩;
>   CT⟨type name⟩ = *record*
>   next: ^CT⟨type name⟩;

8.2. DATA TYPES

```
        value: ⟨type name⟩;
    end;
```

The ⟨type name⟩ may be a node, class, string or scalar type. The set operations defined below allow most operations to be performed without an understanding of the linked list implementation. Programmers should avoid nonprocedural manipulation of sets to insulate themselves from set implementations.

For example, if the IDL declarations file contained a declaration of the form

```
    expression => legalOperations: Set Of operation;
```

then the Pascal declaration file would contain the declaration

```
    type SEToperation = ^CToperation;
        CToperation = record
            next: ^CToperation;
            value: operation
        end;
```

Declarations for all sets of scalar types are found in the generated header file. SETboolean and SETinteger are names for pointers to list cells of types CTboolean and CTinteger, with value types *boolean* and *integer*. SETString, and SETrational are pointers to list cells of types CTString, and CTrational, with value types of *String* and *real*, respectively.

Operations

The IDL translator provides seven set operations for each generated set. In addition, it provides default set routines for each scalar type. The following is a list of the operations that are generated for a sets of flags. Allocation and deallocation of list cells are done by each routine but no allocation or deallocation of the data types is performed.

```
    procedure addSETflag(var aset: SETflag; value: flag);
    function copySETflag (aset: SETflag): SETflag;
    function emptySETflag(aset: SETflag): boolean;
    procedure initializeSETflag(var aset: SETflag);
    function inSETflag(aset: SETflag; value: flag): boolean;
    procedure removeSETflag(var aset: SETflag; value: flag);
    function sizeSETflag (aset: SETflag): integer;
```

Restrictions

As with sequences, each set operation can be named in a restriction specification. An example is

> Restrict Set Of flag To removeSET;

8.2.6 Private Types

IDL private types allow the programmer to use private representation for a particular type. The following sections describe the representation and reader/writer interfacing for private types used with Pascal.

Representation

Private types are specified with up to seven IDL statements which may appear in any order. The form of the first statement is

> Type ⟨private_name⟩;

This statement tells the IDL translator that the type called ⟨private_name⟩ will be a private type rather than a node or class type.

The second and third IDL statements tell the IDL translator where the user-defined representation for the type exists. The form of these statements is:

> For ⟨private_name⟩ Use Package ⟨module_name⟩;
>
> For ⟨private_name⟩ Use Name ⟨name⟩;

The first statement specifies the module name and the second statement specifies the name of the type within the module that will be used internally in the process. The ⟨module_name⟩ specifies a file that contains the declaration of the ⟨private_name⟩. More specifically, the ⟨module_name⟩ will be transformed into the name of a file with an appended suffix of ".**h**", and the IDL declaration file for each Pascal process that uses the ⟨private_name⟩ will be made to **#include** the file specified by the ⟨module_name⟩. Note that an include file will be included in the IDL declaration file only once.

If the second statement is used, then each instance of the ⟨private_name⟩ in the structure declaration is replaced with ⟨name⟩.

One of two statements are required to specify the form of the internal representation of a private type. The following

> For ⟨private_name⟩ Use Internal ⟨type⟩;

8.2. DATA TYPES

is useful when a process does not need to deal with the private type internal representation and can just treat it as an IDL type. The second form

> For ⟨private_name⟩ Use Size ⟨integer⟩ { Bits | Bytes } ;

is used when the internal representation is found in a package. The *Size* variant is redundant when used with the *Internal* variant.

The alignment in main memory, if different than the size, is specified with

> For ⟨private_name⟩ Use Alignment ⟨integer⟩ { Bits | Bytes } ;

The last statement specifies the external representation for the private type. An external representation can be an IDL scalar type or any defined node type. This is the representation that will be used when reading or writing the private type. The form of this statement is

> For ⟨private_name⟩ Use External ⟨type⟩;

Reader/Writer Interfacing

The programmer who implements a private type must define an interface with the reader and writer. The interface is defined in Pascal by the implementor — it provides a way for IDL to read and write the data type without knowing what the implementation is.

This interface takes the form of a separately compiled Pascal file which must be linked into the final process. It must contain definitions for routines used by the reader and writer. Only those routines that are used must be defined; that is, if a private type is only to be written and not read, none of the input routines are needed, and you may omit them. The reverse is true as well, and if the private type is to be neither read nor written, no interface code is needed.

The following interface routines are needed.

- *Input Mapper:* A procedure creating an instance of the internal representation of the private type. Its two arguments are of the external type for the private type and the internal type. The name of the procedure is "⟨external type⟩To⟨internal type⟩".

- *Output Mapper:* A procedure creating an instance of the external representation of the private type. The two arguments are an instance of the internal representation for the private type and the external type. The procedure name is "⟨internal type⟩To⟨external type⟩".

- *Initializer:* A procedure taking as a parameter a private type residing in a newly created node. This procedure initializes the value of the private type. The procedure name is the name of the private type prefixed by "*I*".

- *Finalizer:* A procedure taking as a parameter a private type residing in a node to be deallocated. This procedure frees any external storage associated with the private type. The procedure name is the name of the private type prefixed by "*F*".

You must provide external declarations for these procedures in a file called ⟨private_name⟩.i. For example, if all four procedures were needed for the private type called sourceposition, specified as

```
Type sourceposition;
For sourceposition Use Internal pos;
For sourceposition Use External Integer;
```

You would supply the file **sourceposition.i** with the following contents.

```
procedure integerTopos(IDLfrom: integer; var IDLto: pos); externa
procedure posTointeger(IDLfrom: pos; var IDLto: integer); externa
procedure Isourceposition(var this: pos); external;
procedure Fsourceposition(var this: pos); external;
```

8.2.7 Name-Space Conflicts

An IDL declaration might have node, class, or attribute names that are identical to Pascal keywords. An example would be the use of `real` as a node name. These nodes will be read and written with the names given in the IDL declaration, but you will have to use a modified version of the name in Pascal code. The IDL translator will issue an informative message, as a warning, on the standard error output informing you of the translation and of the new form of the name, which is the name prepended with the letter "T". The modified form of the name will be used wherever the node name is normally prefixed. For example, if the IDL node `real` was modified to `Treal` by the IDL translator, the internal token `KTreal`, and not `Kreal`, would be generated. If a `Seq Of real` were used, then `Treal` would also appear in the generated routines, such as `sizeSEQTreal`.

8.3. PROCESSES

Standard Pascal does not allow the use of underscores in Pascal programs. Should these characters be used in IDL names (e.g., Integer_Constant), an informative error message is printed. The name will appear in the Pascal representation without any underscores (e.g., IntegerConstant). To make the generated Pascal easier to read the programmer should make judicious use of upper and lower case letters.

In both cases, the warning can be avoided through an appropriate representation specification, for example

> *For* real *Use Name* Treal;
> *For* Integer_Constant *Use Name* IntegerConstant;

Warnings concerning underscores in attribute names cannot be avoided.

8.2.8 Sharing

The Pascal data instantiating an IDL record within the memory of a process has the form of a graph. A single node or class may appear multiple times in a traversal of the graph. In input and output, labels are used to resolve such references. Within an IDL process, *sharing detection* in output data is resolved by making two passes over the data record and defining several operations on each node type. The first pass determines which nodes are shared, marking them for the second pass; the second does the output, erasing the first pass's marks as it goes.

Pascal equivalence (the "=" operator) of nodes or classes reduces to a case of pointer equivalence in the Pascal IDL representation. This is an adequate test of equivalence for nodes and classes. For basic IDL types (*Integer*, *Boolean*, and *Rational*) the "=" operator is a valid test for equivalence. Strings may also be compared for equivalence with the "=" operator; they are another case of pointer equivalence. For sets and sequences, the "=" operator may not be used to test equivalence; two sets can contain the same elements and not be equal.

8.3 Processes

IDL processes are associated with Pascal programs. The *Target* clause names the programming language the program will use. The ports correspond to the input and output for the program. Finally, the invariant record represents the collection of data types the program will use. This section describes port representation and functions, storage management for a process, generated files for a process, and the use of the IDL translator.

8.3.1 Ports

Representation

Each port in the IDL specification for a process corresponds to a Pascal *function* generated by the IDL translator. The name used for the port in the IDL specification is the name used for the automatically-generated port function. When the function is called, the appropriate modifications (if any) to the process's invariant record is performed.

Input ports generate functions that return an instance of the root type, through which the entire structure instance may be accessed. These functions take two arguments.

- a value of type `text` specifying from where the data will be read, and

- a boolean value indicating to the caller whether reading of the specified data succeeded.

When an input port is invoked, the file should already be open for reading; an end of file or a top-level pound sign ("#") must be seen at the end of the data, after any amount of white space. Multiple record may be read from the same file if they are separated with pound signs.

Output ports take two arguments, both mandatory.

- a value of type `text` specifying where data is to be written, and

- an instance of the root type indicating the data structure to be written.

A pound sign ("#") is written when the port's writing is complete. The caller is responsible for initially opening the file and finally closing the file. Multiple record may be written sequentially to the file. Output ports use a first pass over the data structure to detect instances of sharing, and a second pass to erase sharing marks and to write the data. The output is in a nested form with labels used only when necessary.

For example, given the declaration

```
Process Test Is
    Target Language Pascal;
    Pre customersin: customers;
    Post billsout: bills;
End
```

two routines will be generated, one for the input port and one for the output port.

8.3. PROCESSES　　　　　　　　　　　　　　　　　　　　　　　　　195

```
function (var f: text; var readerok: boolean): customers;
procedure billsout(var f: text; root: bills);
```

External Format

The external format of a structure associated with a port of a process is selected at translation time by a port representation clause. Every implementation must support the "ASCII External Representation Language", as described in Chapter 6. This is the default output format for any process. Other formats may also be available.

8.3.2 Storage Management

Automatically generated Pascal routines in the IDL code file allocate storage for strings, nodes, list cells, and system data. These routines should be used instead of the Pascal *new* operation.

8.3.3 Restrictions

You may restrict the generated operations for a node or class to a specified set by using restrictions. This is especially useful for decreasing the size of the generated declarations file.

Restrictions are specified in two ways. The first is to restrict the generated operations for a node or class *to* a specified set. The second way is to restrict the generated operations *from* certain operations in the default set of operations. The detailed syntax is given in Chapter 4, and the complete list of operations is given in Appendix B. By default all sequence operations are provided for each generated sequence, all set operations are provided for each generated set, and allocation, deallocation, default initializer, and default finalizer routines are provided for each node type. You should specify which operations from this group are wanted. Invalid operations given in restriction clauses are ignored.

8.3.4 Files

Three files are created by the IDL translator for every process, two header files and an object file. The first header file is named after the process, with a suffix of ".**h**". It contains the type definitions for the process. The second header file is also named after the process, with a suffix of ".**i**". It contains the function and procedure definitions for the process. Finally, the code file is named after the process, but with a suffix of ".**o**". If Version B is specified, a fourth file, with a suffix of "**functions.h**", containing additional functions, is also created. The header files should be textually included in all files that use the data declared in the IDL specification. The object file should be linked into the process along with your code for the process and Pascal interface library code.

8.3.5 Translation of an IDL Process

To translate an IDL specification for a process into an object file and a header files, invoke the program IDLC with one argument, the name of the file containing the IDL declarations for the process. Several files can be processed by the IDL translator in one invocation.

Your Pascal code files (which must #include the generated declarations file for the process) may be compiled after the declaration file is emitted by IDLC. An object code library known as the Pascal interface library must be linked with the generated object files and your object files to produce the final program.

Exercises

8.1 Compare the support of the IDL type model by the runtime system and code generated by IDLC in Pascal with that of C as described in the last chapter.

8.2 Why doesn't Pascal have foreachinSET and foreachinSEQ operations, which *are* supported in C?

Bibliographic Notes

The Pascal programming language is described in Jensen and Wirth [1974].

Lamb [1983] describes a more restricted mapping to Pascal that didn't support classes. Lamb [1987a, 1987b, 1987c] discusses in detail a runtime library consistent with Pascal's strong type checking and gives principles for implementing IDL data structures in C and Pascal. Lie [1984] describes an alternative interface in which generic routines such as attribute accessing and attribute storage perform runtime table lookups to compute the location of the relevant attribute. His runtime system includes automatic garbage collection implemented using reference counting.

Breguet, Grize, and Strohmeier [1985] is a related extension to Pascal, supporting stacks, lists, sets, arrays, and the predefined types vertex, arc, and graph. Modula2+ (Rovner, Levin, and Wick [1985]) includes a limited form of narrowing. Wirth's [1987] Oberon is a Pascal-like language

8.3. PROCESSES

supporting type extensions (Wirth [1988]). This language is similar to the support of IDL classes in Pascal. In particular, the narrowing and widening operators (⟨class name$_1$⟩To⟨class name$_2$⟩) is identical to Wirth's type guard, and the Is⟨class name⟩ operator is identical to Wirth's type test. The major difference is that Wirth also allows classes to be allocated.

The notes on page 170 discuss additional aspects of mapping IDL to a target language.

Chapter 9

Using IDL in a Compiler

While IDL is a general language for specifying arbitrary directed graphs of attributed nodes, it is especially suited to specify the structures passed between tools in a programming environment. This chapter will examine how IDL may be used to specify interphase communication in a simple compiler. We will specify the output of the syntactic and semantic analysis phases, and will implement both phases in C and in Pascal.

The compiler discussed in this chapter concerns the function language introduced in Chapter 3. Specifically, the constant folding phase implemented in that chapter is one of the phases of the compiler. Figure 9.1 shows how the phases fit together.

9.1 The Frontend

In the frontend, the characters in the input are *parsed* according to the syntax of the language, and a *parse tree* corresponding to the input source is constructed. The syntax is usually expressed in BNF; Figure 9.2 provides the syntax for the function language.

The output of the frontend phase will be an IDL instance encoding the parse tree. However, since some elements of the input source, such as the keywords and punctuation, are not of interest to the remaining phases of the compiler, we will omit these elements and instead produce an *abstract syntax tree*. The IDL specification for the abstract syntax tree can be easily extracted from the BNF, and is shown in Figure 9.3 (this structure was introduced in Figure 3.6).

We note several aspects of this structure.

- Only the external representation of the private type source_posi-

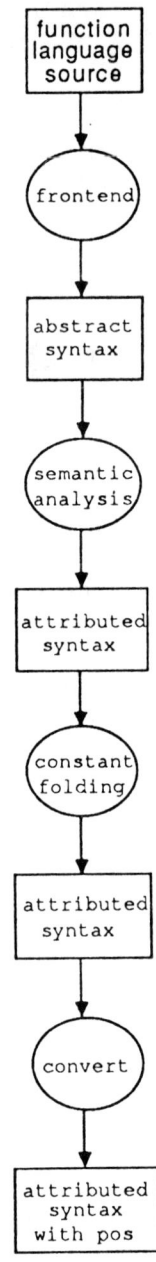

Figure 9.1: Phases of the Function Compiler

9.1. THE FRONTEND

```
⟨program⟩      ::= { ⟨function⟩ }*
⟨function⟩     ::= function ⟨head⟩ '=' ⟨expression⟩ ';'
⟨head⟩         ::= ⟨name⟩ ⟨parameters⟩ ':' ⟨type⟩
⟨parameters⟩   ::= ε | '(' ⟨parameter⟩ { ',' ⟨parameter⟩ }* ')'
⟨parameter⟩    ::= ⟨name⟩ ':' ⟨type⟩
⟨type⟩         ::= integer | real
⟨expression⟩   ::= ⟨expression⟩ '+' ⟨term⟩ | ⟨expression⟩ '-' ⟨term⟩
                 | ⟨term⟩
⟨term⟩         ::= ⟨term⟩ '*' ⟨factor⟩ | ⟨term⟩ '/' ⟨factor⟩ | ⟨factor⟩
⟨factor⟩       ::= '+' ⟨factor⟩ | '-' ⟨factor⟩ | ⟨name⟩
                 | ⟨integer⟩ | ⟨real⟩ | '(' ⟨expression⟩ ')'
```

Figure 9.2: The Syntax for the Function Language

tion is specified. The internal representation will be dealt with when we specify the individual IDL processes.

- Four attributes are lexical in nature and have the prefix "lex_". The remaining attributes are syntactic and have the prefix "syn_". We will later define semantic attributes, which will have the prefix "sem_".

- The possibility of a function having no parameters is accommodated by allowing the sequence syn_parameters to be empty. This is one case where the IDL specification is simpler than the BNF.

- The precedence of the operators need not be specified in the IDL structure, again simplifying the structure.

- The types, binaryoperators and unaryoperators are specified using unattributed nodes. For efficiency, these nodes can later be represented as enumerated types.

- In the abstract syntax tree, certain details, such as the presence of parentheses in ⟨expression⟩s have been omitted. An *unparser* could generate a semantically equivalent program from an instance of abstract_syntax; this program may differ in some minor aspects from the original program from which the instance was generated.

```
1  -- file: specs/functionsyntax.idl                                          1
2  Structure abstract_syntax Root functions Is                                2
3                                                                             3
4     -- private type declaration and type representation information         4
5     Type source_position;                                                   5
6     For source_position Use External Integer;                               6
7                                                                             7
8     identifier        =>  lex_token:       String,                          8
9                           lex_pos:         source_position;                 9
10    functions         =>  syn_func_seq:    Seq Of function;                10
11                                                                           11
12    function          =>  syn_name:        identifier,                     12
13                          syn_return_type: types,                          13
14                          syn_parameters:  Seq Of formal_parameter,        14
15                          syn_definition:  expression;                     15
16    NumParams Assert ForAll f In function Do                               16
17        Size(f.syn_parameters) > 0 Od;                                     17
18    formal_parameter  =>  syn_name:        identifier,                     18
19                          syn_param_type:  types;                          19
20                                                                           20
21    types             ::= int | real;                                      21
22    int =>; real =>;                                                       22
23                                                                           23
24    expression        ::= constant | formal_parameterRef | operation;      24
25    constant          ::= integer_constant | real_constant;                25
26    integer_constant  =>  lex_value:       Integer;                        26
27    real_constant     =>  lex_value:       Rational;                       27
28    formal_parameterRef => syn_name:       identifier;                     28
29    operation         ::= binary_operation | unary_operation;              29
30    binary_operation  =>  syn_op:          binaryoperator,                 30
31                          syn_left:        expression,                     31
32                          syn_right:       expression;                     32
33    binaryoperator    ::= plus | minus | times | divide;                   33
34    plus =>; minus =>; times =>; divide =>;                                34
35    unary_operation   =>  syn_op:          unaryoperator,                  35
36                          syn_argument:    expression;                     36
37    unaryoperator     ::= unaryplus | unaryminus;                          37
38    unaryplus =>; unaryminus =>;                                           38
39                                                                           39
40    -- There are no cross branches in any parse trees                      40
41    NoCrossBranches Assert ForAll n In binary_operation                    41
42        Do (Reach(n.syn_left) Intersect Reach(n.syn_right))                42
43            Same Empty Od;                                                 43
44    -- There are no cycles in any parse trees                              44
45    NoCycles Assert ForAll n In expression Do Not(n Sub Desc(n)) Od;       45
46    -- All expressions are reachable from the root.                        46
47    NoDisconnectedComponents Assert ForAll e In expression Do              47
48        Exists f In Members(Root.syn_func_seq)                             48
49            Do e In Reach(f.syn_definition) Od                             49
50    Od;                                                                    50
51    Define IDesc(n: constant) = Empty;                                     51
52    Define IDesc(n: formal_parameterRef) = Empty;                          52
53    Define IDesc(n: unary_operation) = n.syn_argument;                     53
54    Define IDesc(n: binary_operation) = n.syn_left Union n.syn_right;      54
55    Cyclic Define Desc(n: expression) Returns expression                   55
56        = Reach(IDesc(n));                                                 56
57    Cyclic Define Reach(n: expression) Returns expression                  57
58        = n Union Desc(n);                                                 58
59  End                                                                      59
```

Figure 9.3: The `abstract_syntax` Structure

9.1. THE FRONTEND

The input to the frontend is a character stream, and hence is not specified in IDL. The output is an instance of `abstract_syntax`. The IDL declarations for the frontend process are given in Figures 9.4–9.6. Note that

- The internal representation for the `source_position` private type is specified to be the `pos` node, extracted from the `posdeclaration` structure, shown in Figure 9.7. The external representation was earlier specified to be an *Integer*. Since this aspect is common to both target languages, it is specified in **fe.idl**; the `fe_invariant` structure is imported by both target-language-specific declarations.

- In the C-specific file, the internal representation of the classes containing unattributed nodes, `binaryoperator`, `unaryoperator`, and `types`, is specified to be enumerated to save space. The Pascal target language does not currently support enumerated nodes.

- In the C-specific file, the `int` node is renamed `Tint` to avoid a conflict with the C type *int*.

- In the Pascal-specific file, the `real` and `function` nodes are renamed `Treal` and `Tfunction`, respectively, to avoid a conflict with the Pascal types *real* and *function*.

- These changes only affect the invariant of the `parser` process. If no invariant structure was specified, the IDL translator would have detected the recoverable errors corrected above, and would have taken the same actions in its recovery.

- When the `fe_invariant` structure is imported, those structures that "contribute" to it, namely `abstract_syntax` and `posdeclaration`, are also implicitly imported.

The frontend phase is itself composed of two subphases: one performing lexical analysis and one performing syntactic analysis (also called *parsing*). The parser makes repeated requests of the lexer, each time receiving a single token. Figure 9.8 shows that the tokens can also be specified in BNF. An integer is assigned to each token, except for ⟨white space⟩, which is ignored. The subphase partitioning is not specified in IDL.

Rather than implementing the frontend in C by hand, we use the YACC parser generator, which generates a bottom-up parser in C, and LEX, which generates a lexical analyzer in C. A top-down, recursive descent parser is implemented in Pascal. The next two subsections discuss the parser, in C and in Pascal, respectively. These subsections are independent, and cover the same material in a similar fashion.

204   CHAPTER 9. USING IDL IN A COMPILER

-- *file*: *functionlang/frontend/fe.idl*

Import abstract_syntax From functionsyntax End

Process fe Is
    -- *Pre is tokenized input source*
    Post ParseTreeOut: abstract_syntax;
End

Figure 9.4: The IDL Specification for the fe Process

-- *file*: *functionlang/frontend/C/frontend.idl*

Import fe From fe End

Import posdeclaration From pos End

Structure frontend_invariant From abstract_syntax, posdeclaration Is
    For source_position Use Internal pos;

    For int Use Name Tint;
    For binaryoperator Use Representation Enumerated;
    For unaryoperator Use Representation Enumerated;
    For types Use Representation Enumerated;
End

Process frontend Refines fe Inv frontend_invariant Is
    Target Language C;
End

Figure 9.5: The IDL Specification for the frontend Process for C

9.1. THE FRONTEND

-- *file: functionlang/frontend/Pascal/frontend.idl*

Import fe From fe End

Import posdeclaration From pos End

Structure frontend_invariant From abstract_syntax, posdeclaration Is
    For source_position Use Internal pos;

    For real Use Name Treal;
    For function Use Name Tfunction;
End

Process frontend Refines fe Inv frontend_invariant Is
    Target Language Pascal;
End

Figure 9.6: The IDL Specification for the frontend Process for Pascal

```
1  -- file: specs/pos.idl                                                          1
2                                                                                  2
3  Structure posdeclaration Is                                                     3
4     -- the node that will be used for the external representation                4
5     -- of source_position                                                        5
6     pos =>  charoffset: Integer, -- offset from the first character in the file  6
7             lineoffset: Integer, -- offset from the first character in the line  7
8             linenumber: Integer; -- number of lines; first line is line 0        8
9  End                                                                             9
```

Figure 9.7: The IDL Specification for the pos Node

⟨token⟩   ::= ⟨basic token⟩ | ⟨punctuation⟩ | ⟨white space⟩
⟨basic token⟩   ::= ⟨keyword⟩ | ⟨name⟩ | ⟨integer⟩ | ⟨rational⟩
⟨punctuation⟩   ::= '+' | '-' | '*' | '/' | '(' | ')' | ';' | '='
                    | ':' | ','
⟨white space⟩   ::= ⟨space⟩ | ⟨tab⟩ | ⟨carriage return⟩
⟨keyword⟩   ::= function | integer | real
⟨name⟩   ::= ⟨letter⟩ { ⟨letter⟩ | ⟨digit⟩ | '_' }*
⟨integer⟩   ::= { ⟨digit⟩ }+
⟨rational⟩   ::= { ⟨digit⟩ }+ '.' { ⟨digit⟩ }*
⟨letter⟩   ::= 'a' | ... | 'z' | 'A' | ... | 'Z'
⟨digit⟩   ::= '0' | ... | '9'

Figure 9.8: The Lexical Portion of the Function Language

9.2 The Frontend in C

While the characters in the source file encounter lexical analysis first, we discuss these subphases in the reverse order, starting with syntactic analysis, because of the way in which LEX and YACC interact.

9.2.1 The Parser

The YACC source file for the function language is shown in its entirety in Appendix E.3.1. Here we note only the unusual features; the reader should refer to the appendix for the details.

- YACC requires that the language grammar by LALR(1). Fortunately, the grammar in Figure 9.2 required few changes to satisfy this requirement.

- The IDL node types that will be associated with terminals (tokens) and nonterminals during the parsing are declared in a "%union" clause.

  ```
  %union {
          function    Vfunction;
          identifier  Videntifier;
          ...
  }
  ```

9.2. THE FRONTEND IN C

- The specific types are associated with "%token" or "%type" clauses:

  ```
  %token <Videntifier> IdentifierToken 1
  ...
  %type <Vfunction> _function
  ```

  We also specify the numerical values associated with each token (e.g., 1 for `IdentifierToken`). Nonterminals are distinguished in this particular yacc specification with an initial underscore.

- The correct precedence is achieved by using the `%left` and `%prec` yacc constructs.

- The actions of most productions create a node, set the values of the attributes from the values associated with the symbols on the right hand side of the production, and return the node. In this way, the abstract syntax tree is created in a bottom-up fashion:

  ```
  _expression : _expression PlusToken _expression
              {   binary_operation b;
                  b = Nbinary_operation;
                  b->syn_left = $1;
                  b->syn_op.Vplus = Nplus;
                  b->syn_right = $3;
                  $$.Vbinary_operation = b;
              }
  ```

- Sequences require more care. One action must initialize the sequence; other actions then append new elements to the sequence in the correct order. An example is

  ```
  _parameters      : LParenToken _parameters_list RParenToken
                   { $$ = $2;
                   }
                   ;

  _parameters_list : _parameter
                   {   SEQformal_parameter this;
                       initializeSEQformal_parameter(this);
                       appendrearSEQformal_parameter(this, $1);
                       $$ = this;
                   }
  ```

```
            | _parameters_list CommaToken _parameter
            {   appendrearSEQformal_parameter($1, $3);
                $$ = $1;
            }
            ;
```

- Some of the productions do not create any nodes.

```
_expression : LParenToken _expression RParenToken
            { $$ = $2;
            }
```

- The generated parser calls the routine `yylex` repeatedly, requesting successive tokens. This routine will be implemented in the next section.

- While the private type `source_position` is not explicit in the yacc source, it is there as an attribute of the `identifier` node. Section 9.2.3 will show how private types with differing internal and external representations (here, as a `pos` node and as an `Integer`, respectively) are handled.

9.2.2 The Lexical Analysis Phase

We use LEX to generate the lexer. The lex source file for the function language is shown in its entirety in Appendix E.3.1. Note that

- The numeric constants and the IDL types associated with the tokens are defined in the include file **tokens.h** that is extracted by YACC from the yacc source file. The file **frontend.h** generated by IDLC is also included by the LEX source file.

- The values of the `IdentifierToken`s are of type `identifier`, which has two attributes, `lex_token` and `lex_pos`. The value of the first attribute is an IDL *String*, which is created through the routine `NewString` (`yytext` holds the characters matched by the regular expression). The value of the second attribute is the private type `source_position`, which has as its internal representation the node type `pos`. The values of the attributes of the `pos` node are initialized by counters updated after each token has been processed.

```
/* file: functionlang/frontend/C/main.c */
#include "frontend.h"
#include <stdio.h>
#include "posCconverts.h"

functions thesefunctions;  /* set by yyparse */

main()
{
    if (yyparse()) {
        fprintf(stderr, "frontend: unrecoverable parsing error\n");
        exit(1);
    }
    else {
        ParseTreeOut(stdout, thesefunctions);
        exit(0);
    }
}
```

Figure 9.9: The `main` Function for the Frontend in C

9.2.3 Putting It Together

The `main()` function of the frontend (shown in Figure 9.9) creates the root node, initializes the `syn_func_seq` attribute, and invokes the generated parser. The parser, as a side effect, makes repeated call on the lexer. If the parsing was successful, the abstract syntax tree is written out. The lexer, parser, and main program are compiled separately. The object code is combined to form a single program.

One final portion of the frontend remains to be implemented. Recall that the `source_position` private type had different internal and external representations (the `pos` node and *Integer*, respectively). You must supply conversion routines that are invoked by the code generated by IDLC. Here, only one conversion routine is needed, from `pos` to *Integer*, that will be invoked by the `ParseTreeOut` function. This routine, `posToint`, is provided in the **posCconverts.h** source file, included in **main.c** and shown in Figure 9.10.

9.3 The Frontend in Pascal

The Pascal source for the frontend consists of three files. **main.p**, shown in Figure 9.11, includes the other two files: **lexical.i**, which performs lexical analysis, and **syntactic.i**, which performs the parsing. The latter two files are shown in their entirety in Appendix E.4.1, starting on page 512. In perusing this code, note that

```
/* file: functionlang/specs/posCconverts.h */
/* contains the conversion routines for the private type */
/* source_position, which has two representations: pos and integer.*/

/* source_position is encoded as an integer (31 bits) as follows */
/* 15 bits for character offset in source file */
/* 9 bits for the character offset from the beginning of the line */
/* 7 bits for line number in the source file */
pos intTopos(theint)
int theint;
{
        pos thepos;

        thepos = Npos;

        thepos->charoffset = (theint >> 16) & 0x8FFF;
        thepos->lineoffset = (theint >> 7) & 0x01FF;
        thepos->linenumber = (theint) & 0x007F;

        return (thepos);
}

int posToint(thepos)
pos thepos;
{
        return (((thepos->charoffset & 0x8FFF) << 16) |
            ((thepos->lineoffset & 0x01FF) << 7) |
            ((thepos->linenumber & 0x007F)));
}
```

Figure 9.10: Conversions for source_position in C

```
(* file: functionlang/frontend/Pascal/main.p *)

program parser(input, output);

#include "frontend.h"
#include "frontend.i"
#include "posPconverts.p"
#include "lexical.i"
#include "syntactic.i"

begin (* lexical and syntactic analysis *)
      InitLexer;
      Lexer; (* get initial token *)
      ParseTreeOut(output, Parseprogram); (* create parse tree and write it out *)
end.
```

Figure 9.11: The Main Body for the Frontend in Pascal

9.3. THE FRONTEND IN PASCAL 211

- Tokens are denoted by elements of the enumerated type `tokentype`. The current token is communicated from the lexer to the parser through the global variable `token`.

- Three tokens, `IntegerToken`, `IdentifierToken`, and `RealToken`, are associated with values via the global variable `yylval` (a variable of the same name serves a similar purpose in the C frontend).

- The lexer is a simple finite state machine of four states.

- The values of the `IdentifierToken`s are of type `identifier`, which has two attributes, `lex_token` and `lex_pos`. The value of the first attribute is an IDL *String*, which is created through the routine `NewString` (`thisidentifier` holds the characters matched by the regular expression). The value of the second attribute is the private type `source_position`, which has as its internal representation the node type `pos`. The values of the attributes of the `pos` node are initialized by counters updated after each token has been processed.

- The parser is a recursive descent, top-down parser. Such parsing is possible if the grammar is LL(1). The ⟨expression⟩ and ⟨term⟩ nonterminals in Figure 9.2 were rewritten to those shown below

⟨expression⟩ ::= ⟨term⟩ ⟨X⟩
⟨term⟩   ::= ⟨factor⟩ ⟨Y⟩
⟨X⟩   ::= ϵ | { { '+' ⟨term⟩ } | { '-' ⟨term⟩ } }*
⟨Y⟩   ::= ϵ | { { '*' ⟨factor⟩ } | { '/' ⟨factor⟩ } }*

to satisfy this requirement; the other nonterminals remain as before. Then functions to parse the ⟨program⟩, ⟨parameters⟩, ⟨expression⟩, ⟨term⟩, and ⟨factor⟩ nonterminals were written; the other nonterminals were upmerged into these functions, and hence did not require their own functions. The correct precedence is achieved through the use of intermediate nonterminals (⟨term⟩ and ⟨factor⟩) in the parsing.

- The actions of most functions create a node, call subordinate functions to compute the immediate children of the node, set the values of the attributes with the values returned by the subordinate functions, then return the original node. In this way the abstract syntax tree is computed in a bottom-up fashion.

```
(* file: functionlang/specs/sourceposition.i *)
procedure integerTopos(IDLfrom: integer; var IDLto: pos); external;
procedure posTointeger(IDLfrom: pos; var IDLto: integer); external;
```

Figure 9.12: Pascal Declarations for `source_position` Conversions

- Expressions require more care. The IDL instance constructed for the expression "a*b" is

```
binary_operation[
    syn_op times;
    syn_left formal_parameterRef[name identifier[lex_token "a"]];
    syn_right formal_parameterRef[name identifier[lex_token "b"]];
    ]
```

  `Parseterm` first calls `Parsefactor`, which returns the first `formal_-parameterRef` associated with 'a'. This value is assigned to the `syn_left` attribute of a newly-created `binary_operation` node. `Parsefactor` is then called to compute the value for the `syn_right` attribute. The `binary_operator` node is then returned by `Parseterm`.

- Each of these function calls the routine `Lexer` repeatedly, requesting successive tokens.

- The body of the frontend initializes the lexer, calls `Parseprogram` to generate an abstract syntax tree, then passes the returned value to `ParseTreeOut`, the writer generated by IDLC.

One final portion of the frontend remains to be implemented. Recall that the `source_position` private type had different internal and external representations (the `pos` node and *Integer*, respectively). You must supply conversion routines that are invoked by the code generated by IDLC. Here, only one conversion routine is needed, from `pos` to *Integer*, that will be invoked by the `ParseTreeOut` function. This routine, `posToint`, is declared in the file **sourceposition.i**, shown in Figure 9.12; the body of the procedure is found in the file **posPconverts.p**, included in **main.p** and shown in Figure 9.13.

9.4 Semantic Analysis

This phase performs two tasks

- *name resolution*, in which every use of a name is coupled with its *defining occurrence*, and

9.4. SEMANTIC ANALYSIS

```
(* file: functionlang/specs/posPconverts.p *)
(* contains the conversion routines for the private type *)
(* source-position, which has two representations: pos and integer. *)

(* source-position is encoded as an integer (32 bit signed) *)
(* as follows *)
(* 15 bits for character offset in source file *)
(* 9 bits for the character offset from the beginning of the line *)
(* 7 bits for line number in the source file *)

#include 'sourceposition.i'
procedure integerTopos(* IDLfrom: integer; var IDLto: pos*);
begin
      IDLto := Npos;
      IDLto^.charoffset := (IDLfrom div 65536) mod 32768;
      IDLto^.lineoffset := (IDLfrom div 128) mod 512;
      IDLto^.linenumber := (IDLfrom ) mod 128;
end;

procedure posTointeger(* IDLfrom: pos; var IDLto: integer *);
begin
      IDLto := ((IDLfrom^.charoffset mod 32768) * 65536) +
               ((IDLfrom^.lineoffset mod 512) * 128) +
               (IDLfrom^.linenumber mod 128);
end;
```

Figure 9.13: Conversions for `source_position` in Pascal

- *type checking*, in which the type of each expression is computed and compared with that declared for the result of the function that expression appears in.

Both tasks involve adding information to the abstract syntax tree. In the first task, a reference to the defining occurrence (a `formal_parameter`) is added to each use (a `formal_parameterRef`). In the second task, the type (either `int` or `real`) is added to each `expression`. These additions can easily be specified in IDL by using derivation (Figure 9.14). Attributes have a prefix of "sem_" to identify the phase where they are calculated, and that the meaning of the attributes is partially specified through assertions. The IDL specifications for the semantic analysis phase (Figures 9.15, 9.16 and 9.17) are similar to those for the parser, in that the invariant specifies the internal representation for `source_position` and the name for the `int`, `real` and `function` nodes. Figures 9.18 and 9.19 provide the main bodies of the semantic analysis phase.

As with the other phases, the full source for the secondary functions, in both C and Pascal, is given in Appendixes E.3.2 and E.4.2. In reading this code, note that

- `resolve_exp` is a recursive function that performs a preorder walk of the expression tree, searching for `formal_parameterRef`s to resolve.

```
1  -- file: specs/functionsem.idl
2
3  Import abstract_syntax From functionsyntax End
4
5  Structure attributed_syntax From abstract_syntax Is
6
7      -- additional semantic attributes
8
9      formal_parameterRef => sem_entity:   formal_parameter;
10     CorrectSemEntity Assert ForAll f In formal_parameterRef
11         Do f.syn_name = f.sem_entity.syn_name Od;
12
13     expression         => sem_exp_type: types;
14     CorrectIntConstType Assert ForAll ic In integer_constant
15         Do ic.sem_exp_type Is int Od;
16     CorrectRealConstType Assert ForAll rc In real_constant
17         Do rc.sem_exp_type Is real Od;
18     CorrectFormParamType Assert ForAll f In formal_parameterRef
19         Do f.sem_exp_type = f.sem_entity.syn_param_type Od;
20
21 End
```

Figure 9.14: The `attributed_syntax` Structure

-- *file*: *functionlang/semantic/C/semantic.idl*

```
Import sem From sem End

Structure semantic_invariant From attributed_syntax Is
    For source_position Use Internal Integer;
    For int Use Name Tint;
    For binaryoperator Use Representation Enumerated;
    For unaryoperator Use Representation Enumerated;
    For types Use Representation Enumerated;
End

Process semantic Refines sem Inv semantic_invariant Is
    Target Language C;
End
```

Figure 9.15: The Generic Semantic Analysis Process

9.4. SEMANTIC ANALYSIS

-- *file*: *functionlang/semantic/C/semantic.idl*

```
Import sem From sem End

Structure semantic_invariant From attributed_syntax Is
    For source_position Use Internal Integer;
    For int Use Name Tint;
    For binaryoperator Use Representation Enumerated;
    For unaryoperator Use Representation Enumerated;
    For types Use Representation Enumerated;
End

Process semantic Refines sem Inv semantic_invariant Is
    Target Language C;
End
```

Figure 9.16: The semantic Process for the C Target Language

-- *file*: *functionlang/semantic/Pascal/semantic.idl*

```
Import sem From sem End

Structure semantic_invariant From attributed_syntax Is
    For source_position Use Internal Integer;
    For real Use Name Treal;
    For function Use Name Tfunction;
End

Process semantic Refines sem Inv semantic_invariant Is
    Target Language Pascal;
End
```

Figure 9.17: The semantic Process for the Pascal Target Language

```
/* file: functionlang/semantic/C/main.c */
#include "semantic.h"
#include <stdio.h>

/* the main driver for the expression typing program */
main()
{
        SEQfunction Sfunction;
        function Afunction;
        functions thefunctions;
        types return_type;
        types exp_type;

        /* read in the input data structure */

        thefunctions = inputport(stdin);

        /* for each function, resolve parameter references */

        foreachinSEQfunction(thefunctions->syn_func_seq,
                Sfunction, Afunction) {
           resolve_references(Afunction);
        }

        /* for each function, add types to expressions and check for type */
        /* conflict between function return value and body of function */

        foreachinSEQfunction(thefunctions->syn_func_seq,
                Sfunction, Afunction) {
           expression_type(Afunction->syn_definition);
           return_type = Afunction->syn_return_type;
           exp_type = Afunction->syn_definition.IDLclassCommon->sem_exp_type;

           /* Check result type, permitting integers to be coerced into reals */
           if ((typeof (return_type) == KTint)
                  && (typeof (exp_type) != KTint)) {
              fprintf (stderr,
                  "semantic: function '%s' returns incompatible type\n",
                  Afunction->syn_name->lex_token);
           }
        }

        /* write out the attributed data structure */

        outputport(stdout, thefunctions, TWOPASS);
        exit(0);
}
```

Figure 9.18: The main Function for Semantic Analysis in C

9.4. SEMANTIC ANALYSIS

```
(* file: functionlang/semantic/Pascal/main.p *)

program semantic (input, output);
#include "semantic.h"
#include "sem2.h"

var ATfunction: Tfunction;
    thefunctions: functions;
    returntype: types;
    exptype: types;
    i: integer;
    ReaderOK: boolean;

#include "semantic.i"

(* the main driver for the expression typing program *)
begin
      (* read in the input data structure *)

      thefunctions := inputport(input, ReaderOK);

      if not ReaderOK then halt;

      (* for each function, resolve parameter references *)

      for i := 1 to lengthSEQTfunction(thefunctions^.synfuncseq) do begin
          ATfunction:= ithinSEQTfunction(thefunctions^.synfuncseq, i);
          resolvereferences(ATfunction);
      end;

      (* for each function, add types to expressions and check for type *)
      (* conflict between function return value and body of function *)

      for i := 1 to lengthSEQTfunction(thefunctions^.synfuncseq) do begin
            ATfunction:= ithinSEQTfunction(thefunctions^.synfuncseq, i);

            expressiontype(ATfunction^.syndefinition);
         returntype := ATfunction^.synreturntype;
         exptype := ATfunction^.syndefinition^.semexptype;

         (* Check result type, permitting integers to be coerced into reals *)
         if (returntype^.Etypes = Ktypesint)
            and (exptype^.Etypes <> Ktypesint)
         then writeln('semantic: function', ' ''',
               StringTopacked(ATfunction^.synname^.lextoken),
               ''' returns incompatible type');
      end;

      (* write out the attributed data structure *)

      outputport(output, thefunctions);
end.
```

Figure 9.19: The Main Body of Semantic Analysis in Pascal

- `expression_type` is also a recursive function that performs a preorder traversal of the expression tree. The type of an expression is calculated in a bottom-up fashion, with the `binary_operation` nodes requiring the most effort. If the `expression` is a `constant`, the type of the `expression` is `real` if the `constant` is a `real_constant` and `int` if the `constant` is an `integer_constant`. If the `expression` is a `formal_parameter`, the type of the `expression` is the same as the type of the `formal_parameter`. If the `expression` is an `operation`, the type of the `expression` is the same as the type for the `operation`. The type of a `binary_operation` is `int` if both the left and right `expressions` have type `int`, otherwise it is `real`. The type of a `unary_operation` is the same as the type of the `expression` which makes up its argument.

- Name resolution must be performed before expression typing, so that the type of a `formal_parameterRef` can be determined, by examining the defining occurrence, where the return type declared for the function has been recorded.

- Coercion of integers into reals is accommodated both in the type calculation and in checking the declared result type of each function.

- `foreachinSEQ` and *switch*es on the type of a node are the predominate control structures in the C code. Similarly, *for* loops and *case* statements on the type of a node are the predominate control structures in the Pascal code.

9.5 Constant Folding

This phase is covered in detail in Chapter 3. Again, we note only unusual aspects. The `fold` function is similar to the `expression_type` function in that it performs a preorder traversal of the expression tree, and that it calculates bottom-up. It differs in that it returns an expression tree, the constant-folded version of its argument, which is used to replace its argument in the original expression tree.

9.6 Converting Source Positions

The `abstract_syntax` structure, shown in Figure 9.3, specified that the external representation of the `source_position` private type was an integer. In the invariant of the frontend (Figure 9.4), the internal representation was specified to be the `pos` node, with the `ParseTreeOut` port invoking a

9.7. MERGING IDL PROCESSES

```
1  -- file: functionlang/specs/aswithpos.idl
2
3  Import attributed_syntax From functionsem End
4
5  -- the specification of the pos node
6  Import posdeclaration From pos End
7
8  Structure AS_with_pos From attributed_syntax, posdeclaration Is
9
10   For source_position Use External pos;
11 End
```

Figure 9.20: The IDL Specification for the `AS_with_pos` Structure

user-provided routine to convert each pos node to an integer. Successive phases, semantic analysis and constant folding, had no need for information concerning source positions, and so they retained the encoded integer representation.

In Chapter 11, we examine in detail the XRef language, used to specify cross referencers, such as for programs written in the function language. XRef programs require detailed information about source positions. The AS_with_pos structure (Figure 9.20) expresses the desired information (the pos node itself was given in Figure 9.7), and the convertgen process shown in Figure 9.21 provides the means of computing instances of this structure. As with prior phases, we use refinement to specify target-language-specific aspects (see the process declarations in Figures 9.22 and 9.23).

The source code for the convert process is remarkably simple, consisting of one executable statement (see Figures 9.24 and 9.25). In both cases, the result returned by the reader is immediately fed to the writer. The conversion in the representation of source_position, from *Integer* to pos, occurs as a side effect of the reader (the function inputPort). The reader calls the user-written routine intTopos, provided in the C implementation in the file **posCconverts.h** shown in Figure 9.10, and in the Pascal implementation in the file **posPconverts.p** shown in Figure 9.13. The pos node serves as the internal representation, with the writer (the routine outputPort) simply writing the node out.

When this process is run on the file shown in Figure 3.20 on page 97, the external representation shown in Figure 9.26 is generated.

9.7 Merging IDL Processes

The function language, as presented in this chapter and shown in Figure 9.1, contains four IDL phases. The abstract syntax tree is written out three

-- file: *functionlang/convert/convertgen.idl*

Import attributed_syntax From functionsem End

Import AS_with_pos From aswithpos End

Structure convertgenInv From AS_with_pos Is

    For source_position Use Internal pos;
End

Process convertgen Inv convertgenInv Is
    Pre inputPort: attributed_syntax;
    Post outputPort: AS_with_pos;
    Restrict Seq Of function To initializeSEQ;
End

Figure 9.21: The IDL Specification for the convertgen Process

-- file: *functionlang/convert/C/convert.idl*

Import convertgen From convertgen End

Process convert Refines convertgen Is
    Target Language C;
End

Figure 9.22: The IDL Specification for the convert Process in C

9.7. MERGING IDL PROCESSES

-- file: functionlang/convert/Pascal/convert.idl

```
Import convertgen From convertgen End

Structure convertInv Refines convertgenInv Is
    For function Use Name Tfunction;
    For real Use Name Treal;
End

Process convert Refines convertgen Inv convertInv Is
    Target Language Pascal;
End
```

Figure 9.23: The IDL Specification for the convert Process in Pascal

/* file: functionlang/convert/C/main.c */

```
#include <stdio.h>
#include "convert.h"
#include "posCconverts.h"

main()
{
    outputPort(stdout, inputPort(stdin), TWOPASS);
    exit(0);
}
```

Figure 9.24: The main Function for the convert Process in C

```
(* file: functionlang/convert/Pascal/main.p *)
program convert (input, output);

#include "convert.h"
var ReaderOK: boolean;

#include "convert.i"
#include "posPconverts.p"

begin
     outputPort(output, inputPort(input, ReaderOK));
end.
```

Figure 9.25: The Main Body of the convert Process in Pascal

times and read back in three times before ultimately being written out for the last time by the convert process. While this arrangement is easy to debug, because the intermediate structures are available for viewing, it is severely I/O bound. There are two ways to speed up the compiler significantly without modifying any of the source code. The first is to specify a more efficient port association. This change requires additional lines in the IDL specification, of the form

> For ⟨port_name⟩ Use { ⟨parameter⟩ }$^+$

The second method is to combine all the code into one Unix process, and implement reading and writing of IDL instances by copying in main memory a reference to the root node, a very fast operation. The rest of this section will show how this is done.

Figure 9.27 shows the specification of the one-process variant of the function language compiler. It should be functionally equivalent to the four-process variant, and so should read in the function language source text and generate instances of the AS_with_pos structure.

9.7.1 Into One C Program

Figure 9.28 shows the refined process for the C target language. The internal representation of source_position is also the pos node; there is no need to convert it to an integer and back again later to a pos node. The main program is shown in Figure 9.30; it contains the collected code from the main programs of the various phases, with the port invocations omitted,

9.7. MERGING IDL PROCESSES

```
--   structure attributed_syntax
functions[syn_func_seq <
     function
         [syn_name identifier[lex_token "foo";
                  lex_pos pos[linenumber 1;
                      lineoffset 9;
                      charoffset 9]];
          syn_return_type int;
          syn_parameters <
              L1:formal_parameter[syn_name
                           identifier[lex_token "A";
                              lex_pos pos[linenumber 1;
                                  lineoffset 13;
                                  charoffset 13]
                           ];
                       syn_param_type L2:int]
              >;
          syn_definition binary_operation[
              syn_op times;
              syn_left unary_operation[syn_argument
                  formal_parameterRef[
                      syn_name identifier[lex_token "A";
                          lex_pos pos[linenumber 2;
                              lineoffset 4;
                              charoffset 38]];
                          ];
                      sem_exp_type L2^;
                      sem_entity L1^;
                      ];
                  syn_op unaryminus];
                  sem_exp_type int];
              syn_right integer_constant[lex_value 41;
                  sem_exp_type int];
              sem_exp_type int;
          ];
     ]
>]
#
```

Figure 9.26: Function foo After Constant Folding

-- *file*: *functionlang/oneprocess/all.idl*

Import AS_with_pos From aswithpos End

Process all Is
         -- *Pre is tokenized input source*
         Post outputPort: AS_with_pos;
End

Figure 9.27: The IDL Specification for the all Process

-- *file*: *functionlang/oneprocess/C/onephasecompiler.idl*

Import all From all End

Structure onephase_invariant From AS_with_pos Is
    For source_position Use Internal pos;
    For int Use Name Tint;
    For binaryoperator Use Representation Enumerated;
    For unaryoperator Use Representation Enumerated;
    For types Use Representation Enumerated;
End

Process onephasecompiler Refines all Inv onephase_invariant Is
    Target Language C;
End

Figure 9.28: The IDL Specification for onephasecompiler for C

except for the call to the final outputPort. The routines that main calls are located in the same files comprising the original four-process variant of the compiler: **lex.l**, **parse.y**, **resolve.c**, **typing.c**, and **algorithm.c**. These files are compiled separately and linked to generate the executable program. No source code need be changed.

These files each include a file generated by IDLC that declares the data structures corresponding to the invariant structure for the relevant process. For example, **lex.l** and **parser.y** include the file **frontend.h**, and **resolve.c** includes **semantic.h**. In the one-process variant, there is only one invariant structure, onephase_invariant, that must be used by all the source code. We arrange this by effectively renaming **onephasecompiler.h** to the relevant file, say **semantic.h** when compiling **resolve.c**. To see exactly how this is done, consult the **Makefile** listed in Appendix E.3.5.

9.7.2 Into One Pascal Program

Figure 9.29 shows the refined process for the Pascal target language. The internal representation of source_position is also the pos node; there is no need to convert it to an integer and back again later to a pos node. The main program is shown in Figure 9.31; it contains the collected code from the main programs of the various phases, with the port invocations omitted, except for the call to the final outputPort. The routines that main calls are

9.7. MERGING IDL PROCESSES 225

```
-- file: functionlang/oneprocess/Pascal/onephasecompiler.idl

Import all From all End

Structure onephase_invariant From AS_with_pos Is
    For source_position Use Internal pos;
    For function Use Name Tfunction;
    For real Use Name Treal;
End

Process onephasecompiler Refines all Inv onephase_invariant Is
    Target Language Pascal;
End
```

Figure 9.29: The IDL Specification for `onephasecompiler` for Pascal

located in the same files comprising the original four-process variant of the compiler: **lexical.i**, **syntactic.i**, **resolve.p**, **typing.p**, and **algorithm.p**. These files are included in the main program when it is compiled to generate the executable program. No source code need be changed.

The latter three files each include a file generated by IDLC that declares the data structures corresponding to the invariant structure for the relevant process. For example, **resolve.p** includes **semantic.h**. In the one-process variant, there is only one invariant structure, `onephase_invariant`, that must be used by all the source code. We arrange this by including the generated file **onephasecompiler.h**, then including the various component files (e.g., **resolve.p**). Since **resolve.p** itself includes the file **semantic.h**, we simply create an empty file of that name so that the compilation can proceed. To see exactly how this is done, consult the **Makefile** listed in Appendix E.4.5.

Exercises

9.1 Extend the function language and its compiler to support several parameters of the same type, e.g.,

```
function foo (a, b, c: integer): integer = ... ;
```

9.2 Extend the function language and its compiler to handle the boolean type.

```
/* file: functionlang/oneprocess/C/main.c */

#include "onephasecompiler.h"
#include <stdio.h>
functions thesefunctions;

main()
{
    SEQfunction Sfunction;
    function Afunction;
    functions thefunctions;
    types return_type;
    types exp_type;

    if (yyparse()) {
        fprintf(stderr, "frontend: unrecoverable parsing error\n");
        exit(1);
    }
    else {

        /* for each function, resolve parameter references */

        foreachinSEQfunction(thesefunctions->syn_func_seq,
                Sfunction, Afunction) {
            resolve_references(Afunction);
        }

        /* for each function, add types to expressions and check for type */
        /* conflict between function return value and body of function   */

        foreachinSEQfunction(thesefunctions->syn_func_seq,
                Sfunction, Afunction) {
            expression_type(Afunction->syn_definition);
            return_type = Afunction->syn_return_type;
            exp_type = Afunction->syn_definition.IDLclassCommon->sem_exp_type;

            /* Check result type, permitting integers to be coerced into reals */
            if ((typeof (return_type) == KTint)
                    && (typeof (exp_type) != KTint)) {
                fprintf (stderr,
                    "semantic: function '%s' returns incompatible type\n",
                    Afunction->syn_name->lex_token);
            }
        }

        /* perform constant folding on defining expression */
        foreachinSEQfunction(thesefunctions->syn_func_seq,
                Sfunction, Afunction) {
            fold(&(Afunction->syn_definition));
        }

        /* output the parse tree of the equivalent function */
        outputPort(stdout, thesefunctions, TWOPASS);

        exit(0);
    }
}
```

Figure 9.30: The main Function in C

9.7. MERGING IDL PROCESSES

```
(* file: functionlang/oneprocess/Pascal/main.p *)

program all(input, output);

#include "onephasecompiler.h"
#include "onephasecompiler.i"
#include "sem.h"
#include "const.h"
#include "posPconverts.p"
#include "lexical.i"
#include "syntactic.i"
#include "resolve.p"
#include "typing.p"
#include "algorithm.p"

var ATfunction: Tfunction;
    thefunctions: functions;
    returntype: types;
    exptype: types;
    i: integer;

begin (* lexical and syntactic analysis *)
      InitLexer;
      Lexer; (* get initial token *)
      thefunctions := Parseprogram; (* create parse tree *)

      (* for each function, resolve parameter references *)
      for i := 1 to lengthSEQTfunction(thefunctions^.synfuncseq) do begin
          ATfunction:= ithinSEQTfunction(thefunctions^.synfuncseq, i);
          resolvereferences(ATfunction);
      end;

      (* for each function, add types to expressions and check for type *)
      (* conflict between function return value and body of function *)
      for i := 1 to lengthSEQTfunction(thefunctions^.synfuncseq) do begin
          ATfunction:= ithinSEQTfunction(thefunctions^.synfuncseq, i);
          expressiontype(ATfunction^.syndefinition);
          returntype:= ATfunction^.synreturntype;
          exptype:= ATfunction^.syndefinition^.semexptype;
          (* Check result type, permitting integers to be coerced into reals *)
          if (returntype^.Etypes = Ktypesint)
              and (exptype^.Etypes <> Ktypesint)
          then writeln('semantic: function ',
                  StringTopacked(ATfunction^.synname^.lextoken),
                  ' returns incompatible type');
      end;

      (* perform constant folding on defining expression *)
      for i := 1 to lengthSEQTfunction(thefunctions^.synfuncseq) do begin
          ATfunction:= ithinSEQTfunction(thefunctions^.synfuncseq, i);
          fold(ATfunction^.syndefinition);
      end;

      (* output the parse tree of the equivalent function *)
      outputPort(output, thefunctions);
end.
```

Figure 9.31: The Main Body in Pascal

9.3 The generation of an IDL specification, a LEX lexical analyzer, a Pascal lexical analyzer, a YACC parser, and a top-down recursive descent Pascal parser for the BNF of a language is a fairly mechanical procedure, given the techniques discussed in this chapter. Discuss the desirability of automating this procedure in a compiler-generator tool called FRONTENDGEN.

    a. What are the input(s) and output(s) of FRONTENDGEN?

    b. Are the output(s) always computable from the input(s)?

    c. How would the compile-time space and time of generating an executable version of the parser using FRONTENDGEN compare with generating such a version using LEX, YACC, and IDLC? How would the run time and execution space of the generated frontend compare with that of one generated by hand (via YACC and LEX)?

    d. The frontend must also interface with the user, in terms of invocation argument processing, error messages (and recovery), and listing generation. Do such considerations impact the design of this tool?

9.4 Compare the four-process and one-process variants of the function language compiler, in terms of compile-time space and time and run-time space and time.

Bibliographic Notes

The rules in Section 9.2.1 for writing yacc actions to construct the abstract syntax tree imply that a tool could generate the yacc actions automatically. Park [1988] describes such a tool. Snodgrass and Shannon [1986] describe two extensions to IDL, connections and composite processes, that enable automatic support for the manual activities discussed in Section 9.7. Similar constructs, present in Version 3 IDL, are described by Nestor et al. [1989].

    The distinction between entities and entity references is emphasized by Tennent [1981], who calls the occurrence of an identifier in the declaration of an entity a *binding occurrence* and any other occurrence an *applied occurrence* In DIANA (Goos and Wulf [1981]), the latter is termed a *used occurrence* In our terminology, both kinds of occurrences are *syntactic* entities.

    The LEX and YACC tools and the LL(1) and LALR(1) classes of languages are discussed in many compiler texts, including Aho, Sethi, and Ullman [1986] and Fischer and LeBlanc [1988]. The advice given by

9.7. MERGING IDL PROCESSES

Jones [1988], taken when coding the Pascal version of lexical analysis to achieve better structuring, was contested by Lerche [1988].

Chapter 10

Writing IDL Specifications

In IDL, as in most languages, there are many ways to say similar things. While the IDL translator insists on grammatical correctness, it cares little about style. In this chapter, we provide some elementary guidelines of usage that we find contribute to the readability and maintainability of IDL specifications. Occasionally these guidelines are illustrated from the specifications for the function compiler or for other compilers we have written using IDL. DIANA, an intermediate representation of Ada programs, and CANDLE, the intermediate representation of IDL specifications, are also mentioned occasionally. Further information on CANDLE may be found in Chapter 15, which examines this structure in detail. While following these guidelines will not guarantee a readable specification, and while one can write a readable specification ignoring these guidelines, our experience indicates that keeping these guidelines in mind results in better specifications.

10.1 Coarse Structuring

The first set of guidelines involves structuring the specification.

1. *Use derivation and refinement to partition structures.*

    Derivation and refinement allow the reader to focus on the *differences* between two structures. The `attributed_-syntax` structure adds only two attributes to the `abstract_structure`. These two attributes are the only ones that appear in the specification of `attributed_syntax` (see Figure 9.14).

2. *Use the Import statement to share specifications.*

    In IDL, a series of specifications that depend on each other, through derivation or refinement, can be placed in one file or spread across many files. It usually makes more sense to use more files rather than fewer files, for several reasons. Since most source code control systems (e.g., MAKE, SCCS, and RCS in Unix) operate at the granularity of a file, a change to one of several files will generally trigger less recompilation than if all the IDL specifications were in a single file. Second, the IDL translator will have to do less work in the presence of multiple source files, since only a subset of files required will need to be processed. Finally, reading the specifications can be easier if the specifications are broken into multiple files (but see guideline 3 below).

3. *Use cross references to view the invariant.*

    If guidelines 1 and 2 are followed, the attributes of a node and the members of a class are spread across potentially many specifications and files. In the invariant of the `semantic` process, the `Tint` node name was declared in the `semantic_invariant` structure (in the file **semantic.idl**); the node itself was declared in the `abstract_syntax` structure (in the file **functionsyntax.idl**); and the attribute `sem_exp_type` was declared in still another structure and file: `attributed_syntax` and **functionsem.idl**, respectively. In the code generation process of the IDL translator, about one dozen structures from as many files contribute to the invariant. To write code, the programmer must know which attributes are associated with each class and node. Fortunately, XREF (see Chapter 11) may be employed to obtain this (and other) information in a convenient format (see Appendix E.5). We obtain the advantages of comprehensibility and maintainability through guideline 1, compilation efficiency and readability through guideline 2, and usability through this guideline.

10.1. COARSE STRUCTURING 233

4. *Each succeeding phase should decorate the processed instance with new information in the form of additional attributes, not delete or replace information in this instance.*

    Guideline 1 dictates that the structure specifications are incremental, in that each is defined in terms of another, previously defined structure. The present guideline dictates that (a) each derived structure does not use the without construct (see Section 4.1.4) and (b) the instance produced by a phase contains more information than that read by the phase, that is, that the *instances* are incremental. The justification is that debugging and maintenance are easier when a phase does not corrupt the input structure. If there is some information that is only required by a subset of the phases, the compiler can be debugged using the incremental structures, then, once it is working correctly, it can be recompiled using additional, derived structures that do use the without construct.

5. *When a structure is "grown" in several stages, use prefixes to differentiate the attributes.*

    Attributes with names prefixed with "`lex_`" (for lexical analysis), "`syn_`" (for syntactic analysis), and "`sem_`" (for semantic analysis) appear in the `attributed_syntax` structure. In the CANDLE structure, the prefixes "`rep_`" (for representation analysis) and "`pre_`" (for prelude) also are used. When many similar phases are present, such as separate phases to perform various kinds of optimization, then perhaps a single prefix should be assigned to the collection of phases, with derivation and cross-references (c.f., guideline 3) providing the second order partitioning of names. This was done in the IDLC implementation (see Chapter 17), in which both semantic and representation analysis each consist of two distinct phases.

6. *Use suffixes carefully in attributes names to impart additional information.*

    If the attribute is of a set or sequence type, use a plural name (e.g., `syn_parameters`) or appropriate suffix (e.g., `syn_func_seq`). Suffixes can also be used to indicate the attribute's type (e.g., `lex_pos`, `syn_param_type`).

7. *Employ underscores "_" and capitalization to distinguish portions of an IDL identifier.*

   In guidelines 5 and 6, prefixes and suffixes were distinguished by underscores. Capitalization has the same effect with fewer characters (e.g., `synParameters`, `synFunctionSeq`). As specifications get larger, the need for naming conventions also increases. While we were somewhat inconsistent in the `abstract_syntax` structure (c.f., `formal_parameterRef`, `binary_operation`, and `binaryoperator`), we were much more careful in the 50-page CANDLE specification given in Appendix F.

Guidelines 5, 6 and 7, along with careful selection of the root of the attribute's name, will result in names that are substantially self-documenting (assertions (see guideline 26) and good comments also help).

10.2 Abstract Syntax Trees

The following guidelines apply to structures encoding parse trees or abstract syntax trees.

8. *Annotate sections with comments containing the portion of the BNF associated with each section.*

   Both CANDLE and DIANA follow this guideline, as does the XRef syntax structure (see Section 13.5). Annotations were unnecessary for `abstract_syntax` because of its short length.

9. *Associate each nonterminal appearing on the left hand side of a production in the BNF with a class, or a node if there is only one right-hand side. Associate one "syn_" attribute with each nonterminal, except keywords, on the right-hand side of a production.*

   From the function language

   ⟨expression⟩ ::= ⟨expression⟩ '+' ⟨term⟩
                 | ⟨expression⟩ '-' ⟨term⟩
                 | ⟨term⟩

10.2. ABSTRACT SYNTAX TREES

IDL:
```
expression        ::= operation;
operation         ::= binary_operation;
binary_operation  => syn_op:     binaryoperator,
                     syn_left:   expression,
                     syn_right:  expression;
binaryoperator    ::= plus | minus;
plus => ; minus => ;
```

10. *Do not encode keywords and punctuation.*

   These keywords and punctuation can usually be inferred from the abstract syntax tree.
   From Pascal:

   ⟨for statement⟩ ::= *for* ⟨variable⟩ ' := ' ⟨expression⟩
   { *to* | *downto* } ⟨expression⟩
   do ⟨statement⟩

   IDL:
   ```
   for_statement => syn_control:   variableRef,
                    syn_from:      expression,
                    syn_direction: toOrdownto,
                    syn_to:        expression,
                    syn_statement: statement;
   toOrdownto     ::= to | downto;
   to => ; downto => ;
   ```

   The ':=' punctuation and *do* keyword are not encoded at all in the `for_statement` node. The *to* and *downto* keywords are encoded in the `syn_direction` attribute, which may require as little as one bit of space (see guideline 13) or no additional space (see guideline 18).

11. *Encode precedence implicitly in the abstract syntax tree, thereby eliminating many intermediate nonterminals.*

   The `abstract_syntax` structure does not contain ⟨term⟩ or ⟨factor⟩, even though these nonterminals are required in the BNF.

12. Represent lists of syntactic constructs using IDL sequences. Encode ϵ-productions as empty sequences.

   From the function language

   ⟨parameters⟩ ::= ϵ
   | '(' ⟨parameter⟩ { ',' ⟨parameter⟩ }* ')'

   IDL:

   ```
   function => syn_parameters: Seq Of formal_parameter;
   ```

   Some ϵ-productions are more naturally encoded as classes (see guideline 15).

13. Use enumerated types to encode aspects such as operations and basic types efficiently.

   The following declarations would result in unaryoperators, types, and binaryoperators that require very little space in some implementations.

   ```
   For binaryoperator Use Representation Enumerated;
   For unaryoperator Use Representation Enumerated;
   For types Use Representation Enumerated;
   ```

   Such representations generally should be specified in later refinements of a structure, or in the specification of the invariant of a process (e.g., in fe_invariant in Figure 9.4).

14. Use an enumerated Void node and a class for optional items not in a list.

   From Pascal:

   ⟨ifstmt⟩ ::= IF ⟨expression⟩ THEN ⟨stmt⟩ ⟨elsept⟩
   ⟨elsept⟩ ::= ϵ | ELSE ⟨stmt⟩

   IDL:

   ```
   ifstmt     => syn_else: expression,
                 syn_then: stmt,
                 syn_else: stmtOrVoid;
   stmtOrVoid ::= stmt | Void;
   For Void Use Representation Enumerated;
   ```

The representation clause ensures that Void requires no more space than a node reference.

10.3 Use of Classes

Unlike several other object-oriented languages, IDL allows nodes and classes to have more than one direct superclass. This generality allows classes to be used in a variety of ways. Occasionally a node will have several superclasses, each for a different reason.

There are seven primary occasions when a class is suggested. These will be listed as guidelines.

15. *Use a class when the value of an attribute can be of more than one node type.*

    An example from the abstract_syntax structure is

    ```
    binary_operation => syn_left: expression;
    ```

    Because the value of the syn_left attribute could be an integer_constant, a real_constant, a formal_parameterRef, a unary_operation, or even another binary_operation, we used a class as the attribute type.

16. *Use a class when two or more nodes share a common attribute.*

    An example, from the attributed_syntax structure, is

    ```
    expression => sem_exp_type: types;
    ```

    If the expression class were not used, this one line would have to be replaced with five lines, one each for each member node. Additionally, by using a class, only one recursive descent procedure, taking an expression as an argument, is needed to do the typing. Finally, such classes are useful in maintenance and in later extensions. If a new kind of expression is added to the function language (say, predicates involving And, Or, and Not), it can naturally be made a subclass of expression, and will automatically inherit the sem_exp_type attribute.

17. *Use a class as documentation.*

   In the `abstract_syntax` structure, the line
   `constant ::= integer_constant | real_constant;`

   can be translated to "a `constant` is either an `integer_constant` or a `real_constant`." While this class is not strictly necessary, it nevertheless conveys useful information.

A fourth use of classes was given in guideline 12: Use a class when a clause is optional in the syntax.

18. *Use classes to eliminate attributes.*

   In the XRef language, discussed in detail in Part III, there are three constructs that have similar syntax and meaning.

   ⟨sequence element⟩ ::= *Reorder* ⟨sequence tail⟩
   　　　　　　　　　　| *Unique* ⟨sequence tail⟩
   　　　　　　　　　　| *Intersection* ⟨sequence tail⟩
   ⟨sequence tail⟩　　::= ' (' ⟨sequence⟩ ' , ' ⟨predicate⟩ ') '

   One representation of this syntax in IDL is
   ```
   sequence_element => syn_type:     sequence_type,
                       syn_sequence: sequence,
                       syn_predicate: predicateRef;
   sequence_type   ::= reorder | unique | intersection;
   reorder => ; unique => ; intersection => ;
   For sequence_type Use Representation Enumerated;
   ```

   While this specification uses a class, for the reason given in guideline 13, we can alter the specification slightly, to
   ```
   sequence_element => syn_sequence: sequence,
                       syn_predicate: predicateRef;
   sequence_element ::= reorder | unique | intersection;
   reorder          => ; unique => ; intersection => ;
   ```

   This specification encodes the same information, but with less complexity and in fewer lines. As another example, in the syntax structure from the Pascal for statement, given

10.3. USE OF CLASSES

earlier, one attribute, `syn_direction`, could be replaced with a class:

```
for_statement ::= for_to_statement
                | for_downto_statement;
```

Sometimes all the attributes are eliminated after this guideline is applied, in which case the class can also be enumerated (see guideline 13). As a final note, there is one potential pitfall in applying this guideline: occasionally too much information is removed. For example, the C language allows an increment or decrement operation to precede or follow an expression, with appropriate semantics in each case.

⟨unary exp⟩ ::= ⟨prefix⟩ | ⟨postfix⟩
⟨prefix⟩   ::= '+' '+' ⟨prefix⟩ | '-' '-' ⟨prefix⟩
⟨postfix⟩   ::= ⟨postfix⟩ '+' '+' | ⟨postfix⟩ '-' '-'

Applying the guideline blindly results in

```
expression ::= unaryexp;
unaryexp   => body: expression;
unaryexp   ::= prefix | postfix;
prefix     ::= incr | decr;
postfix    ::= incr | decr;
```

Unfortunately, there is now no way to distinguish between a prefix or postfix expression when examining the syntax tree, since the `incr` and `decr` nodes are each members of both the `prefix` and `postfix` classes! The solution is to use more classes:

```
prefix  ::= preincr | predecr;
postfix ::= preincr | predecr;
```

19. *Use a class when one of the above reasons is anticipated in a derived or refined structure.*

    Guideline 1 and this guideline taken together imply that, when a derived or refined structure is defined, it may be necessary to modify a previously defined ancestor structure, generally to augment the class hierarchy. While these modifications may themselves require changes in the programs that reference these structures, the resulting programs are better organized and more maintainable than if the earlier structures were not modified.

The seventh use of classes is given in Section 10.4.5: use a class to delay computing the value of an attribute when there is insufficient information.

Because these reasons may overlap arbitrarily, the class-subclass structure need not be strictly hierarchical. It turns out that every node and class in the `abstract_syntax` structure has at most one superclass. However, in the CANDLE structure, discussed in detail in Chapter 15, two nodes, `NamedTypeRef` and `Assertion`, have three direct superclasses, and two nodes and one class, `DefInstance`, `AttributeRef`, and `TypeRef`, have two direct superclasses.

10.4 The Symbol Table

A symbol table is a data structure that maps identifiers to values. In IDL terminology, the symbol table associates nodes encoding identifiers with nodes encoding semantic entities. There are various approaches available for specifying the symbol table in IDL. We first examine representations for the components of the symbol table, then discuss the symbol table proper. Guidelines summarizing these issues appear at the end of the section.

10.4.1 Identifiers

The first aspect to consider is the representation of identifiers. An obvious representation is

```
identifier => lex_token: String,
              lex_pos:   source_position;
```

This representation is used in the `abstract_syntax` structure. The runtime system provided in the IDL Toolkit provides special support for values of type *String*. In particular, in both the C and Pascal target languages, value equivalence (denoted with "==" in C and "=" in Pascal) is identical to pointer equivalence. Hence the test of whether two identifiers

```
var a, b: integer;
```

have the same name

```
if (a^.lextoken = b^.lextoken)
```

10.4. THE SYMBOL TABLE

reduces to a simple, efficient pointer equivalence test. The `lex_pos` attribute is important for generating error messages or cross references and ideally should be associated with each syntactic construct (see guideline 20, below). If this attribute is not desired, then the node declaration for an identifier can be replaced with a type representation.

> For identifier Use External String;
> For identifier Use Internal String;

10.4.2 Syntactic and Semantic Entities

A second aspect is representing semantic information about entities named with identifiers present in the source program. It is important to differentiate between syntactic entities and semantic entities. *Syntactic entities* are those nodes encoding the syntactic structure of the source program. The `abstract_syntax` structure has four primary syntactic entities: `function`, `operator`, `identifier`, and `constant` nodes. These nodes will contain "lex_" and "syn_" attributes, such as `lex_pos`. *Semantic entities* are the receptacles for semantic information such as type, extent, scope, address, etc, stored in "sem_" or "code_" attributes. Such nodes play the part of the symbol table in most compilers. Semantic entities for the function language are defined in the `attributed_syntax` structure. Here, there are two semantic entities, `function` and `expression`.

Differentiating syntactic and semantic entities often contributes to the clarity of the specification. For example, in Pascal, many variables can be declared in one declaration.

> ⟨variable declaration⟩ ::= **var** ⟨ident list⟩ ' : ' ⟨type⟩ ' ; '
> ⟨ident list⟩   ::= ⟨ident⟩ { ' , ' ⟨ident⟩ }*

This syntax may be represented in IDL as

```
variableDecl => syn_identifiers: Seq Of identifier,
                syn_type:        typeRef;
```

During semantic analysis, semantic entities, each denoting a variable, are created using information present in the declaration. These variables may be associated with the procedure or function (or the main program) in which they are declared.

```
variableEntity  => sem_name:       String,
                   sem_type:       TypeEntity;
procedureEntity => sem_variables:  Seq Of variableEntity;
```

Some nodes can have two roles, encoding the syntax tree and holding semantic information. In CANDLE, `Attribute` nodes play both roles, yet classes are described syntactically by `subclassProduction` nodes and semantically by `Class` nodes. Generally, a node can play both roles if the language ensures that there is one syntactic definition point for the entity. In the function language, functions are uniquely defined in the syntax. Similarly, the definition point for a variable in Pascal is its declaration. Hence, there is no need to store the name twice; instead, we specify the structure as follows.

```
variableDecl    => syn_variables:   Seq Of variableEntity,
                   syn_type: typeRef;
variableEntity  => syn_ident:       identifier;
```

During semantic analysis, only one attribute is computed.

```
variableEntity  => sem_type:        TypeEntity;
```

On the other hand, there is no single syntactic definition point for an IDL class in an IDL specification; a particular identifier may appear on the left hand side of a class production in many places in a structure specification. In such cases, separating the syntactic and semantic aspects into different nodes, one syntactic entity and potentially several semantic entities, is cleaner.

10.4.3 Entities and Entity References

It is also important to differentiate between *entities* and *entity references*. Each identifier in a parse tree plays one of two roles: it may name an entity being declared, or it may refer to an entity declared, either implicitly or explicitly, elsewhere. Entity references represent identifiers found in the parse tree. Such nodes will contain a `syn_name` attribute, as well as a `sem_entity` attribute specifying the semantic entity referenced by this syntactic entity reference. The `abstract_syntax` structure has one entity reference: the `formal_parameterRef` node. The other semantic entity, `expression`, cannot be referenced by name according to the function language definition. For each kind of entity that can be named in the source program, there should be both a semantic entity node and an entity reference node declared in the IDL structure.

Entities and entity references are handled in various ways, dictated by the syntax and semantics of the source language. In the Pascal fragment,

```
type I = integer;
var a, b: I;
```

10.4. THE SYMBOL TABLE

```
        ...
        a := 3;
```

the first "I" names an entity and the second "I" refers to this entity. The identifier "integer" is an entity reference, specifically to a predefined type. The first occurrence of "a" names an entity, and the second "a" is a reference to that entity. The occurrence of "b" names an entity, a variable of type integer.

Since a type declaration is the definition point for a user-defined type, this parse tree node can be both a syntactic and a semantic entity

```
typeEntity => syn_name:   identifier,
              syn_type:   typeRef;
typeRef    => syn_name:   identifier;
```

in the Pascal syntax structure, and

```
typeRef    => sem_entity: typeEntity;
```

in the Pascal semantic structure. `typeEntity` assumes two roles, that of a syntactic entity containing information about the declaration (the `syn_name` of "I" and the `syn_type` of "integer") and about the type itself (for example, a `rep_size` of 32 bits).

An alternative would be to make the syntactic and semantic entities separate nodes

```
typeDecl   => syn_name:   identifier,
              syn_type:   typeRef;

typeRef    => syn_name:   identifier;
```

in the syntax structure, and

```
typeRef    => sem_entity: typeEntity;

typeEntity => sem_name:    String,
              sem_type:    typeEntity,
              sem_defined: typeDecl;
```

in the semantic structure. This latter approach is, in some ways, conceptually cleaner. It has the disadvantages in this particular situation that it requires more space at compile-time (for two additional attributes) and is slower at compiler execution time (since the additional attributes must be calculated), while encoding no more information than the original structure.

The variable declaration is more complex, in that several variables can be declared to have the same type. This syntactic sugar is easily handled in the syntax specification

```
varDecl    => syn_variables: Seq Of varEntity,
              syn_type:      typeRef;
varEntity => syn_name:       identifier;
```

and in the semantic specification

```
varEntity => sem_type:       typeEntity;
```

The variable entity (`varEntity`) is also both a syntactic and a semantic entity, but the variable declaration (`varDecl`) is purely syntactic. Given the Pascal declarations above, the parser would construct the following parse tree fragment.

```
 1  <T1:typeEntity[
 2      syn_name identifier[lex_token "I"];
 3      syn_type typeRef[syn_name identifier[lex_token "integer"]]
 4      ]
 5  varDecl[
 6      syn_variables <
 7          V1:varEntity[syn_name identifier[lex_token "a"]]
 8          varEntity[syn_name identifier[lex_token "b"]]
 9          >
10      syn_type typeRef[syn_name identifier[lex_token "I"]]
11      ]
12  >
```

In name resolution, the attribute

```
sem_entity P1^
```

would be added to the `typeRef` node in line 3, where `P1` is a label of a predefined `typeEntity` node (with a `syn_name` value of `"integer"`). The attribute

```
sem_type T1^
```

would be added to the `varEntity`s on lines 7 and 8, above, and the attribute

```
sem_entity T1^
```

would be added to the `typeRef` on line 10, above. To specify this process of name resolution formally, we can use two assertions, one specifying that

10.4. THE SYMBOL TABLE

all variable declarations are resolved to the correct type, and one specifying that all type references are resolved correctly.

```
ForAll v In varDecl Do
    ForAll vE In Members(v.syn_variables) Do
        vE.sem_type = v.syn_type.sem_entity
    Od
Od;
ForAll t In typeRef Do
    t.syn_name = t.sem_entity.syn_name
Od;
```

Finally, the last "a" in the Pascal example would be an entity reference, with the assertion specifying that all variable references are resolved correctly.

```
varRef => syn_name:   identifier,
         sem_entity:  varEntity;
ForAll v In varRef Do
    v.syn_name = v.sem_entity.syn_name
Od;
```

and would be resolved in this way

```
varRef[syn_name identifier[lex_token "a"];
    sem_entity V1^]
```

where V1 is a varEntity defined on line 7 of the parse tree fragment above.

A potential problem arises when the parser cannot determine the kind of entity an identifier references. The classic example is the ambiguity between subroutine calls and array accesses in Fortran. The construct

```
A(3)
```

could be either, depending on what type was declared for A. Unfortunately, the parser does not have easy access to that information. The solution is to use classes. The syntactic structure would include

```
ParenRef => syn_name:      identifier,
           syn_arguments: Seq Of expression;
```

The parser need only calculate syn_name, delaying until semantic analysis the computation of sem_entity.

```
ParenRef    => sem_entity: ParenEntity;
ParenEntity ::= arrayEntity | subroutineEntity;
```

10.4.4 Symbol Tables

We have now examined the portions of the parse tree instance that will involved the symbol table, identifiers, syntactic entities, and entity references, as well as the components of symbol tables, semantic entities. There are several approaches to the structure of the symbol table itself.

The symbol table can be either *distributed* throughout the parse tree or *centralized*. In either case, it will be composed of semantics entities (which may, incidentally, also be syntactic entities).

In a distributed symbol table, a table is associated with each scope, for example, with the main program, the procedures, and the functions in a Pascal program, and with the main program, functions, and blocks in a C program. The tables themselves are simply sequences. In Pascal, identifiers can name eight kinds of entities, six of which are listed below (the other two are enumerated constants, which are stored within the typeEntity defining the enumeration, and fields, which are stored within the typeEntity defining the record).

```
Entity ::= constEntity | typeEntity | varEntity
         | labelEntity | procedureEntity | functionEntity;

Scope  ::= program | procedureEntity | functionEntity;
Scope  =>  sem_symbolTable: Seq Of Entity;
```

The entities declared within a particular scope would appear in the sem_symbolTable attribute for that scope.

In a centralized symbol table, we must explicitly encode the scope within the symbol table. One possible approach that defines these entities slightly differently than above is

```
program          =>   sem_symbolTable: ScopeDescriptor;

ScopeDescriptor =>   sem_origin:      Scope;
                     sem_symbolTable: Seq Of Entity;
                     sem_nested:      Seq Of ScopeDescriptor;

Scope           ::=  program | procedureEntity | functionEntity;

Entity          ::=  constEntity | typeEntity | varEntity
                     | labelEntity | procedureEntity
                     | functionEntity;
```

Each ScopeDescriptor, which is a purely semantic entity, contains those entities declared within that scope, and a sequence of nested scopes. The

10.4. THE SYMBOL TABLE

`sem_origin` attribute correlates the `ScopeDescriptor` with a syntactic entity.

These two structure declarations encode exactly the same information, though in slightly different ways that may have a significant influence on the complexity of the algorithms that maintain and search the symbol table. In the `attributed_syntax` structure in Figure 9.14, the symbol table is centralized: it may be found as the `syn_func_seq` attribute of the `functions` node. It is so simple precisely because the function language is simple: there are no nested scopes, and all functions are declared at the top level. In Part III, we will see that XRef has the same lexical scoping as Pascal, and will show how to specify a distributed symbol table as discussed above.

10.4.5 Symbol Table Representation

Regardless of whether the symbol table is centralized or distributed, the representation chosen for the sequences contained in the symbol table can greatly affect the performance of the compiler. Representations such as linked lists, ordered arrays, binary search trees, and hash tables have been proposed. If the desired representation is available, it may be indicated with a representation specification (see Section 4.1.3). Otherwise, the sequence can be replaced with a private type that is implemented and manipulated in exactly the fashion desired.

The following guidelines summarize this approach to representing symbol tables in IDL.

20. *Include a source position attribute with each syntactic construct, especially identifiers.*

    This source position will be useful in generating error messages and cross references.

21. *Differentiate between* syntactic entities *and* semantic entities.

    Often it makes sense for an entity to be both. Semantic analysis will record information, such as the type and number of formal parameters, in the entity.

22. *Differentiate between* entities *and* entity references.

    An entity reference will have a `syn_name` attribute, computed while parsing, and a `sem_entity` attribute, computed during name resolution and referring to an entity.

23. *Use classes creatively to delay computing the value of an attribute if there is insufficient information.*

   A good example is the `ParenEntity` class discussed above.

24. *Choose the representation of the `Seq Of Entity` attribute of the symbol table carefully.*

   Use a representation specification if the desired representation is available in the IDL implementation; otherwise use a private type.

10.5 Attribute Placement

25. *Delay any analysis that is difficult or impossible to do in syntactic analysis until semantic analysis, where there is more information.*

   This was illustrated on page 245, where the parse could not determine easily whether the construct "A(3)" was a subroutine call or an array access. The solution was to make this choice during semantic analysis, as a `sem_entity` attribute.

Modula-2 provides two further examples of this last guideline. In Modula-2, a constant can be equated to a constant expression.

⟨constant declaration⟩ ::= ⟨identifier⟩ '=' ⟨constant expression⟩

However, most parsers have trouble differentiating between ⟨constant expression⟩ and ⟨expression⟩. The solution is to substitute ⟨expression⟩ for ⟨constant expression⟩ in the syntax, and have semantic analysis ensure that the expression can be evaluated at compile-time. More concretely, in the syntax structure

```
ConstantDecl => lex_name: String,
                syn_exp:  expression;
```

and in the semantic structure

```
ConstantDecl => sem_value: Value;
Value        ::= IntegerValue | BooleanValue; -- etc.
BooleanValue => sem_value: Integer;
IntegerValue => sem_value: Boolean;
-- etc.
```

10.5. ATTRIBUTE PLACEMENT

As a second example, Modula-2 identifiers can be prefixed by a series of module names.

⟨qual identifier⟩ ::= ⟨identifier⟩ { '.' ⟨identifier⟩ }*

The "." can also be used for field access in expressions evaluating to a value of a record type.

⟨designator⟩ ::= ⟨qual identifier⟩
{ '.' ⟨identifier⟩ | '[' ⟨expr_list⟩ ']' | '^' }*

During syntactic analysis, it is difficult to tell these two uses of "." apart. The solution is to eliminate record access from the syntax where it causes problems.

⟨designator⟩   ::= ⟨qual identifier⟩ { ⟨designator2⟩ { ⟨designator3⟩ }* }?
⟨qual identifier⟩ ::= ⟨identifier⟩ { '.' ⟨identifier⟩ }*
⟨designator2⟩   ::= '[' ⟨expr_list⟩ ']' | '^'
⟨designator3⟩   ::= ⟨designator2⟩ | '.' ⟨identifier⟩

Note that "." is assumed always to be a quantifier if it follows an ⟨identifier⟩. If it follows a "^" or "]" it is properly considered to be a field access (the second option of ⟨designator3⟩). All syntactically valid programs will be parsed, but some programs will have incorrect parse trees: those that mix identifier qualification and field access in the initial portion of a ⟨designator⟩ (we will see an example shortly).

The structure of the parse tree expressed in IDL is

```
designator    ::= field_access | array_access | pointer
                | qual_ident;
field_access =>  syn_argument_of: designator;
                 syn_field:       FieldRef;
FieldRef     =>  syn_name:        String;
array_access =>  syn_argument_of: designator;
                 dims:            Seq of expression;
pointer      =>  syn_argument_of: designator;
qual_ident   =>  syn_names:       Seq Of String;
```

The parse tree structure allows a series of identifiers to be followed by a field access, but no such parse tree will be generated. As an example, assume that W is a module name, X is a record variable defined in module W, and Y is a field of that record. Also assume that this field is a pointer to another record containing a Z field. The parse tree for "W.X.Y^.Z" will be

```
field_access[syn_field FieldRef[syn_name "Z"];
            syn_argument_of pointer[
                syn_argument_of qual_ident[
                    syn_names <"W" "X" "Y">
                    ]
                ]
            ]
```

This parse tree is incorrect, as it implies that X is a module imported by module W, and that Y is a variable declared in "module" X. However, in semantic analysis, the parse tree is first corrected.

```
field_access[syn_field FieldRef[syn_name "Z"];
            syn_argument_of pointer[
                syn_argument_of field_access[
                    syn_field FieldRef[syn_name "Y"];
                    syn_argument_of qual_ident[
                        syn_names <"W" "X">;
                        ]
                    ]
                ]
            ]
```

Note that X is now considered to be a variable in module W and that ".Y" has been recognized as a field access. We then compute the following attributes in semantic analysis

```
qual_ident  =>   sem_entity: Entity;
Entity      ::=  variableEntity | FieldEntity;  -- etc.
FieldRef    =>   sem_entity: FieldEntity;
```

to arrive at that shown in Figure 10.1.

As a third example, package declarations in Ada allow only a subset of that which can be declared in a package body. The signature (name, parameters, and return type) of a function may be specified in a package declaration; the package body repeats the signature, then follows with the body of the function. Syntactic error recovery is easier if all declarations are accepted by the parser everywhere in the program, and may be present everywhere in the abstract syntax tree. The requirement that the body of a function not appear in a package declaration may then be checked in semantic analysis.

10.5. ATTRIBUTE PLACEMENT

```
field_access[syn_field FieldRef[syn_name "Z";
                                sem_entity L1^];
              syn_argument_of pointer[
                  syn_argument_of field_access[
                      syn_field FieldRef[syn_name "Y";
                                          sem_entity FieldEntity[
                                              lex_name "Y";
                                              ...
                                          ]
                                        ];
                      syn_argument_of qual_ident[
                          syn_names <"W" "X">;
                          sem_entity variableEntity[
                              lex_name "X";
                              ...
                          ]
                      ]
                  ]
              ]
            ]
```

Figure 10.1: The Correct Syntax Tree for "W.X.Y^.Z"

10.6 Invariant Structures

Unless directed otherwise, the IDL translator will automatically compute the invariant structure for each process. This structure will be derived from all of the port structures of the process, and will consist of the union of these structures.

Alternatively, you may supply a process invariant structure rather than using the invariant automatically generated by the IDL translator. This facility allows new nodes and classes that do not appear in any of the other structures referred to by the process to be defined, or attributes and members to nodes and classes already defined in those structures to be added. These new nodes and classes or attributes and members can be used for intermediate calculations within the process without cluttering the external definition of the structures read and written by the process.

You should perform the following steps to derive the invariant data structure from the port structures of the process.

1. Give the new invariant data structure a unique name.

2. For every node or class type for which there is a declaration in only one of the structures used by this process, copy that declaration into the specification for the new invariant structure.

3. For every node for which there are several declarations in the structures used by this process, write a declaration for the node type in the new invariant data structure such that the new declaration has the attributes found in the declarations in the different structures. If two structures have a declaration for the same-named node type and if both declarations have attributes of the same name but these same-named attributes of the same-named node types have different types, then there is an irresolvable conflict. You must either adjust the types of all same-named attributes in same-named nodes in all structures used by the process to be of the same type, or else change the names of the offending attributes or of the offending nodes such that this is no longer true.

4. Add attributes to the existing nodes and/or members to the existing classes or adds new nodes and classes consistent with the rules given for structures above. The properties and usefulness of these added attributes and members will be explained below in the discussion on the purpose of the invariant.

5. Check that the class memberships for the new invariant structure form a forest of nonintersecting trees just as for any other structure. If this

10.7. MISCELLANEOUS

is not true, then you must either change the class structures in the individual port structures and in the invariant structure, or change the names of the offending classes in the individual port structures and in the invariant structure in such a way that this will be true.

Alternatively, if any data structure referred to in a process meets the criteria given above for the invariant data structure, then that structure may be designated as the invariant data structure for the process.

26. *Place process-specific data structures in the invariant.*

    Such data structures should not, by definition, be communicated outside the process. An example is the `cache` node used in the XRef interpreter as illustrated in the IDL structure in Figure 13.5 on page 291. This node, needed during interpretation yet not present in any port structure, is defined as part of the `interpreter_data` invariant structure. If the value *is* needed externally for debugging purposes, a special debug *Post* port, whose structure is the invariant structure, can be specified.

10.7 Miscellaneous

In this last section we give several miscellaneous guidelines.

27. *Use assertions to express additional semantics and constraints of the structure.*

    Often the structural portion of IDL is inadequate for expressing the precise semantics of the data structure. Use assertions to answer the following questions, among others.
    - Can a set or sequence be empty?
    - Is there a maximum size for a set or sequence?
    - How are elements in a sequence ordered? (If they are not in any particular order, why aren't they placed in a set instead?)
    - What property does every element in a set or sequence share?
    - Does the number of actual parameters match the number of formal parameters?
    - Is the information complete? For example, does each type declaration have a corresponding type?

For example, in the `abstract_syntax` structure, we specified that each function have at least one parameter.

    Assert ForAll f In function
      Do Size(f.syn_parameters) > 0 Od;

28. *Isolate target-language-dependent aspects in a derived structure or process.*

    Following this guideline enhances maintainability and sharing of specifications. The generic process specification, shown in Figure 3.9 on page 85, defines the *Pre* and *Post* ports for the `constant_fold` process, as well as the assertions that must be satisfied by this process. The port specifications and assertions define the externally visible behavior of the process, behavior that must be followed by any implementation. The refined processes associated with the C and Pascal implementation of the constant folding process (given in Figures 3.10 and 3.11, on pages 86 and 86, respectively), contain target-specific aspects (including the Target Language clause), yet do not negate any previously-specified aspects. The specification in the **cf.idl** file, and, more importantly, the definition of what constant folding entails, has been shared between the C and Pascal implementations. Aspects that can be delayed include specification of private types (e.g., package, internal representation, external representation), node and class names (e.g., changing the name of the `int` node to `Tint` for C), and target-language-specific attribute and type representations and operations (e.g., enumerated and foreachinSEQ are recognized by C but not by Pascal). The corollary is that target-language-*in*dependent aspects should not appear in a derived structure. Most attribute and type representations and operations (e.g., Size 16 Bites, removeSET) are acceptable to all target languages, and hence should appear in the ancestor structure.

Bibliographic Notes

Symbol table structures are discussed in many compiler texts, including Aho, Sethi, and Ullman [1986]. Fischer and LeBlanc [1988] compare centralized and distributed symbol tables. The Modula-2 language is covered

10.7. MISCELLANEOUS

by Wirth [1983], Ada is defined in Ada [1983], and C is defined in Harbison and Steele [1987] and Kernighan and Ritchie [1988].

Part III

Example: A Cross-Referencer

The first two parts of this book introduced several examples of IDL in a tutorial fashion and defined the language. In this part we present the first of two substantial examples that illustrate the use of IDL. This part will examine the implementation of XREF, a translator and interpreter for XRef, a language in which a cross-referencer is specified. This simple language is introduced in much the same way that IDL was introduced in Parts I and II: we first give a tutorial of the language, followed by a short reference manual. Chapter 13 then discusses how IDL was used in the implementation. Appendix E contains several cross references produced by XREF, along with the relevant XRef specifications.

Chapter 11

An Introduction to XRef

XRef is a language for specifying cross-referencers. Using XRef you can generate cross-reference listings from syntax trees (and other intermediate representations) encoded as IDL instances. An invocation of XREF selects information from an IDL instance, generating a text file that may optionally be run through a text formatter to produce a nicely formatted cross-reference (Figure 11.1). XREF can be used to generate simple cross-references, as will be illustrated in this chapter, or to produce involved ones, such as those in Appendix E.

The following is an example of an XRef program.

```
-- file: functionlang/xref/formal1.xref
--
-- Generates one line per formal, with the name of the formal and the
-- number of the line where that formal is declared
Predicate ascending_names (left, right)
      left.syn_name.lex_token < right.syn_name.lex_token End
"Name\tPosition"
For F In Reorder(Type(Root, formal_parameter), ascending_names) Do

      F.syn_name.lex_token "\t " F.syn_name.lex_pos.linenumber

      "\n\n"
End -- For F
```

When run on the file (shown in Figure 3.20) resulting from compiling the function program

```
function foo(A: integer): integer
      = -A * (28 + 13);
```

the following cross-reference is generated,

CHAPTER 11. AN INTRODUCTION TO XREF

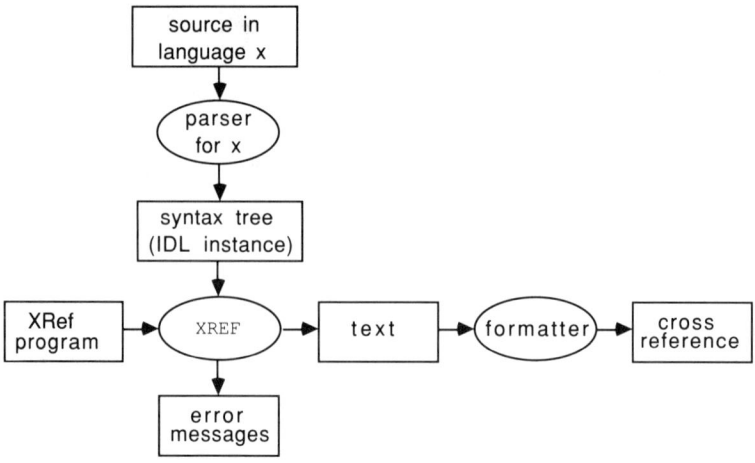

Figure 11.1: Using XREF

Name	Position
A	1

indicating that the formal parameter named "A" is declared on line 1. The process is the same whether a one-line cross-reference such as the above is produced, or whether a complex 20-page cross-reference is generated.

The above example will be explained in this chapter; a more complete definition of the language appears in Chapter 12.

11.1 Tokens

Directives are made up of keywords, user names, and strings. Keywords are case sensitive words defined by the XRef language. All keywords begin with a capital letter and are followed by lower case letters. User names are case sensitive words supplied by the user; by convention, all examples give here will be in lower case. Comments are preceded with "-- " and extend for the rest of the line.

11.2 Basic XRef Primitives

An XRef program defines a sequence of characters extracted from an IDL instance. Some XRef operators define sequences directly while other operators transform one sequence into another sequence. The following sections describe the XRef operators for manipulating sequences that were

11.2. BASIC XREF PRIMITIVES

used in the previous example. After these basic operators are understood, other operators will be discussed, and a more complicated example will be examined.

11.2.1 Strings

The simplest XRef program is

```
"hello world\n"
```

The result of executing this program would be the specified string (the "\n" denotes a newline character). In this example, the output doesn't depend on the contents of the IDL instance.

11.2.2 Root

The result of the *Root* operator:

```
Root
```

is a sequence containing one element, that element being the root node of the IDL instance.

Other primitives transform one sequence into another sequence. The *Root* primitive provides the initial sequence on which these transformation primitives can work.

11.2.3 Type

The *Type* operator searches a portion of an IDL instance and produces a sequence containing all the nodes of the specified type. This search can be specified as follows:

Type(⟨sequence⟩ , ⟨user name⟩)

(a more complex variant of this operator will be discussed in Chapter 12.) The *Type* operator returns a sequence of nodes in a subset of the IDL instance that all are of the specified ⟨user name⟩ type. The subset of the IDL instance to be searched is specified by the ⟨sequence⟩ given to the *Type* operator. The *Type* operator will search the specified nodes and all nodes that are direct or indirect attributes of the specified nodes. If the type of the node matches the ⟨user name⟩ provided, the node will be added to the result sequence. The search continues until all nodes of the specified ⟨sequence⟩ have been examined.

The most common use of the *Type* operator is to search the entire tree by specifying the *Root* operator to produce the starting ⟨sequence⟩.

This was done in the initial example as

`Type(Root, formal_parameter)`

This searches the entire tree for nodes of type `formal_parameter`.

11.2.4 For

The `For` operator provides a way to associate a name with each element of a sequence for use in other operators. `For` operators are invoked as follows.

`For` ⟨iterated name⟩ `In` ⟨sequence⟩ `Do` ⟨operators⟩ `End`

The `For` operator applies the ⟨operators⟩ to each element of the ⟨sequence⟩, replacing all occurrences of ⟨iterated name⟩ by that element. If the ⟨sequence⟩ doesn't contain any elements, an empty sequence results. Within the ⟨operators⟩ of a `For` operator, the ⟨iterated name⟩ will be available for use in references and other sequence operators. The result of the `For` operator is a sequence constructed by concatenating the results of the ⟨operators⟩ of the `For` operator.

11.2.5 References

Simply naming an attribute of a node produces a sequence containing the value of that attribute. Thus, once the nodes of a sequence have been identified by the `Type` operator and associated with an iterated name within a `For` operator, attributes of the node can be selected by a reference of the form

⟨iterated name⟩ . ⟨attribute name$_1$⟩ . $\cdots$. ⟨attribute name$_n$⟩

References are evaluated by starting with the specified node and then locating the attribute of the node with the current name. Once an attribute with the current name has been found, any following attribute names will applied to the node that is the value of that attribute. This searching of nodes continues until all the attribute names have been matched. The result of a reference is a sequence containing the last node visited. An example from the program is `F.syn_name.lex_pos.linenumber`, denoting an integer value.

If the last attribute names an IDL base type such as String or Integer, the result of the reference will be a single element sequence containing the value of that attribute.

11.2.6 Predicates

There are two kinds of predicates: unary and binary. Both return true if the condition in the predicate is satisfied, or false if the predicate is not satisfied. Unary predicates take one argument and binary predicates take two arguments. The following is an example of a binary predicate.

```
Predicate ascending_names (left, right)
    left.syn_name.lex_token < right.syn_name.lex_token End
```

The predicate identifies the attributes of the nodes to be compared. Here, the string names of the formals passed as arguments are compared.

Predicates can compare IDL base types using the comparison operators, ">", "<", ">=", "<=", "^=", and "=". The *Same* operator applies only to nodes, and returns true if the two elements reference the same node. Integers are compared using their value.

In addition to the comparison operators, the boolean operators *And*, *Or*, and *Not* have the usual meaning for combining comparison. Whenever these operators are used, their operands must be fully enclosed in parentheses, preventing any confusion on the precedence of the operators.

11.2.7 The Sorting Operator

The sorting operator, *Reorder*, takes one sequence and returns another sequence containing the same elements but in a sorted order. Before invoking the *Reorder* operator, a predicate must be defined that will determine the order of the elements. *Reorder* takes a binary predicate. The sequence returned by *Reorder* will have the property that any two sequential elements will satisfy the specified binary predicate.

11.2.8 The Example Explained

By this time you should be able to understand what the example at the start of this chapter does. This program searches from the root of the IDL sequence down (that is, the entire tree) for nodes of type `formal_parameter`. This sequence is alphabetized (via *Reorder*). Then for every node, a line of output is produced. Each line contains

> the name of the `formal_parameter`,
> a tab and two spaces,
> the line number where the `formal_parameter` was declared,
> and finally two newline characters.

11.3 Additional Primitives

Other operators exist that will filter elements from sequences and perform set operations. Some of these operators will be briefly examined.

11.3.1 Refining Operators

Once a sequence has been built, two other operators may be used to test and remove unwanted elements. The *Unique* operator tests each element against other elements in the sequence to remove nonunique elements. The *Filter* operator applies a predicate to each element and removes those elements not satisfying the predicate. Both the *Unique* and the *Filter* operator require predefined predicates; *Unique* requires a binary predicate while *Filter* requires a unary predicate. We will see an example shortly of these two operators.

11.3.2 Set Operators

Because sequences are so much like sets, several common set operators have been provided that operate on sequences. These operators include set union, intersection, and difference.

Sequence union doesn't require a separate operator, but can be done, through concatenation, by specifying the sequences side by side.

Sequence intersection is done using the *Intersection* operator. The format is

$$Intersection(\langle sequence_1 \rangle, \langle sequence_2 \rangle, \langle predicate \rangle)$$

The predicate is a binary predicate that determines whether two elements, one from each sequence, are equivalent; if they are equivalent, only one of the elements should be retained in the intersection.

Sequence difference can be done using the *Difference* operator. The format is

$$Difference(\langle sequence_1 \rangle, \langle sequence_2 \rangle, \langle predicate \rangle)$$

The predicate again specifies how to compare the elements to determine equivalence.

The *Extra* function returns the elements of one sequence that do not have corresponding elements in another sequence. The format is

$$Extra(\langle sequence_1 \rangle, \langle sequence_2 \rangle)$$

For example

11.4. A SECOND EXAMPLE   265

```
Extra("a" "b" "c", "1" "2")
```

returns one element, that being "c". This element will be returned because there isn't a corresponding element in the other sequence. Note that no comparison between elements is made.

11.4 A Second Example

Now that we have seen some simple directives, it is time to examine a more complex example. This example uses many of the above primitives. It processes an IDL instances of the `attributed_syntax` structure, discussed in Section 3.2.

```
-- file: functionlang/xref/formal2.xref
--
-- Generates one line per formal, with the name of the formal,
-- the number of the line where the formal parameter is declared and the
-- numbers of the lines where the formal parameter is used

Predicate ascending_names (left, right)
     left.syn_name.lex_token < right.syn_name.lex_token End
Predicate ascending_pos (left, right)
     left.syn_name.lex_pos.linenumber
             < right.syn_name.lex_pos.linenumber End

"Name\tLines\n"

For F In Reorder(Type(Root, formal_parameter), ascending_names) Do

     Predicate same_as_F (this) this.sem_entity Same F End
     Predicate same_line_number (left, right)
        left.syn_name.lex_pos.linenumber
             = right.syn_name.lex_pos.linenumber End

     F.syn_name.lex_token "\t" F.syn_name.lex_pos.linenumber

     For L In Unique(Reorder(Filter(Type(Root, formal_parameterRef),
                                    same_as_F),
                             ascending_pos),
                     same_line_number) Do
        ", " L.syn_name.lex_pos.linenumber End -- For L

     "\n\n"
End -- For F
```

This creates a more typical cross-reference listing that displays the name once and then lists all the locations where the name can be found. When run on the same file, the following is generated

```
Names   Lines
A       1, 2
```

The first part of the processing is identical to the **formal1.xref** program. The *Filter* operator in the inner *For* removes all nodes that don't match the node selected by the outer *For*. This matching is done semantically. The result is that multiple `formal_parameters` with the same name will be individually listed, and only those `formal_parameterRefs` that resolve to a particular `formal_parameter` will be listed with that `formal_parameter`. The inner *For* operator generates the line numbers of the appropriate `formal_parameterRefs`.

11.5 Conclusion

With a little thought and a few lines of XRef, cross-reference listings can be generated from IDL intermediate files. The key is to determine what part of the processing should be done by XREF and what part can better be done by other existing programs. In general all the fancy formatting can be done by the formatter.

Exercise

11.1 Provide a function language program that shows that the **formal2.xref** program matches semantically, rather than syntactically. What change to the XRef program would specify syntactic matching?

Chapter 12

XRef Language Definition

This chapter defines the XRef language, which allows you to write simple programs to extract information from an IDL instance. The extracted information consists of strings contained in the input from which the IDL instance was constructed. Programs can select the strings and specify the order in which they should be displayed. Other strings can be included to control the formatting of the extracted strings. Because of the high-level nature of the XRef programs, a cross-reference listing can be generated with a small program.

XRef provides only minimal text formatting capabilities. If you want listings in an explicit format, you should use a text formatter as a postprocessor. XRef allows text formatting commands to be included as part of the output. This approach minimizes the number of special features that XREF must support.

In this chapter we present the XRef language definition. The first section describes the tokens from which XRef programs are built, and the second section that follows describes the grammer of the XRef programs. The last two sections discuss the meaning of each XRef construct and the scope rules required by the language.

12.1 Lexical Conventions

⟨token⟩   ::= ⟨basic token⟩ | ⟨punctuation⟩ | ⟨white space⟩
⟨basic token⟩   ::= ⟨keyword⟩ | ⟨name⟩ | ⟨string⟩
⟨punctuation⟩   ::= ':' | '=' | '~=' | '<' | '<=' | '>' | '>='
                  | ';' | '(' | ')' | ',' | '.'

⟨white space⟩   ::= ⟨space⟩ | ⟨horizontal tab⟩ | ⟨carriage return⟩
                       | ⟨form feed⟩ | ⟨line feed⟩ | ⟨end of line⟩
                       | '-' '-' ⟨any character except end of line⟩

⟨keyword⟩   ::= And | As | Case | Default | Difference
                       | Do | Else | Empty | End | Extra
                       | Filter | For | Function | In | Is | Head
                       | Intersection | Let | Not | Of | Or
                       | Predicate | Reorder | Root | Same
                       | Tail | Type | Unique

⟨name⟩   ::= ⟨letter⟩ { ⟨letter⟩ | ⟨digit⟩ | '_' }*
⟨string⟩   ::= '"' { ⟨string character⟩ }* '"'
⟨letter⟩   ::= 'a' | ⋯ | 'z' | 'A' | ⋯ | 'Z'
⟨digit⟩   ::= '0' | ⋯ | '9'
⟨string character⟩ ::= ⟨letter⟩ | ⟨digit⟩ | '!' | '#' | '$' | '%'
                       | '>' | ''' | '(' | ')' | '*' | '+' | ','
                       | '-' | '/' | ':' | ';' | '<' | '=' | '>'
                       | '?' | '@' | '[' | '/' | ']' | '^' | '_'
                       | '`' | '{' | '|' | '}' | '.' | ⟨space⟩
                       | '\' 'f' | '\' 'n' | '\' 'r' | '\' 't'
                       | '\' ''' | '\' '\'

The following lexical conventions are observed in XRef programs.

- All XRef programs are run through the C preprocessor. This allows the following C preprocessor commands to be used.

    ```
    #include
    #define
    #ifdef
    #endif
    ```

    Any substitutions done by the preprocessor are strictly textual.

- Break symbols include blanks, comments, and "end-of-line"s. A comment is introduced by double hyphens, "--", and terminated by the end of the line on which they occur. Any number of break symbols may appear between any two ⟨basic token⟩s with no effect. Break symbols may not appear within tokens. Two adjacent ⟨basic token⟩s must be separated by at least one break symbol.

- Reserved words in the XRef programs are all case sensitive. The first letter of every keyword is upper case. All other letters are lower case.

- Identifiers in the XRef programs refer to user-defined quantities such as class or attribute names in the IDL instance, functions, predicates, and iterated values. Identifiers must begin with an alphabetic character (a–z, A–Z) and can include alphabetic, numeric (0–9) characters, and the underscore "_". Identifiers are case sensitive and must match exactly the identifier in the IDL instance. The maximum length of an identifier is implementation dependent, however, a minimum of 56 characters will always be allowed.

- Strings specified in the input programs are copied to output by the XRef facility. These strings have the same syntax as strings found in the C programming language. Strings begin with a '"' and end with the matching '"'. Special characters can be included in a string by prefixing them with a backslash, '\'. The following escape sequences are recognized within a string.

    \f   Form Feed
    \n   New Line
    \r   Carriage Return
    \t   Tab
    \'   Quote
    \\   Backslash

The maximum length of a string is implementation dependent; however, all implementations must support strings containing at least 96 characters.

12.2 XRef Grammar

The extended BNF for XRef is given below in the format described in the preface. Nonterminals of the form "⟨*?*_name⟩" are names in the class *?*.

⟨directives⟩   ::= ⟨body⟩
⟨body⟩   ::= { ⟨declaration⟩ }* ⟨sequence⟩
⟨declaration⟩   ::= ⟨predicate decl⟩ | ⟨function decl⟩

⟨predicate decl⟩   ::= **Predicate** ⟨predicate_name⟩
                         '(' ⟨formals⟩ ')' ⟨predicate⟩ **End**
⟨function decl⟩   ::= **Function** ⟨function_name⟩
                         '(' ⟨formals⟩ ')' ⟨body⟩ **End**
⟨formals⟩   ::= ⟨formal_name⟩ { ',' ⟨formal_name⟩ }*

⟨sequence⟩   ::= { ⟨sequence element⟩ }⁺
⟨sequence element⟩   ::= **Type** '(' ⟨sequence⟩ ',' ⟨node_name⟩
                             { ',' ⟨attribute_name⟩ }? ')'
                         | ⟨function_name⟩ '(' ⟨atoms⟩ ')'
                         | **Extra** '(' ⟨sequence⟩ ',' ⟨sequence⟩ ')'
                         | **Tail** '(' ⟨sequence⟩ ')'
                         | **Reorder** '(' ⟨sequence⟩
                             ',' ⟨binary_predicate_name⟩ ')'
                         | **Filter** '(' ⟨sequence⟩
                             ',' ⟨unary_predicate_name⟩ ')'
                         | **Unique** '(' ⟨sequence⟩
                             ',' ⟨binary_predicate_name⟩ ')'
                         | **Intersection** '(' ⟨sequence⟩ ',' ⟨sequence⟩
                             ',' ⟨binary_predicate_name⟩ ')'
                         | **Difference** '(' ⟨sequence⟩ ',' ⟨sequence⟩
                             ',' ⟨binary_predicate_name⟩ ')'
                         | ⟨atom⟩
                         | ⟨let statement⟩
                         | ⟨case statement⟩
                         | ⟨for statement⟩

12.2. XREF GRAMMAR

⟨let statement⟩   ::= Let ⟨assignments⟩ In ⟨body⟩ End
⟨assignments⟩   ::= ⟨assignment⟩ { ',' ⟨assignment⟩ }*
⟨assignment⟩   ::= ⟨let_variable⟩ '=' ⟨sequence⟩

⟨for statement⟩   ::= For ⟨iterated_name⟩ In ⟨sequence⟩
                       Do ⟨body⟩ End

⟨case statement⟩   ::= Case ⟨atom⟩ As ⟨case_name⟩
                       Of ⟨case branches⟩ End
⟨case branches⟩   ::= { ⟨case branch⟩ }+
                       { Default ':' ⟨body⟩ ';' }?
⟨case branch⟩   ::= ⟨node_name⟩ ':' ⟨body⟩ ';'

⟨atoms⟩   ::= ⟨atom⟩ { ',' ⟨atom⟩ }*
⟨atom⟩   ::= ⟨reference⟩ | ⟨string⟩ | Head '(' ⟨sequence⟩ ')'
⟨reference⟩   ::= { ⟨existing_name⟩ | Root }
                       { '.' ⟨attribute_name⟩ }*

⟨predicate⟩   ::= ⟨atom⟩ ⟨opr⟩ ⟨atom⟩
                     | Empty '(' ⟨sequence⟩ ')'
                     | ⟨predicate_name⟩ '(' ⟨atoms⟩ ')'
                     | Is '(' ⟨atom⟩ ',' ⟨atom⟩ ')'
                     | ⟨paren predicate⟩
                     | ⟨paren predicate⟩ And ⟨paren predicate⟩
                     | ⟨paren predicate⟩ Or ⟨paren predicate⟩
                     | Not ⟨paren predicate⟩
⟨opr⟩   ::= '~=' | '<=' | '>=' | '<' | '>' | '='
                     | Same | In
⟨paren predicate⟩ ::= '(' ⟨predicate⟩ ')'

12.3 Semantics

An XRef program consists of a body. Bodies are also used in functions and in *Let*, *Case* and *For* statements. A body consists of an optional list of declarations followed by a sequence. A sequence consists of one or more elements. There isn't any concatenation operator between successive elements; concatenation is specified implicitly by juxtaposition of the elements. The sequence of values specified by the top level body will be the output of XRef. The elements of the sequence will be printed in a manner dependent on its type, as follows.

IDL base types:	the external ASCII representation of the value
Strings:	the text of the string as given
Nodes:	the type name of the node
Sequence:	the elements of the sequence
Set:	the elements of the set
Private types:	the external representation of the private type

Declaration statements can be predicates or functions. Predicates return either true or false. They are used to compare nodes of the IDL instance to determine membership and ordering in the final output.

A unary predicate makes a decision based on one argument. Other arguments for the decision can be referenced from the invoking environment. Alternatively the predicate itself may contain constants to use for the purposes of comparison. A binary predicate makes a decision based on two arguments.

Functions specify a body to be processed when invoked. A function returns the sequence specified by its body.

12.3.1 Sequence Elements

The following paragraphs describe each ⟨sequence element⟩ in more detail.

Type (⟨sequence⟩, ⟨node_name⟩) returns a sequence derived from the specified sequence. The resulting sequence consists of all nodes that are values of direct or indirect attribute of any element of the specified sequence and have the specified ⟨node_name⟩ type.

Type (⟨sequence⟩, ⟨node_name⟩, ⟨attribute_name⟩) is similar to that of the shortened variant above except that only the attribute name is followed, rather than examining all attributes.

12.3. SEMANTICS

⟨function_name⟩(⟨atoms⟩) returns the result of applying the body of the function to the values of the parameter expressions. One or more atoms must be passed as actuals when invoking a function.

Extra(⟨sequence$_1$⟩, ⟨sequence$_2$⟩) returns a sequence of elements from ⟨sequence$_1$⟩ by skipping one element of ⟨sequence$_1$⟩ for every element of ⟨sequence$_2$⟩. This leave only the extra elements of ⟨sequence$_1$⟩.

Tail(⟨sequence⟩) returns the sequence formed by removing the first element of the specified sequence.

Reorder(⟨sequence⟩, ⟨binary_predicate_name⟩) returns a sequence obtained by reordering the elements of the specified sequence. The order of the resulting sequence will be changed to make the specified "less than" binary predicate true for all pairs of adjacent elements. The action of this operator is undefined if the predicate is not transitive for all elements.

Filter(⟨sequence⟩, ⟨unary_predicate_name⟩) returns a sequence that is a subset of the specified sequence. The resulting sequence will contain only the elements that satisfy the specified unary predicate.

Unique(⟨sequence⟩, ⟨binary_predicate_name⟩) returns a sequence produced by eliminating any nonunique elements from the specified sequence. Uniqueness of the elements is determined by using the specified "equality" predicate to compare the elements. The predicate must be transitive or the result of this function will be undefined.

Intersect(⟨sequence$_1$⟩, ⟨sequence$_2$⟩, ⟨binary_predicate_name⟩) returns a sequence that is a set intersection of ⟨sequence$_1$⟩ and ⟨sequence$_2$⟩. Every element in the resulting sequence satisfies the binary "equality" predicate evaluated on some element of ⟨sequence$_1$⟩ and some element of ⟨sequence$_2$⟩.

Difference(⟨sequence$_1$⟩, ⟨sequence$_2$⟩, ⟨binary_predicate_name⟩) returns a sequence created by performing a set difference between ⟨sequence$_1$⟩ and ⟨sequence$_2$⟩. The resulting sequence consists of elements from ⟨sequence$_1$⟩ such that *no* element of ⟨sequence$_2$⟩ satisfies the binary "equality" predicate.

⟨atom⟩ evaluates to a single IDL type (which may be an IDL sequence or IDL set).

12.3.2 Statements

Statements differ from the other sequence elements in two ways:

- Statements contain a body which can itself contain function and predicate declarations. The other sequence elements cannot contain such declarations directly.

- Statements define one (or in the case of let statements, potentially several) names, which can be referenced (as ⟨existing_name⟩s) in the contained body. The other sequence elements can reference names defined elsewhere, but cannot define them directly.

All three kinds of statements return the sequence generated by evaluating the body. The statements differ in how many times the body is evaluated.

The *Let* statement evaluates each of the sequences, and then evaluates the body. The value of each sequence is available in the body (and in sequences in successive assignments) via the associated let variable.

The *Case* statement returns different sequences depending on the type of the node specified by the atom. Branches of the case define the sequence to be returned for the specified node type. During evaluation of the body, the value of the atom will be available within the body with the specified case name. The default branch handles all cases not otherwise handled by explicit node names.

The *For* statement returns a sequence constructed by concatenating the sequences defined by the for statement body. The body will be evaluated once for each element of the specified sequence. During the evaluation for a given element, that element will be available as the value of the specified ⟨iterated_name⟩.

12.3.3 Atoms

⟨reference⟩ returns a sequence with a single element that is the result of the reference. If the attribute named by the reference is an IDL set or sequence, the result will be a sequence containing the elements in that set or sequence. The distinguished name *Root* denotes the root node of the IDL instance.

⟨string⟩ returns a sequence with the string as a single element.

Head (⟨sequence⟩) returns the first element of the ⟨sequence⟩.

12.4 Predicates

A predicate returns true or false. The predicate can be a simple comparison between two atoms, or can be constructed from several simpler atoms by boolean operators.

⟨atom⟩ ⟨opr⟩ ⟨atom⟩ compares two atoms. Both atoms must resolve to identical types. If the atoms are IDL strings, the comparison will be made as a lexicographic comparison based on the ASCII character set, ignoring case (the *Same* and *In* operators must not be used to compare two IDL strings). If the atoms are IDL integers, the values of the integers will be compared (again, the *Same* and *In* operators do not apply). If the atoms are nodes, the operator must be the *Same* operator which returns true if and only if the nodes are the same node. If the second atom evaluates to an IDL sequence or IDL set, the operator must be the *In* operator that returns true if the value of the first atom an element of the IDL sequence or IDL set. All expressions built from multiple predicates must be fully parenthesized; this prevents any confusion of precedence when reading programs.

⟨predicate_name⟩(⟨atoms⟩) is similar to a function call, except that a boolean result, rather than a sequence, is returned.

Empty(⟨sequence⟩) returns true if the specified sequence contains no elements.

There is one predefined predicate, *Is*, taking two arguments, a node and a string. If the type of the node has a name equal to the string, then *Is* returns true. The following *Filter* operation is equivalent to *Root*.

    `Predicate Use_Is (this) Is(this, "formal_parameter") End`

    `Filter(Type(Root, formal_parameter), Use_Is)`

12.5 Scope Rules

This section describes some of the rules dealing with the names used in XRef programs. Names are defined by function or predicate formals, the let variable of a let statement, the iterated name of a for statement, or the case name of a case statement. The following scope rules will result in a semantic error if violated.

- A predicate declaration makes the specified ⟨predicate_name⟩ visible in the body containing that predicate declaration, but not within the predicate body itself. The type of the predicate is determined by the number of formals given in the definition. When predicates are invoked, the elements of the sequences being manipulated will be available to the predicates as the formals of the predicate definition.

- A function declaration makes the specified ⟨function_name⟩ visible within the body containing the function declaration, but not within the function body itself.

- The names of formals given in function and predicate declarations are visible within the body defined in the function or predicate.

- The name defined by an assignment of a let statement is visible in the sequences of successive assignments and in the body contained in the let statement.

- Names defined by case statements are visible in the bodies defined by the case branches.

- Names defined by a for statement are visible in the body of the for statement.

- An existing name in a reference can be a name defined in a let, case, or for statement.

- Defining a name hides any previous definition of the name. Otherwise, the names visible in a nested body include those visible in the outer body.

Exercises

12.1 XRef includes only string constants. Other kinds of constants, such as integers and booleans, would also be useful. Extend the language definition to handle such constants.

12.2 Add case-sensitive string comparisons to the language definition. Should the other types of comparisons be extended in analogous ways?

12.5. SCOPE RULES 277

12.3 The *Type* construct allows at most one ⟨attribute_name⟩ to be specified. Sometimes more than one such name may be desired.

a. Why are nested invocations of *Type*, such as the following, inadequate?

$$Type(Type(\cdots Type(\langle\text{sequence}\rangle,\langle\text{node\_name}\rangle,\langle\text{attribute\_name}_1\rangle),$$
$$\cdots,$$
$$\langle\text{node\_name}\rangle, \langle\text{attribute\_name}_{n-1}\rangle),$$
$$\langle\text{node\_name}\rangle, \langle\text{attribute\_name}_n\rangle)$$

b. Extend the language definition to allow more than one attribute name in the *Type* construct.

Bibliographic Notes

Lamb [1983] discusses the need for cross references when dealing with large IDL descriptions. Strings in XRef are similar to those in the C language, described by Kernighan and Ritchie [1988].

Chapter 13

xref Implementation

The XREF implementation consists of three major phases. The first phase produces a syntax tree defined using IDL. The second phase takes a syntax tree and "decorates" it by adding information identifying the source position of identifiers. The last phase interprets the attributed syntax tree and applies the operations specified to an IDL intermediate file.

More specifically, Figure 13.1 shows the architecture of the XREF implementation. The input is an XRef source file, which is first run through the standard C preprocessor, then syntactically and semantically analyzed to produce an instance of the `attributed_syntax_tree` structure, which is one of the two inputs of the interpreter. The IDLREAD process converts the input instance to an instance of the generic `IDLdata` structure. The interpreter reads both instances, then walks the `attributed_syntax_tree` instance, generating text as it goes. The portion marked XREF identify the internal organization of the single tool called XREF in Figure 11.1.

In the remaining sections we examine each phase in turn. The IDL specifications for the `syntax_tree` and `attributed_syntax_tree` structures may be found in Sections 13.5 and 13.5, respectively. The IDL specifications for the processes comprising XREF are given throughout this chapter. The source listings are not provided here. Most of the code is a straightforward application of the techniques discussed in Chapter 9. In the present chapter, we point out how the implementation differs from that of the function language compiler.

13.1 The Preprocessor

XREF uses the standard C preprocessor to expand such commands as

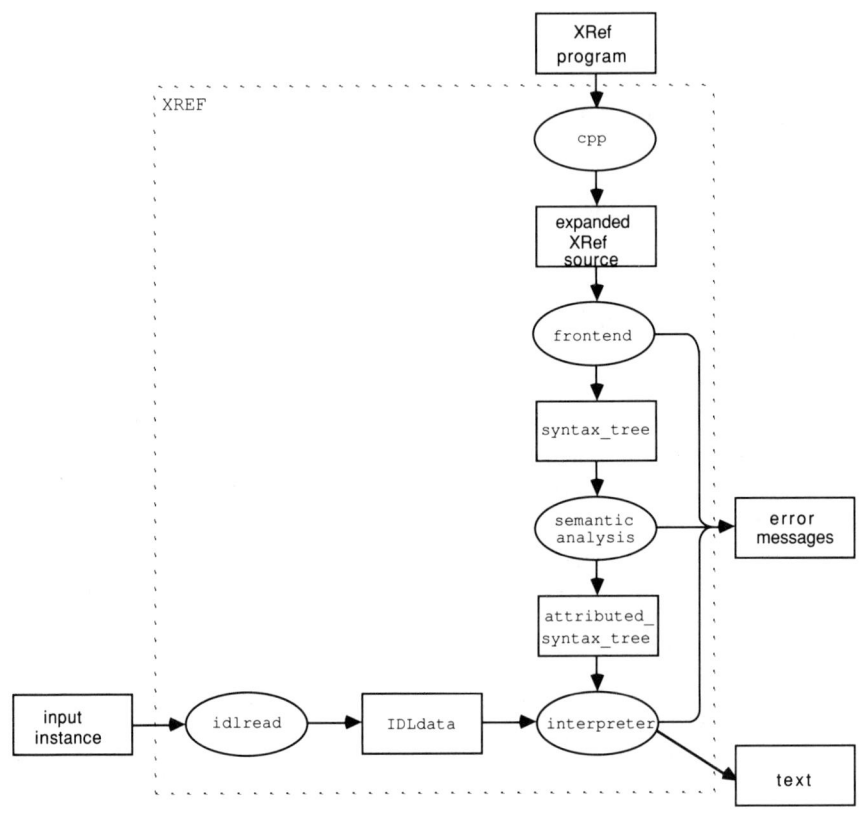

Figure 13.1: XREF Architecture

```
-- file src/xref/frontend/frontend.idl
Import syntax_tree From xrefst End

Process frontend Is
    Target Language C;
-- Pre input: xref source;
    Post write_syntax_tree: syntax_tree;
End
```

Figure 13.2: The `frontend` Process Specification

"#include", "#define", and "#if". The output of the preprocessor contains only the "# ⟨line number⟩ "⟨file name⟩"" directive, indicating where the lines following the directive (up to the next such directive) originated, for example,

```
# 1 "file.xref"
```

These directives are used in the frontend to compute source positions.

13.2 The Frontend

The frontend is broken into two subphases, lexical and syntactic analysis, as in the function language compiler. The `frontend` process declaration is given in Figure 13.2.

13.2.1 Lexical Analysis

The lexical analysis subphase was written using LEX. There were two differences with that of the function language compiler.

- XRef includes string constants, and supports C-style character escapes (e.g., "\n" denotes carriage return).

- XREF uses the C preprocessor to permit macros and included files, somewhat complicating the calculation of the source position, primarily to process the "# ⟨line number⟩" directives.

On the other hand, XRef contains no integer or real constants.

13.2.2 Syntactic Analysis

The parser was written using YACC, as was that of the function language compiler. We followed the mechanical procedure outlined in Section 9.2.1 to write the parser given the BNF for the language. The parser is longer than that of the function language, owing to the longer XRef grammar, but is still similar.

13.2.3 The Syntax Tree Structure

The `syntax_tree` structure was written with the guidelines listed in Chapter 10 in mind, and can be found in Section 13.5. Several points deserve mention.

- The internal and external representations of the source position (called `position` in the specification) were specified to be identical, simplifying matters somewhat.

- Unary and binary predicates were not differentiated at the syntactic level.

  `predicate_declaration => syn_formals: Seq Of local;`

  A unary predicate has a `syn_formals` of size one, while a binary predicate has a `syn_formals` of size two.

- Classes were used for several reasons (see Section 10.3); hence several nodes (e.g., `extra`) have more than one superclass.

- Source positions were recorded for both identifiers (i.e., `user_name`) and string constants.

- There are four semantic entities, `predicate_declaration`, `function_declaration`, `let_variable` and `local`, and three entity references, `predicateRef`, `functionRef`, and `localOrletRef`. The first two semantic entities are also syntactic entities. A `local` may appear in several places: as a formal in predicate and function declarations and as an identifier in the case and for statements. `let_variables` appear, naturally, in let statements. XRef differs from Pascal in that the identifier in these statements is actually a new "variable," defined only within the scope of the statement. Hence, in XRef each statement actually declares a new variable. This distinction will have ramifications in semantic analysis, but, interestingly, not during interpretation of the XRef program. References to locals and to let variables cannot be differentiated during syntactic analysis, since they are

-- file: *src/xref/analyser/analyser.idl*

```
Import attributed_syntax_tree From xrefast End

Process analyser Is
   Target Language C;
   Pre read_syntax_tree: syntax_tree;
   Post write_attributed_tree: attributed_syntax_tree;
End
```

Figure 13.3: The `analyser` Process Specification

both identifiers. They will be differentiated during name resolution in the semantic analysis phase.

- Only four assertions were used, requiring (a) that every predicate have either one or two parameters, (b) that every function declaration have at least one parameter, and (c) that every function call and (d) every predicate call have at least one parameter.

13.3 Semantic Analysis

As with the function language, semantic analysis for XREF involves two activities: name resolution and type checking. However, because of differences between the two languages, both activities differ substantially in the two implementations. In particular, XRef requires a somewhat more sophisticated approach to the symbol table.

The `analyser` process specification is given in Figure 13.3, and the collected `attributed_syntax_tree` structure specification is given in Section 13.5.

13.3.1 Name Resolution

Name resolution involves computing a `sem_entity` attribute for each entity reference. In the function language, there is but one kind of entity reference, `formal_parameterRef`, and but one level of scoping, that of the body of a function. In XRef, there are three kinds of entity references, `predicateRef`, `functionRef`, and `localOrletRef`, and scopes may be nested within bodies of predicates, functions, let statements, case statements, for statements, as well as the main program, which is also a body.

To resolve names, we first compute a distributed symbol table, as a scope node associated with each body.

```
body        => sem_scope:          scope;
scope       => sem_entities:       Seq Of Entity;
               sem_previous_scope: scopeOrVoid;
scopeOrVoid ::= scope | Void;
```

The sem_entities attribute records those entities declared directly in the construct (e.g., a predicate_declaration) containing this body, and the sem_previous_scope attribute refers to the scope of the construct (e.g., a for statement) of the construct containing this enclosing construct.

Name resolution is one-pass, recursive descent, implemented as a collection of procedures, one per type of node in the syntax tree. Each procedure takes as parameters the current scope and a pointer to a node of the appropriate type in the syntax tree. As name resolution proceeds, the sem_entities sequence is accumulated. Using the current scope, name resolution can then calculate the sem_entity attribute.

```
functionRef         => sem_entity: function_declaration;
predicateRef        => sem_entity: predicate_declaration;
localOrletRef       => sem_entity: localOrlet_variable;
localOrlet_variable ::= local | let_variable;
```

Once this is done, the sem_scope attribute of the body node can be discarded, although here it is kept to aid debugging.

Note how the syntactic ambiguity between locals and let variables has been resolved semantically. After syntactic analysis, we have a localOrletRef in either case. After name resolution, the value of the sem_entity is either a local or a let_variable.

Consider the following XRef program, similar to the one discussed in Chapter 11.

```
1
  Predicate ascending_names(left, right)
2
    left.value ¡ right.value End
3
  For name_node In Reorder(Type(Root, user_name),
                ascending names)
  Do
4
```

13.3. SEMANTIC ANALYSIS

      Predicate node_of_name(node)
5
        node.value = name˙node.value *End*
6
     name˙node
  End

In this program there are two bodies: the main program and the for statement. Each will be associated with a scope. Let's simulate name resolution on this XRef program. For purposes of discussion, we will abbreviate the user_name node instance, say the instance

```
user_name[lex_value "ascending_names";
         lex_position position[lex_location 2;
                               lex_cpp_file "book.xref";
                               lex_cpp_location 1]
        ]
```
with the value of the `lex_value` attribute, `"ascending_names"`.

- (We start at position *1* of the program.) A scope is created with the following contents.

  ```
  L1:scope[sem_entities <>;
          sem_previous_scope Void]
  ```

- For each predicate declaration

  - Create a new, temporary scope, containing the local variables in the predicate declaration. This scope should reference the current scope (L1).

    ```
    scope[sem_entries <L2:local[syn_name "left"]
                       L3:local[syn_name "right"]
                      >;
          sem_previous_scope L1^]
    ```

  - (Now at position *2*) Analyze the expression forming the body of the predicate, given this temporary scope. Resolve each entity reference by searching back through the scopes.

    ```
    localOrletRef[syn_name "left";
                  sem_entity L2^]
    localOrletRef[syn_name "right";
                  sem_entity L3^]
    ```

- Add this predicate declaration onto the current scope (L1).

  ```
  L1:scope[sem_entities <
              L4:predicate_declaration[
                  syn_name "ascending_name";
                  syn_formals <...>
                  ]
              >;
          sem_previous_scope Void]
  ```

- Discard the temporary scope for the predicate declaration.

• (At position *3*) Now analyze the body, with L1 as the current scope.

- Analyze the for statement. First analyze the "*In*" expression. Resolve each entity reference, searching back through the scopes.

  ```
  predicateRef[syn_name "ascending_names";
               sem_entity L4^]
  ```

- Create a new scope, containing the local implicitly declared in the for statement. This scope should reference the current scope (L1).

  ```
  L5:scope[sem_entities <L6:local[syn_name "name_node"]>;
           sem_previous_scope L1^]
  ```

- (At position *4*) Analyze the body of the for statement, with L5 as current scope.

  * For each predicate declaration, create a new temporary scope containing its local variables. This scope should reference the current scope (L5).

    ```
    L8:scope[sem_entities <L7:local[syn_name "node"]>;
             sem_previous_scope L5^]
    ```

    At this point, three scopes (L8, L5, and L1) are active.

  * (At position *5*) Analyze the expression forming the body of the predicate, resolving each entity reference by searching back through the scopes.

    ```
    localOrletRef[syn_name "node";
                  sem_entity L7^]
    localOrletRef[syn_name "name_node";
                  sem_entity L6^]
    ```

13.3. SEMANTIC ANALYSIS

The "node" local was found in scope L8, and the "name_node" local was found in scope L5.

* Discard the temporary scope L8.

– Add this predicate onto the current scope (L5).

```
L5:scope[sem_entities <
            L6:local[syn_name "name_node"]
            predicate_declaration[
                syn_name "node_of_name";
                syn_formals <...>;
                ]
            >;
        sem_previous_scope L1^]
```

– (At position *6*) Analyze the statements in the body with L5 as the current scope. Resolve each entity reference.

```
localOrletRef[syn_name "name_node";
              sem_entity L6^]
```

At this point in the program, there are two scopes (L5 and L1), containing a total of three semantic entities.

L5: the local "name_node"
     the predicate_declaration "node_of_name"
L1: the predicate_declaration "ascending_names"

Because the scopes are linked from innermost nesting outward through the sem_previous_scope attribute, a semantic entity can be declared, at an inner scope, with the same name as an entity at an outer scope, and the search given an entity reference with that name will find the inner entity.

Several assertions relating to name resolution are present in the attributed_syntax_tree structure. The ones concerning function, local, and let variable references are straight forward.

```
Assert ForAll f In functionRef Do
        f.syn_name.lex_value = f.sem_entity.syn_name.lex_value Od;

Assert ForAll l In localOrletRef Do
        l.syn_name.lex_value = l.sem_entity.syn_name.lex_value Od;
```

The presence of the predefined predicate *Is* complicates matters only slightly.

```
predicateRef              =>  sem_entity: predicate_declOrPredef;
predicate_declOrPredef  ::=  predicate_declaration
                              | IsPredicate;
IsPredicate =>;

Assert ForAll p In predicateRef Do
       Case E Is p.sem_entity
       predicate_declaration
             Do p.syn_name.lex_value = E.sem_entity.syn_name.lex_value Od
       IsPredicate Do p.syn_name.lex_value = "Is" Od
       Otherwise Do False Od End
Od;
```

13.3.2 Type Checking

In the function language, parameters were typed (either *integer* or *real*) and the type of each expression could be computed during semantic analysis. In XRef, a conscious decision was made not to require type declarations. Instead, types are computed and checked dynamically by the interpreter.

There are two kinds of checks performed during semantic analysis that can be classified as type checking.

- The entity referenced by an entity reference should be of the correct kind: a functionRef should be resolved to a function_declaration, etc. This checking is specified in IDL as

  ```
  functionRef => sem_entity: function_declaration;
  ```

  and is performed during name resolution.

- The correct predicate, either unary or binary, should be used in *Reorder*, etc. This checking is specified in IDL with an assertion.

  ```
  Assert ForAll r In reorder
         Do Case P Is r.syn_predicate.sem_entity
            IsPredicate Do True Od
            Otherwise Do Size(P.syn_formals) = 2 Od End
         Od;
  ```

  and is also performed during name resolution.

In summary, the semantic analysis phase consists of a single, top-down recursive descent traversal of the syntax tree, computing scopes and entity references and making a few checks.

13.3.3 The Interpreter

As shown in Figure 13.1, the interpreter has two inputs. One is the input instance to XREF processed by the IDLREAD process. IDLREAD has a custom reader that is not specific to instances of any particular structure (see the process specification in Figure 13.4). Its writer is a conventional writer produced by the IDL translator, as is both readers of the interpreter.

As an example, if IDLREAD is presented the following instance

```
A[AnAttribute L1:B; AnotherAttribute L1^]
```

it will produce the following instance of the IDLdata structure.

```
nodeDesc[name "A";
         attributes <attrDesc[
                             name "AnAttribute";
                             value L1:nodeDesc[
                                 name "B";
                                 attributes <>;
                                 label "L1"]
                             ]
                    attrDesc[
                             name "AnotherAttribute";
                             value L1^]
                    >;
         label ""]
```

The advantage of using IDLREAD is that the reader for XREF need not be custom generated for the structure of each instance it needs to read. Instead, it always reads an instance of the IDLdata structure.

The IDL specification of the interpreter is shown in Figure 13.5. The interpreter_data structure is specified as the invariant structure for the interpreter process. It defines nodes and sequences that will be used as the interpreter executes. It can optionally be written out during execution to be viewed by other tools, say for debugging the interpreter. Since these attributes are local to the interpreter, they are given an "int_" prefix. The Global.int_body attribute references the root of the attributed syntax tree; the Global.int_data attribute references the root of the input instance. We will examine the remaining attributes and nodes shortly, as we discuss how various operators are implemented.

The interpreter performs the directives by recursively processing the attributed syntax tree. As strings are produced, they are written out; the top level evaluation of the resulting sequence of strings is incremental. As

-- *IDL declaration for the Generic Reader (IDLread)*

```
Structure IDLdata Root nodeDesc Is
    nodeDesc      => name:       String,
                     attributes: Seq Of attrDesc,
                     label:      String; -- may be the null string
    attrDesc      => name:       String,
                     value:      IDLVALUE;
    IDLVALUE      ::= IDLnumber | IDLother;
    IDLnumber     ::= integerDesc | rationalDesc;
    IDLother      ::= booleanDesc | stringDesc | setDesc
                      | sequenceDesc | nodeDesc;
    IDLnumber     => stringRep:  String;

    booleanDesc   => value:      Boolean;
    integerDesc   => value:      Integer;
    stringDesc    => value:      String;
    rationalDesc  => value:      Rational;

    setDesc       => value:      Set Of IDLVALUE;
    sequenceDesc  => value:      Seq Of IDLVALUE;
End

Process IDLread Is
        -- Pre is an instance of an arbitrary IDL structure
        Post idlout: IDLdata;
End
```

Figure 13.4: The IDLread Process Specification

13.3. SEMANTIC ANALYSIS

```
-- file: src/xref/interpreter/interpreter.idl

Import attributed_syntax_tree From xrefast End

-- To record arbitrary IDL values
Import IDLdata From idldata End

Structure interpreter_data Root Global From IDLdata, attributed_syntax_tree Is

    -- global data needed by the interpreter
    Global              =>  int_caches:         Seq Of cache,
                            int_body:           body,
                            int_data:           nodeDesc; -- needed by Root

    -- cache of the result of Type(<sequence>, <node_name>, <attribute_name>)
    -- purely for performance
    cache               =>  int_element:        IDLVALUE, -- element of the sequen
                            int_node_name:      String,
                            int_attribute:      user_nameOrVoid,
                            int_result:         constructed_sequence;

    -- current value of the local variable
    local               =>  int_value:          IDLVALUE;

    -- current value of the let variable
    let_variable        =>  int_value:          constructed_sequence;

    -- sequences of values are used extensively
    constructed_sequence ::= physical_sequence | virtual_sequence;
    physical_sequence   =>  int_values:         Seq Of IDLVALUE;
    virtual_sequence =>; -- append results in value written out
    For virtual_sequence Use Representation Enumerated;

    -- used to optimize the evaluation of Type()
    IDLVALUE            =>  int_type_invocation: Integer;

    For Void Use Name TVoid;
End

Process interpreter Inv interpreter_data Is
    Target Language C;
    Pre read_syntax_tree: attributed_syntax_tree;
    Pre read_user_data: IDLdata;
    -- Post debug: interpreter_data;
End
```

Figure 13.5: The `interpreter` Process Specification

we will see, within various operators, sequences are generated in whole, then scanned and written out.

Each node of the attributed syntax tree is associated with a procedure in the interpreter. This procedure generally has two parameters: the current node in the syntax tree and the current `constructed_sequence` being generated. If the sequence is a `virtual_sequence`, then a concatenation simply outputs the element. On the other hand, if it is a `physical_sequence`, then a concatenation appends the element to `int_values`.

Let us now examine how some of the constructs in XRef are implemented.

- A body is evaluated by calling the relevant routine for each sequence element in turn, passing the `constructed_sequence`.

    ```
    evaluate_body(thisbody, thisseq)
    body thisbody;
    constructed_sequence thisseq;
    {
        sequence_element element;
        SEQsequence_element state;

        foreachinSEQsequence_element(thisbody->syn_sequence->syn_values,
                state,element){
            switch(typeof(element)){
            case Ktype_construct: {evaluate_type_construct(
                    element.Vtype_construct,thisseq);break;}
            case Kfunction_call: {evaluate_function_call(
                    element.Vfunction_call,thisseq);break;}
            ...
        }
    }
    ```

    Notice that declarations in the body are ignored during interpretation.

- The reference operator (the `reference` node in the `attributed_syntax_tree`) first accesses either the node referenced in `Global.int_data`, if the first element of the reference was *Root*, or the node referenced by `syn_local.sem_entity.int_value` (we will see shortly how this attribute is initialized). Then, for each element in the `syn_attributes` of the reference, the attributes of the node are scanned for that element, and, if found, the value is extracted. If the element is not found, an error has been encountered. The value eventually obtained is returned.

- A function call (the `function_call` node in the `attributed_syntax_tree`) first evaluates each of the `syn_actuals` recursively. It then copies each of the values thus computed into the `int_value` attribute of the appropriate element of `syn_function.sem_entity.sem_formals`. For instance, if the function declared as

13.3. SEMANTIC ANALYSIS

>   *Function* f(one) one *End*

were called as

>   f("a")

the first `syn_actual` would evaluate to the string "a", which would then be placed in the only formal, thus

```
L1:local[syn_name "one";
        int_value StringDesc[value "a"]
        ]
```

(we are again abbreviating each `user_name`s to its `lex_value` string). Finally, the `syn_function.sem_entity.syn_value` would be recursively evaluated. Here, the body is a single-entity reference

```
localOrletRef[syn_name "one";
             sem_entity L1^]
```

so its value can be obtained by traversing the `sem_entity` attribute. Predicate calls are handled in an analogous fashion.

- The let construct is easier to implement: each right-hand side is evaluated and the result stored in the `int_value` attribute of the let variable, then the nested body is evaluated.

- A for statement (the `for_statement` node in the `attribute_syntax_tree`) is implemented in a similar fashion, except the body is executed potentially many times. First, the `syn_sequence` is evaluated. Then, for each element of the resulting base sequence, the element is stored in `syn_local.int_value` and the `syn_body` is evaluated, resulting in a final sequence. Since the base sequence may have many elements, many final sequences may result. There are simply concatenated together to form the result of the for statement. As with the `evaluate_body` routine, this concatenation occurs as a side effect of passing the same `constructed_sequence` to each nested invocation.

If the for statement is at the top level, its final `constructed_sequence` (passed in as an argument) will be a `virtual_sequence`, and appends to this sequence will result in the element being printed out.

On the other hand, when evaluating the sequence that the for statement iterates over, its `constructed_sequence` will be a `physical_sequence`, and appends to this sequence will be realized as appends to the `int_values` attribute.

- *Reorder* first evaluates its sequence, then performs an insertion sort, using the binary predicate to determine where each element should be placed in the sequence. Because the ordering can change, this sequence must be a `physical_sequence`.

- The *Type* operator (the `type_construct` in the `attributed_syntax_tree`) takes a sequence, a user name denoting the node type and an optional user name denoting an attribute, and returns a sequence of nodes (a) that are reachable from a node in the sequence (either through all attributes or through the desired attribute) and (b) that are of the specified user name type. First the `syn_sequence` is evaluated. Then, for each element of the resulting base sequence, the reachability search is executed, resulting in a final sequence. As with the for statement, these final sequences are concatenated to form the result of the *Type* operator.

  The reachability search can be expensive to perform. To increase the performance of the interpreter, two simple optimizations were made. First, the results of previous executions of the search are cached in `Global.int_caches`. Each `cache` contains an element of the base sequence, the node name desired, the optional attribute name, and the result of the search. The interpreter first checks the cache; if the entry is not present, then the search is performed and the result recorded in a new cache entry.

  The second optimization involves the representation of a set of values. During the reachability search, we need to determine whether the node just encountered has been processed before. This check, necessary to avoid infinite looping when processing instances containing cycles, uses an auxiliary set. This set is first checked to see if the value has been encountered before. If the value is not in the set, then it is added to the set and analyzed to see what values are reachable from it. This test occurs frequently, and so must be fast. The test may be reduced to a single integer comparison by the following trick. Each evaluation of the *Type* operator is assigned a unique integer (using a counter). We implement the operation of adding a value to the set by storing this integer in `int_type_invocation`. We implement the set membership test by simply comparing the value of this attribute with the integer assigned to the current invocation. Surprisingly, replacing the default set operations with this implementation often lowered execution times by a factor of 10.

13.4 Summary

The XREF architecture is similar to that of a traditional compiler, with the exception that no code is produced; the interpreter directly executes the attributed parse tree. The sizes of the various components are given below. IDLREAD is included since it is part of XREF, as shown in Figure 13.1; it is also a separate process that is used in other tools, notably IDLCHECK, to be discussed in Chapter 18. In this table "n.a." stands for "not applicable". Source lines includes comments, which comprised between 5% and 20% of the lines, depending on whether there was a 23-line header comment, the presence of version history information in the header comment, and individual commenting style, particularly whether comments appeared to the right of executable statements or on dedicated lines.

Component	Source	IDL	Generated	Object Code
	(Lines of Source Code)			(Kilobytes)
XREF		277		
IDLREAD (Pascal)	1,750	32	105	67
frontend (C)	155	9	3185	
Lex	236	n.a.	1424	
Yacc	723	n.a.	1065	
Total	1114	9	5674	107
analyser (C)	549	10	4301	150
interpreter (C)	1268	45	2732	114
Total	4,681	372	12,812	438

XREF is implemented in C, Pascal, Lex, Yacc, and IDL. The latter three are specification languages from which C or Pascal code is automatically generated. The `syntax_tree` and `attributed_syntax_tree`, given below, consists of 277 lines of IDL. The main program of the `frontend` consists of 155 lines of C code; the `frontend` process, shown in Figure 13.2, consists of 9 lines of IDL, from which IDLC generates 3185 lines of C. 72% of the source code of XREF was generated by other tools, from 1331 lines of specifications.

The two primary IDL specifications, for the `syntax_tree` and `attributed_syntax_tree`, follow.

13.5 The Syntax Tree Structure

```
-- file src/xref/specs/syntax_tree.idl

Structure syntax_tree Root body Is

-- lexical information
    user_name              => lex_value:          String,
                              lex_position:       position;

    position               => lex_location:       Integer, -- Absolute file line number
                              lex_cpp_file:       String,  -- original file name
                              lex_cpp_location:   Integer; -- line number in expanded file

    string_constant        => lex_text:           String,
                              lex_position:       position;

-- syntactic structures, first general
    Entity              ::= declaration | localOrlet_variable;
    localOrlet_variable ::= local | let_variable;
    Entity              => syn_name:           user_name;
    local => ;

-- For each Entity, there is an EntityRef
    EntityRef           ::= predicateRef | functionRef | localOrletRef;
    EntityRef           => syn_name:           user_name;
    predicateRef =>; functionRef => ; localOrletRef => ;

-- <directives> ::= <body>
-- <body> ::= { <declaration> }* <sequence>
    body                   => syn_declarations:   Seq Of declaration,
                              syn_sequence:       sequence;

-- <declaration> ::= <predicate decl> | <function decl>
    declaration            ::= predicate_declaration | function_declaration ;

-- <predicate decl> ::= Predicate <predicate_name> '(' <formals> ')'
--                     <predicate> End
-- <formals> ::= <formal_name> { ',' <formal_name> }*
-- (Unary and binary predicates are not differentiated at the syntactic level)
    predicate_declaration => syn_formals:      Seq Of local,
                              syn_value:        expression;
Assert ForAll p In predicate_declaration
    Do Size(p.syn_formals) > 0 and Size(p.syn_formals) <= 2 Od;

-- <function decl> ::= Function <function_name> '(' <formals> ')'
--                    <body> End
    function_declaration => syn_formals:      Seq Of local,
                              syn_value:        body;

Assert ForAll f In function_declaration Do Size(f.syn_formals) > 0 Od;

-- <sequence> ::= { <sequence element> }+
    sequence               => syn_values:      Seq Of sequence_element;

-- <sequence element> ::= <string>
    sequence_element       ::= type_construct |
                               function_call |
                               extra |
                               tail |
                               reorder |
```

13.5. THE SYNTAX TREE STRUCTURE

```
                                  filter |
                                  unique |
                                  intersection |
                                  difference |
                                  atom |
                                  let_construct |
                                  case_statement |
                                  for_statement;
   nested_element         ::= type_construct | tail | reorder | filter | unique;
   nested_element         =>  syn_sequence:          sequence;
   doubly_nested_element  ::= extra |   intersection | difference;
   doubly_nested_element  =>  syn_right_sequence: sequence,
                              syn_left_sequence:  sequence;

-- <sequence element> ::= Type '(' <sequence> ',' <node_name>
--                     { ',' <attribute_name> }? ')'
   type_construct        =>  syn_name:              user_name,
                             syn_attribute:         user_nameOrVoid;
   user_nameOrVoid       ::= user_name | Void;
   Void =>  ;

-- <sequence element> ::= <function_name> '(' <atoms> ')'
-- <atoms> ::= <atom> { ',' <atom> } *
   function_call         =>  syn_function:          functionRef,
                             syn_actuals:           Seq Of atom;
Assert ForAll f In function_call Do Size(f.syn_actuals) > 0 Od;

-- <sequence element> ::= Extra '(' <sequence> ',' <sequence> ')'
   extra =>  ;

-- <sequence element> ::= Tail '(' <sequence> ')'
   tail =>  ;

-- <sequence element> ::= Reorder '(' <sequence> ',' <binary_predicate_name> ')'
   reorder               =>  syn_predicate:         predicateRef;

-- <sequence element> ::= Filter '(' <sequence> ',' <unary_predicate_name> ')'
   filter                =>  syn_predicate:         predicateRef;

-- <sequence element> ::= Unique '(' <sequence> ',' <binary_predicate_name> ')'
   unique                =>  syn_predicate:         predicateRef;

-- <sequence element> ::= Intersection '(' <sequence> ',' <binary_predicate_name> ')'
   intersection          =>  syn_predicate:         predicateRef;

-- <sequence element> ::= Difference '(' <sequence> ',' <sequence> ','
--                     <binary_predicate_name> ')'
   difference            =>  syn_predicate:         predicateRef;

-- <sequence element> ::= Let <assignments> In <body> End
-- <assignments> ::= <assignment> { ',' <assignment> } *
-- <assignment> ::= <let_variable> '=' <sequence>
   let_construct         =>  syn_assignments:       Seq Of let_variable,
                             syn_body:              body;
   let_variable          =>  syn_sequence:          sequence;

-- <sequence element> ::= For <iterated_name> In <sequence> Do <body> End
   for_statement         =>  syn_local:             local,
                             syn_sequence:          sequence,
                             syn_body:              body;
```

```
-- <sequence element> ::= <case statement>
-- <case statement> ::= Case <atom> As <case_name> Of <case branches> End
    case_statement        =>  syn_atom:          atom,
                              syn_local:         local,
                              syn_branches:      Seq Of branch;

-- <case branches> ::= { <case branch> }+ { Default ':' <body> ';' }?
-- <case branch> ::= <node_name> ':' <body> ';'
    branch                =>  syn_key:           user_name_or_default,
                              syn_value:         body;

    user_name_or_default      ::= default_construct | user_name ;
    default_construct =>;

-- <sequence element> ::= <atom>
-- <atom> ::= <reference> | <string> | Head '(' <sequence> ')'
    atom                      ::= reference | string_constant | head;
    head                  =>  syn_sequence:      sequence;

-- <sequence element> ::= <reference>
-- <reference> ::= { <existing_name> | Root } { '.' <attribute_name> }*
    reference             =>  syn_local:         localOrletRefOrRoot,
                              syn_attributes:    Seq Of user_name;
    localOrletRefOrRoot       ::= localOrletRef | Root_construct;
    Root_construct => ;

-- <predicate> ::= <parend predicate>
-- <parend predicate> ::= '(' <predicate> ')'
    expression                ::= unary_op | binary_op | relational_expression
                                | predicate_call | empty_call;

-- <parend predicate> ::= Not <parend predicate>
    unary_op              =>  syn_op_code:       unary_op_code,
                              syn_operand:       expression;

    unary_op_code             ::= not_op;
    not_op =>;

-- <predicate> ::= <parend predicate> And <parend predicate>
--              | <parend predicate> Or <parend predicate>
    binary_op             =>  syn_op_code:       binary_op_code,
                              syn_right_operand: expression,
                              syn_left_operand:  expression;

    binary_op_code            ::= and_op | or_op ;
    and_op =>; or_op =>;

-- <predicate> ::= <atom> <opr> <atom>
-- <opr> ::= '~=' | '<=' | '>=' | ',' | '>' | '=' | Same | In
    relational_expression =>  syn_op_code:       relational_op_code,
                              syn_left_operand:  atom,
                              syn_right_operand: atom;

    relational_op_code        ::= equal_op | not_equal_op | less_than_op |
                                  less_than_or_equal_op | gtr_than_op |
                                  gtr_than_or_equal_op  | same_op | in_op;

    equal_op =>; not_equal_op =>; less_than_op =>; less_than_or_equal_op =>;
    gtr_than_op =>; gtr_than_or_equal_op =>; same_op =>; in_op =>;

-- <predicate> ::= <predicate_name> '(' <atoms> ')'
```

13.6. THE ATTRIBUTED SYNTAX TREE STRUCTURE

```
        predicate_call       =>  syn_predicate:       predicateRef,
                                 syn_actuals:         Seq Of atom;
Assert ForAll p In predicate_call Do Size(p.syn_actuals) > 0 Od;

-- <predicate> ::= Is '(' <atom> ',' <atom> ')'
-- Handled in syntactic analysis as a predicate_call

-- <predicate> ::= Empty '(' <sequence> ')'
    empty_call               =>  syn_sequence:        sequence;

End
```

13.6 The Attributed Syntax Tree Structure

```
-- file: src/xref/specs/xrefast.idl

Import syntax_tree From xrefst End

Structure attributed_syntax_tree From syntax_tree Is

-- Link references with entities
    functionRef              =>  sem_entity:          function_declaration;

-- Predefined functions are resolved correctly
Assert ForAll f In functionRef
    Do f.syn_name.lex_value = f.sem_entity.syn_name.lex_value Od;

    predicateRef             =>  sem_entity:          predicate_declOrPredef;
    predicate_declOrPredef ::= predicate_declaration
                             | IsPredicate;
    IsPredicate =>;

-- The predefined predicates are resolved correctly
Assert ForAll p In predicateRef
    Do Case E Is p.sem_entity
    predicate_declaration Do p.syn_name.lex_value = E.syn_name.lex_value Od
    IsPredicate Do p.syn_name.lex_value = "Is" Od
    Otherwise Do False Od End
Od;

-- The predefined predicates have the correct number of arguments
-- and the rest have one or two arguments
Assert ForAll p In predicate_call
    Do Case E Is p.syn_predicate.sem_entity
    IsPredicate Do Size(p.syn_actuals) = 2 Od
    Otherwise Do Size(p.syn_actuals) = 1 Or Size(p.syn_actuals) = 2 Od End
Od;

-- The correct predicate, either unary or binary, should be used
Assert ForAll r In reorder
    Do Case P Is r.syn_predicate.sem_entity
    IsPredicate Do True Od
    Otherwise Do Size(P.syn_formals) = 2 Od End
Od;
Assert ForAll f In filter
    Do Case P Is f.syn_predicate.sem_entity
    IsPredicate Do False Od
    Otherwise Do Size(P.syn_formals) = 1 Od End
Od;
```

```
Assert ForAll u In unique
    Do Case P Is u.syn_predicate.sem_entity
        IsPredicate Do True Od
        Otherwise Do Size(P.syn_formals) = 2 Od End
Od;
Assert ForAll i In intersection
    Do Case P Is i.syn_predicate.sem_entity
        IsPredicate Do True Od
        Otherwise Do Size(P.syn_formals) = 2 Od End
Od;
Assert ForAll d In difference
    Do Case P Is d.syn_predicate.sem_entity
        IsPredicate Do True Od
        Otherwise Do Size(P.syn_formals) = 2 Od End
Od;

    localOrletRef          =>  sem_entity:        localOrlet_variable;
Assert ForAll l In localOrletRef
    Do l.syn_name.lex_value = l.sem_entity.syn_name.lex_value Od;

-- The let_construct has at least one assignment
Assert ForAll l In let_construct Do Size(l.syn_assignments) >= 1 Od;

-- Identify the scope associated with a body.
    body                   =>  sem_scope:         scope;

    scope                  =>  sem_entities:      Seq Of Entity,
                               sem_previous_scope: scopeOrVoid;
    scopeOrVoid            ::= scope | Void;
For Void Use Representation Enumerated;

-- Identifies a node as the root of tree, i.e., with no previous scope
Assert ForAll b In body
    Do If Not b Same Root
       Then Not b.sem_scope Same Void
       Else True Fi Od;
End
```

Bibliographic Notes

The C preprocessor is described by Harbison and Steele [1987].

Exercises

13.1 Write an example of an XRef program that uses the same name for two different semantic entities at different nesting levels. Run your example through XREF and obtain the attributed syntax tree instance. Verify that the symbol table is correct and that the entity references are resolved correctly.

13.2 Explain the difference in the handling of the distinguished variable name in a for statement between XREF and a Pascal compiler built using

13.6. THE ATTRIBUTED SYNTAX TREE STRUCTURE

IDL. Justify the observation that the XREF interpreter doesn't care which semantics is adopted.

13.3 Identify precisely when a `constructed_sequence` should be a `virtual_sequence` and when it should be a `physical_sequence`.

13.4 Extend the implementation to handle other constants, such as integers and booleans (see Exercise **12.1**).

13.5 Extend the implementation to support case-sensitive string comparisons (see Exercise **12.2**).

13.6 Extend the implementation to allow more than one attribute name in the *Type* construct (see Exercise **12.3**).

13.7 Unlike most languages, XRef does not include a conditional execution construct.

  a. Show how to rewrite the following using available XRef constructs.

   If ⟨predicate⟩ *Then* ⟨sequence⟩ *Else* ⟨sequence⟩ *End*

  b. Extend the implementation to support such a construct directly. What are the efficiency ramifications of this extension?

13.8 XRef permits predicates to have either one or two parameters.

  a. Why were predicates with no parameters disallowed?

  b. Extend the implementation to allow predicates that have more than two parameters.

13.9 XRef requires all predicates to be fully parenthesized.

  a. Why was this restriction imposed?

  b. Extend the implementation to support operators of different precedence.

13.10 XRef does not allow recursive functions. The benefit is that the `local.int_value` attributes may be single-valued.

  a. What would happen during semantic analysis if the user put a direct recursive call (i.e., a function calling itself directly) in an XRef program?

  b. What would happen if the user put an indirect recursive call in an XRef program (such as a function **A** calling a function **B** which in turn calls the original function **A**)?

c. Extend the language definition to support both direct and indirect recursive function calls. Reflect these changes in the IDL specification.

d. Show that the *Extra* construct is not needed given this language extension. What other constructs are superfluous?

e. What would happen if an XRef program containing a recursive call were then interpreted?

f. Modify the interpreter so that it could correctly handle recursion.

g. How can semantic analysis make interpretation more efficient?

h. Answer the above questions for recursive *predicates*.

13.11 XRef is a typeless language. Everything is eventually converted to strings, but the type of a subexpression may be, say, integer one time through a loop and boolean the next time through the loop.

a. What are the benefits of being typeless?

b. What are the drawbacks?

c. How should the types be declared? How should the implementation be augmented if the decision was made to make XRef type-strict?

13.12 The Let statement is often found in applicative languages.

a. Show that this statement is not strictly necessary: that it can be simulated using other constructs of the language. Does your solution maintain correct scoping?

b. Show how the scopes may be manipulated to analyze the following correctly.

```
Let A = ···,
      B = ··· A ···,
      A = ··· B ···
In ··· A ··· B ··· End
```

c. The Let statement can substantially improve performance. Modify **name.xref**, shown in Appendix E.7, so that it doesn't use the Let statement, and run it and the original version on a small CANDLE instance. Why do the run times differ so dramatically?

d. Explain how a sophisticated optimization phase in the XREF compiler could obviate some of the justification of this statement.

Part IV

Example: The IDL Translator

This part gives a final example of using IDL in a software system. The example used is the IDL translator and two associated tools: the assertion checker and syntax tree walker. This example provides a detailed description of a complex system that uses IDL extensively. Chapter 14 provides an overview of the translator. Chapter 15 describes CANDLE, a set of structures used between phases of the translator and with additional tools in the IDL system. Included in this chapter are the design criteria and rationale for CANDLE and a step-by-step description of the creation of a CANDLE instance for a simple IDL specification. Chapter 16 discusses CANDLEWALK, a flexible tool for manipulating the lexical and syntactic information present in a CANDLE instance. Chapter 17 describes the phases of the IDL translator in more detail. Chapter 18 discusses the assertion checker. Appendix F provides the CANDLE structure, and Appendix G explains each assertion checker instruction.

Chapter 14

Overview of the IDL Translator

The IDL translator is composed of six phases. IDL is used to describe the data structures passed between the successive phases of the compiler. Section 14.1 briefly describes the translator. This description focuses on the basic functions of each phase of the translator, the CANDLE structures passed between the successive phases, and the prelude. Section 14.2 gives a more detailed description of the prelude. The prelude defines all predefined types, target languages, operations, assertion definitions, and type representations supported by a particular implementation of a translator. A more detailed examination of the IDL translator is given in Chapter 17.

14.1 IDL Translator Architecture

The architecture for the IDL translator is shown in Figure 14.1. Rectangles denote textual files or instances of IDL structures, with the enclosed text indicating the form of the data. Ovals denote processes accepting one or more inputs and generating one or more outputs. The dotted line delimits the entire translator, which appears to be a single process taking an IDL specification as input and generating source code, object code, and error listings. An IDL declaration of these phases is shown in Figure 14.2.

The IDL Specification is a character stream in the IDL syntax. The Frontend takes an IDL specification, breaks it into tokens, parses the tokens, and produces an abstract syntax tree in the form of an instance of the `CandleSyntax` structure. In addition, this process must record the source position of important tokens, report and recover from any lexical

CHAPTER 14. OVERVIEW OF THE IDL TRANSLATOR

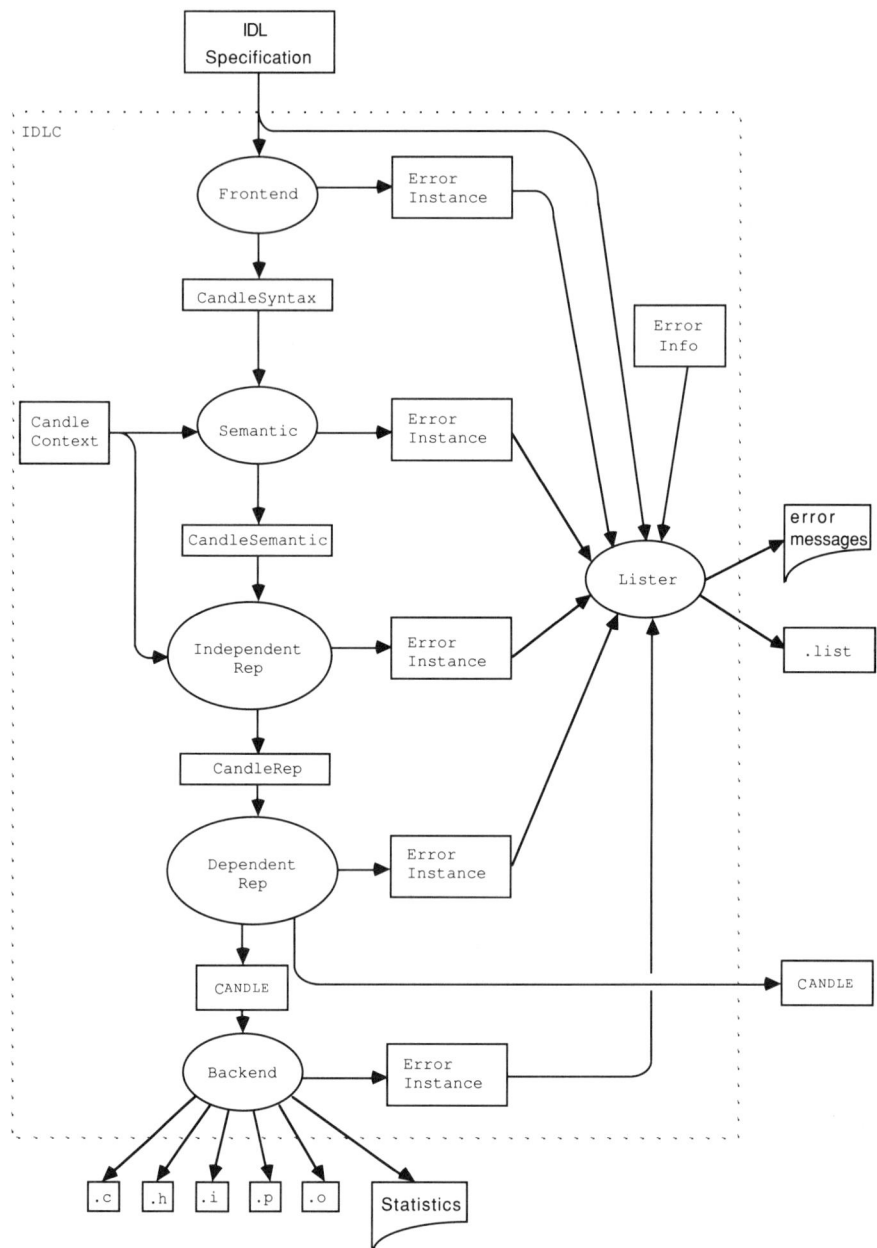

Figure 14.1: Architecture for the IDL Translator

14.1. IDL TRANSLATOR ARCHITECTURE

```
Import CandleContext From CandleContext End

Import ErrorInstance From errinstance End

Import ErrorInfo From errorinfo End

Process Frontend Is
    -- Pre is source text in IDL
    Post OUTParseTree: CandleSyntax;
    Post OUTErrorInstance: ErrorInstance;
End

Process Semantic Is
    Pre INSyntax: CandleSyntax;
    Pre INPrelude: CandleContext;
    Post OUTCandleSem: CandleSemantic;
    Post OUTErrorInstance: ErrorInstance;
End

Process IndependentRep Is
    Pre INCandleSem: CandleSemantic;
    Pre INPrelude: CandleContext;
    Post OUTCandle: CandleRep;
    Post OUTErrorInstance: ErrorInstance;
End

Process DependentRep Is
    Pre INCandleRep: CandleRep;
    Post OUTCandle: Candle;
    Post OUTErrorInstance: ErrorInstance;
End

Process Backend Is
    Pre INCandle: Candle;
    Post OUTErrorInstance: ErrorInstance;
    -- Post is a target-language dependent include file and
    -- readers and writers
End

Process lister Is
    Pre INErr: ErrorInfo;
    Pre INinstances: ErrorInstance;  -- can have any number of these
    -- Post produces listing file
    -- Post produces errors on the user's console
End
```

Figure 14.2: The IDL Specification for IDLC

or syntactic errors, and check for IDL Version 2 conformance if specified. The frontend process uses the compiler tools LEX and YACC for lexical and syntactic analysis. LEX is a tool that generates code to process an input character string and recognize it as a series of tokens. YACC is a tool that generates bottom-up parsers.

The **Semantic** module consists of two parts: the analysis of structures and processes and the analysis of assertions. The main functions for analyzing structures and processes include resolving name references, creating semantic entities, grouping collections of entities, marking duplicates, and correcting recoverable errors. The main functions in analyzing assertions are determining the type of each expression and checking that the assertions and definitions are semantically correct. Assertion and definition checking includes type checking, validity checking of references to types, attributes, and definitions, and checking for legal uses of definitions. Semantic analysis uses information in the *prelude* when resolving names. The prelude is an instance of the **CandleContext** structure and contains all predefined types, target languages, operations, assertion definitions, and type representations supported by a particular translator. The prelude thus allows the semantic analysis algorithms to be both target language independent and independent from predefined entities. The semantic analysis module produces an instance of **CandleSemantic** which is a strict superset of **CandleSyntax**; information is only added, not discarded, during semantic analysis.

The analysis of representational information consists of two phases. The first phase, *independent representation analysis* (**IndependentRep**), is target language independent. This phase uses information in the prelude to resolve operation references in restrictions and type representation references in *For* clauses to operations and representations in the prelude. The result is an instance of **CandleRep** which contains implementation and target-specific information, yet was produced by target-independent algorithms. This **CandleRep** instance is a strict superset of **CandleSemantic**; the analysis does not discard information and therefore is incremental (the desirability of this property is discussed on page 313).

The *dependent representation analysis* phase (**DependentRep**) performs the remainder of the representational analysis. While the processing performed by semantic and independent representation analysis is target independent, that performed by dependent representation analysis is tailored to the specific targets supported by the implementation. This phase performs only two tasks. The first task is to compute the size of node, class, set, and sequence types in the invariant. The second task is to order node and class attributes for space efficiency using a graph coloring algorithm. This ordering may not be necessary for particular target languages. While small in scope, the analysis required can be complex and is closely tied to the target language and architecture. Again, information is not discarded during the analysis, since CANDLE is a strict superset of CandleRep.

CANDLE is the last IDL representation of the initial specification; from it the *code generator* phase (Backend) produces the data declarations, readers, writers, and definitions of internal operations in the target language(s). The code generator phase produces code in either C or Pascal for each process depending on the specified target language in the process declaration.

The Lister processes the error instances from each phase of the translator. The errors are collected and then sorted by source file and source position where the error occurred. The lister then generates a listing file with embedded error messages for each source file containing errors. The error messages also appear on the user's console.

14.2 The Prelude

While the IDL Specification is supplied by the *user* of the translator, the prelude is supplied by the *implementor* of the translator. Its function is similar to that of the standard prelude in Ada, or of the SYSTEM module in Modula-2. Briefly, the prelude defines all predefined types, target languages, operations, assertion definitions, and type representations supported by that particular translator. Some of these components are mandatory, such as the Integer type and a representation for Integers. The prelude, a textual file with a simple syntax, is processed by a prelude translator (either a program or a person) to produce an instance of the CandleContext, also called the "prelude"; the sense the term is intended should be easily discernible. This translation need be done only when the prelude is modified, not each time an IDL specification is compiled.

As discussed briefly in Section 14.1, the prelude provides implementation- and target-language information for use in semantic and independent representation analysis, allowing these phases to use target-independent algorithms yet generate target-specific information. A second benefit of using a prelude is that all portions (syntactic, semantic, and representational) of CANDLE are simplified and better structured when there is no artificial distinction imposed between provided types such as *Integer* and private types. These gains also apply to predefined operations (e.g., cre- ate) and assertion definitions (e.g., Head) that are nominally part of the language definition yet do not appear in CANDLE as distinguished entities. The prelude includes additional aspects unique to the implementation, including specific information on each target language supported. Again, we note the property of incrementality: the prelude is a strict superset of the standard prelude.

Bibliographic Notes

Basic compiler building techniques are discussed by Aho, Sethi, and Ullman [1986]. Lamb [1983] introduced the basic structure of an IDL translator. The IDL translator was used in a comprehensive example by Snodgrass and Shannon [1986].

Chapter 15

The Candle Structure

This chapter describes CANDLE, a *C*ommon *A*ttributed *N*otation for the interface *D*escription *L*anguag*E*. An instance of CANDLE is an intermediate representation of an IDL specification. CANDLE is a common structure on which many IDL tools, including the IDL translator, are based.

Section 15.1 outlines the design principles used in the development of CANDLE. The following section introduces CANDLE by way of an example. The example contains a simple structure and process declaration. Section 15.3 discusses the reasons for some of our design decisions. The design principles and rationale for CANDLE follow the guidelines given in Chapter 10. Indeed, CANDLE can be viewed as a case study in the applications of those guidelines.

Appendix F contains listings of the CANDLE structure and the various structures derived from CANDLE.

15.1 Design Principles

The CANDLE design was based on the experiences during development of previous versions of the IDL translator and on the principles used in the design of DIANA, a *D*escriptive *I*ntermediate *A*ttributed *N*otation for *A*da. The resulting design principles are discussed below.

- CANDLE *is concise.* Powerful constructs in IDL, such as classes, derivation, and refinement, are employed to avoid redundancy. This is a significant improvement over DIANA. As an extreme example, lx_srcpos is used 90 times in DIANA, while a similar attribute is used only twice in CANDLE.

- CANDLE *is representation independent.* Like DIANA, CANDLE is independent of any particular representation. This independence is ensured by using IDL to specify CANDLE. Refinement may be used to specify host specific aspects, such as source position and the representation of comments.

- CANDLE *has the characteristic of regularity of description and notation.* For example, when the value of an attribute is a collection of objects, it is expressed as a sequence or a set. If there need not be an implied ordering and if there are no duplicates, then it is specified to be a set. Otherwise, it is specified to be a sequence, and an assertion is provided that specifies the ordering. Finally, this attribute's name is plural (with a few exceptions). These considerations are applied to each collection of objects.

- CANDLE *is target language independent.* An instance of the CandleContext structure, the prelude, encapsulates all target language specific aspects of an implementation. Predefined types, attribute operations, target representations, and assertion definitions may be found in the prelude. The prelude may also be augmented with target-specific entities.

- *In* CANDLE, *lexical, syntactic, semantic, and representation information is captured.* At the same time, this information is partitioned through derivation.

  - The source position of every significant token is recorded, as is the exact form of all integers and rationals. Provision for storing comments and source file identification is included. CANDLE goes further than DIANA in this regard.

  - A subset of CANDLE, captured in the CandleSyntax structure declaration, contains only syntactic information extracted by standard parsing techniques. The complete structure of the original source specification is retained in CandleSyntax.

  - Another subset of CANDLE, captured in the CandleSymbolTable structure declaration, contains only semantic information computed by standard semantic analysis techniques: name resolution, type checking, and structure derivation and refinement.

  - A third subset of CANDLE, captured in the CandleContext structure declaration, contains only the information present in the prelude instance.

15.1. DESIGN PRINCIPLES

- CandleRep is a minor subset that incorporates information from the prelude, but does not include representation information specific to the target language and not in the prelude.

- Finally, CANDLE includes sufficient information about the runtime representation of the invariant and port structures of each process and each external representation to generate readers and writers, and to display instances residing in main memory or on external storage.

- CANDLE *is efficient to implement.* Because CANDLE is described using IDL notation, an implementation of CANDLE can be automatically produced by the IDL translator. The translator provides alternative representations, for greater efficiency. Node references, rather than nodes, are copied whenever possible during refinement and derivation, thereby achieving a substantial space savings, since pointers require much less space than the nodes they reference. When possible, semantic information is placed in a syntactic node, eliminating the need to create a new semantic node.

- CANDLE *is incremental.* CandleSyntax is the core structure, and contains only syntactic information. The information in CandleSemantic appears in CandleRep or CANDLE as additional attributes and nodes to those in CandleSyntax. Similarly, the representation information also appears in CANDLE as additional attributes and nodes. Finally, when structures are derived or refined from other structures, the CANDLE instance of the source structure need not be modified when creating the CANDLE instance of the target structure. Because it is incremental, CANDLE is amenable to separate compilation and representation on write-once media such as optical disks.

- CANDLE *is useful for many different applications.* Because CANDLE is used for many tools other than the IDL translator, ease of processing for other applications was considered in its design. In particular, it is possible to

    - regenerate the input source file(s) for a specification with complete fidelity via the CANDLEWALK tool (see Chapter 16).

    - generate a pretty-printed IDL specification that is semantically equivalent to the input specification, also via the CANDLEWALK tool.

    - generate an expanded form for a specification that shows the results of derivation, refinement, and propagation.

- identify the line(s) in the source file(s) that contain the declaration of every attribute, node, class, definition, declaration, and assertion, as well as the source position of structures and processes as a whole. If an attribute is inherited, then the declaration in the parent class is also identifiable. This information is declared in the `CandlePos` structure.

- determine the source of every attribute in every node of the invariant and port structures, as well as the elements of sets and sequences.

- determine the position and extent of every attribute in every node.

- provide derived forms of CANDLE that are tailored to specific applications. In particular, a parse tree form (`CandleSyntax`) and a target-language-independent form containing semantic information but not semantic nor runtime representation information (`CandleSymbolTable`) of CANDLE are available. The use of the IDL translator simplifies the derivation of other forms that may be needed.

- provide tradeoffs between size and processing speed when using CANDLE. This again is aided by the IDL translator which allows choices of particular implementations.

- CANDLE *contains a single definition of each IDL entity.* Each definable entity in IDL notation is represented by a node in CANDLE. This allows all information about an entity to be determined at one definition point. When aspects of an IDL entity may be specified in separate places in the IDL source, separate *syntactic* and *semantic* entities are employed. A syntactic entity encodes each place in the source where some aspect is specified, referring to the single semantic entity, where all the semantic information is collected. If there is only one definition point, the entity plays both roles (`Attribute` is an example). As in DIANA, the semantic entities are equivalent to entries in a dictionary or symbol table of a conventional compiler, and are thus found in `CandleSymbolTable`. Entities are discussed further in Section 15.3.

- CANDLE *has a form that can be communicated between cooperating processes.* Like all IDL structures, CANDLE has all the external forms, including ASCII, that are supported by an implementation.

- CANDLE *contains only information typically discovered in syntactic, semantic, and representation analysis.* CANDLE is constructed by

15.2. CONSTRUCTING A CANDLE INSTANCE 315

typical parsing and semantic analysis phases of a compiler. In general, if information could be easily computed (i.e., in a single pass across the instance), it was omitted from CANDLE.

15.2 Constructing a Candle Instance

We have seen *what* CANDLE can do for us, but not *how* it does it. A CANDLE instance describes an IDL structure. In this section, we walk through the process of constructing an instance of the CANDLE structure for the following simple IDL specification.

```
-- a structure declaration
Structure ExampleStructure Root X Is
    X ::= Y |Z;
    X => a: Integer;
    Y => b: X;
    Z => ;
    For X.a Use Representation 16 Bits;
End

-- a process declaration
Process ExampleProcess Is
    Target Language C;
    Pre INex: ExampleStructure;
End
```

15.2.1 The CandleSyntax Instance

The specification is first run through the parser of the IDL translator producing an instance of the CandleSyntax structure whose basic form is shown in Figure 15.1. Line numbers in *italics* are added in this figure so that we may refer to particular parts of the instance. The CandleSyntax instance encodes the syntax tree of the input source, and is a subset of the complete CANDLE instance given in Figures 15.19–15.23 starting on page 338 and illustrated graphically in Figures 15.17 and 15.18 on pages 336–337. The reader is encouraged to compare each instance fragment (such as that given in Figure 15.1) with the entire instance and with its graphical illustration. To aid in this comparison, the starting line number (and label, if available) of each node in the instance are given in the figure (nodes are numbered left-to-right and bottom-to-top on the page). Some labels appear in circles, when it was inconvenient to draw the arc to the node directly. Figure 15.1 references `StructureEntity` node L2, which may be found in the complete instance on line *9* of Figure 15.19 and at the bottom left-hand corner of Figure 15.17. The graphical illustration contains all the nodes and attributes of the CANDLE instance except the `lex_information` attributes on lines *10–15, 165–167,* and *199.*

Before delving into the details of this IDL instance, let us examine its coarse aspects, first examining the line figure (15.17–15.18), and then the ERL instance. The line figure is partitioned into a syntactic portion (the bottom half of the page) and a semantic and representation portion (the top half). Only `lex_` and `syn_` references reside in the syntactic portion. This portion is in the shape of a tree, growing upwards, and rooted at `compilationUnit`. This portion is an instance of CANDLESYNTAX, and is an abstract syntax tree, containing 32 nodes.

The top portion contains all the semantic entities generated during semantic and representation analysis. Included are six `Class` nodes, four `Atomic` nodes (all from the Prelude and all various representations of the `Integer` basic type), four `descriptor` nodes, and 10 miscellaneous nodes. These semantic entities are fairly evenly divided between those associated with the originally specified `ExampleStructure` structure and those associated with the automatically computed `IDLDefaultInv` invariant structure for `ExampleProcess`. The semantic portion serves the role of a symbol table, and is definitely not a tree.

We now examine the ERL instance, shown in Figures 15.19–15.23. The input IDL specification is 13 lines long, or 230 characters; 2 of these lines are comments. The ASCII external representation of the CANDLE instance occupies 287 lines, or 7574 characters, after formatting. This instance contains a total of 75 nodes (56 attributed and 19 unattributed), 241 attributes, 35 sets, 28 sequences, 91 set or sequence elements, and 86 strings, of which 46 are unique and contain a total of 346 characters.

On first glance, it appears that the CANDLE instance is excessively large and inefficient, being over 30 times larger than the original input. This negative impression is incorrect, for several reasons. First, the CANDLE instance should be somewhat larger than the original specification, because more information is explicit. For instance, "X" is used nine times in the specification; that this name in all cases refers to the same class in `ExampleStructure` is represented explicitly in the instance. Indeed, the usefulness of the CANDLE instance is directly a result of this easily accessible information.

Second, the CANDLE instance, when represented in the ERL, is longer in order to make it readable. To ascertain the magnitude of this effect, we compare the information content, as indicated by the size of the instance in main memory, with the size of the instance in ASCII in a file. The

15.2. CONSTRUCTING A CANDLE INSTANCE

(static) average node size, given in Section 15.4, is 98.5 bits. If we assume that the dynamic average node size approximates the static average, then the 75 nodes occupy 925 bytes. A sequence member requires 64 bits, so sequences and sets occupy 728 bytes, assuming all sequences and sets are implemented as linked lists. Strings require another 1034 bytes, for a total of somewhat less than 2700 bytes. Hence, the in-memory representation is about twelve times longer than the input specification, while containing complete syntactic, semantic, and representational information about the specified structures and processes. A reasonable binary encoding would probably require about as much space as the in-memory representation. The ASCII ERL adds a factor of 3. This bulk should be considered as an aid to comprehension and textual processing; other representations can reduce the space significantly, in the case of in-memory and binary encodings, and can eliminate I/O costs, by merging multiple passes into one program, as described in Section 9.7.

The CandleSyntax instance is the first portion of the CANDLE instance to be constructed. It encodes the parse tree of the IDL specification, and uses the techniques discussed in Section 10.2. In particular, each node of the parse tree is represented with an IDL node; references to children of the parse tree node are represented by attributes in the IDL node that reference other IDL nodes. In this presentation of the CandleSyntax instance, we work our way down the tree, examining individual nodes or small subtrees rooted at a node. The full syntax tree can be viewed on the bottom half of Figures 15.17 and 15.18.

The CandleSyntax instance contains one StructureEntity and one ProcessEntity in the *syntactic attribute* syn_body of the compilation-Unit, as shown in Figure 15.1. The *lexical attribute* lex_information on line *3*, is of the private type LexInfo, represented externally in the UNC implementation as a sequence of values of type *String*. Other representations of lexical information, such as storing comments in the nodes where they occur, or storing only the source position of relevant constructs, are certainly possible; this particular representation is discussed because it is the one implemented in IDLC.

The LexInfo sequence contains the lexical information such as comments and white space that appears outside structure and process declarations. In the example, the first element in the sequence contains a comment and a newline character (shown as "~J") since this information appears before the first declaration in the file. A new line and a comment occur between the structure and process declarations, and a single new line appears after the process declaration. Lexical attributes are computed during the lexical phase of the parser and have a prefix of "lex_". Syntactic attributes are computed during the syntactic phase of the parser and have

```
  1     -- structure Candle
  2     compilationUnit[
  3         lex_information <
  4             "-- a structure declaration~J"
  5             "~J~J-- a process declaration~J"
  6             "~J" >;
  7         rep_comptimestamp 1234567;
  8         syn_body <
  9             L2:StructureEntity[···]
164             ProcessEntity[···]
286         >;
287     ]#
```

Figure 15.1: The compilationUnit

a prefix of "syn_". A detailed discussion of the computation and use of lexical and syntactic attributes is given in Chapter 16.

Both StructureEntity and ProcessEntity are examples of *syntactic entities*. A syntactic entity is created during the syntactic analysis phase of the translator. During later phases, information (semantic and representational) is added to this existing entity instead of creating a new entity to hold the union of the syntactic, semantic, and representational information.

All lexical and syntactic information about ExampleStructure is contained in the StructureEntity shown in Figure 15.2. The lexical information is contained in the attributes lex_name and lex_information. The latter sequence contains lexical information such as keywords, punctuation, comments, and white space that appears between tokens whose lexical information is recorded in other attributes of CandleSyntax. In this example, the token identifiers "ExampleStructure" and "X" are recorded in the attributes StructureEntity.lex_name and StructureEntity.syn_root.lex_name, respectively. Therefore the first element in the lex_information sequence contains all characters before "ExampleStructure" and the second element of the sequence contains all characters between "ExampleStructure" and "X". Keywords are recorded because their case can vary and because we wanted to be able to regenerate the source with absolute fidelity. Relaxing this requirement would reduce the space occupied by the lex_information attribute, perhaps substantially. Let us again emphasize that other representations of LexInfo are possible. While this particular representation is costlier in terms of space than other representations not meeting the fidelity constraint, it is

15.2. CONSTRUCTING A CANDLE INSTANCE

nevertheless somewhat less expensive that initially thought. Each unique string is stored only once. In the absence of comments, the same strings (e.g., ";~J   ", " ", ": ", and ";~JEnd") appear repeatedly; these strings are only stored once, and multiple references are used. Secondly there exist techniques that reduce the storage requirements of the standard cases (standard spelling and no comments) to zero; these representations affect the in-memory and binary representations, but not the ASCII ERL.

The syntactic information is contained in the attributes lex_name, syn_root, syn_from, syn_refines, and syn_body. The syn_root attribute contains a reference to the root of the structure if the Root clause is specified or Void if not. In this example, the root *is* specified and references the type X. Therefore the attribute type for syn_root on line *17* is a NamedTypeRef. The syn_from attribute on line *18* contains an empty sequence since the structure is not derived from any structures. Similarly, the syn_refines attribute on line *19* contains Void because the structure is not refined from any structure (syn_refines is not a sequence because a structure can be refined from at most one other structure). The last syntactic attribute, syn_body beginning on line *20*, is a sequence of structureStatements containing one subclassProduction, three attributeProductions, and one attributeRep.

The subclassProduction in Figure 15.3 has two syntactic attributes, syn_class and syn_subclasses. The syn_class attribute on line *22* is a reference to the class X. References to classes, nodes, privates, or basic types are shown by NamedTypeRefs. A NamedTypeRef contains the name of a class or private. We saw another NamedTypeRef in the StructureEntity itself: a reference to the root type on line *17* in Figure 15.2. The syn_subclasses attribute beginning on line *23* is a sequence containing references to the members of X. These members are Y and Z. The white space occurring in this subclassProduction, as well as the other structure statements, is collected in the lex_information attribute of the StructureEntity.

The attributeProductions have two syntactic attributes, syn_class and syn_attributes. As with subclassProductions, syn_class is a reference to a class, in this example X (line *30* of Figure 15.4). At this point in the processing, the IDL translator doesn't yet know that the "X" in this statement is the same "X" encountered in the subclassProduction of Figure 15.3. This correspondence is made later during the semantic analysis phase. syn_attributes is a sequence containing the specified attributes of X. In this example, the attributeProduction contains one Attribute beginning on line *32*.

An Attribute contains one syntactic attribute, syn_type, referencing a type. In this example, the referenced type is the IDL basic type *Integer*

```
 9      L2:StructureEntity[
10          lex_information <
11          "Structure " " Root" " " " Is~J        " " ::=" " |"
12          ";~J         " " =>" ": " ";~J         " " =>" ": "
13          ";~J         " " =>;~J        For "
14          "." " Use " " " " " " ";~JEnd"
15          >;
16          lex_name "ExampleStructure";
17          syn_root NamedTypeRef[lex_name "X"; sem_entity L1^];
18          syn_from <>;
19          syn_refines Void;
20          syn_body <
21              subclassProduction[···]
29              attributeProduction[···]
72              attributeProduction[···]
88              attributeProduction[···]
93              attributeRep[···]
115         >;
163     ]
```

Figure 15.2: The StructureEntity

```
21      subclassProduction[
22          syn_class NamedTypeRef[lex_name "X";···];
23          syn_subclasses <
24              NamedTypeRef[lex_name "Y";···]
25              NamedTypeRef[lex_name "Z";···]
26          >;
28      ]
```

Figure 15.3: The subclassProduction

15.2. CONSTRUCTING A CANDLE INSTANCE

```
29   attributeProduction[
30       syn_class NamedTypeRef[lex_name "X";...];
31       syn_attributes <
32           L5:Attribute[
33               lex_name "a";
34               syn_type L7:NamedTypeRef[lex_name "Integer";...]
68           ]
69       >;
71   ]
```

Figure 15.4: An attributeProduction

(line *34* in Figure 15.4). At this point in the processing, the basic types are not treated any differently from user-defined types.

There are three syntactic attributes in the structure statement attributeRep shown below.

```
93   attributeRep[
94       syn_class NamedTypeRef[lex_name "X";...];
95       syn_attribute AttributeRef[lex_name "a";...];
96       syn_rep RepRef[
97           syn_id <
98               nameToken[lex_name "Representation"]
99               integerToken[lex_externalform "16";...]
100              nameToken[lex_name "Bits"]
101          >;
112      ];
114  ]
```

The attribute syn_rep is a reference to a representation. This reference contains a sequence of tokens naming the representation.

All lexical and syntactic information about the process ExampleProcess is contained in the ProcessEntity, shown in Figure 15.5. The lexical information between recorded tokens, as with the StructureEntity, is stored in the attribute lex_information. The syn_invariant attribute contains a reference to a structure that will be used as the invariant structure for the process if the *Inv* clause is specified or will be Void if the *Inv* clause is not specified. In this example, there is no invariant structure specified (line *169*). The syn_refines attribute on line *170* contains Void since the process is not refined from any processes.

The targetStmt, shown in Figure 15.6, has one syntactic attribute

```
164 ProcessEntity[
165     lex_information <
166         "Process " " Is~J        Target " " " ";~J        Pre
167         ": " ";~JEnd">;
168     lex_name "ExampleProcess";
169     syn_invariant Void;
170     syn_refines Void;
171     syn_body <
172         targetStmt[···]
180         portDefinition[···]
193     >;
285 ]
```

Figure 15.5: The ProcessEntity

```
172 targetStmt[
173     syn_id <
174         nameToken[lex_name "Language"]
175         nameToken[lex_name "C"]
176     >;
179 ]
```

Figure 15.6: The targetStmt

syn_id containing a sequence of tokens identifying the target language to be used for the process.

The portDefinition, shown in Figure 15.7, contains two syntactic attributes, syn_portType and syn_ports. The first syntactic attribute specifies the type (input or output) of the port. The second attribute is a sequence containing the ports that are of this type. Each Port contains a name and a reference to a structure associated with the port.

15.2.2 The CandleSemantic Instance

The Semantic Analysis phase reads in an instance of the CandleSyntax structure and produces an instance of the CandleSemantic structure. The CandleSemantic instance is a superset of the CandleSyntax instance since attributes are added, not deleted.

Six semantic attributes are added to the StructureEntity. These additional attributes are shown on lines *116–162* in Figure 15.8. The sem_root

15.2. CONSTRUCTING A CANDLE INSTANCE

```
180   portDefinition[
181     syn_portType PrePort;
182     syn_ports <
183       L19:Port[
184         lex_name "INex";
185         syn_data StructureRef[
186           lex_name "ExampleStructure";
187         ];
192     ]
193     >;
195   ]
```

Figure 15.7: The portDefinition

attribute points to the type referenced by the syn_root attribute. The NamedTypeRef of the syn_root attribute has an additional attribute sem_entity that also points to this type. Types are discussed later in this section. The attributes sem_assertions, sem_definitions, and sem_types contain sets of the *syntactic entity* Assertion, and of the *semantic entities* Definition and TypeEntity, respectively, that are defined in this structure. A *semantic entity* is an entity that is created during the semantic analysis phases from several constructs in the syntax. For example, a Class entity is created from a collection of attributeProductions and classProductions. The sem_assertions and sem_definitions sets are empty since the structure did not contain any assertions or definitions. The sem_types set contains four types: three Classes and one Atomic. The attribute sem_duplicate contains a boolean value indicating an error condition if this structure is a duplicate structure. In this example, there is no other structure in the specification with the same name. The final semantic attribute sem_corrections contains a sequence of corrections added to make the structure semantically correct. In this example, no corrections were needed.

Classes are created for X, Y, and Z using information in the attributeProductions and subclassProductions with the same syn_class reference. For example, one subclassProduction and one attributeProduction (lines *21-71*) were used to create the Class for X. The NamedTypeRefs referencing X have an additional sem_entity attribute that points to the semantic entity Class for X (Figure 15.9).

The sem_copiedfrom attribute for the Class X has the value Void since the Class is not copied from another structure. The Attributes listed in

```
9     L2:StructureEntity[
17        syn_root NamedTypeRef[lex_name "X";sem_entity L1^];
116       sem_root L1^;
117       sem_assertions { };
118       sem_definitions { };
119       sem_duplicate FALSE;
120       sem_corrections <>;
121       sem_types {
122           L1:Class[···]
135           L3:Class[···]
148           L4:Class[···]
161           L6^
162       };
163   ]
```

Figure 15.8: The Semantic Attributes of StructureEntity

the sem_allattributes sequence are references to the Attributes given in attributeProductions for X. The Classes contained in the sem_subclasses set are those Classes referenced in the syn_subclasses sequence of the subclassProductions for X. In this example, there are two subclasses for X. Finally, the sem_ancestors set contains all the ancestors of a Class. X has no ancestors since it is not referenced in the syn_subclasses sequence of any subclassProduction in the structure.

The Atomic (L4^) contained in the sem_types set of the structure (see Figure 15.8) is from the prelude. The prelude provides semantic entities for the IDL basic types Integer, Boolean, String, and Rational. The NamedTypeRef that references Integer in Figure 15.10 contains a semantic attribute sem_entity pointing to the semantic entity Atomic for Integer.

Attributes contain one semantic attribute, sem_copiedfrom. The value of this attribute for Attribute a in Figure 15.10 is Void since a was not copied from another structure.

The references in the attributeRep statement (shown in Figure 15.11) each have a semantic attribute sem_entity pointing to the particular entity referenced. The AttributeRef on line 95 has a sem_entity field pointing to the Attribute entity for a shown in Figure 15.10. The NamedTypeRef on line 94 has a sem_entity field pointing to the Class entity for X shown in Figure 15.9. The attributeRep statement is further processed in the representation analysis phase.

15.2. CONSTRUCTING A CANDLE INSTANCE

```
21   subclassProduction[
22       syn_class NamedTypeRef[lex_name "X";sem_entity L1^];
23       syn_subclasses <
24           NamedTypeRef[lex_name "Y"; sem_entity L3^]
25           NamedTypeRef[lex_name "Z"; sem_entity L4^]
26       >;
33       sem_duplicate FALSE;
68   ]
29   attributeProduction[
30       syn_class NamedTypeRef[lex_name "X";sem_entity L1^];
31       syn_attributes <
32           L5:Attribute[
33               lex_name "a";
68           ]
69       >;
70       sem_duplicate FALSE;
71   ]
122  L1:Class[
123      sem_name "X";
124      sem_copiedfrom Void;
125      sem_allattributes <L5^>;
126      sem_subclasses {L3^ L4^};
127      sem_ancestors { };
134  ]
```

Figure 15.9: Creating the semantic entity Class

```
32   L5:Attribute[
33       lex_name "a";
34       syn_type L7:NamedTypeRef[lex_name "Integer";sem_entity L8^];
35       sem_copiedfrom Void;
36       sem_duplicate FALSE;
68   ]
43   L8:Atomic[
44       sem_name "Integer";
45       sem_copiedfrom Void;
52   ]
```

Figure 15.10: The Atomic for "*Integer*"

```
 93  attributeRep[
 94     syn_class NamedTypeRef[lex_name "X"; sem_entity L1^];
 95     syn_attribute AttributeRef[lex_name "a";sem_entity L5^];
 96     syn_rep RepRef[
 97        syn_id <
 98           nameToken[lex_name "Representation"]
 99           integerToken[lex_externalform "16"; sem_type L8^]
100           nameToken[lex_name "Bits"]
101        >;
112     ];
113     sem_duplicate FALSE;
114  ]
```

Figure 15.11: The `attributeRep` statement

Seven semantic attributes are added to `ProcessEntity` in Figure 15.12. Several of the semantic attributes correspond to those of the same name for structures; others are unique to processes. The `sem_ports` set contains `Port` entities named in `portDefinition` statements. This set contains the `INex` port from the `portDefinition` in Figure 15.7. The fifth semantic attribute, `sem_target`, points to the `TargetEntity` in the prelude that is referenced by the `targetStmt`. The `sem_entity` field of the `targetStmt` shown in Figure 15.6 also points to this `TargetEntity`. The `syn_id` sequence of the `targetStmt` must match the `sem_id` sequence of the `TargetEntity` node.

The `sem_invariant` attribute contains a `StructureEntity`, created during semantic analysis, which includes all semantic information in the port structures and specified invariant (if any) of the process. All the lexical and syntactic attributes of the new structure are set to empty. In this example, the invariant structure shown below need only contain the semantic information in the structure `ExampleStructure` in Figure 15.8 since this structure is the only port specified and there is no invariant specified. All assertions, definitions, types, and corrections of `ExampleStructure` are added to the new invariant structure.

Each `Class` in the invariant structure is a copy of the corresponding `Class` in `ExampleStructure`. For example, a `Class` for X would be created and information from the corresponding class in `ExampleStructure` (Figure 15.9) would be copied. The newly created class is shown in Figure 15.13.

Each `Attribute` in the new class is a copy from the corresponding `Attribute` in the original class (Figure 15.14). For example, the `Attribute`

15.2. CONSTRUCTING A CANDLE INSTANCE

```
164   ProcessEntity[
168       lex_name "ExampleProcess";
197       sem_invariant StructureEntity[
198           lex_name "IDLDefaultInv";
199           lex_information <>;
200           syn_root Void;
201           syn_from <>;
202           syn_refines Void;
203           syn_body <>;
204           sem_assertions { };
205           sem_definitions { };
206           sem_root Void;
207           sem_types {
208               L11:Class[···]
232               L12:Class[···]
261               L17:Class[···]
274               L6^
275           };
276           sem_duplicate FALSE;
277           sem_corrections <>;
278       ];
279       sem_assertions { };
280       sem_definitions { };
281       sem_ports {L19^};
282       sem_duplicate FALSE;
283       sem_target L20:TargetEntity[sem_id <"C">];
284       sem_corrections <>;
285   ]
```

Figure 15.12: The "ExampleProcess" ProcessEntity

```
208   L11:Class[
209       sem_name "X";
210       sem_copiedfrom L1^;
211       sem_allattributes <
212           L18:Attribute[···]>;
223       sem_subclasses {L12^ L17^};
224       sem_ancestors { };
231   ]
```

Figure 15.13: The Class "X" in the Invariant

```
212 L18:Attribute[
213     lex_name "a";
214     syn_type L7^;
215     sem_copiedfrom L5^;
216     sem_duplicate FALSE;
221 ]
```

Figure 15.14: The Attribute "a" in the Invariant

for a in the new class is copied from the Attribute a in the original class. The values of the syntactic attributes of the new Attribute are references to the values of the syntactic attributes of the original Attribute.

The Atomics in the invariant structure are copies of the Atomics in the copied-from structure only if they do not represent prelude types. In this example, the Atomic is for the prelude type Integer and so a reference to the Atomic is added to the type sequence rather than creating a new copy. This insures that there is only one Integer entity in all structures.

In summary, three kinds of semantic attributes were added during the semantic analysis phase. The attribute sem_entity was added to all references (NamedTypeRef, AttributeRef, StructureRef, etc.) to resolve the name to the named entity. Attributes containing collections of entities such as sem_definitions and sem_assertions for structures and processes were added to group all corresponding entities. As a special case of this kind, attributes containing single entities such as sem_invariant and sem_target for processes were added. Finally, the attributes sem_duplicate and sem_corrections were added to record the error conditions of duplicate structures and processes. In addition, semantic entities such as Class were created during semantic analysis.

15.2.3 The CandleRep Instance

The representation analysis phases augment a CandleSemantic instance with representation information resulting in a CandleRep instance and then a CANDLE instance. There are two phases for representation analysis. The first phase computes *target-dependent information* using *target-independent algorithms* and outputs the CandleRep instance. The purpose of this first phase is to compute all representation information possible only using information in the prelude and therefore using generalized algorithms that will work for any target language.

For each Atomic in each structure, four representation attributes are added: rep_name, rep_internalType, rep_externalType, and rep_-

15.2. CONSTRUCTING A CANDLE INSTANCE

allowedOps. For Atomics representing IDL basic types these attributes are precalculated in the prelude. For Atomics representing user-defined types, these attributes are calculated during the representation analysis phases. The representation attributes precalculated for the IDL basic type *Integer* are shown below.

```
43    L8:Atomic[
44        sem_name "Integer";
45        sem_copiedfrom Void;
46        rep_name "";
47        rep_size 0;
48        rep_alignment 0;
49        rep_internalType Void;
50        rep_externalType Predefined;
51        rep_allowedOps { };
52    ]
```

The representation for *Integer* is incomplete since the attribute rep_internalType contains the value Void and the attributes rep_size and rep_alignment contain the value 0. In general, certain representations will only be complete when they are contained in invariant structures of processes that have a target specified. Specifically, the size and internal representation of integers cannot be determined unless the target language, operating system, and machine on which they are represented are known.

For each Class in each structure, three representation attributes, rep_name, rep_enumerated, and rep_allowedOps are calculated; an example follows.

```
208   L11:Class[
209       sem_name "X";
210       sem_copiedfrom L1^;
225       rep_name "X";
226       rep_enumerated FALSE;
227       rep_allowedOps {ClassOperation[rep_name "typeof"]};
231   ]
```

The value of the rep_name attribute is the same as sem_name unless the name conflicts with one of the target keywords, which are listed in the prelude. The value of the rep_enumerated attribute is true if the Class should be represented as an enumerated type, that is, if a representation clause of the form

    For ⟨class⟩ *Use Representation Enumerated*;

is used for the class. The rep_allowedOps sequence contains the valid operations for the class. The prelude specifies the default set which can then be reduced using restrict statements in a process.

Attributes also have information calculated in this phase: rep_name, rep_descriptor, and rep_allowedOps. The representation attributes for attribute a in Class X in ExampleStructure are shown below.

```
212 L18:Attribute[
213     lex_name "a";
214     syn_type L7^;
215     sem_copiedfrom L5^;
216     sem_duplicate FALSE;
217     rep_name "a";
218     rep_descriptor descriptor[rep_type L6^;
219     ];
220     rep_allowedOps { }
221 ]
```

Recall from Figure 15.10 that the syn_type field of Attribute a contained a NamedTypeRef referencing the IDL basic type *Integer* (L7). Also recall from Figure 15.11 that a has an attributeRep referencing it from the statement

For X.a Use Representation 16 Bits;

The independent representation analysis phase uses this information to change the representation from *Integer* to a new related type represented with 16 bits. Since *Integer* is a type in the prelude, all allowable representations and their relationships are also contained in the prelude. The prelude type represented with 16 bits is an Atomic named bits16, shown below.

```
102 Atomic[
103     sem_name "bits16";
104     sem_copiedfrom L8^;
105     rep_name "";
108     rep_internalType Void;
109     rep_externalType Predefined;
110     rep_allowedOps { };
111 ];
```

The rep_entity field of the associated RepRef is set to this Atomic for bits16 (Figure 15.15).

15.2. CONSTRUCTING A CANDLE INSTANCE

```
 93    attributeRep[
 94        syn_class NamedTypeRef[lex_name "X"; sem_entity L1^];
 95        syn_attribute AttributeRef[lex_name "a";sem_entity L5^];
 96        syn_rep RepRef[
 97            syn_id <...>;
102            rep_entity Atomic[...];
112        ];
114    ]
```

Figure 15.15: An `attributeRep`

The target clauses of a process cause an automatic refinement of all types in the invariant structure during the representation analysis phase. For example, in this example the `Atomic bits16` would be refined to the `Atomic short` since these are the corresponding types in the C target language. This automatic refinement is also calculated using the prelude, and is discussed in Section 15.3.7.

The remainder of the analysis is done in the dependent representation analysis phase. The `CandleRep` instance is communicated between the representation analysis phases.

15.2.4 The CANDLE Instance

The second phase of representation analysis computes target-dependent information such as the size and alignment of a type and the offset of attributes. This computation must often be done with separate algorithms for each target language supported. This phase augments the `CandleRep` instance with additional attributes, creating a CANDLE instance.

One attribute, `rep_comptimestamp`, is computed for the `compilationUnit` which is the root of the CANDLE instance. The type of this attribute is the private type `TimestampType`; it records the time the CANDLE instance was created. This time is also recorded in any code generated from this instance. Tools such as debuggers can then ascertain that a particular CANDLE instance does indeed correspond to a particular executable file.

For each `TypeEntity` in each structure (i.e., `Atomic`, `Class`, `SetOf`, and `SeqOf`), two representation attributes are computed, `rep_size` and `rep_alignment`. In general, these are nonzero only if the target language, operating system, and machine on which they are represented are known.

For `Atomics` representing IDL basic types, the `rep_size` and `rep_alignment` attributes are precalculated in the prelude for each valid target. For example, the representation attributes precalculated for *Integer* with a representation of 16 bits in the C target language are shown below.

```
39    L6:Atomic[
40        sem_name "short";
41        sem_copiedfrom Atomic[···];
60        rep_name "short";
61        rep_size 16;
62        rep_alignment 16;
63        rep_internalType Package[rep_name "ctype"];
64        rep_externalType Predefined;
65        rep_allowedOps { };
66    ];
```

For Atomics representing user-defined types, rep_size and rep_alignment are specified directly using the following representation clauses.

For ⟨atomic⟩ Use Size ⟨integer⟩ { Bits | Bytes };
For ⟨atomic⟩ Use Alignment ⟨integer⟩ { Bits | Bytes };

These values of these two attributes can also be stated indirectly by specifying an internal type with a known size and alignment.

For each Class, SetOf, and SeqOf in each structure, rep_size and rep_alignment are computed using separate algorithms for each target supported. For example, the size of a Class in C is the size of the largest member of the union that represents the class, which is the size of a word pointer on the target operating system and machine. These attributes calculated for the Class X on Unix operating on a DEC VAX 11/780 are shown below.

```
208   L11:Class[
209       sem_name "X";
225       rep_name "X";
226       rep_enumerated FALSE;
227       rep_allowedOps {ClassOperation[rep_name "typeof"]};
228       rep_size 32;
229       rep_alignment 32;
230       rep_typeID 0;
231   ]
```

Each Class also has an additional attribute, rep_typeID, calculated in the second representation analysis phase. As with rep_size and rep_alignment, rep_typeID is computed with separate algorithms for each target supported. In the C target, the rep_typeID for each class in a structure is assigned successive odd integers if the class are enumerated (i.e., rep_enumerated is set to true) and successive even integers otherwise.

15.2. CONSTRUCTING A CANDLE INSTANCE

The descriptor contained in the rep_descriptor field of each Attribute has an additional attribute, rep_offset, added during this phase. In the previous phase, the rep_type field was set to the TypeEntity referenced in syn_type. In this phase, the rep_type can be modified to contain several levels of indirection of descriptors before finally referencing the TypeEntity.

The rep_descriptor field of the Attribute is necessary to provide complete information as to where the attribute resides. In C each node is represented with a single *struct* and hence the indirection path contains a single element. Each rep_descriptor.rep_offset is an integer containing the offset for the corresponding attribute in the *struct*. Each rep_descriptor.rep_type contains the TypeEntity referenced in the syn_type field or to a refined type via a representation clause. The representation attributes for Attribute a in class X in ExampleStructure are shown below.

```
212  L18:Attribute[
213      lex_name "a";
214      syn_type L7^;
215      sem_copiedfrom L5^;
217      rep_name "a";
218      rep_descriptor descriptor[rep_type L6^;
219          rep_offset 32];
220      rep_allowedOps { };
221  ]
```

Since a node is represented in Pascal with multiple *records* (one for attributes of each ancestor class and one for the direct attributes of the node), multiple descriptors are needed. To access an attribute via a value of a node type, index into the node record, follow the indicated pointer(s) until the correct class record is found, then index directly to access the attribute. For a value of a class type, the path will be shorter. For Pascal, the Attribute a in node Z would be represented as shown in Figure 15.16. To access the value of a given a reference to node z, access the pointer at offset 32 bits, and index off of it by 32 bits to obtain the 16 bit value.

The ASCII external representation of the CANDLE instance, as just described, follows. The label numbers, indentation, and line breaks were modified to make the instance more readable. The line numbers were added after the instance had been generated. Figures 15.17 and 15.18 illustrate the instance graphically.

```
Attribute[
    rep_name "a";
    rep_descriptor[
        rep_offset 32;
        rep_type rep_descriptor[
            rep_offset 32;
            rep_type Atomic[
                rep_name "short";
                rep_size 16;
                rep_alignment 16;
            ];
        ];
    ];
]
```

Figure 15.16: The `Attribute` a with Representation Information for Pascal

15.3 Rationale

We have now seen the *what* (Section 15.1) and *how* (Section 15.2) of CANDLE; this section answers the *why* of CANDLE. Specifically, we will move through the CANDLE structure definition, peering closely at the nooks and crannies of this imposing edifice.

15.3.1 Component Structures

The derivation graph for the component structures of CANDLE is shown in Figure 15.24. An arrow from structure A to structure B is read as "structure B is derived from structure A by adding information." A dotted line from structure A to structure B is read "structure B is derived from structure A by removing information via Without statements." Hence, information (e.g., nodes, attributes) is both added and removed from the CANDLE structure to obtain the `CandleContext` structure.

15.3.2 Stylistic Conventions

CANDLE follows the following stylistic conventions to improve the readability of the structure.

- All entities (e.g., `Assertion`, `Attribute`, `Control`) and entity references (e.g., `AssertRef`, `AttributeRef`) are capitalized. All other nodes are not.

15.3. RATIONALE   335

- There are five kinds of attributes defined in CANDLE, *lexical, syntactic, semantic, representation,* and *prelude*. All attributes are prefixed according to when they are determined (the assumed architecture is shown in Figure 14.1). For example, SourcePosition attributes have a prefix of "lex_" since the position is calculated during lexical analysis of the source. Syntactic attributes are prefixed with "syn_". Semantic attributes are prefixed with "sem_". The representation attributes calculated in both subphases of representation analysis are prefixed with "rep_". Finally, the attributes unique to the prelude (Section 14.2) are prefixed with "pre_". Underscores are used only for prefixing.

- Most attributes with a set or sequence type have plural names (e.g., StructureEntity.sem_types). The few attributes with a set or sequence type that do not have plural names instead have names denoting a grouping of elements (e.g., StructureEntity.syn_body).

- Each group of statements in CandleSyntax is preceded by comments giving the syntax, if any, of the statements and are followed by assertions stating the semantics of the statements. The assertion names follow the same naming scheme described above for attributes.

15.3.3 Class Hierarchies

Classes are used throughout the CANDLE structures. There are several reasons for using classes, as discussed in detail in Section 10.3. First, grouping related nodes in a class and putting common information via attributes in the class eliminates redundancy, a common source of errors. Second, even when attribute propagation is not used, grouping related nodes into a class improves readability of the structure by providing additional semantic information in the specification. Third, classes are needed for attributes whose types can be one of several node types. A special case is an optional clause in the syntax. For example, a root of a structure need not be specified, hence the type of the attribute syn_root is the class TypeRefOrVoid containing the two members: TypeRef and Void. Because these reasons may overlap arbitrarily, the class-subclass structure need not be strictly hierarchical. The remainder of this section describes the main class hierarchies in CANDLE, pointing out the rationale for each.

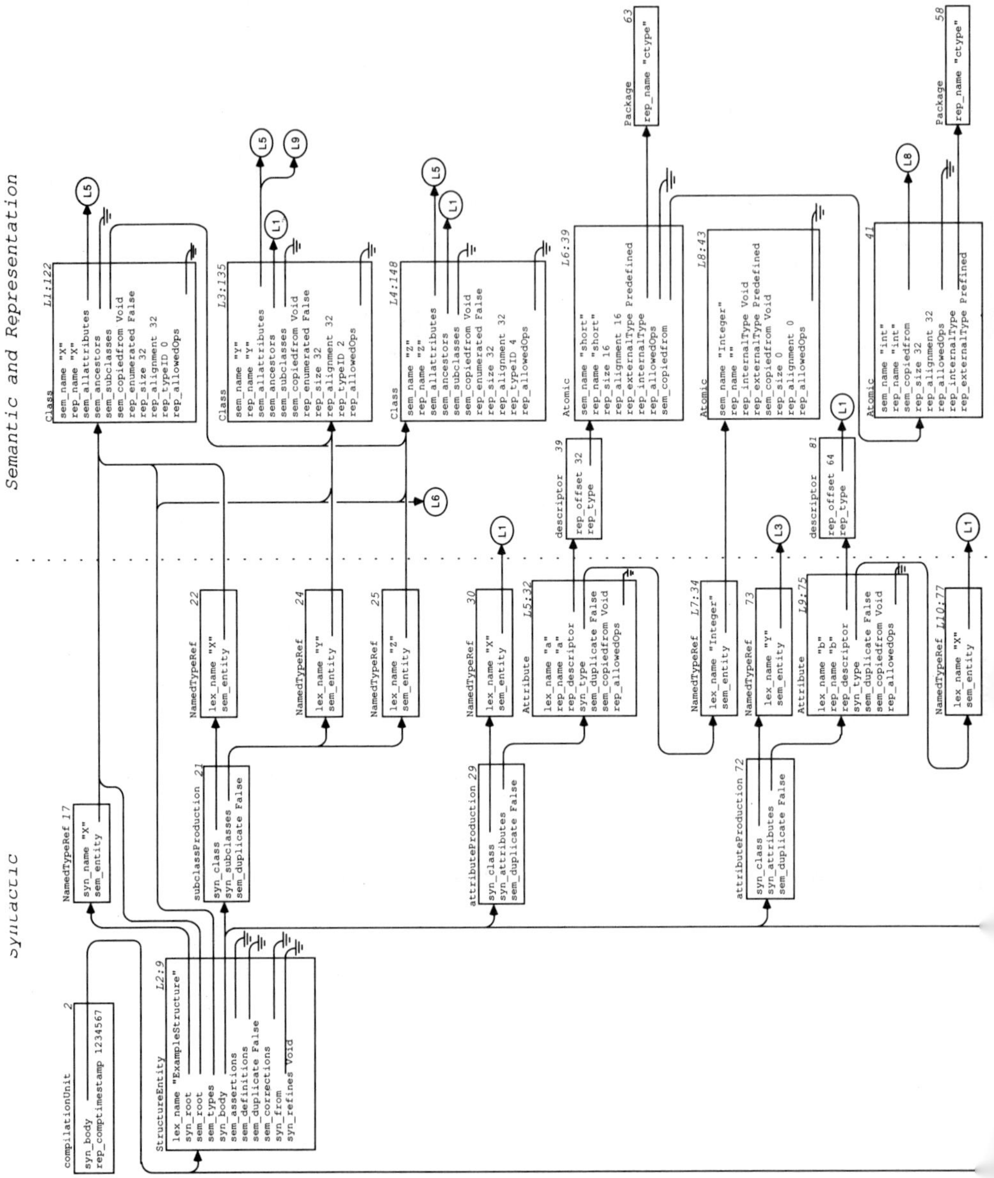

Figure 15.17: A CANDLE Instance, Part 1

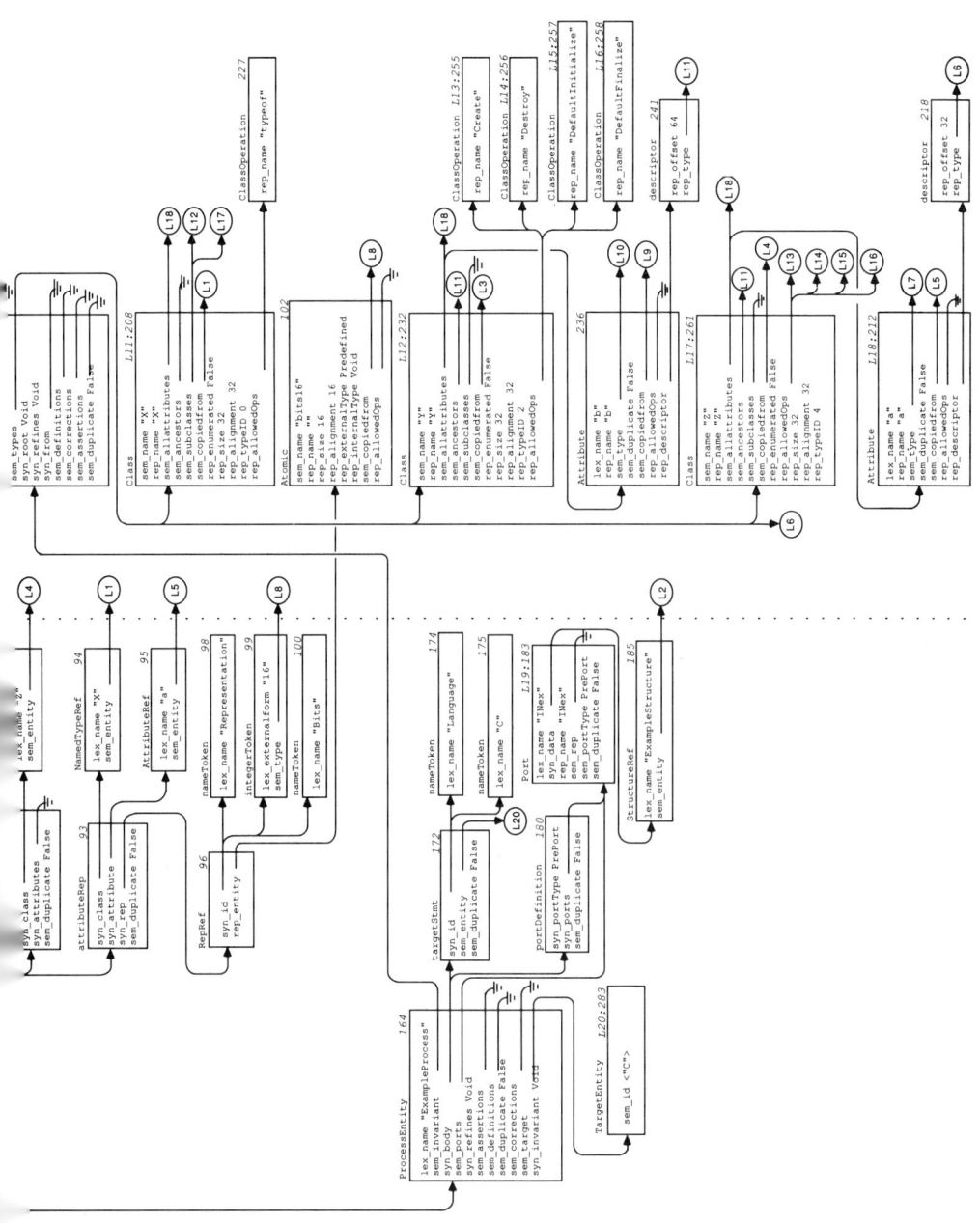

Figure 15.18: A CANDLE Instance, Part 2

```
 1    -- structure Candle
 2    compilationUnit[
 3      lex_information <
 4        "-- a structure declaration~J"
 5        "~J~J-- a process declaration~J"
 6        "~J" >;
 7      rep_comptimestamp 1234567;
 8      syn_body <
 9        L2:StructureEntity[
10          lex_information <
11            "Structure " " " "Root" " " " " Is~J          " " " ::=" " " |"
12            ";~J         " " " =>" " ": " " "; ~J          " " " =>" " ": "
13            ";~J         " " " =>;~J          For "
14            "." " " "Use " " " " " " " " " "; ~JEnd"
15          >;
16          lex_name "ExampleStructure";
17          syn_root NamedTypeRef[lex_name "X"; sem_entity L1^];
18          syn_from <>;
19          syn_refines Void;
20          syn_body <
21            subclassProduction[
22              syn_class NamedTypeRef[lex_name "X"; sem_entity L1^];
23              syn_subclasses <
24                NamedTypeRef[lex_name "Y"; sem_entity L3^]
25                NamedTypeRef[lex_name "Z"; sem_entity L4^]
26              >;
27              sem_duplicate FALSE;
28            ]
29            attributeProduction[
30              syn_class NamedTypeRef[lex_name "X"; sem_entity L1^];
31              syn_attributes <
32                L5:Attribute[
33                  lex_name "a";
34                  syn_type L7:NamedTypeRef[lex_name "Integer";sem_entity L8^];
35                  sem_copiedfrom Void;
36                  sem_duplicate FALSE;
37                  rep_name "a";
38                  rep_allowedOps { };
39                  rep_descriptor descriptor[rep_type L6:Atomic[
40                        sem_name "short";
41                        sem_copiedfrom Atomic[
42                          sem_name "int";
43                          sem_copiedfrom L8:Atomic[
44                            sem_name "Integer";
45                            sem_copiedfrom Void;
46                            rep_name "";
47                            rep_size 0;
48                            rep_alignment 0;
49                            rep_internalType Void;
50                            rep_externalType Predefined;
51                            rep_allowedOps { };
52                          ]
53                          rep_name "int";
54                          rep_size 32;
55                          rep_alignment 32;
56                          rep_allowedOps { };
57                          rep_externalType Predefined;
58                          rep_internalType Package[rep_name "ctype"];
59                        ];
```

Figure 15.19: A CANDLE Instance, Part 1

15.3. RATIONALE 339

```
60              rep_name "short";
61              rep_size 16;
62              rep_alignment 16;
63              rep_internalType Package[rep_name "ctype"];
64              rep_externalType Predefined;
65              rep_allowedOps { };
66            ];
67            rep_offset 32];
68          ]
69        >;
70        sem_duplicate FALSE;
71      ]
72      attributeProduction[
73        syn_class NamedTypeRef[lex_name "Y"; sem_entity L3^];
74        syn_attributes <
75          L9:Attribute[
76            lex_name "b";
77            syn_type L10:NamedTypeRef[lex_name "X"; sem_entity L1^];
78            sem_copiedfrom Void;
79            sem_duplicate FALSE;
80            rep_name "b";
81            rep_descriptor descriptor[rep_offset 64;
82              rep_type L1^];
83            rep_allowedOps { };
84          ]
85        >;
86        sem_duplicate FALSE;
87      ]
88      attributeProduction[
89        syn_class NamedTypeRef[lex_name "Z"; sem_entity L4^];
90        syn_attributes <>;
91        sem_duplicate FALSE;
92      ]
93      attributeRep[
94        syn_class NamedTypeRef[lex_name "X"; sem_entity L1^];
95        syn_attribute AttributeRef[lex_name "a"; sem_entity L5^];
96        syn_rep RepRef[
97          syn_id <
98            nameToken[lex_name "Representation"]
99            integerToken[lex_externalform "16"; sem_type L8^]
100           nameToken[lex_name "Bits"]
101         >;
102         rep_entity Atomic[
103           sem_name "bits16";
104           sem_copiedfrom L8^;
105           rep_name "";
106           rep_size 16;
107           rep_alignment 16;
108           rep_internalType Void;
109           rep_externalType Predefined;
110           rep_allowedOps { };
111         ];
112       ];
113       sem_duplicate FALSE;
114     ]
115   >;
116   sem_root L1^;
117   sem_assertions { };
118   sem_definitions { };
119   sem_duplicate FALSE;
```

Figure 15.20: A CANDLE Instance, Part 2

```
120        sem_corrections <>;
121        sem_types {
122          L1:Class[
123            sem_name "X";
124            sem_copiedfrom Void;
125            sem_allattributes <L5^>;
126            sem_subclasses {L3^ L4^};
127            sem_ancestors { };
128            rep_name "X";
129            rep_enumerated FALSE;
130            rep_typeID 0;
131            rep_allowedOps { };
132            rep_size 32;
133            rep_alignment 32;
134          ]
135          L3:Class[
136            sem_name "Y";
137            sem_copiedfrom Void;
138            sem_allattributes <L5^ L9^>;
139            sem_subclasses { };
140            sem_ancestors {L1^};
141            rep_name "Y";
142            rep_size 32;
143            rep_alignment 32;
144            rep_typeID 2;
145            rep_enumerated FALSE;
146            rep_allowedOps { };
147          ]
148          L4:Class[
149            sem_name "Z";
150            sem_copiedfrom Void;
151            sem_allattributes <L5^>;
152            sem_subclasses { };
153            sem_ancestors {L1^};
154            rep_name "Z";
155            rep_size 32;
156            rep_alignment 32;
157            rep_typeID 4;
158            rep_enumerated FALSE;
159            rep_allowedOps { };
160          ]
161          L6^
162        };
163      ]
164      ProcessEntity[
165        lex_information <
166          "Process " " Is~J      Target " " " ";~J         Pre "
167          ": " ";~JEnd">;
168        lex_name "ExampleProcess";
169        syn_invariant Void;
170        syn_refines Void;
171        syn_body <
172          targetStmt[
173            syn_id <
174              nameToken[lex_name "Language"]
175              nameToken[lex_name "C"]
176            >;
177            sem_entity L20^;
178            sem_duplicate FALSE;
179          ]
```

Figure 15.21: A CANDLE Instance, Part 3

15.3. RATIONALE

```
180         portDefinition[
181           syn_portType PrePort;
182           syn_ports <
183             L19:Port[
184               lex_name "INex";
185               syn_data StructureRef[
186                 lex_name "ExampleStructure";
187                 sem_entity L2^];
188               sem_duplicate FALSE;
189               sem_rep <>;
190               sem_portType PrePort;
191               rep_name "INex";
192             ]
193           >;
194           sem_duplicate FALSE;
195         ]
196       >;
197       sem_invariant StructureEntity[
198         lex_name "IDLDefaultInvar";
199         lex_information <>;
200         syn_root Void;
201         syn_from <>;
202         syn_refines Void;
203         syn_body <>;
204         sem_assertions { };
205         sem_definitions { };
206         sem_root Void;
207         sem_types {
208           L11:Class[
209             sem_name "X";
210             sem_copiedfrom L1^;
211             sem_allattributes <
212               L18:Attribute[
213                 lex_name "a";
214                 syn_type L7^;
215                 sem_copiedfrom L5^;
216                 sem_duplicate FALSE;
217                 rep_name "a";
218                 rep_descriptor descriptor[rep_type L6^;
219                   rep_offset 32];
220                 rep_allowedOps { };
221               ]
222             >;
223             sem_subclasses {L12^ L17^};
224             sem_ancestors { };
225             rep_name "X";
226             rep_enumerated FALSE;
227             rep_allowedOps {ClassOperation[rep_name "typeof"]};
228             rep_size 32;
229             rep_alignment 32;
230             rep_typeID 0;
231           ]
```

Figure 15.22: A CANDLE Instance, Part 4

```
232         L12:Class[
233           sem_name "Y";
234           sem_copiedfrom L3^;
235           sem_allattributes <L18^
236             Attribute[
237               lex_name "b";
238               sem_duplicate FALSE;
239               sem_copiedfrom L9^;
240               syn_type L10^;
241               rep_descriptor descriptor[rep_type L11^;
242                 rep_offset 64];
243               rep_name "b";
244               rep_allowedOps { }
245             ]
246           >;
247           sem_subclasses { };
248           sem_ancestors {L11^};
249           rep_name "Y";
250           rep_enumerated FALSE;
251           rep_size 32;
252           rep_alignment 32;
253           rep_typeID 2;
254           rep_allowedOps {
255             L13:ClassOperation[rep_name "Create"]
256             L14:ClassOperation[rep_name "Destroy"]
257             L15:ClassOperation[rep_name "DefaultInitialize"]
258             L16:ClassOperation[rep_name "DefaultFinalize"]
259           };
260         ]
261         L17:Class[
262           sem_name "Z";
263           sem_copiedfrom L4^;
264           sem_allattributes <L18^>;
265           sem_subclasses { };
266           sem_ancestors {L11^};
267           rep_name "Z";
268           rep_enumerated FALSE;
269           rep_size 32;
270           rep_alignment 32;
271           rep_typeID 4;
272           rep_allowedOps {L13^ L14^ L15^ L16^};
273         ]
274         L6^
275       };
276       sem_duplicate FALSE;
277       sem_corrections <>;
278     ];
279     sem_assertions { };
280     sem_definitions { };
281     sem_ports {L19^};
282     sem_duplicate FALSE;
283     sem_target L20:TargetEntity[sem_id <"C">];
284     sem_corrections <>;
285   ]
286 >;
287 ]#
```

Figure 15.23: A CANDLE Instance, Part 5

15.3. RATIONALE

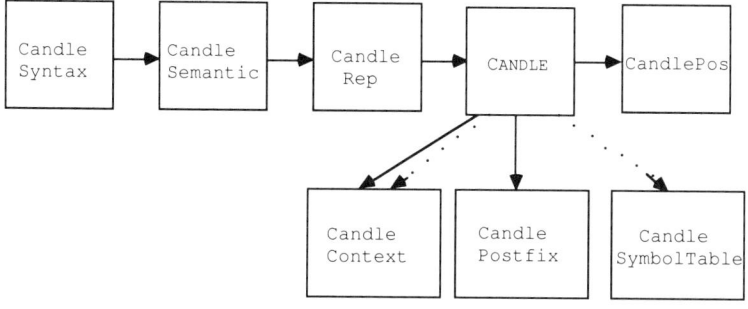

Figure 15.24: Structure Derivation Graph for CANDLE

Two main hierarchies are `statement` and `Entity`, shown below, where the types at the most indented level are nodes and the types at the other levels are classes.

```
statement                        Entity
   structureStatement               SyntacticEntity
      atomicDecl                       Assertion
      attributeRep                     Attribute
      production                       CaseName
         subclassProduction            Control
         attributeProduction           Formal
      typeRepDecl                      DefInstance
      withoutClause                       IDLDefInstance
      Assertion                              cyclicdef
      DefInstance                            noncyclicdef
   processStatement                       PrivateDefInstance
      portAssociation               Port
      portDefinition                StructureOrProcess
      restriction                      StructureEntity
         attributeRestriction          ProcessEntity
         typeRestriction           SemanticEntity
      targetStmt                       Definition
      Assertion                        TypeEntity
      DefInstance                         NamedType
                                             Atomic
                                             Class
                                          SetOrSeq
                                             SetOf
                                             SeqOf
```

The `processStatement` and `structureStatement` classes are subclasses of `statement` because they share a common attribute `sem_duplicate`. The `structureStatement` and `processStatement` classes exist to group together all possible statements for structures and processes, respectively.

The `Entity` class exists for documentation purposes. An entity can be a syntactic or semantic entity. `SyntacticEntity`s share one common attribute, `lex_name`, through the `Identifier` superclass, discussed below. In addition, syntactic entities share the property that they are defined during the syntactic phase of the translator.

Subclasses of `SemanticEntity` share one common attribute, `sem_name`, and share the property that they are defined during the semantic phase of the translator.

Two nodes appear more than once: `Assertion` and `DefInstance`. These

15.3. RATIONALE

nodes exist in both because assertions and definitions can be specified in both process and structure declarations. It would be redundant to have two different types of assertions and definitions, one type for structures and a second type for processes, since the information in each type would be identical. Also, for documentation purposes, we want assertions and definition versions (previously termed "instances") to appear in both structures and processes since they are processed the same way in the translator.

One node is shared between the `statement` and `Entity` hierarchies: `Assertion`. This node is a member of both `statement` and `SyntacticEntity` since the `statement` is the definition point for the `Assertion` entity. The other syntactic entities are defined by only a portion of a `statement` (e.g., `Attribute`), and hence are not in the `statement` hierarchy. The semantic entities are defined by multiple `statements` (e.g., `Class`) or are predefined in the prelude (e.g., `Atomics` for basic types).

The other main hierarchies are `Identifier`, `TypeRef`, and `otherToken`, also shown below.

```
Identifier                         TypeRef
    SyntacticEntity                    NamedTypeRef
    nameToken                          SetOrSeqRef
    EntityReference                        SetRef
        AssertRef                          SeqRef
        AttributeRef
        AttributeRef               otherToken
        compUnitRef                    integerToken
        DefineRef                      rationalToken
        DefInstanceOrDefineRef         stringToken
        ExpNameRef
        NamedTypeRef
        OperRef
        PortRef
        ProcessRef
        StructureRef
        StructureOrProcessRep
```

In these hierarchies, `NamedTypeRef` is shared. `NamedTypeRef` is a member of `Identifier` because it has an attribute in common with the other nodes in the class, `lex_name`. `NamedTypeRef` is a member of `TypeRef` because it can be one of the node types of an attribute, for example

    typeRepDecl => syn_type: TypeRef;

`NamedTypeRef` also is a member of `TypeRef` for documentation purposes:

TypeRef is a reference to a type and NamedTypeRef is a reference to a named type, and therefore is a subclass of a type reference.

SyntacticEntity, and all of its subclasses, are shared between Entity and Identifier.

In these hierarchies, AttributeRef, TypeRef, and NamedTypeRef are shared by the hierarchies AttributeOrAllAttributes, TypeOrAllTypes, and ClassOrAllClasses, respectively.

AttributeOrAllAttributes	TypeOrAllTypes	ClassOrAllClasses
AttributeRef	TypeRef	NamedTypeRef
AllAttributes	AllTypes	AllClasses

These three minor hierarchies are used as types when an attribute value can be one of two types. Other minor hierarchies are ?OrError (e.g., ClassOrError) and ?OrVoid (e.g., AttributeOrVoid). These hierarchies contain shared subclasses from the three main hierarchies: Entity, Entity-Reference, and TypeRef. As should be clear from this discussion, permitting only one hierarchy would have required significant modifications to CANDLE, at the expense of clarity.

15.3.4 Entities

There are two kinds of entities in CANDLE, syntactic and semantic. Syntactic entities have a single definition point in the syntax of the specification. There is adequate information in the syntax at the definition to build the entity. For example, an Attribute has a single definition point in an attributeProduction, as shown in Figure 15.25. All additional semantic and representation information (e.g., sem_entity and sem_representation) about the attribute is added to this syntactic entity (Figure 15.26) during semantic analysis rather than creating a new semantic entity.

Semantic entities have several definition points in the syntax or are defined in the prelude. Semantic analysis combines this information to build the entity. For example, a Class entity is constructed from a sequence of subclassProductions and attributeProductions shown in Figure 15.27. All additional information about the Class is added to this constructed entity rather than to a definition point of the entity. Each definition point has a reference to this entity.

Although an Atomic has a single definition point atomicDecl in the syntax, it is a semantic entity because Atomics for basic types exist in the prelude. In addition, representation information for each Atomic associated with a private type exists in the prelude. For example, an Atomic entity for a private type is constructed from an atomicDecl, several typeRepDecls,

15.3. RATIONALE

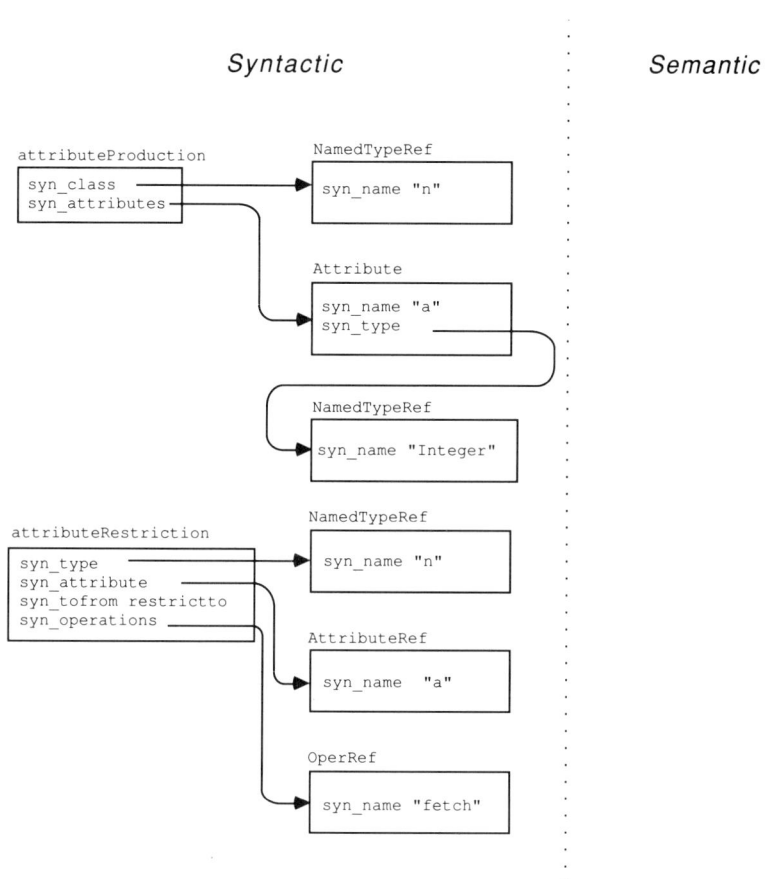

n => a: *Integer*;
Restrict n.a *To* fetch;

Figure 15.25: An Example of the SyntacticEntity Attribute

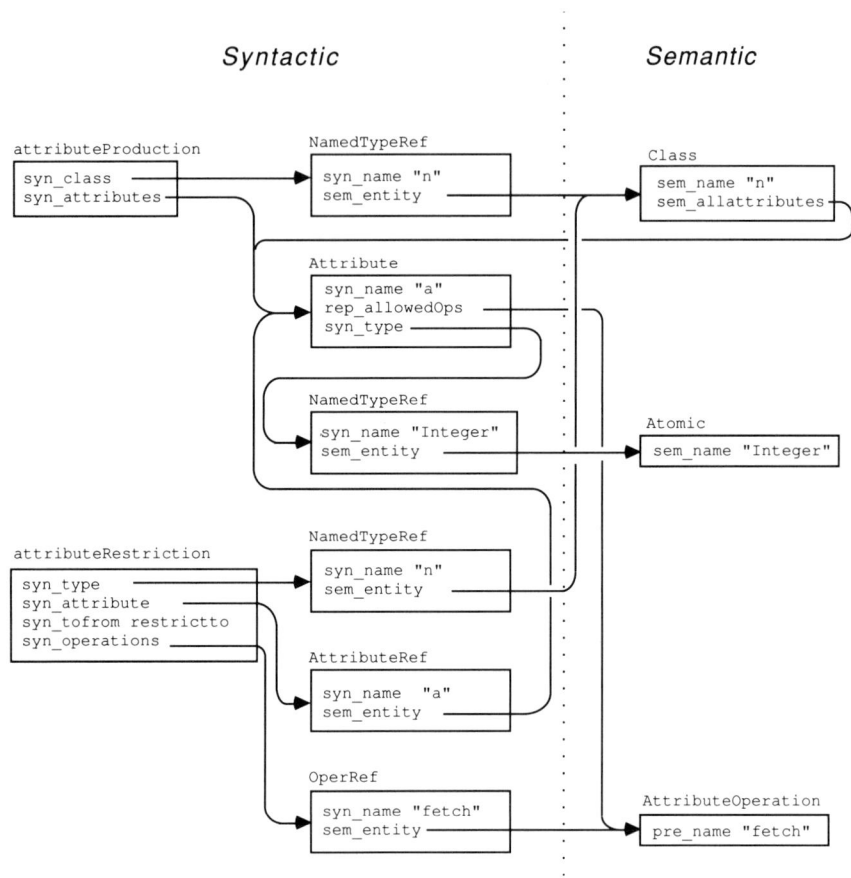

```
n => a: Integer;
Restrict n.a To fetch;
```

Figure 15.26: An Example of the Augmented SyntacticEntity Attribute

15.3. RATIONALE

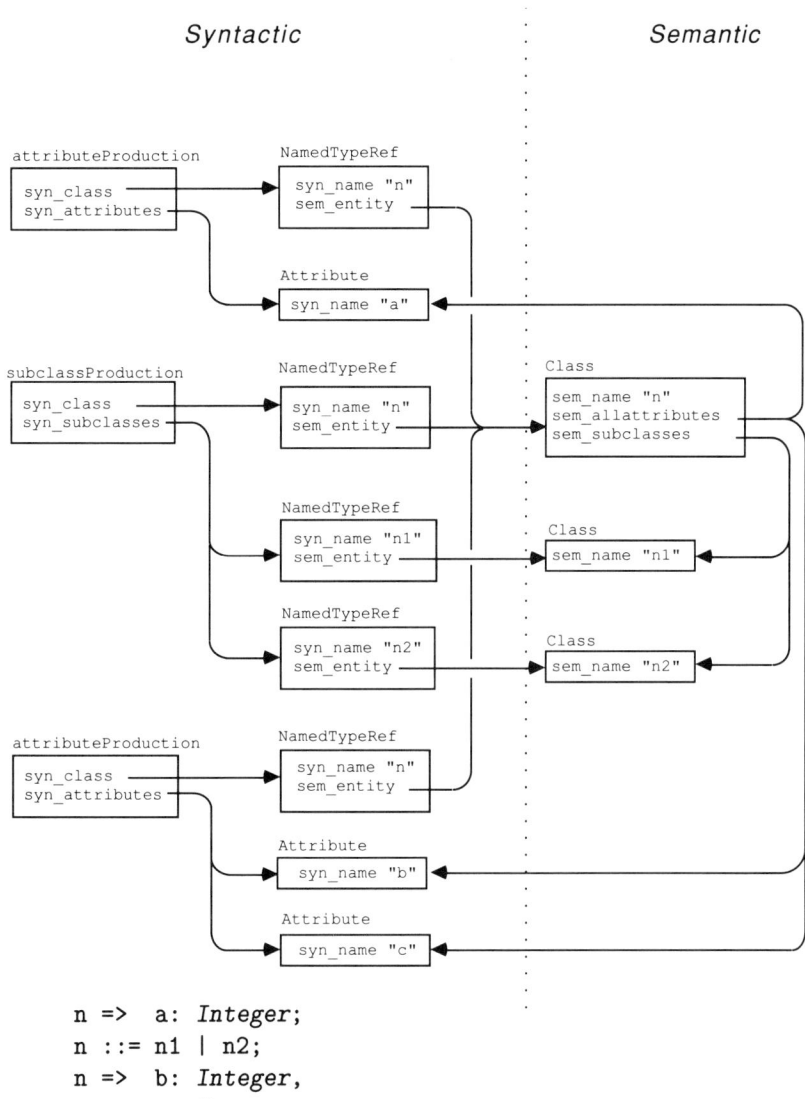

```
n => a: Integer;
n ::= n1 | n2;
n => b: Integer,
     c: Integer;
```

Figure 15.27: An Example of the SemanticEntity Class

and prelude representation information. This is shown in Figure 15.28.

15.3.5 Treatment of Errors

There are six categories of errors that can occur when processing an IDL specification.

1. A *fatal error* is serious enough to abort processing of the specification. If a fatal error occurs, no CANDLE structure and no target code is produced. There can be at most one fatal error during processing. An example is a write error occurring when the target code file is being produced.

2. A *severe error* is an error that can cause incorrect target code and from which the translator cannot recover. If one or more severe errors occur, no target code is produced. The CANDLE instance is still produced, but some of the assertions may not be satisfied, since some analysis may not be complete. An example will be given shortly.

3. A *recoverable error* is an error that is corrected by adding the appropriate information to CANDLE. The CANDLE instance and the target code are still produced. An example will be given shortly.

4. A *warning* indicates a possible error. The primary difference between a warning and a recoverable error is that the recovery action for a warning is always to ignore the error or inconsistency, while the recovery action for a recoverable error is to add information to fix the error or inconsistency. There is no limit to the number of warnings that can occur. Several examples will be given.

5. An *extension* indicates a feature being used that is not compatible with IDL notation. An example is the use of a target clause when IDL Version 2 conformance checking is requested; the target clause is not supported in IDL Version 2, but is supported in IDL87.

6. A *comment* in the listing file indicates poor style in the IDL specification file. An example is using an identifier identical to an IDL keyword except for case. If IDL Version 2 conformance is checked, such identifiers are valid, but confusing, and hence their use is considered poor style.

Warnings, recoverable errors, and severe errors are all indicated in CANDLE. Three types of warning errors can occur. The first occurs when the entity for a reference is not found. Here, the `sem_entity` attribute

15.3. RATIONALE

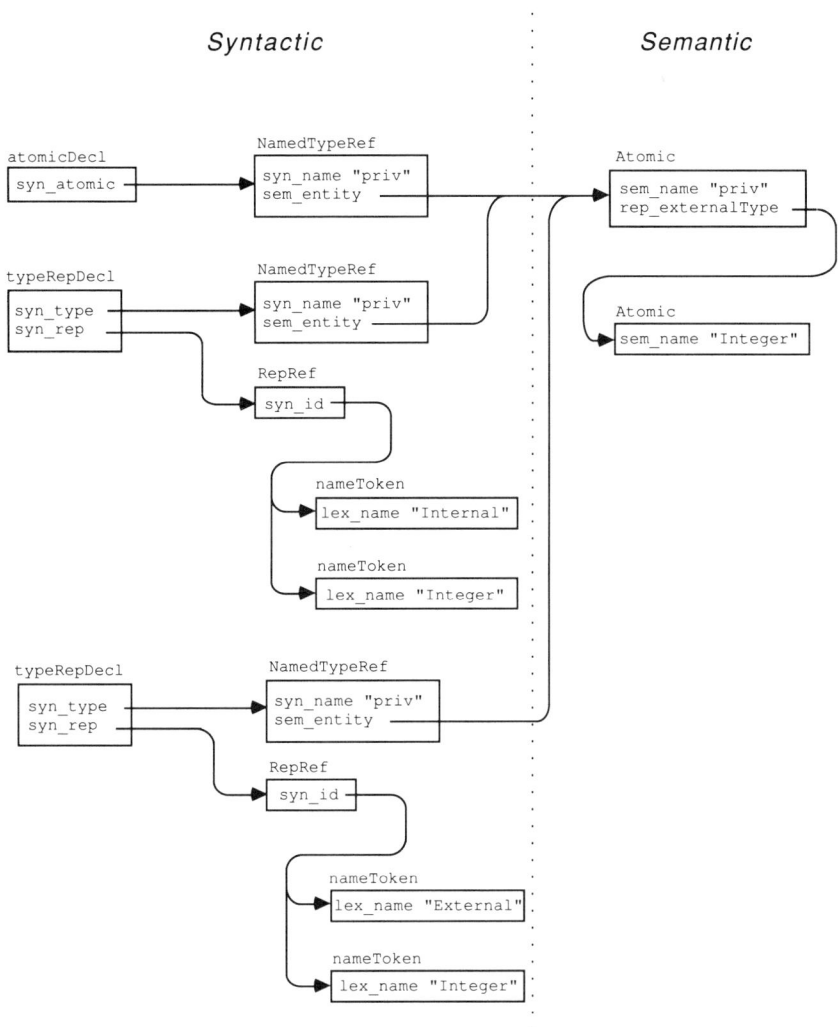

```
Type priv;
For priv Use Internal Integer;
For priv Use External Integer;
```

Figure 15.28: An Example of the SemanticEntity Atomic

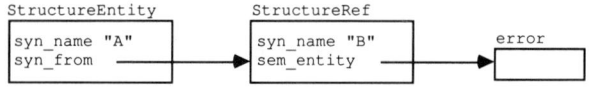

```
1| Structure A From B Is
         ^1
**   1 Warning 105: Ancestor structure not found.
2| End
```

Figure 15.29: Example of a Reference Not Found

of the reference is set to Error and the statement containing the reference is ignored. An example is an ancestor structure that is not found (Figure 15.29).

The second type occurs when an illegal statement is encountered. The semantic attributes are set to Error and the statement is ignored. An example is a withoutClause in a nonderived structure (Figure 15.30).

The third type of warning is signaled when a duplicate entity is encountered. Here, the duplicate is ignored and the sem_duplicate attribute is set to TRUE. An example is a duplicate Attribute in a Class (Figure 15.31).

Recoverable errors are indicated by adding an additional statement to the sem_corrections attribute of a StructureEntity or ProcessEntity. An example is a subclass not being defined for a class. A new attribute-Production is created and added to StructureEntity.sem_corrections (Figure 15.32).

Severe errors are recorded in the semantic attributes of StructureEntitys and ProcessEntitys. An example is a cycle in the class hierarchy relation. The cycle can be determined using the sem_types attribute of the StructureEntity and the sem_subclasses attribute of the Classes (Figure 15.33).

15.3.6 Name Resolution

An IDL specification file contains entities introduced by a declaration that binds a name to the entity. Uses of the name always refer to the entity. In CandleSyntax, the name appears as an EntityReference containing a lexical attribute lex_name. CANDLE adds a semantic attribute sem_entity. The value of this attribute is a reference either to the entity named by lex_name or to an Error if the reference cannot be resolved (see Section 15.3.5).

15.3. RATIONALE

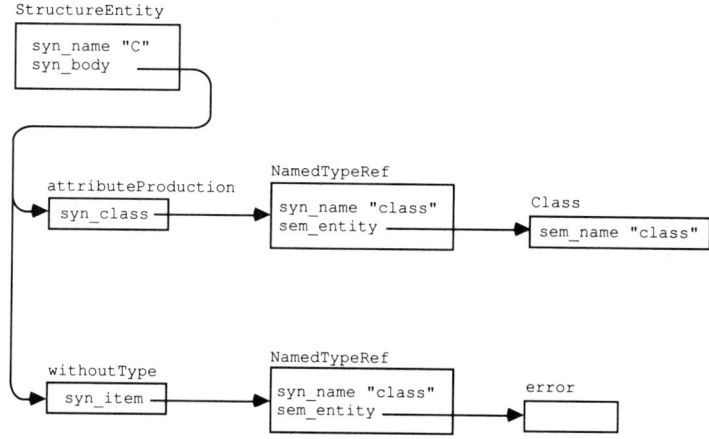

```
1| Structure C Is
2|    class =>;
3|    Without Type class;
      ^1
**  1 Warning 102: Nonderived structure cannot have
**    a Without clause.
4| End
```

Figure 15.30: An Example of an Illegal Statement

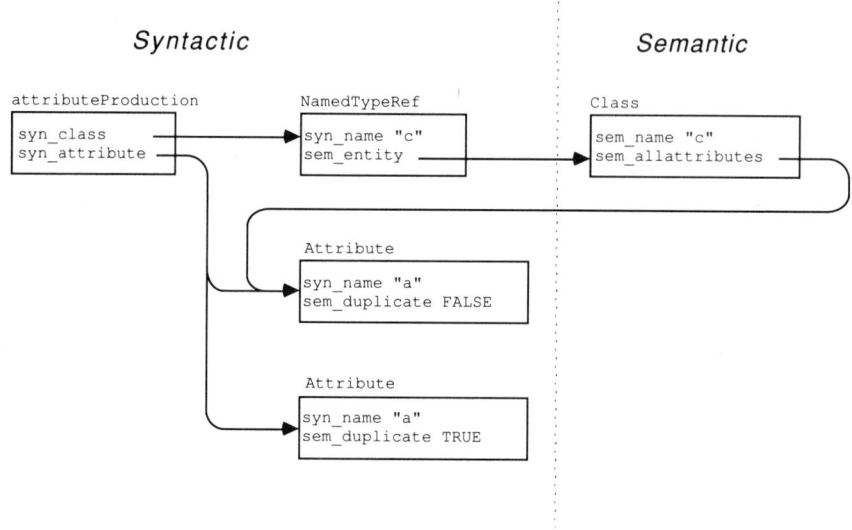

```
2| c => a: Integer,
3|    a: Integer;
      ^1
**  1 Warning 274: Duplicate attribute in production.
```

Figure 15.31: An Example of a Duplicate Attribute

15.3. RATIONALE

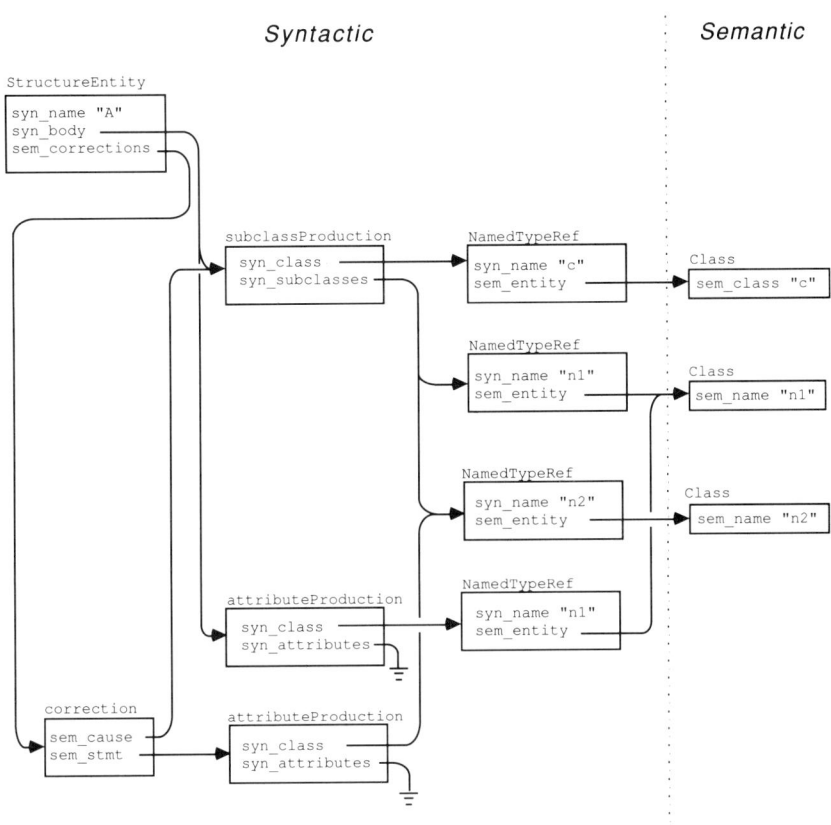

```
1|  Structure A Root c Is
2|      c ::= n1 | n2;
                    ^1
**      1 Recoverable Error 200: Creating new node type for
**        unknown type.
3|      n1 =>;
4|  End
```

Figure 15.32: An Example of the Correction of a Recoverable Error

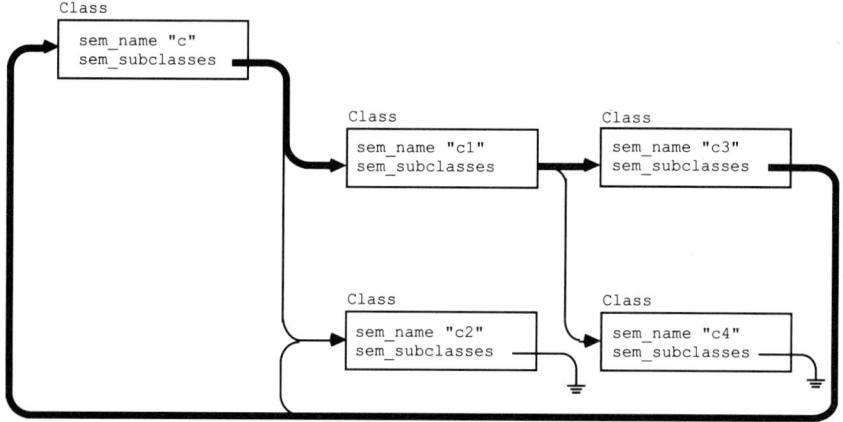

```
 2|    c   ::= c1 | c2;
 3|    c1  ::= c3 | c4;
 4|    c3  ::= c  | c2;
**    1 Severe Error 226: Class hierarchy has a cycle containing c
**    1 Severe Error 226: Class hierarchy has a cycle containing c
**    1 Severe Error 226: Class hierarchy has a cycle containing c
```

Figure 15.33: An Example of a Severe Error

15.3. RATIONALE

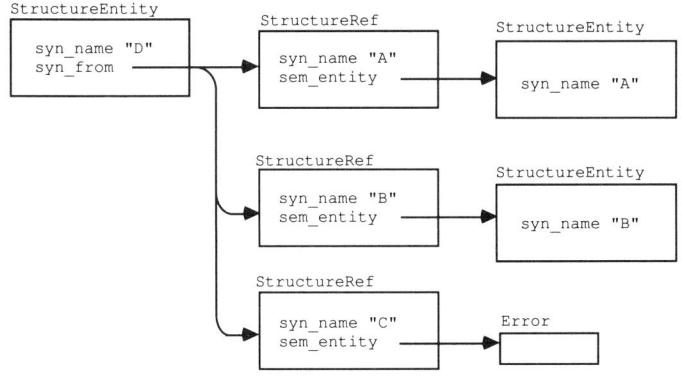

```
1| Structure D From A, B, C Is
                  ^1
**   1 Warning 105: Ancestor structure not found.
End
```

Figure 15.34: Name Resolution for **StructureRefs**

The kind of entity referenced can usually be determined by the context of the name. Hence, **EntityReference** in CANDLE is a class containing a subclass for each type of named entity reference. Each subclass has a **sem_entity** attribute with the type of the corresponding entity or **Error**. For example, names listed after a *From* keyword in a structure declaration would be **StructureRefs** each with a **sem_entity** attribute pointing to a **StructureEntity** or **Error** (Figure 15.34).

When the type of a reference cannot be determined during syntactic analysis (e.g., an identifier naming either a structure or a process in an import statement), all such references are combined into one (e.g., **StructureOrProcessRef**) and distinguished in semantic analysis via its **sem_entity** attribute:

```
StructureOrProcessRef =>   sem_entity: StructureOrProcess;
StructureOrProcess    ::= StructureEntity | ProcessEntity;
```

This use of classes is discussed further in Section 10.3.

15.3.7 Types

Types in CANDLE consist of node, class, private, basic, and structured types. Node and class types are represented by **Class** entities. The difference is that a node is represented by a **Class** entity with an empty sem_subclasses set. Private and basic types are represented by Atomic entities. Atomic entities for private types are created during semantic analysis. Atomic entities for basic types exist in the prelude. A structured type is a set or sequence of a Class or Atomic. Sets are represented by SetOf entities and sequences are represented by SeqOf entities.

A Class is constructed from a sequence of subclassProductions and attributeProductions. The subclasses and attributes of the productions are combined to form the sem_subclasses set and sem_attributes sequence for the Class (Figure 15.35).

The representation for the Class in the target language consists of the target name for the Class, a set of allowed operations, and an indication of whether the Class should be represented as an enumerated type. The target name is the same as the Class name unless the name is a keyword in the target language in which case the target name would be the Class name with an added prefix. The set of allowed operations specifies how variables with a type of the Class can be used in source programs.

An Atomic type is a prelude type or a user-defined private type. The Atomics in the standard prelude are the IDL basic types *Integer*, *Boolean*, *String*, and *Rational*. The prelude also contains special representations for these types in the target language. For example, the prelude would include the following:

```
L1:Atomic[
    lex_name "Integer";
    rep_name "Integer";
    rep_size 0;
    rep_alignment 0;
    rep_internalType Void;
    rep_externalType Predefined;
    rep_allowedOps { };
]
```

The rep_externalType of Predefined causes the target-dependent representation phase to treat this private type specially.

Additional representations are also present in the prelude to support various representation clauses. As an example, the representations shown in Figure 15.36 are supported for *Integer* in the target language C are present. The first representation is the default. From the statements in the *user's* IDL specification

X => a: *Integer*,
    b: *Integer*;
For X.a *Use Representation* Unsigned;
For X.a *Use Representation* 8 Bits;

15.3. RATIONALE

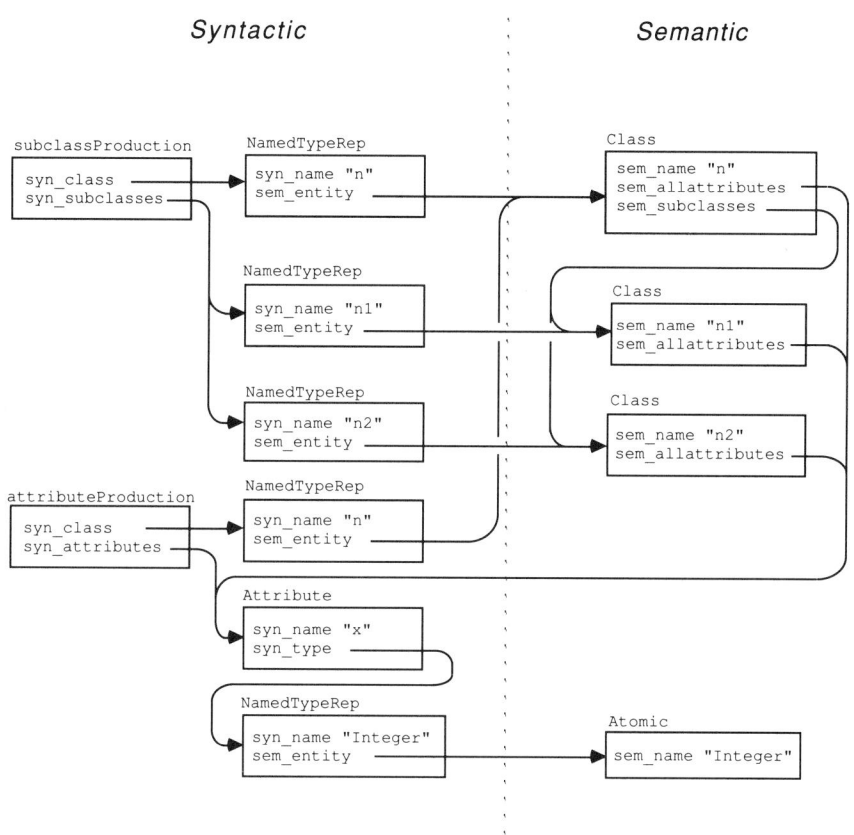

```
n ::= n1 | n2;
n =>  x: Integer;
```

Figure 15.35: Construction of a Class

```
        L2:Atomic[
            sem_name "int";
            rep_name "int";
            rep_size 32;
            rep_alignment 32;
            rep_internalType Package[rep_name "Ctype"];
        ]
        L3:Atomic[
            sem_name "unsigned char";
            rep_name "uchar";
            rep_size 8;
            rep_alignment 8;
            rep_internalType Package[rep_name "Ctype"];
        ]
```

Figure 15.36: Several Integers Representations from the Prelude

the representation analysis phase will generate

```
        Attribute[
            lex_name "a";
            syn_type NamedTypeRef[
                lex_name "Integer";
                sem_entity L1^]
            rep_descriptor descriptor[rep_type L3^;
                rep_offset 32];
        ]
        Attribute[
            lex_name "b";
            syn_type NamedTypeRef[
                lex_name "Integer";
                sem_entity L1^];
            rep_descriptor descriptor[rep_type L2^;
                rep_offset 40];
        ]
```

syn_type.sem_entity is the language-independent integer type L1, whereas the rep_type is the specific, language-dependent type (L2 or L3) chosen by the representation phases.

15.3. RATIONALE

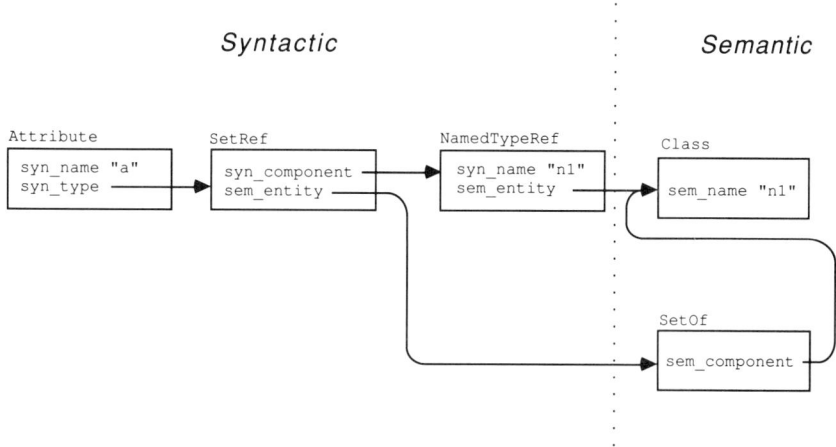

n => a: *Set Of* n1;

Figure 15.37: Creation of a Structured Type

A user-defined private `Atomic` is constructed from an `atomicDecl` statement and from representation clauses (Figure 15.28) using representation information in the prelude. The `Atomic` entity is declared at the point of the `atomicDecl` statement. The internal type of an `Atomic` can be specified using a package. The name of the package gives the file identifier where the concrete representation of the `Atomic` can be found. An `Atomic` can instead be represented with an existing type; in that case, the internal representation for the `Atomic` would be the same as the representation for the existing type.

Structured types exist in the prelude or are created when they are used as the type of an attribute (see Figure 15.37). For each structured type, the representation attributes include the size and alignment of the structured type in the target language, the representation of the structured type, and the allowed operations for the type.

Type resolution is similar to name resolution. The type of an attribute or expression is denoted syntactically as a `TypeRef`. A `TypeRef` can be a set reference, a sequence reference, or a named type (`Class` or `Atomic`) reference. The `sem_entity` field of the reference is resolved to a type in the structure or `Error`. In Figure 15.38 the `sem_entity` is set to `Error` since there is no type "*Set Of* f" in the structure.

A "*" is a special symbol which can reference any number of any kind of entity. The set of entities it resolves to is determined by semantics of the

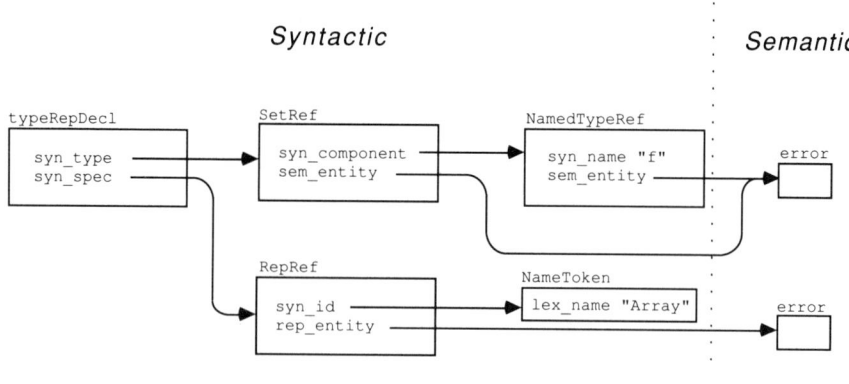

```
1| For Set Of f Use Array;
    ^1
**  1 Warning 151: Type not found in representation
**    clause.
```

Figure 15.38: Type Resolution

statement. For example, in the restriction clause shown in Figure 15.39, "*" resolves to the set of all sequence types in the structure since the named operation appendfrontSEQ is a sequence operation.

In the separate restriction clause shown in Figure 15.40, "*" resolves to the set of all classes in the structure since the named operation Create is a class operation.

15.3.8 Propagation

Attributes in a class are propagated to its descendants. There exists only one copy of the Attribute that is shared between the class and its descendants. For example, if the class C propagated the a attribute to its descendants N1 and N2, only one copy of the a attribute would exist (see Figure 15.41). Note that, in this example, attributes b and c are not shared.

The propagated attribute is combined with the existing attributes in the descendant and any inconsistencies are flagged. For example, an existing attribute with the same name as the propagated attribute would result in a duplicate attribute error.

15.3. RATIONALE

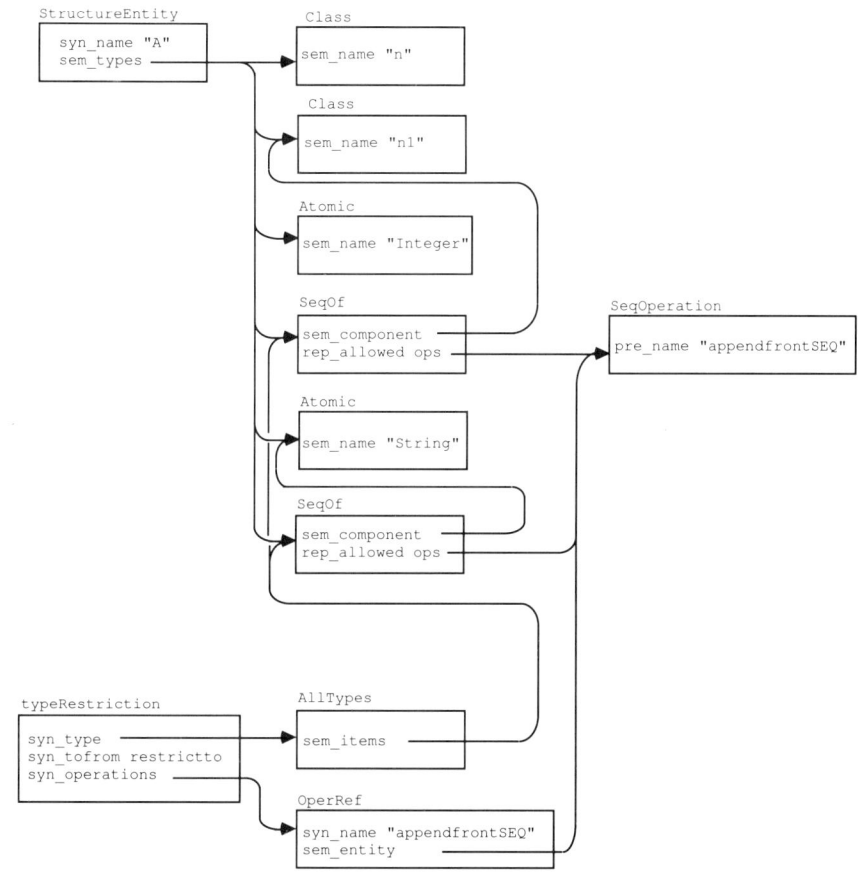

*Restrict * To* appendfrontSEQ;

Figure 15.39: Resolution of "*" for Sequences

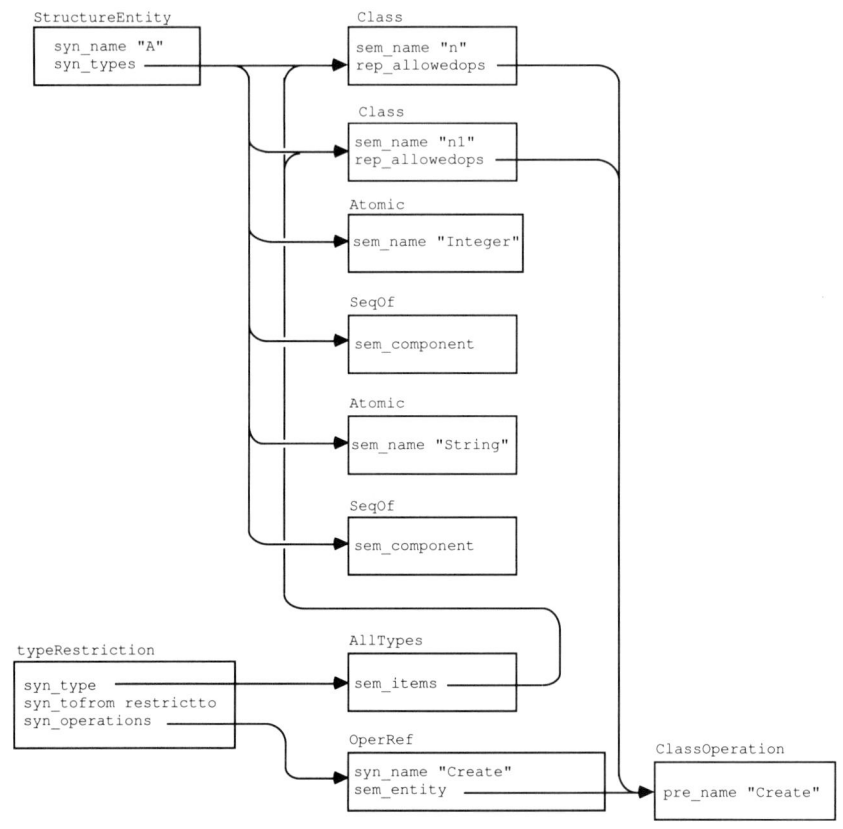

Restrict * To Create;

Figure 15.40: Resolution of "*" for Classes

15.4. STATISTICS ON THE SPECIFICATION

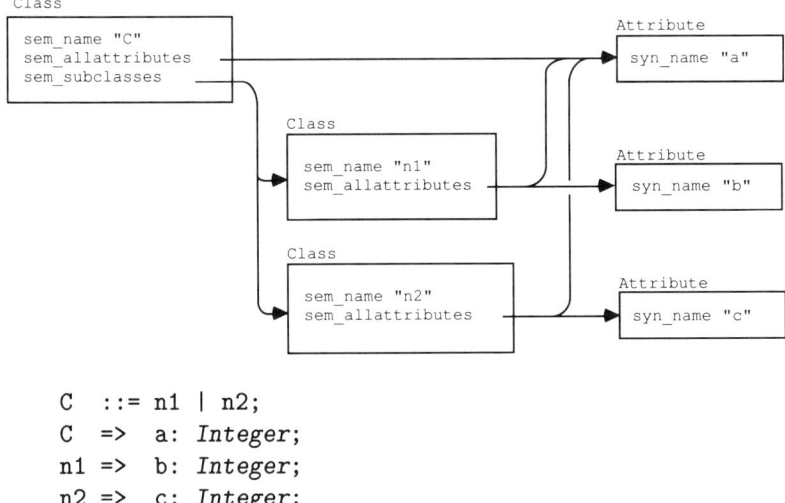

```
C   ::= n1 | n2;
C   =>  a: Integer;
n1  =>  b: Integer;
n2  =>  c: Integer;
```

Figure 15.41: Propagation

15.3.9 Derivation and Refinement

When a structure is derived or refined from other structures, all information from the ancestor structures is added to the structure before any of the structure statements are processed. The information in the new structure is either copied by reference or by value. In general, syntactic attributes are copied by reference and semantic attributes are copied by value (this aspect is discussed further in Section 17.3.5, below).

Refined structures add special representation information to a structure. Multiple representation clauses for a type are allowed if they are compatible. For example, an *Integer* type can be refined to the C type **short** and then refined again to the C type **unsigned short**. This refinement is legal because the C type **unsigned short** is a refinement of the C type **short**, which is in turn a refinement of the C type for *Integer*.

15.4 Statistics on the Specification

We conclude with two sets of statistics, the first consisting of counts of lines of IDL specifications, and the second generated by the **-ps** option of IDLC.

Component	Lines of Code
CandleSyntax	334
CandleSemantic	122
CandleRep	51
CANDLE	14
CandleContext	142
UNCCandle	11
CandlePos	29
UNCCandlePos	8
SubTotal	711
CandlePostfix	37
CandleSymbolTable	39
UNCCandle...	120
Total	831

The first set of structures are in some sense *public*, because they contribute to structures generated by tools: UNCCandle by IDLC and UNCCandlePos by CANDLEWALK. The second set of structures are generally used internally by the tools.

The CANDLE structure, including all the ancestor structures, contains 115 node types, 72 class types, 12 sets, 19 sequences, 150 distinct attributes, and two private types. Interestingly, the Rational basic type does not appear in CANDLE, although rational constants may appear in CANDLE specifications. CANDLE does include a String attribute, lex_externalform, to record the characters comprising a Rational constant. The smallest node is 32 bits long (1 word on most machines) and contains no attributes; the average node is 98.5 bits long (3.1 words) and contains 2.21 attributes (after attribute propagation from classes); and the largest node is 392 bits long (13 words) and contains 12 attributes. We conclude from these static statistics that most nodes are small. The average attribute size is 30.11 bits, indicating a preponderance of one word attributes.

Bibliographic Notes

CANDLE is a major redesign of the IDLAbstractTree, IDLsymbolTable, and TranslatorData structures described by Lamb [1983]. The **descriptor** nodes used to specify the location of attributes, which may be several levels of indirection away from the primary record, are a simplification of *data descriptors*, developed by Holt [1987] from *value descriptors* defined by Wilcox [1971]. In particular, for **descriptor** nodes the base of an analogous

15.4. STATISTICS ON THE SPECIFICATION

data descriptor is assumed to be the primary record denoting the node or class, and no concept of index is supported, although indexing is implied by the array representation of sets and sequences.

CANDLE is similar to DIANA in that both are intermediate representations expressed in IDL (Goos et al. [1983]). DIANA is to Ada [1983] what CANDLE is to IDL, and what IVAN (Gilman [1986]) is to VHDL (Shahdad et al. [1985]). The LexInfo representation chosen for IDLC, that of a sequence of strings, has the advantage that the exact placement of comments is captured in the CANDLE instance; such is not the case for Ada comments represented in DIANA instances (Butler and Evans [1983]). DIANA also assumes a few minor normalizations that prevent exact fidelity of the encoded representation; CANDLE assumes no normalizations. The original definition of DIANA did not employ classes fully; Revision 4 of DIANA, by McKinley and Schaefer [1986] and Lamb [1988] is more effective in its use of class. Howell et al. [1988] and Smith et al. [1988] describe how DIANA may be used as a standard for a multi-vendor programming environment for Ada. The implementation of Anna and related tools is based on DIANA (Luckham, Neff, and Rosenblum [1987]), as is a test environment generator implemented by Besson and Queyras [1987]. The design principles listed in Section 15.1 derive from those of DIANA. Other, lower level intermediate representations, providing explicit addressing schemes and requiring a run-time support package, have also been proposed by Appelbe and Dismukes [1982] and by Roubine and Teller [1982]. Lamb [1983] describes alternatives to the ASCII ERL, and discusses the improvements they elicit to file size and to I/O costs, ranging over factors of 5 and 25, respectively.

RDL, the representation description language used in DOSE, also has a specification of itself in its own notation (Feiler and Kaiser [1983]), as does the Mini IDL system described by Nestor et al. [1989]. Lie [1984] uses an IDL structure roughly equivalent to a significantly reduced version of CANDLE to describe all internal data. Various routines, such as the reader, writer, and garbage collector, use instances of this structure.

Prefixing an instance (in the ASCII External Representation) with the CANDLE instance that describes it (also in the ASCII External Representation) results a self-describing database for information exchange results, as defined by Mark and Roussopoulos [1987]. In this context, the CANDLE instance is the schema, and a CANDLE instance of the CANDLE structure would be the meta-schema.

CANDLE's incremental nature may be exploited using techniques Lamb [1987c] developed for efficiently supporting graph deltas.

Cook [1988] has implemented IDLVIEW, an interactive tool for displaying IDL instances within an executing process that interprets the data structures in main memory using information in the CANDLE instance.

Chapter 16

candlewalk Implementation

CANDLEWALK traverses the syntax tree embedded in a CANDLE instance, performing an action at each node of the tree (see Figure 16.1). By using different actions, CANDLEWALK can achieve different results, while still following the same traversal strategy.

We discuss CANDLEWALK for several reasons. First, this program provides an excellent example of how syntax trees encoded as IDL instances may be traversed. Second, it illustrates how information computed by one tool (the IDL translator) may be profitably used by another tool. Third, this discussion provides an opportunity to examine the CANDLE structure from another point of view, thereby augmenting the material in the previous chapter. Finally, CANDLEWALK was used to produce Appendix F.

In the next section we describe the tree traversal algorithm at the core of CANDLEWALK, and discuss one set of actions, those necessary to reconstitute the original source from a CANDLE instance. Later sections will examine other sets of actions. An IDL specification of CANDLEWALK is given in Figure 16.2.

16.1 Regenerating the IDL Source

One design rationale for CANDLE was that it capture all the lexical and syntactic information present in the input specification. There are only four lexical attributes in CANDLE.

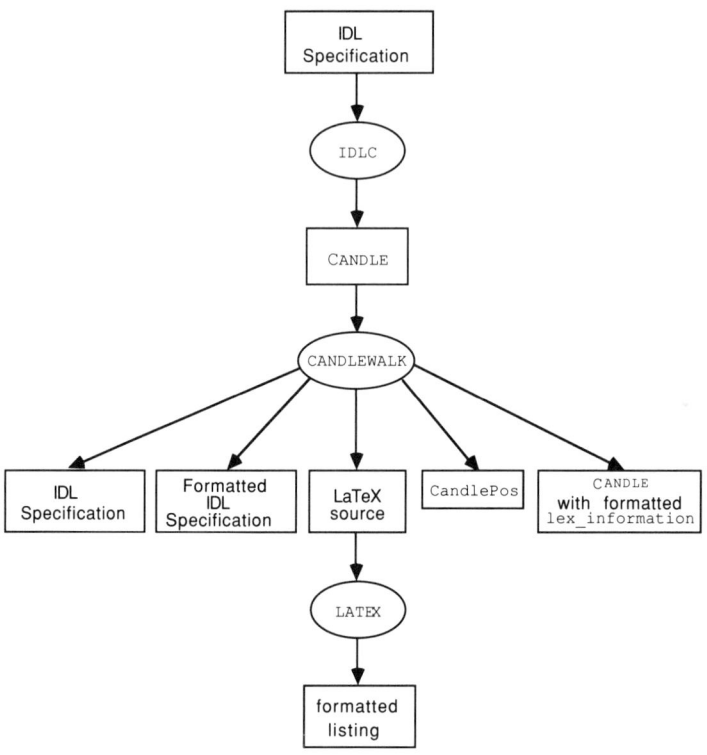

Figure 16.1: How CANDLEWALK Is Used

16.1. REGENERATING THE IDL SOURCE

```
Import UNCCandlePos From UNCCandlePos End

Structure walkInv From UNCCandlePos Is

    compilationUnit => inv_filenumber: Integer,
                       inv_filename:   String;

    For LexInfo Use Internal Seq Of String;
End

Process candlewalk Inv walkInv Is
    Target Language C;
    Pre input: UNCCandle;
    Post Candleout: UNCCandle;
    Post posout: UNCCandlePos;
    -- another Post is textual output of specification
End
```

Figure 16.2: IDL Specification of CANDLEWALK

```
Identifier => lex_name: String;
```
Gives the characters composing an identifier.

```
otherToken => lex_externalform: String;
```
Gives the characters composing an integer constant (`integerToken`), a rational constant (`rationalToken`) or string constant (`stringToken`).

```
Declaration => lex_information: LexInfo;
```
Gives the characters occurring between entities described lexically by the attributes above.

```
compilationUnit => lex_information: LexInfo;
```
Gives the characters occurring between declarations.

The `LexInfo` private type is given an external representation of `Seq Of String`; each implementation is free to put whatever information it deems useful into this sequence of character strings. The information recorded by the IDL translator, discussed in the next chapter, is in some sense maximal, in that every character of the source text may be found in a value of one of these four attributes. Each declaration (`StructureEntity`, `ProcessEntity`, and `ImportDecl`) records the characters before, between, and after identifiers and integer, rational, and string constants. Analogously, the one compilation unit (`compilationUnit`) in a CANDLE instance records the characters before, between, and after the declarations occurring in the specification. An example of these attributes is discussed in Section 15.2.1.

The ordering of the strings in this sequence is *infix*: the characters before a given construct appear first, followed by the characters within the construct, followed by the characters found after the construct. Hence, the characters appear in `lex_information` in the same order they appear in the source text.

Since every character is recorded, it is possible to regenerate the original specification text using a single infix traversal over the syntax tree. This traversal can be implemented as a collection of recursive descent routines, each associated with a node type of the syntax tree. The main routine of CANDLEWALK, implemented in C, is shown below (a simplified version is illustrated here; CANDLEWALK consists of some 2400 lines of C source code).

```
#include <stdio.h>
#include "candlewalk.h"

SEQLexInfo restlexinfo;

main(argc, argv)
int argc;
char *argv[];
{
        compilationUnit compUnit;
        FILE *inputfp;
        SEQDeclaration SDecl;
        Declaration ADecl;

        inputfp = fopen(argv[1], "r");
        compUnit = input(inputfp);
        restlexinfo = compUnit->lex_information;
        ProcessNextLexInfo;
        foreachinSEQDeclaration(compUnit->syn_body, SDecl, ADecl) {
            switch (typeof(ADecl)) {
            case KImportDecl:
                ProcessImportDecl(ADecl.VImportDecl);
                break;
            case KStructureEntity:
                ProcessStructureEntity(ADecl.VStructureEntity);
                break;
            case KProcessEntity:
                ProcessProcessEntity(ADecl.VProcessEntity);
                break;
            }
            ProcessNextLexInfo;  /* after previous decl */
        }
}
```

The main routine simply reads in the CANDLE instance, initializes the global variable `restlexinfo`, then processes each declaration in turn, thereby handling the `compilationUnit` node. Routines for the `ImportDecl` and

16.1. REGENERATING THE IDL SOURCE

```
void ProcessImport(this)
ImportDecl this;
{
    SEQLexInfo copyrestlexinfo;
    SEQStructureOrProcessRef SS;
    StructureOrProcessRef SPspec;

    copyrestlexinfo = restlexinfo;
    restlexinfo = this->lex_information;
    ProcessNextLexInfo; /* import... */
    foreachinSEQStructureOrProcessRef(import->syn_specs, SS, SPspec) {
        ProcessIdentifier((Identifier)SPspec);
        ProcessNextLexInfo; /* from ... or , */
    }
    ProcessIdentifier((Identifier)this->syn_compUnit);
    ProcessNextLexInfo; /* ..end */
    restlexinfo = copyrestlexinfo;
}
void ProcessProcessEntity(this)
ProcessEntity this;
{
    SEQLexInfo copyrestlexinfo;
    SEQprocessStatement Spst;
    processStatement Apst;

    copyrestlexinfo = restlexinfo;
    restlexinfo = this->lex_information;
    ProcessNextLexInfo; /* Process.. */
    ProcessIdentifier((Identifier)this);
    if (typeof(this->syn_invariant) == KStructureRef){
        ProcessNextLexInfo; /* Inv.. */
        ProcessIdentifier(this->syn_invariant.VIdentifier);
    }
    if (typeof(this->syn_refines)==KProcessRef){
        ProcessNextLexInfo; /* Refines.. */
        ProcessIdentifier(this->syn_refines.VIdentifier);
    }
    ProcessNextLexInfo; /* Is */
    foreachinSEQprocessStatement(this->syn_body, Spst, Apst){
        ProcessStatement(Apst);
        ProcessNextLexInfo;
    }
    restlexinfo = copyrestlexinfo;
}
```

Figure 16.3: The `ProcessImport` and `ProcessProcessEntity` Routines

ProcessEntity nodes are shown in Figure 16.3. Since `restlexinfo` is a global variable, the old value must be saved (in `copyrestlexinfo`) and later restored when temporary changes are made to it, as in `ProcessImport`. The characters associated with the immediate node are always directly handled by the routine; characters associated with children nodes in the syntax tree are handled by other routines. Hence, the `main` routine calls `ProcessProcessEntity`, which in turn calls `ProcessStatement`, which in turn calls routines associated with children nodes of `processStatement`.

There are three actions that parameterize the effect of the infix traversal of CANDLEWALK: processing the next `LexInfo` string sequence, processing an `Identifier`, and processing an `otherToken`. For regenerating the IDL source, the C functions shown below suffice.

```
void ProcessNextLexInfo()
{
    SEQString currentlexinfo;
    retrievefirstSEQString(restlexinfo, currentlexinfo);
    fprintf(stdout, currentlexinfo);
    removefirstSEQString(restlexinfo);
}

void ProcessIdentifier(this)
Identifier this;
{
    fprintf(stdout, this.IDLclassCommon->lex_name);
}

void ProcessOther(this)
otherToken this;
{
    fprintf(stdout, this->lex_externalform);
}
```

`ProcessNextLexInfo` removes the first element from `restlexinfo` and prints it; the remaining functions print out the name or external representation of the node passed as a parameter.

The recursive nature of the traversal is best illustrated with the `ProcessExpression` routine, shown in Figure 16.4. This routine assumes that the characters preceding the expression have already been printed. These characters may include the first keyword in the expression (e.g., the *ForAll* keyword) or the operator of a unary expression (e.g., "-"). In a typical inorder fashion, the left subtree is first printed recursively (e.g., `exp.Vbinary->syn_left`), followed by the characters between the left and right subtrees, via `ProcessNextLexInfo`, including the operator, followed by the right subtree (e.g., `exp.Vbinary->syn_right`).

16.1. REGENERATING THE IDL SOURCE

```
void ProcessExpression(exp)
expression exp;
{
    SEQexpressionPair Sep;
    expressionPair ep;
    SEQexpression Sexp;
    expression Anexp;
    switch (typeof(exp)) {
    case Kconditional: /* "If" was processed previously */
        ProcessExpression(exp.Vconditional->syn_test);
        ProcessNextLexInfo; /* "Then" */
        ProcessExpression(exp.Vconditional->syn_then);
        foreachinSEQexpressionPair(exp.Vconditional->syn_orif, Sep, ep){
            ProcessNextLexInfo; /* "Orif" */
            ProcessExpression(ep->syn_test);
            ProcessNextLexInfo; /* "Then" */
            ProcessExpression(ep->syn_then); }
        ProcessNextLexInfo; /* "Else" */
        ProcessExpression(exp.Vconditional->syn_else);
        break;
    case Kforallq:
    case Kexistsq: /* "ForAll" and "Exists" was processed previously */
        ProcessIdentifier(exp.Vquantifier.IDLclassCommon->syn_control.VIdentifier);
        ProcessNextLexInfo; /* "In..." */
        ProcessExpression(exp.Vquantifier.IDLclassCommon->syn_set);
        ProcessNextLexInfo; /* "Do" */
        ProcessExpression(exp.Vquantifier.IDLclassCommon->syn_body);
        break;
    case Kbinary:
        ProcessExpression(exp.Vbinary->syn_left);
        ProcessNextLexInfo; /* operator */
        ProcessExpression(exp.Vbinary->syn_right);
        break;
    case Kunary: /* operator was processed previously */
        ProcessExpression(exp.Vunary->syn_body);
        break;
    case Kdotted:
        ProcessExpression(exp.Vdotted->syn_left);
        ProcessNextLexInfo; /* . */
        ProcessIdentifier(exp.Vdotted->syn_right.VIdenfitifer);
        break;
    case KExpNameRef:
        ProcessIdentifier(exp.VIdentifier);
        break;
    case KintegerToken:
    case KrationalToken:
    case KstringToken:
        ProcessOther(exp.VotherToken);
        break;
    /* Other cases (Kapplication, KportExpression, KemptyExp, */
    /* KtrueExp, KfalseExp, KrootExp, KExpSetRef, */
    /* and KExpSeqRef) omitted */
}
```

Figure 16.4: The ProcessExpression Routine

As an example, the expression illustrated below

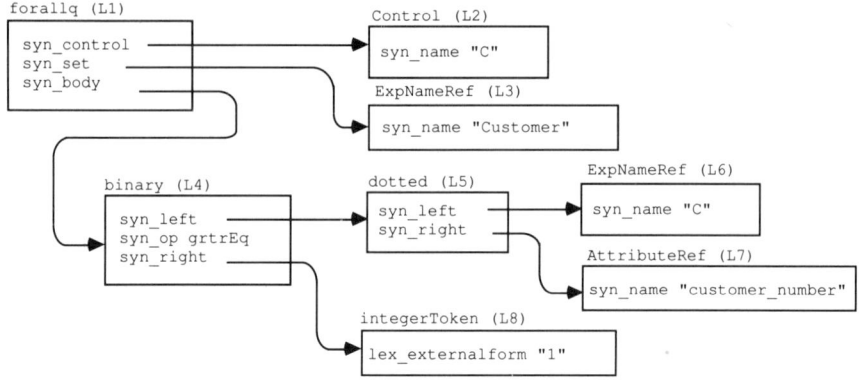

corresponds to the assertion

   ForAll C *In* Customer *Do* C.customer_number >= 1 *Od*;

When ProcessExpression is called, the characters "ForAll␣" have already been printed, and the restlexinfo sequence stands at

   <"␣In␣" "␣Do␣" "." "␣>=␣" "␣Od;···" ··· >

We show the spaces explicitly as "␣". The following calling sequence occurs.

```
ProcessExpression(L1)
     case Kforallq
     ProcessIdentifier(L2)
         output "C"
     ProcessNextLexInfo
         output "␣In␣"
     ProcessExpression(L3)
         case KExpNameRef
         ProcessIdentifier(L3)
             output "Customer"
     ProcessNextLexInfo
         output "␣Do␣"
     ProcessExpression(L4)
         case Kbinary
         ProcessExpression(L5)
             case Kdotted
             ProcessExpression(L6)
```

```
            case KExpNameRef
            ProcessIdentifier(L6)
                output "C"
            ProcessNextLexInfo
                output "."
            ProcessIdentifier(L7)
                output "customer_number"
        ProcessNextLexInfo
            output "␣>=␣"
        ProcessExpression(L8)
            case KintegerToken
            ProcessOther(L8)
                output "1"
```

Once the expression has been printed, the `restlexinfo` sequence stands at

<"␣0d;···" ··· >

The "*0d*" keyword will be printed by the routine that invoked `PrintExpression` in the first place. Note that it is imperative that `ProcessNextLexInfo` be called at exactly the right times. If the syntax tree traversal and the sequence stored in `restlexinfo` ever became unsynchronized, the output would be totally scrambled.

16.2 Generating Formatted Source

The `ProcessNextLexInfo` action to regenerate the CANDLE source, given on page 374, does not interpret the characters in `currentlexinfo`; these characters are simply written out. However, by removing tabs and inserting tabs and spaces in appropriate positions, CANDLEWALK can instead be used to generate a pretty-printed version of the IDL source. The formatting performed by CANDLEWALK includes the following.

- All attribute and class productions are indented one tab stop.
- The '::=' and '=>' symbols are lined up.
- The attribute types are lined up.
- This alignment is computed on a per-structure basis.
- Tab stops (whose setting can be specified when CANDLEWALK is invoked) apply for all lines except those involved in attribute or class productions.

```
int processingmode, /* =0 if normal mode*/
    characternumber;

void ProcessNextLexInfo()
{
    SEQString currentlexinfo;
    int i;

    retrievefirstSEQString(restlexinfo, currentlexinfo);
    if (processingmode == 0) {
        for(i=0; i<strlen(currentlexinfo); i++) {
            if (currentlexinfo[i] == "\t") {
                /* process tab */
            }
            else if (currentlexinfo[i] == "\n") {
                characternumber = 0;
                fprintf(stdout, "\n");
            }
            else {
                characternumber = characternumber + 1;
                fprintf(stdout, currentlexinfo[i]);
            }
        }
    }
    else /* process portion of an attribute or class production */;
    removefirstSEQString(restlexinfo);
}

void ProcessIdentifier(this)
Identifier this;
{
    characternumber = characternumber
            + strlen(this.IDLclassCommon->lex_name);
    fprintf(stdout, this->lex_name);
}

void ProcessOther(this)
otherToken this;
{
    characternumber = characternumber + strlen(this->lex_externalform);
    fprintf(stdout, this->lex_externalform);
}
```

Figure 16.5: Actions for Formatting the CANDLE Source

One design decision was that no newline characters were to be added or removed, thereby ensuring that each statement resided on the same line after formatting.

To format the source, CANDLEWALK makes the same tree traversal discussed in the previous section. There are four changes necessary to cause the output to be formatted.

1. The `ProcessStructureEntity` routine is modified to make an additional traversal of the parse tree rooted at that `StructureEntity`, computing at each attribute and class production the longest left-hand side and the longest attribute name within the structure.

2. The routines associated with attribute and class productions must record in a global variable `processingmode` the fact that such a production is currently being emitted (actually, the position within the production must also be recorded).

3. The `ProcessNextLexInfo` action must interpret the `currentlexinfo` value according to the value of the `processingmode` global variable (Figure 16.5). If an attribute or class production is not being emitted, then tab characters are converted into the required number of spaces, computed from the specified tab stops and the current character position. If such a production is being emitted, then some of the spaces and tab stops are ignored, and additional spaces generated to line things up correctly.

4. The other actions must maintain the global variable `characternumber`.

`ProcessNextLexInfo` becomes somewhat complex, because it must contend with newline characters and comments appearing in arbitrary places within the production.

In summary, the recursive descent traversal needs only to be slightly modified, and the `ProcessNextLexInfo` action modified substantially, to pretty-print the IDL source.

16.3 Variants of Formatted Source

CANDLEWALK supports two variants achieved through minor changes to the approach described in the previous section. The first variant produces LaTeX source, with embedded LaTeX commands. The following formatting is specified in the LaTeX source.

- IDL keywords (e.g., *ForAll*) are put in *slanted typewriter font*.

- IDL comments are put in *italics*.

- A macro call is placed at the beginning of each line, with the page and line numbers as parameters (e.g., \SPA{2}{4}). The SPA macro must be separately defined, perhaps evaluating to the empty string.

- A similar macro call is placed at the end of each line (e.g., \SPB{2}{4}).

- Some characters that are normally interpreted in particular ways by LaTeX are replaced with macro calls (e.g., '{' is replaced with "{\char'173}").

- Tabs are replaced with "\>."

- LaTeX commands are generated to set the tab stops appropriately.

All these transformations are performed in the `PrintNextLexInfo` action. The result, when run through the LaTeX formatter, will look like the listings given in Appendix F.

Another variant of the formatted source produces a CANDLE instance, rather than source text. The calculations to line up "::=", "=>", and attribute types are still performed, but instead of printing out the resulting string, this string replaces the string in `lex_information` from which it was computed. This change is realized by `ProcessNextLexInfo` appending this new string onto a sequence stored in the global variable `newlexinfo`. The three routines `ProcessImport`, `ProcessStructureEntity`, and `Process-ProcessEntity`, as well as the `main` routine, then store the `newlexinfo` sequence back into the `lex_information` attribute. The output is the modified CANDLE instance. Of course, this instance could be later printed by simply regenerating the source via a second invocation of CANDLEWALK.

16.4 Calculating Source Positions

The source position (i.e., page and line number) of each identifier is not stored explicitly in a CANDLE instance. However, by counting the number of newline characters and form feeds occurring before the identifier, the source position can be calculated using information that *is* stored in the CANDLE instance. CANDLEWALK can calculate an instance of `CandlePos` (shown in Appendix F) from a CANDLE instance by using the actions shown in Figure 16.6. CANDLEWALK can also compute the source positions of identifiers found in imported structures present in other source files, by walking the syntax tree referenced in

   ImportDecl.syn_spec.sem_entity.syn_body

16.5. SUMMARY

```
int filenumber = 1,
    pagenumber = 1,
    linenumber = 1;
void ProcessNextLexInfo()
{
    String currentlexinfo;
    int i;

    retrievefirstSEQString(restlexinfo, currentlexinfo);
    for (i=0; i<strlen(currentlexinfo); i++) {
        if (currentlexinfo[i] == "\l") pagenumber = pagenumber + 1;
        else if (currentlexinfo[i] == "\n") linenumber = linenumber + 1;
        else /* do nothing */
        }
    removefirstSEQString(restlexinfo);
}
void ProcessIdentifier(this)
Identifier this;
{
    MakeSourcePosition(&this.IDLclassCommon->lex_srcpos);
}
void ProcessOther(this)
otherToken this;
{
    /* do nothing */
}
void MakeSourcePosition(thispointer)
SourcePosition *thispointer;
{
    if (*thispointer==NULL) (*thispointer) = NSourcePosition;
    (*thispointer)->lex_file = filenumber;
    (*thispointer)->lex_page = pagenumber;
    (*thispointer)->lex_line = linenumber;
}
```

Figure 16.6: Actions for Computing the Source Position

The resulting CandlePos instance can then be processed by XREF to generate concordances. Since the formatted listings and the concordances were generated from the same CANDLE instance, they are more likely to be consistent.

16.5 Summary

By executing different actions on a recursive descent traversal of the syntax tree embedded in a CANDLE instance, CANDLEWALK can do the following tasks.

- regenerate the original IDL source text;

- produce a pretty-printed version of the IDL source;

- generate a version of the IDL source to be formatted by LaTeX;

- generate a CANDLE instance with formatted `lex_information` attributes; and

- generate a CANDLE instance in which every identifier has an additional `lex_srcpos` attribute indicating the source position of the identifier.

The sizes for CANDLEWALK are given below. As with most IDL processes, the generated code far exceeds the user-written code (here, the generated code is 87% of the total).

Component	Source	IDL	Generated	Object Code
	(Lines of Source Code)			(Kilobytes)
CANDLEWALK (C)	2,356	629	14,375	366
Total				433

Bibliographic Notes

Persch [1983] and Butler and Evans [1983] describe formatters for Ada programs similar in design to CANDLEWALK, yet using DIANA. The latter formatter encapsulates many of the details of formatting in a separate Ada package, an approach that closely resembles the actions found in CANDLEWALK. Lie [1984] describes an implementation of a general unparser based on IDL.

Cameron [1988] advocates passing the actions as procedure parameters to the pretty-printer routine. Rubin [1983] provides details on how the parse tree traversal may be automated. Lamport [1986] defines the LaTeX document production system.

Chapter 17

idlc Implementation

This chapter provides an example of the use of IDL in a large and complex software system, that of the IDL translator for the IDL toolkit (IDLC). The IDL translator maps the IDL constructs into code fragments and declarations in the target language for a particular target operating system and machine. It also optionally generates a CANDLE instance of the input specification, thereby providing the raw information for tools such as XREF, CANDLEWALK, and IDLCHECK. This translator exhibits complexity similar to that of compilers for modern programming languages such as Pascal or C, yet differs from these compilers because of the declarative nature of IDL. Hence, while the overall organization of IDLC follows closely that of these compilers, the details of the phases differ, sometimes significantly. For this reason, and because IDLC illustrates the proper use of IDL in a large tool, we discuss in detail the techniques and algorithms employed in IDLC.

Throughout this chapter, we refer to conformance to IDL Version 2. IDL Version 2 is the IDL language syntax and semantics as it is defined in the 1982 IDL Formal Description. The IDL language processed by IDLC is a modification of this language as several features have been added or changed. Conformance to IDL Version 2 can be checked by specifying a command line option to IDLC. Conformance checking is necessary so that IDL specifications based on IDL Version 2, such as DIANA, can be processed by IDLC.

We had several goals in mind for the implementation of the IDL translator. The most important goals were readability, extensibility, ease of implementation, and providing for IDL Version 2 conformance. A less important goal was efficiency, since this goal could be achieved by continually refining the translator over the later versions.

As mentioned briefly in Chapter 14, IDLC is based on the architecture depicted in Figure 14.1. The first section of this chapter gives an overview of the implementation and explains how and why it differs from the architecture of Figure 14.1. The following sections describe the various phases of the translator. We discuss the specific algorithms used in IDLC, and motivate the various design decisions. While the discussion is relevant to those wishing to implement their own IDL translator, it is descriptive of one particular implementation, rather than prescriptive of such implementations in general. The final section discusses the strengths and weaknesses of the translator architecture and implementation.

17.1 Implementation Overview

The IDLC architecture, depicted in Figure 17.1, differs from the architecture shown in Figure 14.1 in three minor ways. These differences, expressible in IDL via derivation, are an example of code sharing in IDL. In this case, the entire IDL architecture specification, as given in Figure 14.2, has been utilized in the specification of the IDLC architecture.

The first difference is that the specific data structures passed between the various phases of IDLC are altered versions of the CANDLE structures described in Chapter 15. The derivation graph for these structures is shown below.

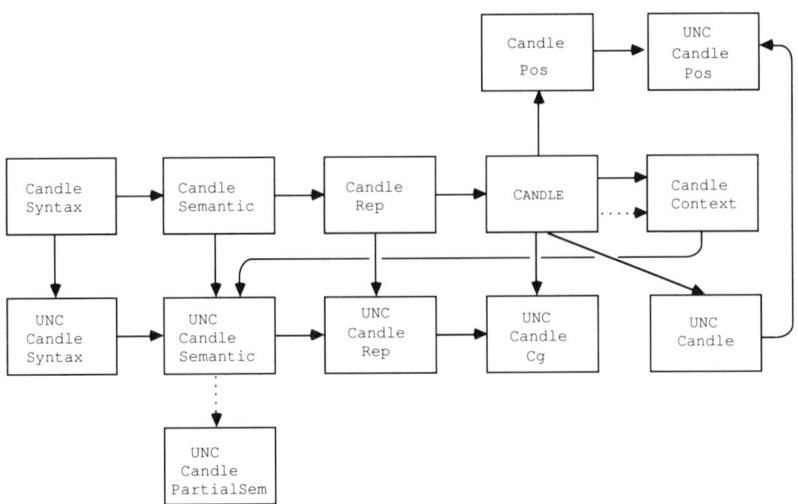

This graph should be compared with Figure 15.24. As with the other figure, an arrow from structure A to structure B is read as "structure B is derived from structure A by adding information" and a dotted line from structure A

17.1. IMPLEMENTATION OVERVIEW

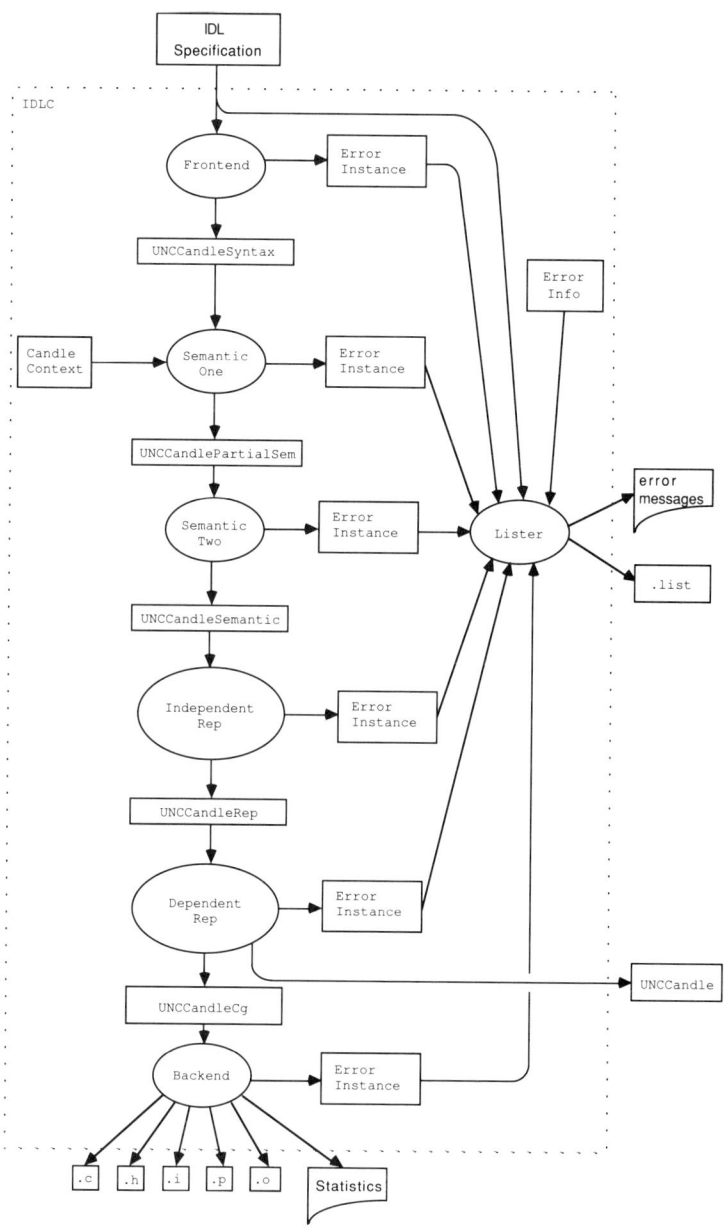

Figure 17.1: IDLC Architecture

to structure B is read "structure B is derived from structure A by removing information via Without statements." For example, UNCCandleSemantic is derived from three structures: UNCCandleSyntax, CandleSemantic, and CandleContext (the IDL Toolkit was implemented at the University of North Carolina, hence the prefix UNC).

IDLC uses different structures than the CANDLE structures for three reasons. The first reason is that, since CANDLE is implementation-independent, no external representations for the private types LexInfo and TimestampType are provided. UNCCandle, the structure computed by IDLC, specifies the external representations as *Seq Of String* and *Integer*, respectively. Second, the CANDLE structures are abstract structures in that the internal representation of private types is not specified. The UNCCandle... structures augment the CANDLE structures with the concrete information necessary to represent the private types internally. For example, the private type LexInfo is represented internally as a *Seq Of String* in all processes of IDLC.

The final reason for using separate structures is that the phases of IDLC use similar information not contained in the Candle structures. Rather than recalculate this information in each phase, it is passed along via UNCCandle structures to later phases until it is no longer needed. An example is the position of important tokens in the source file. Each phase may need this information to report errors. Rather than having each phase recalculate the position from the private type LexInfo, the position is calculated once in the frontend and passed along to the later phases.

The second difference between the initial architecture and IDLC's architecture is that the semantic analysis process is split into two processes, one to analyze the structures and processes and the second to analyze the assertions. We partitioned the process to enable two people to implement the different phases of semantic analysis.

A third difference is that, rather than the prelude being read by each of these phases, it is read in once by the first SemanticAnalysis phase. The relevant information is retained in the UNCCandleSemantic structure and passed to the second SemanticAnalysis phase and to the Independent Representation Analysis phase. This approach also provides a solution to another problem, discussed in Section 17.8. The UNC structure is a strict superset of the original structure, that is, no Without clauses are used.

No IDL translator existed when we started implementing IDLC, yet we wanted to use IDL in the implementation. Version 1.0 of IDLC was bootstrapped by manually writing macros describing the declarations and readers and writers. The declaration files and reader/writer code files were then generated by a macro processor. This initial version of IDLC only supported

17.1. IMPLEMENTATION OVERVIEW

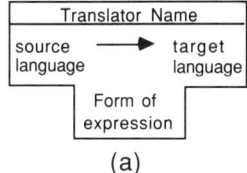

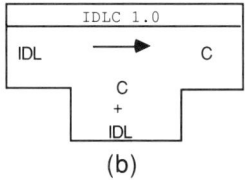 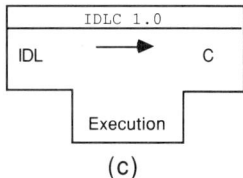

Figure 17.2: T Diagrams

a subset of IDL. In particular, assertions, classes and nodes with multiple super-classes, restrictions, and refined processes were not supported. Successive versions of IDLC were bootstrapped first by using the previous version of IDLC and then using the current version after this version stabilized. This process may be visualized using T diagrams as shown in Figure 17.2. Each T diagram illustrates the application of a translator on a program in the source language, producing a program in the target language. A prototype T diagram is given in Figure 17.2a. Figure 17.2b shows IDLC 1.0 in source code form and Figure 17.2c shows the same translator in execution. The source and target languages are identical, but the form of expression is not. Figure 17.3 illustrates how an execution of IDLC 1.0 was obtained, and how IDLC 1.0 was used to compile IDLC 2.0. IDLC 2.0 supported nonhierarchical classes and restrictions. IDLC 3.0 added refined processes, and was the first version to support CANDLE. IDLC 4.0 added support for Pascal and assertions.

The CANDLE structures use assertions extensively. The assertions were useful for providing a precise explanation of the CANDLE structures for tool builders. Unfortunately, the assertion checker was not yet available during the implementation, and the assertions in CANDLE have not yet been debugged.

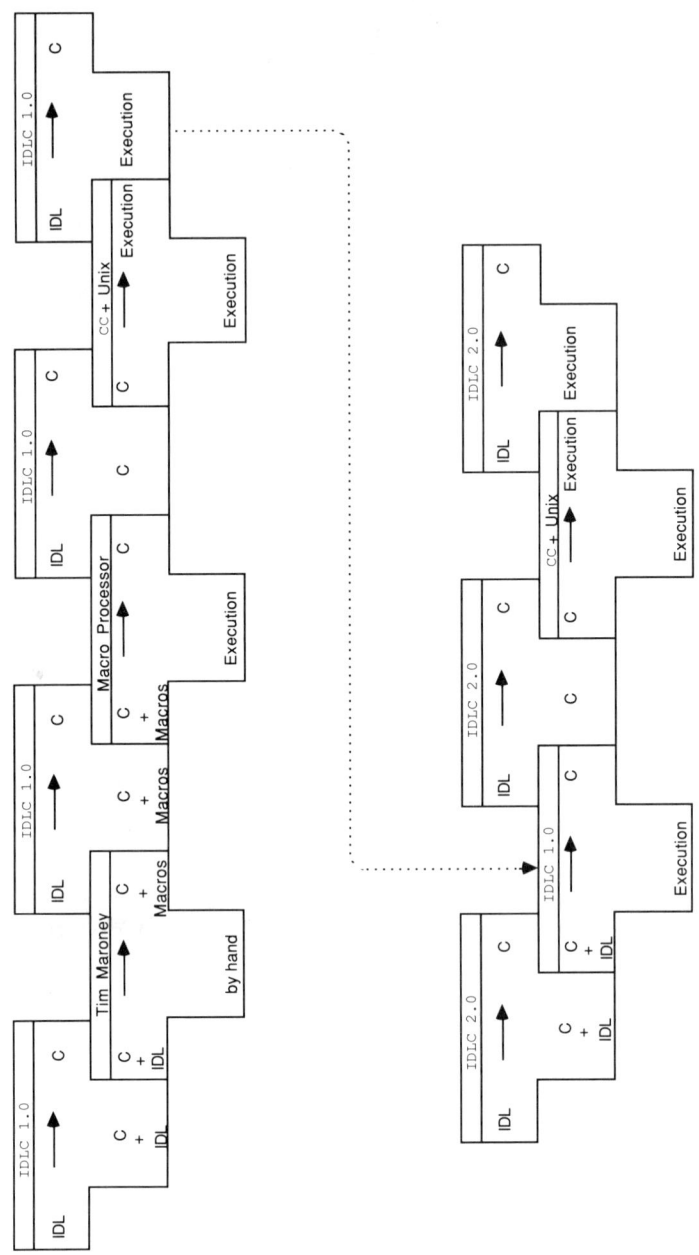

Figure 17.3: Bootstrapping IDLC

17.2 The Frontend

The main functions of the frontend are to recognize identifiers and symbols, verify that the syntax is correct, and build the UNCCandleSyntax structure. In addition, the process must record the source position of important tokens, report and recover from any lexical or syntactic errors, and check for IDL Version 2 conformance if specified.

The frontend uses the LEX and YACC compiler tools for lexical and syntactic analysis, respectively (as does the function language compiler discussed in Chapter 9). Although hand-written analyzers could be more efficient, the compiler tools were used to generate the analyzers for ease of implementation. In the following, we mention only unusual or noteworthy aspects of the frontend.

In the lexical analyzer, the actions for each token encountered keep track of the current character count as well as the start position of the previous token processed. The current character count is necessary so that all identifiers and syntactic constructs requiring a source position in UNCCandleSyntax will have the necessary information. The start position of the last token processed must be retained so that error messages can point to the starting character of the offending token without worrying about any white space encountered after the token was recognized.

The generated lexical analyzer differentiates between identifiers and keywords and checks for IDL Version 2 conformance of keywords. The latter involves testing that the case of keywords matches the IDL Version 2 specifications. Keywords are stored alphabetically in a table, both in IDL Version 2 format and in all lower case. Each time an identifier is recognized, a binary search on the keyword table is performed. The comparison step involves converting the identifier to lower case and then comparing it with the lower case version of the keyword. If there is no match, the token constant for "identifier" is returned.

If a match is found, there are several possibilities. If IDL Version 2 conformance is not specified, the lexical analyzer returns the token constant for the corresponding keyword. If IDL Version 2 conformance *is* specified, the original form of the identifier is also compared with the IDL Version 2 format of the keyword (the first character is in upper case and the remaining characters are in lower case, except for the keywords *ForAll* and *OrIf*). If the identifier matches exactly, the lexical analyzer returns the token constant for the corresponding keyword, otherwise the analyzer returns the token constant for "identifier" and prints an error message indicating that an identifier is the same as a keyword except for case.

The parser was built using YACC. The parser builds the **UNCCandleSyntax** structure, checks for IDL Version 2 grammar conformance, and recovers from syntactic errors. Error recovery is necessary so that multiple distinct errors can be flagged.

Building the `UNCCandleSyntax` structure is straightforward since the structure is based on the BNF for IDL. The structure is built bottom-up as the statements and declarations are recognized, as described in Section 9.2.1. Conformance to IDL Version 2 grammar is checked by adding additional rules for each construct with a differing syntax. Certain grammar rules are flagged as illegal when conformance is not specified, including features that have been deleted or replaced by new constructs. Similarly, other rules are flagged as illegal when conformance is specified.

The error recovery used is that provided by YACC, and consequently is somewhat primitive. In general, if an error is encountered while processing a structure or process statement, the parser scans forward to the next "*;*", "*End*", or end-of-file. All characters from the previous "*;*" (or from the "*Is*" keyword if there is no previous statement) to the current character are stored in the `lex_info` attribute in the `errorstatement` node. The parser then continues processing the input. If an error is encountered when processing a structure or process declaration but not within a statement, the parser scans forward to the next "*End*" or end-of-file. All characters from the end of the previous declaration or from the beginning of the file are stored in the attribute `lex_info` in the `errordeclaration` node. The parser then continues processing the input. This error recovery strategy is admittedly unsophisticated but suffices for the purposes of the translator since it allows the entire input to be processed even in the presence of errors. The strategy also allows for later error recovery extensions. For example, a future version of IDLC could process the `lex_info` attribute to see which construct it most closely matched and then be able to provide a fix for the error.

After the complete `UNCCandleSyntax` structure is built, a writer routine is called to pass this structure to the next phase of the translator.

17.3 Semantic Analysis

There are two processes concerned with semantic analysis, one for the analysis of structures and processes and one for the analysis of assertions. Semantic analysis of structures, processes, and assertions involves the following tasks.

- Resolve names.

- Creat semantic entities.

17.3. SEMANTIC ANALYSIS

- Collect similar entities.
- Handle errors.

Each task calculates various attributes in the `UNCCandleSemantic` structure. We now briefly describe each task and list the attributes it calculates. Details of structure and process analysis follow this overview.

Name resolution associates an entity or entities with a single name, a name clause (e.g., *Seq Of* ⟨name⟩), or the special symbol "*". Each reference is associated with a reference node. Reference nodes for single names and name clauses have a `sem_entity` attribute which contains a pointer to the appropriate entity if the entity is found or to the `error` node if the entity is not found. Reference nodes for the symbol "*" have an attribute `sem_items` which is a set of the appropriate entity. If no appropriate entities are found, the set is empty.

Creating semantic entities involves collecting the appropriate syntactic constructs together to determine the relevant information and then building the new node. The following semantic entities are created during semantic analysis.

```
arbitrary      SeqOf
Atomic         SetOf
Class          singleton
Definition
```

For example, to create a `Class` semantic entity, all `subclassProductions` and `attributeProductions` referencing the class are collected together, then the class entity is built.

Another task of semantic analysis is calculating attributes referencing semantic entities, either a single entity or a collection of entities. The former are represented by attributes with a node, class, or atomic type. The single entity attributes calculated are

```
Attribute.sem_copiedfrom
collection.sem_type
Control.sem_owner
Definition.sem_resulttype
expression.sem_type
Port.sem_portType
ProcessEntity.sem_target
SetOrSeq.sem_component
TypeEntity.sem_copiedfrom
```

The `sem_portType` attribute of a `Port`, for example, is calculated using the type in the `portDefinition`. The multiple entity attributes calculated are

```
Attribute.sem_reps
Class.sem_allattributes
Class.sem_ancestors
Class.sem_subclasses
Definition.sem_overload
ProcessEntity.sem_ports
StructureEntity.sem_types
StructureOrProcess.sem_assertions
StructureOrProcess.sem_definitions
TypeEntity.sem_reps
```

The `sem_allattributes` attribute is calculated by collecting all attributes in all `attributeProductions` referencing a particular `Class`.

The final function is error handling. There are three ways in which errors are handled in semantic analysis. The first is concerned with setting unresolved references to `error` (described in Section 15.3.5). The second is marking duplicates. Duplicates will be explained in more detail in Section 17.3.3. The third kind is correcting recoverable errors. There are two attributes calculated for this, `sem_duplicate` and `sem_corrections`.

17.3.1 Overview of Structure and Process Analysis

The main steps for analyzing structures and processes are as follows.

1. Read in the prelude and the `UNCCandleSyntax` instance.

2. Process import clauses.

3. Sort the structures and processes into processing order.

4. Analyze each structure.

5. Analyze each process.

6. Write out the `UNCCandleSemantic` instance.

The readers and writer for steps 1 and 6 are generated automatically by IDLC.

After the prelude and `UNCCandleSyntax` instances are read in, each import declaration in `compilationUnit.syn_body` is processed. Import declarations are processed recursively. Each import declaration contains a file reference and a sequence of structure and process references. The file name is sent to the frontend, which returns an instance of the `UNCCandleSyntax` structure. All import declarations in this structure are then processed. Next, name resolution is performed for the structure and process references

17.3. SEMANTIC ANALYSIS

using the corresponding UNCCandleSyntax structure for the import declaration. A file referenced in multiple import declarations will be sent to the frontend only once. This procedure continues until all import declarations have been processed.

An extension to IDLC could support separate compilation of IDL specifications. Here, the CANDLE instance associated with the file name (with the suffix ".Cdl") would be read in if it was newer in modification date than the corresponding IDL file (⟨filename⟩.idl), otherwise a CANDLE instance for the IDL file would be created by executing IDLC on the IDL file.

17.3.2 Ordering the Structures and Processes

Once the import declarations have been processed, the structures and processes are sorted based on the following dependency relations.

- A derived or refined structure is analyzed after all the structures from which it is derived (the syn_from attribute) or refined (the syn_refines attribute).

- A refined process is analyzed after all the processes from which it is refined (the syn_refines attribute).

- A process is analyzed after all its port structures and after its invariant structure.

To meet these dependency relations, all structures are analyzed before any processes (other sort orders are possible). The structures are sorted so that a derived or refined structure appears after any structures named in its syn_from or syn_refines attributes. The processes are sorted so that a refined process appears after the process named in its syn_refines attribute. Circular dependency relations are not allowed and result in a fatal error.

Duplicate structures and processes are marked as such during sorting. For each set of structures with the same name, only one structure in the set will not be marked as a duplicate and therefore will be considered as the (one) correct structure. The choice of this "correct" structure from the set is arbitrary. An analogous approach is used for a set of processes with the same name.

After sorting is complete, all structures are analyzed in order followed by all processes in order.

17.3.3 Structure Analysis

The steps in semantically analyzing structure declarations are

- resolve names of ancestor structures,
- resolve without clauses,
- perform name resolution on productions,
- resolve the root name,
- perform name resolution on attribute and type representations, and
- collect assertions and definitions.

Each step will be discussed in turn.

Ancestor Structure Resolution

The structure analysis phase first checks if the structure is derived or refined. It is an error if a structure is both derived and refined (combined derivation and refinement is allowed in IDL Version 2; IDLC does not permit this even when conformance is specified). A derived structure has a nonempty syn_from sequence and a refined structure has a nonvoid syn_refines attribute:

```
StructureEntity => syn_from:     Seq Of StructureRef,
                   syn_refines:  StructureRefOrVoid;
```

Within each dependent structure, name resolution is performed for each ancestor structure named by a StructureRef. After name resolution, all information in the ancestor structure(s) is copied to the dependent structure. Copying is described in further detail in Section 17.3.5.

Without Clauses

The next step is to process withoutClauses for derived structures, checking first that nonderived structures do not contain them. Processing withoutClauses involves name resolution, the deletion of the semantic entities Assertion, Definition, or TypeEntity from their respective sets sem_assertions, sem_definitions, and sem_types in a StructureEntity, and the deletion of Attributes or subclasses from the sem_attributes or sem_subclasses sets contained in a Class.

17.3. SEMANTIC ANALYSIS

Deleting Assertions, Definitions, and TypeEntitys is straightforward. These types of deletions are specified by withoutAssert, withoutDefine, and withoutType nodes, respectively, each of which has an attribute syn_item that is a reference to the corresponding entity.

```
withoutAssert  => syn_item: AssertRef;
withoutDefine  => syn_item: DefineRef;
withoutType    => syn_item: TypeRef;
```

The entity reference is first resolved, then the entity (if found) is deleted from the set sem_assertions, sem_definitions, or sem_types.

Deleting attributes or subclasses is slightly more involved in the presence of "*". These deletions are specified by withoutAttribute or withoutSubclass nodes, each of which has an attribute syn_lefthandside that is either a reference to a single Class or a reference to all classes denoted by "*".

```
withoutProduction ::= withoutAttribute | withoutSubclass;
withoutProduction => syn_lefthandside: ClassOrAllClasses;
withoutAttribute  => syn_righthandside:AttributeOrAllAttributes;
withoutSubclass   => syn_righthandside:ClassOrAllClasses;
```

A withoutAttribute also has an attribute syn_righthandside that is either a reference to a single attribute or to all attributes, denoted by "*". Similarly, a withoutSubclass has an attribute syn_righthandside that is either a reference to a single subclass or to all subclasses, of the class denoted by "*". The "*" resolves to different sets depending on the context. If it appears on the left hand side, it will resolve to all classes in the structure. If it appears on the right hand side, it will either resolve to all attributes of all classes on the left hand side for a withoutAttribute or it will resolve to all subclasses of all classes on the left hand side for a withoutSubclass. After name resolution, the attributes or classes are deleted from their respective sets: Class.sem_allattributes or Class.sem_subclasses.

Productions and Type Declarations

The next step in the structure analysis phase is the processing of productions. There are two types of productions, subclassProductions that add subclasses and attributeProductions that add attributes.

```
production           ::= subclassProduction | attributeProduction;
production           => syn_class:      NamedTypeRef;
subclassProduction   => syn_subclasses: Seq Of NamedTypeRef;
attributeProduction  => syn_attributes: Seq Of Attribute;
Attribute            => syn_type:       TypeRef;
```

Each production has an attribute syn_class that is a reference to a Class in the structure. If the Class does not exist when processing the production, a new `Class` is created and added to the structure's `sem_types` set. This new `Class` serves as the defining entity for the type (defining entities are discussed in Chapter 15). For `subclassProductions`, all subclasses listed in `syn_subclasses` are added to the class temporarily as references. These cannot be resolved until all the productions have been processed since they may refer to classes not yet created. For `attributeProductions`, all attributes listed in `syn_attributes` are added to the `sem_allattributes` sequence of the class. The type references in each `Attribute.syn_type` are not resolved yet since all types have not yet been added at this point.

After `productions` are processed, the phase then creates `Atomics` for each `atomicDecl`.

```
atomicDecl => syn_atomic:    NamedTypeRef,
              sem_duplicate: Boolean;
```

Each new `Atomic` is added to the structure's `sem_types` set. These `Atomics` serve as the defining entity. Duplicate private declarations are now detected and flagged as errors.

The phase then performs name resolution for the subclass references in each `Class` and for the type references in each `Attribute`. Each subclass reference must resolve to a node or class rather than a private type since private types cannot be members of a class. Any sets or sequences referenced via a `SeqRef` or `SetRef` in an `Attribute` but not already existing are created and added to the structure's `sem_types` set. `NamedTypeRefs` can refer to names in the structure or IDL types found in the prelude. Any `NamedTypeRefs` that name a type not in the structure will have a new `Class` created and added to the structure's `sem_types` as an error recovery. In addition, a `correction` node is created and added to the structure `sem_corrections` sequence.

```
correction => sem_stmt:  statement,
              sem_cause: statement;
```

The `sem_cause` attribute of the `correction` points to the `subclassProduction` or `attributeProduction` that contains the unresolved reference. The `sem_stmt` attribute points to an `attributeProduction` created for the new `Class`.

After name resolution in productions is completed, the phase checks for cycles in the class hierarchy. A class is part of a cycle if it can be reached via its `sem_subclasses` set. A cycle is flagged as a serious error. If there are no cycles, the classes are sorted from most inclusive to least inclusive: class C_1 appears before class C_2 if C_2 is a subclass of C_1. Attributes are then propagated from classes to their subclasses. Attributes with identical names propagated to the same node are flagged as errors.

17.3. SEMANTIC ANALYSIS

Root Name Resolution

At this point, all types in the structure have been created. The next step is to perform name resolution for the root clause of the structure if given. A `StructureEntity` has two attributes relating to the structure root.

```
StructureEntity => syn_root: TypeRefOrVoid,
                   sem_root: TypeEntityOrVoid;
```

The attribute `syn_root` is Void if no root was specified in the structure declaration, otherwise it is a `TypeRef`. If the root clause is given, the `TypeRef` is resolved to the corresponding type in the structure. This type is then assigned to the `sem_root` attribute. If the root clause is not given and the structure is derived or refined, the root can be inherited from an ancestor structure. If the structure is refined, the `sem_root` attribute is set to the type named in the `sem_root` attribute of the ancestor structure. This is guaranteed to exist in the refined structure since no without clauses are allowed. If the structure is derived, the `sem_root` attribute is set to the type named in the first ancestor structure in the `syn_from` sequence that has a root that has not been deleted in the derived structure.

If the `sem_root` attribute is not Void, a reachability check is performed. This check uses a recursive procedure marking each type reachable through the following attributes.

```
StructureEntity =>  syn_root:           TypeRefOrVoid,
                    sem_types:          Seq Of TypeEntity;
Class           =>  sem_allattributes:  Seq Of Attribute,
                    sem_subclasses:     Set Of Class,
                    sem_ancestors:      Set Of Class;
Attribute       =>  syn_type:           TypeRef;
TypeRef         =>  sem_entity:         TypeEntityOrError;
SetOrSeq        =>  sem_component:      NamedType;
```

The marking begins with the root of the structure and marks all types reachable through attributes, subclasses, or ancestor classes. The reachability check then tests all types in `StructureEntity.sem_types` to see if they have been marked. Those that are not marked are not reachable from the root. A warning message is printed for each unreachable type.

Representation Name Resolution

At this point, name resolution is performed for `attributeReps` and `typeRepDecls`. The relevant attributes are shown below.

```
attributeRep => syn_class:     NamedTypeRef,
                syn_attribute: AttributeRef,
                syn_rep:       RepRef;
typeRepDecl => syn_type:       TypeRef,
               syn_spec:       RepRef;
```

For `attributeRep`s the references are resolved for the `syn_class` and `syn_-attribute` fields. The corresponding `RepRef` is then added to the `sem_reps` sequence of the attribute resolved to. For `typeRepDecl`s the reference is resolved for the `syn_type` field and the corresponding `RepRef` is added to the `sem_reps` sequence of the type resolved to.

```
Attribute  => sym_reps: Seq Of RepRef;
TypeEntity => sem_reps: Seq Of RepRef;
```

No representation analysis is done for the `RepRef`s of attributes or types during semantic analysis. They are simply collected in an ordered sequence for later processing. The `sem_reps` field is present in `UNCCandleSemantic` but not in `CandleSemantic` since it can be easily calculated.

Collecting Assertions and Definitions

The last step of the structure analysis phase adds the `Assertions` and `Definitions` to the structure's `sem_assertions` and `sem_definitions` sets. Assertions and definitions must be added in the first semantic analysis process rather than the second so that `withoutAsserts` and `withoutDefines` can be processed. `Assertions` are added directly to the structure's `sem_assertions` set. `DefInstances` (i.e., versions) with the same name are collected in the `sem_overload` set of a newly created `Definition`. The new `Definition` is then added to the structure's `sem_definitions` set. Further analysis of assertions and definitions is left for the second semantic analysis process.

17.3.4 Process Analysis

The basic steps of process analysis are

- create the invariant structure,
- perform refinement,
- perform name resolution and type checking on port declarations,
- analyze the invariant structure,

17.3. SEMANTIC ANALYSIS

- perform name resolution of the target, and
- collect process assertions and definitions.

Create The Invariant Structure

The process analysis phase first creates a new structure for the invariant of the process regardless of whether an invariant structure is specified. A new structure must be created even if an invariant structure is specified so that the invariant structure of the process is local to the process. The target of a process causes an implicit refinement of the invariant structure of the process so the structure may not be valid for other processes, with different targets, that reference it. The new structure is added to the sem_invariant attribute of the process.

```
ProcessEntity => syn_invariant: StructureRefOrVoid,
                 sem_invariant: StructureEntity;
```

If an invariant clause is given, name resolution is performed for the StructureRef given in syn_invariant. All the information from the named invariant is then copied to the new structure in sem_invariant. Structure copying is described in the next section.

Perform Refinement

A refined process has a nonempty syn_refines attribute:

```
ProcessEntity => syn_refines: ProcessRefOrVoid;
```

If this attribute is not Void, the ancestor process must be located. The process, the ports, the invariant structure, and the target are copied from the ancestor process to the refined process. For each port in the ancestor process, a new Port entity is created and added to the sem_ports attribute of the refined process. The lex_name and syn_data attributes of the port are copied as references. All information in the sem_invariant structure of the ancestor process is copied to the sem_invariant structure of this process.

Analyze Port Declarations

The ports are added next. Each portDefinition in ProcessEntity.syn_body defines one or more ports.

```
portDefinition => syn_portType: PortType,
                  syn_ports:    Seq Of Port;
```

```
Port            => syn_data:       StructureRef,
                   sem_portType:   PortType,
                   sem_duplicate:  Boolean;
```

Each `Port` in `syn_ports` has an attribute `sem_portType` that is assigned the value of the `syn_portType` in the `portDefinition`. A `Port` is added to the `sem_ports` set of the process if all the following criteria are met.

- The structure referenced in the `StructureRef` of `Port.syn_data` must be a structure in `compilationUnit.syn_body` or a structure imported in an `ImportDecl` in `compilationUnit.syn_body`.

- The structure found must have a root, that is, the `sem_root` attribute of the structure must not be `Void`.

- No other port in the `sem_ports` set can have the same name. If a port with the same name already exists, the port being tested is marked as a duplicate.

Analyze Invariant Structure

Once port declarations are analyzed, all types in the port structures are checked for existence in the invariant structure of the process. There are four possibilities.

1. The port type does not exist in the invariant structure. Here, the type is copied and added to the invariant.

2. The port type exists in the invariant structure but is a different type. This results in a severe error.

3. The port type exists in the invariant but the invariant type does not contain all the information in the port type. the extra information is added to the invariant type. For example, if the port type contains extra attributes, these are added to the invariant type.

4. The port type exists in the invariant and the invariant type contains a superset of the information in the port type. No additional processing for this port type is needed.

After the port structure information is added to the invariant, the invariant is analyzed as a structure. The member references and attribute type references are resolved; the class hierarchy is checked for cycles; the class attributes are propagated to subclasses; and the root reference is resolved if given. If the invariant contains a root, reachability is checked. Neither a root nor reachability is required for the invariant since presumably no traversing from the root is required as in port structures.

17.3. SEMANTIC ANALYSIS

Perform Name Resolution of the Target

The next step is to perform name resolution for any `targetStmts`. If the named `TargetEntity` is located in the prelude it is attached to the `sem_entity` attribute of the `targetStmt` and also to the `sem_target` attribute of the `ProcessEntity`. If it is not found, the `sem_entity` of the `targetStmt` is set to `Error`. Multiple target statements may appear within a process declaration provided they are compatible as determined by the prelude. Specific details are beyond the scope of this book, but in general, each successive target statement must not conflict with previous target statements. For example, the two target clauses

```
Target Language C;
Target Operating System Unix;
```

are compatible, but the two statements

```
Target Language C;
Target Language Pascal;
```

conflict, since they each specify a separate language.

Collecting Assertions and Definitions

The last step of the process analysis phase adds the assertions and definitions to the process's `sem_assertions` and `sem_definitions` sets, similar to the same step in structure analysis. Assertions are added directly to the process' `sem_assertions` set. `DefInstances` (i.e., versions) with the same name are collected in the `sem_overload` set of a newly created `Definition`, which is then added to the process' `sem_definitions` set. Again, further analysis of assertions and definitions is left for the second semantic analysis phase.

17.3.5 Copying Structures

Copying during semantic analysis is a time-consuming task. There are two types of copying operations: copying values and copying references. Copying values usually requires allocating space for the new object and therefore can be expensive in both space and time. Copying by reference usually involves only a pointer assignment and so is fast. One way to make this tradeoff would be to copy all objects except primitive objects (i.e., integers, rationals, etc.) as references. Unfortunately, this approach is not always feasible. For example, in the derivation of structures, attributes can be added to classes inherited from ancestor structures. If the classes were copied by reference to the new structure, attribute additions to the class in the derived structure would also affect the class in the ancestor structure.

Our approach instead is to copy as much as possible by reference, and copy the rest by value. Specifically, we always copy syntactic attributes as references and copy semantic attributes by reference whenever possible and by value only when required for correctness. Semantic attributes can be copied by reference rather than value when there is no possibility that they will be changed in later phases. For example, the sem_name attribute of a class can be copied as reference since it will not be changed in representation analysis. If sem_name conflicts with a target keyword, a new prefixed form of the name is assigned to rep_name rather than changing sem_name.

The first step is to copy all types contained in the ancestor structure to the dependent structure. All assertion information is then copied, a task discussed below.

We refer to the type being copied as the *original type* and the resulting type in the dependent structure as the *destination type*. There are several considerations to keep in mind when copying types. First, for a derived structure, which may have several ancestor structures, there may be several originating types with the same name from different ancestor structures. These must be combined correctly to form the destination type. Second, Without clauses may delete some parts of the result of copying so certain information should not be copied until after Without clauses have been processed. For example, propagated attributes should not be copied since the original attribute of the class may be deleted with a Without clause. Finally, since information may be added or deleted from the destination type, we must use value copying rather than reference copying.

Only Classes and Atomics are copied. Sets and sequences are added after processing Without clauses to ensure that if the attribute that defines them is deleted, they will not exist in the dependent structure. When copying a Class or Atomic we first check if a type with the same name (added from a previous ancestor structure) already exists in the dependent structure. If not, a new Class or Atomic is allocated and added to the sem_types set of the dependent structure.

Copying Classes

Copying Classes is a two-step process. The first step involves allocating a new Class, copying the name and attributes, and setting the sem_copied-from attribute to the originating type. The second step builds the subclass and ancestor sets by setting the appropriate references to the newly created classes from the first step.

17.3. SEMANTIC ANALYSIS

```
Class => sem_name:         String,
         sem_allattributes: Seq Of Attribute,
         sem_subclasses:   Set Of Class,
         sem_ancestors:    Set Of Class,
         sem_copiedfrom:   ClassOrVoid,
```

The name can be copied as a reference even though it is a semantic attribute since it is guaranteed not to be modified. The attribute sequence is copied and all nonpropagated attributes are copied. Copying **Attributes** involves copying the name and type reference and setting the **sem_copiedfrom** field to the attribute that is copied from.

```
Attribute => lex_name:       String,
             syn_type:       TypeRef,
             sem_copiedfrom: AttributeOrVoid,
```

The name and type are copied as references since they are syntactic attributes. This means that the entity of the type reference will point to the type in the ancestor structure rather than the dependent structure. However, during representation analysis, a **rep_type** attribute is added to each **Attribute** that will point to a type in the dependent structure.

Copying Atomics

When copying **Atomics**, the name is copied as a reference and the **sem_copiedfrom** field is set to the originating type. **Atomics** representing IDL basic types such as *Boolean* and *Integer* are *always* copied as references. This ensures that there is only one of each predefined type throughout all the structures in a **compilationUnit**. No structure can modify a predefined type so there is no reason to ever re-allocate these types. Any representation clauses allowed for predefined types will result in another predefined type in the prelude rather than changing the first type.

If a type with the same name is already contained in the dependent structure then one of five actions is taken based on a comparison of the existing type and the ancestor type.

1. If the existing type and the ancestor type are not both **Class**es or are not both **Atomics** a conflicting type error is reported and the new type is not added.

2. If both types are **Class**es and the existing type is a node (i.e. contains no subclasses) and the new type is a class (i.e. contains one or more subclasses), then an error of trying to promote a node to a class is reported and the new type is not added.

3. If the types are not both from the same definition point, a conflicting type error is reported. The definition point of a type is found by following the `sem_copiedfrom` attribute until an ancestor type is found that is not copied from any other type. Actions 1 and 2 are more specific examples of this action.

4. If both types are `Atomics` and they are from the same definition point, then the representation information of the ancestor type is added to the representation information of the existing type. This involves concatenating the `sem_rep` sequences of the two types. No representation analysis is done at this point; the `RepRefs` are simply added to the sequence as references.

5. If both types are nodes or both types are classes, then the attributes, subclasses, and representations of the ancestor type are added to the existing type. Duplicate attributes are flagged if they are not from the same definition point. The definition point of an `Attribute` is found by following the `sem_copiedfrom` field until an `Attribute` is found that is not copied from any other `Attribute`. Duplicate attributes not from the same definition point are also checked for type conflict, a further indication that there may be an error. Subclasses are temporarily added as references since the class they refer to may not yet be added to the structure. Finally, the `sem_rep` sequences of both types are concatenated and attached to the existing type.

After all `Classes` and `Atomics` are copied, the temporary subclass references in the `Classes` are resolved.

Copying Assertion Information

The second step, after all the types have been copied, is to copy the assertion information. This involves copying both the assertions and definitions. Only named assertions are copied and these are copied as references, unless we are processing a refined structure, in which case all assertions are copied. If an `Assertion` exists in several ancestor structures, then only one copy is added to the dependent structure. A new `Definition` is allocated for each ancestor definition if a definition with the same name does not already exist in the dependent structure. All `DefInstances` (i.e., versions) are added to `Definition.sem_overload` as references. Since `Assertions` and `DefInstances` are copied as references, any type references in internal expressions will reference types in the ancestor structure rather than in the dependent structure.

17.3.6 Semantic Analysis of Assertions

Semantic analysis of assertions involves the following tasks.

- Resolve names.
- Analyze definitions.
- Check types.

Name resolution involves associating names found in the expressions of assertions and definitions with the control variable, formal argument, type, or definition entity they reference. Definition analysis concerns overloading and distinguishes between cyclic and noncyclic definitions. Finally, type checking ensures that no run time type errors will occur. These three tasks are explained in detail below.

Name Resolution

Control variables, formal arguments, type expressions with no port specified, and parameterless definition references are recognized by the parser only as identifiers. Semantic analysis must resolve these identifiers to the appropriate entities before typing them.

A quantifier (`ForAll` or `Exists`) is *active* if its body is currently being typed. Active quantifiers are kept on a stack. When a name is encountered, it is checked against the control names for all active quantifiers. If no match is found, the name is then checked against the names of all formal arguments in the definition whose body is currently being typed. If the name is still not bound, the names of all definitions that have no parameters are searched. If this fails, the name is assumed to be a type expression. The structure is searched for a node that has the same name as the name the analyzer is attempting to bind. If no such node exists, the search for a binding is stopped and a semantic error is reported.

Applications are examined to determine which definition they refer to. The parser does not distinguish between applications of the language-supplied definitions `Members`, `Head`, `Tail`, `Size`, and `Type` and user-defined definitions. Semantic analysis does make this distinction, and for user-defined definitions determines which definition (and if possible, which version) the application refers to. Applications must also refer to a declared definition, and the types of the actual arguments in the application must match the types of some instance of the definition or the union of the instances.

For example, the following overloaded definition utilizing types declared in the billing example in Chapter 2 may be specified.

```
Define CodeOf(c: commercial_customer) = c.industry_code;
Define CodeOf(c: state_customer) = c.state_code;
Define CodeOf(c: federal_customer) = c.agency_code;
```

The following assertions using this definition are both semantically correct.

```
Assert ForAll c In state_customer Do CodeOf(c) >= 1 Od;
Assert ForAll c In Customer Do CodeOf(c) >= 1 Od;
```

The first assertion is correct because the actual argument is of type `state_customer`, which is the type of the formal argument of one instance. The second assertion is also correct because, although there is no single version whose formal argument type matches the actual argument's type (Customer), the union of the formal types (`commercial_customer`, `state_customer`, and `federal_customer`) includes the actual argument type. Here, the union of the instance formal types is exactly the actual argument type.

Definition Analysis

First, overloading of user-defined definitions is checked. Versions of the same definition must be distinguishable by the types of their formal arguments. For example, the definition

```
Define CodeOf(c: Customer) = c.customer_number;
Define CodeOf(c: commercial_customer) = c.industry_code;
```

is semantically incorrect. The versions are not distinguishable because an argument of type `commercial_customer` matches both versions. At run time the assertion checker would not know which version to apply.

The ordering of the definitions for the type checking is determined by creating and analyzing a directed call graph. Definitions are nodes in this graph, and an arc from definition A to definition B states that definition A calls definition B. A depth-first search is performed on the call graph to determine if any of the noncyclic definitions are indeed in a cycle. If so, and if a cyclic identical call, with the identical arguments as in a previous call, is possible, the definition is reclassified as cyclic.

A reverse topological sort is then performed on the call graph. This provides the order in which the definitions must be typed. The definition typed first is that which calls no other definition. This definition is removed from the call graph, possibly rendering another definition with no out arcs. This process continues until only those definitions that occur in cycles remain. These definitions are either recursive or cyclic.

17.3. SEMANTIC ANALYSIS

Recursive definitions are then typed. For each such definition, as much typing as possible is performed. *ForAll* and *Exists* may be typed immediately. *Case* and *If* statements may be typed if any of their constituent expressions can be typed. Eventually this process will type at least one definition in each recursive cycle, which will break the cycle and allow all the definitions originally in the cycle to be typed. If a cycle still exists among recursive definitions, these definitions would call each other endlessly at runtime; in this situation a compile time type error is reported.

Finally, cyclic definitions are typed. A cyclic definition must return an object collection, but semantic analysis must determine the type of the objects in the collection. Since the body of a cyclic definition may include cyclic identical calls, it might be difficult to determine the return type automatically in semantic analysis, so the language definition requires that the return type for the definition be specified by the user.

Type Checking

Definitions are typed, followed by assertions. For each root expression contained in a definition or assertion, a depth-first traversal is performed. Leaf expressions are typed before expressions closer to the root of the expression tree. The root (the definition or assertion body) is typed last.

Expressions in the assertion language may have as types integer, rational, string, boolean, node, class, set or sequence of any of the above types, and object collection. For object collections, semantic analysis must determine the (one) type of the objects in the collection, to prevent runtime type errors. If the semantic analyzer cannot be certain that the types of the parts of an expression will be correct at runtime, and an error is returned. For example, the assertion

```
Assert ForAll c In Customer Do
    c.industry_code = 10
Od;
```

contains the control variable c iterating over all nodes of type Customer. Although the node commercial_customer has an attribute called industry_code, not *all* Customer nodes do. Therefore, the semantic analyzer cannot be certain without sophisticated flow analysis that the control variable will have the named attribute. An object missing an attribute would cause a runtime error, and so the above assertion is semantically incorrect.

The type checker is conservative in its analysis. There are cases where it can be proven that no type error is possible at runtime, yet semantic analysis will still flag it as an error. The following assertion will result in a type error.

```
Assert ForAll c In Customer Do
    If Type(c) Same commercial_customer
        Then c.industry_code = 10
    Else True
    Fi
Od;
```

In this particular situation, the *Case* construct is useful. The following assertion is type correct according to IDLC.

```
Assert ForAll c In Customer Do
    Case c2 Is c
        commercial_customer Do c2.industry_code = 10 Od
    Otherwise True
    End
Od;
```

There are two kinds of object collections, singleton collections and arbitrary collections. A *singleton collection* is known at compile-time to contain exactly one object. Singleton collections may act as values in expressions. The most common examples are dot expressions, such as c.customer_number. One use denotes an integer value which can be used in arithmetic expressions. Another use of the same expression may denote the collection containing the customer number.

An *arbitrary collection* may contain more than one object. For example, the expression

```
c.customer_number Union c.industry_code
```

results in an arbitrary collection containing two integers (if they are distinct). Unlike singleton collections, arbitrary collections are not allowed as operands of value operators. One task of type checking is to ensure that all value operators are applied only to singleton collections.

Type checking must also ensure that compatible value types are used as operands. For example, a string value should not be used as an operand to the multiplication operator or to the *Not* operator.

Finally, the last task of type checking is to ensure that the types of actual parameters in an application identify one and only one of the versions of the corresponding definition and that all versions of the same definition return the same type.

17.4 Independent Representation Analysis

The main steps for independent representation analysis are as follows.

1. Read in the `UNCCandleSemantic` instance.

2. Determine the representations of the types used in the specification.

3. Check for name conflicts with target keywords.

4. Determine the allowed operations for types and attributes.

5. Write out the `UNCCandleRep` instance.

The reader and writers for steps 1 and 5 are generated by IDLC.

17.4.1 Type Representations

The representation for types is determined using information in the prelude. The prelude provides the implementation and target language information necessary to allow target-independent algorithms to perform target-specific actions. An indepth discussion of the prelude is beyond the scope of this book, but an overview is appropriate. The prelude contains, for each target language, the syntax and the actions for each allowed representation clause in the target, as well as those allowed for any target. An *action* is the name of a task to be performed by the translator. Representation clauses are grouped within each target according to the type they can refine. For example, the IDL basic type `Integer` could have an associated set of representation clauses that would allow it to be represented as a 1, 2, or 4 bytes integer in the C target language. There is also a set of representation clauses associated with general types such as user-defined private types. The example that follows illustrates actions taken while interpreting representation clauses.

The calculation of the representation attributes for a type is a series of refinements, each associated with a `RepRef` in `TypeEntity.sem_rep`. For invariant structures, a final refinement is implicitly specified by the target of the process. Each valid representation specified in a `RepRef` is located in the prelude. The particular refinement applied to the type indicated by the representation is also specified in the prelude. This is best explained with an example. Assume that private type `SourcePos` and the following representation specifications have been given.

> *Type* SourcePos;
> *For* SourcePos *Use Size* 2 *Bytes*;
> *For* SourcePos *Use External Integer*;
> *For* SourcePos *Use Package* position;

An Atomic with a sem_reps sequence containing 3 RepRefs is created during semantic analysis. At the start of the representation analysis process, the representation attributes are initialized to default values.

```
Atomic[
    sem_name "SourcePos";
    sem_reps < RepRef[...] RepRef[...] RepRef[...] >;
    rep_size 0;
    rep_alignment 0;
    rep_internalType Void;
    rep_externalType Void;
]
```

The action for the first representation statement (i.e., the first For statement) is specified in the prelude along with the syntax of the representation statement. This action sets the size of the Atomic to the size specified in the representation clause, thereby refining the Atomic to a more concrete type since the size is now defined.

```
Atomic[
    sem_name "SourcePos";
    sem_reps < RepRef[...] RepRef[...] RepRef[...] >;
    rep_size 16;
    rep_alignment 0;
    rep_internalType Void;
    rep_externalType Void;
]
```

The action associated with the second representation statement (also specified in the prelude) is to set the external type to the type specified in the clause.

```
Atomic[
    sem_name "SourcePos";
    sem_reps < RepRef[...] RepRef[...] RepRef[...] >;
    rep_size 16;
    rep_alignment 0;
    rep_internalType Void;
    rep_externalType Atomic[sem_name "Integer"; ...];
]
```

Finally, the action associated with the third representation statement is to set the internal type to the indicated package as specified in the clause.

17.4. INDEPENDENT REPRESENTATION ANALYSIS

```
Atomic[
    sem_name "SourcePos";
    sem_reps < RepRef[···] RepRef[···] RepRef[···] >;
    rep_size 16;
    rep_alignment 0;
    rep_internalType Package[rep_name "position"];
    rep_externalType Atomic[sem_name "Integer"; ···];
]
```

Assuming `SourcePos` existed in the invariant structure of a process it would be further refined if the process had a target. Once the explicit representation statements have been processed, the defaults are applied. For example, the external representation of a private type, if not specified, defaults to the internal representation, and the alignment of a private type defaults to its size.

```
Atomic[
    sem_name "SourcePos";
    sem_reps < RepRef[···] RepRef[···] RepRef[···] >;
    rep_size 16;
    rep_alignment 16;
    rep_internalType Package[rep_name "position"];
    rep_externalType Atomic[sem_name "Integer"; ···];
]
```

After the representation attributes have been calculated for all types, the `rep_type` fields of attributes are calculated. If the `sem_reps` field of the `Attribute` is empty then the `rep_type` field is set to the type named in `syn_type`. If the `sem_reps` field is not empty, refinements are made to the type named in `syn_type` for each `RepRef` in `sem_reps`. The resulting type is then assigned to `Attribute.rep_type`.

17.4.2 Name Conflicts

The next step after determining representations is to check for name conflicts with the target language for invariant types. Each target in the prelude contains a list of keywords. Each type name is checked against all keywords. If the name is the same as a keyword a prefix is added and the newly constructed name is assigned to the `rep_name` field of the type, otherwise the original name is assigned to the `rep_name` field. Since "SourcePos" does nto conflict with either C nor Pascal keywords, the `rep_name` in this case would also be "SourcePos".

17.4.3 Allowed Operations

Allowed operations are next determined for each type in process invariants as follows.

1. The default set of operations is assigned to the type.

2. The `Restrict To` statements for the type are processed by collecting the operations of the default set that are named in the statements, thereby effecting a set intersection. If there are no `Restrict To` clauses, the default set remains the same.

3. The `Restrict From` clauses for the type are processed by subtracting each operation named in a statement from the set of operations.

This sequence of steps follows directly from the semantics of restriction given in Section 4.2.5. The resulting set of operations is then assigned to the type.

17.5 Dependent Representation Analysis

The steps for dependent representation analysis are as follows.

1. Read in the `UNCCandleRep` instance.

2. Determine the sizes of the types.

3. Order the attributes within the nodes and classes.

4. Write out the `UNCCandle` and CANDLE instances.

These tasks are part of the dependent representation analysis because they may require special code for each target.

17.5.1 Determine Type Sizes

Sizes for types are determined first. Sizes for `Atomics` can be specified with representation statements, but sizes for classes, nodes, sets, and sequences must be calculated by this phase. The alignment defaults to the size, if not specified, and vice versa.

17.5.2 Order Attributes

Attributes are then ordered for nodes and classes. A graph coloring algorithm is used to minimize the unused space in nodes. This algorithm utilizes information concerning an attribute's representation size, its representation alignment, and the other attributes it must coexist with in a node or class. This ordering is only performed for specific targets that rely on the ordering of the attributes for efficient accessing through classes. Each class attribute must appear in the same position in each node that is a member of the class. Because of nodes and classes with multiple super-classes, this may require adding unused fields to some nodes. This algorithm is used for the C target language, where class attributes are located with node attributes, but not for the Pascal target language, where class attributes are located in separate record(s) from node attributes.

The algorithm is best explained through an example. Assume that the following IDL specification is being processed:

```
A ::= B | C;
D ::= C;
A => a: Integer;
B => b: Integer;
C => c: Integer;
D => d: Integer,
     e: Integer;
For C.c Use Representation 8 Bits;
For D.e Use Representation 16 Bits;
```

The class hierarchy for this specification is shown below.

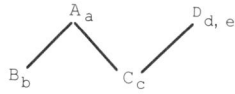

The attributes directly associated with a node or class are shown in a subscript to the node or class name.

First, all the attributes are collected into a set by scanning through all the nodes of the structure (recall that attributes have been propagated). Here, the set contains the attributes $\{a, b, c, d, e\}$. Next, an attribute conflict graph is constructed. This undirected graph contains an arc between attributes x and y if x and y *conflict*, i.e., cannot be overlapped in memory because they both reside in a particular node. The conflict graph for the example is shown in Figure 17.4. This graph is represented by associating with each attribute the set of attributes reachable via a single arc in the

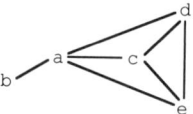

Figure 17.4: A Conflict Graph

conflict graph. An attribute y is contained in the set of reachable attributes for attribute x if x and y co-reside in at least one node of the IDL structure. Here the sets are:

a: {b, c, d, e}
b: {a}
c: {a, d, e}
d: {a, c, e}
e: {a, c, d}

The attributes are sorted in order from greatest to least number of conflicting attributes: a, e, d, c, b, and the attributes are positioned in this order, using best-fit among the free areas not occupied by conflicting attributes positioned earlier, and consistent with the representation size and alignment constraints. Attributes in the Pascal target language are also positioned using best-fit; fewer conflicts result, because class attributes are not colocated with node attributes. The prelude provides the representation size and alignment for the basic types; type representation statements provide this information for private types. Figure 17.5 shows the free areas before each attribute is positioned. For attribute a (size 32 bits, alignment 32 bits), no other attributes have been positioned, so there is one free area. Attribute a is positioned in bits 32–63. For attribute e (size 16 bits, alignment 16 bits), the best fit in the one free area is in bits 64–79 (bit 64 is aligned on a 16 bit boundary). For attribute d (size 32 bits, alignment 32 bits), the best fit in the one free area consistent with the alignment is in bits 96–127. For attribute c (size 8 bits, alignment 8 bits), the best fit in the two free areas is in bits 80–95. Finally, for attribute b (size 32 bits, alignment 32 bits, conflicting only with attribute a), the best fit in the one free area is in bits 64–79.

The code generation phase will use these attribute positions. Figure 17.6 shows where each attribute appears in the nodes and classes of the example.

17.5. DEPENDENT REPRESENTATION ANALYSIS

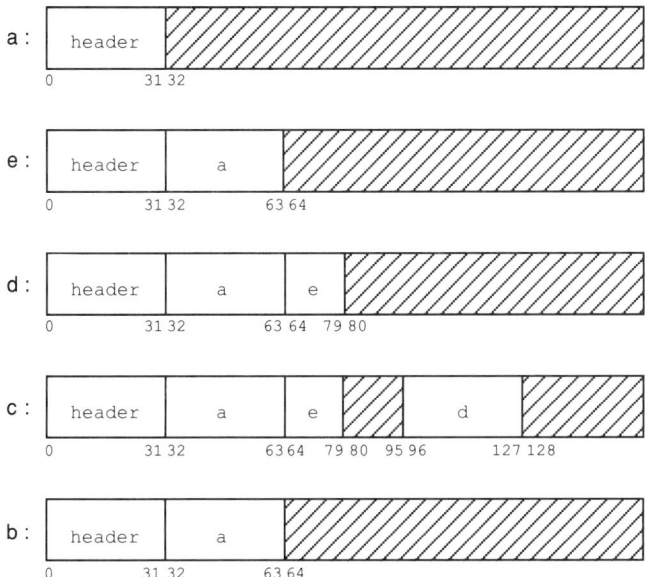

Figure 17.5: Free Areas in Attribute Positioning

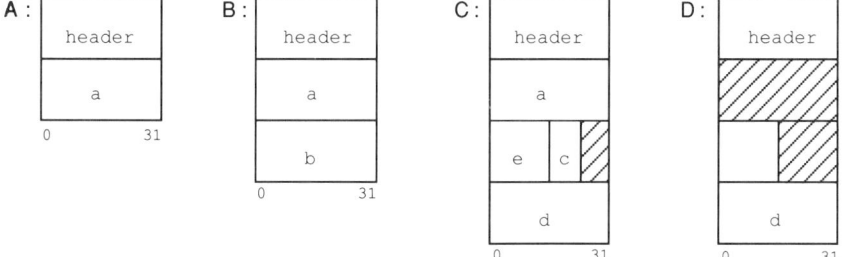

Figure 17.6: Attribute Positioning in Nodes and Classes

The attributes are sorted from greatest to least number of conflicting attributes to ensure that class attributes, which will conflict with all attributes declared for subclasses of that class, are placed near the top of the class, necessitating fewer free areas. This occurs in the example except for attribute c, a node attribute that is placed before the class attribute d due to alignment constraints. Another benefit of this sort order is that, in the absence of multiple superclasses for a node, the attributes will be positioned so that there are no free areas, except where necessitated because of alignment constraints.

17.6 Code Generation

The code generator is the simplest conceptually of all processes in IDLC, although it takes the longest time to run due to the compilation step. The steps for code generation are

1. Read the UNCCandle instance.

2. Calculate additional attributes, to be used in the next step.

3. Generate the code.

4. Optionally output static statistics concerning the specification.

5. Compile the code.

After the UNCCandle instance is read, the additional attributes needed in code generation are calculated. These include the set of ports that each attribute and type is contained in, the indirect descendants of a class, and the alphabetic ordering of the nodes. The information calculated depends on the target of the process. For example, the C target requires alphabetic ordering of nodes to support an efficient reader; the Pascal target does not have this requirement.

Generating target language code is straightforward, once the desired output code has been designed. Each target language is associated with a procedure in the code generator. For each process, several walks of the CANDLE structure are performed to output the declarations and procedures in the necessary order for the target. If the optional statistics flag is specified, an additional walk of the CANDLE structure collects the desired information.

The final step is to compile the code, placing any error messages in a listing file. Often this step dominates all the other steps put together in terms of compilation time. An optional flag specifies that the generated code should not be compiled. One use of this flag is to allow the use of tools that compare the generated code with its previous version, and avoid recompiling those outputs that haven't changed significantly.

17.7 Error Handling

Error handling for each process of the translator is performed by the LISTER program. LISTER is a generic process that can handle error messages from an arbitrary number of passes in a translator. If any errors occur in a source file, a listing file with embedded error messages is created. The error messages and surrounding source lines are also printed on your terminal. Additional information, such as the number of each type of error, is printed at the end of each listing.

All information about errors for IDLC is collected in a single file (termed ErrorInfo), from which the LISTER extracts the error messages themselves and from which a separate utility generates appropriate sections of the user manual for IDLC. Since the error messages generated by the LISTER and the list of errors given in the user manual are generated from a single file, they are guaranteed to be consistent.

Each process in IDLC sends the LISTER a sequence of error instances. Each instance contains an error number, a source position where the error occurred, and any arguments for the error message. These instances are then sorted by file and source position. The corresponding error message is found in the error information file, combined with any arguments given, and embedded in the listing file.

17.8 Evaluation

We first summarize the architecture and discuss the strengths and weaknesses of the translator architecture and implementation. We next describe the advantages and limitations of IDL encountered during development of the translator.

The IDLC architecture is a traditional one, despite the declarative nature of the source language. The sizes for the various components is given below. The LISTER is included, since it is part of IDLC, as shown in Figure 17.1; it is also a separate process that is used in other compilers. In this table, "n.a." stands for "not applicable". Source lines includes comments, which comprised between 5% and 20% of the lines, depending on whether there was a 23-line header comment, the presence of version history information in the header comment, and individual commenting style, particularly whether comments appeared to the right of executable statements or on dedicated lines.

Component	Source	IDL	Generated	Object Code
	(Lines of Source Code)			(Kilobytes)
IDLC (C)		694		
frontend	406	28	7897	
Lex	479	n.a.	1237	
Yacc	1425	n.a.	2011	
Total	2310	28	11145	176
semantic	6493	110	19667	436
semassert	2903	61	18277	410
rep	3828	91	19371	411
backend	7165	99	9430	318
LISTER (C)	1,443	100	1,380	99
Total	24,142	1,183	79,270	1,850

IDLC is implemented in C, Lex, Yacc, and IDL. The initial 694 lines of IDL code refers to the CANDLE specification, which is common to all phases; the other line counts refer to the the individual phases (the process specification and perhaps an invariant structure specification).

Lex, Yacc, and IDL are specification languages from which C code, comprising 76% of the 104,595 lines of source code, is automatically generated. However, these figures are artificially inflated by the multiple (*Unix*) process implementation. If we combined all the IDL processes into one Unix process, as was discussed in Section 9.7, we would not require any readers or writers, and the generated code from the IDL specifications would be on the order of 5,900 lines of C, resulting in a total of 34,400 lines of source code, with the generated code comprising 26%. This change would also dramatically reduce both the object code size and the runtime. On the other hand, we haven't been compelled to make this change, because the execution time to compile the generated C code usually exceeds that processing the IDL specification. If we reduced the execution time of processing the IDL specification to no time, which is clearly impossible, we would still have reduced the execution time for IDLC as a whole by less than half.

The decision to break the translator into many phases and to use the various CANDLE structures between phases had many advantages related to development and testing. Each main function of the translator could be developed and tested independently. The ASCII external representation

17.8. EVALUATION

allowed viewing of the output of each phase. The writers provided a test to see if attributes contained legal types.

There were also advantages to using the various CANDLE structures between phases. The incremental synthesis of information was beneficial for such tasks as error reporting. For example, if an error is detected in a Representation Analysis phase, the internal data structure contains the syntactic and lexical information necessary to point to the exact token in the source file that contains the error. Using the prelude allows the Semantic Analysis and Independent Representation Analysis phases to be target-independent. Finally, the code is simpler and better structured since predefined types and definitions need not be distinguished from user-defined types and definitions until the target dependent representation phase.

One weakness of the architecture, caused by a subtle limitation in the model underlying the ASCII External Representation Language, is that the model does not contain a provision for identifying unique objects. Each time a structure instance is written out by an ASCII writer, it exists as a separate instance. Even when the exact instance is written twice, the two versions are treated as separate instances. The same problem exists when reading an instance twice which results in two identical copies in main memory. Ideally, the reader should recognize that the instances are identical and simply return a pointer to the first instance read when reading in the second instance.

This problem affected the IDL translator when using the prelude. The prelude is read in by two separate phases, Semantic Analysis and Representation Analysis (see Figure 14.1). The information in the prelude instance read by the Representation Analysis phase would be treated as separate from the prelude information already contained in the CandleSemantic structure. Conceptually, this information should be the same. For example, the node in the prelude corresponding to the *Integer* data type would appear as two nodes after the prelude is read in the second time. This creates problems when testing if a type is the *Integer* type in the prelude. Testing for object equivalence is no longer sufficient: the values of several attributes of the two objects must be examined to determine object equivalence.

We considered two different solutions to this problem. The first solution was to check manually the prelude for object equivalence when reading it the second time. We decided that this solution required excessive implementation effort since it would involve changing the equivalence maintenance code each time a change to the prelude was made, as the translator implementation evolved. The second solution was used in a development version of IDLC. We derived a structure that was a union of CandleSemantic and CandleContext (the structure that describes the prelude). An instance of this derived structure was passed between the Semantic Analysis and the Representation Analysis phases rather than an instance of the CandleSemantic structure alone (see Figure 17.1). After the implementation of the translator was stable we used a different approach: we combined the two phases into one process by passing pointers to the CandleSemantic and CandleContext instances rather than writing them externally and then reading them back in again. Since IDLC does not currently support pointer-passing ports, the combining of the two phases was done by hand, using techniques discussed in Section 9.7. We combined initialization functions and wrote a new main routine that called the driver functions of the two phases.

Bibliographic Notes

The lexical analyzer uses LEX (Chang [1985] and Lesk [1975]). The parser is based on YACC (Johnson [1975] and Thorvaldsdottir [1985]). The basic algorithms of the IDL translator are discussed, in less detail, by Lamb [1983]. The node positioning algorithm is a variant of that described by Ambler and Trawick [1983], which itself is a variant of Chaitin's register allocation algorithm, described in Chaitin et al. [1981] and Chaitin [1982]. The graph K-colorability problem at the core of attribute positioning (Section 17.5.2) is NP-complete (Karp [1972]). We use the standard greedy heuristic (Aho, Hopcroft, and Ullman [1983]) and best-fit (Knuth [1973]) to achieve a running time of $O(nm^2)$, where n is the number of node types and m is the maximum number of attributes (direct and propagated) associated with a node type (the conflict graph calculation dominates). For the CANDLE specification, $n = 115$ and $m = 12$.

The T diagrams used in Figure 17.2 were introduced by Bratman [1961].

Chapter 18

idlcheck Implementation

IDLCHECK takes as input a CANDLE instance of an IDL process specification and input and output instances in the ASCII External Representation resulting from an execution of that process, and produces an error log indicating which assertions were violated for the given instances (see Figure 2.17 on page 67). The internal architecture of IDLCHECK is shown in Figure 18.1. Parsing and semantic analysis of assertions occurs in IDLC, producing a CANDLE instance containing the analyzed assertions. The code generator takes this instance and augments it with a few attributes, the most important of which is a sequence of byte codes attached to each assertion and definition. Finally, the interpreter executes these byte codes and generates an error log via the LISTER indicating which assertions were violated for the given instances.

The implementation of IDLCHECK exhibits many similarities with that of XREF (c.f., Chapter 13). The input to the interpreter is an attributed syntax tree in both cases. However, there is no code generator in XREF; the attributed syntax tree is directly interpreted. In IDLCHECK the attribute syntax tree is not interpreted directly; instead, the postfix byte codes contained in specific attributes are interpreted.

An important aspect of assertion checking is generating a complete and accurate error log. The error log should maximize the useful information while minimizing the irrelevant information, so that the precise reason an assertion failed can be determined.

This chapter looks at these three tasks, code generation, interpretation, and error log generation, in detail.

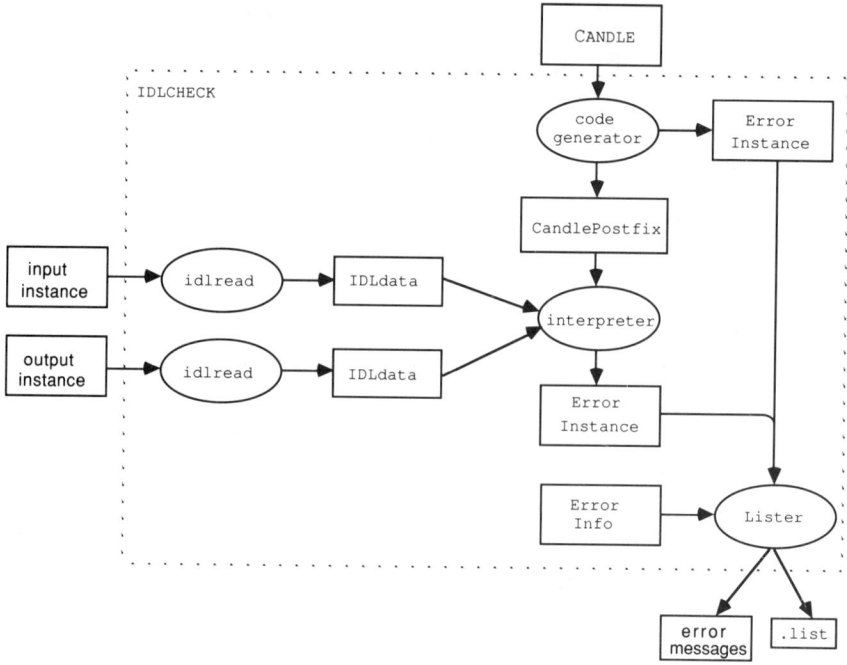

Figure 18.1: The Architecture of IDLCHECK

18.1 Code Generation

Code generation is implemented as a top-down traversal of the abstract syntax tree of each assertion, generating postfix code bottom-up. The postfix code is semantically equivalent to the attributed expression tree representation of the assertion body, and is represented as an array of one-byte integers. Appendix G contains a detailed description of each byte code. We will illustrate the use of these byte codes through three examples.

The assertion

```
Assert Size(Root.list) = 2 And
       Head(Root.list) Sub Government_customer;
```

results in the following postfix code (the number in parentheses is the index of the instruction). Some instructions require more than one byte.

18.1. CODE GENERATION

Instruction		Integer Code(s)
(1)	root	8
(2)	dot	63 1 0
(5)	setorseqorcoll_size	55
(6)	integer	2 1 0
(9)	num_equal	32
(10)	root	8
(11)	dot	63 1 0
(14)	head	52
(15)	typeExpression	9 1 0
(18)	subset	14
(19)	and	20
(20)	endAssertion	66

Each instruction is represented by a one byte integer, except for those instructions that must reference additional information. Such instructions cannot be coded in one byte. For example, the dot operator has an attribute name, which can be any string. Type expressions have a type reference; there may be many type references. Applications have a definition reference, and there may also be many definitions. Integer, string, and rational tokens refer to far more possibilities than can be encoded in one byte. To deal with these attributes, five arrays (i.e., IDL *Seq*s) are associated with each structure or process. The code generator places string names, types, definitions, integers, and rationals into these arrays. The generated code contains two-byte pointers (low-order byte followed by high-order byte) into these arrays. This allows for more than 64,000 distinct objects of each type. In the above example, dot has an index into the string name array where the name "list" will be found. The type instruction has an index into the type array. Finally, the integer instruction has an index into the integer table.

String Array
(1) "list"

Type Array
(1) Government_customer

Definition Array
no entries

Integer Array
(1) 2

Rational Array
no entries

Interpretation of the code proceeds sequentially starting at index 1 of the postfix code. An evaluation stack keeps track of the interpretation. Some instructions (e.g., Root, integer, type) result in a value being pushed on the evaluation stack. Other instructions pop the appropriate number of arguments and push the result. For example, size pops one value off the evaluation stack and pushes the size of that value. The And instruction pops two values, and pushes *True* if the conjunction is true, *False* otherwise. All assertions are ended by the instruction endAssertion. This instruction pops the result, either *True* or *False*, off of the evaluation stack and returns this value.

An *If* expression such as in the following assertion

```
Assert If Size(Root.list) = 3
    Then Head(Root.list).name = "AT&T"
    Else True Fi;
```

is implemented with jump instructions.

Instruction		Integer Code(s)
(1)	root	8
(2)	dot	63 1 0
(5)	setorseqorcoll_size	55
(6)	integer	3 1 0
(9)	num_equal	32
(10)	jfalse	50 28 0
(13)	root	8
(14)	dot	63 1 0
(17)	head	52
(18)	dot	63 2 0
(21)	string	4 3 0
(24)	str_equal	26
(25)	jump	48 29 0
(28)	true	5
(29)	endAssertion	66

String Array	Type Array	Definition Array
(1) "list"	*no entries*	*no entries*
(2) "name"		
(3) "AT&T"		

Integer Array	Rational Array
(1) 3	*no entries*

The instruction jfalse jumps to the location specified in the next instruction if the top of the evaluation stack is *False*, which is popped in either case.

18.1. CODE GENERATION

The instruction jump is an unqualified jump. The extra bytes after the jump instructions are absolute indexes in the code array where execution should continue, implying that each assertion or definition must require no more than approximately 65,000 instructions.

Quantifiers (*ForAll* or *Exists*) generate two instructions: one to set up the quantifier and one to clean up at the end. The quantifier expression

Assert ForAll c *In* Customer *Do* c.customer_number >= 1 *Od*;

would result in the code

Instruction		Integer Code(s)
(1)	typeExpression	9 1 0
(4)	forall	57 14 0
(7)	control	61 1
(9)	dot	63 1 0
(12)	integerone	1
(13)	num_grtrEq	31
(14)	endForAll	59 7 0
(17)	endAssertion	66

String Array
(1) "customer_number"

Type Array
(1) Customer

Definition Array
no entries

Integer Array
(1) 1

Rational Array
no entries

The two extra bytes after the forall instruction represent an absolute index in the code array where the quantifier ends, the endForAll instruction. The two extra bytes after the endForAll instruction represent an absolute index in the code array where the quantifier begins. The extra byte after the control instruction is the control's nesting level, which is the nesting depth of the quantifier to which the control variable belongs; a nesting level of 1 denotes the current nesting level. The type instruction will create the collection of all nodes in the structure of type Customer. The forall instruction sets up the execution of the quantifier body by placing the collection on the quantifier collection stack, and incrementing the control stack offset. It then pushes TRUE and branches directly to the endForAll instruction. The endForAll instruction pops the evaluation stack. If the result is *False*, then the forall is false, and the interpretation of the forall is stopped. If the result is *True*, the current object in the collection is removed, and control returns to the instruction indexed by endForAll (i.e., the instruction immediately following the original forall). If the collection is now empty, then the quantifier is satisfied. The control instruction takes an object in the collection of Customers and pushes it onto the evaluation stack. The body of the quantifier is then executed.

Detailed explanations and examples of interpretation of code are provided in the next section. Special considerations in code generation will now be discussed.

Many instructions may take several different types of operands. For example, the equality operator may compare operands of type node, integer, rational, string, boolean, set, or sequence. The code generator examines the types of the operands of each operator and generates an instruction specific to those types of operands. For example, the expression "c.customer_number >= 1" results in the instruction num_grtrEq, denoting the greater-than-or-equal-to relation on numeric operands (integers or rationals). The expression "c.name = "AT&T"" in the second example results in the instruction str_equal, denoting the equality relation on string operands. During execution, the interpreter does not have to examine the types of the operands.

If an assertion is not satisfied, the assertion checker prints in the assertion failure log information about the values of intermediate expressions leading to the unsatisfied assertion. The assertion failure log generator walks down the expression tree (in a prefix manner), and requires access to information about the result values of expressions which are interpreted in a postfix manner (see Section 18.3). To make this possible, the code generator saves in each node of the expression tree an index in the generated code array where that expression's code ends. It is at this point that the result of the expression is known (e.g., see Figure 18.3).

18.2 Interpretation

The code generation phase of the assertion checker creates a sequence of interpreter instructions for each assertion and the body of each IDL definition version. The interpreter can be viewed as a virtual machine executing these instructions. The interpreter executes each assertion in StructureOrProcess.sem_assertions in turn. The program counter for the interpreter is an index into the code array of a particular assertion.

There are several auxiliary data structures used by the interpreter: the *runtime stack*, the *quantifier collections stack*, and the *control stack*. We describe each below.

The interpreter machine makes heavy use of a runtime stack to store intermediate results. Each instruction the machine encounters in the array

18.2. INTERPRETATION

results in some action involving the runtime stack and sometimes further actions involving a stack of collections maintained to interpret quantifier instructions.

A quantifier specifies a collection of objects over which its control variable will iterate. The quantifier collections stack contains the collections for all active quantifiers. An active quantifier is one whose body is being executed. As quantifiers are encountered during interpretation, the iteration collections for the quantifiers are pushed onto the quantifier collections stack. When a quantifier has been interpreted, it is no longer active and its iteration collection is popped from the quantifier collections stack. If no quantifiers are currently being interpreted, the quantifier collections stack will be empty. The collection associated with a quantifier that has just been interpreted is always the top collection in the quantifier collections stack, since the most recently completed quantifier is the most deeply nested.

A control stack is used in the interpretation of control variables. The control stack contains objects or collections, and is implemented as an array. When a control variable reference is encountered, the object or collection in the control stack at the position pointed to by the control's level attribute is pushed onto the runtime stack. The value of the control variable associated with a quantifier is pushed when that quantifier is first evaluated (in **forall** or **exists**), and popped when the quantifier completes (in **endForAll** and **endExists**).

The control stack also holds the values for formals during definition invocation. When a definition is invoked (termed an *application*), the values of the arguments are popped off the runtime stack and pushed onto the control stack, thereby constructing an activation record on the control stack. Similarly, on activation return (**return**), the values of the formals are popped off the stack.

We now trace the contents of the runtime and control stacks as two different assertions are interpreted.

The first example is the assertion given on page 422. Initially, the runtime stack and control stack are empty. Figure 18.2 shows the state of the runtime stack after the execution of each operation. Objects are identified by their labels, which are identifiers beginning with the character 'L' and followed by one or more digits. Sets and collections are enclosed in curly brackets ("{ }"). Sequences are enclosed in pointed brackets ("< >"). The control and quantifier collections stacks are not used in interpreting this assertion (there are no quantifiers or applications), so these stacks are not shown.

The execution proceeds as follows ("TOS" refers to Top-Of-(runtime)-Stack and the number in parentheses is the index of the instruction).

(1)	root	Push the root object of the structure.
(2)	dot	Pop the stack. Push the list attribute of TOS.
(5)	size	Pop the stack. Push the size of TOS.
(6)	integer	Push the integer 2.
(9)	num_equal	Pop the stack twice. Push *False* since $2 \neq 3$.
(10)	root	Push the root object of the structure.
(11)	dot	Pop the stack. Push the list attribute of TOS.
(14)	head	Pop the stack. Push the head of TOS.
(15)	type	Push the collection of all Government_customer nodes.
(18)	subset	Pop the stack twice. Push *False* since L2 is not a subset of L3 L4.
(19)	and	Pop the stack twice. Push *False* since both value popped are *False*.
(20)	endAssertion	Pop the stack. Return TOS, which is *False* as the result of the interpretation. End the assertion interpretation.

The third example, given on page 425, contains a quantifier. Figure 18.3 displays the state of the runtime and control stacks after executing each instruction. The quantifier collections stack, while important, is not shown. The execution proceeds as follows.

(1)	type	Push the collection of all Customer nodes.
(4)	forall	Pop the runtime stack. Place this TOS on the end of the quantifier collections stack. Push TRUE onto the runtime stack, since this operation is considered true until proven false. Resume control at index 14.
(14)	endForAll	Pop the runtime stack. Since TOS is true, remove another object from the Customers collection, found at the top of the quantifier collections stack, and replace the object in the control stack at level 1 with the new object. Resume control at index 7.
(7)	control	Push the object found in the control stack at level 1.

18.2. INTERPRETATION

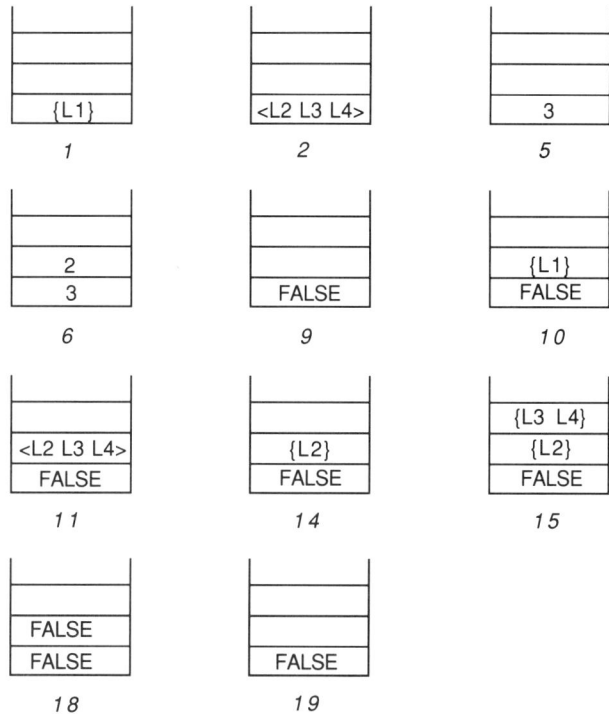

Figure 18.2: Execution Trace of the First Example

(9) dot Pop the runtime stack. Push the customer_-number attribute of TOS onto the runtime stack.
(12) integerone Push the integer 1 onto the runtime stack.
(13) num_grtrEq Pop the runtime stack twice. Push TRUE onto the runtime stack since $1 \geq 1$.
(14) endForAll Pop the runtime stack. Since TOS is true, remove another object from the Customers collection, found at the top of the quantifier collections stack, and replace the object in the control stack at level 1 with the new object. Resume control at index 7.
(7) control Push the object found in the control stack at level 1.
(9) dot Pop the runtime stack. Push the customer_-number attribute of TOS onto the runtime stack.

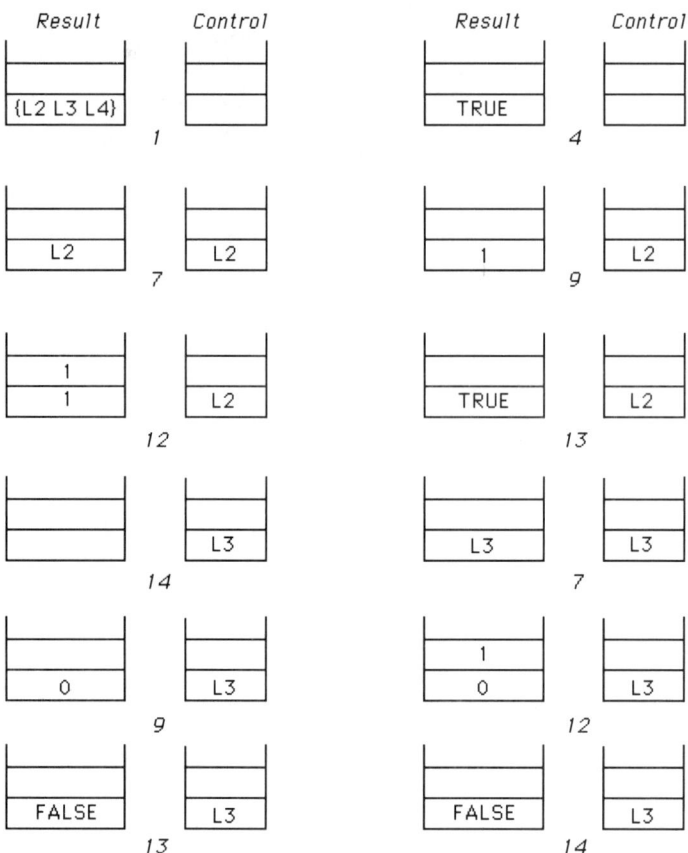

Figure 18.3: Trace of Execution of the Third Example

(12)	integerone	Push the integer 1 onto the runtime stack.
(13)	num_grtrEq	Pop the runtime stack twice. Push FALSE onto the runtime stack since $0 \not\geq 1$.
(14)	endForAll	Pop the runtime stack. Since TOS is false, push FALSE onto the runtime stack. Pop the quantifier collections stack. The quantifier is not satisfied.
(17)	endAssertion	Pop the stack. Return TOS, which is *False* as the result of the interpretation. End the assertion interpretation.

The object for which the quantifier failed is still in the control stack. This is useful in producing the assertion failure log, as will now be discussed.

18.3 Error Log Generation

When the assertion checker finds that an assertion has not been satisfied, it prints in the assertion log the values of the intermediate expressions in the unsatisfied assertion. The assertion log is designed to contain information that could be useful in discovering why the assertion was not satisfied, yet not contain so much irrelevant information that the useful information is hidden.

The assertion failure log is generated through a preorder traversal of the expression tree. The traversal depends on the availability of certain information saved during code generation and interpretation.

During code generation, each subexpression is associated with a pointer to the position in the code array where that expression's code ends. It is at this position that the interpreter determines the result of that subexpression, since the code is postfix. Whenever the interpreter stacks a result on the run stack, it also saves this result in a result array. This array is the same size as the code array, but holds run stack entries, not instructions. The result is stored in the result array at the same index as the instruction that produced the result is stored in the code array. Thus, a subexpression in the tree points not only to the end of its code in the code array, but also to the position in the result array where the value of its result is stored.

Figure 18.4 illustrates the relationships between the various data structures for the assertion on page 422. Solid lines denote descendant node relationships in the expression tree, while dotted lines denote that the expression contains the index in the code array of the indicated instruction.

As the assertion failure log routine traverses the expression tree, it decides whether to print information about each subexpression. Information about a subexpression is printed if that subexpression was not satisfied, unless it is part of a negation (**Not**), in which case the subexpression is printed if it is satisfied. Determining whether a subexpression was satisfied involves looking in the result array at the position saved during code generation.

Results of nonboolean subexpressions are also saved in the result array. Information about these subexpressions is printed if the subexpression is part of an unsatisfied expression (or satisfied if part of a negation).

To improve readability, the error message is indented. Information about an expression is indented by a number of levels equal to the depth of the expression in the tree. In addition, the value of an expression is preceded by the symbol '>' (interpreted as "because") if the expression is farthest left at its level, and by the symbol '&' (interpreted as "and") if the expression follows another expression at the same level. The output produced for the above assertion, if the assertion was not satisfied and both operands of the conjunction were false, is as follows.

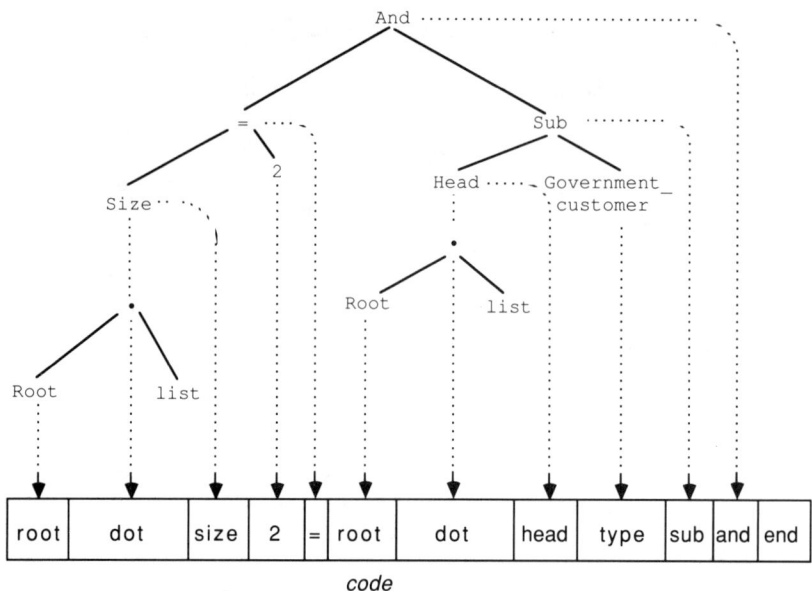

Figure 18.4: Error Log Generation for the First Example

```
Assertion is false.
> And not satisfied.
   > Equality not satisfied.
      Size is 3
         > .list is {< L2 L3 L4 >}
            > Root is {L1 }
   & Subset not satisfied.
      > Head is {L2 }
         > .list is {< L2 L3 L4 >}
            > Root is {L1 }
      & Government_customer is {L4 L3}
```

18.3. ERROR LOG GENERATION

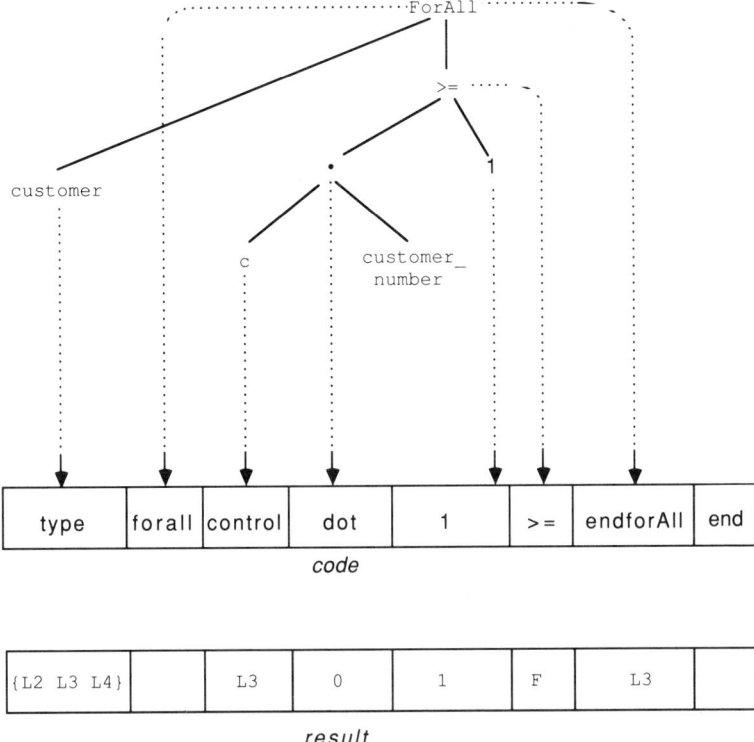

Figure 18.5: Error Log Generation for the Third Example

Quantifier operators (*ForAll* and *Exists*) are handled a little differently. The quantifier expression contains the index of the end of quantifier instruction. The result of the quantifier execution is placed in the result array at this index by the end of quantifier instruction. The end of quantifier instruction also places the object that caused the quantifier to be false (in a *ForAll*) or to be true (in an *Exists*) in the result array at the succeeding index. Figure 18.5 illustrates these relationships for the assertion on page 425; the error message would be as follows.

```
Assertion is false.
   > ForAll not satisfied for c = L3.
      > Greater than or equal not satisfied.
         > .customer_number is 0.
```

18.4 Summary

IDLCHECK is composed of four processes, as illustrated in Figure 18.1. The sizes for these components is given below. LISTER and IDLREAD also appear in IDLC and XREF, respectively.

Component	Source	IDL	Generated	Object Code
	(Lines of Source Code)			(Kilobytes)
IDLCHECK		532		
assertcode (C)	1081	27	13701	301
check (C)	4291	74	7533	193
LISTER (C)	1443	100	1380	99
IDLREAD (Pascal)	1750	32	105	67
Total	8,565	765	22,719	660

The 532 lines of IDL specifications refer to CANDLE. The comments concerning inflation of generated code due to the multi-process architecture made in Section 17.8 also apply here.

Bibliographic Notes

Lamb [1983] formulated the design of an assertion checker and investigated efficiency issues in that context. He also proved the correctness of the computation rule for cyclic definitions: that it will result in the fixed point and that it will terminate. The Eiffel implementation will check assertions at runtime if requested by the user (Meyer [1988]).

Part V

Appendices

Appendix A

Glossary

ancestor process A process from which another process is refined.

ancestor structure A structure from which another structure is derived or refined.

application The invocation of a version of a definition with specific values for the formal parameters.

assertion The IDL construct stating a predicate to be satisfied by all instances of the structure in which it appears, or by the instances input or output by the process in which it appears.

ASCII ERL The ASCII External Representation Language. This language is used for representing instances of IDL-specified data structures externally to a process.

atomic type A node, class, or private type, as contrasted with a basic or structured type.

attribute A named value whose domain is specified by its type. Attributes are collected together into nodes.

attribute finalization function A function called before a node is freed to finalize the values of the attributes of that node.

attribute production The IDL construct that associates attributes with a node or class; denoted by the "=>" symbol.

attribute propagation The process whereby the members of a particular class inherit the attributes of that class.

attribute representation The IDL construct that specifies some aspect of the implementation of an attribute.

attributed node A node that contains at least one attribute.

base process A process not refined from another process.

base structure A structure not derived or refined from another structure.

basic type One of the following four attribute types directly supported by IDL: *Boolean*, *Integer*, *Rational*, and *String*.

boolean type The domain of values true and false.

CANDLE A Common Attributed Notation for the interface Description LanguagE: an intermediate structure specified in IDL of IDL notation.

CANDLEWALK A process provided in the IDL Toolkit that traverses the syntax tree embedded in a CANDLE instance, performing an action at each node of the tree.

centralized symbol table A monolithic symbol table containing information on all the symbols in the source program; contrast with distributed symbol table.

class A grouping of identified nodes and other classes.

class hierarchy The tree or acyclic directed graph denoting the subclass relation, where an arc from a to b states that b is a direct subclass of a.

class inheritance The process whereby the members of a particular class are also considered to be members of any class to which the first class belongs.

class production The IDL construct that associates subclasses and nodes with a class; denoted by the "::=" symbol.

collection A typed set of IDL objects manipulated by assertions.

collection type The one type associated with a collection used by an assertion or definition.

cyclic definition A definition in a group of definitions that call each other. Their use in the assertion language is restricted.

APPENDIX A. GLOSSARY 439

definition An IDL construct analogous to a function in conventional programming languages. It may take parameters, and returns a value or collection.

derivation The definition of a new structure by specifying modifications and additions to an existing structure.

dependent process A process refined from another process.

dependent structure A structure derived or refined from another structure.

DIANA A Descriptive Intermediate Attributed Notation for Ada; an intermediate structure specified in IDL of an Ada program.

direct class member A node or class that appears on the right-hand side of a class production for that class.

derives-ancestor structure A derives-parent of the structure, or a derives-ancestor of the derives-parent of the structure.

derives-parent structure A structure appearing in the From clause of the specification of another structure.

distributed symbol table A table scattered through the parse tree, with portions generally associated with each scope; contrast with centralized symbol table.

entity A syntactic or semantic entity.

entity reference An identifier in a source program that names an object (entity) declared elsewhere in the program.

enumerated type Domain of distinct values, each of which is represented with a unique integer.

external type An IDL type in which the value of the private type is encoded in the external representation of the structure containing the private type.

external representation The representation of a type or structure instance outside of a process' internal state in main memory, either written through a post port or created manually.

externally-adequate structure A structure in which all types have a specified or implicit external representation.

IDL The Interface Description Language. This language is used for writing specifications of data structures and processes.

IDL specification The data structures and processes expressed in IDL.

IDL Toolkit A set of tools developed at the University of North Carolina to manipulate specifications expressed in IDL; includes CANDLEWALK, IDLC, IDLCHECK, IDLREAD, and XREF.

IDL type An atomic, basic, or structured type.

IDL Version 1 The original definition of IDL, completed in August, 1981.

IDL Version 2 The standard definition of IDL, as defined by Nestor, Lamb, and Wulf in June, 1982.

IDL Version 3 A new language designed by Nestor.

IDL87 The minor modification and extension of IDL Version 2 that is accepted by IDLC. Appendix B lists the differences between the two languages.

IDLC The IDL translator in the IDL Toolkit; performs syntactic and semantic checking of an IDL specification, generating readers, writers, and internal data structure and routine declarations in several target languages.

IDLCHECK A process provided in the IDL Toolkit that identifies assertions not satisfied by the input and output instances of a particular execution of an IDL process.

IDLREAD A process provided in the IDL Toolkit that converts an instance of any IDL structure into an instance of IDLdata, a specific IDL structure.

import specification The IDL construct that brings in declarations from a separate file.

indirect class member A node or class that does not appear on the right-hand side of a class production for the class but that is a member of the class by class inheritance.

input mapper A function in the target language converting the internal representation of the external type of the private type to an instance of the internal representation of the private type.

APPENDIX A. GLOSSARY 441

instance of a structure Data that conforms to the restrictions defined by the structure specification.

instantiation The declarations and routines produced by the IDL translator given a process specification.

integer type The domain of whole numbers, both positive and negative.

internal representation The representation of the value of a type or structure instance in a process' internal state in main memory, either created in main memory or read through a pre port.

internally-adequate structure A structure in which all types have a specified or implicit internal representation.

invariant The structure that describes the representation of IDL nodes within the running process.

iterator A name in a quantifier that takes on successive values of the collection.

linear representation A sequence encoding a more complex data structure, such as a directed graph.

more general If node or class A is a subclass of class B, then B is more general than A. Also, the `Rational` type is more general than the `Integer` type.

name resolution The process by which entities are associated with entity references.

narrowing Assignment of a value of a class type to a variable or attribute whose type is contained in that class.

node A data type that is a named grouping of attributes.

node initialization function A function called when a node is created to initialize the values of the attributes of that node.

overloaded definition A definition that has more than one version. Each version applies to a different type of argument(s).

output mapper A function in the target language converting the internal representation of the private type to the internal representation of the external type of the private type.

plain class A class that contains at least one attributed node.

port An association between an IDL-specified data structure and a name for the IDL-supplied reader or writer.

port association The IDL construct that specifies some aspect of the external representation associated with a port.

port prefix A type name or `Root` prefixed with the name of a port and ":".

pre port The IDL construct specifying a conversion of an instance of a specified structure from an external representation to an internal representation.

predefined definition The IDL definitions `Head`, `Members`, `Size`, `Tail`, and `Type`.

post port The IDL construct specifying a conversion of an instance of a specified structure from an internal representation to an external representation.

prelude An instance of the `CandleContext` structure that contains all predefined types, target languages, operations, assertion definitions, and type representations supported by IDLC.

private definition A definition whose body is expressed directly in the target language.

private type An implementation-specific data structure, generally with a user-supplied internal representation.

process The IDL abstraction of a computation.

quantifier An assertion that iterates over the objects in a collection. There are two variants — `ForAll` and `Exists`.

rational type The domain of all rational numbers, that is, those numbers that can be expressed as a ratio of two whole numbers.

refinement The definition of a new structure or process that is a more detailed representation of the old structure.

refines-ancestor A refines-parent of a structure or process, or a refines-ancestor of the refines-parent of the structure or process.

refines-parent A structure or process appearing in the Refines clause of the specification of another structure or process.

APPENDIX A. GLOSSARY

restriction The IDL construct that provides information about the operations a process may perform on objects of an IDL type.

root A distinguished object from which all others in the structure instance can be reached.

reachable An IDL type that may be traced from the root through attribute types or class membership.

semantic entity A node containing semantic information about an object in the source program.

sequence type The domain of ordered sequences of value of either an atomic or basic type.

set type The domain of unordered sets of values of either an atomic or basic type, without duplication of values.

singleton collection A collection that is guaranteed to contain exactly one object.

string type The domain of ordered sequences of ASCII characters.

structure A named grouping of IDL types.

structured type The `Set Of` and `Seq Of` attribute types provided by IDL.

subclass A class contained in the indicated class.

superclass A class containing the indicated node or class.

syntactic entity A node in the parse tree or syntax tree encoding a portion of the syntactic structure of the source program.

target language The programming language for which the IDL translator is to generate code from the IDL specification of the process.

type A symbol that specifies a domain (set) of values.

type checking The process by which type entities are associated with expressions and checked for conformance with the language definition.

type representation The IDL construct that specifies some aspect of the implementation of a type.

unattributed class A class that contains no attributed nodes.

unattributed node A node that contains no direct or propagated attributes.

version of a definition A specific body of a definition associated with particular type(s) for the argument(s).

white space Comments, tab characters, and newline characters separating lexical tokens in a source program.

widening Assignment of a value of a node or class type to a variable or attribute whose type is a superclass of that node or class.

XREF A translator and interpreter provided in the IDL Toolkit for the XRef language.

XRef A language in which cross-referencers are specified.

Appendix B

IDL Syntax

In this appendix we list the syntax of IDL as accepted by IDLC and the other tools in the IDL Toolkit. This language, termed *IDL87* because it first became available in Spring, 1987, is a modification of the current "standard" definition of IDL, termed *IDL Version 2*. All differences between the two languages are listed in Section B.4 and B.5. The differences are partitioned into *syntactic* and *semantic* differences, then divided further into the categories of *restrictions* to IDL Version 2, *modifications* to IDL Version 2, and *extensions* to IDL Version 2. Restrictions are the most critical, because they may invalidate existing IDL specifications. Modifications may require changes to the specification before it can be processed by IDLC. Most of the changes to IDL Version 2 are extensions. The restrictions are small in number and are limited in scope; we list ways of modifying the specification to bring it into accordance with the restrictions.

IDLC supports a conformity switch that will instruct it to recognize only IDL Version 2 constructs. This switch should be used when processing specifications written in IDL Version 2.

B.1 Lexical Conventions

The BNF for the lexical tokens in an IDL specification is as follows.

⟨token⟩   ::= ⟨basic token⟩ | ⟨punctuation⟩ | ⟨white space⟩
⟨basic token⟩   ::= ⟨keyword⟩ | ⟨name⟩ | ⟨integer⟩ | ⟨rational⟩
                       | ⟨string⟩
⟨punctuation⟩   ::= ':' | '=' | '<' | '>' | '~' | '+' | '-' | '*'

| '/' | ';' | '|' | '(' | ')' | ',' | '.'

⟨white space⟩ ::= ⟨space⟩ | ⟨horizontal tab⟩ | ⟨carriage return⟩
| ⟨form feed⟩ | ⟨line feed⟩ | ⟨end of line⟩
| '-' '-' { ⟨comment character⟩ }* ⟨end of line⟩

⟨keyword⟩ ::= And | Assert | Case | Cyclic | Define
| Do | Else | Empty | End | Exists
| False | Fi | For | ForAll | From
| If | Import | In | Intersect | Inv
| Is | Not | Od | Of | Or
| OrIf | Otherwise | Post | Pre | Process
| Psub | Refines | Restrict | Returns
| Root | Same | Seq | Set | Structure
| Sub | Target | Then | To | True
| Type | Union | Use | Without

⟨name⟩ ::= ⟨letter⟩ { ⟨letter⟩ | ⟨digit⟩ | '_' }*
⟨integer⟩ ::= { '+' | '-' }? ⟨unsigned integer⟩
⟨unsigned integer⟩ ::= { ⟨digit⟩ }+
⟨rational⟩ ::= { '+' | '-' }? ⟨unsigned rational⟩
⟨unsigned rational⟩ ::= ⟨basic rational⟩
| { ⟨unsigned integer⟩ | ⟨basic rational⟩ } '/'
    { ⟨unsigned integer⟩ | ⟨basic rational⟩ }
⟨basic rational⟩ ::= ⟨unsigned integer⟩ '.' ⟨unsigned integer⟩
    { ⟨exponent⟩ }?
| ⟨unsigned integer⟩ { '.' ⟨unsigned integer⟩ }
    ⟨exponent⟩
| ⟨unsigned integer⟩ '#' ⟨based⟩ { '.' ⟨based⟩ }
    '#' { ⟨exponent⟩ }?
⟨exponent⟩ ::= 'E' ⟨integer⟩
⟨based⟩ ::= { ⟨digit⟩ | 'A' | 'B' | 'C' | 'D' | 'E' | 'F' }
⟨string⟩ ::= '"' { ⟨string character⟩ }* '"'
⟨letter⟩ ::= 'a' | ⋯ | 'z' | 'A' | ⋯ | 'Z'

B.1. LEXICAL CONVENTIONS

⟨digit⟩ ::= '0' | ⋯ | '9'
⟨single string char⟩ ::= ⟨letter⟩ | ⟨digit⟩ | '!' | '#' | '$' | '%'
| '&' | ''' | '(' | ')' | '*' | '+' | ','
| '-' | '.' | '/' | ':' | ';' | '<' | '='
| '>' | '?' | '@' | '[' | '\' | ']' | '^'
| '_' | '`' | '{' | '|' | '}' | '.' | ⟨space⟩
⟨string character⟩ ::= '"' '"' | '~' ⟨single string char⟩ | '~' '~'
| ⟨single string char⟩
⟨comment character⟩ ::= ⟨single string char⟩ | '"' | '~'
| ⟨horizontal tab⟩

The following lexical conventions are observed in an IDL specification:

- Break symbols include blanks, comments, and "end-of-line"s. A comment is introduced by double hyphens, '--', and terminated by an ⟨end of line⟩. Any number of break symbols may appear between any two ⟨basic token⟩s with no effect. Break symbols may not appear within tokens. Two adjacent ⟨basic token⟩s must be separated by at least one break symbol.

- Identifiers consist of a letter followed by a sequence of letters, digits, or underscore characters. Identifiers with identical spelling except for the case of their letters are considered distinct. The predefined types **Boolean**, **Integer**, **Rational**, and **String** are considered to be identifiers, not reserved words.

- Reserved identifiers (i.e., keywords) in the IDL syntax have by convention the first letter of each word capitalized, and all other letters in lower case, for example, '**Structure**' ('**ForAll**' is the one exception). However, reserved identifiers are *not* case sensitive, so any capitalization alternative is acceptable.

- The ⟨rational⟩ literal can be used to represent any rational number. The form i/j is the rational number produced by dividing i by j. The form with the "#" can be used to represent numbers in any base between 2 and 16. The first ⟨unsigned integer⟩ gives the base in base 10 and must have a value between 2 and 16. The next part gives the value in that base. The exponent is given in base 10 and specifies the power of the base by which the number is to be multiplied. Representations that specify the same rational value (e.g., "1/2" and "0.5") are considered to be equivalent.

- The ⟨string⟩ literal can represent any ASCII string. It may directly contain blanks and the ASCII printing characters, except """ and "~". Each of the other ASCII characters is represented by a two character escape sequence. The character """ is represented by "~"". The nonprinting characters with octal values 0, 1, ..., 37 are represented by the escape sequences "~@", "~A", ..., "~_" (i.e. the control-shift equivalents of a standard ASCII keyboard). The character "~" is represented by "~~". The character whose octal value is 177 is represented by "~|".

B.2 IDL Grammar

The extended BNF for IDL87 is given below in the format described in the preface. Nonterminals of the form "⟨?_name⟩" are names of kind ?. Most of these names are self-explanatory. ⟨atomic_name⟩ identifies a class, node or private type; ⟨class_node_name⟩ identifies a class or node; ⟨def_name⟩ identifies an assertion definition; and ⟨control_name⟩ identifies the name appearing in a **ForAll** or **Exists** clause. "⟨name⟩"s are names that are in one of several kinds. Several IDL constructs are implementation-specific, in that the validity of specific instances of that construct is determined by each implementation. In such cases, which will be clearly identified, we will specify how the IDL Toolkit handles the construct.

⟨specification⟩   ::= { ⟨import decl⟩ | ⟨structure decl⟩
                            | ⟨process decl⟩ }*

⟨import decl⟩   ::= **Import** { ⟨str_name⟩ | ⟨process_name⟩ }
                            { ',' { ⟨str_name⟩ | ⟨process_name⟩ } }*
                            From ⟨file_name⟩ **End**

⟨structure decl⟩   ::= **Structure** ⟨str_name⟩ { **Root** ⟨type⟩ }?
                            { **Refines** ⟨str_name⟩ }?
                            { **From** ⟨str_name⟩ { ',' ⟨str_name⟩ }* }?
                            Is { ⟨structure stmt⟩ ';' }* **End**

⟨structure stmt⟩   ::= ⟨production⟩ | ⟨type decl⟩ | ⟨without clause⟩
                            | ⟨attribute rep⟩ | ⟨type rep⟩ | ⟨assertion stmt⟩

B.2. IDL GRAMMAR

⟨production⟩ ::= ⟨attribute production⟩ | ⟨class production⟩

⟨attribute production⟩ ::= { ⟨node_name⟩ | ⟨class_name⟩ } '=>'
{ ⟨attribute⟩ { ',' ⟨attribute⟩ }* }?

⟨attribute⟩ ::= ⟨attribute_name⟩ ':' ⟨type⟩

⟨class production⟩ ::= ⟨class_name⟩ '::='
{ ⟨class_node_name⟩ { '|' ⟨class_node_name⟩ }* }?

⟨type decl⟩ ::= **Type** ⟨private_name⟩

⟨atomic type⟩ ::= **Boolean** | **Integer** | **Rational** | **String**
| ⟨atomic_name⟩

⟨type⟩ ::= ⟨atomic type⟩ | { **Seq** | **Set** } **Of** ⟨atomic type⟩

⟨without clause⟩ ::= **Without** ⟨without item⟩ { ',' ⟨without item⟩ }*

⟨without item⟩ ::= **Assert** { ⟨assertion_name⟩ | '*' }
| **Define** { ⟨def_name⟩ | '*' }
| **Type** ⟨type⟩
| { ⟨atomic_name⟩ | '*' } { '=>' | '::=' }
{ ⟨name⟩ | '*' }?

⟨attribute rep⟩ ::= **For** ⟨name⟩ '.' ⟨attribute_name⟩
Use { ⟨parameter⟩ }+

⟨parameter⟩ ::= ⟨name⟩ | ⟨integer⟩ | ⟨rational⟩ | ⟨string⟩

⟨type rep⟩ ::= **For** ⟨type⟩ **Use** { ⟨parameter⟩ }+

⟨process decl⟩ ::= **Process** ⟨process_name⟩
{ **Refines** ⟨process_name⟩ }?

⟨process stmt⟩

⟨port definition⟩
⟨port⟩

⟨port assoc⟩

⟨target⟩

⟨restriction⟩

⟨assertion stmt⟩
⟨assertion⟩

⟨expression⟩
⟨1op⟩
⟨1exp⟩
⟨2op⟩
⟨2exp⟩
⟨3exp⟩

⟨3op⟩

⟨4exp⟩

{ **Inv** ⟨str_name⟩ }?
Is { ⟨process stmt⟩ ';' }* **End**

::= ⟨port definition⟩ | ⟨port assoc⟩ | ⟨target⟩
    | ⟨restriction⟩ | ⟨assertion stmt⟩

::= { **Pre** | **Post** } ⟨port⟩ { ',' ⟨port⟩ }*
::= ⟨port_name⟩ ':' ⟨str_name⟩

::= **For** ⟨port_name⟩ **Use** { ⟨parameter⟩ }+

::= **Target** { ⟨parameter⟩ }+

::= **Restrict** { ⟨type⟩ | '*' }
    { '.' { ⟨attribute_name⟩ | '*' } }?
    { **To** | **From** }
    ⟨oper_name⟩ { ',' ⟨oper_name⟩ }*

::= ⟨assertion⟩ | ⟨definition⟩
::= { ⟨name⟩ }? **Assert** ⟨expression⟩

::= ⟨1exp⟩ | ⟨expression⟩ ⟨1op⟩ ⟨1exp⟩
::= **Or** | **Union**
::= ⟨2exp⟩ | ⟨1exp⟩ ⟨2op⟩ ⟨2exp⟩
::= **And** | **Intersect**
::= { **Not** }? ⟨3exp⟩
::= ⟨4exp⟩ | ⟨3exp⟩ ⟨3op⟩ ⟨4exp⟩
    | ⟨4exp⟩ **Is** ⟨atomic type⟩
::= '=' | '~=' | '<' | '<=' | '>' | '>='
    | **In** | **Same** | **Psub** | **Sub**
::= { ⟨4op⟩ }? ⟨5exp⟩ | ⟨4exp⟩ ⟨4op⟩ ⟨5exp⟩

B.2. IDL GRAMMAR

```
⟨4op⟩               ::= '+' | '-'
⟨5exp⟩              ::= ⟨primary exp⟩ | ⟨5exp⟩ ⟨5op⟩ ⟨primary exp⟩
⟨5op⟩               ::= '*' | '/'
⟨primary exp⟩       ::= { ⟨port_name⟩ ':' }? ⟨type⟩ | ⟨literal⟩
                      | '(' ⟨expression⟩ ')'
                      | ⟨primary exp⟩ '.' ⟨attribute_name⟩
                      | ⟨def_name⟩ '(' ⟨actuals⟩ ')'
                      | ⟨if exp⟩ | ⟨quantified exp⟩ | ⟨case exp⟩
                      | ⟨class_name⟩ '(' ⟨expression⟩ ')'

⟨literal⟩           ::= True | False | { ⟨port_name⟩ ':' }? Root
                      | Empty | ⟨integer⟩ | ⟨rational⟩ | ⟨string⟩
                      | ⟨control_name⟩ | ⟨formal_name⟩ | ⟨case_name⟩

⟨actuals⟩           ::= ⟨expression⟩ { ',' ⟨expression⟩ }*

⟨if exp⟩            ::= If ⟨expression⟩ Then ⟨expression⟩
                          { OrIf ⟨expression⟩ Then ⟨expression⟩ }*
                          Else ⟨expression⟩ Fi

⟨quantified exp⟩    ::= { ForAll | Exists } ⟨control_name⟩
                          In ⟨expression⟩ Do ⟨expression⟩ Od

⟨case exp⟩          ::= Case ⟨case_name⟩ Is ⟨expression⟩
                          { ⟨case select⟩ }* { ⟨case other⟩ }? End
⟨case select⟩       ::= ⟨atomic type⟩ Do ⟨expression⟩ Od
⟨case other⟩        ::= Otherwise Do ⟨expression⟩ Od

⟨definition⟩        ::= ⟨private definition⟩ | ⟨IDL definition⟩
⟨private definition⟩ ::= Define ⟨def_name⟩ { ⟨formals⟩ }? Returns ⟨type⟩
⟨IDL definition⟩    ::= { Cyclic }? Define ⟨def_name⟩ { ⟨formals⟩ }?
                          { Returns ⟨type⟩ }? '=' ⟨expression⟩
```

⟨formals⟩   ::= '(' ⟨formal⟩ { ',' ⟨formal⟩ }* ')'
⟨formal⟩   ::= ⟨formal_name⟩ ':' ⟨type⟩

B.3 Implementation-defined Aspects

Several productions in the syntax involve ⟨parameter⟩s or ⟨oper_name⟩s that are implementation defined. Below we list the possibilities for IDL87 that are supported for all languages. Other variants are also supported; consult Appendices C and D for details on C and Pascal, respectively. The names found in ⟨parameter⟩s and ⟨oper_name⟩s are not case sensitive, except for identifiers used as parameters (e.g., ⟨name⟩ in 'For ⟨type⟩ Use Name ⟨name⟩'), which like other identifiers, are case sensitive.

B.3.1 Target Languages

There are at least two possibilities for target languages

> Target Language C;
>
> Target Language Pascal;

Various target modifiers may also be required.

> Target Language Version { ⟨parameter⟩ }$^+$;
> Target Operating System { ⟨parameter⟩ }$^+$;
> Target Operating System Version { ⟨parameter⟩ }$^+$;
> Target Machine { ⟨parameter⟩ }$^+$;
> Target Machine Version { ⟨parameter⟩ }$^+$;
> Target Runtime { ⟨parameter⟩ }$^+$;
> Target Runtime Version { ⟨parameter⟩ }$^+$;

B.3.2 Representation Specifications

The first representation applies to all types.

> For ⟨type⟩ Use Name ⟨name⟩;

Use ⟨name⟩ internally, to avoid name conflicts with target language keywords.

B.3. IMPLEMENTATION-DEFINED ASPECTS

> For ⟨type⟩ Use Representation ⟨integer⟩ { Bits | Bytes } ;

Specify the amount of space to be allocated for this type. Only particular sizes are permitted; even *int* varies from machine to machine and compiler to compiler. The default size varies by type, and is undefined for private types. The *Representation* variant is also applicable to attributes as well as to ⟨type⟩s. This statement cannot be used for node or class types.

> For ⟨private_name⟩ Use External ⟨type⟩;
> For ⟨private_name⟩ Use Internal ⟨type⟩;
> For ⟨private_name⟩ Use Package ⟨module_name⟩;
> For ⟨private_name⟩ Use Name ⟨name⟩;
> For ⟨private_name⟩ Use Size ⟨integer⟩ { Bits | Bytes } ;
> For ⟨private_name⟩ Use Alignment ⟨integer⟩ { Bits | Bytes } ;

The first form is used to specify the ⟨type⟩ that will encode the value of the ⟨private_name⟩ when written out to an external representation; this ⟨type⟩ cannot be a private type. The second clause is used to specify the representation type used with an IDL process. The third clause specifies the package (e.g., the include file for C and Pascal) that defines the private type. The name used internally for the private type can be specified with the fourth clause, which substitutes ⟨name⟩ for all occurrences of the ⟨private_name⟩ in the generated code. The last two clauses are used to specify the size and alignment of the internal representation.

B.3.3 Port Associations

There is at least one kind of reader or writer port:

> For ⟨port_name⟩ Use ASCII External Representation;

This is the default.

B.3.4 Restrictions

The restrict clause specifies a subset of the ⟨oper⟩s allowed on particular objects. The valid ⟨oper⟩s are implementation and language specific. Appendices C and D list the ⟨oper⟩s that are relevant for C and Pascal, respectively.

B.4 Syntactic Differences

For those readers familiar with IDL Version 2, we list the differences between that version and IDL87.

- **Restriction:**

IDL Version 2:

⟨type⟩   ::= Boolean | Integer | Rational | String
                   | ⟨atomic_name⟩
                   | { Seq | Set } Of ⟨type⟩

IDL87:

⟨atomic type⟩   ::= Boolean | Integer | Rational | String
                   | ⟨atomic_name⟩
⟨type⟩   ::= ⟨atomic type⟩ | { Seq | Set } Of ⟨atomic type⟩

Sets of sets (and sets of sequences, etc.) are not be allowed.

Reason for change: You may declare a node, which then has one attribute, that is the secondary set. The presence of a node allows new attributes to be added later, making maintenance easier. Also, a straightforward implementation is easier to produce without sets of sets, and a sophisticated implementation can optimize away the node should there be only the one set attribute.

- **Modification:**

IDL Version 2:

Keywords are case sensitive.

IDL87:

Keywords are not case sensitive.

Reason for change: Most users find case insensitivity of both keywords and identifiers more natural. However, in both IDL Version 2 and IDL87, only

B.4. SYNTACTIC DIFFERENCES

identifiers remain case sensitive. This is a natural choice in part because both target languages are case sensitive.

- **Extension and Restriction:**

IDL Version 2:

⟨structure decl⟩ ::= **Structure** ⟨str_name⟩ { **Root** ⟨atomic_name⟩ }$^?$
{ **Refines** ⟨str_name⟩ { ',' ⟨str_name⟩ }* }$^?$
{ **From** ⟨str_name⟩ { ',' ⟨str_name⟩ }* }$^?$
Is { ⟨structure stmt⟩ ';' }* **End**

IDL87:

⟨structure decl⟩ ::= **Structure** ⟨str_name⟩ { **Root** ⟨type⟩ }$^?$
{ **Refines** ⟨str_name⟩ }$^?$
{ **From** ⟨str_name⟩ { ',' ⟨str_name⟩ }* }$^?$
Is { ⟨structure stmt⟩ ';' }* **End**

Structures may not be refined from multiple structures in IDL87. The root can be an arbitrary type.

Reason for change: Refinement from more than one base structure was not well defined in IDL Version 2, and so is disallowed. To get a similar effect, use derivation from multiple structures. Structure declarations need not contain any structure statements, if the structure is simply the union of the From structures. Finally, we could not see any pressing reason to restrict the root type.

- **Modification and Extension:**

IDL Version 2:

⟨without item⟩ ::= **Assert** ⟨assertion_name⟩ | ⟨name⟩
| { ⟨atomic_name⟩ | '*' } { '=>' | '::=' }
{ ⟨name⟩ }$^?$

IDL87:

⟨without item⟩ ::= **Assert** { ⟨assertion_name⟩ | '*' }
                  | **Define** { ⟨def_name⟩ | '*' }
                  | **Type** ⟨type⟩
                  | { ⟨atomic_name⟩ | '*' } { '=>' | '::=' }
                    { ⟨name⟩ | '*' }?

Examples:

IDL Version 2:

```
Without SourcePosition;
Without a => ;
Without b ::= ;
```

IDL87:

```
Without Type SourcePosition;
Without Type a;
Without Type b;

Without Define CheckType;
Without Node => *;
Without Assert *;
```

(The last three examples cannot be expressed in IDL Version 2).

Reason for change: The keywords *Define* and *Type* were already used elsewhere in the language, and are included here to be unambiguous about what is being removed and to be consistent with the use of the keyword *Assert*. "*Without Assert **" is used to remove all assertions from a specification; "*Without Define **" has a similar semantics. "*Without Type **" is not allowed because the structure would be reduced to the empty structure, which is not useful.

B.4. SYNTACTIC DIFFERENCES

- **Modification and Extension:**

IDL Version 2:

⟨attribute rep⟩	::= *For* ⟨type reference⟩ *Use* ⟨type⟩
⟨type reference⟩	::= ⟨name⟩ '.' ⟨attribute_name⟩
	{ '(' ⟨integer⟩ ')' }?
⟨type rep⟩	::= *For* ⟨private_name⟩ *Use* ⟨use type⟩
⟨use type⟩	::= ⟨type⟩	⟨package type⟩	*External* ⟨type⟩
⟨package type⟩	::= ⟨package_name⟩ '.' ⟨type_name⟩

IDL87:

⟨attribute rep⟩	::= *For* ⟨name⟩ '.' ⟨attribute_name⟩
	Use { ⟨parameter⟩ }$^+$
⟨parameter⟩	::= ⟨name⟩	⟨integer⟩	⟨rational⟩	⟨string⟩
⟨type rep⟩	::= *For* ⟨type⟩ *Use* { ⟨parameter⟩ }$^+$

Examples:

IDL Version 2:

```
For a.b Use short;
For sourceposition Use Integer;
For c Use External Integer;
For d Use CPackage.int;
```

IDL87:

```
For a.b Use Representation 16 Bits;
For sourceposition Use Type Integer;
For c Use External Integer;
For d Use Package CPackage;
For d Use Name int;

For float Use Name real;
For b.c Use Representation 7 Bits;
For b.c Use Representation Unsigned;
For d Use Size 8 Bits;
For d Use Alignment 8 Bits;
```

(The last five examples cannot be expressed in IDL Version 2.)

Reason for change: The optional level number (' (' ⟨integer⟩ ') ') is unnecessary when sets of sets are disallowed and so was eliminated. ⟨parameter⟩s are used to extend the syntax to include additional implementation specific details. ⟨type⟩ is used rather than ⟨private_name⟩ to permit representations for classes, nodes, sets and sequences to be specified. The alternative is to associate each attribute having a particular set of sequence type with a private type, and then associate that private type with a representation. This is undesirable for software maintenance considerations. The *Type* keyword is used elsewhere, and so is not a new keyword. The inconsistent "." in "⟨package_name⟩ . ⟨type_name⟩" was eliminated.

- **Modification and Extension:**

IDL Version 2:

```
⟨restriction⟩        ::= Restrict ⟨name⟩ { To | From }
                         ⟨oper⟩ { ',' ⟨oper⟩ }*
⟨oper⟩               ::= ⟨node oper⟩ | ⟨attribute oper⟩
⟨node oper⟩          ::= Create | Destroy | ⟨name⟩
⟨attribute oper⟩     ::= { Fetch | Store } '(' ⟨name list⟩ ')'
```

IDL87:

```
⟨restriction⟩        ::= Restrict { ⟨type⟩ | '*' }
                         { '.' { ⟨attribute_name⟩ | '*' } }?
                         { To | From }
                         ⟨oper_name⟩ { ',' ⟨oper_name⟩ }*
```

Examples:

IDL Version 2:

    `Restrict Anode To Create;`

    `Restrict Anode To Fetch(Attr1, Attr2), Store(Attr1);`

IDL87:

B.4. SYNTACTIC DIFFERENCES

```
Restrict Anode To Create;

Restrict Anode.Attr1 To Fetch, Store;
Restrict Anode.Attr2 To Store;

Restrict Anode.* From Delete;
Restrict *.srcpos From Increment;
Restrict * From Delete;
```

(The last three examples cannot be expressed in IDL Version 2.)

Reason for change: A class or attribute has associated with it a default set of allowed operations. Therefore, you should be allowed to permit (*"Restrict To"*) a subset of these operations or disallow (*"Restrict From"*) a subset of these operations. *"Create"*, *"Destroy"*, *"Fetch"*, and *"Store"* do not need to be distinguished from other named operations, and hence do not need to be keywords (see below). Attribute references should be the same as in the For statement for consistency. The "*" construct was added for shorthand and for consistency with the Without statement.

- **Extension:**

IDL Version 2:

⟨class production⟩   ::= ⟨class_name⟩ ' ::= ' ⟨class_node_name⟩
          { ' | ' ⟨class_node_name⟩ }*

IDL87:

⟨class production⟩   ::= ⟨class_name⟩ ' ::= ' { ⟨class_node_name⟩
          { ' | ' ⟨class_node_name⟩ }* }?

A class production with an empty right-hand side defines a class named ⟨class_name⟩ with no subclasses specified as yet.

Reason for change: Since a node is not allowed to change into a class, there needed to be some way to specify that an identifier was a class, even if no subclasses were available at the time the identifier was declared.

- **Extension:**

IDL Version 2:

⟨process decl⟩ ::= *Process* ⟨process_name⟩
　　　　　　　　　{ *Refines* ⟨process_name⟩ }$^?$
　　　　　　　　　{ *Inv* ⟨str_name⟩ }$^?$
　　　　　　　　　Is { ⟨process stmt⟩ ';' }$^+$ *End*

IDL87:

⟨process decl⟩ ::= *Process* ⟨process_name⟩
　　　　　　　　　{ *Refines* ⟨process_name⟩ }$^?$
　　　　　　　　　{ *Inv* ⟨str_name⟩ }$^?$
　　　　　　　　　Is { ⟨process stmt⟩ ';' }* *End*

A process declaration may have an empty statement list.

Reason for change: A process declaration with no process statements is useful for debugging when target code is to be produced for the invariant but not for any readers or writers.

- **Extension:**

IDL Version 2:

⟨port assoc⟩ ::= *For* ⟨port_name⟩ *Use* ⟨name⟩

IDL87:

⟨port assoc⟩ ::= *For* ⟨port_name⟩ *Use* { ⟨parameter⟩ }$^+$

The parameters present in a port expression is now a sequence.

Reason for change: The port association is a straight-forward extension, and is included partially for consistency with type representation declarations.

B.4. SYNTACTIC DIFFERENCES

- **Extension:**

IDL Version 2:

None

IDL87:

⟨target⟩   ::= **Target** { ⟨parameter⟩ }⁺

The target statement specifies the format of the generated code.

Reason for change: This clause is required when the IDL translator can generate code in more than one target language (e.g., C and Pascal).

- **Extension:**

IDL Version 2:

⟨specification file⟩   ::= { ⟨structure decl⟩ | ⟨process decl⟩ }*

IDL87:

⟨specification file⟩   ::= { ⟨import decl⟩ | ⟨structure decl⟩
                              | ⟨process decl⟩ }*

⟨import decl⟩   ::= **Import** { ⟨str_name⟩ | ⟨process_name⟩ }
                              { ',' { ⟨str_name⟩ | ⟨process_name⟩ } }*
                              From ⟨file_name⟩ **End**

Examples:

IDL Version 2:

None

IDL87:

   Import SymbolTable **From** St **End**;

Reason for change: The import clause was added to eliminate the need for multiple copies of a specification. The complete file name is derived from ⟨file name⟩ in a system-specific manner.

- **Extension:**

IDL Version 2:

> *None*

IDL87:

> ⟨3exp⟩ ::= ⟨4exp⟩ Is ⟨atomic type⟩

Examples:

IDL Version 2:

> `Type(x) Sub Y;`

IDL87:

> `x Is Y`

Reason for change: The form "`Type(x) Sub Y`" is expected to occur often. The formal meaning of the above construct is to assert that the collection containing all objects of the same type as x is a subset of the collection containing all objects of the same type as Y. The object x is usually a control variable or formal argument, and the object Y is usually a type expression. A user would more likely wish to assert that the type of the object x *is* Y.

- **Extension:**

IDL Version 2:

> *None*

IDL87:

> ⟨primary exp⟩ ::= ⟨class_name⟩ '(' ⟨expression⟩ ')'

B.4. SYNTACTIC DIFFERENCES

Examples:

IDL Version 2:

　None

IDL87:

　　A(B)

The ⟨expression⟩ is considered to be of type ⟨class_name⟩ while type checking. ⟨class_name⟩ must be a superclass of the type of ⟨expression⟩.

Reason for change: In the example, A and B are classes, with A a superclass of B. The expression "B", denotes the collection of all nodes in the class B. "A(B)" coerces the collection to be of type A.

- **Extension:**

IDL Version 2:

　None

IDL87:

⟨case exp⟩	::=	Case ⟨case_name⟩ Is ⟨expression⟩ { ⟨case select⟩ }* { ⟨case other⟩ }? End
⟨case select⟩	::=	⟨atomic type⟩ Do ⟨expression⟩ Od
⟨case other⟩	::=	Otherwise Do ⟨expression⟩ Od

Examples:

IDL Version 2:
```
Define IDesc(e:exp) =
    If Type(e) Sub leaf
        Then Empty
    Else If Type(e) Sub inner
        Then e.leaf Union x.right Fi;
End;
```
IDL87:

```
Define IDesc(e:exp) = Case x Is e
    leaf Do Empty Od
    inner Do x.left Union x.right Od End
End;
```

⟨case_name⟩ is bound to the first ⟨expression⟩ and is local to the case expression. If the type of ⟨name⟩ is the first ⟨type⟩ (e.g., `leaf`), then the associated ⟨expression⟩ (e.g., `Empty`) is evaluated. Inside the ⟨expression⟩, ⟨name⟩ is typed to the ⟨type⟩. Hence, inside "`x.left Union x.right`", x is typed to `inner`. If the type of ⟨name⟩ doesn't match any of the specified ⟨type⟩s, then the ⟨expression⟩ in ⟨case other⟩ is evaluated.

Reason for change: This change is also required by the strong typing in the assertion language. "`e.left`" is permitted only when the type of `e` is `leaf`. The IDL Version 2 example above would result in a type error, because `e` has a type of `exp`. No type error occurs in the IDL87 example.

- **Extension in the ASCII ERL:**

IDL Version 2:

⟨ASCII rep⟩ ::= ⟨reference⟩ { ⟨label⟩ ':' ⟨node⟩ }*

IDL87:

⟨ASCII rep⟩ ::= ⟨reference⟩ { ⟨label⟩ ':' ⟨node⟩ }* { '#' }?

Examples:

IDL Version 2:

    a[value 3]

IDL87:

    a[value 3]#

An instance in the ASCII External Representation Language may be optionally terminated with a "#".

Reason for change: If there are multiple instances in a single file, there needs to be a way to separate them.

- **Extension in the ASCII ERL:**

IDL Version 2:

⟨attributes⟩ ::= ⟨attribute⟩ { ';' ⟨attribute⟩ }*

IDL87:

⟨attributes⟩ ::= ⟨attribute⟩ { ';' ⟨attribute⟩ }* { ';' }?

Examples:

IDL Version 2:

    a[value 3]

IDL87:

    a[value 3;]

The value of the final attribute of a node in the ASCII External Representation Language can be optionally followed by a ";".

Reason for change: If instances are written manually in the ASCII ERL, the absence of a terminating semi-colon on the last attribute should not be required.

B.5 Semantic Differences

As with the syntactic differences, we divide the semantic differences into restrictions and extensions. Many semantic aspects of IDL Version 2 were unclear in the original definition; some of the confusion was avoided by omitting various features, such as derivation in concert with refinement. As restrictions have more impact, since they may invalidate existing specifications, they are presented first.

B.5.1 Restrictions

- Derivation may not be combined with refinement in a ⟨structure decl⟩. This combination, while allowed in IDL Version 2, was not well defined. To get a similar effect, first apply derivation and then refinement.

- Typing in the assertion language in IDL87 was tightened up to permit full compile-time type checking.
  - In IDL87, object collections are typed with a single node, class, structured or basic type. In IDL Version 2, collections could be composed of objects of a variety of types.
  - In IDL Version 2, dot qualification of an object collection containing only node objects (⟨primary exp⟩ . ⟨attribute_name⟩) produces an object collection consisting of the objects that are associated with the specified attribute of all these nodes. In IDL87, the node or class associated with the collection's type must have the ⟨attribute_name⟩ associated with it as an attribute.
  - Overloaded definitions must return the same type, with some implicit coercions supported.
  - The two operands of Union, Intersection, Same, Sub, and PSub must be of the same type, with some implicit coercions supported.
- IDL Version 2 permitted the conversion of classes to nodes or nodes to classes via derivation. In IDL87, nodes and classes remain nodes or classes. For nodes that need to be converted to classes, specify them initially as classes. For classes that need to be converted to nodes, define a new class that has the eventual node as a subclass.
- In IDL Version 2, if a root clause is omitted in a structure declaration, it is copied from a refines ancestor if there is one; otherwise it is copied from a derived structure that has a root. In IDL87, the root of the first ancestor structure that is still present (i.e., has not been deleted by a without clause) is made the root of the derived structure.

B.5.2 Extensions

- The following are keywords in IDL Version 2, and thus may not be declared as user-defined identifiers: Boolean, Create, Destroy, External, Fetch, Integer, Rational, Store, and String. These identifiers are *not* keywords in IDL87 and thus may be declared as user-defined identifiers. The same holds for Internal and Package and the ⟨name⟩s found in the ⟨attribute rep⟩, ⟨port assoc⟩, ⟨restriction⟩, ⟨target⟩ and ⟨type rep⟩ clauses.
- The Members function may take either a set or a sequence object as an argument and returns the collection of objects in that set or sequence. In IDL Version 2, Members took only a set as an argument.

B.5. SEMANTIC DIFFERENCES

- The *Size* function may take an object collection or a sequence as the argument as well as sets. In IDL Version 2, *Size* took only a set as the argument.

- The *In* operator may take a collection or sequence as its right operand as well as a set. In IDL Version 2, *In* took only a set as its right operand.

- In IDL Version 2, all structures must have a root. In IDL87, only port structures need have a root. If desired, reachability checks for the invariant (which in the process can catch typographic errors) may be requested by defining a root, thereby triggering the reachability checking.

Bibliographic Notes

The "standard" definition of IDL is Nestor, Lamb, and Wulf [1982]. A new language, IDL Version 3, also incorporated some of the changes described here, has been described by Nestor et al. [1989].

Appendix C

C Interface Details

This appendix describes details of the mapping from IDL to the C programming language and the runtime support provided for C programs, as supported in the IDL Toolkit.

To specify C, use

>   *Target Language C;*

There are two versions available.

>   *Target Language Version A;*
>   *Target Language Version B;*

C.1 Prefixes

In generating the include files, IDLC prefixes certain letters to the names employed in the IDL specification. In this appendix, such prefixes are emphasized by using a slanted font. The prefixes that are used internally should not be used directly.

A⟨name⟩	typedef name for an array (A) of type ⟨name⟩; used internally
C⟨name⟩	type name for the cell (C) type for a list of ⟨name⟩ used in sets and sequences of ⟨name⟩; used internally
CA⟨class_name⟩	type name for the **struct** containing the attributes for ⟨class_name⟩ (i.e., Class Attributes)

CP⟨class_name⟩	type name for the pointer to the **struct** containing the attributes for ⟨class_name⟩ (i.e., Class Pointer)
D⟨node_name⟩	name of the storage deallocation (D) macro generated for the node ⟨node_name⟩
F⟨node_name⟩	name of the user-written attribute storage finalization (F) function for the attributed node ⟨node_name⟩; called just before the node is deallocated
F⟨private_name⟩	name of the user-written finalization (F) function for ⟨private_name⟩; called just before the node containing this private type is deallocated
I⟨node_name⟩	name of the user-written attribute initialization (I) function for the node ⟨node_name⟩
I⟨private_name⟩	name of the user-written interface function (i.e., Input) that returns an instance of the internal representation of the private type ⟨private_name⟩
IDL⟨anything⟩	reserved for the runtime library; used internally
K⟨node_name⟩	name of the integer constant associated with the attributed or unattributed node ⟨node_name⟩
L⟨name⟩	typedef name for the list (L) type of ⟨name⟩; used internally
N⟨node_name⟩	name of the storage allocation macro (i.e., New) generated for the node ⟨node_name⟩
R⟨node_name⟩	name of the C **struct** (i.e., Record) for a node with the name ⟨node_name⟩; used internally
SEQ⟨name⟩	typedef name for a sequence (SEQ) of ⟨name⟩
SET⟨name⟩	typedef name for a set (SET) of ⟨name⟩
T⟨keyword⟩	new IDLC generated name (i.e., new Type) for the C keyword ⟨keyword⟩
V⟨member_name⟩	name of the field of a **union** (i.e., Variant) for a class with member ⟨member_name⟩

C.2 Representations

IDLC maps the various IDL declarations into C data declarations. Here we give the C analogues of IDL declarations for scalar, node, class, set, sequence, and private types. Many of the details are not relevant to most users of IDL, and are included here only for completeness.

C.2.1 Scalar Types

The IDL *Boolean* data type is mapped into the new C *Boolean* data type with values *TRUE* and *FALSE*. The IDL *Integer* data type is usually mapped into the C *int* data type, unless a type representation clause is used. Similarly, the IDL *Rational* data type is usually mapped into the C *float* data type. Finally, the IDL *String* data type is mapped into a new C String data type.

```
typedef char *String;
typedef char Boolean;
#define TRUE 1
#define FALSE 0
```

C.2.2 Node Types

The IDL specification

$$\langle \text{node\_name} \rangle \Rightarrow \langle \text{attribute}_1 \rangle : \langle \text{type}_1 \rangle,$$
$$\langle \text{attribute}_2 \rangle : \langle \text{type}_2 \rangle,$$
$$\vdots$$
$$\langle \text{attribute}_n \rangle : \langle \text{type}_n \rangle;$$

will generate the following C declarations.

```
struct R⟨node_name⟩ {
        IDLnodeHeader IDLhidden;
        ⟨type1⟩ ⟨attribute1⟩;
        ⟨type2⟩ ⟨attribute2⟩;
            .
            .
            .
        ⟨typen⟩ ⟨attributen⟩;
};
typedef struct R⟨node_name⟩ *⟨node_name⟩;
#define K⟨nodename⟩ ⟨even integer⟩
```

Enumerated nodes, that cannot contain attributes, are specified with a for clause.

> For ⟨node_name⟩ Use Enumerated;

and generate the following C declarations.

> typedef int ⟨node_name⟩
> #define K⟨node_name⟩ ⟨odd integer⟩

C.2.3 Class Types

The IDL specification

> ⟨class_name⟩ ::= ⟨node name$_1$⟩
> | ⟨node name$_2$⟩
> ...
> | ⟨node name$_n$⟩ ;

(where ⟨class_name$_i$⟩ can be used in place of ⟨node name$_i$⟩) will generate the following C declarations.

> typedef struct CA⟨class_name⟩ * CP⟨class_name⟩;
> typedef union {
>   int IDLinternal;
>   CP⟨classname⟩ IDLclassCommon;
>   ⟨node name$_1$⟩ V⟨node name$_1$⟩;
>   ⟨node name$_2$⟩ V⟨node name$_2$⟩;
>   ...
>   ⟨node name$_n$⟩ V⟨attribute$_n$⟩;
> } ⟨class_name⟩;
> struct CA⟨class⟩ {
>   IDLnodeHeader IDLhidden;
>   ⟨type$_1$⟩ ⟨attribute$_1$⟩;
>   ⟨type$_2$⟩ ⟨attribute$_2$⟩;
>   ...
>   ⟨type$_n$⟩ ⟨attribute$_n$⟩;
> };

Place holders in the CA⟨class⟩ *struct*, of the form

> char placeholder⟨integer⟩[⟨integer⟩];

may be necessary if a node or subclass of the class has multiple superclasses.

C.2. REPRESENTATIONS

C.2.4 Sequences

The IDL specification

⟨node_name⟩ => ⟨attribute⟩: Seq Of ⟨type⟩;

will generate the following C declarations by default (i.e, a linked list representation).

```
typedef struct ⟨unique label⟩ {
        struct ⟨unique label⟩ *next;
        ⟨type⟩ value;
} C⟨type⟩, *L⟨type⟩;
#define SEQ⟨type⟩ L⟨type⟩
```

An array representation is also possible.

```
typedef struct {
    int size;
    int length;
    ⟨type_name⟩ * array;
} A⟨type_name⟩;
#define SEQ⟨type_name⟩ A⟨type_name⟩
```

C.2.5 Sets

The IDL specification

⟨node_name⟩ => ⟨attribute⟩: Seq Of ⟨type⟩;

will generate the following C declarations by default (i.e., a linked list).

```
#define SET⟨type⟩ L⟨type⟩
```

where L⟨type⟩ is as defined above.

An array implementation is also available.

```
#define SET⟨type⟩ A⟨type⟩
```

where A⟨type⟩ is as defined above.

Finally, a bitvector representation is available for sets of integers. The storage for bitvectors is allocated directly in the **struct** representing the node.

SETInteger ⟨attribute_name⟩[⟨set size⟩];

where SETInteger is **defined** to be an **int** and the ⟨set size⟩ is calculated so that there is at least one bit for each element in the set.

C.2.6 Private Types

The IDL specification

> *Type* ⟨private type⟩;
> *For* ⟨private type⟩ *Use Package* ⟨package_name⟩;
> *For* ⟨private type⟩ *Use Internal* ⟨internal type⟩;
> *For* ⟨private type⟩ *Use Name* ⟨name⟩;

will generate the following C declarations.

> #include "⟨package_name⟩.h"
> *typedef* ⟨name⟩ ⟨private type⟩;

The other three representation clauses for private types

For ⟨private type⟩ *Use Size* ⟨integer⟩ { *Bits* | *Bytes* } ;
For ⟨private type⟩ *Use Alignment* ⟨integer⟩ { *Bits* | *Bytes* } ;
For ⟨private type⟩ *Use External* ⟨type⟩;

are used by IDLC in attribute ordering and in generating the port routines.

C.3 Runtime Support Routines

The following routines and macros for manipulating data are provided by the IDL C interface. The routines and macros have been grouped under the data types or structures that they manipulate. An entry for a procedure consists of the calling format of the procedure followed by a description of its purpose and use. Unless indicated otherwise, these routines and macros are available in Versions A and B of the C target language.

C.3.1 Strings

The `String` data type was defined to preserve the single-value semantics of IDL basic types. Because there is only one object with each value, pointer equality can be used for object equality.

```
String NewString(Ccharstring)
char *Ccharstring;
```

> Returns a pointer to the newly allocated `String` with the same contents as `Ccharstring`. The contents of `Ccharstring` are copied, so `Ccharstring` may be safely deallocated, if desired.

```
char *StringToChar(IDLstring)
String IDLstring;
```

C.3. RUNTIME SUPPORT ROUTINES

Returns a pointer to a newly allocated C character string with the same contents as `IDLstring`.

C.3.2 Nodes

void *D*⟨node_name⟩ (n)
⟨node_name⟩ n;

> Deallocates the instance of ⟨node_name⟩ referenced by n. Since no check is made for membership of the instance in other data structures, pointers to the freed instance of a ⟨node_name⟩ can be left "dangling."

⟨node_name⟩ *N*⟨node_name⟩

> Returns a pointer to a newly allocated instance of ⟨node_name⟩. This function does the default initialization of the attributes of the new instance.

⟨attribute type⟩ ⟨attribute_name⟩Of⟨node_name⟩ (n)
⟨node_name⟩ n;

> Available only in Version B. This routine extracts the value of the attribute ⟨attribute_name⟩ of the argument node. The ⟨attribute name⟩ must be associated with ⟨node_name⟩, perhaps through a superclass via propagation.

⟨class_name⟩ ⟨node_name⟩To⟨class_name⟩ (n)
⟨node_name⟩ n;

> Available only in Version B. This routine *widens* the argument node to be of type ⟨class_name⟩, which must be a superclass of ⟨node_name⟩. This is a type conversion; no code is actually generated.

C.3.3 Classes

int typeof(c)
⟨class_name⟩ c;

> Every ⟨node_name⟩ has a unique integer associated with it that is symbolically represented as "K⟨node_name⟩". This function returns the type of the node instance contained in c.

⟨attribute type⟩ ⟨attribute_name⟩Of⟨class_name⟩ (c)
⟨class_name⟩ c;

> Available only in Version B. This routine extracts the value of the attribute ⟨attribute_name⟩ of the argument node. The ⟨attribute name⟩ must be associated with ⟨class_name⟩, perhaps indirectly from a superclass via propagation.

⟨class_name$_2$⟩ ⟨class_name$_1$⟩To⟨class_name$_2$⟩ (c)
⟨class_name$_1$⟩ c;
extern void ConversionError(FromClass, ToClass);
char *FromClass, *ToClass;

> Available only in Version B. If ⟨class_name$_1$⟩ is a subclass of ⟨class_name$_2$⟩, then this routine *widens* the argument node to be of type ⟨class_name$_2$⟩. This is a type conversion; no code is actually generated. On the other hand, if ⟨class name$_1$⟩ is a superclass of ⟨class_name$_2$⟩, then this routine *narrows* the argument node to be of type ⟨class_name$_2$⟩. If the argument node is not a member of ⟨class_name$_2$⟩, then the routine ConversionError will be invoked, with the names of the participating classes as arguments. This macro is generated only if ⟨class_name$_1$⟩ and ⟨class_name$_2$⟩ shared at least one node type.

⟨node_name⟩ ⟨class_name⟩To⟨node_name⟩ (c)
⟨class_name⟩ c;

> Available only in Version B. This is a special case of the narrowing operation disussed above. This macro is generated only if ⟨node name⟩ is contained in ⟨class_name⟩.

Boolean Is⟨class_name$_1$⟩ (c)
⟨class_name$_2$⟩ c;

> Available only in Version B. This macro is generated if ⟨class name$_1$⟩ shares one or more node types with any other class. Returns *TRUE* if the type of the node instance referenced in c is a member of ⟨class_name$_1$⟩.

C.3.4 Sets

In this section, ⟨type_name⟩ can be replaced by Boolean, *int*, *float*, *double*, String, or any user-defined ⟨node_name⟩ or ⟨class_name⟩. These routines apply regardless of the representation assigned to the set using a for

C.3. RUNTIME SUPPORT ROUTINES

clause (however, all sets of a particular type must have the same representation). Allocation and deallocation of list cells (in the linked list implementation) are done by each routine but no allocation or deallocation of the data types is performed except for the `float` data type. When comparing data types, two instances of node and class data types are considered to be equal if they occupy the same physical storage and two scalar data types are equal if they have the same value.

```
void addSET⟨type_name⟩ (Aset, Amember)
SET⟨type_name⟩ Aset;
⟨type_name⟩ Amember;
```

> Adds the instance of ⟨type_name⟩ referenced by `Amember` to the set referenced by `Aset`. Attempts to add instances of ⟨type_name⟩ that are already present in the set have no effect.

```
SET⟨type_name⟩ copySET⟨type_name⟩ (Aset)
SET⟨type_name⟩ Aset;
```

> Returns a copy of the set `Aset`. Only the set is copied; the elements themselves are not copied.

```
Boolean emptySET⟨type_name⟩ (Aset)
SET⟨type_name⟩ Aset;
```

> Returns a Boolean `TRUE` if the set referenced by `Aset` is empty. Otherwise it returns a Boolean `FALSE`.

```
foreachinSET⟨type_name⟩ (Aset, traversalset, Amember)
SET⟨type_name⟩ Aset, traversalset;
⟨type_name⟩ Amember;
```

> This macro provides an iterator over each element in a set. If it is directly followed by a compound statement of the target language, it will execute that compound statement once for each element in the set referenced by `Aset`. A pointer to the current ⟨type_name⟩ of the set is presented in `Amember` for use in the compound statement. The compound statement may not add elements to or delete elements from the set, though it may alter their values. The `traversalset` argument holds information regarding the current position in the traversal; you should not reference it. `foreachinSET⟨type_name⟩`'s may be nested, but each nested occurrence must have its own distinct `traversalset`.

void initializeSET⟨type_name⟩ (Aset)
SET⟨type_name⟩ Aset;

> Initializes the set referenced by Aset to empty.

Boolean inSET⟨type_name⟩ (Aset, Amember)
SET⟨type_name⟩ Aset;
⟨type_name⟩ Amember;

> Searches the set of ⟨type_name⟩ referenced by Aset for the instance of ⟨type_name⟩ referenced by Amember and returns a Boolean TRUE if that search succeeds, otherwise it returns a Boolean FALSE.

void removeSET⟨type_name⟩ (Aset, Amember)
SET⟨type_name⟩ Aset;
⟨type_name⟩ Amember;

> Removes the instance of ⟨type_name⟩ referenced by Amember from the set referenced by Aset. Attempts to remove instances of ⟨type_name⟩ that are not present in the set have no effect.

int sizeSET⟨type_name⟩ (Aset)
SET⟨type_name⟩ Aset;

> Returns the number of elements in the set Aset.

C.3.5 Sequences

In this section, ⟨type_name⟩ can be replaced by Boolean, *int*, *float*, *double*, String, or any user-defined ⟨node_name⟩ or ⟨class_name⟩ appearing as a sequence in the IDL specification. These routines apply regardless of the representation assigned to the sequence using a for clause (however, all sequences of a particular type must have the same representation). Allocation and deallocation of list cells (in the linked list representation) are done by each routine but no allocation or deallocation of the data types is performed except for the data types of *float* and *Integer*. When comparing data types, two instances of node and class data types are considered to be equal if they occupy the same physical storage and two scalar data types are equal if they have the same value.

void appendfrontSEQ⟨type_name⟩ (Aseq, Amember)
SEQ⟨type_name⟩ Aseq;
⟨type_name⟩ Amember;

C.3. RUNTIME SUPPORT ROUTINES

> Adds the instance of ⟨type_name⟩ referenced by Amember to the front of the sequence referenced by Aseq. Adding instances of ⟨type_name⟩ that are already present in the sequence will result in duplicate entries.

```
void appendrearSEQ⟨type_name⟩ (Aseq, Amember)
SEQ⟨type_name⟩ Aseq;
⟨type_name⟩ Amember;
```

> Adds the instance of ⟨type_name⟩ referenced by Amember to the rear of the sequence referenced by Aseq. Adding instances of ⟨type_name⟩ that are already present in the sequence will result in duplicate entries.

```
SEQ⟨type_name⟩ copySEQ⟨type_name⟩ (Aseq)
SEQ⟨type_name⟩ Aseq;
```

> Returns a copy of the sequence Aseq. Only the sequence is copied; the elements themselves are not copied.

```
Boolean emptySEQ⟨type_name⟩ (Aseq)
SEQ⟨type_name⟩ Aseq;
```

> Returns a Boolean *TRUE* if the sequence referenced by Aseq is empty. Otherwise it returns a Boolean *FALSE*.

```
foreachinSEQ⟨type_name⟩ (Aseq, traversalseq, Amember)
SEQ⟨type_name⟩ Aseq, traversalseq;
⟨type_name⟩ Amember;
```

> This macro provides an iterator over each element in a sequence. If it is directly followed by a compound statement of the target language, it will execute that compound statement once for each element in the sequence referenced by Aseq. A pointer to the current ⟨type_name⟩ of the sequence is presented in Amember for use in the compound statement. The compound statement may not add elements to or delete elements from the sequence, though it may alter their values The traversalseq argument holds information regarding the current position in the traversal; you should not use it. foreachinSEQ's may be nested, but each nested occurrence must have its own distinct traversalseq.

void initializeSEQ⟨type_name⟩ (Aseq)
SEQ⟨type_name⟩ Aseq;

> Initializes the sequence referenced by Aseq to empty.

Boolean inSEQ⟨type_name⟩ (Aseq, Amember)
SEQ⟨node type⟩ Aseq;
⟨node type⟩ Amember;

> Searches the sequence of ⟨type_name⟩ referenced by Aseq for the instance of ⟨type_name⟩ referenced by Amember and returns a Boolean *TRUE* if that search succeeds. Otherwise it returns a Boolean *FALSE*.

void ithinSEQ⟨type_name⟩ (Aseq, index, Amember)
SEQ⟨type_name⟩ Aseq;
int index;
⟨type_name⟩ Amember;

> Retrieves the ith instance of ⟨type_name⟩ given by index from the sequence referenced by Aseq and assigns it to Amember. If the sequence does not contain index number of elements, Amember is assigned *NULL*. The instance is not actually removed from the sequence.

int lengthSEQ⟨type_name⟩ (Aseq)
SEQ⟨type_name⟩ Aseq;

> Returns the number of elements in the sequence Aseq.

void orderedinsertSEQ⟨type_name⟩ (Aseq, Amember, comparison)
SEQ⟨type_name⟩ Aseq;
⟨type_name⟩ Amember;
Boolean (*comparison)();

> Adds the instance of ⟨type_name⟩ referenced by Amember to the sequence referenced by Aseq in the order dictated by the user-supplied comparison function referenced by comparison. The comparison function, which takes two arguments of type ⟨type_name⟩, should return Boolean *TRUE* if the instance of ⟨type_name⟩ referenced by the second argument should be inserted in the sequence *before* the current instance of ⟨type_name⟩ referenced by the first argument. Otherwise, the function should return Boolean *FALSE*. Adding instances of ⟨type_name⟩ that are already present in the sequence will result in duplicate entries.

C.3. RUNTIME SUPPORT ROUTINES 481

```
void removeSEQ⟨type_name⟩ (Aseq, Amember)
SEQ⟨type_name⟩ Aseq;
⟨type_name⟩ Amember;
```

> Removes from the sequence referenced by **Aseq** the *first* instance of ⟨type_name⟩ referenced by **Amember**. Attempts to remove instances of ⟨type_name⟩ that are not present in the sequence have no effect.

```
void removefirstSEQ⟨type_name⟩ (Aseq)
SEQ⟨type_name⟩ Aseq;
```

> Removes the instance of ⟨type_name⟩ from the front of the sequence pointed to by **Aseq**. Attempts to remove instances of ⟨type_name⟩ from an empty sequence have no effect.

```
void removelastSEQ⟨type_name⟩ (Aseq)
SEQ⟨type_name⟩ Aseq;
```

> Removes the instance of ⟨type_name⟩ from the rear of the sequence pointed to by **Aseq**. Attempts to remove instances of ⟨type_name⟩ from an empty sequence have no effect.

```
void retrievefirstSEQ⟨type_name⟩ (Aseq, Amember)
SEQ⟨type_name⟩ Aseq;
⟨type_name⟩ Amember;
```

> Retrieves the first instance of ⟨type_name⟩ from the sequence referenced by **Aseq** and assigns it to **Amember**. If the sequence is empty, **Amember** is assigned *NULL*. The instance is not actually removed from the sequence.

```
void retrievelastSEQ⟨type_name⟩ (Aseq, Amember)
SEQ⟨type_name⟩ Aseq;
⟨type_name⟩ Amember;
```

> Retrieves the last instance of ⟨type_name⟩ from the sequence referenced by **Aseq** and assigns it to **Amember**. If the sequence is empty, **Amember** is assigned *NULL*. The instance is not actually removed from the sequence.

```
void sortSEQ⟨type_name⟩ (Aseq, comparison)
SEQ⟨type_name⟩ Aseq;
Boolean (*comparison)();
```

Sorts the sequence referenced by `Aseq` in the order dictated by the user-supplied comparison function referenced by `comparison`. The comparison function, which takes two arguments of type ⟨type_name⟩, should return Boolean *TRUE* if the instance of ⟨type_name⟩ referenced by the second argument should be inserted in the sequence *before* the current instance of ⟨type_name⟩ referenced by the first argument. Otherwise, the function should return Boolean *FALSE*.

SEQ⟨type_name⟩ `tailSEQ`⟨type_name⟩ `(Aseq)`
SEQ⟨type_name⟩ `Aseq;`

Returns the remainder of the sequence after the first instance of ⟨type_name⟩. If the sequence is empty, returns *NULL*.

C.3.6 Input Ports

A port declared with

    Pre ⟨port_name⟩: ⟨structure_name⟩;

will generate the following function.

    ⟨root type_name⟩ ⟨port_name⟩ (f)
    FILE *f;

This function reads an IDL data structure from the file referenced by `f` and returns a reference to its root. The file should already be open for reading; an end of file or a trailing pound sign ("#") must be present at the end of the data.

C.3.7 Output Ports

A port declared with

    Post ⟨port_name⟩: ⟨structure_name⟩;

will generate the following function.

    void ⟨port_name⟩ (f,n)
    FILE *f;
    ⟨root type_name⟩ n;

This function writes the instance references by `n` to the file `f`. This file should already be opened for writing; a pound sign ('#') will be written into the file at the end of the data structure.

C.4 Representation Specifications

The following are the representation specifications supported in addition to those listed in Appendix B. Each is described in detail in the indicated section.

For Integer Use Representation Unsigned;

See Section 7.2.1.

For ⟨node_name⟩.⟨attribute_name⟩ *Use Representation* ⟨integer⟩ *Bits;*

See Section 7.2.1.

For ⟨node_name⟩.⟨attribute_name⟩ *Use Representation* ⟨integer⟩ *Bytes;*

See Section 7.2.1.

For Rational Use Double Precision;

See Section 7.2.1.

For ⟨node_name⟩ *Use Representation Enumerated;*

See Section 7.2.2.

For ⟨class_name⟩ *Use Representation Enumerated;*

See Section 7.2.2.

For { Set | Seq } Of ⟨type_name⟩ *Use Representation Array;*

See Sections 7.2.4 and 7.2.5.

For Set of Integer Use Representation Bitvector;

See Section 7.2.5.

For { Set | Seq } Of ⟨type_name⟩ *Use Maximum* ⟨integer⟩ *Elements;*

See Sections 7.2.4 and 7.2.5.

For ⟨private_name⟩ *Use Alignment* ⟨integer⟩ *{ Bits | Bytes };*

See Section 7.2.6.

For ⟨private_name⟩ *Use Size* ⟨integer⟩ *{ Bits | Bytes };*

See Section 7.2.6.

C.5 Restrictions

There are four kinds of operations that may appear in the restriction specifications for C processes, each associated with a macro or function.

- Default node initialization and finalization routines.

$$\langle \text{oper} \rangle ::= \mathit{DefaultInitialize} \mid \mathit{DefaultFinalize}$$

If one of these operations is *not* present, then you must provide a function that performs application-specific initialization or finalization (see Section 4.1.3).

- Node operations.

$$\langle \text{oper} \rangle ::= \mathit{Create} \mid \mathit{Destroy}$$

See Section 7.2.2.

- Sequence operations.

$$\begin{aligned}\langle \text{oper} \rangle ::=\ & \mathit{appendfrontSEQ} \mid \mathit{appendrearSEQ} \mid \mathit{copySEQ} \\ & \mid \mathit{emptySEQ} \mid \mathit{foreachinSEQ} \mid \mathit{inSEQ} \\ & \mid \mathit{initializeSEQ} \mid \mathit{ithinSEQ} \mid \mathit{lengthSEQ} \\ & \mid \mathit{orderedinsertSEQ} \mid \mathit{removefirstSEQ} \mid \mathit{removelastSEQ} \\ & \mid \mathit{removeSEQ} \mid \mathit{retrievefirstSEQ} \mid \mathit{retrievelastSEQ} \\ & \mid \mathit{sortSEQ} \mid \mathit{tailSEQ} \end{aligned}$$

Each sequence macro is associated with an ⟨oper⟩. If an operation is present, the associated macro will be generated (see Section 7.2.4).

- Set operations.

$$\begin{aligned}\langle \text{oper} \rangle ::=\ & \mathit{addSET} \mid \mathit{copySET} \mid \mathit{emptySET} \mid \mathit{foreachinSET} \\ & \mid \mathit{initializeSET} \mid \mathit{inSET} \mid \mathit{removeSET} \\ & \mid \mathit{sizeSET} \end{aligned}$$

Each set macro is associated with an ⟨oper⟩. If an operation is present, the associated macro will be generated (see Section 7.2.5).

Appendix D

Pascal Interface Details

This appendix describes details of the mapping from IDL to the Pascal programming language and the runtime support provided for Pascal programs, as supported in the IDL Toolkit.

To specify Pascal, use

> `Target Language Pascal;`

There are two versions available.

> `Target Language Version A;`
> `Target Language Version B;`

D.1 Prefixes

In generating the include files, the IDL translator prefixes certain letters to the names employed in the IDL specification. In this appendix, such prefixes are emphasized by using a slanted font. The prefixes that are used internally should not be used directly.

CQ ⟨name⟩	type name for the cell (C) type for a list of ⟨name⟩ used in sequences (Q) of ⟨name⟩; used internally
CT ⟨name⟩	type name for the cell (C) type for a list of ⟨name⟩ used in sets (T) of ⟨name⟩; used internally
D ⟨node_name⟩	name of the storage deallocation (D) procedure generated for the node ⟨node_name⟩

$E\langle$name$\rangle$	name of the tag in the variant record for the node or class with the name $\langle$name$\rangle$; used internally
$F\langle$node_name$\rangle$	name of the user-written attribute storage finalization (F) procedure for the attributed node $\langle$node_name$\rangle$; called just before a node is deallocated
$F\langle$private_name$\rangle$	name of the user-written finalization (F) procedure for $\langle$private_name$\rangle$; called just before the node containing this private type is deallocated
$I\langle$node_name$\rangle$	name of the user-written attribute initialization (I) function for $\langle$node_name$\rangle$
$I\langle$private_name$\rangle$	name of the user-written interface procedure that initializes (i.e., Input) an instance of the internal representation of the private type $\langle$private_name$\rangle$
$IDL\langle$anything$\rangle$	reserved for the runtime library; used internally
$K\langle$class_name$\rangle\langle$node_name$\rangle$	name of the enumeration constant (K) associated with the $\langle$node_name$\rangle$ used in $\langle$class_name$\rangle$
$K\langle$node_name$\rangle$	name of the integer constant (K) encoding the type of the node or class; used internally
$N\langle$node_name$\rangle$	name of the storage allocation procedure (i.e., New) generated for the node $\langle$node_name$\rangle$
$P\langle$class_name$\rangle$	name of the field whose value points (P) to the record R$\langle$class name$\rangle$
$Q\langle$class_name$\rangle$	Enumerated type containing these subclasses and nodes of $\langle$class name$\rangle$; used internally
$R\langle$name$\rangle$	name of the Pascal *record* (R) for a node or class with the name $\langle$name$\rangle$; used internally
$SEQ\langle$name$\rangle$	type name for a sequence (SEQ) of $\langle$name$\rangle$
$SET\langle$name$\rangle$	type name for a set (SET) of $\langle$name$\rangle$
$T\langle$keyword$\rangle$	new name generated by the IDL translator (i.e., a new Type) for the Pascal keyword $\langle$keyword$\rangle$

V⟨member_name⟩   name of the field of a variant (V) record for a
                        class with member ⟨member_name⟩

D.2 Representations

The IDL translator maps the various IDL declarations into Pascal data declarations. Here we give the Pascal analogues of IDL declarations for scalar, node, class, set and sequence types. Many of the details are not relevant to most users of IDL, and are included here only for completeness.

D.2.1 Scalar Types

The IDL *Boolean* data type is mapped into the Pascal *boolean* data type. The IDL *Integer* data type is usually mapped into the Pascal *integer* data type, unless a type representation clause is used, in which case a subrange of integer may be used. Similarly, the IDL *Rational* data type is usually mapped into the Pascal *real* data type. Finally, the IDL *String* data type is mapped into a new Pascal *String* data type.

```
type String = ^record
       length: integer;
       chars:  array [1..512] of char
       end;
```

D.2.2 Node and Class Types

Both nodes and classes are represented explicitly in Pascal, with pointers linking the representation. The IDL specification

$$
\begin{array}{l}
\langle \text{class\_name}_1 \rangle ::= \langle \text{class\_name}_2 \rangle; \\
\langle \text{class\_name}_2 \rangle ::= \langle \text{node\_name} \rangle \\
\qquad\qquad\qquad | \ \langle \text{node name}_2 \rangle \\
\qquad\qquad\qquad \ldots \\
\qquad\qquad\qquad | \ \langle \text{node name}_n \rangle; \\
\\
\langle \text{node\_name} \rangle \ \Rightarrow \ \langle \text{attribute}_1 \rangle: \ \langle \text{type}_1 \rangle, \\
\qquad\qquad\qquad\quad \langle \text{attribute}_2 \rangle: \ \langle \text{type}_2 \rangle, \\
\qquad\qquad\qquad\quad \ldots \\
\qquad\qquad\qquad\quad \langle \text{attribute}_n \rangle: \ \langle \text{type}_n \rangle; \\
\\
\langle \text{class\_name}_1 \rangle \ \Rightarrow \ \langle \text{attribute}_{n+1} \rangle: \ \langle \text{type}_{n+1} \rangle, \\
\langle \text{class\_name}_2 \rangle \ \Rightarrow \ \langle \text{attribute}_{n+2} \rangle: \ \langle \text{type}_{n+2} \rangle,
\end{array}
$$

will generate the following Pascal declarations.

```
const K⟨node_name⟩ = ⟨even integer⟩;
type Q⟨class_name₁⟩ = (K⟨class name₁⟩⟨class_name₂⟩);
⟨class_name₁⟩ = ^R⟨class_name₁⟩;
Q⟨class_name₂⟩ = (K⟨class_name₂⟩⟨node name₁⟩,
                  K⟨class_name₂⟩⟨node name₂⟩, ···
                  K⟨class_name₂⟩⟨node nameₙ⟩);
⟨class_name₂⟩ = ^R⟨class_name₂⟩;
⟨node_name⟩ = ^R⟨node_name⟩;

R⟨class_name₁⟩ = record
            IDLhidden: IDLnodeHeader;
            ⟨attributeₙ₊₁⟩: ⟨typeₙ₊₁⟩;
            case E⟨class_name₁⟩: Q⟨class_name₁⟩ of
                K⟨class_name₁⟩⟨class_name₂⟩:
                        (V⟨class name₂⟩: ⟨class_name₁⟩);
            end;

R⟨class_name₂⟩ = record
            IDLhidden: IDLnodeHeader;
            P⟨class_name₁⟩: ⟨class_name₁⟩;
            ⟨attributeₙ₊₂⟩: ⟨typeₙ₊₂⟩;
            case E⟨class_name₂⟩: Q⟨class_name₂⟩ of
                K⟨class_name₂⟩⟨node_name₁⟩:
                        (V⟨node name₁⟩: ⟨node_name₁⟩);
                ...
                K⟨class_name₂⟩⟨node_nameₙ⟩:
                        (V⟨node nameₙ⟩: ⟨node_nameₙ⟩);
            end;

R⟨node_name⟩ = record
            IDLhidden: IDLnodeHeader;
            P⟨class_name₁⟩: ⟨class_name₁⟩;
            P⟨class_name₂⟩: ⟨class_name₂⟩;
            ⟨attribute₁⟩:   ⟨type₁⟩;
            ⟨attribute₂⟩:   ⟨type₂⟩;
            ...
            ⟨attributeₙ⟩:   ⟨type₁⟩;
            end;
```

D.2. REPRESENTATIONS

D.2.3 Sequences

The IDL specification

⟨node_name⟩ => ⟨attribute⟩: *Seq Of* ⟨type⟩;

will generate a linked list representation.

```
type SEQ⟨type⟩ = record
      next: ^SEQ⟨type⟩;
      value: ⟨type⟩;
end;
```

D.2.4 Sets

The IDL specification

⟨node_name⟩ => ⟨attribute⟩: *Seq Of* ⟨type⟩;

will generate a linked list representation.

```
type SET⟨type⟩ = record
      next: ^SEQ⟨type⟩;
      value: ⟨type⟩;
end;
```

D.2.5 Private Types

The IDL specification

Type ⟨private type⟩;
For ⟨private type⟩ *Use Package* ⟨package_name⟩;
For ⟨private type⟩ *Use Internal* ⟨internal type⟩;
For ⟨private type⟩ *Use Name* ⟨name⟩;

will generate the following Pascal declarations

```
#include "⟨package_name⟩.h"
type ⟨name⟩ = ⟨private type⟩;
```

The other three representation clauses for private types

For ⟨private type⟩ *Use Alignment* ⟨integer⟩ { *Bits* | *Bytes* } ;
For ⟨private type⟩ *Use Size* ⟨integer⟩ { *Bits* | *Bytes* } ;
For ⟨private type⟩ *Use External* ⟨type⟩;

are used by the IDL translator in attribute ordering and in generating the port routines.

D.3 Runtime Support Routines

The following routines for manipulating data are provided by the IDL Pascal interface. The routines have been grouped under the data types or structures that they manipulate. An entry for a procedure consists of the calling format of the procedure followed by a description of its purpose and use. Unless indicated otherwise, these routines are available in Versions A and B of the Pascal target language.

D.3.1 Strings

The String data type was defined to preserve the single-value semantics of IDL basic types. Because there is only one object with each value, pointer equality can be used for object equality.

function NewString(length: *integer*;
    value: *packedArrayType*): String;

> Returns a pointer to the newly allocated String with the same contents as value. The contents of value are copied, so value may be safely deallocated, if desired.

procedure FreeString(var ThisString: String);

> Frees the storage used by the specified string.

function StringAppend(source, added: String): String;

> Appends added onto the end of the source, and returns the result.

function StringLength(stringInstance: String): *integer*;

> Extracts the length of the stringInstance.

function StringTopacked(value: *String*): packedArrayType;

> Extracts the characters from the String.

D.3.2 Nodes

function $N\langle\text{node\_name}\rangle$: $\langle\text{node\_name}\rangle$;

> Returns a pointer to a newly-allocated instance of ⟨node_name⟩. This function does the default initialization of the attributes of the new instance.

procedure $D\langle\text{node\_name}\rangle$(n: ⟨node_name⟩);

> Deallocates the instance of ⟨node_name⟩ referenced by n. Since no check is made for membership of the instance in other data structures, pointers to the freed instance of a ⟨node_name⟩ can be left "dangling."

function ⟨attribute_name⟩Of⟨node name⟩(n: ⟨node_name⟩):
  ⟨attribute type⟩;

> Available only in Version B. This routine extracts the value of the attribute ⟨attribute_name⟩ of the argument node. The ⟨attribute name⟩ must be associated with ⟨node_name⟩, perhaps through a superclass via propagation.

function ⟨node_name⟩To⟨class_name⟩(n: ⟨node_name⟩): ⟨class_name⟩;

> Available only in Version B. This routine *widens* the argument node to be of type ⟨class_name⟩, which must be a superclass of ⟨node_name⟩.

D.3.3 Classes

function ⟨attribute_name⟩Of⟨class_name⟩(c: ⟨class_name⟩):
  ⟨attribute type⟩;

> Available only in Version B. This function extracts the value of the attribute ⟨attribute_name⟩ of the argument node. The ⟨attribute name⟩ must be associated with ⟨class_name⟩, perhaps indirectly from a superclass via propagation.

function $\langle\text{class\_name}_1\rangle$To$\langle\text{class\_name}_2\rangle$(c: $\langle\text{class\_name}_1\rangle$): $\langle\text{class\_name}_2\rangle$;
procedure ConversionError(FromClass, ToClass: String);

> Available only in Version B. If $\langle\text{class\_name}_1\rangle$ is a subclass of $\langle\text{class\_name}_2\rangle$, then this function *widens* the argument node to be of type $\langle\text{class\_name}_2\rangle$. On the other hand, if $\langle\text{class name}_1\rangle$

is a superclass of ⟨class_name₂⟩, then this function *narrows* the argument node to be of type ⟨class_name₂⟩. If the argument node is not a member of ⟨class_name₂⟩, then the procedure ConversionError will be invoked, with the names of the participating classes as arguments. This function is generated only if ⟨class_name₁⟩ and ⟨class_name₂⟩ shared at least one node type.

function ⟨class_name⟩To⟨node_name⟩(c: ⟨class_name⟩): ⟨node_name⟩

Available only in Version B. This is a special case of the narrowing operation disussed above. This function is generated only if ⟨node_name⟩ is contained in ⟨class_name⟩.

D.3.4 Sets

In this section, ⟨type_name⟩ can be replaced by boolean, integer, real, String, or any user-defined ⟨node_name⟩ or ⟨class_name⟩. These routines apply regardless of the representation assigned to the set using a for clause. Allocation and deallocation of list cells (in the linked list implementation) are done by each routine. When comparing two instances of node and class data types are considered to be equal if they occupy the same physical storage and two scalar data types are equal if they have the same value.

procedure addSET⟨type_name⟩(var Aset: SET⟨type_name⟩;
    Amember: ⟨type_name⟩);

Adds the instance of ⟨type_name⟩ referenced by Amember to the set referenced by Aset. Attempts to add instances of ⟨type_name⟩ that are already present in the set have no effect.

function copySET⟨type_name⟩(Aset: SET⟨type_name⟩): SET⟨type_name⟩;

Returns a copy of the set Aset. Only the set is copied; the elements themselves are not copied.

function emptySET⟨type_name⟩(Aset: SET⟨type_name⟩): boolean;

Returns true if the set referenced by Aset is empty. Otherwise it returns false.

procedure initializeSET⟨type_name⟩(var Aset: SET⟨type_name⟩);

Initializes the set referenced by Aset to empty.

D.3. RUNTIME SUPPORT ROUTINES 493

function inSET⟨type_name⟩(Aset: SET⟨type_name⟩;
         Amember: ⟨type_name⟩): *boolean*;

> Searches the set of ⟨type_name⟩ referenced by Aset for the instance of ⟨type_name⟩ referenced by Amember and returns true if that search succeeds, otherwise it returns false.

procedure removeSET⟨type_name⟩(var Aset: SET⟨type_name⟩;
         Amember: ⟨type_name⟩);

> Removes the instance of ⟨type_name⟩ referenced by Amember from the set referenced by Aset. Attempts to remove instances of ⟨type_name⟩ that are not present in the set have no effect.

function sizeSET⟨type_name⟩(Aset: SET⟨type_name⟩): *integer*;

> Returns the number of elements in the set Aset.

D.3.5 Sequences

In this section, ⟨type_name⟩ can be replaced by *boolean*, *integer*, *real*, String, or any user-defined ⟨node_name⟩ or ⟨class_name⟩ appearing as a sequence in the IDL specification. These routines apply regardless of the representation assigned to the sequence using a for clause. Allocation and deallocation of list cells (in the linked list representation) are done by each routine but no allocation or deallocation of the data types is performed except for the data types of *float* and *Integer*. When comparing data types, two instances of node and class data types are considered to be equal if they occupy the same physical storage and two scalar data types are equal if they have the same value.

procedure appendfrontSEQ⟨type_name⟩(var Aseq: SEQ⟨type_name⟩;
         Amember: ⟨type_name⟩);

> Adds the instance of ⟨type_name⟩ referenced by Amember to the front of the sequence referenced by Aseq. Adding instances of ⟨type_name⟩ that are already present in the sequence will result in duplicate entries.

procedure appendrearSEQ⟨type_name⟩(var Aseq: SEQ⟨type_name⟩;
         Amember: ⟨type_name⟩);

> Adds the instance of ⟨type_name⟩ referenced by Amember to the rear of the sequence referenced by Aseq. Adding instances of ⟨type_name⟩ that are already present in the sequence will result in duplicate entries.

function copySEQ⟨type_name⟩(Aseq: SEQ⟨type_name⟩): SEQ⟨type_name⟩;

   Returns a copy of the sequence Aseq. Only the sequence is copied; the elements themselves are not copied.

function emptySEQ⟨type_name⟩(Aseq: SEQ⟨type_name⟩): *boolean*;

   Returns *true* if the sequence referenced by Aseq is empty. Otherwise it returns *false*.

procedure initializeSEQ⟨type_name⟩(var Aseq: SEQ⟨type_name⟩);

   Initializes the sequence referenced by Aseq to empty.

function inSEQ⟨type_name⟩(Aseq: SEQ⟨node type⟩;
                Amember: ⟨node type⟩): *boolean*;

   Searches the sequence of ⟨type_name⟩ referenced by Aseq for the instance of ⟨type_name⟩ referenced by Amember and returns *true* if that search succeeds. Otherwise it returns *false*.

function ithinSEQ⟨type_name⟩(Aseq: SEQ⟨type_name⟩;
                index: *integer*): ⟨type_name⟩;

   Retrieves the ith instance of ⟨type_name⟩ given by index from the sequence referenced by Aseq. If the sequence does not contain index number of elements, *null* is returned. The instance is not actually removed from the sequence.

function lengthSEQ⟨type_name⟩(Aseq: SEQ⟨type_name⟩): *integer*;

   Returns the number of elements in the sequence Aseq.

procedure orderedinsertSEQ⟨type_name⟩(var Aseq: SEQ⟨type_name⟩;
                Amember: ⟨type_name⟩;
                function comparison: *boolean*);

   Adds the instance of ⟨type_name⟩ referenced by Amember to the sequence referenced by Aseq in the order dictated by the user-supplied comparison function referenced by comparison. The comparison function, which takes two parameters of type ⟨type_name⟩, should return *true* if the instance of ⟨type_name⟩ referenced by the second parameter should be inserted in the sequence *before* the current instance of ⟨type_name⟩ referenced by the first parameter. Otherwise, the function should return *false*. Adding instances of ⟨type_name⟩ that are already present in the sequence will result in duplicate entries.

D.3. RUNTIME SUPPORT ROUTINES

procedure removeSEQ⟨type_name⟩(*var* Aseq: SEQ⟨type_name⟩;
           Amember: ⟨type_name⟩);

Removes from the sequence referenced by Aseq the *first* instance of ⟨type_name⟩ referenced by Amember. Attempts to remove instances of ⟨type_name⟩ that are not present in the sequence have no effect.

procedure removefirstSEQ⟨type_name⟩(*var* Aseq: SEQ⟨type_name⟩);

Removes the instance of ⟨type_name⟩ from the front of the sequence pointed to by Aseq. Attempts to remove instances of ⟨type_name⟩ from an empty sequence have no effect.

procedure removelastSEQ⟨type_name⟩(*var* Aseq: SEQ⟨type_name⟩);

Removes the instance of ⟨type_name⟩ from the rear of the sequence pointed to by Aseq. Attempts to remove instances of ⟨type_name⟩ from an empty sequence have no effect.

function retrievefirstSEQ⟨type_name⟩
           (Aseq: SEQ⟨type_name⟩): ⟨type_name⟩;

Retrieves the first instance of ⟨type_name⟩ from the sequence referenced by Aseq. If the sequence is empty, *null* is returned. The instance is not actually removed from the sequence.

function retrievelastSEQ⟨type_name⟩
           (Aseq: SEQ⟨type_name⟩): ⟨type_name⟩;

Retrieves the last instance of ⟨type_name⟩ from the sequence referenced by Aseq. If the sequence is empty, *null* is returned. The instance is not actually removed from the sequence.

procedure sortSEQ⟨type_name⟩(*var* Aseq: SEQ⟨type_name⟩;
           function comparison: *boolean*);

Sorts the sequence referenced by Aseq in the order dictated by the user-supplied comparison function referenced by **comparison**. The comparison function, which takes two parameters of type ⟨type_name⟩, should return *true* if the instance of ⟨type_name⟩ referenced by the second parameter should be inserted in the sequence *before* the current instance of ⟨type_name⟩ referenced by the first parameter. Otherwise, the function should return *false*.

function `tailSEQ`⟨type_name⟩`(Aseq:` `SEQ`⟨type_name⟩`):` `SEQ`⟨type_name⟩`;`

Returns the remainder of the sequence after the first instance of ⟨type_name⟩. If the sequence is empty, returns `null`.

D.3.6 Input Ports

A port declared with

Pre ⟨port_name⟩: ⟨structure_name⟩;

will generate the following function.

function ⟨port_name⟩`(var f: text):` ⟨root type_name⟩;

This function reads an IDL data structure from the file referenced by `f` and returns a reference to its root. The file should already be open for reading; an end of file or a trailing pound sign ("#") must be present at the end of the data.

D.3.7 Output Ports

A port declared with

Post ⟨port_name⟩: ⟨structure_name⟩;

will generate the following function:

procedure ⟨port_name⟩`(var f: text; root:` ⟨root type_name⟩`);`

This procedure writes the instance references by n to the file f. This file should already be opened for writing; a pound sign ('#') will be written into the file at the end of the data structure.

D.4 Representation Specifications

The following are the representation specifications supported in addition to those listed in Appendix B. Each is described in detail in the indicated section.

For Integer Use Representation Unsigned;

See Section 8.2.1.

For ⟨node_name⟩.⟨attribute_name⟩ *Use Representation* ⟨integer⟩ *Bits;*

See Section 8.2.1.

For ⟨node_name⟩.⟨attribute_name⟩ *Use Representation* ⟨integer⟩ *Bytes;*

See Section 8.2.1.

For ⟨private_name⟩ *Use Alignment* ⟨integer⟩ { *Bits* | *Bytes* };

See Section 8.2.6.

For ⟨private_name⟩ *Use Size* ⟨integer⟩ { *Bits* | *Bytes* };

See Section 8.2.6.

D.5 Restrictions

There are four kinds of operations that may appear in the restriction specifications for Pascal processes, each associated with a function.

- Default node initialization and finalization routines.

    ⟨oper⟩ ::= *DefaultInitialize* | *DefaultFinalize*

    If one of these operations is *not* present, then you must provide a function that performs application-specific initialization or finalization (see Section 8.2.2).

- Node operations.

    ⟨oper⟩ ::= *Create* | *Destroy*

    See Section 8.2.2.

- Sequence operations.

    ⟨oper⟩ ::= *appendfrontSEQ* | *appendrearSEQ* | *copySEQ*
    | *emptySEQ* | *inSEQ* | *initializeSEQ*
    | *ithinSEQ* | *lengthSEQ* | *orderedinsertSEQ*
    | *removefirstSEQ* | *removelastSEQ* | *removeSEQ*
    | *retrievefirstSEQ* | *retrievelastSEQ*
    | *sortSEQ* | *tailSEQ*

Each sequence procedure or function is associated with an ⟨oper⟩. If an operation is present, the associated procedure or function will be generated (see Section 8.2.4).

- Set operations.

$$\langle \text{oper} \rangle ::= \text{addSET} \mid \text{copySET} \mid \text{emptySET}$$
$$\mid \text{initializeSET} \mid \text{inSET} \mid \text{removeSET}$$
$$\mid \text{sizeSET}$$

Each set procedure or function is associated with an ⟨oper⟩. If an operation is present, the associated procedure or function will be generated (see Section 8.2.5).

Appendix E

Function Language Compiler

This appendix contains the code for the function language compiler described in Chapters 3 and 9. Both the C and Pascal code are given. This compiler has four phases:

- the frontend, which reads in the characters of the source program, tokenizes this input, syntactically analyzes the input, and generates a syntax tree;

- the semantic analysis phase, which resolves names and performs type checking, writing out an attributed syntax tree;

- the constant folding phase, which reads in the attributed syntax tree, simplifies those operations applied to constants, and writes out another, presumably faster-executing instance of the same function, and

- the convert phase, which replaces the encoded form of the source position (as an integer) with an instance of the **pos** node.

A single-phase variant, functionally equivalent to the four-phase variant, is also defined.

The directory structure for this examples, showing all source files, is given in Figure E.1. Names ending with '/' are subdirectories. The figure number (or starting page number) of all listings provided in this book are indicated. Most of the **Makefile**s are not given; they generally have the structure of **oneprocess/C/Makefile**, given on page 509.

functionlang/
  Makefile
  specs/
    functionsyntax.idl (3.6,9.3)
    functionsem.idl (3.8,9.14)
    pos.idl (9.7)
    posCconverts.h (9.22)
    posPconverts.h (9.23)
    sourceposition.i (9.12)
    aswithpos.idl (9.20)
  frontend/
    Makefile
    fe.idl (9.4)
    C/
      Makefile
      frontend.idl (9.5)
      main.c (9.9)
      lex.l (p. 501)
      parser.y (p. 503)
    Pascal/
      Makefile
      frontend.idl (9.6)
      main.p (9.11)
      lexical.i (p. 512)
      syntactic.i (E.4.1)
  semantic/
    Makefile
    sem.idl (9.15)
    C/
      Makefile
      semantic.idl (9.16)
      main.c (9.18)
      resolve.c (p. 507)
      typing.c (p. 508)
    Pascal/
      Makefile
      semantic.idl (9.17)
      main.p (9.19)
      resolve.p (p. 520)
      typing.p (p. 521)
  test/
    foo.in (3.4)
    bar.in (3.5)
  constantfold/
    Makefile
    cf.idl (3.9)
    C/
      Makefile
      constant_fold.idl (3.9)
      main.c (3.12)
      algorithm.c (3.15–3.16)
    Pascal/
      Makefile
      constant_fold.idl (3.11)
      main.p (3.14)
      algorithm.p (3.17–3.18)
  convert/
    Makefile
    convertgen.idl (9.21)
    C/
      Makefile
      convert.idl (9.22)
      main.c (9.24)
    Pascal/
      Makefile
      convert.idl (9.23)
      main.p (9.25)
  oneprocess/
    Makefile
    all.idl (9.27)
    C/
      Makefile (p. 509)
      onephasecompiler.idl (9.28)
      main.c (9.30)
    Pascal/
      Makefile (p. 523)
      onephasecompiler.idl (9.29)
      main.p (9.31)

Figure E.1: Directory Structure for Function Language Compiler

E.1 Language Definition

The syntax for the function language is given in Figure 3.2 on page 73 (and repeated in Figure 9.2 on page 201). The lexical portion of the syntax is given in Figure 9.8 (page 206).

E.2 The IDL Specifications

The `abstract_syntax` structure is given in Figure 3.6 (page 76) and repeated in Figure 9.3 (page 202). The `attributed_syntax` structure is given in Figure 3.8 (page 78) and repeated in Figure 9.14 (page 214). The `pos` node is specified in Figure 9.7 (page 205); the `AS_with_pos` structure is given in Figure 9.20 (page 219).

The generic IDL specifications for the processes in the two variants are given in Figures 9.4 (page 204: **fe.idl**), 9.15 (page 214: **sem.idl**), 3.9 (page 85: **cf.idl**), 9.21 (page 220: **convertgen.idl**), and 9.27 (page 223: **all.idl**).

E.3 The Implementation in C

E.3.1 The Frontend

As discussed in Chapter 9, LEX and YACC were used to generate the frontend. The process specification for this phase is given in Figure 9.5 (page 204). The `main` function for this phase is given in Figure 9.9 (page 209). The conversion routines for the `sourceposition` private type are given in Figure 9.10 (page 210). The listings for the Lex input file (**lex.l**) and Yacc input file (**parser.y**) follow.

```
%{/* file: functionlang/frontend/C/lex.l */
#include "frontend.h"
#include "tokens.h"

int linecount = 1,
    charoffset = 0,
    linestart = 0;  /* character offset of first character of this line */
%}

%%
"+"         { charoffset+=1; return (PlusToken); }
"-"         { charoffset+=1; return (MinusToken); }
"*"         { charoffset+=1; return (TimesToken); }
"/"         { charoffset+=1; return (DivideToken); }
"("         { charoffset+=1; return (LParenToken); }
")"         { charoffset+=1; return (RParenToken); }
";"         { charoffset+=1; return (SemiToken); }
"="         { charoffset+=1; return (EqualToken); }
":"         { charoffset+=1; return (ColonToken); }
","         { charoffset+=1; return (CommaToken); }
```

```
[0-9]+       {
             int this;
             charoffset += yyleng;
             sscanf(yytext,"%d",&this);
             yylval.Vinteger_constant = Ninteger_constant;
             yylval.Vinteger_constant->lex_value = this;
             return (IntegerToken);
             }
[0-9]+"."[0-9]* {
             float this;
             charoffset += yyleng;
             sscanf(yytext,"%f",&this);
             yylval.Vreal_constant = Nreal_constant;
             yylval.Vreal_constant->lex_value = this;
             return (RealToken);
             }
[a-zA-Z][a-zA-Z0-9_]* {
             if (strcmp(yytext,"function")==0) {
                 charoffset += yyleng;
                 return (functionKeyword);
             }
             else if (strcmp(yytext,"integer")==0) {
                 charoffset += yyleng;
                 return (integerKeyword);
             }
             else if (strcmp(yytext,"real")==0) {
                 charoffset += yyleng;
                 return (realKeyword);
             }
             else {
                 identifier n;
                 n = Nidentifier;
                 n->lex_token = NewString(yytext);
                 n->lex_pos = Npos;
                 n->lex_pos->charoffset = charoffset;
                 n->lex_pos->lineoffset = charoffset - linestart;
                 n->lex_pos->linenumber = linecount;
                 yylval.Videntifier = n;
                 charoffset += yyleng;
                 return (IdentifierToken);
             }
             }
[ \t]*       { /* white space */
             charoffset+=yyleng;
             }
\n           { /* more white space */
             linecount += 1;
             charoffset += 1;
             linestart = charoffset;
             }
%%
```

E.3. THE IMPLEMENTATION IN C

```
%{/* file: functionlang/frontend/C/parser.y */
#include "frontend.h"
#include <stdio.h>
functions thesefunctions;
%}
/* types associated with grammar symbols */
%union{
function Vfunction;
identifier Videntifier;
integer_constant Vinteger_constant;
real_constant Vreal_constant;
SEQformal_parameter Vparameters;
formal_parameter Vformal_parameter;
expression Vexpression;
types Vtypes;
}

/* token declarations */
%token <Videntifier> IdentifierToken 1
%token <Vinteger_constant> IntegerToken 2
%token <Vreal_constant> RealToken 3
/* keywords */
%token functionKeyword 4
%token integerKeyword 5
%token realKeyword 6
/* punctuation */
%token PlusToken 7
%token MinusToken 8
%token TimesToken 9
%token DivideToken 10
%token LParenToken 11
%token RParenToken 12
%token SemiToken 13
%token EqualToken 14
%token ColonToken 15
%token CommaToken 16
/* precedence */
%left PlusToken MinusToken
%left TimesToken DivideToken
%left UMINUS
/* types */
%type <Vfunction> _function
%type <Vparameters> _parameters
%type <Vparameters> _parameters_list
%type <Vformal_parameter> _parameter
%type <Vexpression> _expression
%type <Vtypes> _type
%%

_program : /* empty */
    {
        thesefunctions = Nfunctions;
        initializeSEQfunction(thesefunctions->syn_func_seq);
    }
    |   _program _function
    {
        appendrearSEQfunction(thesefunctions->syn_func_seq, $2);
    }
    ;
```

```
_function : functionKeyword IdentifierToken _parameters
           ColonToken _type EqualToken _expression SemiToken
      {
           function thisfunction;
           thisfunction = Nfunction;
           thisfunction->syn_name = $2;
           thisfunction->syn_parameters = $3;
           thisfunction->syn_return_type = $5;
           thisfunction->syn_definition = $7;
           $$ = thisfunction;
      }
      ;
_parameters :  /* empty */
      {
           SEQformal_parameter this;
           initializeSEQformal_parameter(this);
           $$ = this;
      }
      |    LParenToken _parameters_list RParenToken
      {
           $$ = $2;
      }
      ;

_parameters_list : _parameter
      {
           SEQformal_parameter this;
           initializeSEQformal_parameter(this);
           appendrearSEQformal_parameter(this, $1);
           $$ = this;
      }
      |    _parameters_list CommaToken _parameter
      {
           appendrearSEQformal_parameter($1, $3);
           $$ = $1;
      }
      ;

_parameter : IdentifierToken ColonToken _type
      {
           formal_parameter this;
           this = Nformal_parameter;
           this->syn_name = $1;
           this->syn_param_type = $3;
           $$ = this;
      }
      ;

_type integerKeyword
      {
           $$.VTint = NTint;
      }
      |    realKeyword
      {
           $$.Vreal = Nreal;
      }
      ;
```

E.3. THE IMPLEMENTATION IN C

```
_expression : IntegerToken
        {
            $$.Vinteger_constant = $1;
        }
    |   RealToken
        {
            $$.Vreal_constant = $1;
        }
    |   IdentifierToken
        {
            formal_parameterRef p;
            p = Nformal_parameterRef;
            p->syn_name = $1;
            $$.Vformal_parameterRef = p;
        }
    |   _expression PlusToken _expression
        {
            binary_operation b;
            b = Nbinary_operation;
            b->syn_left = $1;
            b->syn_op.Vplus = Nplus;
            b->syn_right = $3;
            $$.Vbinary_operation = b;
        }
    |   _expression MinusToken _expression
        {
            binary_operation b;
            b = Nbinary_operation;
            b->syn_left = $1;
            b->syn_op.Vminus = Nminus;
            b->syn_right = $3;
            $$.Vbinary_operation = b;
        }
    |   _expression TimesToken _expression
        {
            binary_operation b;
            b = Nbinary_operation;
            b->syn_left = $1;
            b->syn_op.Vtimes = Ntimes;
            b->syn_right = $3;
            $$.Vbinary_operation = b;
        }
    |   _expression DivideToken _expression
        {
            binary_operation b;
            b = Nbinary_operation;
            b->syn_left = $1;
            b->syn_op.Vdivide = Ndivide;
            b->syn_right = $3;
            $$.Vbinary_operation = b;
        }
    |   PlusToken _expression %prec UMINUS
        {
            unary_operation u;
            u = Nunary_operation;
            u->syn_argument = $2;
            u->syn_op.Vunaryplus = Nunaryplus;
            $$.Vunary_operation = u;
        }
```

```
        |   MinusToken _expression %prec UMINUS
        {
            unary_operation u;
            u = Nunary_operation;
            u->syn_argument = $2;
            u->syn_op.Vunaryminus = Nunaryminus;
            $$.Vunary_operation = u;
        }
        |   LParenToken _expression RParenToken
        {
            $$ = $2;
        }
        ;
%%

yyerror(s)
char *s;
{
    fprintf(stderr, "frontend: %s\n",s);
    exit(1);
}

yywrap()
{
    return (1);
}
```

E.3.2 The Semantic Analysis Phase

The process specification for this phase is given in Figure 9.16 on page 215.
The main program in C is shown in Figure 9.18 (page 216). The listings for
the name resolution (**resolve.c**) and typing (**typing.c**) source files follow.

```
/* file: functionlang/semantic/C/resolve.c */

#include "semantic.h"
#include <stdio.h>

/* the procedure for resolving parameter references */

resolve_references(thefunction)
function thefunction;
{
    resolve_exp(thefunction->syn_definition, thefunction->syn_parameters);
}

resolve_exp(the_exp, theparameters)
expression the_exp;
SEQformal_parameter theparameters;
{
    SEQformal_parameter Sp;
    formal_parameter Aformal_parameter;

    switch (typeof(the_exp)) {
    case Kinteger_constant:
        break;

    case Kreal_constant:
        break;

    case Kformal_parameterRef:
        foreachinSEQformal_parameter(theparameters, Sp, Aformal_parameter) {
            if (Aformal_parameter->syn_name->lex_token
                    == the_exp.Vformal_parameterRef->syn_name->lex_token) {
                the_exp.Vformal_parameterRef->sem_entity = Aformal_parameter;
                break;
            }
        };
        break;

    case Kbinary_operation:
        resolve_exp(the_exp.Vbinary_operation->syn_left, theparameters);
        resolve_exp(the_exp.Vbinary_operation->syn_right, theparameters);
        break;

    case Kunary_operation:
        resolve_exp(the_exp.Vunary_operation->syn_argument, theparameters);
        break;

    default:
        fprintf(stderr, "resolve: invalid type in switch\n");
    }
}
```

```c
/* file: functionlang/semantic/C/typing.c */

#include "semantic.h"
#include <stdio.h>

/* the procedure for expression typing */
expression_type (the_exp)
expression the_exp;
{
    expression left_exp;  /* for de-referencing left exp of binary op */
    expression right_exp; /* for de-referencing right exp of binary op */
    expression arg_exp;   /* for de-referencing argument of unary op */
    types left_type;
    types right_type;
    types arg_type;
    types result_type;

    switch (typeof(the_exp)) {
    case Kinteger_constant:
        the_exp.Vinteger_constant->sem_exp_type.VTint = NTint;
        break;

    case Kreal_constant:
        the_exp.Vreal_constant->sem_exp_type.Vreal = Nreal;
        break;

    case Kformal_parameterRef:
        the_exp.Vformal_parameterRef->sem_exp_type =
            the_exp.Vformal_parameterRef->sem_entity->syn_param_type;
        break;

    case Kbinary_operation:
        left_exp = the_exp.Vbinary_operation->syn_left;
        right_exp = the_exp.Vbinary_operation->syn_right;
        expression_type(left_exp);
        expression_type(right_exp);
        left_type = left_exp.IDLclassCommon->sem_exp_type;
        right_type = right_exp.IDLclassCommon->sem_exp_type;

        switch (typeof (the_exp.Vbinary_operation->syn_op)) {
        case Kplus:
        case Kminus:
        case Ktimes:
            if ((typeof (left_type) != KTint) || (typeof (right_type) != KTint)
                result_type.Vreal = Nreal;
            else
                result_type.VTint = NTint;
            break;

        case Kdivide:
            result_type.Vreal = Nreal;
            break;

        default:
            fprintf (stderr,
                    "typing: unknown binary operator\n");
            break;
        }
        the_exp.Vunary_operation->sem_exp_type = result_type;
        break;
    case Kunary_operation:
        arg_exp = the_exp.Vunary_operation->syn_argument;
```

E.3. THE IMPLEMENTATION IN C

```
            expression_type(arg_exp);
            arg_type = arg_exp.IDLclassCommon->sem_exp_type;

            if (typeof (arg_type) != KTint)
                result_type.Vreal = Nreal;
            else
                result_type.VTint = NTint;

            the_exp.Vunary_operation->sem_exp_type = result_type;
            break;

        default:
            fprintf(stderr, "typing: unknown expression type\n");
        }
    }
}
```

E.3.3 The Constant Folding Phase

The IDL specification and C source files for this phase were given in Chapter 3. The process specification is shown in Figure 3.10 (page 86). There are two source files, a driver program (**main.c**) and the constant folding algorithm (**algorithm.c**). These are given in Figures 3.12 (page 89) and 3.15 (page 92) and 3.16 (page 93), respectively.

E.3.4 The Convert Phase

The process specification for this phase is given in Figure 9.22 (page 220). The C source file for this process is particularly simple, and is given in Figure 9.24 (page 221).

E.3.5 One-Process Variant

The process specification for this combined phase is given in Figure 9.28 (page 224). The C source file for this process is shown in Figure 9.30 (page 226); it includes or is linked with many of the C source files discussed above. The **Makefile** is particularly interesting, and so is given below.

```
# file: functionlang/oneprocess/C/Makefile
SRC = main.c ../../frontend/C/parser.y ../../frontend/C/lex.l \
      ../../semantic/C/resolve.c ../../semantic/C/typing.c \
      ../../constantfold/C/algorithm.c
OBJ = main.o parser.o lex.o resolve.o typing.o algorithm.o
LIBDIR = /usr/softlab/lib
BINDIR = /usr/softlab/bin
TEST = ../../test
LIB = $(LIBDIR)/libidl.a
IDLC = $(BINDIR)/idlc -g
SPECS = ../../specs
CC = /bin/cc
MV = /bin/mv
RM = /bin/rm -f
```

```
CFLAGS = -g

examples : funccomp
        $(RM) $(TEST)/foo.foldedposC2.aer $(TEST)/bar.foldedposC2.aer
        /bin/time funccomp < $(TEST)/foo.in > $(TEST)/foo.foldedposC2.aer
        /bin/time funccomp < $(TEST)/bar.in > $(TEST)/bar.foldedposC2.aer

funccomp : $(OBJ) onephasecompiler.h $(LIB)
        $(CC) $(CFLAGS) -o funccomp $(OBJ) onephasecompiler.o $(LIB)

main.o : main.c onephasecompiler.h
        $(CC) $(CFLAGS) -c main.c

parser.c tokens.h : ../../frontend/C/parser.y
        $(YACC) -d ../../frontend/C/parser.y
        $(MV) y.tab.c parser.c
        $(MV) y.tab.h tokens.h

parser.o : parser.c frontend.h
        $(CC) $(CFLAGS) -c parser.c

lex.o : lex.c frontend.h tokens.h
        $(CC) $(CFLAGS) -c lex.c

lex.c : ../../frontend/C/lex.l
        $(LEX) ../../frontend/C/lex.l
        $(MV) lex.yy.c lex.c

frontend.h : onephasecompiler.h
        $(RM) frontend.h
        ln onephasecompiler.h frontend.h

resolve.o : resolve.c semantic.h
        $(CC) $(CFLAGS) -c resolve.c

resolve.c : ../../semantic/C/resolve.c
        $(RM) resolve.c
        ln ../../semantic/C/resolve.c

typing.o : typing.c semantic.h
        $(CC) $(CFLAGS) -c typing.c

typing.c : ../../semantic/C/typing.c
        $(RM) typing.c
        ln ../../semantic/C/typing.c

semantic.h : onephasecompiler.h
        $(RM) semantic.h
        ln onephasecompiler.h semantic.h

algorithm.o : algorithm.c constant_fold.h
        $(CC) $(CFLAGS) -c algorithm.c

algorithm.c : ../../constantfold/C/algorithm.c
        $(RM) algorithm.c
        ln ../../constantfold/C/algorithm.c

constant_fold.h : onephasecompiler.h
        $(RM) constant_fold.h
        ln onephasecompiler.h constant_fold.h
```

E.3. THE IMPLEMENTATION IN C

```
onephasecompiler.h : onephasecompiler.idl \
        $(SPECS)/functionsem.idl $(SPECS)/functionsyntax.idl \
        $(SPECS)/pos.idl ../all.idl
    $(IDLC) -v -I$(SPECS) -I.. -C onephasecompiler.Cdl onephasecompiler.idl

Clean :
    $(RM) *.o onepasscompiler.c *.list *.Cdl \
        frontend.h pos.h tokens.h main.out lex.c \
        resolve.c typing.c semantic.h \
        algorithm.c constantfold.h onephasecompiler.h onephasecompiler.o
```

E.4 The Implementation in Pascal

E.4.1 The Frontend

The process specification for this phase is given in Figure 9.6 (page 205). The conversion routines for the sourceposition private type declared in Figure 9.12 (page 212) and are given in Figure 9.13 (page 213). The main body of this phase is given in Figure 9.11 (page 210). The listings for the lexical analysis portion (**lexical.i**) and syntactic portion (**syntactic.i**) are given below.

(* file: functionlang/frontend/Pascal/lexical.i *)

```
const maxidentifierlength = 128;

type tokenType = (endoffileToken,
        (* binary operators *)
            PlusToken, MinusToken, TimesToken, DivideToken,
        (* unary operators *)
            UnaryMinusToken, UnaryPlusToken,
        (* punctuation *)
            LParenToken, RParenToken, SemiToken, EqualToken,
            ColonToken, CommaToken,
        (* keywords *)
            functionKeyword, integerKeyword, realKeyword,
        (* tokens with values *)
            IntegerToken, IdentifierToken, RealToken);

var     token: tokenType; (* current token, set by lexer *)
        lasttoken: tokenType;
        yylval: record case tokenType of
            IntegerToken: (Vintegerconstant: integerconstant);
            IdentifierToken: (Videntifier: identifier);
            RealToken: (Vrealconstant: realconstant);
            end;
        linecount, charoffset, linestart: integer; (* source position *)
        thischar: char; (* computed by GetChar *)

procedure GetChar;
begin
        charoffset := charoffset + 1;
        if eof(input)
        then thischar := chr(0)
        else if eoln(input)
        then begin
            thischar := chr(12);
            readln;
            linecount := linecount + 1;
            linestart := charoffset;
            end
        else read(thischar)
end;
procedure Lexer;
var
        fracdigits,     (* number of digits seen to the right *)
                        (* of a decimal point *)
            identifierlength,
            i,          (* temporary *)
            thisint: integer;    (* constants accumulated *)
```

E.4. THE IMPLEMENTATION IN PASCAL 513

```pascal
        thisreal: real;
        thisidentifier: packed array [1..maxidentifierlength] of char;
        n: identifier;
        thispat: packedArrayType;
procedure MakeInteger;
var i: integerconstant;
begin
        i := Nintegerconstant;
        i^.lexvalue := thisint;
        yylval.Vintegerconstant := i;
        token := IntegerToken;
end;

procedure MakeReal;
var r: realconstant;
        i: integer;
begin
        r := Nrealconstant;
        for i := 1 to fracdigits do thisreal := thisreal / 10;
        r^.lexvalue := thisint + thisreal;
        yylval.Vrealconstant := r;
        token := RealToken;
end;

begin (* Lexer *)
        lasttoken := token;
        for i := 1 to maxidentifierlength do
            thisidentifier[i] := ' ';
        while (thischar = ' ') or (thischar = chr(9))
            or (thischar = chr(11)) or (thischar = chr(12))
        do GetChar; (* skip white space *)
        if thischar = chr(0)
        then token := endoffileToken
        else if thischar = '+'
        then begin
            if lasttoken in [RParenToken, IntegerToken, IdentifierToken, RealToken]
                then token := PlusToken
                else token := UnaryPlusToken;
            GetChar end
        else if thischar = '-'
        then begin
            if lasttoken in [RParenToken, IntegerToken, IdentifierToken, RealToken]
                then token := MinusToken
                else token := UnaryMinusToken;
            GetChar end
        else if thischar = '*'
        then begin token := TimesToken; GetChar end
        else if thischar = '/'
        then begin token := DivideToken; GetChar end
        else if thischar = '('
        then begin token := LParenToken; GetChar end
        else if thischar = ')'
        then begin token := RParenToken; GetChar end
        else if thischar = ';'
        then begin token := SemiToken; GetChar end
        else if thischar = '='
        then begin token := EqualToken; GetChar end
        else if thischar = ':'
        then begin token := ColonToken; GetChar end
        else if thischar = ','
        then begin token := CommaToken; GetChar end
```

APPENDIX E. FUNCTION LANGUAGE COMPILER

```
       else if thischar in ['0'..'9']
       then begin (* saw a number *)
           thisint := ord(thischar) - ord('0');
           GetChar;
           while thischar in ['0'..'9']
           do begin
               thisint := thisint * 10 + ord(thischar) - ord('0');
               GetChar;
               end;
           if thischar = '.'
           then begin
               fracdigits := 0;
               thisreal := 0;
               GetChar;
               while thischar in ['0'..'9']
               do begin
                   fracdigits := fracdigits + 1;
                   thisreal := thisreal * 10 + ord(thischar) - ord('0');
                   GetChar;
                   end;
               MakeReal;
               end
           else MakeInteger;
           end
       else if thischar in ['a'..'z', 'A'..'Z']
       then begin (* identifier *)
           identifierlength := 1;
           thisidentifier[identifierlength] := thischar;
           GetChar;
           while thischar in ['a'..'z', 'A'..'Z', '0'..'9', '_']
           do begin
               if identifierlength < maxidentifierlength
               then identifierlength := identifierlength + 1;
               thisidentifier[identifierlength] := thischar;
               GetChar;
               end;
           if thisidentifier = 'function'
           then token := functionKeyword
           else if thisidentifier = 'integer'
           then token := integerKeyword
           else if thisidentifier = 'real'
           then token := realKeyword
           else begin
               n := Nidentifier;
               with n^ do begin
                   thispat := ' ';
                   for i := 1 to identifierlength do
                       thispat[i] := thisidentifier[i];
                   lextoken := NewString(identifierlength, thispat);
                   lexpos := Npos;
                   lexpos^.charoffset := charoffset;
                   lexpos^.lineoffset := charoffset - linestart;
                   lexpos^.linenumber := linecount;
                   end;
               yylval.Videntifier := n;
               token := IdentifierToken
               end
           end
       else begin
           writeln(output, 'frontend: illegal character encountered, with',
               ' ASCII value ', ord(thischar), '.');
           halt;
```

E.4. THE IMPLEMENTATION IN PASCAL 515

```
            end
end (* Lexer *);

procedure InitLexer;
begin
      linecount := 1;
      charoffset := 0;
      linestart := 0;
      token := endoffileToken;
      GetChar;
end;
```

APPENDIX E. FUNCTION LANGUAGE COMPILER

```
(* file: functionlang/frontend/Pascal/syntactic.i *)

procedure error;
begin
      writeln(output, 'frontend: unrecoverable parsing error');
      halt;
end;

procedure Next(desired: tokenType);
begin
      if token = desired
      then Lexer
      else error;
end;

function Parseexpression: expression; forward;

function Parsefactor: expression;
var tempunaryoperation: unaryoperation;
      tempformalparameterRef: formalparameterRef;
      tempunaryplus: unaryplus;
      tempunaryminus: unaryminus;
begin
      if token = UnaryPlusToken
      then begin
         Lexer;
         tempunaryoperation := Nunaryoperation;
         tempunaryplus := Nunaryplus;
         tempunaryoperation^.synop := tempunaryplus^.Punaryoperator;
         tempunaryoperation^.synargument := Parsefactor;
         Parsefactor := tempunaryoperation^.Poperation^.Pexpression;
         end
      else if token = UnaryMinusToken
      then begin
         Lexer;
         tempunaryoperation := Nunaryoperation;
         tempunaryminus := Nunaryminus;
         tempunaryoperation^.synop := tempunaryminus^.Punaryoperator;
         tempunaryoperation^.synargument := Parsefactor;
         Parsefactor := tempunaryoperation^.Poperation^.Pexpression;
         end
      else if token = IdentifierToken
      then begin
         tempformalparameterRef := NformalparameterRef;
         tempformalparameterRef^.synname := yylval.Videntifier;
         Parsefactor := tempformalparameterRef^.Pexpression;
         Lexer;
         end
      else if token = IntegerToken
      then begin
         Parsefactor := yylval.Vintegerconstant^.Pconstant^.Pexpression;
         Lexer;
         end
      else if token = RealToken
      then begin
         Parsefactor := yylval.Vrealconstant^.Pconstant^.Pexpression;
         Lexer;
         end
      else if token = LParenToken
      then begin
         Lexer;       (* go past left parenthesis *)
         Parsefactor := Parseexpression;
```

E.4. THE IMPLEMENTATION IN PASCAL

```
              if token <> RParenToken then error;
              Lexer;        (* go past right parenthesis *)
              end;
end;

function Parseterm: expression;
var leftfactor: expression;
    newbinary: binaryoperation;
    newtimes: times;
    newdivide: divide;
begin
      leftfactor := Parsefactor;
      while (token = TimesToken) or (token = DivideToken)
      do begin
         newbinary := Nbinaryoperation;
         newbinary^.synleft := leftfactor;
         if token = TimesToken
         then begin
              newtimes := Ntimes;
              newbinary^.synop := newtimes^.Pbinaryoperator;
              end
         else begin
              newdivide := Ndivide;
              newbinary^.synop := newdivide^.Pbinaryoperator;
              end;
         Lexer;     (* go past operator *)
         newbinary^.synright := Parsefactor;
         leftfactor := newbinary^.Poperation^.Pexpression
         end;
      Parseterm := leftfactor;
end;

function Parseexpression (* : expression *);
var leftterm: expression;
    newbinary: binaryoperation;
    tempplus: plus;
    tempminus: minus;
begin
      leftterm := Parseterm;
      while (token = PlusToken) or (token = MinusToken)
      do begin
         newbinary := Nbinaryoperation;
         newbinary^.synleft := leftterm;
         if token = PlusToken
         then begin
              tempplus := Nplus;
              newbinary^.synop := tempplus^.Pbinaryoperator;
              end
         else begin
              tempminus := Nminus;
              newbinary^.synop := tempminus^.Pbinaryoperator;
              end;
         Lexer;     (* go past operator *)
         newbinary^.synright := Parseterm;
         leftterm := newbinary^.Poperation^.Pexpression;
         end;
      Parseexpression := leftterm;
end;

function Parseparameters: SEQformalparameter;
var thisSEQfp: SEQformalparameter;
    thisfp: formalparameter;
```

```
            tempint: int;
            tempTreal: Treal;
begin
        initializeSEQformalparameter(thisSEQfp);
        if token = LParenToken
        then begin
            Lexer;
            while token = IdentifierToken do begin
                thisfp := Nformalparameter;
                appendrearSEQformalparameter(thisSEQfp, thisfp);
                with thisfp^ do begin
                    synname := yylval.Videntifier;
                    Lexer;
                    Next(ColonToken);
                    if token = integerKeyword
                    then begin
                        tempint := Nint;
                        synparamtype := tempint^.Ptypes;
                        end
                    else if token = realKeyword
                    then begin
                        tempTreal := NTreal;
                        synparamtype := tempTreal^.Ptypes;
                        end
                    else error;
                    Lexer;
                    if token = CommaToken
                    then Lexer
                    end
                end (* while *);
            Next(RParenToken);
            end;
        Parseparameters := thisSEQfp;
end;

function Parseprogram: functions;
var thesefunctions: functions;
        thisfunction: Tfunction;
        newint: int;
        newTreal: Treal;
begin
        thesefunctions := Nfunctions;
        initializeSEQTfunction(thesefunctions^.synfuncseq);
        while token = functionKeyword do begin
            thisfunction:= NTfunction;
            appendrearSEQTfunction(thesefunctions^.synfuncseq, thisfunction);
            with thisfunction^ do begin
                Lexer;
                if token <> IdentifierToken then error;
                synname := yylval.Videntifier;
                Lexer;
                synparameters := Parseparameters;
                Next(ColonToken);
                if token = integerKeyword
                then begin
                    newint := Nint;
                    synreturntype:= newint^.Ptypes;
                    end
                else begin
                    newTreal := NTreal;
                    synreturntype:= newTreal^.Ptypes;
                    end;
```

E.4. THE IMPLEMENTATION IN PASCAL

```
                Lexer;
                Next(EqualToken);
                syndefinition := Parseexpression;
                Next(SemiToken);
                end
            end (* while *);
        Parseprogram:= thesefunctions
end;
```

E.4.2 The Semantic Analysis Phase

The process specification for this phase is given in Figure 9.17 on page 215. The main program in Pascal is shown in Figure 9.19 (page 217). The listings for the name resolution (**resolve.p**) and typing (**typing.p**) source files follow.

(* file: functionlang/semantic/Pascal/resolve.p *)

```
#include "semantic.h"
#include "semantic.i"
#include "sem2.h"

procedure resolveexp(var theexp: expression;
                     var theparameters: SEQformalparameter);
var Aformalparameter: formalparameter;
    i: integer;
begin
    case theexp^.Eexpression of
    Kexpressionconstant: (* do nothing *);
    KexpressionformalparameterRef:
        for i := 1 to lengthSEQformalparameter(theparameters) do begin
            Aformalparameter := ithinSEQformalparameter(theparameters, i);
            if Aformalparameter^.synname^.lextoken
               = theexp^.VformalparameterRef^.synname^.lextoken
            then theexp^.VformalparameterRef^.sementity := Aformalparameter;
            end;
    Kexpressionoperation: case theexp^.Voperation^.Eoperation of
        Koperationbinaryoperation: begin
            resolveexp(theexp^.Voperation^.Vbinaryoperation^.synleft,
                       theparameters);
            resolveexp(theexp^.Voperation^.Vbinaryoperation^.synright,
                       theparameters);
            end;
        Koperationunaryoperation:
            resolveexp(theexp^.Voperation^.Vunaryoperation^.synargument,
                       theparameters);
        end
    end
end;

(* the procedure for resolving parameter references *)

procedure resolvereferences(*var thefunction: function*);
begin
    resolveexp(thefunction^.syndefinition, thefunction^.synparameters);
end;
```

E.4. THE IMPLEMENTATION IN PASCAL 521

```
(* file: functionlang/semantic/Pascal/typing.p *)

#include "semantic.h"
#include "sem2.h"
#include "semantic.i"

(* the procedure for expression typing *)
procedure expressiontype(*var theexp: expression*);
var    leftexp: expression;   (* for de-referencing left exp of binary op *)
       rightexp: expression;  (* for de-referencing right exp of binary op *)
       argexp: expression;    (* for de-referencing argument of unary op *)
       lefttype: types;
       righttype: types;
       argtype: types;
       resulttype: types;
       tempint: int;
       tempTreal: Treal;
begin
       case theexp^.Eexpression of
       Kexpressionconstant: case theexp^.Vconstant^.Econstant of
           Kconstantintegerconstant: begin
               tempint := Nint;
               theexp^.semexptype:= tempint^.Ptypes;
               end;
           Kconstantrealconstant: begin
               tempTreal := NTreal;
               theexp^.semexptype:= tempTreal^.Ptypes;
               end;
           end;

       KexpressionformalparameterRef:
           theexp^.semexptype:=
               theexp^.VformalparameterRef^.sementity^.synparamtype;

       Kexpressionoperation: case theexp^.Voperation^.Eoperation of
           Koperationbinaryoperation: begin
               leftexp := theexp^.Voperation^.Vbinaryoperation^.synleft;
               rightexp := theexp^.Voperation^.Vbinaryoperation^.synright;
               expressiontype(leftexp);
               expressiontype(rightexp);
               lefttype:= leftexp^.semexptype;
               righttype:= rightexp^.semexptype;
               case theexp^.Voperation^.Vbinaryoperation^.synop
                                        ^.Ebinaryoperator of
               Kbinaryoperatorplus: if (lefttype^.Etypes <> Ktypesint)
                       or (righttype^.Etypes <> Ktypesint)
                   then begin
                       tempTreal := NTreal;
                       resulttype:= tempTreal^.Ptypes;
                       end
                   else begin
                       tempint := Nint;
                       resulttype:= tempint^.Ptypes;
                       end;
               Kbinaryoperatorminus: if (lefttype^.Etypes <> Ktypesint)
                       or (righttype^.Etypes <> Ktypesint)
                   then begin
                       tempTreal := NTreal;
                       resulttype:= tempTreal^.Ptypes;
                       end
                   else begin
                       tempint := Nint;
```

```
                    resulttype:= tempint^.Ptypes;
                    end;
                Kbinaryoperatortimes: if (lefttype^.Etypes <> Ktypesint)
                        or (righttype^.Etypes <> Ktypesint)
                    then begin
                        tempTreal := NTreal;
                        resulttype:= tempTreal^.Ptypes;
                        end
                    else begin
                        tempint := Nint;
                        resulttype:= tempint^.Ptypes;
                        end;
                Kbinaryoperatordivide: begin
                    tempTreal := NTreal;
                    resulttype:= tempTreal^.Ptypes;
                    end;
                end;
            theexp^.semexptype:= resulttype;
            end;
        Koperationunaryoperation: begin
            argexp := theexp^.Voperation^.Vunaryoperation^.synargument;
            expressiontype(argexp);
            argtype:= argexp^.semexptype;
            if argtype^.Etypes <> Ktypesint
            then begin
                tempTreal := NTreal;
                resulttype:= tempTreal^.Ptypes;
                end
            else begin
                tempint := Nint;
                resulttype:= tempint^.Ptypes;
                end;
            theexp^.semexptype:= resulttype;
            end;
        end;
    end
end;
```

E.4.3 The Constant Folding Phase

The IDL specification and Pascal source files for this phase were given in Chapter 3. The process specification is shown in Figure 3.11 (page 86). There are two source files, a driver program (**main.p**) and the constant folding algorithm (**algorithm.p**). These are given in Figures 3.14 (page 90) and 3.17 (page 94) and 3.18 (page 95), respectively.

E.4.4 The Convert Phase

The process specification for this phase is given in Figure 9.23 (page 221). The Pascal source file for this process is particularly simple, and is given in Figure 9.25 (page 222).

E.4.5 One-Process Variant

The process specification for this combined phase is given in Figure 9.29 (page 225). The Pascal source file for this process is shown in Figure 9.31 (page 227); it includes many of the Pascal source files discussed above. The **Makefile** is particularly interesting, and so is given below.

```
# file: functionlang/oneprocess/Pascal/Makefile
SRC = main.p
OBJ = main.o
LIBDIR = /usr/softlab/personal/shannon/idl3.4/lib#!!!lib
BINDIR = /unc/shannon/bin#!!!/usr/softlab/bin
TEST = ../../test
LIB = $(LIBDIR)/libidlP.a #!!!$(LIBDIR)/idlvlib.o $(LIBDIR)/idlvlib.a
IDLC = $(BINDIR)/idlc
SPECS = ../../specs
PC = pc
MV = /bin/mv
RM = /bin/rm -f

PFLAGS = -I$(SPECS) -g

examples : funccomp
        $(RM) $(TEST)/foo.foldedposP2.aer $(TEST)/bar.foldedposP2.aer
        /bin/time funccomp < $(TEST)/foo.in > $(TEST)/foo.foldedposP2.aer
        /bin/time funccomp < $(TEST)/bar.in > $(TEST)/bar.foldedposP2.aer

funccomp : $(OBJ) onephasecompiler.h $(LIB)
        $(PC) $(PFLAGS) -o funccomp $(OBJ) onephasecompiler.o $(LIB)

main.o : main.p onephasecompiler.h ../../frontend/Pascal/lexical.i \
           ../../frontend/Pascal/syntactic.i resolve.p typing.p sem.h \
           algorithm.p const.h
        touch frontend.h frontend.i semantic.h semantic.i sem2.h
        touch constant_fold.h constant_fold.i const2.h
        $(PC) $(PFLAGS) -I../../frontend/Pascal -c main.p

resolve.p : ../../semantic/Pascal/resolve.p
        $(RM) resolve.p
        ln -s ../../semantic/Pascal/resolve.p resolve.p

typing.p : ../../semantic/Pascal/typing.p
        $(RM) typing.p
        ln -s ../../semantic/Pascal/typing.p typing.p

sem.h : ../../semantic/Pascal/sem2.h
        $(RM) sem.h
        ln -s ../../semantic/Pascal/sem2.h sem.h

algorithm.p : ../../constantfold/Pascal/algorithm.p
        $(RM) algorithm.p
        ln -s ../../constantfold/Pascal/algorithm.p algorithm.p

const.h : ../../constantfold/Pascal/const2.h
        $(RM) const.h
        ln -s ../../constantfold/Pascal/const2.h const.h

onephasecompiler.h : onephasecompiler.idl \
          $(SPECS)/functionsem.idl $(SPECS)/functionsyntax.idl \
          $(SPECS)/pos.idl ../all.idl
        $(IDLC) -v -I$(SPECS) -I..  -C onephasecompiler.Cdl onephasecompiler.idl
```

```
Clean :
    $(RM) *.o onephasecompiler.h onepasscompiler.p *.list *.Cdl \
        frontend.h frontend.i pos.h main.out \
        resolve.p typing.p semantic.h semantic.i sem.h sem2.h \
        algorithm.p constant_fold.h constant_fold.i const.h const2.h
```

E.5   Function Language Cross Referencers

Two cross referencers for the function language were implemented in XRef in Chapter 11: that shown on page 259 and that shown in Figure 11.4 on page 265.

E.6   Specification Concordances

In this section we provided various concordances for the IDL specifications used in the function language implementation discussed in Chapters 3 and 9. Included are the abstract_syntax, attributed_syntax, pos, and AS_with_pos structures. The XRef specifications generating the concordances are given in the next section. When a source position is given, it is in the form *page:line*, with an optional structure name (e.g., Pos 205:17), if space allows. The structure name is abbreviated, with the following correspondences.

abstract_syntax	→	Syntax (p. 76 and 202)
attributed_syntax	→	Semant (p. 78 and 214)
posdeclaration	→	PosDecl (p. 219)
AS_with_pos	→	WithPos (p. 205)

E.6.1   Names

This section lists all the names appearing in the function language specification, except for attributes, which are covered in later sections. The kind of name (whether assertion, class, control, definition, formal, node, parameter, private type (either predefined such as *String* or user-defined), or private definition) is indicated in square brackets ("[ ]") if not a set or sequence, in curly brackets ("{}") if a set, and in angle brackets ("<>") if a sequence. The source position of all occurrences is also given, and may be split across multiple lines.

Name	Kind	Spec	Position
abstract_syntax	[structure]	Semant	214:5
		Syntax	202:2

E.6. SPECIFICATION CONCORDANCES 525

AS_with_pos	[structure]	WithPos	219:8
attributed_syntax	[structure]	WithPos	219:8
		Semant	214:5
binaryoperator	[class]	Syntax	202:30, 202:33
binary_operation	[node]	Syntax	202:29, 202:30, 202:41, 202:54
constant	[class]	Syntax	202:24, 202:25, 202:51
Desc	[definition]	Syntax	202:45, 202:58
divide	[node]	Syntax	202:33, 202:34
expression	[class]	Semant	214:13
		Syntax	202:15, 202:24, 202:31, 202:32, 202:36
			202:45, 202:47, 202:55, 202:57
External	[parameter]	Syntax	202:6
formal_parameter	[node]	Semant	214:9
		Syntax	202:14, 202:18
formal_parameterRef	[node]	Semant	214:9, 214:10, 214:18
		Syntax	202:24, 202:28, 202:52
function	[node]	Syntax	202:10, 202:12, 202:16
functions	[node]	Syntax	202:2, 202:10
identifier	[node]	Syntax	202:8, 202:12, 202:18, 202:28
IDesc	[definition]	Syntax	202:56
int	[node]	Semant	214:15
		Syntax	202:21, 202:22
Integer	[private]	Syntax	202:26
		PosDecl	205:6, 205:7, 205:8
Integer	[parameter]	Syntax	202:6
integer_constant	[node]	Semant	214:14
		Syntax	202:25, 202:26
members	[priv. def]	Syntax	202:48
minus	[node]	Syntax	202:33, 202:34
operation	[class]	Syntax	202:24, 202:29
plus	[node]	Syntax	202:33, 202:34
pos	[parameter]	WithPos	219:10
pos	[node]	PosDecl	205:6
posdeclaration	[structure]	WithPos	219:8
		PosDecl	205:3

Rational	[private]	Syntax	202:27
Reach	[definition]	Syntax	202:42, 202:42, 202:49, 202:56
real	[node]	Semant	214:17
		Syntax	202:21, 202:22
real_constant	[node]	Semant	214:16
		Syntax	202:25, 202:27
Seq Of formal_parameter	<node>	Syntax	202:14
Seq Of function	<node>	Syntax	202:10
Size	[priv. def]	Syntax	202:17
source_position	[private]	WithPos	219:10
		Syntax	202:5, 202:6, 202:9
String	[private]	Syntax	202:8
times	[node]	Syntax	202:33, 202:34
types	[class]	Semant	214:13
		Syntax	202:13, 202:19, 202:21
unaryminus	[node]	Syntax	202:37, 202:38
unaryoperator	[class]	Syntax	202:35, 202:37
unaryplus	[node]	Syntax	202:37, 202:38
unary_operation	[node]	Syntax	202:29, 202:35, 202:53

E.6.2 Attributes

This section lists all the attributes appearing in the CANDLE specification, along with their type and source position of each use, with the source position of the definition of the attribute given in bold. As they are ordered alphabetically, all attributes with an identical prefix are grouped together. Some attributes (e.g., lex_value) are repeated; these are actually different attributes with the same name.

Name	**Type**	**Spec**	**Position**
charoffset:	Integer	PosDecl	**205:6**
lex_pos:	source_position	Syntax	**202:9**
lex_token:	String	Syntax	**202:8**
lex_value:	Rational	Syntax	**202:27**
lex_value:	Integer	Syntax	**202:26**
linenumber:	Integer	PosDecl	**205:8**

E.6. SPECIFICATION CONCORDANCES

lineoffset:	Integer	PosDecl	**205:7**
sem_entity:	formal_parameter	Semant	**214:9**, 214:11, 214:19
sem_exp_type:	types	Semant	**214:13**, 214:15, 214:17, 214:19
syn_argument:	expression	Syntax	**202:36**, 202:53
syn_definition:	expression	Syntax	**202:15**, 202:49
syn_func_seq:	Seq Of function	Syntax	**202:10**, 202:48
syn_left:	expression	Syntax	**202:31**, 202:42, 202:54
syn_name:	identifier	Syntax	**202:12**
syn_name:	identifier	Semant Syntax	214:11 **202:18**
syn_name:	identifier	Semant Syntax	214:11 **202:28**
syn_op:	unaryoperator	Syntax	**202:35**
syn_op:	binaryoperator	Syntax	**202:30**
syn_parameters:	Seq Of formal_parameter	Syntax	**202:14**, 202:17
syn_param_type:	types	Semant Syntax	214:19 **202:19**
syn_return_type:	types	Syntax	**202:13**
syn_right:	expression	Syntax	**202:32**, 202:42, 202:54

E.6.3 Attribute Productions

This section lists all the attributes for each class and node. Propagated attributes are identified by a "**P**"; their source position refers to where they were associated with a superclass. Unattributed nodes and classes are also listed, for completeness, although source positions do not appear with unattributed classes. Structure names are also omitted, due to lack of space.

Node or Class	**Attribute**	**Type**	**Position**
binaryoperator	=> ;		
binary_operation	=> sem_exp_type: syn_left: syn_op: syn_right:	types expression binaryoperator expression	**P** 214:13 202:31 202:30 202:32
constant	=> sem_exp_type:	types	**P** 214:13

```
divide              => ;                                            202:34

expression          => sem_exp_type:    types                       214:13

formal_parameter    => syn_name:        identifier                  202:18
                       syn_param_type:  types                       202:19

formal_parameterRef => sem_entity:      formal_parameter            214:9
                       sem_exp_type:    types                     P 214:13
                       syn_name:        identifier                  202:28

function            => syn_definition:  expression                  202:15
                       syn_name:        identifier                  202:12
                       syn_parameters:  Seq Of formal_parameter     202:14
                       syn_return_type: types                       202:13

functions           => syn_func_seq:    Seq Of function             202:10

identifier          => lex_pos:         source_position             202:9
                       lex_token:       String                      202:8

int                 => ;                                            202:22

integer_constant    => lex_value:       Integer                     202:26
                       sem_exp_type:    types                     P 214:13

minus               => ;                                            202:34

operation           => sem_exp_type:    types                     P 214:13

plus                => ;                                            202:34

pos                 => charoffset:      Integer                     205:6
                       linenumber:      Integer                     205:8
                       lineoffset:      Integer                     205:7

real                => ;                                            202:22

real_constant       => lex_value:       Rational                    202:27
                       sem_exp_type:    types                     P 214:13

times               => ;                                            202:34

types               => ;

unaryminus          => ;                                            202:38

unaryoperator       => ;

unaryplus           => ;                                            202:38

unary_operation     => sem_exp_type:    types                     P 214:13
                       syn_argument:    expression                  202:36
                       syn_op:          unaryoperator               202:35
```

E.7 XRef Specifications

In this section we give the XRef programs that generated the previous concordances.

```
-- file: CandleXRef/name.xref
-- Creates a concordance of all names.
Function nameof (this)
      Case this As N Of
            Atomic: N.sem_name;
            Class:  N.sem_name;
            Definition: N.sem_name;
            PrivateDefInstance: N.syn_def.lex_name;
            SeqOf:  N.sem_name;
            SetOf:  N.sem_name;
            Default: N.lex_name;
            End -- Case this
      End -- function

Function fileof (this)
      Case this As R Of
      SeqRef: R.syn_component.lex_srcpos.lex_file ;
      SetRef: R.syn_component.lex_srcpos.lex_file ;
      Default: R.lex_srcpos.lex_file ;
      End
End

Function pageof (this)
      Case this As R Of
      SeqRef: R.syn_component.lex_srcpos.lex_page ;
      SetRef: R.syn_component.lex_srcpos.lex_page ;
      Default: R.lex_srcpos.lex_page ;
      End
End

Function lineof (this)
      Case this As R Of
      SeqRef: R.syn_component.lex_srcpos.lex_line ;
      SetRef: R.syn_component.lex_srcpos.lex_line ;
      Default: R.lex_srcpos.lex_line ;
      End
End

Predicate ascending_file (left, right)
      Head(fileof(left)) < Head(fileof(right)) End
Predicate ascending_page (left, right)
      Head(pageof(left)) < Head(pageof(right)) End
Predicate ascending_line (left, right)
      Head(lineof(left)) < Head(lineof(right)) End

#define Sort(this) Reorder(Reorder(Reorder(this, ascending_line), \
            ascending_page), \
            ascending_file)

Predicate is_structure (this) Is(this, "StructureEntity") End
Predicate same_name (left, right) Head(nameof(left)) = Head(nameof(right)) End
Predicate is_Class (this) Is(this, "Class") End
Predicate same_seqof (left, right)
      left.sem_component.sem_name = right.sem_component.sem_name End
Predicate is_ControlRef (this) Is(this.sem_entity, "Control") End
Predicate is_FormalRef (this) Is(this.sem_entity, "Formal") End
```

```
Predicate is_PrivateDefInstance (this)
    Is(this.sem_entity, "PrivateDefInstance") End
Predicate is_cyclicdef (this) Is(this.sem_entity, "cyclicdef") End
Predicate is_noncyclicdef (this) Is(this.sem_entity, "noncyclicdef") End
Predicate is_ClassRef (this) Is(this.sem_entity, "Class") End
Predicate is_AtomicRef (this) Is(this.sem_entity, "Atomic") End
Predicate is_StructureRef (this) Is(this.sem_entity, "StructureEntity") End
Predicate same_seq (left, right)
    left.syn_component.sem_entity.sem_name
        = right.syn_component.sem_entity.sem_name End
Predicate same_set (left, right)
    left.syn_component.sem_entity.sem_name
        = right.syn_component.sem_entity.sem_name End
Predicate ascending_names (left, right)
    Head(nameof(left)) < Head(nameof(right)) End

Let StructDefs = Filter(Root.syn_body, is_structure),
    Assertions = Unique(For D In Head(StructDefs) Do
            D.sem_assertions End, same_name),
    Atomics = Unique(Type(For D In Head(StructDefs) Do
                D.sem_types End, Atomic) ,
            same_name),
    Controls = Unique(Type(For D In Head(StructDefs) Do
            D.sem_assertions D.sem_definitions End,
            Control) ,
        same_name),
    Formals = Unique(Type(For D In Head(StructDefs) Do
            D.sem_assertions D.sem_definitions End,
            Formal) ,
        same_name),
    PrivateDefInstances = Unique(Type(Head(StructDefs), PrivateDefInstance),
            same_name),
    cyclicdefs = Unique(Type(Head(StructDefs), cyclicdef), same_name),
    noncyclicdefs = Unique(Type(Head(StructDefs), noncyclicdef), same_name),
    nameTokens = Unique(Type(Root, nameToken), same_name),
    Structures = Unique(Type(Root, StructureEntity), same_name),

    SyntacticEntities = Assertions Atomics Controls Formals
        PrivateDefInstances cyclicdefs noncyclicdefs nameTokens
        Structures,

    Classes = Filter(For D In Head(StructDefs)
            Do D.sem_types End ,
        is_Class),
    SeqOfs = Unique(Type(For D In Head(StructDefs) Do
            D.sem_types End, SeqOf) ,
        same_seqof),
    SetOfs = Unique(Type(For D In Head(StructDefs) Do
            D.sem_types End, SetOf) ,
        same_seqof),

    SemanticEntities = Classes SeqOfs SetOfs,

    AllAssertion = Sort(Assertions Type(Root, AssertRef)),
    AllControl = Sort(Controls Filter(Type(Root, ExpNameRef), is_ControlRef)),
    AllFormal = Sort(Formals Filter(Type(Root, ExpNameRef), is_FormalRef)),
    AllPrivateDefInstance = Sort(PrivateDefInstances
        Filter(Type(Root, ExpNameRef), is_PrivateDefInstance)
        Type(Root, DefInstanceOrDefineRef)),
    Allcyclic = Sort(cyclicdefs Filter(Type(Root, ExpNameRef), is_cyclicdef)
            Type(Root, DefInstanceOrDefineRef)),
    Allnoncyclic = Sort(noncyclicdefs
```

E.7. XREF SPECIFICATIONS 531

```
                  Filter(Type(Root, ExpNameRef), is_noncyclicdef)
                  Type(Root, DefInstanceOrDefineRef)),
      AllClass = Sort(Filter(Type(Root, ExpNameRef) Type(Root, NamedTypeRef),
                  is_ClassRef)),
      AllAtomic = Sort(Filter(Type(Root, ExpNameRef) Type(Root, NamedTypeRef),
                  is_AtomicRef)),
      SeqRefs = Sort(Type(Root, SeqRef)),
      SetRefs = Sort(Type(Root, SetRef)),
      AllStructure = Sort(Structures Unique(Filter(Type(Root, StructureRef),
                  is_StructureRef), same_name))
In
Predicate same_pos (left, right) ((Head(fileof(left)) = Head(fileof(right)))
                  And (Head(pageof(left)) = Head(pageof(right))))
                  And (Head(lineof(left)) = Head(lineof(right))) End
Predicate is_node(this) Empty(this.sem_subclasses) End
Predicate is_class(this) Not (Empty(this.sem_subclasses)) End

Function print_seq_of_atomic (this)
      Case this As that Of
      Class: For N In Filter(that, is_node)
                  Do "{\\smalltt <}node{\\smalltt >}" End
                        For C In Filter(that, is_class)
                  Do "{\\smalltt <}seq of class{\\smalltt >}" End;
            Default: "{\\smalltt <}private{\\smalltt >}";
            End
End
Function print_set_of_atomic (this)
      Case this As that Of
      Class: For N In Filter(that, is_node)
                  Do "{\]smalltt\\char'173}node{\\smalltt\\char'175}" End
                        For C In Filter(that, is_class)
                  Do "{\\smalltt\\char'173}class{\\smalltt\\char'175}" End;
            Default: "{\\smalltt\\char'175}private{\\smalltt\\char'175}";
            End
End

#define GenRefs(this) \
"\\smalltt\\>" \
For GenR2 In this Do \
      "\\PosB{" fileof(GenR2) "}{" pageof(GenR2) "}{" \
      lineof(GenR2) "}\\relax\n" \
      End

For One In Head(For S2 In Head(StructDefs) Do S2.lex_srcpos.lex_file End) Do
For N In Reorder(SyntacticEntities SemanticEntities, ascending_names) Do

      Predicate same_name_as_N (this)
            (Head(nameof(this)) = Head(nameof(N)))
            And (Not (this.lex_srcpos.lex_file < One))
            End
      Predicate same_seq_as_N (this)
            (this.syn_component.sem_entity.sem_name = N.sem_component.sem_name)
            And (Not (this.syn_component.lex_srcpos.lex_file < One))
            End

      nameof(N) "\\>\\smallrm "

      Case N As R Of
            Assertion: "[assertion]"
                  GenRefs(Filter(AllAssertion, same_name_as_N));
            Atomic: "[private]" -- print_atomic(R)
```

```
                    GenRefs(Unique(Filter(AllAtomic, same_name_as_N), same_pos));
          Class: For N In Filter(R, is_node) Do "[node]" End
                 For C In Filter(R, is_class) Do "[class]" End
                    GenRefs(Unique(Filter(AllClass, same_name_as_N), same_pos));
          Control: "[control]"
                    GenRefs(Filter(AllControl, same_name_as_N));
          Formal: "[formal]"
                    GenRefs(Filter(AllFormal, same_name_as_N));
          PrivateDefInstance: "[priv. def]"
                    GenRefs(Filter(AllPrivateDefInstance, same_name_as_N));
          cyclicdef: "[definition]"
                    GenRefs(Filter(Allcyclic, same_name_as_N));
          noncyclicdef: "[definition]"
                    GenRefs(Filter(Allnoncyclic, same_name_as_N));
          nameToken: "[parameter]"
                    GenRefs(Filter(nameTokens, same_name_as_N));
          SeqOf: print_seq_of_atomic(R.sem_component)
                    GenRefs(Unique(Filter(SeqRefs, same_seq_as_N), same_pos));
          SetOf: print_set_of_atomic(R.sem_component)
                    GenRefs(Unique(Filter(SetRefs, same_seq_as_N), same_pos));
          StructureEntity: "[structure]"
                    GenRefs(Filter(AllStructure, same_name_as_N));
          End -- Case

      "\\PosEnd\n"
        End -- For N
End -- For One
End -- Let
```

E.7. XREF SPECIFICATIONS

```
-- file: CandleXRef/attribute.xref
-- Creates a concordance of all attribute declarations for classes and nodes

Predicate ascending_names (left, right) left.sem_name < right.sem_name End

Predicate att_ascending_names (left, right) left.lex_name < right.lex_name End

Predicate is_Class(this) Is(this, "Class") End

Predicate is_structure(this) Is(this, "StructureEntity") End

For C In Reorder(Filter(For D In Filter(Root.syn_body, is_structure)
                    Do D.sem_types End,
                is_Class),
        ascending_names) Do
    Predicate has_attributes(this) Not (Empty(this.sem_allattributes)) End

    Predicate has_no_attributes(this) Empty(this.sem_allattributes) End

    Predicate same_attribute(left, right) left.lex_name = right.lex_name End

    "\\>" C.sem_name "\\>=>\\>"
            -- Case 1: C is unattributed
            For C2 In Filter(C, has_no_attributes) Do
            Predicate correct_production (this)
                (Empty(this.syn_attributes))
                    And (this.syn_class.sem_entity.sem_name = C2.sem_name) End
    ";"
            -- should find at most one S
            For S In Filter(Type(Root, attributeProduction), correct_production) Do
            "\\>\\>\\>\\PosS{"
            S.syn_class.lex_srcpos.lex_file
            "}{" S.syn_class.lex_srcpos.lex_page
            "}{" S.syn_class.lex_srcpos.lex_line
            "}"
            End
    "\\\\n"
    End -- C2

            -- Case 2: C has attributes
            For C2 In Filter(C, has_attributes) Do
            Let Superattrs = Unique(For Super In C.sem_ancestors Do
                        Super.sem_allattributes End,
                            same_attribute) In
            For Att In Reorder(C.sem_allattributes, att_ascending_names) Do
                Att.lex_name ":\\>" Att.syn_type.sem_entity.sem_name "\\>"
                    For Rem In Intersection(Superattrs, Att, same_attribute)
                    Do "{\\smallbf P}" End
                    "\\>\\PosS{" Att.lex_srcpos.lex_file
                    "}{" Att.lex_srcpos.lex_page
                    "}{" Att.lex_srcpos.lex_line "}\\\\n\\>\\>\\>"
                    End -- Att
            End -- Let
    End -- C2
    "\\kill\n\\\\n"
End -- C (class)
```

```
-- file: CandleXRef/allattr.xref

-- Creates a concordance of all attributes

Predicate is_structure(this) Is(this, "StructureEntity") End

-- i.e., they were copied from the same attribute
Predicate same_attribute (left, right)
    ((left.lex_srcpos.lex_line = right.lex_srcpos.lex_line) And
        ((left.lex_srcpos.lex_page = right.lex_srcpos.lex_page) And
         (left.lex_srcpos.lex_file = right.lex_srcpos.lex_file)))
    End

#define Attributes Unique(Type(For D In Filter(Root.syn_body, is_structure) \
            Do D.sem_types End, \
            Attribute), \
        same_attribute)

Predicate ascending_names (left, right) left.lex_name < right.lex_name End

For A In Reorder(Attributes, ascending_names) Do

    Predicate same_name_as_A (this) this.lex_name = A.lex_name End
    Predicate ascending_file (left, right)
        left.lex_srcpos.lex_file < right.lex_srcpos.lex_file End
    Predicate ascending_page (left, right)
        left.lex_srcpos.lex_page < right.lex_srcpos.lex_page End
    Predicate ascending_line (left, right)
        left.lex_srcpos.lex_line < right.lex_srcpos.lex_line End
    Predicate same_as_A (this) same_attribute(this, A) End
    Predicate ref_same_as_A (this) same_attribute(this.sem_entity, A) End

    A.lex_name ":\\>" A.syn_type.sem_entity.sem_name "\\>"

    -- rely on fact that Reorder is stable
    For R In Reorder(Reorder(Reorder(A Filter(Type(Root, AttributeRef),
                    same_name_as_A),
                ascending_line),
            ascending_page),
        ascending_file) Do
        Case R As R2 Of
            Attribute: For R3 In Filter(R2, same_as_A) Do
                "\\PosD{" R2.lex_srcpos.lex_file "}{"
                R3.lex_srcpos.lex_page "}{"
                R3.lex_srcpos.lex_line "}" End;
            AttributeRef: For R3 In Filter(R2, ref_same_as_A) Do
                "\\PosB{" R3.lex_srcpos.lex_file "}{"
                R3.lex_srcpos.lex_page "}{"
                R3.lex_srcpos.lex_line "}" End;
        End -- Case R

    End -- For R(eference)
    "\\PosEnd\n"
End -- For A (ttribute)
```

Appendix F

The Candle Specification

This appendix contains the CANDLE specification. Specifications for the requisite and associated structures follow: CandleSyntax, CandleSemantic, CandleRep, CANDLE, CandlePos, CandleContext, and CandleSymbolTable. The UNC-specific structures UNCCandle and UNCCandlePos are also given. The relationship among all of these structures is discussed in Chapter 15.

F.1 The CandleSyntax Structure

```
-- file src/specs/Candle/CandleSyntax.idl
Structure CandleSyntax Root compilationUnit Is
-- Part 1: Introduction
  -- Private types
    -- comments and file information
    Type LexInfo;
  -- Global structure
    -- <specification> ::= { <structure entity> | <process entity> }+
    compilationUnit        => lex_information:  LexInfo,
                              syn_body:         Seq Of Declaration;

    Declaration            ::= ImportDecl | StructureOrProcess;
    Declaration            => lex_information:  LexInfo;

    StructureOrProcess     ::= StructureEntity | ProcessEntity;
    ImportDecl             => syn_specs:        Seq Of StructureOrProcessRef,
                              syn_compUnit:     compUnitRef;

    statement              ::= structureStatement | processStatement;
```

```
-- Part 2: Structure Declarations
--   <structure entity> ::= Structure <name>
--**      { Root <type> }?
--**      { Refines <name> }?
--       { From <name list> }?
--   Is { <structure stmt> ; }* End
--   <name list> ::= <name> { ", <name> }*
    StructureEntity            =>  syn_root:          TypeRefOrVoid,
                                   syn_refines:       StructureRefOrVoid,
                                   syn_from:          Seq Of StructureRef,
                                   syn_body:          Seq Of structureStatement;

--   <structure stmt> ::= { <production> | <atomic decl> |
--     <attribute rep> | <type rep decl> |
--     <without clause> | <assertion> | <definition instance> }
    structureStatement         ::= production | atomicDecl
                                   | attributeRep | typeRepDecl |
                                   withoutClause | Assertion | DefInstance ;

--   <production> ::= <subclass production> | <attribute production>
--   <subclass production> ::= <name> "::= <name> { "| <name> }*
--   <attribute production> ::= <name> => { <attribute> { ", <attribute> }* }?
--   <attribute> ::= <name> : <type>
    production                 ::= subclassProduction | attributeProduction;
    production                 =>  syn_class:         NamedTypeRef; -- class added to

    subclassProduction         =>  syn_subclasses:    Seq Of NamedTypeRef;

    attributeProduction        =>  syn_attributes:    Seq Of Attribute;
    Attribute                  =>  syn_type:          TypeRef;

--   <atomic decl> ::= Type <name>
    atomicDecl                 =>  syn_atomic:        NamedTypeRef;

--   <attribute type rep> ::= For <attribute reference> Use <parameters>
--   <attribute reference> ::= <name> . <name>
--   <parameters> ::= { <parameter> }+
    attributeRep               =>  syn_class:         NamedTypeRef,
                                   syn_attribute:     AttributeRef,
                                   syn_rep:           RepRef;
    RepRef                     =>  syn_id:            Seq Of parameter;
--   <parameter> ::= <name> | <integer> | <rational> | <string>
    parameter                  ::= nameToken | otherToken;

--** <type rep decl> ::= For <type> Use <parameters>
    typeRepDecl                =>  syn_type:          TypeRef,
                                   syn_spec:          RepRef;

--   <without clause> ::= Without <without item> { , <without item> }*
--** <without item> ::= Assert { <name> | "* }
--**     Define { <name> | "* }
--**     Type <type> |
--**{ <name> | "* } { -> | ::= } { <name> | "* }
    withoutClause              =>  syn_list:          Seq Of withoutItem;
    withoutItem                ::= withoutAssert | withoutDefine | withoutType
                                   | withoutProduction;
```

F.1. THE CANDLESYNTAX STRUCTURE

```
withoutAssert              =>   syn_item:           AssertRef;
withoutDefine              =>   syn_item:           DefineRef;
withoutType                =>   syn_item:           TypeRef;
withoutProduction          ::=  withoutSubclass | withoutAttribute;

withoutProduction          =>   syn_lefthandside:   ClassOrAllClasses;
withoutSubclass            =>   syn_righthandside:  ClassOrAllClasses;
withoutAttribute           =>   syn_righthandside:  AttributeOrAllAttributes;

ClassOrAllClasses          ::=  NamedTypeRef | AllClasses;
AttributeOrAllAttributes   ::=  AttributeRefs | AllAttributes;
AllClasses =>;
AllAttributes =>;
```

-- Part 3: Process Declarations

```
-- <process entity> ::= Process <name> {Inv <name>}?
--      {Refines <name>}? Is
--      { <process statement> }* End
ProcessEntity              =>   syn_refines:        ProcessRefOrVoid,
                                syn_invariant:      StructureRefOrVoid,
                                syn_body:           Seq Of processStatement;

-- <process statement> ::= {<port definition> |
--   <assertion> | <definition instance> |
--   <port assoc> | <target stmt> | <restriction> }
processStatement           ::=  portDefinition | Assertion | DefInstance |
                                portAssociation | targetStmt | restriction;

-- <port definition> ::= {Pre | Post}? <port> { , <port> }*
-- <port> ::= <name> : <name>

portDefinition             =>   syn_portType:       PortType,
                                syn_ports:          Seq Of Port;
PortType                   ::=  PrePort | PostPort ;
PrePort =>;
PostPort =>;
Port                       =>   syn_data:           StructureRef;

-- <port assoc> ::= For <name> Use <parameters>
portAssociation            =>   syn_port:           PortRef,
                                syn_rep:            RepRef;

--** <target stmt> ::= Target <parameters>

targetStmt                 =>   syn_id:             Seq Of parameter;

--** <restriction> ::= Restrict { <type reference> | <attribute reference> }
--**<toOrfrom> <oper list>
--** <type reference> ::= { <type> | "*" }
--** <attribute reference> ::= { <name> | "*" } ". { <name> | "*" }
--** <toOrfrom> ::= { To | From }
--** <oper list> ::= <opername> { ", <opername> }*

restriction                ::=  typeRestriction | attributeRestriction;
restriction                =>   syn_type:           TypeOrAllTypes,
                                syn_tofrom:         restrictToOrFrom,
                                syn_operations:     Seq Of OperRef;
restrictToOrFrom           ::=  restrictto | restrictfrom;
restrictto =>; restrictfrom =>;
```

```
                    typeRestriction =>;
                    attributeRestriction       =>  syn_attribute:      AttributeOrAllAttributes;

                    TypeOrAllTypes             ::= TypeRef | AllTypes;
                    AllTypes => ;

-- Part 4: Assertions

    -- <assertion> ::= {<name>}? Assert <expression>

                    Assertion                  =>  syn_body:           expression;

    -- <definition instance> ::= <cyclic define> | <private define> | <define>
    -- <define> ::= Define <name> { <formals> }? = <expression>
    -- <private define> ::= Define <name> { <formals> }? Returns <type>
    -- <cyclic define> ::= Cyclic <define> Returns <type>
    -- <formals> ::= (<formal> {,<formal>}*)
    -- <formal> ::= <name> : <type>

                    DefInstance                ::= IDLDefInstance | PrivateDefInstance;
                    DefInstance                =>  syn_def:            DefineRef,
                                                   syn_list:           Seq Of Formal;

                    IDLDefInstance             ::= cyclicdef | noncyclicdef;
                    IDLDefInstance             =>  syn_body:           expression;
                    cyclicdef                  =>  syn_returnType:     TypeRef;
                    noncyclicdef =>;
                    PrivateDefInstance         =>  syn_returnType:     TypeRef;

                    Formal                     =>  syn_type:           TypeRef;

    -- <expression> ::= <conditional> | <quantifier> | <binary> | <unary> |
    --          <application> | <dotted> | <portExpression> |
    --          <expref> | <literal> | <caseExp>
                    expression                 ::= conditional | quantifier | binary | unary
                                                   | application | dotted | portExpression |
                                                   expRef | literal | caseExp;

    -- <conditional> ::= If <expression> Then <expression>
    --      { OrIf <expression> Then <expression> }*
    --      Else <expression> Fi
                    conditional                =>  syn_test:           expression,
                                                   syn_then:           expression,
                                                   syn_orif:           Seq Of expressionPair,
                                                   syn_else:           expression;

                    expressionPair             =>  syn_test:           expression,
                                                   syn_then:           expression;

    -- <quantifier> ::= { ForAll | Exists } <name> In <expression>
    --          Do <expression> Od

                    quantifier                 ::= forallq | existsq;
                    forallq =>; existsq =>;
                    quantifier                 =>  syn_control:        Control,
                                                   syn_set:            expression,
                                                   syn_body:           expression;
                    Control =>;                    --a syntactic entity

    -- <binary> ::= <expression> <binary op> <expression>
    -- <binary op> ::= {And | Or | Union | Intersect | + | - |
```

F.1. THE CANDLESYNTAX STRUCTURE 539

```
--              * | / | < | <= | > | >= | = | ~= | Same |
--              In | Sub | Psub }
binary                      =>   syn_left:          expression,
                                 syn_right:         expression,
                                 syn_op:            binaryOp;

binaryOp                    ::=  andOp | orOp | unionOp | isOp | intersectOp |
                                 plus | minus | times | divide |
                                 less | lessEq | greater |
                                 grtrEq | equal | notEqual | sameOp |
                                 inSet | subset | propSubset;
andOp =>; orOp =>; unionOp =>; isOp =>; intersectOp =>;
plus =>; minus =>; times =>; divide =>;
less =>; lessEq =>; greater =>;
grtrEq =>; equal =>; notEqual =>; sameOp=>;
inSet =>; subset =>; propSubset =>;

-- <unary> ::= <unary op> <expression>
-- <unary op> ::= { + | - | Not }
unary                       =>   syn_body:          expression,
                                 syn_op:            unaryOp;
unaryOp                     ::=  UnaryPlus | UnaryMinus | notOp;
UnaryPlus =>; UnaryMinus =>; notOp =>;

-- <application> ::= <name> ( { <expression> }* )
application                 =>   syn_instance:      DefInstanceOrDefineRef,
                                 syn_arguments:     Seq Of expression;

-- <dotted> ::= <expression> . <name>
dotted                      =>   syn_left:          expression,
                                 syn_right:         AttributeRef;

-- <port expression> ::= <name> : <type>
portExpression              =>   syn_portName:      PortRef,
                                 syn_type:          TypeRef;

--<expref> ::= <name> | {Set | Seq} Of <name>
expRef                      ::=  ExpSetSeqRef | ExpNameRef;
ExpSetSeqRef                ::=  ExpSetRef | ExpSeqRef;
ExpSetSeqRef                =>   syn_component:     NamedTypeRef;
ExpSetRef =>;
ExpSeqRef =>;

-- <literal> ::= <integer> | <rational> | <string> | <root>
--             | Empty | True | False
literal                     ::=  otherToken | rootExp | emptyExp | trueExp |
                                 falseExp;
emptyExp =>; trueExp =>; falseExp =>;

-- <caseExp>   ::= Case <case_name> Is <expression>
--                { <case select> }* { <case other> }? End
-- <case select> ::= <type> Do <expression> Od
-- <case other> ::= Otherwise Do <expression> Od
caseExp                     =>   syn_casename:      CaseName,
                                 syn_exp:           expression,
                                 syn_select:        Seq Of case_select,
                                 syn_otherwise:     expressionOrVoid;
case_select                 =>   syn_type:          TypeRef,
                                 syn_exp:           expression;

-- <root> ::= {<portname> :}? Root
rootExp                     =>   syn_portName:      PortRefOrVoid;
```

APPENDIX F. THE CANDLE SPECIFICATION

```
-- Part 5: Miscellaneous
    otherToken              ::= integerToken | rationalToken | stringToken;
    otherToken              => lex_externalform:  String;

    integerToken => ;
    rationalToken => ;
    stringToken => ;

    -- Identifiers have a lex_name attribute
    Identifier              ::= SyntacticEntity | EntityReference | nameToken;
    Identifier              => lex_name:          String;
    nameToken => ;

    Entity                  ::= SyntacticEntity;
    SyntacticEntity         ::= Assertion | Attribute | CaseName | Control
                                | Formal | DefInstance | Port |
                                StructureOrProcess;

    EntityReference         ::= AssertRef | AttributeRef | AttributeRefs |
                                compUnitRef | DefineRef |
                                DefInstanceOrDefineRef | ExpNameRef |
                                NamedTypeRef | OperRef | PortRef |
                                ProcessRef | StructureRef |
                                StructureOrProcessRef;
    AssertRef => ;
    AttributeRef => ;
    AttributeRefs =>;
    CaseName =>;
    compUnitRef =>;
    DefineRef => ;
    DefInstanceOrDefineRef =>;
    ExpNameRef =>;
    OperRef => ;
    PortRef => ;
    ProcessRef => ;
    StructureRef => ;
    StructureOrProcessRef =>;

    -- <type> ::= <name> | { Seq | Set } Of <name>
    TypeRef                 ::= SetOrSeqRef | NamedTypeRef ;
    SetOrSeqRef             ::= SetRef | SeqRef;
    SetOrSeqRef             => syn_component:    NamedTypeRef;
    SetRef =>;
    SeqRef =>;
    NamedTypeRef =>;

    AttributeOrVoid         ::= Attribute | Void;
    expressionOrVoid        ::= expression | Void;
    intOrVoid               ::= integerToken | Void;
    nameOrVoid              ::= nameToken | Void;
    PortRefOrVoid           ::= PortRef | Void;
    ProcessRefOrVoid        ::= ProcessRef | Void;
    stringOrVoid            ::= stringToken | Void;
    StructureOrVoid         ::= StructureEntity | Void;
    StructureRefOrVoid      ::= StructureRef | Void;
    TypeRefOrVoid           ::= TypeRef | Void;
    Void =>;
End
```

F.2 The `CandleSemantic` Structure

-- *file*: *src/specs/Candle/CandleSemantic.idl*

```
Import CandleSyntax From CandleSyntax End

Structure CandleSemantic Root compilationUnit From CandleSyntax Is

-- Part 1: Introduction

    StructureOrProcess      =>  sem_duplicate:      Boolean,
                                sem_definitions:    Set Of Definition,
                                sem_assertions:     Set Of Assertion;

    statement               =>  sem_duplicate:      Boolean;

-- Part 2: Structures

    StructureEntity         =>  sem_root:           TypeEntityOrVoid,
                                sem_types:          Set Of TypeEntity,
                                sem_corrections:    Seq Of correction;

    correction              =>  sem_stmt:           statement,
                                sem_cause:          statement;

    Attribute               =>  sem_duplicate:      Boolean,
                                sem_copiedfrom:     AttributeOrVoid;

    Class                   =>  sem_allattributes:  Seq Of Attribute,
                                sem_ancestors:      Set Of Class,      --direct
                                sem_subclasses:     Set Of Class;      --direct

    AllClasses              =>  sem_items:          Set Of Class;
    AllAttributes           =>  sem_items:          Set Of Attribute;

-- Part 3: Process Declarations

    ProcessEntity           =>  sem_invariant:      StructureEntity,
                                sem_target:         TargetOrVoid,
                                sem_ports:          Set Of Port,
                                sem_corrections:    Seq Of correction;
                  -- additions from recoverable errors

    Port                    =>  sem_portType:       PortType,
                                sem_duplicate:      Boolean,
                                sem_rep:            Seq Of RepRef;

    -- the target statement specifies the TargetEntity
    targetStmt              =>  sem_entity:         TargetOrError;
    TargetEntity            =>  sem_id:             Seq Of String;

    AllTypes                =>  sem_items:          Set Of TypeEntity;

-- Part 4: Assertions

    Definition              =>  sem_overload:       Set Of DefInstance,
                                sem_resulttype:     AssertTypeOrError;

    expression              =>  sem_type:           AssertTypeOrError;

    AssertType              ::= TypeEntity | collection;
```

APPENDIX F. THE CANDLE SPECIFICATION

```
    Expname                    ::= Formal | CaseName | Control | Definition |
                                   DefInstance | NamedType;

    CaseName                   =>  sem_owner:           caseExp;

    Control                    =>  sem_owner:           quantifier;

    --an object set expression
    collection                 ::= singleton | arbitrary;
    collection                 =>  sem_type:            TypeEntityOrError;
    singleton =>; arbitrary=>;
-- Part 5: Miscellaneous
    Entity                     ::= SemanticEntity;
    SemanticEntity             ::= Definition | TypeEntity;
    SemanticEntity             =>  sem_name:            String;

    -- TypeRefs are resolved to TypeEntities
    TypeEntity                 ::= SetOrSeq | NamedType;
    TypeEntity                 =>  sem_copiedfrom:      TypeEntityOrVoid;
    SetOrSeq                   ::= SetOf | SeqOf;
    SetOrSeq                   =>  sem_component:       NamedType;
    SetOf =>; SeqOf =>;
    NamedType                  ::= Atomic | Class;
    Atomic =>;

    AssertRef                  =>  sem_entity:          AssertOrError;
    AttributeRef               =>  sem_entity:          AttributeOrError;
    AttributeRefs              =>  sem_items:           Set Of Attribute;
    DefineRef                  =>  sem_entity:          DefineOrError;
    DefInstanceOrDefineRef     =>  sem_entity:          DefInstanceDefineOrError;
    ExpNameRef                 =>  sem_entity:          ExpnameOrError;
    ExpSetRef                  =>  sem_entity:          SetOrError;
    ExpSeqRef                  =>  sem_entity:          SeqOrError;
    PortRef                    =>  sem_entity:          PortOrError;
    ProcessRef                 =>  sem_entity:          ProcessOrError;
    StructureRef               =>  sem_entity:          StructureOrError;
    StructureOrProcessRef      =>  sem_entity:          StructureProcessOrError;
    TypeRef                    =>  sem_entity:          TypeEntityOrError;

    AssertOrError              ::= Assertion | error;
    AssertTypeOrError          ::= AssertType | error;
    AtomicOrError              ::= Atomic | error;
    AttributeOrError           ::= Attribute | error;
    DefineOrError              ::= Definition | error;
    DefInstanceDefineOrError   ::= DefInstance | Definition | error;
    ExpnameOrError             ::= Expname | error;
    FormalOrError              ::= Formal | error;
    PortOrError                ::= Port | error;
    ProcessOrError             ::= ProcessEntity | error;
    SeqOrError                 ::= SeqOf | error;
    SetOrError                 ::= SetOf | error;
    StructureOrError           ::= StructureEntity | error;
    StructureProcessOrError    ::= StructureOrProcess | error;
    TargetOrError              ::= TargetEntity | error;
    TypeEntityOrError          ::= TypeEntity | error;
    error =>;

    TargetOrVoid               ::= TargetEntity | Void;
    TypeEntityOrVoid           ::= TypeEntity | Void;
End
```

F.3 The `CandleRep` Structure

-- *file*: *src/specs/Candle/CandleRep.idl*

Import CandleSemantic From CandleSemantic End

Structure CandleRep From CandleSemantic Is

```
    Attribute              =>  rep_allowedOps:   Set Of AttributeOperation,
                               rep_name:         String,
                               rep_descriptor:   descriptor;

    descriptor             =>  rep_type:         descriptorOrTypeEntity;
    descriptorOrTypeEntity ::= descriptor | TypeEntity;

    Port                   =>  rep_name:         String;

    Operation              ::= SetOperation | SeqOperation | ClassOperation
                               | AttributeOperation | AtomicOperation;
    Operation              =>  rep_name:         String;
    SetOperation =>;
    SeqOperation =>;
    ClassOperation =>;
    AttributeOperation =>;
    AtomicOperation =>;

    TypeEntity             =>  rep_name:         String;

    SetOf                  =>  rep_allowedOps:   Set Of SetOperation;
    SeqOf                  =>  rep_allowedOps:   Set Of SeqOperation;

    Class                  =>  rep_enumerated:   Boolean,
                               rep_typeId:       Integer,
                               rep_allowedOps:   Set Of ClassOperation;

    Atomic                 =>  rep_internalType: InternalType,
                               rep_externalType: ExternalType,
                               rep_allowedOps:   Set Of AtomicOperation;

    InternalType           ::= TypeEntity | Package | Void;
    Package                =>  rep_name:         String;
    ExternalType           ::= TypeEntity | Predefined | Void;
    Predefined =>;

    SetOrSeq               =>  rep_package:      String,
                               rep_numelements:  SetSeqSize;
    SetSeqSize             ::= integerToken | anynumber;
    anynumber =>;

    OperRef                =>  rep_entity:       OperationOrError;
    RepRef                 =>  rep_entity:       TypeEntityOrError;

    OperationOrError       ::= Operation | error;
```

End

F.4 The CANDLE Structure

-- *file*: *src/specs/Candle/Candle.idl*

```
Import CandleRep From CandleRep End

Structure Candle From CandleRep Is

    compilationUnit =>   rep_comptimestamp: TimestampType;
    Type TimestampType;

    descriptor       =>  rep_offset:        Integer;  --in bits

    TypeEntity       =>  rep_size:          Integer,
                         rep_alignment:     Integer;
End
```

F.5 The UNCCandle Structure

-- *file*: *src/specs/Candle/UNCCandle.idl*

```
Import Candle From Candle End

Structure UNCCandle From Candle Is

        -- specify representations for private types
        For LexInfo Use External Seq Of String;
        For TimestampType Use External Integer;

End
```

F.6 The CandlePos Structure

-- *file*: *src/specs/Candle/CandlePos.idl*

```
Import Candle From Candle End

Structure CandlePos From Candle Is

        -- files will be numbered arbitrarily, but not stocastically
        SourcePosition => lex_file:   Integer,
                          lex_page:   Integer,
                          lex_line:   Integer,
                          lex_column: Integer; -- within the line

        Identifier     => lex_srcpos: SourcePosition;

        -- The source position is either uninitialized or correctly set
        Assert ForAll s In SourcePosition Do
            If s.lex_file = 0 -- i.e., uninitialized
            Then s.lex_page = 0 And s.lex_line = 0
            Else s.lex_page >= 1 And s.lex_line >= 1
            Fi Od;

        -- The source position for all copied attributes is identical
        Assert ForAll a In Attribute Do
            Case a2 Is a.sem_copiedFrom
                Void Do True Od
                Attribute Do a.lex_srcpos = a2.lex_srcpos Od
            End Od;
End
```

F.7 The `UNCCandlePos` Structure

-- *file src/specs/Candle/UNCCandlePos.idl*

Import UNCCandle From UNCCandle End

Import CandlePos From CandlePos End

Structure UNCCandlePos From UNCCandle, CandlePos Is
End

F.8 The `CandleContext` Structure

-- *file: src/specs/Candle/CandleContext.idl*

Import Candle From Candle End

```
Structure CandleContext Root Context From Candle Is

    Context                 =>  pre_targets:          Seq Of TargetType,
                                pre_types:            Seq Of PreludeType,
                                pre_definitions:      Set Of Definition;
    PreludeType             ::= TypeEntity | AnyClass | AnyNode | AnyPrivate
                                | AnySet | AnySeq;
    PreludeType             =>  pre_statetransitions: Seq Of StateTransition;
    AnyPrivate =>; AnySet =>; AnySeq =>;
    AnyClass                ::= AnyAttrClass | AnyUnattrClass;
    AnyAttrClass =>; AnyUnattrClass =>;
    AnyNode                 ::= AnyAttrNode | AnyUnattrNode;
    AnyAttrNode =>; AnyUnattrNode =>;

    StateTransition         =>  pre_transition:       transition,
                                pre_nextstate:        PreludeType;
    transition              =>  pre_id:               Seq Of Idparameter,
                                pre_actions:          Seq Of ActionType;

    Idparameter             ::= Idnameparameter | Idintegerparameter
                                | Idrationalparameter;
    Idnameparameter         ::= nameValue | nameSpec;
    Idintegerparameter      ::= integerRange | integerValue | integerSpec;
    Idrationalparameter     ::= rationalRange | rationalValue | rationalSpec;

    nameValue               =>  pre_name:             String;
    integerValue            =>  pre_integer:          Integer;
    rationalValue           =>  pre_rational:         Rational;
    nameSpec =>;
    integerSpec =>;
    rationalSpec =>;
    integerRange            =>  pre_low:              Integer,
                                pre_high:             Integer,
                                pre_actual:           Integer;
    rationalRange           =>  pre_low:              Rational,
                                pre_high:             Rational,
                                pre_actual:           Rational;

    ActionType              ::= copy | assign;
    copy                    ::= newcopy | copytransitions;
    newcopy =>; copytransitions =>;
    assign                  ::= assignName | assignExternal | assignInternal |
                                assignPackage | assignType | assignSize |
```

```
                              assignAlignment | assignEnum |
                              assignsetseqPackage | assignsetseqnumelems;

    assignName              => pre_param:              Idnameparameter;
    assignPackage           => pre_param:              Idnameparameter;
    assignSize              => pre_param:              Idintegerparameter;
    assignAlignment         => pre_param:              Idintegerparameter;
    assignEnum =>;
    assignsetseqPackage     => pre_param:              Idnameparameter;
    assignsetseqnumelems    => pre_param:              Idintegerparameter;

    assignExternal          ::= assignExternalSet | assignExternalSeq |
                                assignExternalNamedType;
    assignExternal          => pre_param:              Idnameparameter;
    assignExternalSet =>; assignExternalSeq =>;
    assignExternalNamedType =>;
    assignInternal          ::= assignInternalSet | assignInternalSeq |
                                assignInternalNamedType;
    assignInternal          => pre_param:              Idnameparameter;
    assignInternalSet =>; assignInternalSeq =>;
    assignInternalNamedType =>;
    assignType              ::= assignSet | assignSeq | assignNamedType;
    assignType              => pre_param:              Idnameparameter;
    assignSet =>; assignSeq =>; assignNamedType =>;

    TargetType              ::= TargetEntity | AnyTarget;
    TargetType              => pre_targettransitions: Seq Of TargetTransition;
    AnyTarget =>;

    TargetEntity            => pre_types:              Set Of TypeEntity,
                                pre_refinedtypePrs:    Seq Of RefinedTypePair,
                                pre_setOps:            Set Of SetOperation,
                                pre_seqOps:            Set Of SeqOperation,
                                pre_atomicOps:         Set Of AtomicOperation,
                                pre_classOps:          Set Of ClassOperation,
                                pre_nodeOps:           Set Of ClassOperation,
                                pre_attributeOps:      Set Of AttributeOperation
                                pre_keywords:          Set Of String;
    RefinedTypePair         => pre_targetIndependent:  TypeEntity,
                                pre_targetDependent:   TypeEntity;

    TargetTransition        => pre_id:                 TargetId,
                                pre_nextstate:         TargetEntity;
    TargetId                => pre_params:             Seq Of Idparameter;

    Without AllAttributes,
        AllClasses,
        Assertion,
        atomicDecl,
        Attribute => rep_allowedOps,
        Attribute => rep_name,
        Attribute => rep_descriptor,
        AttributeOrAllAttributes,
        attributeProduction,
        attributeRep,
        attributeRestriction,
        ClassOrAllClasses,
        compilationUnit,
        correction,
        Declaration,
        ImportDecl,
        LexInfo,
```

F.9. THE CANDLESYMBOLTABLE STRUCTURE

```
            OperRef => rep_entity,
            Port,
            portAssociation,
            portDefinition,
            PortType,
            PostPort,
            PrePort,
            production,
            ProcessEntity,
            processStatement,
            rationalToken,
            RepRef,
            restrictfrom,
            restriction,
            restrictto,
            restrictToOrFrom,
            statement,
            StructureEntity,
            StructureOrProcess,
            structureStatement,
            subclassProduction,
            targetStmt,
            TimestampType,
            typeRepDecl,
            typeRestriction,
            withoutAssert,
            withoutDefine,
            withoutClause,
            withoutItem,
            withoutProduction,
            withoutSubclass,
            withoutType,
            withoutAttribute;
End
```

F.9   The CandleSymbolTable Structure

-- *file: src/specs/Candle/CandleSymbolTable.idl*

Import Candle From Candle End

Structure CandleSymbolTable From Candle Is

--without syntactic only attributes
```
      Without AllAttributes,
              AllClasses,
              AttributeOrAllAttributes,
              attributeProduction,
              attributeRep,
              attributeRestriction,
              ClassOrAllClasses,
              LexInfo,
              portAssociation,
              portDefinition,
              ProcessEntity => syn_body,
              processStatement,
              production,
              restriction,
              restrictfrom,
```

```
            restrictto,
            restrictToOrFrom,
            statement,
            StructureEntity => syn_body,
            structureStatement,
            subclassProduction,
            targetStmt,
            typeRepDecl,
            typeRestriction,
            withoutAssert,
            withoutAttribute,
            withoutClause,
            withoutDefine,
            withoutItem,
            withoutProduction,
            withoutSubclass,
            withoutType;
End
```

Appendix G

idlcheck Instructions

This appendix describes the instructions of the assertion checker virtual machine. The instructions are grouped according to their general function and the type of their operands. On the left is the name of the instruction. The number preceding the instruction is the integer code for that instruction. On the right is a verbal description of the instruction. Below the instruction name is a notational description of the runtime stack before and after execution of the instruction. Only the relevant portion of the stack (the top few elements) is shown. Some instructions have attributes as well as stack operands. Attributes, with type specified after a colon, are in parentheses to the right of the instruction. Attributes are represented in the code array as two byte integers, which index an array containing the attribute itself. In the remainder of this appendix, whenever *stack* is mentioned, only the relevant portion at the top of the evaluation stack is meant.

The stack before execution is represented on the left of the description. This is followed by a colon, followed by a representation of the stack after execution of the instruction. Each representation of the stack is enclosed within angle brackets ("⟨ ⟩"). Within brackets, the stack grows toward the top from left to right. Individual operands are separated by commas; vertical bars specify exclusive alternatives (one or the other value, but not both). The operand closest to the right bracket ("⟩") is the top-of-stack (TOS). The operand to the left of TOS is TOS−1. Brackets that do not enclose any operands represent an empty evaluation stack.

The following type abbreviations are used.

int	*Integer*
rat	*Rational*

str	*String*	
bool	*Boolean*	
set	*Set Of* ⟨anything⟩	
seq	*Seq Of* ⟨anything⟩	
node	A node of any type	
num	int | rat	
value	num | str | bool | set | seq | node	
coll	A collection of any type	
ver	A definition or version of a definition	
type	An IDL type name	

When 'int' appears as an attribute, it denotes an index into the integer array. Similarly, 'rat', 'str', 'ver', and 'type' denote indices into the rational, string, definition, and type arrays, respectively. No other type abbreviation may appear as an attribute.

G.1 Literals

0 integerzero Push the integer 0.
⟨⟩ : ⟨int⟩

1 integerone Push the integer 1.
⟨⟩ : ⟨int⟩

2 integer(i:int) Push the integer i.
⟨⟩ : ⟨int⟩

3 rational(r:rat) Push the rational r.
⟨⟩ : ⟨rat⟩

4 string(s:str) Push the string s.
⟨⟩ : ⟨str⟩

5 true Push *True*.
⟨⟩ : ⟨bool⟩

6 false Push *False*.
⟨⟩ : ⟨bool⟩

7 empty
⟨⟩ : ⟨coll⟩

Push the empty collection.

8 root
⟨⟩ : ⟨node⟩

Push the collection containing only the root node object of the structure in which the root appears.

9 typeExpression(*t*:type)
⟨⟩ : ⟨coll⟩

Push the collection containing all objects with the type specified by *t*. The objects are taken from the structure in which the typeExpression is found.

G.2 Binary Operators

Infix Operators

10 root(*portname*:str)
⟨⟩ : ⟨node⟩

Push the collection containing only the root node object of the structure associated with the port specified by *portname*.

**11 portExpression
(*pn*:str,*t*:type)**
⟨⟩ : ⟨coll⟩

Push the collection containing all objects with the type specified by *t*. The objects are taken from the structure associated with the port specified by *pn*.

Collection Binary Operators

12 union
⟨coll, coll⟩ : ⟨coll⟩

Collection union. Push the union of collections TOS and TOS − 1.

13 intersect
⟨coll,coll⟩ : ⟨coll⟩

Collection intersection. Push the intersection of collections TOS and TOS − 1.

14 subset
⟨coll,coll⟩ : ⟨bool⟩

Collection subset. Push the Boolean result of TOS − 1 ⊆ TOS.

15 propsubset
⟨coll,coll⟩ : ⟨bool⟩

Collection proper subset. Push the Boolean result of TOS − 1 ⊂ TOS.

Arithmetic Binary Operators

16 plus
⟨num,num⟩:⟨num⟩

Addition. Add TOS to TOS − 1 and push the result. If either of the operands is rational, the result will be rational; otherwise, the result will be integer.

17 minus
⟨num,num⟩:⟨num⟩

Subtraction. Subtract TOS from TOS − 1 and push the result. If either of the operands is rational, the result will be rational; otherwise, the result will be integer.

18 times
⟨num,num⟩:⟨num⟩

Multiplication. Multiply TOS by TOS − 1 and push the result. If either of the operands is rational, the result will be rational; otherwise, the result will be integer.

19 divide
⟨num,num⟩:⟨num⟩

Division. Divide a TOS into TOS − 1 and push the result. If either of the operands is rational, the result will be rational; otherwise, the result will be integer.

Boolean Binary Operators

20 and
⟨bool,bool⟩:⟨bool⟩

Boolean AND. Push the Boolean result of TOS − 1 ∧ TOS.

21 or
⟨bool,bool⟩:⟨bool⟩

Boolean OR. Push the Boolean result of TOS − 1 ∨ TOS.

Relational Operators on Strings

These operations are based on the lexicographic comparison of TOS − 1 and TOS, as defined by the standard ASCII ordering.

22 str_less
⟨str,str⟩:⟨bool⟩

Less-than relation. If TOS − 1 is lexicographically less than TOS, push *True*; otherwise, push *False*.

23 str_lessEq
⟨str,str⟩:⟨bool⟩

Less-than-or-equal relation. If TOS − 1 is lexicographically less than or equal to TOS, push *True*; otherwise, push *False*.

G.2. BINARY OPERATORS

24 str_greater
⟨str,str⟩ : ⟨bool⟩

Greater-than relation. If TOS − 1 is lexicographically greater than TOS, push *True*; otherwise push *False*.

25 str_grtrEq
⟨str,str⟩ : ⟨bool⟩

Greater-than-or-equal relation. If TOS − 1 is lexicographically greater than or equal to TOS, push *True*; otherwise push *False*.

26 str_equal
⟨str,str⟩ : ⟨bool⟩

Equivalence relation. If TOS − 1 is lexicographically equivalent to TOS, push *True*; otherwise push *False*.

27 str_notEqual
⟨str,str⟩ : ⟨bool⟩

Nonequivalence relation. If TOS − 1 is not lexicographically equivalent to TOS, push *True*; otherwise push *False*.

Relational Operators on Integers and Rationals

28 num_lessEq
⟨num,num⟩ : ⟨bool⟩

Less-than-or-equal relation. Push the Boolean result of TOS − 1 ≤ TOS.

29 num_less
⟨num,num⟩ : ⟨bool⟩

Less-than relation. Push the Boolean result of TOS − 1 < TOS.

30 num_greater
⟨num,num⟩ : ⟨bool⟩

Greater-than relation. Push the Boolean result of TOS − 1 > TOS.

31 num_grtrEq
⟨num,num⟩ : ⟨bool⟩

Greater-than-or-equal relation. Push the Boolean result of TOS − 1 ≥ TOS.

32 num_equal
⟨num,num⟩ : ⟨bool⟩

Equivalence relation. Push the Boolean result of TOS − 1 =TOS.

33 num_notEqual
⟨num,num⟩ : ⟨bool⟩

Nonequivalence relation. Push the Boolean result of TOS − 1 ≠ TOS.

Relational Operators on Booleans

34 bool_equal
⟨bool,bool⟩ : ⟨bool⟩

Equivalence relation. If TOS and TOS − 1 are both *True* or both operands are *False*, push *True*; otherwise push *False*.

35 bool_notEqual
⟨bool,bool⟩ : ⟨bool⟩

Nonequivalence relation. If TOS and TOS − 1 are both *True* or both operands are *False*, push *False*; otherwise push *True*.

Relational Operators on Sets

36 set_equal
⟨set,set⟩ : ⟨bool⟩

Equivalence relation. If TOS and TOS−1 contain exactly the same objects, push *True*; otherwise push *False*.

37 set_notEqual
⟨set,set⟩ : ⟨bool⟩

Nonequivalence relation. If TOS and TOS − 1 do not contain exactly the same objects, push *True*. Otherwise push *False*.

Relational Operators on Sequences

38 seq_equal
⟨seq,seq⟩ : ⟨bool⟩

Equivalence relation. If TOS and TOS−1 contain exactly the same objects in the same order, push *True*. Otherwise push *False*.

39 seq_notEqual
⟨seq,seq⟩ : ⟨bool⟩

Nonequivalence relation. If TOS and TOS − 1 do not contain exactly the same objects in the same order, push *True*; otherwise push *False*.

Relational Operators on Node Objects

40 node_equal
⟨node,node⟩ : ⟨bool⟩

Equivalence relation. If TOS and TOS − 1 are the same object, push *True*; otherwise push *False*.

41 nodenotEqual
⟨node,node⟩ : ⟨bool⟩

Nonequivalence relation. If TOS and TOS − 1 are not the same object, push *True*; otherwise push *False*.

Miscellaneous Relational Operators

42 same
⟨coll,coll⟩ : ⟨bool⟩

Equivalence relation for collections. If TOS and TOS − 1 contain exactly the same objects, push *True*. Otherwise push *False*.

43 inSet
⟨num|str|bool|node,set⟩ : ⟨bool⟩

Set inclusion. If TOS − 1 is a member of TOS, push *True*; otherwise push *False*.

44 inSeq
⟨num|str|bool|node,seq⟩ : ⟨bool⟩

Sequence inclusion. If TOS − 1 is a member of TOS, push *True*; otherwise push *False*.

G.3. UNARY OPERATORS

45 inCollection
⟨num|str|bool|node,coll⟩:
⟨bool⟩

Collection inclusion. If TOS − 1 is a member of TOS, push `True`; otherwise push `False`.

G.3 Unary Operators

46 unaryMinus
⟨num⟩:⟨num⟩

Unary minus. Multiply TOS -1 and push the result. The type of TOS will remain the same.

47 not
⟨bool⟩:⟨bool⟩

Boolean negation. If TOS is `True`, push `False`. If TOS is `False`, push `True`.

Jumps

48 jump(*loc*:int)
⟨⟩:⟨⟩

Jump to the location in the code array indexed by *loc*.

49 jtrue(*loc*:int)
⟨bool⟩:⟨⟩

Jump to the location in the code array indexed by *loc* if TOS is `True`.

50 jfalse(*loc*:int)
⟨bool⟩:⟨⟩

Jump to the location in the code array indexed by *loc* if TOS is `False`.

G.4 Miscellaneous Instructions

51 members
{⟨set⟩|⟨seq⟩}:⟨coll⟩

Push the collection containing the objects contained in TOS.

52 head
⟨seq⟩:⟨value⟩

Push the first object in TOS.

53 tail
⟨seq⟩:⟨seq⟩

Push the sequence obtained by deleting the first in object in TOS.

54 str_size
⟨str⟩:⟨int⟩

Push the number of characters in TOS.

55 setorseqorcoll_size
⟨set|seq⟩:⟨int⟩

Push the number of objects contained in TOS.

56 type
⟨coll⟩ : ⟨coll⟩

For each object in TOS, create a collection containing all objects of the same type as the object in TOS. Push the union of these collections.

57 forall(*loc*:int)
⟨coll⟩ : ⟨⟩

Remove the first object of TOS and push this value onto the quantifier collections stack. Increment the control stack offset. Push `True` onto the runtime stack, since this operation is considered true until proven otherwise. Jump to the location in the code array indexed by *loc*.

58 exists(*loc*:int)
⟨coll⟩ : ⟨⟩

Remove the first object of TOS and push this value onto the quantifier collections stack. Increment the control stack offset. Push `False` onto the runtime stack, since this operation is considered false until proven otherwise. Jump to the location in the code array indexed by *loc*.

59 endForAll(*return*:int)
⟨bool⟩ : ⟨bool⟩|⟨⟩

If TOS is `False`, pop the quantifier collections stack, decrement the control stack offset, and push `False`. If TOS is `True` and the top entry of the quantifier collections stack is empty, pop the quantifier collections stack, decrement the control stack offset, and push `True`. If TOS is `True` and the top entry of the quantifier collections stack is nonempty, pop the runtime stack, remove the first object of the top entry of the quantifier collections stack, place it in the control stack at the current offset-1, and jump to the position in the code indexed by *return*.

G.4. MISCELLANEOUS INSTRUCTIONS

60 endExists(*return*:int)
⟨bool⟩:⟨bool⟩|⟨⟩

If TOS is *True*, pop the quantifier collections stack, decrement the control stack offset, and push *True*. If TOS is *False* and the top entry of the quantifier collections stack is empty, pop the quantifier collections stack and push *False*. If TOS is *False* and the top entry of the quantifier collections stack is nonempty, pop the runtime stack, remove the first object of the top entry of the quantifier collections stack, place it in the control stack at the current offset-1, and jump to the position in the code indexed by *return*.

61 control(*level*:int)
⟨⟩:⟨value⟩

Push the object located in the control stack indexed by current offset + *level*.

62 formArg(*pos*:int)
⟨⟩:⟨value⟩

Push the object located in the definition's argument list at position *pos*.

63 dot(*attr*:str)
⟨coll⟩:⟨coll⟩

Push the collection containing all objects that are associated with the attribute (specified by the name attr) of all objects in TOS. For each object in TOS, there will be exactly one object in the result collection.

64 application
(*v*:ver,*i*:int)
⟨{value}^{i}⟩:⟨value|coll⟩

If v is a definition, then determine which version of the referenced definition applies to this application, by matching number and types of actual arguments with number and types of formal arguments. Evaluate the version specified by v, applied to the correct number of arguments (specified by i) at the top of the stack. Push the result returned by the evaluation.

65 return
⟨⟩:⟨⟩

Signals the end of a definition evaluation. Return TOS.

66 endAssertion
⟨bool⟩:⟨⟩

If TOS is *True*, the assertion is *True*. If TOS is *False*, the assertion is *False*. Report the result.

67 cyclicapplication ⟨v:ver,i:int⟩ ⟨{value}^{i}⟩:⟨value|coll⟩	First determine the version from v, as in a normal application (see **application**, above). Then search through the call stack, looking for a previous application with the same parameters. If found, then return the current return value (initially, the empty collection). Otherwise, evaluate the version specified by v, applied to the correct number of arguments (specified by i) at the top of the stack. Push the result returned by the evaluation.
68 cyclicreturn ⟨⟩:⟨⟩	Signals the end of a cyclic definition evaluation. Compare TOS with the current return value. If they are identical, then return TOS. Otherwise, the current return value becomes the TOS unioned with the previous value of the current return value, and a jump to the first element of the code array is performed to reevaluate the version.
69 is ⟨type,node type⟩:⟨bool⟩	If TOS and TOS $-$ 1 are the same type, push *True*; otherwise push *False*.
70 casename ⟨coll⟩:⟨⟩	Remove the first object of TOS and place it in the control stack at the current offset. Increment the offset.

Bibliographic Notes

The format used here was taken from the description of the UCSD Pascal P-code machine, by SofTech Microsystems [1981].

Appendix H
Answers to Exercises

The preface suggests that you attempt to solve the exercises yourself before looking up the answer here.

1.1 Pt is generated from the original source file, or from commands given to the structure editor. Pr-std is specific to the pretty-printer, and hence is independent of the other data structures. Apt is probably a superset of Pt. Fg and Tcs are subsets of Apt. The information in Rel is derived from that of Apt (by the Code process), but is in a substantially different form. Core is probably simpler in form, but similar in information content, to Rel. We will see in Chapter 4 how to make these statements precise in IDL.

1.2 This language is infinite, and is composed of sentences with three components. The first is one of { "aIs::=d", "aIs::=e", "aIs::=", "bIs::=d", "bIs::=e", "bIs::=" }, the second is one of { "f", "ff", "fff", ...}, and the third may absent or be one of { "g", "gg", "ggg", ...}. For example, "bIs::=efffggggg" is one valid sentence.

2.1 bill_list is reachable because it is the root type; bill is reachable through bill_list, Customer through bill_list.list, commercial_customer and Government_customer through Customer, and state_customer and federal_customer through Government_customer.

2.2 The following macros were generated for the billing process: 12 node identifiers, 24 user-visible and 48 internal node allocators and destroyers, 72 set and sequence operations, 31 node and 14 class attribute accessors, 11 widening, 11 narrowing, and 4 Is macros, for a total of 227 macros, in addition to the more than two dozen process-independent macros. The accessor, widening, narrowing, and Is macros (a total of 71 macros) are generated by target language **Version B**.

3.1 It's easy to confuse the concepts of class hierarchy and parse tree, because there are strong similarities.

- Both are trees (usually, but see Section 10.3).
- Both result from specifications of the form

    x ::= y | z

    which can be read "an x is either a y or a z."

However, there are also significant differences.

- The class hierarchy is actually a *directed acyclic graph*, while the parse tree instance is a true *tree*.
- A parse tree is an *instance* of an IDL structure. The class hierarchy is a *property* of an IDL structure.
- A parse tree contains *instances* of IDL *nodes*. The class hierarchy describes relationships between *nodes* and *classes*.
- The arcs of a parse tree are specified as *attributes* in an IDL specification. The arcs of the class hierarchy are specified as *subclasses* in an IDL specification.

3.2 If the function itself was folded to a constant value (i.e., if the function's body did not contain any references to the formal parameters), then calls to the function could be replaced with the constant itself.

4.1 An integer value i can be expressed as the ratio of integers i and 1. A fixed point value $i.j$, where the integer j is stored in a field of integral width k and is of integral base b, can be expressed as the ratio of the integers $i \cdot b^k + j$ and b^k. A floating point value $i \exp e$, where i is stored in a field of integral width k with integral exponent e and integral base b, can be expressed as the ratio of integers $i \cdot e^b$ and b^k.

4.2 The operations given in the problem informally state that (1) only the A, B, and C operations should be generated for the entity; (2) the C operation should not be generated for the entity; and (3) only the A and C operations should be generated for the entity. The analysis is ($\{A, B, C, D\} \cap \{A, C\}) - \{C\} = \{A\}$. Hence, only the A operation would be generated (B is disallowed by (3), C by (2), and D by (1) and by (3)).

4.3 The file **C/constant_fold.idl** imports the constant_fold process from **cf.idl**, shown in Figure 3.9, which imports the attributed_syntax structure from **functionsem.idl**, shown in Figure 3.8, which imports the abstract_syntax structure from **functionsyntax.idl**, shown in Figure 3.6.

5.1 All are examples of 5.78125×10^1.

5.2 "*Assert Exists* ..." can fail only once, if no object satisfies the predicate. "*Assert ForAll* ... "can fail many times, once for each object that doesn't satisfy the predicate. In IDLCHECK, all other assertions can fail just once, if their predicate is not satisfied, although a more sophisticated analysis could often generate multiple failures in the presence of embedded *ForAll* expressions.

6.1 The initial character may be '-' to start a comment or negative integer or rational constant, an alphabetic character to start a node, label, or boolean constant, a '"' to start a string constant, a numeric character or '+' to start a rational or integer constant, a '{' to start a set, or a '<' to start a sequence, or 66 characters out of the 128 possible. The final character may be ⟨end of line⟩, a '#' to end the instance or a rational constant, a numeric character to end an integer constant, rational constant, or node name, an alphabetic character to end a node name or boolean constant, a ']' to end a node, a '}' to end a set, a '>' to end a sequence, a '_' to end a node name, or a '^' to end a reference, or 69 characters, out of the 128 possible.

6.2 The non-printing characters (ASCII values 0 through 32 and 127), except for ⟨horizontal tab⟩ (value 9) and ⟨end of line⟩ (generally ⟨linefeed⟩ (value 10) and/or ⟨carriage return⟩ (value 13)) are not permitted anywhere in an ERL instance. Hence, 31 ASCII characters out of 128 possible are not permitted.

7.1 To eliminate the assertion failure, add the following representation specification to the **customers** structure.

    For Customers.balance *Use Double Precision*;

7.2 The runtime libraries (and code generated by IDLC) are quite similar in their support of the IDL type model. The differences are

- C implements nodes as single *struct*s, whereas Pascal requires multiple *record*s, linked with pointers, to support widening and narrowing. This difference is hidden when the **Version B** macros are used.

- Given a variable of a class type, C requires the field selection .IDL-classCommon to access a class attribute; in Pascal the attribute may often be accessed directly. This difference is hidden when the **Version B** macros are used.

- Support for *String*s in Pascal is somewhat awkward, because Pascal does not directly support character strings, as does C.

- Pascal requires multiple levels of indirection to access some attributes; this difference is hidden when the `Version B` macros are used.

- C has a special enumerated representation for unattributed nodes and classes; Pascal does not.

- C has a macro `typeof` to determine the node type, while Pascal uses the 'E' fields to determine the subclass type.

8.1 See the answer to exercise **7.1**.

8.2 Operations in C are generally implemented as macros. The `foreachinSET` and `foreachinSEQ` operations are macros that expand to the initial part of a *for* statement. Operations in Pascal have the stronger requirement that they be supportable as routines, since most Pascal implementations do not support macros.

9.1 The BNF would be changed as follows.

⟨parameter⟩ ::= ⟨name⟩ { ',' ⟨name⟩ }* ':' ⟨type⟩

An analogous change in the Yacc specification would be necessary. No change to the `abstract_syntax` structure, and hence to the rest of the compiler, would be required.

9.2 An extended version of the function language compiler that supports booleans is available with the IDL Toolkit. The required changes are small, but pervasive.

Lexical analysis — Six keywords are added.

⟨keyword⟩ ::= `boolean` | `true` | `false` | `and` | `or` | `not`

Syntactic Analysis — A new type and its associated constants are added.

⟨type⟩   ::= `boolean`
⟨expression⟩ ::= ⟨expression⟩ `or` ⟨term⟩
⟨term⟩   ::= ⟨term⟩ `and` ⟨factor⟩
⟨factor⟩   ::= `true` | `false` | `not` ⟨expression⟩

The `abstract_syntax` structure must be similarly augmented.

```
types              ::= bool;
bool               => ;
constant           ::= boolean_constant;
boolean_constant   ::= true_constant | false_constant;
true_constant      => ;
false_constant     => ;
binaryoperator     ::= andop | orop;
andop              => ;
orop               => ;
unaryoperator      ::= unarynot;
unarynot           => ;
```

Semantic Analysis — Adding a boolean type does not affect name resolution. The attributed_syntax structure is augmented with an assertion.

CorrectBoolConstType *Assert ForAll* bc *In* boolean_constant
    Do bc.sem_exp_type *Is* bool *Od*;

Type checking, shown in Appendix E.3.2, has additional cases for the new operators and constants.

Constant folding — This phase, as shown in Figures 3.15–3.18, on pp. 92–95, requires additional cases.

Convert — This phase is unaffected.

9.3 FRONTENDGEN would be useful only if the problems discussed in (d), below, were adequately solved.

a. The input to FRONTENDGEN would be a two-level BNF specification, one level giving the lexical structure and one level giving the syntactic structure (the tool could possibly extract the lexical and syntactic structures directly from a one-level BNF specification). The BNF should support iteration ({}*) and alteration ({ | }), as well as optional clauses ({}?). The outputs would be Lex and Yacc specifications, if C output were desired, or a lexical analyzer and recursive descent parser, if Pascal output were desired. Also output would be an IDL specification of the abstract syntax tree to be computed by the generated parser.

b. The lexical structure would have to be Type 3 (a regular grammar) and the syntactic structure would have to be LALR(1) or LL(1), for C and Pascal, respectively.

564   APPENDIX H. ANSWERS TO EXERCISES

c. The compile-time time would be longer than the manual approach, because FRONTENDGEN would duplicate much of the processing of LEX and YACC. The compile-time space would be equivalent in the two approaches. The runtime space and time of the generated frontend should be similar to that of one generated by hand, since in many cases the code would be identical.

d. Details of the user interface significantly complicate the design of FRONTENDGEN. The considerations listed in the question are usually handled in the manual approach with special-purpose C or Pascal code. Mechanisms must be designed to allow such code to be inserted by FRONTENDGEN into the code *it* generates, or the behavior of this code must be specified in a declarative fashion in the input to FRONTENDGEN.

9.4 The runtime space for the `frontend`, `semantic`, `constant_fold`, and `convert` phases in Pascal are 77, 122, 122, and 124 kilobytes on a Sun-3 workstation, respectively, or a total of 445 kb. For the one-process variant, the size is 85 kb, or a factor of 5 less. For C, the totals are 346 kb and 71 kb, respectively, or almost a factor of 5 less. The total execution time for the four-process variant in Pascal on a 300-line function language program was 80.5 seconds (on a Sun-3/60); for the one-process variant the runtime was 7.2 seconds, or a factor of 11 less. The execution times for the C processes on the same input file were 10.6 and 4.1 seconds, respectively, or a factor of 2 less. The differences between the four- and one-process variants can be attributed to the reading and writing of intermediate representations, which require much code and execution time.

11.1 The following function program

```
function foo(A : integer) : integer
       = A;
function bar(A : integer) : integer
       = A;
```

will generate the following output when run through **formal2.xref**.

```
Name    Lines
A       1, 2

A       3, 4
```

On the other hand, if matching were done syntactically, the following would have been generated instead.

```
Name    Lines
A       1, 2, 4

A       3, 2, 4
```

If syntactic matching were desired, the predicate same_as_F would be written as

Predicate same_as_F (this)
this.sem_entity.syn_token.lex_token = F.syn_token.lex_token End

12.1 The lexical conventions could be extended with the following.

⟨keyword⟩   ::= *False* | *True*
⟨basic token⟩ ::= ⟨integer⟩
⟨integer⟩   ::= { '+' | '-' }? { ⟨digit⟩ }+

In the syntax, the following needs to be added.

⟨atom⟩ ::= ⟨integer⟩ | *True* | *False*

12.3 A *Type* construct with multiple attribute names cannot be simulated in XRef.

a. A nested invocation of *Type* imposes an ordering on the attributes to be following, and also results in nodes returned by the intermediate *Type* expressions being of the wrong type. To use an example on the function language's abstract_syntax structure, assume we want all constants accessible through syn_left and syn_right attributes. The following expression appears initially to do the trick.

*Type(Type(Type(Root, binary_operation),
        constant, syn_left),
    constant, syn_right)*

From the inner-most invocation of *Type*, we get all the binary_- operation nodes. Going one level out, the next invocation of *Type* will return a sequence of constant nodes, which certainly do not have an syn_right attributes. Hence the outer-most invocation of *Type* will return no objects. Even if the types somehow worked out, only nodes that were values of syn_right that were themselves values of syn_left would be returned. In the following function

```
function a (b: integer): integer = a + 3;
```

the constant 3 would not be returned.

b. The required change to the syntax is minimal.

⟨sequence element⟩ ::= *Type* ' (' ⟨sequence⟩ ' , ' ⟨node_name⟩
     { ' , ' ⟨attribute_name⟩ }* ') '

13.1 We can modify the example given in Section 13.3.1 to demonstrate the name resolution in XRef: change the name of the second predicate to ascending_names and the line after point *6* to

Filter(name_node, ascending_names(name_node))

This changes the scope L5 to

```
L5:scope[sem_entities <L6:local[syn_name "name_node"]
                      L8:predicate_declaration[
                              syn_name "ascending_names";
                              syn_formals <...>;
                              ]
                      >;
          sem_previous_scope L1^]
```

The entity references after point *6* would then be resolved as follows

```
localRef[syn_name "name_node"; sem_entity L6^]
predicateRef[syn_name "ascending_names"; sem_entity L8^]
```

since L8^ appears in scope L5, which is searched before scope L1, whereas the entity reference after point *3* would remain as before:

```
predicateRef[syn_name "ascending_name"; sem_entity L4^]
```

since the current scope at this point is still L1.

13.2 The difference between Pascal and XRef in their for statements is one of scoping. In Pascal, the distinguished variable ⟨iterated_name⟩ must be previously declared. In XRef, a new variable is implicitly declared, with a scope of the body of the for statement. The scope of a previously declared variable of that same name does not include the for statement. One practical ramification is that the last value of this variable outside the for statement is available in Pascal but not in XRef. The correct scoping must be maintained during name resolution in semantic analysis. However, once a reference is associate with its sem_entity (which entity is determined by the scope rules), the interpreter accesses this entity when needed, not caring which particular local it is.

13.3 A constructed_sequence should be a virtual_sequence only if its elements should appear in the output in exactly the order found in the sequence. A virtual sequence is preferred, since it requires less time and space to manage. Clearly the top level sequence in body should be virtual. This sequence is passed down to the operators appearing in the body. The remainder of the occurrences of ⟨sequence⟩ listed in Section 12.2 are implemented as physical sequences, although it may be possible to implement *Head*, *Tail*, and *Empty* with virtual sequences.

13.4 Boolean and integer constants can be easily added. The **parse_tree-.idl** specification, the lexical analyzer, and the syntactic analyzer could be easily extended.

```
atom               ::= integer_constant | true_constant
                       | false_constant;
integer_constant => lex_value: Integer;
true_constant    => ;
false_constant   => ;
```

The semantic analyzer and interpreter require even fewer changes.

13.6 Two changes to the implementation are necessary to support multiple attribute names in the *Type* construct. First, the reachability search must be extended to consider each attribute name. Second, the cache must include all the attribute names in its key.

13.7 The question suggests two possible approaches to implementing an if construct.

a. The if construct can be implemented as a macro.

```
#define if(test, then, else) \
    Predicate Y(this) test End \
    Predicate Z(this) Not(Y(this)) End \
    For X In Filter(Root, Y) \
    Do then End \
    For X In Filter(Root, Z) \
    Do else End
```

b. The macro implementation is quite inefficient. It evaluates the predicate twice, calls two helper predicates, and calls *Filter* twice. A direct implementation of *If* would not exhibit this excessiveoverhead.

13.8 Loosening the constraint on the number of predicate parameters is straight-forward.

a. Predicates with no parameters may be replaced with the boolean constants true or false, or with a macro defined to be true or false (see Exercise **13.4**).

b. The frontend already supports predicates with more than two parameters. Semantic analysis need only to check that the number of formals and actuals correspond. In the interpreter, the handling of an arbitrary number of parameters for predicate invocation is identical to that for function invocation.

13.9 Full parenthesization is mildly controversial.

a. Fully parenthesized expressions reduce the need to remember the precedence of the operators, and are justified if the language will be used infrequently, as is probably the case with XRef.

b. Only the Yacc specification would need to be changed to support precedence.

13.10 Recursive calls could be supported, with the cost of additional complexity in the implementation.

a. Since the function declaration is added to the scope *after* semantic analysis of the function body, a direct recursive call in function A cannot be resolved, unless a previous declaration of A had already been processed. In the first case, a semantic error would be detected; in the second case, the call to A would be resolved, but it would not be a direct recursive call.

b. Assume without loss of generality that the declaration for A appeared before the declaration for B. Function B's call of function A could be resolved, but B's call of A could not, because B had not yet been declared. Hence, a semantic error would be signaled.

c. One way to support recursive calls would be to add a forward declaration, as in Pascal.

⟨declaration⟩ ::= *Function* ⟨function_name⟩
          '(' ⟨formals⟩ ')' *Forward*

This extension results in two defining occurrences for function declarations. To handle this, separate the syntactic (declarative) and semantic aspects of functions, in the `parse_tree` structure

```
SyntacticEntity      ::= declaration | local;
SyntacticEntity      => syn_name:  user_name;
function_declaration => syn_value: bodyOrVoid;
bodyOrVoid           ::= body | Forward;
Forward              => ;
```

and in the `attributed_parse_tree` structure

```
SemanticEntity ::= predicate | function | local;
SemanticEntity => sem_name:    user_name;
predicate      => sem_formals: Seq Of local,
                  sem_value:   expression;
function       => sem_formals: Seq Of local,
                  sem_value:   body;
```

These semantic entities would be constructed as the declarations were processed, and would appear in scopes (the declarations would no longer appear in scopes).

```
scope => sem_entities: SemanticEntity;
```

d. *Extra* can be implemented as a recursive function, using *if*, as defined in Exercise **13.7**.

Function Extra (one, two) *Forward*;
Function Extra (one, two)
    if(*Empty*(*Tail*(two), *Tail*(one),
        Head(one) *Extra*(*Tail*(one), *Tail*(two));

Unique, *Intersection*, and *Difference* are also superfluous once recursive functions are available, except that their direct support in the interpreter significantly increases their efficiency over a recursive function implementation.

e. The program would be interpreted, but the results would probably be incorrect. When a call was made to a function while another call to that same function was still in effect, the values of `local.int_value` would be corrupted.

f. For the values of the formal parameters, the solution is straightforward: keep a sequence of values around.

```
local => int_values: Seq Of IDLVALUE;
```

Whenever a function is called, the new values for the parameters are pushed onto the `int_values` sequence. At the same time, the values of the locals within the case and for statements must also be saved. These locals may be found by scanning the `sem_scope` of the function's body. On function return, these sequences of values must be popped.

g. Recursive functions could be differentiated from nonrecursive functions, as the latter can be called more efficiently (no stacks of values are needed). Locals appearing after the recursive call need not be saved across calls. The relevant locals in a recursive function should be collected together as another semantic attribute.

```
functionEntity => sem_stacked_locals: Seq Of local;
```

h. The answers are similar for recursive predicates.

13.11 The lack of types is also mildly controversial.

a. The benefits of being typeless are that the user need not declare a type and that the restriction that every expression have a single type is not imposed.

b. The drawbacks are that the type is not identified explicitly in the XRef program and that some errors, such as trying to add two boolean values, are detected not at compile time but at runtime.

13.12 The *Let* construct is useful both for linguistic and performance reasons.

a. Let A = ··· In ··· A ··· End

can be written instead as

```
#define A ···
··· A ···
```

In a nested *Let* statement with overlapping identifiers, the scope rules will not be followed correctly, unless some of the identifiers are changed so that they no longer overlap.

b. We will mark each identifier and expression with a subscript to differentiate them, and will show the scopes explicitly, shifted to the left.

$$\text{Let } A_1 = \cdots_2,$$
$$A_1 = \cdots_2$$
$$B_1 = \cdots_3 A_1 \cdots_4,$$
$$A_1 = \cdots_2$$
$$B_1 = \cdots_3 \cdots_2 \cdots_4$$
$$A_2 = \cdots_5 B \cdots_6$$
$$B_1 = \cdots_3 \cdots_2 \cdots_4$$
$$A_2 = \cdots_5 \cdots_3 \cdots_2 \cdots_4 \cdots_6$$
$$\text{In } \cdots_7 A_2 \cdots_8 B_1 \cdots_9 \text{ End}$$

which evaluates to

$$\cdots_7 \cdots_5 \cdots_3 \cdots_2 \cdots_4 \cdots_6 \cdots_8 \cdots_3 \cdots_2 \cdots_4 \cdots_9$$

c. The run times differ so dramatically because the expressions in the *Let* statements are being reevaluated over and over again.

d. If the XREF compiler did common subexpression elimination as well as code motion out of loops (e.g., For), then temporaries could cache intermediate values, and the *Let* statement would not be justified by performance considerations. Such a statement might still be useful as a linguistic device.

Bibliography

Ada [1983]. *Reference Manual for the Ada Programming Language.* ANSI/-MIL-STD-1815A Edition. United States Department of Defense, Washington, D.C.

Aho, A.V., R. Sethi, and J.D. Ullman [1986]. *Compilers: Principles, Techniques, and Tools.* Reading, Massachusetts: Addison-Wesley Publishing Company.

Aho, A.V., J.E. Hopcroft, and J.D. Ullman [1983]. *Data Structures and Algorithms.* Reading, Massachusetts: Addison-Wesley Publishing Company.

Allman, E.P., G. Held, and M. Stonebraker [1976]. *Embedding a Data Manipulation Language in a General Purpose Programming Language*, in *Proceedings of the Conference on Data Abstraction, Definition, and Structure*, ACM-SIGPlan-SIGMod. Salt Lake City, Utah: ACM, March, pp. 25–35.

Ambler, A. and R. Trawick [1983]. *Chaitin's Graph Coloring Algorithm as a Method for Assigning Positions to Diana Attributes. ACM SIGPlan Notices*, 18, No. 2, February, pp. 37–38.

ANSI [1977]. *ANSI X3.4-1977 Code for Information Exchange.*

Appelbe, B.F. and G.J. Dismukes [1982]. *An Operational Definition of Intermediate Code for Implementing a Portable Ada Compiler*, in *Proceedings of the AdaTEC Conference on Ada*, Association for Computing Machinery. Arlington, Virginia: ACM, October, pp. 266–274.

Archer, J.E., Jr. and M.T. Devlin [1986]. *Rational's Experience Using Ada for Very Large Systems*, in *Proceedings of the First International Conference on Ada Programming Language Applications for the NASA Space Station*, Houston, Texas: June, pp. B.2.5.1–B.2.5.11.

Atkinson, M.P. [1977]. *IDL: A Machine-independent Data Language*. *Software Practice and Experience*, 7, November, pp. 671–684.

Atkinson, M.P., K.J. Chisholm, and W.P. Cockshott [1982]. *PS-algol: an algol with a persistent heap*. *ACM SIGPlan Notices*, 17, No. 7, pp. 24–31.

Avakian, A., S.G. Harandhvala, J. Horn, and B. Knobe [1982]. *The Design of an Integrated Support Software System*, in *Proceedings of the Symposium on Compiler Construction*, Boston, Massachusetts: June, pp. 308–317.

Barstow, D.R., H.E Shrobe, and E. Sandewall [1984]. *Interactive Programming Environments*. New York, New York: McGraw-Hill Book Company.

Bershad, B.N., D.T. Ching, E.D. Lazowska, J.O. Sanislo, and M. Schwartz [1987]. *A Remote Procedure Call Facility for Interconnecting Heterogeneous Computer Systems*. *IEEE Transactions on Software Engineering*, SE-13, No. 6, August, pp. 880–894.

Besson, M. and B. Queyras [1987]. *GET: A Test Environment Generator for Ada*, in *Proceedings of the Ada-Europe International Conference*, Stockholm, Sweden, May, reprinted in *Ada Components: Libraries and Tools*, S. Tafvelin, editor. Paris: Cambridge University Press, pp. 237–250.

Birrell, A.D. and B.J. Nelson [1984]. *Implementing Remote Procedure Calls*. *ACM Transactions on Computer Systems*, 2, No. 1, February, pp. 39–59.

Birrell, A.D., M.B. Jones, and E.P. Wobber [1988]. *A Simple and Efficient Implementation for Small Databases*. Technical Report 24. Digital Systems Research Center, Palo Alto, California.

Birtwistle, G.M., O.-J. Dahl, B. Myhrhaus, and K. Nygaard [1973]. *Simula Begin*. Philadelphia, Pennsylvania: Auerbach Publishers, Inc.

Biyani, V. [1987]. *An Efficient Runtime System for IDL*. Master's Thesis. University of North Carolina at Chapel Hill, October.

Bobrow, D.G. [1986]. *CommonLoops: Merging Lisp and Object-Oriented Programming*, in *Proceedings of Object-Oriented Programming Systems, Languages and Applications Conference (OOPSLA '86)*, Association for Computing Machinery. Portland, Oregon: September, pp. 17–29.

Borning, A.H. and D.H.H. Ingalls [1982]. *Multiple Inheritance in Smalltalk-80*, in *Proceedings of AAAI-82*, August, pp. 234–237.

Bratman, H. [1961]. *An Alternate Form of the "UNCOL Diagram"*. *Communications of the ACM*, 4, No. 3, March, p. 142.

Breguet, P., F. Grize, and A. Strohmeier [1985]. *SARTEX A Programming Language for Graph Processing*. *ACM SIGPlan Notices*, 20, No. 1, January, pp. 11–19.

Brosgol, B.M. [1980]. *Tcol-ada and the 'middle end' of the PQCC Ada compiler*, in *Proceedings of the Symposium on the Ada Programming Language*, ACM SIGPlan. Boston, Massachusetts: December, pp. 101–112.

Brosgol, B.M., J.M. Newcomer, D.A. Lamb, D.A. Levine, M.S. Van Deusen and W.A. Wulf [1980]. *Tcol Ada: Revised Report on An Intermediate Representation for the Preliminary Ada Language*. Technical Report CMU-CS-80-105. Computer Science Department, Carnegie Mellon University, Pittsburgh, Pennsylvania, February.

Butler, K.J. [1983]. *DIANA Past, Present, and Future*, in *Lecture Notes in Computer Science Ada Software Tools Interfaces*, Ed. G.T. Goos and J. Hartmanis. Workshop, Bath, England. New York: Springer-Verlag, pp. 3–22.

Butler, K.J. and A. Evans, Jr. [1983]. *A Diana-Driven Pretty-Printer for Ada*. Technical Report TL 83-3. Tartan Laboratories, Pittsburgh, Pennsylvania, February.

Cameron, R.D. [1988]. *An Abstract Pretty Printer*. IEEE Software, 5, No. 6, November, pp. 61–67.

Chaitin, G.J., M.A. Auslander, A.K. Chandra, J. Cocke, M.E. Hopkins and P.W. Markstein [1981]. *Register Allocation via coloring*. Computer Languages, 6, pp. 47–57.

Chaitin, G.J. [1982]. *Register Allocation and Spilling via Graph Coloring*, in *Proceedings of the ACM SIGPlan '82 Symposium on Compiler Construction*, Boston, Massachusetts: June, pp. 98–105.

Chamberlin, D.D., J.N. Gray, and I.L. Traiger [1975]. *Views, Authorization, and Locking in a Relational Data Base System*, in *AFIPS Conference Proceedings*, AFIPS. Anaheim, California, pp. 425–430.

Chang, A.M. [1985]. *A Lex Tutorial*. SoftLab Document 19. Computer Science Department, University of North Carolina at Chapel Hill, December.

Chou, F.C. and M. Ganapathi [1983]. *Intermediate Languages in Compiler Construction—A Bibliography*. ACM SIGPlan Notices, 18, No. 11, November, pp. 21–23.

Clarke, L.A., J.C. Wileden, and A.L. Wolf [1986]. *Graphite: A Meta-Tool For Ada Environment Development*, in *Proceedings of the International Conference on Ada Applications and Environments*, Miami Beach, Florida, IEEE Computer Society Press, April, pp. 81–90.

Clemm, G.M. [1986]. *The Odin System: An Object Manager for Extensible Software Environments*. Ph.D. Dissertation. CU-CS-314-86. Department of Computer Science, University of Colorado at Boulder, February.

Cockshott, W.P., M.P. Atkinson, K.J. Chisholm, P. Bailey and R. Morrison [1984]. *Persistent Object Management Systems*. Software–Practice and Experience, 14, pp. 49–71.

Conradi, R., T.M. Didriksen, and A. Lie [1986]. *IDL as a Data Description Language for a Programming Environment Database*. EPOS 15. Division of Computer Science, University of Trondheim, Norway, July.

BIBLIOGRAPHY

Cook, R.E. [1988]. *A Tool for Viewing IDL Data Structures.* Master's Thesis. Computer Science Department, University of North Carolina at Chapel Hill, April.

Cox, B.J. [1986]. *Object-oriented Programming: An Evolutionary Approach.* Reading, Massachusetts: Addison-Wesley Publishing Company.

Curry, G., L. Baer, D. Lipkie, and B. Lee [1982]. *Traits: An Approach to Multiple Inheritance Subclassing*, in *Proceedings of the ACM-SIGOA Conference on Office Automation Systems*, June.

Dausmann, M., S. Drossopoulou, G.T. Goos, G. Persch, and G. Winterstein [1980]. *AIDA Introduction and User Manual.* Technical Report Nr. 38/80. Universitæt Karlsruhe, FRG.

DeRemer, F. and H.H. Kron [1976]. *Programming-in-the-Large vs. Programming-in-the-Small. IEEE Transactions on Software Engineering*, SE-2, No. 2, June, pp. 80–86.

DeSchon, A.L. [1986]. *A Survey of Data Representation Standards.* RFC-971. Information Sciences Institute, USC, Los Angeles, California, January.

Dixon, G.N. and S.K. Shrivastava [1987]. *Exploiting Type Inheritance Facilities to Implement Recoverability in Object Based Systems*, in *Proceedings of the Sixth Symposium on Reliability in Distributed Software and Database Systems*, IEEE. Williamsburgh, Virginia: March.

Feiler, P.H. and G.E. Kaiser [1983]. *Display-Oriented Structure Manipulation in a Multi-Purpose System*, in *CompSac Fall '83*, IEEE.

Feiler, P.H., F. Jalili, and J.H. Schlichter [1986]. *An Interactive Prototyping Environment for Language Design*, in *Proceedings of the Hawaii International Conference on System Sciences-19*, January.

Feiler, P.H. [1987]. *Relationship between IDL and Structure Editor Generation Technology. ACM SIGPlan Notices*, 22, No. 11, November, pp. 87–95.

Fischer, C.N. and R.J. LeBlanc, Jr. [1988]. *Crafting a Compiler.* Menlo Park, California: Benjamin/Cummings Publishing Company.

Frailey, D.J. [1979]. *An Intermediate Language For Source and Target Independent Code Optimization.* ACM SIGPlan Notices, 14, No. 8, August, pp. 188–198.

Ganapathi, M., C.N. Fischer, S.J. Scalpone, and K.C. Thompson [1981]. *Linear Intermediate Representation for Portable Code Generation.* Computer Science Technical Report 435. University of Wisconsin at Madison, September.

Garlan, D.B. [1986]. *Views for Tools in Integrated Environments*, in *Advanced Programming Environments, Proceedings of an International Workshop*, Ed. T.M. Didriksen, R. Conradi, D.H. Wanvik. Lecture Notes in Computer Science. Trondheim, Norway: Springer-Verlag, June, pp. 314–343.

Garlan, D.B. [1987a]. *Views for Tools in Integrated Environments.* Ph.D. Dissertation. Technical Report CMU-CS-87-147. Computer Science Department, Carnegie Mellon University, Pittsburgh, Pennsylvania, May.

Garlan, D.B. [1987b]. *Extending IDL to Support Concurrent Views.* ACM SIGPlan Notices, 22, No. 11, November, pp. 95–107.

Gersting, J., K. Kinsley, N. McDonald, J. North, M. Sastry and E. Stull [1988]. *Reference Model for DBMS User Facility.* SIGMod Record, 17, No. 2, June, pp. 23–52.

Giannini, P. [1986]. *A Formal Semantics for IDL.* Technical Report CMU-CS-86-150. Department of Computer Science, Carnegie Mellon University, Pittsburgh, Pennsylvania, September.

Gilman, A.S. [1986]. *VHDL—The Designer Environment.* IEEE Design and Test, 3, No. 2, April, pp. 42–47.

Goldberg, A.J. and D. Robson [1983]. *Smalltalk-80: The Language and its Implementation.* Reading, Massachusetts: Addison-Wesley Publishing Company.

Goos, G.T. and W.A. Wulf [1981]. *Diana Reference Manual.* Technical Report CMU-CS-81-101. Computer Science Department, Carnegie Mellon University, Pittsburgh, Pennsylvania, March.

Goos, G.T., W.A. Wulf, A. Evans, Jr. and K.J. Butler [1983]. *DIANA An Intermediate Language for Ada*. Vol. 161 of Lecture Notes in Computer Science. Heidelberg, FRG: Springer-Verlag.

Gutknecht, J. [1986]. *Separate Compilation in Modula-2: An Approach to Efficient Symbol Files*. Software, 3, No. 6, November, pp. 29–38.

Gutknecht, J. [1987]. *Compilation of Data Structures: An New Approach to Efficient Modula-2 Symbol Files*. Technical Report. Institut fur Informatik, ETH, Zurich, Switzerland.

Harbison, S.P. and G.L. Steele, Jr. [1987]. *C: A Reference Manual*. Software Series. Englewood Cliffs, New Jersey: Prentice-Hall.

Harrison, M.P. [1983]. *DIANETTE—A Pragmatic Variant of DIANA*, in *Lectures Notes in Computer Science Ada Software Tools Interfaces*, Ed. G.T. Goos and J. Hartmanis. Workshop, Bath, England: Springer-Verlag, pp. 48–59.

Herlihy, M.P. and B.H. Liskov [1982]. *A Value Transmission Method for Abstract Data Types*. ACM Transactions on Programming Languages and Systems, 4, No. 4, October, pp. 527–551.

Holt, R.C. [1987]. *Data Descriptors: A Compile-Time Model of Data and Addressing*. ACM Transactions on Programming Languages and Systems, 9, No. 3, July, pp. 367–389.

Howell, C.C., D.H. Gill, A. Harrison, D.S. Hough, T.S. Reed, and T.J. Smith [1988]. *An Ada Interface to DIANA for Inter-Tool Communication*, in *Proceedings of the Washington Ada Symposium*, Washington, DC Chapter of the ACM, June, pp. 19–23.

Intermetrics, Inc. [1980]. *Intermetrics LS system description*. Technical Report IR 536. Cambridge, Massachusetts, August.

Intermetrics, Inc. [1981]. *Draft computer program development specification for the Ada integrated environment: Program integration facilities*. Technical Report IR 681. Cambridge, Massachusetts, March.

Intermetrics, Inc. [1985]. *IDL Primer*. Technical Report IR-MD-071. Bethesda, Maryland, May.

Jensen, K. and N.E. Wirth [1974]. *Pascal User Manual and Report*. Heidelberg, FRG: Springer-Verlag.

Johnson, S.C. [1975]. *Yacc—Yet Another Compiler-Compiler*. Computer Science Technical Report No. 32. Bell Laboratories, New Jersey, July.

Jones, D.W. [1988]. *How (Not) to Code a Finite State Machine*. ACM SIGPlan Notices, 23, No. 8, August, pp. 19–22.

Jones, M.B. and R.F. Rashid [1986]. *Mach and Matchmaker: Kernel and Language Support for Object-Oriented Distributed Systems*, in *Proceedings of the Conference on Object-Oriented Programming Systems, Languages and Applications*, Ed. N. Meyrowitz. Association for Computing Machinery. Portland, Oregon: IEEE, November, pp. 67–77.

Kaiser, G.E. and P.H. Feiler [1982]. *Generation of Language-Oriented Editors*. Technical Report. Siemens Corporate Research and Support, Inc., Princeton, New Jersey, August.

Karp, R.M. [1972]. *Reducibility Among Combinatorial Problems*, in Complexity of Computer Computations. New York: Plenum Press, pp. 85–103.

Kastens, U., B. Hutt and E. Zimmermann [1982]. *GAG: A Practical Compiler Generator*. Vol. 141 of Lecture Notes in Computer Science. Heidelberg, FRG: Springer-Verlag.

Kernighan, B.W. and D.M. Ritchie [1988]. *The C Programming Language*. Second edition. Software Series. Englewood Cliffs, New Jersey: Prentice Hall.

Kirchgässner, W., G. Persch, and J. Uhl [1987]. *Structural Analysis of Large Ada Systems*, in *Proceedings of the Ada-Europe International Conference*, Stockholm, Sweden, May, reprinted in *Ada Components: Libraries and Tools*, S. Tafvelin, editor. Paris: Cambridge University Press, pp. 170–180.

Knuth, D.E. [1968]. *Semantics of Context-Free Languages*, in *Mathematical Systems Theory*. New York: Springer-Verlag. Vol. 2. pp. 127–145.

Knuth, D.E. [1973]. *Fundamental Algorithms*. Vol. 1, Second Edition. Reading, Massachusetts: Addison-Wesley Publishing Company.

Krogdahl, S. [1984]. *An Efficient Implementation of Simula Classes with Multiple Prefixing*. Research Report No. 83. ISBN 82-90230-82-6. Institute of Informatics, University of Oslo, June.

Lamb, D.A. [1983]. *Sharing Intermediate Representations: The Interface Description Language*. Ph.D. Dissertation. Computer Science Department, Carnegie Mellon University, Pittsburgh, Pennsylvania, May.

Lamb, D.A. [1986]. *Adding Map Types to IDL*. Technical Report. Department of Computing and Information Science, Queen's University, Kingston, Ontario, May.

Lamb, D.A. [1987a]. *Generating Interface Packages, Readers and Writers from IDL Descriptions*. Technical Report 87-190. Department of Computing and Information Science, Queen's University, Kingston, Ontario, April.

Lamb, D.A. [1987b]. *IDL: Sharing Intermediate Representations*. ACM Transactions on Programming Languages and Systems, 9, No. 3, July, pp. 297–318.

Lamb, D.A. [1987c]. *Using Graph Deltas to Implement Programming Support Libraries*. Technical Report 87-197. Department of Computing and Information Science, Queen's University, Kingston, Ontario, August.

Lamb, D.A. [1987d]. *Implementation Strategies for DIANA Attributes*. ACM SIGPlan Notices, 22, No. 11, November, pp. 44–54.

Lamb, D.A. [1988]. *Revising DIANA '83*. External Technical Report ISSN-0836-0227-88-239. Department of Computing and Information Science, Queen's University, Kingston, Ontario, November.

Lamb, D.A. and R. Dawes [1988]. *Testing for Class Membership in Multi-Parent Hierarchies*. Information Processing Letters, 28, No. 1, May, pp. 21–25.

Lamport, L. [1986]. *LaTeX User's Guide and Reference Manual*. Reading, Massachusetts: Addison-Wesley Publishing Company.

Lerche, R.A. [1986]. Letter to the Editor. *SIGPlan Notices*, 23, No. 12, December, pp. 12–13.

Lesk, M.E. [1975]. *Lex—A Lexical Analyzer Generator*. Computer Science Technical Report No. 39. Bell Laboratories, New Jersey, October.

Leverett, B.W., R.G.G. Cattell, S.O. Hobbs, J.M. Newcomer, A.H. Reiner, B.R. Schatz, and W.A. Wulf [1980]. *An Overview of the Production Quality Compiler-Compiler Project*. IEEE Computer, 13, No. 8, August, pp. 38–49.

Leverett, B.W. [1982]. *Topics in Code Generation and Register Allocation*. Technical Report CMU-CS-82-130. Computer Science Department, Carnegie Mellon University, Pittsburgh, Pennsylvania, July.

Lewi, J., K. De Vlaminck, J. Huens, and M. Huybrechts [1979a]. *A Programming Methodology in Compiler Construction, Part 1: Concepts*. New York, New York: North-Holland Publishing Co.

Lewi, J., K. De Vlaminck, J. Huens, and M. Huybrechts [1979b]. *A Programming Methodology in Compiler Construction, Part 2: Implementation*. New York, New York: North-Holland Publishing Co.

Lie, A. [1984]. *An IDL Based Structure Editor*. Master's Thesis. Division of Computer Science, University of Trondheim, Norway, December.

Luckham, D.C., R. Neff, and D.S. Rosenblum [1987]. *An Environment for Ada Software Development Based on Formal Specification*. Ada Letters, VII, No. 3, May, pp. 94–106.

Maier, D., J.H. Stein, A.N. Otis, and A. Purdy [1986]. *Development of an Object-Oriented DBMS*, in *First Annual Conference On Object-Oriented Programming Systems, Languages and Applications*, Association for Computing Machinery. Portland, Oregon: September, pp. 472–482.

McKinley, K.L. and C.F. Schaefer [1986]. *Diana Reference Manual, Draft Revision 4*. Technical Report IR-MD-078. Intermetrics, Inc., Bethesda, Maryland, May.

Mark, L. and N. Roussopoulos [1987]. *Information Interchange between Self-Describing Databases. Data Engineering*, 10, No. 3, September, pp. 46–52.

Marshall, H.F. [1982]. *The Linear Graph Package, A Compiler Building Environment. ACM SIGPlan Notices*, 17, No. 6, June, pp. 294–300.

Meyer, B. [1988]. *Object-oriented Software Construction.* New York, New York: Prentice Hall.

Mitchell, J.G., W.J. Maybury, and R.E. Sweet [1979]. *Mesa Language Manual Version 5.0.* Technical Report CSL-79-3. Xerox Palo Alto Research Center, Palo Alto, California, April.

Morgan, C.R. [1987]. *Introduction*, in *ACM SIGPlan Notices Special Issue on the Interface Description Language*, 22, No. 11, November, pp. 1–3.

Moss, J.E.B. and S. Sinofsky [1988]. *Managing Persistent Data with Mneme: Designing a Reliable, Shared Object Interface*, in *Proceedings of the Second International Workshop on Object Oriented Data Bases.* Germany: September.

Narayanaswamy, K. and W.S. Scacchi [1987]. *A Database Foundation to Support Software System Evolution. Journal of Systems & Software*, 7, No. 1, pp. 37–49.

Nestor, J.R. and M.A. Beard [1981]. *Front End Generator System*, in Computer Science Research Review. Pittsburgh, Pennsylvania: Carnegie Mellon University, pp. 75–92.

Nestor, J.R., W.A. Wulf, and D.A. Lamb [1981]. *IDL—Interface Description Language, Revision 1.0.* Technical Report CMU-CS-81-139. Computer Science Department, Carnegie Mellon University, Pittsburgh, Pennsylvania, August.

Nestor, J.R., W.A. Wulf, and D.A. Lamb [1982]. *IDL—Interface Description Language—Formal Description—Draft Revision 2.0.* Internal Document. Computer Science Department, Carnegie Mellon University, Pittsburgh, Pennsylvania, June.

Nestor, J.R., B. Mishra, W.L. Scherlis, and W.A. Wulf [1983]. *Extensions to Attribute Grammars.* TL 83-36. Tartan Laboratories, Inc., Pittsburgh, Pennsylvania, April.

Nestor, J.R., J.M. Newcomer, P. Giannini, and D.L. Stone [1989]. *IDL: The Language and Its Implementation.* Englewood Cliffs, New Jersey: Prentice-Hall (in press).

Newcomer, J.M., R.G.G. Cattell, D.L. Dill, P.N. Hilfinger, S.O. Hobbs, B.W. Leverett, A.H Reiner, B.R. Schatz, and W.A. Wulf [1980]. *PQCC Implementor's Handbook.* Department of Computer Science, Carnegie Mellon University, Pittsburgh, Pennsylvania.

Newcomer, J.M. [1986]. *IDL: Past Experience and New Ideas,* in *Proceedings of the International Workshop on Advanced Programming Environments,* IFIP WG 2.4. Trondheim, Norway: June.

Newcomer, J.M. [1987a]. *Tool Interface Technology.* Technical Report SEI-87-TR-7-ESD-TR-87-108. Software Engineering Institute, Carnegie Mellon University, Pittsburgh, Pennsylvania, March.

Newcomer, J.M. [1987b]. *Efficient Binary I/O of IDL Objects. ACM SIGPlan Notices,* 22, No. 11, November, pp. 35-43.

Notkin, D.S., A.P. Black, E.D. Lazowska, H.M. Levy, J.O. Sanislo, and J. Zahorjan [1988]. *Interconnecting Heterogeneous Computer Systems. Communications of the ACM,* 31, No. 3, March, pp. 258-273.

Ottenstein, K.J. [1984]. *Intermediate Program Representations in Compiler Construction: A Supplemental Bibliography. ACM SIGPlan Notices,* 19, No. 7, July, pp. 25-27.

Park, J.C.H. [1988]. *y+: A Yacc Preprocessor for Certain Semantic Actions. ACM SIGPlan Notices,* 23, No. 6, June, pp. 97-106.

Payton, T.F., S.E. Keller, J.M. Perkins, and S.P. Mardinly [1983]. *The DIANA Interfacer,* in *Lecture Notes in Computer Science Ada Software Tools Interfaces,* Ed. G.T. Goos and J. Hartmanis. Workshop, Bath, England: Springer-Verlag, pp. 88-103.

Persch, G., G. Winterstein, M. Dausmann, S. Drossopoulou, and G.T. Goos [1980]. *AIDA Reference Manual.* Technical Report Nr. 39/80. Universitæt Karlsruhe, FRG, November.

Persch, G. [1983]. *The Use of Diana in Compilers, Language Transformers, Formatters, and Debuggers,* in *Lecture Notes in Computer Science Ada Software Tools Interfaces,* Ed. G.T. Goos and J. Hartmanis. Workshop, Bath, England: Springer-Verlag, pp. 76–87.

Persch, G. and M. Dausmann [1983]. *The Intermediate Language Diana: Design and Implementation,* in *Lecture Notes in Computer Science Ada Software Tools Interfaces,* Ed. G.T. Goos and J. Hartmanis. Workshop, Bath, England: Springer-Verlag, pp. 23–34.

Persch, G. [1987]. *Editing IDL Data Structures. ACM SIGPlan Notices,* 22, No. 11, November, pp. 79–86.

Purtilo, J.M. [1985]. *Polylith: An Environment to Support Management of Tool Interfaces,* in *Proceedings of the ACM SIGPlan '85 Symposium on Language Issues in Programming Environments,* Seattle, Washington: July, pp. 12–18.

Purtilo, J.M. [1986]. *A Software Interconnection Technology to Support Specification of Computational Environments.* Ph.D. Dissertation. Department of Computer Science, University of Illinois at Urbana-Champaign, September.

Quinn, M.E. [1982]. *The Ada Breadboard Compiler: The DIANA Package.* Technical Report. Bell Laboratories, New Jersey.

Reiss, S.P. [1984]. *An Approach to Incremental Compilation. ACM SIGPlan Notices,* 19, No. 6, June, pp. 144–156.

Reiss, S.P. [1985]. *PLUM—A Data Management Package.* Technical Report. Department of Computer Science, Brown University, Providence, Rhode Island, April.

Reps, T.W. and T. Teitelbaum [1987]. *Language Processing in Program Editors. IEEE Computer,* 20, No. 11, November, pp. 29–40.

Rosenblum, D.S. [1985]. *A Methodology for the Design of Ada Transformation Tools in an DIANA Environment. IEEE Software*, 2, No. 2, March, pp. 24–33.

Roubine, O. and J. Teller [1982]. *LOLITA—A Low Level Intermediate Language for Ada*, in *Proceedings of the AdaTEC Conference on Ada*, Arlington, Virginia: ACM, October, pp. 251–260.

Rovner, P.D., R. Levin, and J. Wick [1985]. *On Extending Modula-2 for Building Large, Integrated Systems*. Technical Report 3. Digital Systems Research Center, Palo Alto, California, January.

Rubin, L.F. [1983]. *Syntax-directed Pretty Printing—A First Step Towards a Syntax-Directed Editor. IEEE Transactions on Software Engineering*, SE-9, No. 2, March, pp. 119–127.

Sankar, S., D.S. Rosenblum, and R.B. Neff [1985]. *An Implementation of Anna*, in *Proceedings of the Ada International Conference on Ada in Use*, Ed. J.G.P. Barnes and G.A. Fisher, Jr. Association for Computing Machinery. Paris: Cambridge University Press, May, pp. 285–296.

Schmidt, J. [1977]. *Some High Level Language Constructs for Data of Type Relation. ACM Transactions on Database Systems*, 2, No. 3, September, pp. 247–261.

Shahdad, M., R. Lipsett, F.E. Marschner, K.C. Sheehan, H. Cohen, R. Waxman and D. Ackley [1985]. *VHSIC Hardware Description Language. IEEE Computer*, 18, No. 2, February, pp. 94–103.

Shannon, K.P. and R.T. Snodgrass [1986]. *Mapping the Interface Description Language Type Model into C*. SoftLab Document 25. Computer Science Department, University of North Carolina at Chapel Hill, March.

Simpson, R.T. [1982]. *The ALS ADA Compiler Front End Architecture*, in *Proceedings of the Ada TEC Conference on Ada*, Association for Computing Machinery. Arlington, Virginia: October, pp. 98–106.

Smith, T.J., D.H. Gill, A. Harrison, D.S. Hough, C.C. Howell and T.J. Reed [1988]. *A Standard Interface to Programming Environment Information*, in *Proceedings of the 1988 Ada-Europe International Conference*,

Munich. Cambridge, England: Cambridge University Press, June, pp. 251–262.

Snodgrass, R.T. and K.P. Shannon [1986]. *Supporting Flexible and Efficient Tool Integration*, in *Proceedings of the International Workshop on Advanced Programming Environments*, IFIP WG 2.4. Trondheim, Norway: Springer-Verlag, June, pp. 290–313.

Snodgrass, R.T. [1987]. *Displaying IDL Instances. ACM SIGPlan Notices*, 22, No. 11, November, pp. 10–17.

Snodgrass, R.T. and K.P. Shannon [1988]. *Type Extension in IDL*. Soft-Lab Document 37. Computer Science Department, University of North Carolina at Chapel Hill, December.

SofTech Microsystems, Inc. [1981]. *UCSD p-System Internal Architecture Guide*. Version IV.0 edition. San Diego, California.

Stone, D.L. and J.R. Nestor [1987]. *IDL: Background and Status. ACM SIGPlan Notices*, 22, No. 11, November, pp. 5–9.

Stonebraker, M. and L.A. Rowe [1984]. *Database Portals: A New Application Program Interface*, in *Proceedings of the Conference on Very Large Databases*, Singapore: ACM, August.

Stroustrup, B. [1986]. *The C++ Programming Language*. Reading, Massachusetts: Addison-Wesley Publishing Company.

Sun Microsystems, Inc. [1987]. *External Data Representation Standard, Version 2*. RFC-1014. Mountain View, California, June.

Sun Microsystems, Inc. [1988]. *Remote Procedure Call Protocol Specification, Version 2*. RFC-1057. Mountain View, California, June.

Taft, S.T. [1982]. *DIANA as an Internal Representation in an ADA-IN-ADA Compiler*, in *Proceedings of the Ada TEC Conference on Ada*, Association for Computing Machinery. Arlington, Virginia: October, pp. 261–265.

Tennent, R.D. [1981]. *Principles of Programming Languages*. Series in Computer Science. London, England: Prentice-Hall International.

Terwilliger, R.B. and R.H. Campbell [1988]. *PLEASE: Executable Specifications for Incremental Software Development.* Journal of Systems and Software (to appear).

Thorvaldsdottir, H. [1985]. *A yacc Tutorial.* SoftLab Document 12. Computer Science Department, University of North Carolina at Chapel Hill, August.

Tichy, W.F. [1979]. *Software Development Control Based on Module Interconnection,* in *Proceedings of the Fourth International Conference on Software Engineering,* Munich, West Germany: September, pp. 29–41.

Uhl, J. [1983]. *A Formal Definition of DIANA,* in *Lecture Notes in Computer Science Ada Software Tools Interfaces,* Ed. G.T. Goos and J. Hartmanis. Workshop, Bath, England: Springer-Verlag, pp. 35–47.

Ullman, J.D. [1982]. *Principles of Database Systems, Second Edition.* Potomac, Maryland: Computer Science Press.

Varadarajan, S. [1988]. *Using IDL in a Heterogeneous Environment.* Master's Thesis. Computer Science Department, University of North Carolina at Chapel Hill, August.

Waite, W.M. and G.T. Goos [1984]. *Compiler Construction.* New York: Springer-Verlag.

Warren, W.B., J.S. Kickenson, and R.T. Snodgrass [1987]. *A Tutorial Introduction to Using IDL. ACM SIGPlan Notices,* 22, No. 11, November, pp. 18–34.

Wasserman, A. [1979]. *The Data Management Facilities of PLAIN,* in *Proceedings of ACM SIGMod International Conference on Management of Data.* Boston, Massachusetts: June, pp. 60–70.

Wetherell, C.S. [1982]. *The Ada Breadboard Compiler: An Overview.* Technical Report. Bell Laboratories, New Jersey.

Wilcox, T.R. [1971]. *Generating Machine Code for High-Level Programming Languages.* Ph.D. Dissertation. Computer Science Department, Cornell University, Ithaca, New York.

Wileden, J.C., A.L. Wolf, C.D. Fisher, and P.L. Tarr [1988]. *PGRAPHITE: An Experiment in Persistent Typed Object Management*, in *Proceedings of the Third Symposium on Software Development Environments*, Boston, Massachusetts: November, pp. 130-142.

Wirth, N.E. [1983]. *Programming in Modula-2, 2nd Edition*. Texts and Monographs in Computer Science. New York, New York: Springer-Verlag.

Wirth, N.E. [1987]. *From Modula to Oberon and The Programming Language Oberon*. Technical Report 82. Institut fur Informatik, ETH, Zurich, Switzerland, September.

Wirth, N.E. [1988]. *Type Extensions*. ACM Transactions on Programming Languages and Systems, 10, No. 2, April, pp. 204–214.

Wolf, A.L., L.A. Clarke, and J.C. Wileden [1985]. *Ada-Based Support for Programming-in-the-Large*. IEEE Software, 2, No. 2, March, pp. 58–71.

Wolf, A.L., L.A. Clarke, and J.C. Wileden [1989]. *The AdaPIC Toolset: Supporting Interface Control and Analysis Throughout the Software Development Process*, IEEE Transactions on Software Engineering, SE-14, No. 3, March.

Wolfe, M.I. [1981]. *The Ada Language System*. IEEE Computer, 14, No. 6, June, pp. 37–45.

Wulf, W.A., D.B. Russell, and A.N. Habermann [1971]. *Bliss: A Language for System Programming*. Communications of the ACM, 14, December, pp. 780–790.

Wulf, W.A. [1980]. *PQCC: A Machine-Relative Compiler Technology*. Technical Report CMU-CS-80-144. Department of Computer Science, Carnegie Mellon University, Pittsburgh, Pennsylvania, September.

Wulf, W.A., R. Levin, and S.P. Harbison [1981]. *Hydra/C.mmp: An Experimental Computer System*. New York, New York: McGraw-Hill Book Company.

Zorn, B.G. [1985]. *Experiences with Ada Code Generation*. Technical Report UCB/CSD 85/249. University of California, Berkeley, June.

Author Index

Page numbers associated with secondary authors indicate where their article was referenced.

A

Ackley, David, 14, 367, 586
Aho, Alfred V., 15, 102, 228, 254, 310, 420, 573
Allman, Eric P., 127, 573
Ambler, Arol, 420, 573
Appelbe, Bill F., 367, 573
Archer, James E., Jr., 14, 574
Atkinson, Malcolm P., 127, 144, 574, 576
Auslander, Marc A., 420, 576
Avakian, A., 14, 125, 144, 574

B

Baer, L., 69, 577
Bailey, Peter J., 127, 576
Barstow, David R., 14, 574
Beard, Margaret Anne, 14, 583
Bershad, Brian N., 15, 574
Besson, M., 367, 574
Birrell, Andrew D., 15, 144, 574
Birtwistle, Graham M., 69, 575
Biyani, Vikram, xv, 144, 171, 575
Black, Andrew P., 15, 584
Bobrow, Daniel Gureasko, 69, 575
Borning, Alan H., 69, 575
Bratman, Harvey, 420, 575
Breguet, P., 196, 575
Brosgol, Benjamin M., 125, 575
Buneman, O. Peter, 127

Butler, Kenneth Jennings, 14, 125, 170, 171, 367, 382, 575, 579

C

Cameron, Robert D., 382, 576
Campbell, Roy H., 139, 588
Cattell, Roderic Gregory G., 125, 144, 170, 582, 584
Chaitin, Gregory John, 420, 576
Chamberlin, Donald D., 127, 576
Chandra, Ashok Kumar, 420, 576
Chang, Allen Mi, 420, 576
Ching, D. T., 15, 574
Chisholm, K. J., 127, 574, 576
Chou, Frederick C., 102, 576
Clarke, Lori Ann, 14, 126, 171, 576, 589
Clemm, Geoffrey M., 576
Cocke, John, 420, 576
Cockshott, W. P., 127, 574, 576
Cohen, H., 14, 367, 586
Conradi, Reidar, 15, 576
Cook, Ralph Ellsworth, xv, 367, 577
Cox, Brad J., 69, 144, 577
Curry, G., 69, 577

D

Dahl, Ole-Johan, 69, 575

AUTHOR INDEX

Dausmann, Manfred, 125, 577, 585
Dawes, Robin W., 171, 581
De Vlaminck, Karel, 138, 582
DeRemer, Frank, 14, 577
DeSchon, Annette L., 144, 577
Devlin, Michael T., 14, 574
Didriksen, Tor M., 15, 576
Dill, David L., 125, 144, 170, 584
Dismukes, Gary J., 367, 573
Dixon, G. N., 127, 577
Drossopoulou, Sophia, 125, 577, 585

E

Evans, Arthur, Jr., xv, 170, 171, 367, 382, 575, 579

F

Feiler, Peter Hermann, 15, 367, 577, 580
Fischer, Charles N., 102, 228, 254, 577, 578
Fisher, Charles D., 127, 589
Frailey, Dennis J., 102, 578

G

Ganapathi, Mahadevan, 102, 576, 578
Garlan, David B., 127, 578
Gersting, Judith L., 127, 578
Giannini, Paola, 14, 15, 126, 171, 228, 367, 467, 578, 584
Gill, Dorothy Helen, xv, 14, 144, 171, 367, 579, 586
Gilman, Alfred S., 14, 367, 578
Goldberg, Adele J., 69, 144, 578
Goos, Gerhard T., 14, 102, 125, 126, 170, 171, 228, 367, 577–579, 585, 588
Gray, Jim N., 127, 576
Grize, Francois, 196, 575
Gutknecht, J., 144, 579

H

Habermann, A. Nico, 125, 589
Harandhvala, Sam G., 14, 125, 144, 574
Harbison, Samuel P., 144, 170, 255, 302, 579, 589
Harrison, Annelle, 14, 144, 171, 367, 579, 586
Harrison, M. P., 14, 579
Held, Gerard, 127, 573
Herlihy, Maurice Peter, 144, 579
Hilfinger, Paul N., 125, 144, 170, 584
Hobbs, Steven O., 125, 144, 170, 582, 584
Holt, Richard C., 366, 579
Hopcroft, John E., 420, 573
Hopkins, Martin E., 420, 576
Horn, J., 14, 125, 144, 574
Hough, David S., 14, 144, 171, 367, 579, 586
Howell, Charles Clement, xv, 14, 144, 171, 367, 579, 586
Huens, Jean, 138, 582
Hutt, Brigitte, 138, 580
Huybrechts, Michel, 138, 582

I

Ingalls, Daniel Henry Holmes, 69, 575

J

Jalili, Fahimeh, 127, 577
Jensen, Kathleen, 196, 580
Johnson, Stephen Curtis, 420, 580
Jones, Douglas W., 229, 580
Jones, Michael B., 15, 144, 574, 580

K

Kaiser, Gail E., 127, 367, 577, 580
Karp, Richard Manning, 420, 580

Kastens, Uwe, 138, 580
Keller, Steven E., 138, 584
Kernighan, Brian W., 170, 255, 277, 580
Kickenson, Jerry Scott, xiii, 70, 588
Kinsley, Katheryn C., 127, 578
Kirchgässner, Walter, 14, 580
Knobe, Bruce, 14, 125, 144, 574
Knuth, Donald Ervin, 138, 420, 580, 581
Krogdahl, Stein, 69, 581
Kron, H. H., 14, 577

L

Lamb, David Alex, xiv, 14, 15, 70, 125, 126, 144, 170, 171, 196, 277, 310, 366, 367, 420, 434, 440, 467, 575, 581, 583
Lamport, Leslie, 382, 581
Lazowska, Edward D., 15, 574, 584
LeBlanc, Richard Joseph, Jr., 228, 254, 577
Lee, B., 69, 577
Lerche, Robert A., 229, 582
Lesk, Michael E., 420, 582
Leverett, Bruce W., 14, 125, 144, 170, 582, 584
Levin, Roy, 139, 144, 196, 586, 589
Levine, David A., 125, 575
Levy, Henry M., 15, 584
Lewi, Johan, 138, 582
Lie, Anund, xv, 15, 69, 144, 171, 196, 367, 382, 576, 582
Lipkie, Daniel E., 69, 577
Lipsett, Roger, 14, 367, 586
Liskov, Barbara H., 144, 579
Luckham, David C., 14, 367, 582

M

Maier, David, 127, 582
Mardinly, Susan P., 138, 584
Mark, L., 367, 583
Markstein, P. W., 420
Maroney, Thomas, xiv
Marschner, F. Erich, 14, 367, 586
Marshall, H. F., 125, 583
Maybury, William J., 14, 583
McDonald, Nancy H., 127, 578
McKinley, Kathryn L., 367, 582
Meyer, Bertrand, 69, 139, 144, 434, 583
Mishra, Bhubaneswar, 138, 584
Mitchell, James G., 14, 583
Morgan, C. Robert, 126, 583
Morrison, R., 127, 576
Moss, J. Eliot B., 127, 583
Myhrhaus, B., 69, 575

N

Narayanaswamy, K., 14, 583
Neff, Randall B., 14, 139, 367, 582, 586
Nelson, Bruce J., 15, 574
Nestor, John R., xiv, 14, 15, 70, 126, 138, 170, 171, 228, 367, 440, 467, 583, 584, 587
Newcomer, Joseph M., xv, 14, 15, 125, 126, 144, 170, 171, 228, 367, 467, 575, 582, 584
North, J., 127, 578
Notkin, David S., 15, 584
Nygaard, Kristen, 69, 575

O

Otis, Arthur N., 127, 582
Ottenstein, Karl J., 102, 584

P

Park, Joseph C. H., 228, 584
Payton, Teri F., 138, 584
Perkins, J. Michael, 138, 584
Persch, Guido, 14, 15, 125, 382, 577, 580, 585
Purdy, A., 127, 582
Purtilo, James M., 14, 585

Q

Queyras, B., 367, 574
Quinn, Margaret E., 14, 171, 585

R

Rashid, Richard F., 15, 580
Reed, Teresa S., 14, 144, 171, 367, 579, 586
Reiner, Andrew H., 125, 144, 170, 582, 584
Reiss, Steven Peter, 171, 585
Reps, Thomas Williams, 15, 585
Ritchie, Dennis M., 170, 255, 277, 580
Robson, David, 69, 144, 578
Rosenblum, David S., 14, 139, 367, 582, 586
Roubine, Olivier, 367, 586
Roussopoulos, Nicholas, 367, 583
Rovner, Paul David, 139, 196, 586
Rowe, Lawrence A., 127, 587
Rubin, Lisa F., 382, 586
Russell, D. B., 125, 589

S

Sandewall, Erik, 14, 574
Sanislo, Jan O., 15, 574, 584
Sankar, Sriram, 139, 586
Sastry, Mudi, 127, 578
Scacchi, Walter S., 14, 583
Scalpone, Stephen J., 102, 578
Schaefer, Carl F., 367, 582
Schatz, Bruce R., 125, 144, 170, 582, 584
Scherlis, William L., 138, 584
Schlichter, Johann H., 127, 577
Schmidt, Joachim, 127, 586
Schwartz, M., 15, 574
Sethi, Ravi, 15, 102, 228, 254, 310, 573
Shahdad, Moe, 14, 367, 586
Shannon, Karen Palermo, xiii, 127, 171, 228, 310, 586, 587
Shapiro, Michael Andrew, xiv
Sheehan, Kellye C., 14, 367, 586
Shrivastava, S. K., 127, 577
Shrobe, Howard E., 14, 574
Simpson, Richard T., 14, 586
Sinofsky, S., 127, 583
Smith, Thomas Jacob, 14, 144, 171, 367, 579, 586
Snodgrass, Richard Thomas, xiii, 15, 70, 127, 144, 171, 228, 310, 586–588
Steele, Guy L., Jr., 170, 255, 302, 579
Stein, Jacob H., 127, 582
Stone, Donald L., xv, 14, 15, 126, 171, 228, 367, 467, 584, 587
Stonebraker, Michael, 127, 573, 587
Strohmeier, Alfred, 196, 575
Stroustrup, Bjarne, 69, 587
Stull, Edward, 127, 578
Sweet, Richard E., 14, 583

T

Taft, S. Tucker, 171, 587
Tarr, Peri L., 127, 589
Teitelbaum, Tim, 15, 585
Teller, Joachim, 367, 586
Tennent, Richard D., 228, 587
Terwilliger, Robert B., 139, 588

Thompson, Keith C., 102, 578
Thorvaldsdottir, Helga, 420, 588
Throop, Dean Darwin, xiv
Tichy, Walter F., 14, 588
Traiger, Irving L., 127, 576
Trawick, Robert J., 420, 573

U

Uhl, Jürgen, 14, 139, 580, 588
Ullman, Jeffrey David, 15, 102, 127, 228, 254, 310, 420, 573, 588

V

Van Deusen, Mary S., 125, 575
Varadarajan, Sundar, xv, 15, 144, 588

W

Waite, William McCastline, 102, 588
Warren, William Bizzell, xiv, 70, 588
Wasserman, Anthony, 127, 588
Waxman, Ronald, 14, 367, 586
Wetherell, Charles S., 171, 588
Wick, John D., 139, 196, 586
Wilcox, Thomas R., 366, 588
Wileden, Jack C., 14, 126, 127, 171, 576, 589
Winterstein, Georg, 125, 577, 585
Wirth, Niklaus Emil, 14, 69, 127, 139, 171, 196, 197, 255, 580, 589
Wobber, Edward P., 144, 574
Wolf, Alexander Lee, 14, 126, 127, 171, 576, 589
Wolfe, Martin I., 14, 589
Wulf, William Allan, xiv, 14, 15, 70, 125, 138, 144, 170, 171, 228, 367, 440, 467, 578, 579, 582–584, 589

Z

Zahorjan, John, 15, 584
Zimmermann, Erich, 138, 580
Zorn, Benjamin G., 14, 589

Index

Page numbers in bold face (e.g., **123**) indicate where a technical term or feature is defined.

= operator, **132**
~= operator, **132**
~, *see* ASCII external representation language escape character

A

A (array) prefix, C, **469**
abstract data type, **4**, 5, 9, 98, 105, 106, 144, 171, 579
abstract modeling, **5**
abstract process specification, **106**
abstract specification, **20**, **106**
abstract structure specification, **106**, 123, *see also* structure, concrete specification
abstract syntax tree, 75, 77, 102, **199**
  creating, 207, 211, 212, 228
  example, 201, 316
  use in code generation, 422
action, **409**
active quantifier, **405**, 427
Ada Breadboard Compiler, 171, 585, 588
Ada Group Ltd., 14
Ada language, xi, 14, 22, 125, 126, 138, 171, 231, 255, 309, 367, 382, 439, 573–576, 579, 580, 582, 586, 587

Ada language, 589
  package, 98, 122, 171, 250, 382
addSET operation
  C, **484**
  Pascal, **498**
addSET routine
  C, **477**
  C example, 164
  Pascal, **492**
  Pascal example, 189
AIDA, 125, 577, 585
alignment
  analysis in IDLC, 329, 331, 332, 414
  attribute, 150, 178
  default, 332, 412
  in the prelude, 361
  private type, 113, 165, 191
    default, 411
    example, 453, 457
allocation, 6, 44, 50, 401, 453
  array, 161
  C, 169
  class, 171, *see also* class type, allocation
  data type, 161, 164, 187, 189, 477, 478, 493

597

allocation, *cont.*
  list cell
    C, 161, 164, 169, 477, 478
    Pascal, 187, 189, 492, 493
  Pascal, 195
  register, 420, 576, 582
allocation function, *see* node allocation routine for Pascal
allocation macro, *see* node allocation routine for C
ancestor process, 33, **437**
ancestor structure, **108**, 254, 357, 365, 402, **437**, 439
  analysis in IDLC, 394
  name resolution, 394
  not found, 352
  root, 466
And assertion operator, 36, **132**
  example, 36
  IDLCHECK instruction, **552**
  IDLCHECK instruction example, 423
And XRef operator, 263
Anna, 138, 367, 586
ANSI, 144, 573
appendfrontSEQ operation, 12, 362
  C, **484**
  example, 363
  Pascal, **497**
appendfrontSEQ routine
  C, **478**
  example, 161, 187
  Pascal, **493**
appendrearSEQ operation
  C, **484**
  Pascal, **497**
appendrearSEQ routine
  C, **479**
  example, 161, 187
  Pascal, **493**
application, 558, *see* definition application

applied occurrence, **228**
arbitrary collection, **408**
array representation, 160
  dynamic-sized fixed-storage, **160**
  sequence, 160
  set, 160
  size, 161
ASCII, 63, 143, 144, 561
  lexicographic ordering, 132, 275, 552
  string, 110, 132, 443, 448
ASCII ERL, **131**, **437**, *see also* ASCII external representation language
ASCII external representation, 453
  origin, 144
ASCII external representation language, 60, 63, 119, 141–144, 169, 195, **437**
  alternatives, 367
  escape character (~), 63, 110, 448
  example, 63, 64, 91, 97
  extension, 464, 465
  origin, 126
  use with IDLCHECK, 421
assertion, 4, 253, **437**
  example, 170, 283, 376, 563
  extension, 455
  in derivation, 114
  in process refinement, 121
  in process specification, 117
  in structure refinement, 115
  in the invariant, 118, 326
  in the prelude, 305, 309
  removing, 115, 395, 456
  two of the same name, 114
assertion checker, xi, xiii, 5, 101, 126, 303, 434, *see also* IDLCHECK
assertion failure log, 426, 430, 431

INDEX 599

assertion language, 101
    analysis in IDLC, 308, 398, 401, 404–408
    definition, 129–139
    example, 34–43, 79–84
    formal semantics, 126
    strong typing, 464, 466
atomic type, 391, **437**, 449, 454, 462
attribute, 5, 20, 63, **437**
    alignment, 150, 178
    conflict graph, **413**
    default finalization, 120
        C, 169, 484
        Pascal, 179, 195, 497
        Pascal example, 180
    default value, 178
    deletion, 152
    example, 22, 25, 75, 77
    finalization routine, 120, **437**
        C, 151, **152**, 157, 470
        Pascal, **179**, 486, 497
    indirect, 261, 272
    prefix, *see* `lex_`, `pre_`, `rep_`, `sem_`, `syn_`
    propagation, **437**
    representation, 147, **438**
    restriction, 24
        average size in CANDLE, 366
    syntax, 20, 25
attribute conflict, **413**
attribute initialization, *see* node type initialization routine
attribute production, **20**, 25, **437**
attributed node, **147**, **438**, *see also* node, attributed
attributed parse tree, 3, 295, *see also* attributed syntax tree

B

base process, **120**, **438**
base structure, **438**

basic type, **22**, 36, 45, 51, 63, 110, 167, 319, **438**, 443, 466
    in the prelude, 414
    `Boolean`, *see* boolean type
    `Integer`, *see* integer type
    `Rational`, *see* rational type
    `String`, *see* string type
Bell Laboratories, 14
binding occurrence, **228**
bitvector representation, 163, 483
boolean expression, 36
boolean type, 22, 45, 51, 110, 135, 146, 174, **438**, 563
    example, 25
    `False` literal, 146
    initial value, 120
    literal, 131
        analysis in XREF, 567
    operator, **132**, *see also* `And` operator, `Is` operator, `Not` operator, `Or` operator, `=` operator, `~=` operator
    representation, 146, 174
    `True` literal, 146
    XRef literal, 568
Britton-Lee, 127
Burroughs Corporation, 14

C

`C` (cell) prefix, C, **469**
C++ language, 69, 127, 587
`CA` (class attribute) prefix, C, **469**
CANDLE structure, 231, 311–367, 420, **438**, 535–548
    average node size, **366**
    use in CANDLEWALK, 369–382
    use in IDLCHECK, 421
    use in IDLC, 383–420
    use with IDLCHECK, 84
CANDLEWALK tool, xiii, 303, 366, 369–383, **438**

Case assertion operator, 81, **136**, 463
    example, 79, 288
    type checking in IDLC, 407
Case XRef statement, **274**
centralized symbol table, **246**, 254, **438**, 439
class, **23**, **109**, **438**
    example, 77
class inheritance, **438**
class production, **23**, **438**
class type
    alignment
        analysis in IDLC, 332
    allocation, 197
    allocation routine
        C, 155, 156
        Pascal, 183, 184
    as set type, 163
    attribute, 155, 181
    deallocation routine
        C, 155, 156
        Pascal, 184
    direct member, **439**
    enumerated, 124, 149, 236, 483
        analysis in IDLC, 329, 332, 358
        example, 149, 203, 236, 238
    example, 25
    hierarchy, 102, **438**
    indirect member, 29, 416, **440**
        assigning attributes, 25
    member, **23**
        direct, **24**
        indirect, **24**
    membership inheritance, 24, 87
    plain, **153**, **181**, **441**
        common attribute, 155, 181
        representation, 153, 181
    sharing, 167, 193

class type, *cont.*
    size
        analysis in IDLC, 332
    type information, 184
    typeof macro, **156**
    unattributed, 149, **153**, 156, **181**, **443**, 527
    enumerated representation, 562
    representation, 156, 181, 203
collection, **41**, 82, 131–137, 425–427, **438**, 441, 442, 466, 550, 551, 555
    empty, **42**, 131, 551, 558
    example, 41, 428
    iteration over a, 427
collection type, 37, 131, 135–137, 391, 407, **438**
    arbitrary, 408
    binary operators, **133**
        IDLCHECK instructions, **551**
    comparison operator, *see Same* operator
        IDLCHECK instruction, **554**
    example, 425
    IDL Version 2, 466
    IDL87, 466
    inclusion operator
        IDLCHECK instruction, **555**
    infix operator, 131, 132
        IDLCHECK instruction, **551**
    intersection operator, *see Intersect* operator
    prefix operation, **135**, **556**
    proper subset operator, *see PSub* operator
    singleton, **133**, **135**, 391, **443**
    subset operator, *see Sub* operator
    union operator, *see Union* operator

INDEX 601

collection-returning definition, *see* definition, returning a collection
comments, 234
    IDL, 35, 380, 447, 561
    in listing file, 350
    in CANDLE, 335
    placement, 367
    representation, 312, 317
    XRef, 268
CommonLoops language, 69, 70, 575
concrete specification, **106**, *see also* abstract specification
conflict graph
    example, 414
constant, *see* literal
`copySEQ` routine
    C, **479**
    example, 187
    Pascal, **494**
`copySET` operation
    C, **484**
    Pascal, **498**
`copySET` routine
    C, **477**
    C example, 164
    Pascal, **492**
    Pascal example, 189
`CP` (class pointer) prefix, C, 155, **470**
`CQ` (sequence cell) prefix, Pascal, **485**
create, *see also* node type allocation routine
`Create` operation, 120, 458, 459, 466
    C, **484**
    example, 150, 177, 342, 362, 364, 458, 459
    Pascal, **497**
`CT` (set cell) prefix, Pascal, **485**

cyclic application, *see* definition, cyclic application
cyclic definition, *see* definition, cyclic
cyclic identical call, **137**, 406, 407

D

`D` (deallocate) prefix
    C, 151, **470**
    Pascal, 179, **485**
data descriptor, **366**, 579
deallocation, 474
    class, *see* class type, deallocation
    data type, 161, 164, 187, 189, 477, 478, 493
    list cell
        C, 161, 164, 477, 478
        Pascal, 187, 189, 492, 493
    node, *see* node type deallocation routine, private type deallocation routine
    private type, *see* private type finalization routine
deallocation function, *see* node deallocation routine for Pascal
deallocation macro, *see* node deallocation routine for C
declaration, **77**
default
    alignment, 332, 412
        private type, 411
    external representation, **113**, 116, 453
        private type, 411
    finalization, *see* node type default finalization, private type default finalization routine
    in `Case` statement, 271, 274
    initialization, *see* node type default initialization

default, *cont.*
   integer
      size, 163
   integer type
      C, 111
   internal representation, **113**
   invariant structure, 316
   operations, 119, 120, 125, 330, 412, 459
      sequence, *see* sequence operations, default
      set, *see* set operations, default
   output format
      C, **169**
      Pascal, **195**
   representation, 358, 411
   Runtime Version
      C, **84**
      Pascal, **87**
   sequence representation
      C, **159**
      Pascal, **186**
   set type
      size, **163**
   site-specific, 143
   size, 332, 412, 453
   target, 118
   target language
      version, **145**, **173**
   type, 110
`DefaultFinalize` operation, 120
   C, **484**
   C example, 152
   example, 342
   Pascal, **497**
   Pascal example, 180
`DefaultInitialize` operation, 120
   C, **484**
   example, 150, 151, 178, 342
   Pascal, **497**

defining occurrence, **212**, 213, 218, 569
definition array, 423
definition point, 314, 345, 346, 404
definition, assertion, 114, **130**, **439**, 448
   analysis in IDLC, 308
   application, 133, 405, 408, 423, 427, **437**, 557, 558
      IDLCHECK instruction, **557**
   cyclic, **83**, 84, **137**, 138, 344, **438**
      analysis in IDLC, 405, 406
      example, 83
      restrictions on, 83, 434
      typing in IDLC, 407
   cyclic application
      IDLCHECK instruction, **558**
   formal parameter, 132, 135, 557
   in process refinement, 121
   in the invariant, 326
   in the prelude, 305, 309
   in without clause, 115
   instructions for, 421
   invocation, **133**, *see* definition application
   noncyclic, **137**, 344
      analysis in IDLC, 405, 406
   overloaded, **80**, 137, 138, **441**
      analysis in IDLC, 406
      example, 80, 82, 406
      return type, 466
   predefined, 419, **442**
   private, **137**, **442**
   recursive, 40, 81
      typing in IDLC, 407
   return type, 137
   returning a collection, 41, 42
   returning a value, 39
   two of the same name, 114, 404

definition, assertion, *cont.*
   typing in IDLC, 406
   value returning
      example, 39
   version of a, **80**, **444**, 550
      example, 80, 82
   return type, **137**, 408
   IDLCHECK instructions for, 426
deletion, *see* deallocation
dependent process, **439**
dependent structure, **108**, 394, **439**
derivation, **30**, 100, 101, **108**, 231, **439**
   analysis in IDLC, 365
   combined with refinement, 394, 455, 465
   example, 30, 77, 213
derivation graph, **334**, 384
derived structure, 77
derives relation, **114**
derives* relation, **114**
derives-ancestor structure, **114**, **439**
derives-parent structure, **114**, **439**
descendant classes, representation, 153
`descriptor` node, 366
`Destroy` operation, 120, 458, 459, 466, *see also* node type deallocator routine
   C, **484**
   example, 151, 179, 342
   Pascal, **497**
destroyer, *see* node type deallocator routine
DIANA, 14, 125, 126, 139, 171, 228, 231, 311, 312, 383, **439**, 578, 582, 585
   attribute positioning, 573
   lexical information, 312
   pretty-printer based on, 382, 575

Difference XRef operator, 264, **273**, 569
direct class member, **24**
directed acyclic graph, 560
distributed symbol table, **246**, 254, 438, **439**

E

E (enumeration) prefix, Pascal, 181, **486**
Eiffel language, 69, 70, 138, 144, 434
empty collection, **42**, 131, 551, 558
Empty operator, 42, **131**
   IDLCHECK instruction, **551**
`emptySEQ` operation
   C, **484**
   Pascal, **497**
`emptySEQ` routine
   C, **479**
   example, 161, 187
   Pascal, **494**
`emptySET` operation
   C, **484**
   Pascal, **498**
`emptySET` routine
   C, **477**
   C example, 164
   Pascal, **492**
   Pascal example, 189
entity, 228, **242**, 344, **439**
   defining, 396
   duplicate, 352
   semantic, **314**
      example, 282, 323
   syntactic, **314**
      example, 282, 318
entity reference, 228, **242**, **247**, **439**
   example, 282
   name resolution, 283, 300, 352, 441

entity reference, *cont.*
  name resolution in IDLC, 391
  type checking, 288
enumerated class, *see* class type, enumerated
enumerated node, *see* node type, enumerated
enumerated type, **439**
Equel language, 127
escape character (~), 63, 110, 448
escape sequence, XRef, 269, 281
Exists operator, **136**, 442
  analysis in IDLCHECK, 425, 433
  analysis in IDLC, 405
  example, 36, 80
  failure, 138, 561
  type checking in IDLC, 407
  IDLCHECK instruction, **556**, 557
external data representation, *see* ASCII External Representation Language, XDR
external format, 32, 169, 195, *see also* ASCII External Representation Language
external representation, **439**
  default, **113**, 453
externally-adequate structure, **439**
Extra XRef operator, **273**, 302, 569
  example, 265

F

F (finalize) prefix
  C, 152, 166, **470**
  Pascal, 179, 192, **486**
False
  ASCII External Representation, 142
  assertion literal, 40, **131**
    example, 79
    IDLCHECK instruction, **550**

False, *cont.*
  C constant, 22, 45, 146, 471
  jump if, IDLCHECK instruction, **555**
false, Pascal constant, 174
Fetch operation, 458, 459, 466
  example, 347, 459
Filter XRef operator, 264, **273**
  example, 275
finalizer, *see* attribute finalization routine, private type finalization routine
font conventions, 12
for clause, *see* type representation, port association
For XRef operator, 262, 272, **274**
  example, 284
ForAll operator, **136**, 442
  analysis in IDLCHECK, 425, 433
  analysis in IDLC, 405
  example, 36, 83
  failure, 138, 561
  type checking in IDLC, 407
  IDLCHECK instruction, **556**
  example, 425
foreachinSEQ macro
  C, **479**
  example, 161
foreachinSEQ operation
  C, **484**
foreachinSET macro
  C, **477**
  C example, 164
foreachinSET operation
  C, **484**
formal parameter of a definition, *see* definition formal parameter
Fortran language, 125, 245
FreeString routine, **490**
function language, **71**

INDEX 605

G

garbage collection, 171, 196, 367
GemStone system, 127
generated file, 50, 60, 170, 195, 225
graph delta, 144, 367, 581

H

Head assertion operator, **133**, 135, 309, 405, 442
   example, 39, 41, 422
   IDLCHECK instruction, **555**
      example, 423
Head XRef operator, **274**

I

I (initialize) prefix
   C, 150, 166, **470**
   Pascal, 178, 192, **486**
IBM Corporation, xv
IDL, **439**
   history, 125
   prefix
      C, **470**
      Pascal, **486**
   specification, **440**
   translator, *see* IDLC
   Version 1, 126, **440**
   Version 2, 126, 350, **440**, **445**, 454
   Version 3, 15, 126, 171, 228, **440**, 467
iDL, 127
IDL Toolkit, xi, xii, **1**, 11, 103, **440**
   availability, xiii
IDL type, **131**, **440**
IDL87, 350, **440**, **445**, 448, 452
   versus IDL Version 2, 454–467

IDLC, **440**
   default behavior, 44, 51
   example invocation, 44, 51, 84
   implementation, 305–309, 383–420
   process, 307
   usage, 43, 170, 196
IDLCHECK, **440**
   example invocation, 66
   implementation, 421–434
   instruction, 12, 549–558
IDLclassCommon field, 155
   example, 87
IDLdata structure, 279, 289, **290**, **440**
   example, 289
IDLREAD, 279, 289, **290**, 295, 434, **440**
   example, 289
import specification, 33, **121**, 232, **440**, 461
   analysis in IDLC, 392
   example, 84, 122, 307
In (inclusion) assertion operator, **132**, 467
   IDLCHECK instruction, **554**
In (inclusion) XRef operator, 275
indirect attribute, 261, 272
indirect class member, **24**, 29, 416
   assigning attributes, 25
infix, **372**
initializer, *see* attribute initialization routine, private type initialization routine
`initializeSEQ` operation
   C, **484**
   Pascal, **497**

initializeSEQ routine
  C, **480**
  example, 161, 187
  Pascal, **494**
initializeSET operation
  C, **484**
  Pascal, **498**
initializeSET routine
  C, **478**
  C example, 164
  Pascal, **492**
  Pascal example, 189
input mapper, *see* private type input mapper
input port, 168, *see* port, input
inSEQ operation
  C, **484**
  Pascal, **497**
inSEQ routine
  C, **480**
  example, 161, 187
  Pascal, **494**
inSET operation
  C, **484**
  Pascal, **498**
inSET routine
  C, **478**
  C example, 164
  Pascal, **493**
  Pascal example, 189
instance of a structure, **440**
  external representation, **439**
  internal representation, **441**
instantiation, **441**
int_ prefix, 289
integer array, 423
integer type, **441**
  default
    C, 111
    literal, 131
      analysis in XREF, 567

integer type, *cont.*
  literal
    analysis in CANDLEWALK, 371
    ASCII External Representation, 142
    IDLCHECK instruction, **550**
  representation, 146, 174
  size, 453
Intermetrics, Inc., 14, 70, 125, 144, 579
internal representation, **441**
  default, **113**, 116
internally-adequate structure, **441**
Intersect assertion operator, **134**, 466
  IDLCHECK instruction, **551**
Intersection XRef operator, 264, 273, 569
invariant structure, **31**, **441**
  default, 316
Is assertion operator, **132**, 139, 462
  example, 39, 41
  IDLCHECK instruction, **558**
Is XRef operator, **275**, 287
Is⟨class name⟩ predicate, **159**, 171, 197, **476**, 559
iteration collection, 427
iterator, **36**, **441**
ithinSEQ operation
  C, **484**
  example, 162, 188
  Pascal, **497**
ithinSEQ routine
  C, **480**
  example, 161, 187
  Pascal, **494**
IVAN, 14, 367

INDEX 607

K

K (constant) prefix
  C, 147, **470**
  Pascal, 176, 181, **486**

L

L (list) prefix, C, **470**
lengthSEQ operation
  C, **484**
  example, 162, 188
  Pascal, **497**
lengthSEQ routine
  C, **480**
  example, 162, 187
  Pascal, **494**
Let XRef statement, **274**, 302
lex_ prefix, 201, 317, 335
LG, **125**, 126
linear representation, **441**
linked-list representation, 159, 186, 188
list cell
  allocation
    C, 161, 164, 169, 477, 478
    Pascal, 187, 492, 493
  deallocation
    C, 161, 164, 477, 478
    Pascal, 187, 189, 492, 493
  literal
    boolean, *see* boolean type literal
    integer, *see* integer type literal
    rational, *see* rational type literal
    string, *see* string type literal
local variable initialization, 150

M

Members operator, 405, 442
  IDLCHECK instruction, **555**
Mesa language, 14, 69, 583

Modula-2 language, 14, 144, 254, 309, 579, 586, 589
  constant expression, 248
Modula-2+ language, 586
  Typecase statement, 139
more general, **134**, **441**
multiple views, **101**

N

N (new) prefix
  C, 150, **470**
  Pascal, 177, **486**
name conflict, 166, 192, 329, 402
name resolution, **212**, **441**, *see also* entity reference, name resolution
narrowing, **441**, 476, 492
National Science Foundation, xv
newline character
  in XRef string literal, 261
  in CANDLE instance, 317
  manipulation in CANDLEWALK, 379
NewString routine, 147
node, **20**
  example, 23
node deletion, *see* node type deallocation routine
node type, 5, 20, 147, 175, **441**
  alignment
    analysis in IDLC, 332
  allocation
    C, 166, 169
    C example, 91
    Pascal, 179, 195
    Pascal example, 56
  allocation routine
    C, 69, 120, 149–151, 156, 169, 470, **475**
    Pascal, 177, 178, 486, **491**
  as sequence type, 159, 186
  as set type, 163

node type, *cont.*
    attribute deletion, 152, 157
    attribute representation, 147
    attributed, **147**, 153, **175**, 181,
        438
    deallocation
        C, 169
        Pascal, 195
    deallocation routine, 120
        C, 69, 120, 149, 151, 470,
            475
        Pascal, 177, 179, 485, **491**
    default finalization, 152
        C, 484
        C example, 152
        Pascal, 497
    default initialization
        C, **120**, 150, 151, 169, 475,
            484
        C example, 151
        Pascal, **178**, 195, 497
        Pascal example, 178
    enumerated, 148, 236, 472, 483,
        see also unattributed
        example, 236
    example, 22, 25, 30, 75, 77
    finalization routine, *see* attribute
        finalization routine
    initialization routine, **441**
        C, 45, 120, **150**, 169, 470,
            484
        C example, 45
        Pascal, **178**, 486, 497
        Pascal example, 52
    null, 181
    representation, 147, 175
        attributed, 175
    sharing, 167, 193
    size
        analysis in IDLC, 150, 178,
            332

node type, *cont.*
    size
        average attribute in
            CANDLE, 366
        syntax, 20
        token constant, 147–149, 175,
            176
        unattributed, **147**, 153, **175,
            176**, 181, 316, **444**, 470,
            527
        enumerated representation,
            45, 148, 562
        example, 26, 77, 201
        representation, 176, 181
        value in XRef program, 272
noncyclic definition, *see* definition,
    noncyclic
Not assertion operator, 36, **132**,
    408, 431
    example, 83
    IDLCHECK instruction, **555**
Not XRef operator, 263
    example, 567

O

Oberon language, 196, 589
object code library, 170, 196
object collection type, **131**, *see
    also* collection
Objective-C language, 69, 70, 144
occurrence
    applied, 228
    binding, **228**
    defining, **212**, 213, 218, 569
    used, **228**
operation, *see also* create, destroy,
    defaultfinalize, defaultini-
    tialize, fetch, store
Or assertion operator, 36, 130, **132**
    IDLCHECK instruction, **552**
Or XRef operator, 263

orderedinsertSEQ operation
    C, **484**
    Pascal, **497**
orderedinsertSEQ routine
    C, **480**
    example, 162, 187
    Pascal, **494**
OrIf operator, 40, **41**, 135
output format, default
    C, **169**
    Pascal, **195**
output mapper, *see* private type output mapper
output port, 168, 194
overloaded definition, *see* definition, overloaded

P

P (pointer) prefix, Pascal, **486**
P-code, 558
package, **112**, *see also* Ada language package, private type, package
parse tree, 1, 75, 98, 102, **199**, 560, *see also* syntax tree
    containing the symbol table, 439
    example, 77
    function language, 81
    traversal, 379, 382
parsing, **203**
PascalR language, 127
pass, 6
passivation, **144**
phase, 1
pickling, **144**
PL/1 language, 22, 125
plain class, **153**, **181**, **441**, *see also* class type, plain
Plain language, 127
port, **31**, **117**, 167, 193, **441**
    example, 32

port, *cont.*
    external representation
        default, 453
    input, 168, 194
    mode
        twopass, 168, 194
    name, 32
    output, 168, 194
    post, 31, **442**
    pre, 31, **442**
    prefix, **38**, **442**
    syntax, 31
port association, **119**, **442**
Portals language, 127
post port, **442**
pre port, **442**
pre_ prefix, 335
predefined definition, *see* definition, predefined
Predicate, XRef, 263, 272, 275, 276, 568
    analysis in XREF, 293
    example, 263, 275, 565
prefix, 45, 51, 402, 411
    C, 469, 470
    Pascal, 485–487
prelude, **308**, **442**
private definition, *see* definition, private
private type, 77, **109**, 164, 190, **442**
    alignment, 113, 165, 191
        default, 411
        example, 453, 457
    deallocation, *see* private type finalization routine
    example, 77, 409
    external representation, 254, **439**, 453
        default, 411
        example, 409, 457
    external type, **439**

private type, *cont.*
   finalization routine
     C, 151, **166**, 470
     Pascal, 179, 192, 486
   initialization routine
     C, 150, **166**
     Pascal, 178, 192, 486
   input mapper, **440**
     C, **166**
     Pascal, **191**
   internal representation, 165, 190, 254, **441**, 453, 489
     example, 457
   module for, 165, 190
   name, 453, 489
     example, 457
   output mapper, **441**
     C, **166**
     Pascal, **191**
   package, **112**, 113, 121, 165, 254, 453, 474, 489
     example, 409, 457
   reader/writer interfacing, 166, 191
   size, 113, 165, 191
     default, 453
     example, 409, 453, 457
   value in XRef program, 272
process, **30**, 167, 193, **442**
   abstract specification, **106**
   base, **438**
   concrete specification, 106, 117, 123
   example, 32
   instance, **105**
   instantiation, **441**
   invariant structure, 168, 193, **441**
   port representation, 168, 194
   refined, **33**, **442**
   refines-ancestor, **442**
   refines-parent, **442**

process, *cont.*
   syntax, 31
   translation, 170, 196
programming environment, **1**
PS-Algol language, 127
PSub (proper subset) operator, **134**, 466
   IDLCHECK instruction, **551**

Q

Q prefix, Pascal, 181, **486**
quantifier, **35**, **442**
quantifier collections stack, 426–430, 556, 557

R

R (record) prefix
   C, 147, **470**
   Pascal, 175, **486**
rational array, 423
rational type, 12, **442**
   constant, 366
   literal, 131, 447
     analysis in CANDLEWALK, 371
     ASCII External Representation, 142
     example, 138
     IDLCHECK instruction, **550**
   representation, 146, 174
Rational, Inc., 14
reach, **82**
reachable, **29**, **443**
recursive definition, *see* definition, recursive
reference, **77**
refined process, **33**
refinement, **107**, **442**
   analysis in IDLC, 365
   combined with derivation, 394, 455, 465
   structure, 30, 115

refines* relation, **114**
refines-ancestor relation, **114**, **442**
refines-parent relation, **114**, **442**
refines relation, **113**
register allocation, 420, 582
remote procedure call, 15
`removefirstSEQ` operation
    C, **484**
    Pascal, **497**
`removefirstSEQ` routine
    C, **481**
    example, 162, 188
    Pascal, **495**
`removelastSEQ` operation
    C, **484**
    Pascal, **497**
`removelastSEQ` routine
    C, **481**
    example, 162, 188
    Pascal, **495**
`removeSEQ` operation
    C, **484**
    Pascal, **497**
`removeSEQ` routine
    C, **481**
    example, 162, 188
    Pascal, **495**
`removeSET` operation
    C, **484**
    Pascal, **498**
`removeSET` routine
    C, **478**
    C example, 164
    Pascal, **493**
    Pascal example, 189
Reorder XRef operator, 263, **273**
    analysis in XREF, 294
    example, 284
`rep_` prefix, 335
representation
    attribute, 147
    attributed node, 147, 175

representation, *cont.*
    boolean, 146, 174
    external, **439**
    integer, 146, 174
    internal, **441**
    plain class, 153, 181
    private type, 164, 190
    rational, 174
    sequence, 159, 186
    set, 162, 188
    string, 146, 174
    unattributed class, 156, 181
    unattributed node, 148, 176
Research Systems, Inc., 127
restriction, **442**
`retrievefirstSEQ` operation
    C, **484**
    Pascal, **497**
`retrievefirstSEQ` routine
    C, **481**
    example, 162, 188
    Pascal, **495**
`retrievelastSEQ` operation
    C, **484**
    Pascal, **497**
`retrievelastSEQ` routine
    C, **481**
    example, 162, 188
    Pascal, **495**
return type, **137**
Root assertion operator, 40, **131**, **134**, 135, **442**, *see also* port prefix
    analysis in IDLCHECK, 423
    example, 35, 79
    IDLCHECK instruction, **551**
    example, 423
Root XRef operator, 261, **274**
    analysis in XREF, 292
    example, 262, 284
root, of a structure, *see* structure root

Runtime Version, 12, **452**
  A, 84, 87
    example, 118
  B, 152, 158, 180, 185
  default
    C, **84**
    Pascal, **87**

S

Same (collection comparison) operator, **134**, 135, 466
  example, 83, 408
Same (comparison) XRef operator, 263, 275
sem_ prefix, 201, 213, 335
semantic entity, **241**, 247, **443**,
    see also entity, semantic
SEQ (sequence) prefix
  C, **470**
  Pascal, 187, **486**
sequence type, **443**
  alignment
    analysis in IDLC, 332
  array representation, 160
  default representation, **167**
    C, **159**, **186**
  linked-list representation, 159, 186
  operations, 160, 161, 187
    default set of, 162, **169**, 188, **195**
  scalar types in, 160
  size
    analysis in IDLC, 332
    value in XRef program, 272
SET prefix
  C, 163, **470**
  Pascal, **486**
set type, **443**
  alignment
    analysis in IDLC, 332
  array representation, 163

set type, *cont.*
  default representation, **167**
    C, **162**
  linked-list representation, 162, 188
  of class, 163
  of integer, 163
  of node, 163
  of rational, 163
  operations, 164, 189
    default set of, 189, **195**, 295
  scalar types in, 187, 189
  size
    analysis in IDLC, 332
    value in XRef program, 272
sharing, 167
  detection, **193**
Simula language, 23, 69, 575, 581
singleton collection, **135**
singleton collection type, **133**, 391, **408**, **443**
size
  analysis in IDLC, 331, 332, 414
  array representation, 161
  attribute, 146
  default, 332, 412, 453
  in the prelude, 361
  integer type, 453
    default, 163
  node
    analysis in IDLC, 150, 178
  private type, 113, 165, 191, 453
    example, 457
Size operator, **133**, 405, 442, 467
  example, 35, 254
  IDLCHECK instruction, 423, **555**
    example, 424
sizeSET operation
  C, **484**
  Pascal, **498**

INDEX

sizeSET routine
   C, **478**
   C example, 164
   Pascal, **493**
   Pascal example, 189
Smalltalk language, 23, 69, 70, 144, 575, 578
SofTech Microsystems, Inc., 14, 558, 587
SoftLab Project, xiii, xv
Software Engineering Institute, xv
sortSEQ operation
   C, **484**
   Pascal, **497**
sortSEQ routine
   C, **481**
   example, 162, 188
   Pascal, **495**
Sperry Univac, 14
storage management, 169
Store operation, 458, 459, 466
   example, 459
string name array, 423
string type, **443**
   allocation
      C, 147, 474
      Pascal, 175, **490**
   constant, 37
   deallocation routine
      Pascal, **490**
   literal, 37, 132, 448
      analysis in CANDLEWALK, 371
      ASCII External Representation, 142
      IDLCHECK instruction, **550**
   representation, 146, 174
   value in XRef program, 272
   XRef constant, 276
StringAppend routine, 175, **490**
StringLength routine, 175, **490**
StringToChar routine, 147
StringTopacked routine, 175, 490
structure, 20, **26**, **443**
   abstract specification, **106**, 123, *see also* concrete specification
   base, **438**
   concrete specification, 106, *see also* abstract specification
   derivation, *see* derivation
   derived, 77
   derives-ancestor, **439**
   derives-parent, **439**
   example, 26
   externally-adequate, **439**
   instance, **105**, **441**
   internally-adequate, **441**
   invariant, **441**
   refined, **442**
   refinement, 30
   refines-ancestor, **442**
   refines-parent, **442**
   root, 29, **108**, **443**, 455
      analysis in IDLC, 319, 397, 400
      in derivation, 466
      in IDL87, 467
      in refinement, 466
      in the ASCII External Representation, 63, **143**
      inheritance, **116**
structured type, **22**, **443**
Sub (subset) operator, **134**, 466, **551**
   example, 83
   IDLCHECK instruction
      example, 423
subclass, **443**
Sun Microsystems, Inc., 15, 144, 587
superclass, **158**, **443**
symbol table, 8, 19, 98, 100, 144, 162, 188, 254, 314

symbol table, *cont.*
   centralized, 254, **438**, 439
   distributed, 254, 438, **439**
   XREF, 300
   XREF, 283
syn_ prefix, 318, 335
syntactic entity, **241**, 247, **443**,
     see also entity, syntactic
syntax tree, *see also* abstract syntax tree

T

T (type) prefix
   C, 167, **470**
   Pascal, 192, **486**
Tail assertion operator, 40, **133**,
   405, 442
   example, 39
   IDLCHECK instruction, **555**
Tail XRef operator, 273
   example, 569
tailSEQ operation
   C, **484**
   Pascal, **497**
tailSEQ routine
   C, **482**
   example, 162, 188
   Pascal, **496**
target, **117**, 461
   analysis in IDLC, 321, 331, 399
   default, 118
   in the prelude, 409
   language, **32**, **443**, 452
     C example, 118
     in the prelude, 309
     syntax, 32
     version, **452**
     Version A example, 145, 173
     Version B, 34, 47, 53, 69, 560
     Version B example, 118, 145, 173

target, *cont.*
   machine, **452**
     Vax example, 118
     version, **452**
   name conflict, 401, 411, 452
   name resolution in IDLC, 401
   operating system, **452**
     4.2 BSD Version example, 118
     Unix example, 118
     version, **452**
   runtime system, **452**
   runtime version, *see* Runtime Version
Tartan Labs, 14
Tcol, 125, 575
token constant, 147, 175
toolkit, *see* IDL Toolkit
tree, **82**, 560
True
   ASCII External Representation, 142
   assertion literal, **131**
     example, 36
     IDLCHECK instruction, **550**
   C constant, 22, 45, 146, 471
   in IDLCHECK, 424
   jump if, IDLCHECK instruction, **555**
true, Pascal constant, 174
twopass port mode, 168, 194
type, **22**, **443**
   boolean, **438**
   collection, **438**, *see also* collection type
   domain, **5**, 22, 99, 106, 437
   enumerated, **439**
   external representation, **439**
   integer, **441**
   internal representation, **441**
   private, **442**
   rational, **442**

type, *cont.*
  sequence, **443**
  set, **443**
  string, **443**
  structured, **22**, **443**
type array, 423
Type assertion operator, **135**, 405, 442, 462
  IDLCHECK instruction, **551**, **556**
  example, 423
type checking, **213**, **443**
type representation, **111**, 146, 148, **443**
  example, 112, 149
Type XRef operator, 261, **272**, 277, 301
  analysis in XREF, 294
  example, 262, 275, 284
typeof macro, 45, 47, 156

U

unattributed class, **153**, **181**, **443**, *see also* class type, unattributed
unattributed node, **147**, **176**, **443**, *see also* node type, unattributed
UNC prefix, 386
Union operator, 130, **134**, 466
  IDLCHECK instruction, **551**
Unique XRef operator, 264, **273**, 569
unparser, **201**
used occurrence, **228**

V

V (variant) prefix
  C, 88, 153, **470**
  Pascal, 177, 181, **487**
value descriptor, **366**
value-returning definition, *see* definition, returning a value
Verdix, 14

version, *see* definition, version of
VHDL, 14, 367, 578
VHSIC Hardware Description Language, *see* VHDL

W

white space, **444**
widening, 133, **157**, **444**, 475, 476, 491, *see also* narrowing

X

XDR, 15, 144
XRef, **444**
XREF process, **444**